HISTORY OF
ENGLISH LITERATURE
1660–1837

HISTORY OF ENGLISH LITERATURE 1660–1837

Martin S. Day, *Ph.D.*

*Professor of English
at the University of Houston*

A COLLEGE COURSE GUIDE

DOUBLEDAY & COMPANY, INC., GARDEN CITY, NEW YORK,

Library of Congress Catalog Card Number 63-18042
Copyright © 1963 by Doubleday & Company, Inc.
All Rights Reserved
Printed in the United States of America

Preface

This volume examines the course of English literature from the restoration of Charles II in 1660 to the accession of Queen Victoria in 1837. The periods covered here are the Restoration, the Age of Enlightenment (neoclassicism), the era of the French Revolution, and the Romantic Movement.

The first volume of this series of three traces English literature from its beginnings to 1660. The concluding work extends the survey of English literature from 1837 to the present. All three volumes attempt to provide for everyone interested in English literature a succinct, factual introduction to the works of every notable writer in our language in the British Isles.

Major figures are treated at some length, even to their minor writings. Also, if the writings of any author present special difficulties requiring more thorough explication, his works are discussed here in great detail. Correspondingly, those authors who present few problems in interpretation receive relatively less space. Therefore, length of scrutiny is not in itself a measure of an author's importance.

Lesser writers are considered in sufficient fashion to show their contribution to, and revelation of, their age. Where desirable, quite minor writers are considered in order to demonstrate the scope and variety of a period or a genre. Background material in history, cultural conditions, and development of the language is provided in order to orient the reader and to set each author in his milieu. In order to offer the maximum amount of information about the literary works themselves, footnotes and bibliographies have been omitted.

The goal has been to achieve as much usefulness and thoroughness as possible. For each significant literary work the reader will find:

(1) THE CIRCUMSTANCES OF PUBLICATION, DATE, SOURCE, ETC. Every attempt has been made to offer the latest and most accurate information. Dating presents somewhat of a problem before the adoption of the Gregorian calendar by the English-speaking peoples in 1752. Old Style (O.S.) dates until 1752 were eleven days off in chronology and started the New Year on the vernal equinox in March. As far as

possible, dating throughout this volume conforms to New Style (N.S.), our present calendar.

The dates in parentheses after a work should be read in the following manner: *the date in italic type is the work's date of composition, and the date in roman type is the date of publication.* Thus (*1742*, 1748) means that the work was written in 1742 but not first printed until 1748. Unless otherwise stated, this dating scheme holds true for dramas as well as other literary forms, since plays of this era regularly saw print at the time of first performance.

(2) BRIEF SUMMARIES. The reader is specifically informed about the exact contents of a work so that plot and characters are clearly understood. The summaries, except for wholly minor pieces, commence new paragraphs but appear in the same size of type as the biographical and other data which precede them.

(3) ANALYSES. Instead of rhapsodizing or censuring, this book seeks to explain what an author said and meant in each piece of writing. Interpretations hew as closely as possible to what seems the author's actual intent. Where other interpretations are likely, they are indicated.

While the divisions of the book are generally based upon chronological historical or cultural periods, those literary or art forms of special interest or importance to the period under discussion have been kept separate. It is therefore possible in using this series of books to follow the development of a major art form (such as the novel or the essay) from its beginnings to the present by tracing it through the table of contents.

A pronunciation key has been provided where any difficulty in pronunciation might occur. Sounds follow standard Middle American:

cat, dāte, bär, âsk, bāre

bet, bē, pér

din, dīne

dot, dōte, prŏve, bôre

but, brūte, bùll

þ as in then, th as in thin

Though the author's indebtednesses are too numerous to detail, he wishes most especially to acknowledge the invaluable assistance of Lawrence W. Lamm and Harry L. Wagner of Copeland & Lamm, Inc.

Houston, Texas   MARTIN S. DAY
April 1963

Contents

PART TWO

The Revolutionary Era and the Romantic Movement

HISTORY OF
ENGLISH LITERATURE
1660–1837

Part One

THE ENLIGHTENMENT
AND THE
RISE OF NEOCLASSICISM

Chapter 1

The Restoration and the
Age of Dryden (1660–1700)

BACKGROUND INFORMATION

MAJOR HISTORICAL EVENTS. After the execution of Charles I
in 1649, Parliament abolished the monarchy and the House of Lords
and proclaimed England "a Commonwealth or Free State." However,
the real power lay with the victorious army headed by Oliver Cromwell
(1599–1658). Cromwell tried to mediate between the army and Parliament, without success, and in 1653 he cleared Parliament with
Roundhead Musketeers, dissolved the Council of State, and began five
and a half years of personal rule that ended with his death in 1658. In
1653 he was proclaimed "Lord Protector of the Commonwealth of
England, Scotland, and Ireland."

Cromwell's government was fiercely Protestant (Puritan) in religion
and therefore austere—even scrupulously honest—in administration. It
passed sumptuary laws (to prevent extravagance in private life by
limiting expenditure for food, clothing, etc.) of a rigor previously
unknown in English history, and though at times it was brutally repressive, as in the "pacification" of Ireland, England enjoyed more
freedom of discussion in religious questions than before. Although even
at this distance in time the roles of Cromwell and of the Protectorate
are controversial, it may be said that he was one of England's ablest
rulers, and one of the world's most remarkable dictators. Cromwell's
failure was his inability to provide a constitutional basis for his government, and so at his death he was briefly succeeded by his incompetent
son, Richard, who fell before a military junta within eight months.

The exiled Charles II, son of the executed Charles I, who had fled to France after his fruitless attempt to overthrow Cromwell, was requested by the triumphant junta to resume the throne of England. On May 29, 1660, he was tumultuously welcomed to his capital, and the era of the Restoration began.

The first Parliament of Charles II, triumphantly royalist, enacted repressive measures known as the Clarendon Code (although Clarendon personally opposed many of these acts). Chief among these was the Act of Conformity (1662), which required all clergy, college fellows, and schoolmasters to belong to the Anglican Church; those who refused were termed Nonconformists, a word ever since applied in England to Protestants outside of the Established Church.

Then a series of disasters occurred in rapid succession. After initial naval victories in the war with Holland (1664–67), the English were humiliated by bold Dutch forays up the Thames; the royal docks at Chatham were set afire and the flagship of the English fleet, the *Royal Charles,* was towed off ignominiously. From this low ebb the British Navy was to rise under its modern founder, Samuel Pepys, Secretary of the Admiralty.

London in 1665 was devastated by bubonic plague, the worst epidemic since the Black Plague of the 14th century. In the next year London was virtually destroyed by the Great Fire, which forever eliminated the London of the Middle Ages and of Shakespeare's days. In the still smoldering ruins of the old Gothic cathedral of St. Paul's, Sir Christopher Wren set as the mark for the center of his projected new Baroque cathedral of St. Paul's the fragment of a tombstone appropriately reading "Resurgens" ("I shall rise again"). And finally, in 1666, an uprising by Scottish Covenanters against episcopacy (the government of the Church by bishops) was quickly suppressed.

Seeking a scapegoat for their grievous setbacks, in 1667 the English impeached and exiled Clarendon, the king's chief minister. Rule now fell into the hands of five ministers, the *Cabal,* from their initials (*C*lifford, *A*rlington, *B*uckingham, *A*shley, *L*auderdale). Although not responsible to Parliament, this ministry foreshadowed the later English cabinet. Political parties were forming in the two major factions: Tory (originally an Irish term of reproach) in the court faction, followers of the Cavaliers and supporters of the royal prerogative; and Whig (originally a Scottish term of reproach) in the country faction, followers of the former parliamentarians, and advocates of representative rule. These latter were not radicals or democrats, however, but for the most part merchants, and the representation they desired was more designed to give their class a voice in the government than to espouse the cause of democracy.

Sir William Temple, Swift's patron, negotiated a triple alliance of England, Holland, and Sweden in 1668, but it was vitiated by the secret treaty of Dover between Charles II and Louis XIV in 1670. The Treaty of Dover forced England into a war with its supposed ally, Holland, from 1672 to 1674, an act that disgruntled a large section of the English population.   *POPISH PLOT*

At last the Restoration Parliament began to oppose Charles II. Irritated by the conversion to Roman Catholicism of James, Duke of York, the king's brother and heir, Parliament in 1673 passed the Test Act, requiring all officeholders to be Anglicans. To insure the Protestant succession, Temple arranged the marriage of James's Protestant daughter, Mary, to William of Orange (Dutch branch of the royal family) in 1677. In 1678 Titus Oates's false report of a gigantic Roman Catholic plot resulted in a religious frenzy giving rise to the Papists' Disabling Act, which banned Roman Catholics from Parliament until its repeal in 1829. The next year, however, the passing of the Habeas Corpus Act achieved one of the notable steps in English law. Habeas Corpus is a writ by a judge directing someone who is detaining another to produce the detained one at a specified place at a specified time for a specified purpose. It is considered a safeguard against illegal imprisonment.

The 1679 rebellion of the Scottish Covenanters, treated in Sir Walter Scott's *Old Mortality,* was only one of the series of Scottish Presbyterian rebellions against English episcopacy which were to terminate in the Glorious Revolution of 1688. The English elections of 1679, the first genuine party elections in English history, were almost pitched battles. In 1683 two plots against Charles II were revealed. On the death of Charles II in 1685, the new monarch, his brother James II, became the first Roman Catholic ruler of England since "Bloody Mary." The Duke of Monmouth, illegitimate son of Charles II, proclaimed himself king in 1685 but was soundly defeated at the battle of Sedgmoor. Monmouth and his supporter, the Earl of Shaftesbury, play the title roles in Dryden's poem *Absalom and Achitophel.*   *Glorious*

The new king's tactless attempts to aid English Roman Catholics *Revo-* drove the Anglican Tories into co-operation with the opposition Whigs. *lution* The birth of a son to James in 1688 and the consequent threat of a continued royal line of Roman Catholics forced Parliament to action.

Leading Whigs and Tories petitioned William, Mary's husband, to save England. Upon William's landing, the nation rallied behind him, and James II, throwing the Great Seal of England into the Thames, fled to France. In the "Bloodless Revolution" (also termed the "Glorious Revolution") the English people established the principle that they (or at any rate Parliament) could choose England's ruler.

England's only joint rulers of history were William and Mary (she died in 1694 and William died in 1702). It was William's determination to ruin France, and to that end he forced England into a bloody and expensive war (1689–97). The national debt was thereby started in 1693 with a modest million-pound borrowing. The next year saw the founding of the Bank of England, the first English joint stock bank. The Bank of England, which in twelve days raised £1,200,000 from the public to prosecute the war, began the issuance of bank notes, which are to this day the English currency. The world's first true stock exchange, the London Stock Exchange, was established in 1689. With the death of the exiled James II in 1701, his son, James Edward ("The Old Pretender"), was proclaimed King of Great Britain and Ireland by Louis XIV. However, it was Anne, younger sister of Mary and a Protestant, who succeeded to the throne at William's death in 1702.

CULTURAL CONDITIONS. Throughout Western society the end of the 17th century marked the true beginning of the era in which we still live. The 18th century, the first stage of this period, is often referred to as the Enlightenment. Although the masses still clung to older patterns, the intellectual and ruling classes had accepted a "scientific," rationalistic, materialistic viewpoint. Religious wars were over, the rulers permitted no more public trials of witches, the pseudo-sciences such as astrology and alchemy no longer interested intellectuals, and thinking men (including many of the clergy) sought to establish society and human conduct upon a secular instead of religious basis. Order was a desire of the Enlightenment as much as it had been of any previous age, but the order sought was a rational secular order. What appealed to the universal experience of mankind and the intelligent comprehension of the world by refined gentlemen was what appealed to the Enlightenment. Poetry and all other literature descended from the prophet's eloquence to coffeehouse conversation.

In trying to reconstitute society after the interregnum of the Commonwealth, the public leaders at the close of the 17th century wanted tolerance instead of acrimonious controversy, calm instead of excitement, reason instead of religious fanaticism. Church and State had suffered such violence that they could not be rebuilt upon the old foundations. Commonsense, gentility, secular reason, and the scientific mind were to be the new bases for structuring human society.

Fundamental to the new age was its neoclassic temper. This was not the austere neoclassicism of Milton's *Samson Agonistes,* but rather a bland, urbane manner much like that of Horace of antiquity. For more than a century the ideal in thought and spirit was a clear, simple, dignified (but not pompous) expression, informed by a gentleman's reason and polish.

From this neoclassic base the age moved in two divergent directions. When it sought the grand and monumental style it employed the Classical Baroque. As in Milton's *Paradise Lost,* the Classical Baroque offered the gigantic and magnificently formal—in short, the overpowering. Much of Dryden's poetry is Baroque, and especially Baroque is the heroic drama of the period. Later, when the age sought a light and fine style, it employed the Rococo. The Rococo is an aristocratic elegance and sophisticated artificiality, delighting in informal gaiety, insouciant wit, and charming trifling.

Belletristic writing of the Restoration was still an aristocratic prerogative. Therefore, literary men without ancestral income had to look to patrons who would support them. Readers of Restoration literature usually misinterpret the era, thinking the entire age to be dissolute and immoral. However, the infamous Restoration indecencies were the revels of the very few clustered about Charles II, and rarely has the contrast between popular and aristocratic standards been so apparent, for *The Term Catalogues* (a bookseller's list of available titles published several times a year) reveal that the overwhelming mass of printed matter during the Restoration consisted of sober, edifying, but dull works of piety. The amoral works of the literati, notably the Restoration comedy, clearly demonstrate a transitional stage of society, which was casting adrift from the religious anchorage of the past and which had not yet re-established itself upon a basis of secular ethics and philosophy.

In addition to literature, this was one of the great ages in the history of art in England. Sir Christopher Wren (1632–1723), the nation's most illustrious architect, masterfully designed modest structures in neoclassic fashion and large ones, like St. Paul's, in Classical Baroque. Grinling Gibbons (1648–1721) was England's most skillful wood carver, too accomplished to have any effective imitators and bequeathing even to our day perhaps the world's most exquisite carvings of flowers and foliage. By general consent, Henry Purcell (1658–95) is considered England's greatest native composer. (Handel, although a naturalized English citizen, was German by birth.) At the age of seventeen Purcell composed *Dido and Aeneas,* probably the finest and most artistically successful opera by an Englishman.

The economic foundation of this society was still essentially the soil. Dr. Charles Davenant, writing about trade in 1688, estimated that five sixths of the population was agricultural, and the estimated acreage under cultivation was very close to the present-day figure. The landed gentry were the masters of the soil. Perhaps in an attempt to forget their peril under the Commonwealth and to assert their dynastic grasp of the land, they started a great building program, dotting the English countryside with their mansions, trim neoclassic structures for the moderately well-to-do; and vast, drafty Baroque edifices for the rich. In 1701 Sir John Vanbrugh started construction of Castle Howard, Yorkshire, for the Earl of Carlisle. When it was completed in 1714, an awed visitor remarked that the laundry court where the servants washed clothes would do credit to the Roman emperor Diocletian.

The greatest boost to industry came from skilled immigrants, chiefly French Huguenots. A naturalization edict by Charles II in 1681, renewed by James II in 1685, caused at least eighty thousand persons, mostly expert artisans, to settle in England between 1670 and 1690.

LANGUAGE. Not merely in England, but throughout Western society, and notably in France, the earlier Renaissance drive to enrich vocabulary was superseded in this age by efforts at refinement and regulation of language. In place of a bookish standard, the language of polite conversation (with its emphasis on clarity and precision) was set as the standard. Chief spokesman for the new spirit was Dryden, who artfully attributed the innovation to Charles II, the monarch who "first awakened the dull and heavy spirits of the English from their natural reservedness; loosened them from their stiff forms of conversation, and made them easy and pliant to each other in discourse."

Dryden stigmatized the luxuriant puns of Shakespeare and Jonson as "meanness of expression." He brushed aside the grammar and syntax of Shakespeare and Fletcher as no more than one could expect from such popular writers; he was distressed to point out many cases of "false grammar" in Jonson, "a most judicious writer." In his 1676 version of *Hamlet,* Davenant improved Shakespeare's English, substituting "Peace be with his soul" for "God a mercy on my soul" and "meet Ophelia here" for "here affront Ophelia." Less rigorous writers of the age still muddled their *who* and *whom,* failed to make subject and verb always agree, and blithely doubled negatives; but Dryden wrote in essentially the grammatical pattern approved nowadays by textbooks and schoolteachers.

In his dedication to *The Rival Ladies* (1664), Dryden called for an English Academy that, like its model, the French Academy (founded 1635), would frame rules for the language, pass authoritatively upon the admission of words and their meaning, and prescribe good usage in dictionaries and grammars. The proposal had been advanced as early as 1617 by Edmund Bolton. Dryden lent his great prestige to the idea, but in spite of its later support from Swift and others, such an academy was never established. The nearest realization of an English Academy was the Royal Society of London, founded in 1662, but linguistic study never became more than a minor portion of its activities. This group and the "Invisible College," founded by the distinguished chemist Robert Boyle in 1625, preached the New Science, which carefully eschewed theology and metaphysics and proclaimed scientific findings in "a clear and naked style approaching mathematical plainness." Today's total separation of technical writing from literary writing had not developed as yet, and the scientific conciseness and precision of these men strongly affected all writers.

The first scientific study of English appeared in *Grammatica Linguae Anglicanae* (1653), by John Wallis. Although written in Latin, it discarded the entire incubus of Latin terminology for English and studied our language inductively; e.g. Wallis determined the use of *shall* and *will* from observation of hundreds of conversations and printed works. *An Essay towards a Real Character, and a Philosophical Language* (1668), by John Wilkins, likewise broke with the Latin tradition and sought a scientific basis for analyzing language.

Apparently Hoole's *New Discovery of the Old Art of Teaching School* (1660) is the first book to recommend English literature as the basis for academic study of literature. In *Some Thoughts concerning Education* (1690), John Locke advocated writing themes in English instead of Latin, and also the study of "things that are well writ in English" instead of only Latin readings. Some Dissenting academies substituted English training instead of a strict indoctrination in the classics, notably Newington Green under Charles Morton, later of Harvard College, in Massachusetts.

A Key to the Art of Letters (1700), by A. Lane, drops the apologies of earlier English grammarians (who usually claimed to write for the fair sex or foreigners) and boldly asserts that Englishmen should first and foremost study and know English, learning any foreign tongue by applying to it their knowledge of English. Lane seems to be the first educator to ascribe to English the prominence in learning that it now holds in the English-speaking world.

The tendencies of the age, especially the drive for "correctness," resulted in a great circumscription of the language, especially a remarkable narrowing of vocabulary. Even though French influence was notably high at the century's end, far fewer French words were absorbed into English in the last forty years of the 17th century than in the first forty years. The rather limited vocabulary therefore threw undue burdens upon many words: both *wit* and *nature* had to carry a wide variety of meanings, and today's reader should not blame Dryden or his successor, Pope, for ambiguities thrust upon them by current usage.

DRYDEN AND HIS WORKS

John Dryden (1631–1700). John Dryden modestly minimized his own biography. He was born at Aldwinkle, Northamptonshire, of a staunchly Puritan family. He was educated at Westminster School and Cambridge. After receiving his degree in 1654, he settled in London. Originally a parliamentarian, he went over to the royalist and Anglican side at the Restoration. In 1662 he was elected to the Royal Society, in which he took a prominent role. In the next year he was married above his station to Lady Elizabeth Howard.

For the next fifteen years his chief income was from the drama. From 1670 to 1688 he was poet laureate and historiographer royal; he gave the laureateship a position of topical and popular voice it has never known since, except under Tennyson.

Soon after the accession of Roman Catholic James II in 1685, Dryden became a convert to Roman Catholicism. After the Bloodless Revolution he remained a Roman Catholic and thereby lost his official sinecures. His pen had to be his livelihood in his last years, which were ones of decidedly limited financial circumstances.

Although one of England's greatest poets—he was highly praised throughout the 18th century and also by Byron in the 19th—Dryden has suffered with modern readers for the following reasons:

(1) He has been accused of being a political and religious weathervane, changing his affiliations opportunistically to suit incumbent

patronage. Certainly many men of his age were facile turncoats, and Dryden's conversions are chronologically a bit too advantageous not to be suspect. But it must be noted that he loyally clung to his last religious stand, Roman Catholicism, even though it meant considerable sacrifice. Also, the direction of his changes remained constant. The intellectual history of Dryden shows him growing distrustful of the populace in politics, thus moving toward Tory conservatism; and because he was, in his own words, "naturally inclined to skepticism in philosophy," he was led by his mistrust of man's power to know and to judge properly to seek absolute authority in the Church. This reliance upon faith rather than reason for religious truth is theologically termed *fideism*.

(2) A great deal of Dryden's work was written frankly for money; this is especially true of his comedies, which pander to current taste as much as those of his fellows. However, when Dryden wrote as he wanted, he produced in *All for Love* one of the greatest English tragedies since Shakespeare.

(3) Much of his work is "occasional" and has hence lost interest now that the event that generated it has largely been forgotten. It was a remarkable ability, however, that could immortalize Shadwell and Monmouth to later ages that care nothing for the originals.

(4) The most distinguishing characteristic of Dryden is the virtual absence of the sensuous and emotional qualities in his writings. To those who make such qualities the touchstone of literature, Dryden will have little appeal. Dryden's is the poetry of eloquence and intellectual statement; it is a criticism of life remarkably impersonal, even editorial. He seeks the reader's favor, not by a rich outpouring of emotion, but by his control and discipline. Dr. Samuel Johnson saw Dryden as the creator of the "new versification" and extolled him: "There was . . . before the time of Dryden no poetical diction, no system of words at once refined from the grossness of domestic use, and free from the harshness of terms appropriated to particular arts." Broadly speaking, Dryden was the great advocate and exemplar of the poetic ideal that would govern English poetry until the brink of the 19th century.

The Poetry

Of all the great English poets, Dryden was the slowest to mature poetically and find his own voice. "Upon the Death of the Lord Hastings" (a classmate of Dryden's at Westminster), written in 1650, is a wrenched piece of Mannerism, with one of literature's most preposterous conceits upon smallpox pustules. The "Heroick Stanzas" (1659), on Cromwell's death, and "Astraea Redux" (1660), on the Restoration of Charles II, seem strained hackwork; both display a Hobbesian dread of political and social chaos and praise their widely different subjects as the givers of order and peace. Dryden's first poetic period was terminated by "Annus Mirabilis" (1667) in stanzas about the Dutch war and the Great Fire of London, with an eloquent tribute to the scientific research of the Royal Society. From then until 1681 Dryden's efforts were largely in the drama. His second poetic period (1681–87) offers the great satires and religious poems. His last poetic period (1687–1700) is concerned chiefly with translations.

PANEGYRIC AND ELEGY. Dryden first found his poetic self in the panegyric, notably in "To My Honour'd Friend, Dr. Charleton" (1663), which gracefully praised that man's important but now superseded theories upon the ancient ruins of Stonehenge. Here Dryden displays his marvelous ability to say in verse exactly the right thing in smooth and conversational language. Throughout his subsequent career Dryden was to be the English master of such panegyrics, as in "To My Dear Friend Mr. Congreve" (1694), in which he acknowledges his own inferiority in comic drama to Congreve. Similarly, Dryden excelled in the elegy. "To the Memory of Mr. Oldham," with dignity and poise, adroitly uses classic allusions to eulogize the satirist, dead at twenty-nine.

SATIRE. Dryden is probably the greatest English satirist in verse, certainly of satire in the Juvenalian manner. Since all satire is humorous ridicule and rebuke containing a demand for correction, it flourishes most strongly in an era of sharp critical analysis when religious standards are superseded by social standards. Because the admonishings of the preacher are no longer able to enforce social conformity, the weapon of social laughter is employed. Horatian satire is debonair, focusing on foibles and minor failings. Juvenalian satire is invective *a violent reproach* satire magisterially denouncing gross sins. While essentially Juvenalian, Dryden's satire is peculiarly Baroque, grand, impressive, blandly superior, and devastatingly condemnatory.

Mac Flecknoe; or, A Satire upon the True-Blew-Protestant Poet, T. S. (1682) was written in 1678 and circulated about the court and literary London. Thomas Shadwell was a minor contemporary poet and dramatist who in his plays, *Virtuoso* (1676) and *History of Timon of Athens* (1678), had slightly referred to Dryden. Dryden's satire arose less from anger than from the chance of displaying his wit against a convenient butt. The form of the work is mock-heroic, treating a trivial subject in pseudo-majestic fashion. It jokingly proclaims Shadwell the monarch of the kingdom of dullness. Richard Flecknoe (d. 1678) was a wholly obscure versifier who probably had a hand in early attacks upon Dryden. The "Mac," of course, is the Celtic patronymic, suggested by Shadwell's brief Irish residence.

In sonorous tones Dryden has Flecknoe designate Shadwell as his successor to the rule of inanity. Dryden here displays his first superb mastery of the heroic couplet. The mock solemnity of *Mac Flecknoe* and its sparkling epigrammatic wit set a fashion that English poetic satire sought to emulate for more than a century. *The Medal of John Bayes* (1682), a satire against Dryden probably by Shadwell, apparently triggered the publication of *Mac Flecknoe*. In life, Shadwell had the last laugh because he succeeded Dryden as poet laureate in 1689, but to all later ages the name of Shadwell has been remembered almost solely because of Dryden's satire.

Absalom and Achitophel (Part I, 1681) was written for Charles II and was published a few days before judgment was to be pronounced in the trial of the Earl of Shaftesbury, the Ashley of the Cabal. Shaftesbury, who supported the claims of Monmouth to the throne against the Roman Catholic Duke of York (later James II), was imprisoned in 1681 on charges of high treason. Dryden, then poet laureate, was trying to sway opinion against Shaftesbury. On the face of it, Dryden's work is a noble heroic poem based upon the biblical story of Absalom's rebellion against his father, David (2 Samuel, xv–xviii). Actually, the contemporary English political scene is the subject; Dryden attacks Shaftesbury by putting him in the guise of Achitophel, the priest who misguided Absalom. Dryden presumably was influenced by the anti-Catholic *Achitophel or the Picture of a Wicked Politician* (1627), by Nathaniel Carpenter, by the pro-Catholic *Naboth's Vineyard: or, the Innocent Traitor* (1679), by John Caryll, against the judges of the "Popish plot," and especially by Thomas D'Urfey's *The Progress of Honesty* (1680), in which Shaftesbury is specifically pictured as Achitophel.

Actually, no action really occurs in Dryden's poem; the speech of David (Charles II) quashes the rebellion before it can start. The poem's excellence lies in its series of masterful portraits: Absalom (Monmouth), Zimri (Buckingham), Corah (Titus Oates), and, best of all, Achitophel (Shaftesbury). Realizing that he must be cautious, Dryden indicts only one real villain, Shaftesbury. Every vignette, however, is an unforgettable etching of wit and shrewd judgment in the <u>style of Baroque mock grandeur.</u> Dryden's position is Tory conservative, demanding the retention of traditional monarchy while eschewing Shaftesbury's desire for a ruler subject to the popular will. Although one of the greatest satires in English, Dryden's poem failed in its immediate object. Shaftesbury was acquitted by a Whig jury. A year later, when he was about to be indicted again, this time by a Tory jury who would not acquit him, he fled to Holland, where he died.

The Second Part of Absalom and Achitophel (1682) was largely written by Nahum Tate (1652–1715), who became poet laureate in 1692. Dryden revised this continued abuse of the Whigs and inserted two excellent satiric portraits of Whig versifiers: Shadwell (Og) and Elkanah Settle (Doeg). Settle (1648–1724) had tried to reply to the first part of *Absalom and Achitophel;* for his pains he secured satiric immortality in the Dryden-Tate poem and later in Pope's *Dunciad.*

The Medall, A Satyre against Sedition (1682) was induced by a commemorative medal struck in honor of Shaftesbury's acquittal. On one side the medal bore the face of Shaftesbury; on the other appeared a view of London, the Bridge, and the Tower with the sun rising to dispel clouds and "Laetamur" ("Rejoice") inscribed about the edge. More somber than the previous satires, the poem further excoriates Shaftesbury. Conservatively attacking democratic concepts of government, Dryden contends that only a "rightful monarch," wholly independent of popular sentiment, can subdue faction and maintain a peaceful country. This and the previous satires display concern with the minutiae of everyday politics on one hand and, on the other, a searching of political principles only possible when the system of modern political parties was first emerging.

<u>ARGUMENTATIVE RELIGIOUS VERSE</u>. Dryden's powerful contributions here demonstrate: (1) the intertwining of religion and politics in the era; (2) the neoclassic concern for universal and social faith instead of the intensely personal religious experience of the earlier devotional poets; (3) the search for faith by an intelligent mind in a time of mounting skepticism.

Religio Laici ("A Layman's Religion") (1682) was immediately occasioned through the translation (1682) by Henry Dickinson, a personal friend of Dryden's, of *Histoire Critique du Vieux Testament,* from a Roman Catholic priest, Richard Simon. Simon's work sought to undermine the Protestant reliance upon the scriptures by demonstrating the original unreliability of Old Testament texts and the subsequent faults of all translations.

Dryden's reply is couched essentially in the spirit of Anglican Latitudinarianism; he was still a member of the Established Church. The Bible, he asserts, "in all things needful to salvation," is clear enough; any obscurities are "not necessary to salvation." There are two enemies to this reasonable faith: the Papists, who "kept the Scriptures from us" and assume "the pretense of infallibility," and the Fanatics (Puritans and other nonconformists), who claim "what amounts to an infallibility in the private spirit" and use scripture for seditious purposes. If the Bible puzzles us, turn to the Patristic writers. If reason clashes with faith, silence and peace are the best responses. What sounds like a drab theological disputation is transmuted, as Gray said, into "thoughts that breathe and words that burn."

The Hind and the Panther (1687) appeared after Dryden's conversion to Roman Catholicism. Rather incongruously, it adopts the form of a beast fable, picturing Hind (Roman Catholic Church), Panther (Anglican Church—"fairest creature of the spotted kind"), Bear (Independents), Wolf (Presbyterians), Hare (Quakers), Ape (Freethinkers). The Hind and the Panther elaborately discuss religious matters, with dialectical victory accorded the Hind. Dryden, unusual for a recent convert, is calm and balanced, a moderate English Roman Catholic, rightfully fearful that the efforts of James II to support Roman Catholicism would cause a violent anti-Catholic reaction. Even though much of the political and theological discussion of the poem is uninteresting to modern readers, no other English poet can discuss religion so well and in such adroit, flexible, perfectly phrased couplets.

TRANSLATIONS. The need for money persuaded Dryden in his later years to devote much of his time and talent to extensive translations, which were then published between 1684 and 1711. Greek poetry was only slightly touched upon by his translations of Theocritus and excerpts from Homer, while most of his effort consisted of translations of Latin poets: Ovid, Horace, Lucretius, Juvenal, Persius, Vergil. He also translated portions of Boccaccio and Chaucer. Such enormous labor inevitably produced unevenness, but never incompetence. While modern readers are usually distressed by the Chaucer paraphrases, where Dryden's Baroque elaboration seems inappropriate, the translation of Vergil's *Aeneid* (1697) is especially good, for Dryden's spirit was strongly Vergilian. His effective capturing of the ancient Augustan manner was to color English attitudes toward antiquity during most of the following century.

LYRICS. Dryden's lyrics are, for the most part, scattered throughout his dramas. They are characterized by stronger dance rhythms than their Elizabethan and earlier 17th-century models. The poet tends more to follow the lead of the music or to emulate musical effects verbally. Speed and strength are Dryden's lyric forte, but he was also capable of delicacy and subtlety. One of his very last works, *The Secular Masque* (1700), performed a few weeks before his death, contains in the Song of Momus, which bids adieu to the 17th century and heralds the new 18th century, one of his most haunting lyrics. Not until the Romantics would English literature again produce such a great lyricist.

ODES. Dryden's imitation of musical effects in verse reaches its zenith in two pseudo-Pindaric odes, "A Song for St. Cecilia's Day" (1687) and "Alexander's Feast: or, The Power of Music" (1697). In theme he was following a 17th-century fashion of poetic praise for music on St. Cecilia's Day (November 22). In the earlier poem Dryden cleverly imitates the sounds of trumpet, flute, and violin; he sees music as the symbol of divine harmony, accompanying the Day of Judgment as it did the Day of Creation. The latter poem is one of the most lavish displays of virtuosity in the language. To show the effects of various types of music upon Alexander the Great, the poet runs the gamut from sweet amatory music to martial strains, in each case perfectly suiting line and cadence to the musical effects. Pope lavishly extols this poem in *Essay on Criticism*. However, Dryden's finest achievement in the pseudo-Pindaric ode is "To the Pious Memory of the Accomplisht Young Lady Mrs. Ann Killigrew" (1686), a eulogy in the grand manner, completely filled with rhetorical splendor. The indecency of Restoration literature is severely condemned in this poem. Dr. Johnson termed this the greatest ode in English. Almost its equal is the pseudo-Pindaric paraphrase of the Horatian Ode 29 from Book III (1685), with its majestic assertion of confidence in a life of peaceful, calm moderation.

The Prose   *3.90*

Dryden's prose style does not contain the usual Baroque heightening of his major verse, but rather displays a sure neoclassic manner perfectly adapted to effective prose. His chief characteristics in prose are:

(1) "Correctness." To Dryden and later neoclassicists, this was not

a mere absence of grammatical errors but a positive coherence and unity of expression.

(2) <u>Clarity and simplicity</u>. No previous English prose reads with the deceptive ease and grace of Dryden's. Exactly what the neoclassicists sought, this is art concealing art. The elaborate rhetorical devices of Milton and Browne are absent. Never artificially balanced, his sentences cunningly vary phrases and clauses with a sense of inevitable flow.

(3) <u>Graceful movement</u>. Dryden's prose never surprises or puzzles. Unobtrusive connectives bear the reader on without any feeling of break. References and allusions are not ornamental but wholly natural.

(4) <u>Conversational ease.</u> The effect of Dryden's prose is such that the reader feels that he is being talked to, not at. Pedantry and eccentricity are eschewed in favor of the conversational style of gentlemen—refined, dignified, never stilted, never slovenly.

"<u>Dryden</u> may be properly considered as the <u>father of English criticism</u>," asserted Dr. Johnson. With minor exceptions, Dryden's prose consists of literary criticism. No previous writer in English was so concerned with criticism or produced such an impressive body of it. He truly inaugurated the critical approach toward English letters and bequeathed the tradition to later ages. His chief work in this genre is:

Of Dramatick Poesie, An Essay (1665, 1688) appears in dialogue form, one suggested by continental critics such as the French Chapelain, Sarrasin, Desmarets, and the Spanish De Molina. The form permitted a full discussion of opposing views without demanding a definitive conclusion.

The picturesque opening is upon the lower Thames in June 1665 as the Dutch navy is pounding the English. When the cannonades diminish, four gentlemen consider the literary position of English drama. Crites (Sir Robert Howard, Dryden's brother-in-law) argues for the pre-eminence of the ancients and sees "the greatest man of the last age, Ben Jonson," as leaning wholly upon classical drama. Eugenius (Lord Buckhurst) claims that modern playwrights have improved upon the ancients. Lisideius (Sir Charles Sedley) asserts that the French have surpassed the English in the drama, maintaining that contemporary French playwrights have avoided the absurdities of the English tragi-comedy and the bare chronicle plays of Shakespeare, which unnaturally crowd many years into a few hours. The French carefully select the significant points and develop them searchingly.

Neander (Dryden) boldly defends the English drama as more life-like and "natural" than the French. The English can match the French "regularity," as note Jonson's *Epicoene*, and in Dryden's scrutiny of this play there follows the first significant piece of detailed practical criticism in English. Beaumont and Fletcher are praised for their "imitation of the conversation of gentlemen." Shakespeare is hailed as "the largest and most comprehensive soul of all modern, and perhaps ancient, poets." Jonson is "the most learned and judicious of dramatists." Neander asserts: "Jonson I admire, but I love Shakespeare." Crites favors blank verse, while Neander supports riming dramatic verse.

Although different viewpoints are presented, the work favors the eloquent vindication of the English drama. Dryden's fundamental critical position is one that considers refined taste superior to any rigid critical yardstick, and resemblance and relevance to life superior to artifice.

With the exception of this famous essay, Dryden's other criticism takes the form of prefaces or dedications for his printed works. In the earlier period, up to 1674, his concern is chiefly with immediate specific problems in the dramas he is writing—imitation of Renaissance English and contemporary French dramatists or the heroic couplet for tragedy.

Dryden's great critical period ranges from 1674 to 1685, when he lifts his sights to consider the broader critical concepts. In the preface to *The State of Innocence* (1674), his operatic version of *Paradise Lost,* Dryden considers the nature of epic poetry and asserts that Milton combines Homeric loftiness of mind with Vergilian elevation of language. "The Grounds of Criticism in Tragedy," prefacing his adaptation (1679) of Shakespeare's *Troilus and Cressida,* contains the first significant and detailed analysis in English of Aristotle's concept of tragedy. Dryden contends that the traditions of Shakespeare and Fletcher should be emulated as far as they are consistent with the principles of Aristotle, Longinus, and Horace.

Translation of Ovid's Epistles (1680) is prefaced by an examination of current theories about translation; Dryden favors creative translation where the spirit, not the letter, of the original is communicated in another tongue. In the lively dedication to *The Spanish Friar* (1681), he supports tragi-comedy as nature's mixture of serious and comic, and urges the coherent structure of an entire play against mere brilliant excerpts.

After 1685 his critical prefaces are chiefly occasioned by his translations. The dedication to *Examen Poeticum* (1693) defends the English drama against the ancients and the modern continentals alike, and discusses all too briefly his own principles of versification. "A Discourse concerning the Original and Progress of Satire," prefacing his translation of Juvenal and Persius in 1693, considers the nature and role of satire, although in this work the aging writer is prolix and in places boring. The preface to *Fables, Ancient and Modern* (1700) is in some respects the crown of Dryden's criticism, for it heralds the modern rediscovery of Chaucer and displays a penetrating analysis of Chaucer's poetic achievement, even though Dryden was ignorant of Chaucerian pronunciation. Dryden could not help but feel that Chaucer's verse failed to scan. His ignorance of Chaucer's sounding the final "e" in a word, for instance, would lead him to find Chaucer's lines unaccountably short. His admiration for Chaucer's other qualities must therefore have been all the greater to offset this seeming defect.

The total mass of Dryden's criticism constitutes one of the most impressive of such efforts in our language. Its dominant qualities set the style of English literary criticism ever since: tolerance and universality of taste, and balanced and sane judgment founded upon intrinsic importance of the work examined and its resemblance to genuine life problems.

DRYDEN'S DRAMATIC WORKS. Dryden was the master of tragedy in his age, and he also made no small contribution to comedy, though in that field he had keen competition. However, in order that we may present a complete picture of the drama of the time, we will discuss Dryden's plays along with those of other playwrights in the following section on the Restoration drama.

THE RESTORATION OF THE PUBLIC THEATER

The Puritan closing of the theaters in 1642 meant the virtual but not the absolute disappearance of the English drama for eighteen years. All through the Commonwealth period, dramas were performed in the private residences of country gentlemen, with some actors even attempting public performances. In 1648 Fletcher's *Bloody Brother* was being staged at the surreptitiously reopened Cockpit; parliamentarian soldiers effectively ended this rashness by imprisoning the actors and confiscating their costumes. A more successful circumvention of the authorities consisted of *drolls,* brief excerpts from the Renaissance drama that could be quickly presented at a fair or festival and completed before a raid could be launched.

Sir William Davenant (the only playwright to practice both before and after the Commonwealth) was permitted to produce *The Siege of Rhodes,* usually termed the first English opera, at Rutland House in 1656 under the guise of "story sung in recitative music." But the theatrical tradition was essentially broken and most actors of the Caroline stage were dead, old, out of practice, or fixed in other employment when the Restoration gave the theater a new birth.

One of the first actions of Charles II upon his resumption of the throne in 1660 was the granting of two patents, assigning the monopoly of London theatrical performances to the King's Company, headed by Thomas Killigrew (the elder), and to the Duke of York's Company, under Sir William Davenant. Killigrew had an acting troupe performing in make-shift quarters early in November 1660. In 1663 he erected a playhouse in Covent Garden, the first of several famous theaters upon that site. Davenant got his company started by mid-November 1660; it played at various places until finally it settled at Drury Lane in 1673.

THE AUDIENCE. While the Caroline theater had been dominated by the court, the Restoration theater was wholly the court's preserve. The Merry Monarch himself had re-created the theater, and it was largely in his image. He was the first English monarch who regularly attended the public theater, even though he had his own private theater at Whitehall. Charles II personally interested himself in the preparation of scripts and in the running of the acting companies; he frequently lent state robes for stage performances; and he dearly loved the actresses.

The spectators at the two theaters were exclusively courtiers and their hangers-on. Two theaters were therefore quite sufficient for the metropolis of London, and the managers bitterly lamented the meager patronage. Performances were occasionally canceled because of inadequate attendance, and the opening presentation of Dryden's *All for Love* in 1677 drew only 249 paid admissions. The best seats cost four shillings, the poorest twelve pence. Courtesy permitted a gallant, on the pretense of "looking for a friend," to see one act without charge. Performances started at three-thirty or four in the afternoon.

The aristocrats looked upon the playhouse as a social assembly where they had an opportunity to disport themselves. Pepys recounts in his diary the brilliant wit displayed in front of him by Sir Charles

Sedley and his own annoyance at being interrupted by the players' voices.

THE PHYSICAL THEATER. Although linked with the Caroline drama, Davenant was the chief force in bringing about the abandonment of the Renaissance English stage in favor of the continental, especially the French, stage. The theaters were wholly indoors. The apron, or forestage, still projected into the audience but was cut to seventeen feet or less. The curtain was an innovation of Davenant's, as were painted backdrops also. Seldom permitted any longer upon the stage itself, the gallants were still prominently on display in boxes set on either side of the apron. The smaller theaters for a smaller audience encouraged an intimate drama unlike the panoramic effect of the Renaissance theater.

THE ACTORS. The limited patronage necessitated small professional companies and therefore plays with relatively few roles. The acting company approximated a modern repertory company. Financial underwriting and profits were for the management, and the performers were salaried. Boy apprentices had vanished, but a few males took women's roles, notably Edward Kynaston, who impressed Pepys as about the "most handsome woman" the diarist had seen. Mrs. Margaret Hughes may have been the first English actress, taking the role of Desdemona with Killigrew's company in 1660.

THE PLAYWRIGHTS. Writing Restoration drama conveyed more court prestige than ready money. Shadwell apparently was the best rewarded, receiving £130 for The Squire of Alsatia (1688). Dryden also did well financially, but there were no longer the stables of professional writers of the Elizabethan age. Most of the dramatists were aristocratic gentlemen, or else hacks seeking to tickle aristocratic palates.

Restoration Comedy

All comedy of the era was bawdy but not in the earthy fashion of the Elizabethans. As our time with its reaction to Victorianism has discovered, the aftermath of Puritanism and prudery usually manifests itself in smirking, self-conscious indecency, and the Restoration went out of its way to flaunt Commonwealth and Puritan principles. Bedroom and assignation scenes were blatant and adultery was a commonplace representation.

Romantic comedy of Shakespeare's type was hardly appreciated. Pepys says of A Midsummer Night's Dream that it was "the most insipid ridiculous play" he had ever seen. Continental models were frequent, but the greatest influence from the past was that of Ben Jonson, and occasionally the Restoration comedy produced a comedy of humors in the Jonsonian style.

It is the comedy of manners, however, that most people think of when they talk about "Restoration comedy." Adumbrated by the Caroline comedy of manners, this genre was brought to its fullest form by the courtly wits of the Restoration. It is a peculiarly rococo form of art.

Life to the gallants of Charles II's court was itself a "pleasant comedy" with marriage a "main design" relieved by "underplots." The gentleman does have a host of love affairs and mistresses, but he is never plagued with love itself. Marriage is an alliance which he maintains no more resolutely than Charles II did his alliances. The sole battleground and preoccupation of this gallant is the boudoir. The fine lady who figures in this battle of wits and sex is equally independent and adventuresome. When finally brought to marriage, she insists upon elaborate provisos to maintain her "dear liberty."

The clash of male gallant with high-spirited womankind provides the opportunity for scintillating wit and badinage, unsullied by the vulgarity of warm attachment. Probably this comedy was essentially an accurate reflection of this limited society, except that life could never be as brilliantly witty as this art.

Sir George Etherege (or **Etheredge**) (eth'er-ēj) (c. 1634–1691). Sir George Etherege has his early years cloaked in obscurity. His parentage is not certain, and it is not known whether he was born in England or in Bermuda. Apparently he resided with the exiled court in France and returned to enjoy the unbridled life of a Restoration rake. Pepys disliked *The Comical Revenge* (1664), but this Etherege play in virtually all respects inaugurated the Restoration comedy of manners. A disreputable street brawl in 1676 which cost a man's life forced Etherege and the notorious Lord Rochester to leave the country, but by 1685 Etherege was an English diplomat in Germany, shocking the burghers with his indecent conduct. The Revolution of 1689 cost him his post, and he drifted to Paris, where his last years proved as obscure as his earlier ones.

The Man of Mode; or, Sir Fopling Flutter (1676)—Comedy of Manners. This, Etherege's third and last play, has become the symbol of the entire genre, singled out by Steele in *The Spectator* for special condemnation. Though Molière's *Les Précieuses Ridicules* suggested some of its scenes, this prose comedy derives largely from actual Restoration life.

The central character, Dorimant, is casting off an old flame, Mrs. Loveit, is currently conducting an affair with Bellinda, and is very much interested in Harriet. Harriet is intended for young Bellair, who, however, is drawn to Emilia. Dorimant fobs off Mrs. Loveit on Sir Fopling Flutter, and young Bellair encourages Harriet and Dorimant. Dissimulation surrounds all the characters until the tangle is straightened out and the couples, Emilia and young Bellair, Harriet and Dorimant are to be wed.

Dorimant (usually believed a portrait of Rochester) provided the model for hosts of subsequent stage gallants. While his conduct may seem altogether reprehensible to moralists, Etherege obviously interprets him as the contemporary hero. Dorimant is an adept in the heartless world that rates a man by his amatory conquests. His suave and easy manner, his sparkling wit, and his genteel refusal "to betray a lady" after he has ruined her are supposed to be highly admirable. Sir Fopling Flutter likewise was the model for a multitude of imitations, being the prototype of the empty-headed fool of fashion. In the Restoration code, Flutter is the failure because clothes and outward show monopolize him completely, while Dorimant is the success because of his numerous conquests. So far as there is a "moral," Dorimant has indulged in superficial sexual triumphs purely for vanity, while Harriet astutely guides him into expressing his natural drives through marriage, though the new Dorimant is not asked to be a "Fanatick" or to abandon the London social world for the dreary countryside. Most importantly, however, the play provides constant opportunity for polished repartee and sophisticated witticisms, with Dorimant's friend Medley (probably based on Sir Charles Sedley) existing solely for his scintillating and devastating remarks.

Thomas Shadwell (c. 1642–1692). Born in Norfolk, Thomas Shadwell was educated at Cambridge and the Inner Temple. His plays were coarse and, contrary to Dryden's report, often witty. He succeeded Dryden as historiographer royal and poet laureate in 1689. Shadwell, as we have mentioned before, was probably the most financially successful of the Restoration dramatists. Among his most famous plays are *Epsom Wells* (1672), *The Squire of Alsatia* (1688), and the one we will discuss, *Bury Fair*.

Bury Fair (1689)—Comedy of Humors. This work shows clear indebtedness to Jonson's *Bartholomew Fair,* but the bustle of the fair is here only a fascinating backdrop.

Gertrude, essentially a sensible young woman, determines to reform her lover before marriage; and Wildish, after protestations of rakish gallantry, gracefully yields to the force of true love and promises reformation. Lady Fantast, affecting high style, is gulled into marrying La Roche, a French barber. The curtain falls upon a double wedding.

However, the real interest here lies in a collection of "humours" characters, the gulls and confidence men of the age. Oldfox "pretends to have been one of Ben Jonson's sons." Bellamy, a country friend of Wildish, praises rural virtues over those of London and foreshadows the change of moral tone at the turn of the century.

William Wycherley (wich'er-li) (c. 1640–1716). William Wycherley was born at Clive near Shrewsbury. In his youth he resided in France, mingling with the literati and becoming a Roman Catholic convert. He returned for a brief residence at Oxford and thence proceeded to the Middle Temple. His high reputation in drama and gay Restoration society enabled him to marry the widow of the Earl of Drogheda in 1680, but at her death attendant lawsuits resulted in his imprisonment. James II rescued him from prison and pensioned him, but Wycherley's later years witnessed a decline in powers and spirit. Apparently to thwart a greedy nephew, Wycherley remarried eleven days before his death. He was frequently extolled as "manly" or "brawny" Wycherley.

The Country Wife (c. *1672,* pub. 1675)—Comedy of Manners. This play was the first great success in the Restoration comedy of manners. It is indebted to Molière's *L'École des Femmes* with some obligation to the *Eunuchus* of Terence.

An aging, conceited roué, Pinchwife, had married a naïve country girl, Margery, hoping that her ignorance will keep her faithful. Pinchwife's incessant talk of cuckolding implants the idea in his friends' minds, especially in the mind of Horner. Pinchwife disguises Margery as a boy; Horner interprets this as concealment of a wench and therefore fair game for flirtation. Pinchwife forces Margery to write a letter rebuffing Horner, but she adroitly substitutes a love letter. Pinchwife wants his sister Alithea to bribe Horner into leaving Margery alone; disguised as Alithea, Margery is thrust upon Horner by Pinchwife. With the connivance of his physician, Horner has announced his impotence from overstimulation. His friends feel that their wives are therefore safe in his hands, and Horner cuckolds them all, particularly in the famous "china" scene. The ladies compel Margery to join in the lies to the husbands and agree that Horner is impotent. Everyone goes away satisfied. In the sub-plot Alithea drops her jealous and greedy fiancé Sparkish for Harcourt, Horner's friend.

In this play jealousy and suspicion bring the very disaster they fear. Every step that the perturbed Pinchwife takes to prevent his cuckolding brings him that much closer to it. The country wife herself, like her soiled sisters, is not innocent at all; hers is solely the purity of the ignorant. She had not succumbed simply because she had not had opportunity. Hazlitt asserted: "Mrs. Margery Pinchwife is a character that will last for ever" with her amalgam of "self-will, curiosity, art, and ignorance."

Moralists obviously object, but the "china" scene is unsurpassed in English literature for its sardonic, risqué comedy. Nonetheless, there is an undercurrent, as in the Russian classic, Nicolai Gogol's *Inspector General,* of terrifying corruption and emptiness beneath the surface laughter. In the society Wycherley depicts, love has vanished; all that remains are erotic charades; indeed, it has been suggested that Wycherley is really a Puritan masquerading as a Restoration rake. The sub-plot is no real riposte, for Alithea discards Sparkish on the basis of his jealousy and desire for her fortune; the sub-plot is therefore no criticism of the society but a mere parallel to the Pinchwife-type jealousy.

The Plain Dealer (1674, pub. 1677) delighted James II and caused him to save the fortunes of the imprisoned playwright. In this drama Wycherley adapts Shakespeare's *Twelfth Night*—even to the point of using the name Olivia—and also Molière's *Le Misanthrope.*

Manly, a sea captain, returns from fighting the Dutch, only to find that the one woman he trusted, Olivia, is married, is carrying on with a mob of admiring dandies, and is unwilling to refund to him the money he had entrusted to her. Observing Olivia's desire for his cabin boy, Manly sends the youth to her, and intends to substitute himself in the assignation, thinking to gain revenge upon Olivia by overpowering her sexually. Her husband appears, however, and turns out to be Vernish, the only man that Manly had trusted. The cabin boy is revealed to be Fidelia, a girl in disguise, who had thus been able to follow Manly, whom she worships. The sea captain marries Fidelia.

In the sub-plot Manly's lieutenant, Freeman, seeks to marry the rich Widow Blackacre, a monomaniac about lawsuits. Discovering the widow's gross defrauding of her son, Freeman blackmails her into settling a sizable annuity upon him.

Dryden termed this play "one of the most bold, most general, and most useful satires which has ever been presented on the English theatre." Manly is the voice of savage indignation, denouncing every perfidy of the age. On this basis the playwright may be considered a moralist attacking the Restoration inadequacies. Such an interpretation is clouded, however, by the sub-plot.

While Manly receives the reward of Fidelia, a woman who completely adores him and is a rich heiress in the bargain, Freeman gains his reward by the very duplicity that Manly berates. Freeman is the successful rake-hero at the game of social pretense and trickery. Manly is a new creation for the drama of the age, an innately good man at variance with the social pattern. One can truthfully state that Manly's is the greater reward, but his Fidelia is incongruous, a Shakespearean heroine out of her element. The employment of the name Olivia is an obvious comparison between the wholesome world of the Renaissance comedy and the reality of an Olivia in the seamy Restoration world. The Widow Blackacre, that demon for litigation, is one of the great "humours" characters of English drama.

Sir John Vanbrugh (van'bru, van'bruk, or van-brog') (1664–1726). The grandson of a Flemish merchant, John Vanbrugh was a refugee from the Spanish persecutions in the Low Countries. He studied art in Paris and spent 1690–92 in French prisons as an English spy. Drama was subsidiary to his work as an architect. He built Haymarket Theatre in 1705 and designed magnificent country mansions such as Castle Howard and Blenheim Palace. His government posts included Comptroller of the Board of Works and Garter King of Arms. He was knighted in 1714.

The Relapse (1696)—Comedy of Manners. A sequel and rejoinder to Colley Cibber's play, *Love's Last Shift, The Relapse* was supposedly written in six weeks. The critic Jeremy Collier, who was a clergyman, bitterly assailed the play on moral grounds.

Loveless, bored with faithful Amanda, conducts an affair with her cousin Berinthia. Worthy seeks to assault Amanda's virtue. The faithful wife maintains her virtue in spite of a torrid seduction scene, and Loveless is once again reformed. Lord Foppington (formerly Sir Novelty Fashion) is tricked out of his bride, Miss Hoyden, by his brother, Young Fashion, in a loosely joined sub-plot that is actually more interesting than the main plot.

In reply to Collier, Vanbrugh dubiously claimed that the play was a dramatic sermon on the text "Lead us not into temptation." Basically this is a farcical Restoration drama, but its significant differences are: (1) the maintenance of virtue; (2) sensibility and emotional feeling instead of the brittle wit of his predecessors. The Etherege model is decidedly modified, as Vanbrugh lacks the detached amusement of his masters. Cibber proved a great success as Lord Foppington, "the personification of the foppery and folly of dress and appearance in full feather," according to Hazlitt.

The Provok'd Wife (1697) is Vanbrugh's masterpiece. Lady Brute is married to the cowardly and irascible Lord Brute. She is tempted by Constant, while her niece, Belinda, captures the fancy of Constant's friend, Heartfree. Lady Fanciful, angered by Constant's attentions to Lady Brute, tries to brew mischief, but is foiled. Lady Brute remains faithful to Lord Brute, and Belinda marries Heartfree.

Vanbrugh is on the verge of domestic drama in this play, especially in the great scene where Sir John Brute and Lady Brute bare their mutual antipathy. Sir John Brute, though in no way admirable, is one of the most memorable characters in English drama. The wit of the play is almost equal to that of the great Congreve, and the well-knit plot is the author's best.

William Congreve (1670–1729). William Congreve was born at Bardsey near Leeds. His parents moving shortly thereafter to Ireland, he was educated at Kilkenny (where Swift was a schoolmate) and at Trinity College, Dublin. For Mrs. Bracegirdle, one of the loveliest actresses of the age and the object of his affections, Congreve wrote exceedingly brilliant roles in each of his four plays. His literary fame brought him lucrative government posts, especially the secretaryship of Jamaica from 1714. Reputedly, after his death, another of his flames, the Duchess of Marlborough, had seated at her table a life-size wax automaton resembling Congreve, complete in every detail even to his fashionable ailment of gout.

Before his final masterpiece, Congreve wrote three brilliant comedies: *The Old Bachelor* (1693), which achieved great popularity; *The Double Dealer* (1694); and *Love for Love* (1695), which was very popular in its day and has been revived many times since.

The Way of the World (1700) was termed "the unequalled and unapproached masterpiece of English comedy" by Swinburne, while Lytton Strachey considered it "among the most wonderful and glorious creations of the human mind." It is the unquestioned masterwork of Restoration drama, at least the equal of Molière, to whom it is greatly indebted.

Lady Wishfort, in addition to her own estates, controls the property of Mrs. Fainall, her daughter, and Millamant, her niece. Mrs. Fainall's former lover, Mirabell, is now interested in Millamant. Mirabell disguises his servant Waitwell (already married) as a nobleman, hoping for his marriage to Lady Wishfort. Then, on the threat of telling the world how she was duped, Mirabell can blackmail Lady Wishfort into giving him Millamant and her property.

Learning of his wife's former relations with Mirabell, Fainall threatens full revelation unless all property is signed over to him. The sweethearts, Millamant and Mirabell, come to an agreement, but it appears that their fortunes are ruined. Mirabell, however, produces a deed from Mrs. Fainall before her marriage that conveys all her property to Mirabell. Triumphant in law and in the ways of the world, Mirabell is united to Millamant.

The world of the play's title is the narrow, circumscribed world of St. James's Park, the chocolate house, and the mansion of Lady Wishfort (the three locales of the drama). The way of the world is falseness and pretense, typified by the wholly unloving marriage of the Fainalls. However, Millamant and Mirabell are trying to build a true marriage instead of a feigned one. Congreve and his intelligent pair realize the absurdity of contemplating their union as the romantic heroes and heroines of Shakespeare do theirs. They must accept the realities of the current world. While Millamant has always been chaste, Mirabell has been a rake, but as a more cerebral Dorimant, he shall in the future direct his natural desires within the socially necessary form of marriage. Millamant is one of the greatest women of the stage. She is a wit, a woman of the world, but she is moral, and determined to remain so. Virtually every critic has fallen under her unique spell: a thoroughly captivating worldly-wise woman.

Both Mirabell and Millamant must play the game of the deceitful world to achieve their marriage, and they play it without approval and without protests. They stipulate rational and wholly possible terms for a companionable and genteel marriage partnership.

In their elegant and polite conversations Millamant and Mirabell rise above the badinage of the comedy of manners to the universality of complexity and sadness in human relationships. The fourth act of the drama is usually conceded as one of the finest in the English theater. All the comic themes are drawn together and adroitly clashed with each other, while the climax of the lovers' scene of marriage stipulations remains virtually unequaled. It is remarkable how Congreve employs every hackneyed device of the genre yet lifts the whole to originality and freshness. Yet perhaps the finest aspect of the drama is its language. No other English drama sustains throughout such brisk, sparkling dialogue.

Congreve in 1692 published his novel, *Incognita; or, Love and Duty Reconcil'd,* which he may have written as early as the age of seventeen. It is a brief comedy of errors set in Florence. For a lark, two young men exchange their names, and in the resultant confusion they fall in love with the young ladies their families want them to marry, but the mix-ups from disguise of names result in fearful misunderstandings before the concluding explanation. Needless to say, they are all properly paired at the end of the story.

Colley Cibber (sib'er) (1671–1757). The son of a Danish sculptor practicing in England, Colley Cibber began acting about 1690, and from 1711 to 1732 he was one of the managers of Drury Lane. Because he was a devoted Whig, he was made poet laureate in 1730. His success in the roles of empty-headed fops caused many to brand him as vapid and lent credence to Pope's portrayal of him as a dunce. His autobiography, *Apology for the Life of Mr. Colley Cibber, Comedian* (1740), provides invaluable information on contemporary dramatic life.

Love's Last Shift (1696)—Comedy of Manners. This work is a Restoration comedy for four acts and a "sentimental comedy" in the concluding act.

For eight years Amanda has been separated from her roué husband, Loveless. When her husband returns from abroad, he fails to recognize her. The "shift" is suggested by Young Worthy. Amanda presents herself to Loveless as a mistress, and the next day he is a reformed character, convinced that the happy life can be found only in the arms of a virtuous wife.

Congreve declared that the play "had only in it a great many Things that were like Wit, that were in reality not Wit." Cibber's forte is farce. The audience could enjoy conventional cynicism for most of the drama with a sop to morality at the end. Cibber starred in the role of Sir Novelty Fashion, a foolish fop. Vanbrugh's *The Relapse,* which has already been discussed, was written in the same year as a non-sentimental answer to this play.

George Farquhar (fär'ker) (1678–1707). A clergyman's son, George Farquhar was born in Londonderry, Ireland. After studies at Trinity College, Dublin, he worked as a proofreader and then as an actor. Accidentally wounding a fellow actor, he vowed never to act again. He came to London about 1697 and proved one of the most fertile of contemporary dramatists until his early death in poverty. His wife tricked him into marriage in 1703 on the pretense of being an heiress, but Farquhar apparently harbored no resentment against her.

The Recruiting Officer (1706)—Comedy of Manners. This play may have been based upon the author's brief military experience under the Earl of Orrery during the War of the Spanish Succession.

Sergeant Kite is recruiting at Shrewsbury and also pimping for his superior, Captain Plume. One of the recruits is Sylvia Ballance, in love with the captain and pursuing him disguised as a boy. In the end it is her recruiting that proves successful. Another recruiting officer, Captain Brazen, seeks the wealthy Melinda but is tricked into marrying Melinda's maid.

London is here abandoned for a provincial atmosphere. While the men play at being Restoration rakes, all the characters maintain a vigor and realism alien to the older comedy of manners. The immoral figures and scenes display coarseness rather than insouciant Restoration artificiality. The diversity of events gives the feel of the great world apart from the West End salons. Sylvia is Farquhar's most charming heroine, and Sergeant Kite vies with Captain Bobadil for the title of English drama's best comic soldier. Implicit is the criticism of a selfish, morally weak society.

The Beaux' Stratagem (1707)—Comedy of Manners. This work was the last and most successful play by Farquhar, and he died during its first run.

Aimwell and Archer are the beaux, and their stratagem is to recoup their lost fortunes by marrying rich country girls near Litchfield by means of a complicated imposture. Archer weds Dorinda, daughter of Lady Bountiful. Aimwell almost seduces Mrs. Sullen, but she is saved because a gang of thieves breaks into the house. The heroes subdue the ransackers, and Mrs. Sullen and her churlish husband agree to divorce. Aimwell is to be her next husband.

This play really represents the last of the Restoration comedies of manners. It is conceived in brilliant artificiality, but it is spiced with shrewd realism also. Mrs. Sullen conventionally derogates rural life, but Dorinda skillfully supports the country. Significantly, the heroes must demonstrate courage and honor, not merely fashionable repartee, to emerge victorious. Farquhar has adapted the Restoration man to the tastes of a middle-class audience, which prizes virtue above debonair graces.

Another unique creation in the work is the figure of Lady Bountiful, who is no Lady Wishfort but a kindly, affectionate old woman, foolish only in her attachment to the boorish Sullen, her son. Her name has become a part of the language. Also, a number of the minor characters are delightful: Cherry, the romping daughter of the innkeeper; Scrub, the doltish servant of Sullen; and Gibbet, the glib highwayman. Farquhar shows a lively humanity and a racy gusto.

After Farquhar the comedy of manners withered. A modified form was the "genteel comedy," which substituted social foibles and drawing-room discussions for the wit and bedroom scenes of the earlier drama. This effeminate rococo genre apparently started with Cibber's *The Double Gallant* (1707), but it never produced any memorable works.

Heroic and Neoclassic Tragedy

It seems inconceivable that the audience for the Restoration comedy was the same audience that witnessed the contemporary heroic tragedy. In the comedy we find the rakehell, constantly philandering about London with a bon mot on his lips. In the tragedy we see the superhero, arrayed in gorgeous clothes, enmeshed in the inevitable conflict of exalted, Platonic love with sacred duty. These were the exaggerated and impossible heroics of an essentially unheroic age.

Credit for the standard form of the Restoration heroic tragedy is given by Dryden to Roger Boyle, Earl of Orrery (1621–79), whose *Henry V* was written in 1661–62, first acted in 1664, and published in 1668. The pattern is the theme of love versus honor, placed in grandiose, non-contemporary settings, with rhetorical sentiments spoken in heroic couplets.

Representing the search for balance of a reconstructing society, Restoration drama presented the extremes of baroque in the heroic tragedy and rococo in the comedy of manners. The balance was found in the neoclassic tragedy. The influences were ancient Greek and Latin drama, Jonson's tragedies, and especially the classic 17th-century French plays. Again Roger Boyle, in unperformed dramas he had written in the 1660's, apparently gave the cue for the neoclassic tragedy.

In essence, the 17th-century neoclassic drama maintained many of the conventions of the heroic tragedy: the theme of love versus honor, the great heroic figure, and the resounding rhetoric. It differed from this drama chiefly in emphasizing: (1) locales of classic Greece or Rome or more familiar continental locales as against the exotic Orient and elsewhere of the heroic tragedy; (2) characterization and plotting more approximating plausibility; (3) observance of the "rules" (unities of time, place, and action; decorum); and (4) blank verse instead of heroic couplets. The English neoclassic drama never went as far as the great contemporary French classic drama of Racine and Corneille except in a stilted attempt like Thomas Rymer's *Edgar; or the English Monarch* (1678), which was never acted.

John Dryden (1631–1700). Dryden wrote the most memorable of the heroic tragedies, and was, indeed, the most accomplished tragedian of the age in both the heroic and the neoclassic tragedy. His nondramatic works are discussed earlier in the chapter.

The Indian Queen (*1664*, pub. 1665)—Heroic Tragedy. John Dryden and Sir Robert Howard (1626–98), Dryden's brother-in-law, wrote this work jointly. It was performed six months before Boyle's drama, and actually set the stage tradition for heroic tragedy. The play attempts to exemplify Dryden's definition: "an heroic play ought to be an imitation, in little, of an heroic poem; and, consequently . . . love and valour ought to be the subject of it." Source of the work is *Polexandre* (1629), by Gomberville; such "heroic romances" in French were one of the chief influences upon the English heroic drama.

Montezuma, a general serving the Peruvian Inca, has soundly defeated the Mexicans. Rebuffed when seeking the hand of Orazia, the Inca's daughter, he leads the Mexicans against his former troops, scores a sensational victory, and captures both the Inca and Orazia. Complications develop as the usurping queen of Mexico, Zempoalla, falls in love with Montezuma, and Traxalla, Zempoalla's general, is smitten with Orazia. After inflated disquisitions on love and honor, the real queen of Mexico appears, Amexia, who turns out to be Montezuma's mother. Conveniently ennobled, the hero marries Orazia while all lesser characters perish.

As always in this genre, the primary consideration was spectacle; *The Indian Queen* luxuriated in lavishly colorful costumes and wildly exotic backdrops—all bizarrely non-authentic. The remoteness of the settings permitted bombastic histrionics that would have been palpably absurd in Pall Mall. The characters are in fact altogether too grand and grandiloquent for viewers to identify with. There is no character development, and a notable feature of this type of tragedy is the customary survival of the main pair of lovers while the corpses of lesser characters litter the stage. When Pepys witnessed this play, he praised it as "a most pleasant show, and beyond my expectation."

The popularity of *The Indian Queen* induced Dryden alone to prepare a sequel, *The Indian Emperor*, in the next year. The desirability of another display of the magnificent garments and sumptuous backdrops was also a strong incitement to the sequel. Dryden recognized the difficulty of undertaking a sequel, pointing out that from the previous drama there survived "but two of the considerable Characters alive."

The Conquest of Granada by the Spaniards (*1670*, pub. 1672) —Heroic Tragedy. Of the five rimed heroic tragedies by Dryden himself, this may be the greatest and, as T. S. Eliot contends, the masterpiece of the genre. It was possibly influenced by Madeleine de Scudéry's *Almahide*.

In 1491 the last Moorish stronghold in Spain is being besieged. The weak Moorish king of Granada, Boabdelin, can hardly control his own quarreling subjects. The scheming Lyndaraxa, ambitious to be queen (Nell Gwyn enacted the role!), is fomenting trouble when Almanzor mysteriously appears to unite the Granadans against the Spaniards. Lyndaraxa promises to wed Abdalla if he will kill his brother, Boabdelin. Boabdelin's weakness causes him to be unjust to Almanzor, who therefore sides with Abdalla to cast out the king. Boabdelin's betrothed, Almahide, attracts both Almanzor and Zulema, Lyndaraxa's brother. When the usurping Abdalla favors Zulema's suit, Almanzor brings back Boabdelin, and Abdalla must flee to the Spanish camp. Boabdelin will not grant his own betrothed to Almanzor, who thereupon sadly goes into exile.

All the features of the heroic tragedy are here, from exotic scenery to grand oratory about love and honor, but Dryden does rise above these conventions to something approximating romantic poetic drama. His story concerns what historically was the last dying gasp of medieval chivalry, and Dryden senses those days of expiring grandeur. There is some real poetry and some generation of real sympathy for Almanzor. In its portrayal of a heroic figure trapped by love, this play parallels Restoration comedy, for Almanzor's love is physical as well as Platonic. The drama itself and its prefatory "Essay of Heroique Plays" constitute the best justification for the genre. In *Almanzor and Almahide* (*1671*, pub. 1672) the lovers are finally united.

Aureng-Zebe (*1675*, pub. 1676)—Heroic Tragedy. This work was Dryden's last heroic tragedy. It was derived from François Bernier's

Histoire, and, remotely, the account deals with the contemporary Mongol emperors of India. In the prologue Dryden declared himself "weary of his long-lov'd Mistris, Rhyme." The play displays far less bombast than most of its fellows, and the rimed couplet is treated with greater freedom than in previous Dryden dramas.

All for Love; or, The World Well Lost (1678)—Neoclassic Tragedy. John Dryden admits in the preface to this work that "the unities of time, place, and action are more exactly observed than perhaps the English theatre requires." While endeavoring to imitate the ancients, he believes their models too meager for English tragedy, which calls for greater compass. While he admires the meticulous French, he considers them lacking in the genius animating the English stage. Dryden professes to emulate "the divine Shakespeare," and, "to perform more freely," he discards the heroic couplet in favor of blank verse.

Dryden compresses the familiar Antony and Cleopatra story into action covering a few hours, and presents all scenes in Alexandria. Shakespeare's Ventidius and Enobarbus are condensed into one character, Ventidius, who is the voice of honor and duty. The acts move with mechanical precision. In the first, Ventidius rouses the lovelorn Antony to martial valor, but the glamorous, enticing Cleopatra turns the tables in the next. The mounting tension of the succeeding acts climaxes with Antony's sacrifice of all for the Eygptian beauty. Unlike Shakespeare, Dryden times Antony's death just shortly before Cleopatra's death and final curtain. Octavius and in fact all characters unessential to the love and honor theme are excluded.

No dramatist can outdo Shakespeare on his own ground, for not even the Dryden mastery of language can match the Bard's majesty. However, no other play upon a Shakespearean theme comes as close to rivalry as Dryden's does. Dryden's Antony is no "bully" from the heroic tragedy but a convincing man caught in the tangles of love, a love he knows is unwise but which he cannot escape. Bluff, direct Ventidius is a great Roman without any statuesque quality, a characterization Shakespeare would have admired. Dryden's Cleopatra has all the loveliness and grandeur of womanhood, but she is not the volatile and developing heroine of Shakespeare. Comparison is unfair, for the romantic tragedy of the Renaissance is a world away from the concentrated, perfectly tailored and symmetrical neoclassicism of the Restoration. The Dryden play is a masterpiece of its type and perhaps the greatest English tragedy in the period following the Renaissance.

Marriage-à-la-Mode (c. *1672,* pub. 1673)—Comedy. This play is a strange mixture of Spanish intrigue and Fletcher tragicomedy. This type derived essentially from the plays of the Spanish playwright Calderón, and emphasized ingenious reversals. With lesser dramatists this genre often degenerated to farce. Although Dryden thought comedy to be "inferior to all other sorts of dramatic writing," he was influential in shaping the comedy of manners. Among his own comedies he preferred *Marriage-à-la-Mode.*

In Sicily, Rhodophil, bored with his wife Doralice, seeks Melantha as a mistress. His friend Palamede returns home to wed an unknown bride (Melantha, as one would suspect), but is infatuated with Doralice. The double intrigue is constantly in danger of discovery, but all works out to unite the proper parties. In the sub-plot the shepherd Leonidas, in love with the shepherdess Palmyra, is proclaimed the long-lost prince of Sicily and ordered to marry the aristocratic Amalthea. After suitable mix-ups of identity, Leonidas is proved an actual king (not the prince) and Palmyra is a genuine princess. True lovers are joined together.

The sub-plot of "love and honor" is not well dovetailed with the main plot, and its plea for "reformation" is not very convincing. The main plot is cleverly handled, with witty dialogue. The chief characters speak and act by the code of the comedy of manners.

The powerful influence of Beaumont and Fletcher insured the continued writing of tragicomedy. Most of these works are hardly distinguishable from the heroic tragedy except for the absence of corpses. Four of Dryden's plays fall into this category, and his last drama, *Love Triumphant; or, Nature Will Prevail* (1694) was a tragicomedy.

Thomas Otway (1652–1685). Born at Trotton, Sussex, Thomas Otway was educated at Westminster School and Oxford. His first play, *Alcibiades* (1675), gained him the attention of Lord Rochester and caused him to fall in love with the leading lady, the beautiful Mrs. Barry. Otway's chagrin when Mrs. Barry became Rochester's mistress impelled him to enlist with British troops in Holland, 1678–79. Returning to London, he wrote his masterpiece with its great acting role for his idol, Mrs. Barry. His death is variously attributed to starvation or liquor.

Venice Preserved; or, A Plot Discovered (1682)—Neoclassic Tragedy. This play takes its account from César Vichard's *Le Conjuration des Espagnols contre Vénise* (1674, translated 1675), but, like

Dryden's *Absalom and Achitophel,* the work is really an attack directed at Shaftesbury.

Venetian Senator Priuli bitterly resents the elopement of his daughter Belvidera with Jaffeir. Jaffeir, thus slighted, joins the conspiracy against Venice, pledging his wife as evidence of his good faith. One of the conspirators, the villainous Renault, attacks her, but she escapes. She persuades Jaffeir to reveal the plot on the condition that the conspirators will not be slain. When the plotters (including Jaffeir's noble and faithful friend Pierre) are tried and condemned to death, Jaffeir is agonizingly self-reproachful and threatens Belvidera's life unless she can induce her father to intercede for the condemned men. She fulfills the mission, but too late. In a corruscating finale, Jaffeir commits suicide, and Belvidera goes mad and then dies of a broken heart.

With this play, English drama marks an end and a beginning. *Venice Preserved* has the last touches of the Renaissance poetic fire in verse and characterization. Jaffeir is the last of the heroic figures torn between love and honor, and the tearing is shrewdly and realistically plotted. The psychological complexity and penetration of the work quite exceed that of Dryden's *All for Love.* Otway's concern is for man's capacity for feeling, especially for self-torture, and the most powerful scenes are detailed analyses of emotional entanglement. The essential domesticity of the tragedy foreshadows the 18th-century drama. It is not the revolt against tyranny but marital and filial love that dominate the play. Belvidera is one of the great heroines of the English drama, strong in affection, personality, and character. Neoclassic elements are admittedly meager, but the spirit of heroic tragedy as well as its form has been thoroughly eliminated.

Nathaniel Lee (c. 1653–1692). Nathaniel Lee had an obscure origin, though we know that he studied at Westminster School and Cambridge. After college graduation in 1668, he delighted Lords Buckingham and Rochester with his striking appearance and gifted speech, but nervousness caused his failure as an actor. For his second play, *Sophonisba* (1675), Purcell wrote music for the stage for the first time. Madness (a favorite subject in Lee's plays) seized the dramatist in 1684 and compelled his confinement until 1689. His death was supposedly from intoxication. Another play, *Oedipus (1678,* pub. 1679), is a transitional piece, essentially heroic drama but with the appearance of classicism.

The Rival Queens; or, The Death of Alexander the Great (1677)— Neoclassic Tragedy. This work derives chiefly from Sir Charles Cotterell's translation (1652) of *Cassandre,* by La Calprenède, with additional help from other classical historians.

Alexander, conqueror of the world, is the object of contention between his first wife, Roxana, and his second wife, Statira, but evil portents will not frighten the egotistical monarch. Roxana stabs Statira, and Cassander (one of a group of conspirators) poisons Alexander. The mighty ruler expires after a titanic mad scene.

The many good acting roles of this drama insured its popularity on the English stage even into the 19th century. The men are all manly and martial, and the women are wildly passionate. In its frenetic spirit this is certainly not a neoclassical play, but it marks the transition between the heroic and the neoclassical drama. Blank verse here supplants heroic couplets, the figures are historical and classical, the "rules" are generally observed, and the love-versus-honor theme is not the central plot. Platonic love, an inevitable factor in heroic tragedy, is overpowered by swelling passion in *The Rival Queens.* With all its inflation, the drama captures the feel of a Greek youth intoxicated with Oriental splendor and a sense of his own might. Later versions of the drama interpolated the famous song "See the conquering hero come" in the second act.

George Villiers, Duke of Buckingham (1628–1687). George Villiers, with Martin Clifford, Thomas Sprat, and possibly Samuel Butler, fashioned in 1663 a ludicrous burlesque of the pompous heroic tragedy. Davenant and Sir Robert Howard were the chief targets then. The script circulated in manuscript for the amusement of the court and London literati. Over the intervening years, Dryden emerged as the greatest practitioner of heroic tragedy, and in 1671 his play *The Conquest of Granada* caused the chief ridicule of the burlesque to be directed against him. Actually at least seventeen contemporary dramas are "hit" at one place or another, but today's reader will find them all quite obscure except for Dryden's works.

The Rehearsal (1671, pub. 1672) is one of the greatest mock-heroic dramas of the English stage, with no prior equal except Beaumont's *Knight of the Burning Pestle.*

City man Johnson takes his country visitor Smith to a stage rehearsal for a new play by Mr. Bayes (Dryden as poet laureate wearing the bays). Part of the humor arises from the wry comments of Johnson and Smith, but most of it springs from the burlesque of the heroic drama of Bayes. The plot is so horribly complex and confused that the actors cannot follow it. Fancy costuming, scenery, and dances are Bayes's chief concerns; for pieces of dramatic writing, he simply plagiarizes from his fellow playwrights. Bravura speeches pop up without warning or motivation. The love-and-honor conflict is mocked in a long formal debate by an actor about which boot should go on first. There are some cruel satires of Dryden's own verses, and Almanzor (from *Conquest of Granada*) is satirized as the farcical Drawcansir. Eventually everyone walks out on Mr. Bayes in disgust.

All the weak aspects of the heroic tragedy are gaily lampooned: the fantastically inflated speeches, the comparisons stretched to the breaking point, the lack of probability and verisimilitude, the quibbling over minutiae, and the interminable baroque debates between love and honor. The "Zimri" of *Absalom and Achitophel* devastates at least six plays of Dryden in wild parody. The heroic tragedy was not crushed by this sally, but, as proof of the burlesque's intrinsic delight, it survived on the English stage well into the 18th century, after the heroic tragedy had itself died out.

The Beginning of English Opera

The late 17th century was the most active period in the history of opera composed in English, and with *Psyche* (1675), Shadwell inaugurated the main line of 17th-century English opera. This work went one step further than the heroic tragedy and exploited the unreal world of mythology and classic legend. Dryden contributed such operas as *Albion and Albanius* (1685) and *King Arthur* (1691), but the greatest of the English operas with the previously mentioned *Dido and Aeneas* (1689), with music by Henry Purcell and libretto by Nahum Tate. As Dryden stated in the preface to *Albion and Albanius,* the proper figures in opera were to be "supernatural, as Gods and Goddesses, and Heroes which at least are descended from them, and are in due time to be adopted into their number." Scenic effects for such spectacles outdid even the heroic tragedy; in addition to sumptuous backdrops, elaborate machines were necessary for the effects of characters flying about the stage or mysteriously appearing and disappearing.

William Davenant (or **D'Avenant**) (dăv′e-nent) (1606–1668). The one significant bridge between Renaissance and Restoration drama is William Davenant. Once thought to have been the natural son of Shakespeare, he was almost certainly the son of an Oxford innkeeper. During his second year (1662) in Lincoln College his father died, and Davenant entered the service of the Duchess of Richmond and later that of Fulke Greville. He composed masques for the royal court and, in 1638, succeeded Jonson as poet laureate. During the civil wars he supported the royalist cause and was forced to flee to France. Setting out in 1650 on a diplomatic mission to America for the exiled Stuarts, Davenant was captured by an English ship and languished in jail for some time. After his release, he privately produced shows in noble houses. The dramas he wrote before the closing of the theaters are discussed in a companion volume to this book which treats English literature to 1660.

Davenant's unfinished epic poem *Gondibert* (1651) is not intrinsically important, but its grandiose effects of ethical magnificence and poetic justice herald the baroque heroic tragedy to follow. In heroic quatrains this epic dwells upon the contest of love and ambition as Lombard princes Gondibert and Oswald vie for the hand of Princess Rhodalind.

Siege of Rhodes was the prototype of the heroic tragedy as well as its own specific genre, the English opera. It opened after the Restoration in 1661 and was long included in the repertoire. The theme is typically love versus honor, and the main characters are the grandiloquent Turk, Soliman the Magnificent, and the Sicilian Duke Alphonso, both of whom are within the besieged Rhodes. Heroic couplets are used extensively with lyric measures interwoven.

During the 1660's much of Shakespeare's work was turned into opera, Dryden and Davenant co-operating in 1667 to produce an operatic version of *The Tempest*.

OTHER POETRY OF THE PERIOD

Verse Satire

Theoretically this era considered the greatest literary genres to be tragic drama and epic poetry. Dryden and Otway indeed succeeded in tragic drama, but in spite of some woeful attempts, this period and the following age never produced a notable epic. After Milton the heroic age was dead. Inverted heroism in poetry was inevitable, and the age found its natural level in satire. Dryden justified satire as a sort of epical, heroic verse. The Ages of Dryden and Pope are the pre-eminent epochs of English satire.

Charles Cotton (1630–1687). Charles Cotton was born at Beresford, Staffordshire. He is best known for his continuation of Walton's *Com-*

pleat Angler (fifth edition, 1676) and his translation of Montaigne's *Essays* (1685).

Scarronides; or, The First Book of Virgil Travestie (1664; addition of the fourth book in 1670) was closely patterned after the *Virgile Travesti* (1648) of Paul Scarron. Travesty is a low, specific burlesque that closely follows the subject matter of a grand and serious work but treats it in vulgar fashion. A little of this kind of humor is amusing, but the late 17th century and most of the 18th century could enjoy astonishingly lengthy doses of line-by-line travesties of literary monuments. Apparently an unheroic age incapable of producing the great epic found compensation in mockery of the classic epics it most admired.

Samuel Butler (1612–1680). Born at Strensham, Worcestershire, Samuel Butler was educated at King's School, Worcester. During the Commonwealth he was employed by the Presbyterian Sir Samuel Luke. In 1661 he was steward of Ludlow Castle for the Earl of Carbery, Lord President of Wales. He is eulogized upon his monument for plucking "the mask from pious hypocrisy."

Hudibras (Part I, 1663; Part II, 1664; Part III, 1678) is an unfinished series of over ten thousand lines of rollicking doggerel in rough octosyllabics.

Part I tells of the epic struggle of Presbyterian colonel Hudibras and his squire Ralpho, an Independent in religion, to stop bear-baiting in a "western" town. After initial triumphs, they are bested and cast in prison. Hudibras becomes enamored with the desirable real estate of a widow and vows to gain her hand.

Parts II and III relate the woeful misadventures of Hudibras in trying to win the widow. He has a memorable battle royal with a Rosicrucian seer, Sidrophel, and is universally pummeled and humiliated.

But the story is unimportant. It is nothing but the flimsiest framework for blistering attacks upon the Puritans, including irreverent portraits, wildly comic imbroglios, and crude buffoonery. Cocking an eye at *The Faerie Queene,* Butler limns a burlesque knight (often thought to be Sir Samuel Luke but undoubtedly broader in application) who is the epitome of Hypocrisy. All human sins and follies manifest themselves as sub-species of hypocrisy. The meter, diction, and style of the work combine in "diminution," the picturing of everything about the Puritans in the most undignified fashion possible; the reader's inevitable response toward the victim is utter contempt. Topically, the satire caught the Restoration man-in-the-street's desire for humorous sallies against the vanquished Roundheads. But to the learned, it had and still has brilliant sallies against theological logic-chopping, pedantry, the absurdity of some of the New Science, and all forms of fanaticism. Butler's mastery has since caused *hudibrastics* to become a generic term for the use of doggerel verse (octosyllabic couplets) in a low general burlesque, imitating not a specific work, as travesty does, but a whole category of pretentious writings, which are treated in a vulgarized manner. The name of Hudibras is derived from *The Faerie Queene*, that of Ralpho from *The Knight of the Burning Pestle*. Don Quixote and Sancho Panza are distant models, and, like Cervantes, Butler laughs away the world of heroism and chivalric pretense in one of literature's greatest comic poems.

The General Remains in Prose and Verse of Mr. Samuel Butler (*1668*, 1759) contains "The Elephant in the Moon," a verse satire upon the Royal Society and the New Science. Butler reveals himself as a strange combination, a complete conservative and a complete skeptic. Also included in this work are satiric prose "characters" in the tradition of Sir Thomas Overbury and John Earle. Withering are the portraits of "The Quaker," "A Modern Politician," "The Henpect Man."

John Oldham (1653–1683). Born at Shipton Moyne, Gloucestershire, John Oldham was educated at Tetbury Grammar School and Oxford. Poems he wrote while teaching at Croydon School attracted the attention of Rochester, who helped set up Oldham as a London wit. His premature death was caused by smallpox.

Satyrs upon the Jesuits (1681) was a great topical success during the furor over the "Popish Plot." Oldham's heroic couplets constitute a dramatic monologue supporting Whig and Protestant viewpoints against Tories and Roman Catholics. Graceful, neatly constructed, and occasionally quite witty, this work established Oldham as the age's greatest formal satirist next to Dryden, in contrast to the informal slapdash of Cotton and Butler.

Court Poetry

Butler and Oldham were condescendingly patronized as "professional" poets by the courtiers. Gentlemen of the court, heirs of the Cavalier poets, still produced amateur verse as a sign of their gentility. This was the last age when graceful poetic accomplishments were considered an aristocratic perquisite.

John Wilmot, second **Earl of Rochester** (1647–1680). Born at Ditchley, Oxfordshire, John Wilmot succeeded his father to the earldom at eleven and started writing verse at thirteen. After wide travels in Europe and a spell of fighting the Dutch in 1665, he joined a notorious circle of Restoration rakes, including Sedley, Dorset, and Buckingham. Despite his youth, Rochester was famed as the most dissolute man of his era. Also famed as a wit and satirist, he proved a fickle patron to several poets, including Dryden. Debauchery brought him to an early death. A sizable portion of his poetry is obscene, and apparently none of his verse was authorized for publication. Rochester was several times banished from the court because of his blunt and filthy political satire against Charles II, royal advisers, and royal mistresses; but the brilliant wit was always quickly pardoned. His printable lyrics show all the skill, grace, and artificiality of the Cavalier poets. Had he lived, his mastery of the heroic couplet and his searching intellectuality might have made him one of England's notable poets.

Satyr against Mankind (*1675,* 1679) is the fullest expounding in English of "theriophily," i.e. theoretical intellectual belief in animals' superiority to man. Instead of the Renaissance pride in mental powers, Rochester, completely skeptical of reason, proclaims man the most stupid of creatures. Man is more murderous and cruel than other animals, his highly cherished reason only leads him into errors, and beasts possess true wisdom instead of man's folly. Instinct provides a moderate self-sufficiency for animals that is impossible in "reasoning" man. The source seems to be Boileau's Eighth Satire with suggestion also from Montaigne.

Upon Nothing (1711) is the ultimate expression in English of cynicism and skepticism at the expense of all sober and self-important philosophers and theologians. Rochester carries the skeptical materialism of Hobbes to its logical conclusion of nullity and meaninglessness. Dr. Johnson termed this his lordship's "strongest effort," perhaps sensing that such profound pessimism could well turn a powerful intellect toward fideism. This might account for Rochester's famed conversion just five weeks before his death.

In "Allusion to Horace's 10th Satyr of the First Book," Rochester produced the first significant example of what would be common poetic practice for over a century. Broadly imitating a classic work, he modernizes it by extensive contemporary allusions. Rochester defends Jonson and Shakespeare against detractors, praises Etherege and Butler as well as his fellow court poets, but refuses to be "blindly partial" to Dryden.

Sir Charles Sedley (1639–1701). Sir Charles Sedley took an active role in Restoration politics and a hectic role in Restoration debauchery. He wrote several plays that were well received at the time but that have since been virtually forgotten. Rochester usurped Sedley's position as the most disreputable man in London, but Rochester and posterity had to agree that Sedley was the master of *vers de société*. He transformed this type of verse from the gay Cavalier freedom to the artificial lilt and gaiety of the salon and drawing room. His collected poems in 1702 established him as one of the very best light poets of the 17th century.

Charles Sackville, Baron Buckhurst, sixth **Earl of Dorset,** first **Earl of Middlesex** (1638–1706). Charles Sackville was a friend and patron of poets such as Dryden and Prior. His caustic satire induced Rochester to term him "the best Good Man with the worst-natur'd Muse." Time, however, has remembered him almost solely for "Song Written at Sea" (1664), a rollicking piece of light verse.

John Sheffield, third **Earl of Mulgrave,** first **Duke of Buckingham and Normanby** (1648–1721). John Sheffield experienced a stormy political life but displayed for the era remarkable freedom from indecency in his writings. His prose *Essay on Satire* (1679) was mistakenly ascribed to Dryden, who consequently suffered a street assault from Rochester's bullies. His heroic couplet *Essay upon Poetry* (1682) foreshadows in viewpoint but not in technical skill the *Essay on Criticsm* by Pope. Sheffield also amused himself in his free moments from guiding the national destiny by inditing facile society verse.

Wentworth Dillon, fourth **Earl of Roscommon** in Ireland (c. 1633–1685). Wentworth Dillon was unstained by the scandal associated with his fellow peers. In 1680 he translated Horace's *Ars Poetica* into blank verse. In *Essay on Translated Verse,* in heroic couplets, he formulated the concept of "poetic diction" more fully expounded and exemplified in the next century. He is famed as the first critic to praise *Paradise Lost.*

PROSE WRITINGS OF THE LATER SEVENTEENTH CENTURY

The essay had not as yet developed into a major form of expression in this age, and the literary criticism was mainly based on neoclassic principles, the chief proponent of which was Thomas Rymer. Jeremy Collier, however, concentrated his attack on the current improprieties of the public stage. The Elizabethan tradition of prose fiction developed by Lyly, Greene, Nashe, Sidney, and others had died out by the latter part of the 17th century, to be replaced by the influence of the contemporary French prose romance. Mrs. Aphra Behn was the only notable practitioner of this form. However, the real emergence of the novel together with a discussion of all its sources will be treated in a later chapter devoted exclusively to that subject.

In the realm of private papers and diaries, the most commanding figure of the age is the inimitable Samuel Pepys. It is chiefly from his diary that we obtain an extremely minute view of the life of that period and also an up-to-that-time unparalleled revelation of the inner thoughts of a fellow human being. The other diaries and histories of this time, while not nearly so self-revealing as Pepys's, nevertheless do present a wide and detailed picture of contemporary life.

While the religious writings of the era did not produce a major work, the fields of physical science and speculative philosophy were represented by two of England's greatest prodigies, Isaac Newton and John Locke.

Literary Criticism, Essays, and Prose Fiction

Thomas Rymer (1641–1713). Thomas Rymer was called to the bar at Gray's Inn (1673). In 1692 he succeeded Shadwell as historiographer royal. His greatest achievement was *Foedera,* a monumental compilation of English historical documents in twenty volumes, finally completed and published in 1735. Romantics tended to see the neoclassic critic as a cold rationalist, mercilessly insistent upon the strict observance of the "rules." However, the only such critic in English history was Rymer, who went to the logical extreme that some contemporary French critics espoused. No other English critic ever went so far.

The Tragedies of the Last Age (1677) and *Short View of Tragedy* (1692) insist that "Reason" should wholly govern poetic fancy: "Those who object against reason are the Fanatics of poetry, are never to be saved by their good works." Hence, proclaims Rymer, in Spenser's *Faerie Queene* "all is fanciful and chimerical, without any uniformity, without any foundation in truth; his poem is perfect Fairy-land." Only Rymer and George Bernard Shaw (the latter more facetiously than seriously) among English critics have roundly denounced Shakespeare. In the *Short View,* Rymer, wholly literal and prosaic, finds of *Othello* "the tragical part plainly none other than a Bloody Farce, without salt or savour." Rigorously intent upon "decorum" that always paints soldiers as "open-hearted, frank, plain-dealing," Rymer condemns the character of Iago as "against common sense and Nature." Butler in verse and Dryden in prose (preface to *All for Love*) contested Rymer's severity. Yet this limited critic practically inaugurated the detailed study of literary texts and invented the famous phrase "poetical justice," with all its connotations of wrenching reality to make everything turn out as if devised by an ideal world. Though now a curiosity, Rymer was a potent critical force for over a century.

Jeremy Collier (1650–1726). Jeremy Collier was a Nonjuring cleric, one who refused to take the oath of allegiance to William and Mary after 1688. He suffered persecution and imprisonment, being branded an outlaw in 1696. In 1713 he was consecrated a bishop by the Nonjurors, a sect that became extinct later in the 18th century.

Short View of the Immorality and Profaneness of the English Stage (1698) takes its title and its spirit from Rymer, but it is even less able to discriminate art from life. Collier assumes that whenever a debauchee or criminal is portrayed in writings or on the stage, it is *ipso facto* a glorification of debauchery and crime. Any slighting reference to a clergyman piques him, and he forbids the mention of any church or of the Bible (Foppington's "Sunday is a vile day," from Vanbrugh's *Relapse,* made Collier indignant) in a comedy. The strictures on the theater's indecencies carry much truth, but the contemporary stage was already itself eliminating much of the bawdy. Dryden admitted that Collier had "taxed him justly" at points, but in doing so, he had displayed a narrow, rancorous mind and a desire to reduce literature to the efficacy of sugar candy.

Sir William Temple (1628–1699). A native Londoner, Sir William Temple, one of the notable essayists of the period, was educated at Cambridge under Cudworth. Traveling in France, he met the beautiful and intelligent Dorothy Osborne in 1648, and he married her in 1654. After service in the Irish Parliament, Temple pursued a distinguished diplomatic career from 1665 until 1681, negotiating many of England's significant treaties and alliances, and arranging in 1677 for the union of William and Mary. In 1681 he voluntarily retired to devote his remaining life to study and writing. From 1689 his secretary was Jonathan Swift.

Though not a profound thinker, Temple is stimulating, especially as another pioneer of "modern" style. With an editor's exaggeration Swift declared: "This author has advanced our English tongue to as great perfection as it can well bear." Dr. Johnson extolled Temple as "the first writer who gave cadence to English prose." Lamb termed his style "plain, natural chit-chat," which is closer to a just evaluation of Temple's easy, unaffected, lucid phrasing.

"Essay upon the Original and Nature of Government" (*1672*, 1680) objected to the social-contract theory of Hobbes and Locke, theorizing, as many modern thinkers do, that national governments arose as extensions of paternal and patriarchal rule.

"Upon Ancient and Modern Learning" (1690) introduced England to the quarrel then raging in France of "the ancients vs. the moderns." Not until the dazzling regime of the "Sun King," Louis XIV, were voices of Western society raised, like that of Charles Perrault, to claim that modern culture could equal or surpass that of antiquity. Temple's essay favoring the ancients is not notable for its content, for he was not that conversant with classical literature. Immediately, however, by his off-hand praise of the *Letters of Phalaris*, he prodded Richard Bentley (1662–1742) to study the ancient work and, in Bentley's *Dissertation on the Epistles of Phalaris* (1697), proving the epistles spurious, to produce the first great piece of textual scholarship in English. Later Temple's position was to be espoused in *The Battle of the Books* (1704), by Swift. Temple's significant pronouncement in the essay is his denial of the idea of progress, when the idea was first gaining credence in England. He believed in the existence of a cyclical pattern of physical and historic change; man and his essential problems were, are, and will remain fundamentally unaltered and unchanged.

"Upon the Gardens of Epicurus; or, Of Gardening" (*1685*, 1690) is a most persuasive and ingratiating picture of the joys of retirement, the simple pleasures of rural life, and the preoccupation with the eternal rhythm of growing things. Of course, it is a wealthy gentleman farmer, not a dirt farmer, who speaks. Perhaps no one else in English is so much the epitome of gracious, respectable Epicureanism. The development of English gardens for several generations was influenced by this essay.

Memoirs (1692) was the first significant work in a now familiar genre: the record of great national and international affairs considered in retirement by a notable public figure who was instrumental in their development. As always, Temple is distinguished by easy grace and dignified, cadenced prose. Apparently this work was motivated by a desire to gain English sympathy for King William. The other memoirs and histories of this period will be discussed later in this chapter.

Sir George Savile, Marquis Of Halifax (1633–1695). Halifax was famed as the most intellectual courtier of his age. He served on numerous diplomatic missions and held many high offices. He was one of the leading figures to support William and Mary against James II. Throughout troubled times he was the prime example of moderation. Dryden saw his literary virtues as "piercing wit and pregnant thought." We might also note his bland, easy manner and his epigrammatic effectiveness. Instead of the personal tone and discursiveness of Cowley and Temple, Savile speaks generally from a distance, always to the point.

The New-Year's-Gift: or, Advice to a Daughter (1688, fifteen editions by 1765) is sage counsel to a young lady in the midst of a naughty world. Halifax is not asking a reform of the way of the world but urges keeping one's integrity amidst its pitfalls. Here a nubile daughter may learn how best to deal with improper advances and later, if need be, with a willful and drunken husband.

The Character of a Trimmer (1688) was induced by an attack upon Halifax in *The Observator* (1684). The periodical sneeringly labeled Halifax as a "trimmer," trimming his position as expedient to circumstances. In a pamphlet long circulating in manuscript, Halifax made the term one of praise. Here is the justification of the Revolution of 1688 and, more broadly, the classic avowal of the English confidence in moderation and reasonable compromise. In a smiling and witty finale, Halifax asserts that from climate to laws England is naturally a Trimmer.

The Character of King Charles II (*1685*, 1750) may be the ultimate in the 17th-century "Characters." All aspects of the Merry Monarch are dissected without rancor or omission. Always moderate, Halifax does not ask human conduct to be impossibly righteous; rather, he is acid where applicable, laudatory where permissible.

Mrs. Aphra Behn ("The Incomparable Astrea") (af'ra bāne) **(1640–1689).** Aphra Behn also spelled her first name "Afra," "Aphara," and "Ayfara"; and her statements about her career are equally various and more dubious. Her maiden name (Amis or Johnson) is not certain, and questionable also is her claim to residence in Surinam during her youth. Marriage to a Dutch merchant, Behn, was a brief experience c. 1658. She claimed to have spied for Charles II in Antwerp during the Dutch war, without adequate recognition or recompense from English authorities. What is sure is her authorship of fifteen plays between 1671 and 1689, in which her propensity for obscenity equals that of her male competitors. She wrote poetry as well, but it was from drama and prose fiction that she was able to achieve the distinction of being the first woman in English history to make her living by the pen. Her high-sounding nickname, which she used as a signature for her dispatches as a spy, was taken from the heroic romances that she emulated in several volumes, but her one claim to fame is:

Oroonoko; or, The Royal Slave (1688), presented as fact, the Surinam portions supposedly experienced by the narrator. The eyewitness presentation and realistic details give an unprecedented air of authenticity to an English fiction.

Negro prince Oroonoko of Coromantien marries the lovely Imoinda, but his lecherous grandfather, the King, forces Imoinda into the royal harem. When Oroonoko secretly visits his wife, the King sells Imoinda into slavery and tells Oroonoko that she is dead. Kidnaped by an English merchantman, Oroonoko is sold as a slave to a Dutch master in Surinam. There he finds Imoinda, whom he thought dead. Rather than see their child born in slavery, Oroonoko leads a rebellion of the slaves. The craven slaves desert when their masters counterattack. Oroonoko surrenders when promised no punishment, but the white Governor goes back on his pledged word. Oroonoko manages to decapitate Imoinda rather than have her ravished. Stoically he endures living dismemberment.

Thomas Southerne dramatized this novel in 1696, and it inaugurated for English the "Noble Savage" theme in the novel. This primitivistic concept of the savage's superiority to civilized man was to reoccur throughout hundreds of 18th- and 19th-century works. The simple but exemplary Negro would shortly be reintroduced in *Robinson Crusoe* and much later would appear in *Uncle Tom's Cabin*. Humanitarianism was to employ Oroonoko in the fight against slavery.

Famous Diaries, Letters, Memoirs, and Histories

Samuel Pepys (pēps or peps, pips, pep'is) (1633–1703). Born the son of a London tailor, Samuel Pepys studied at St. Paul's School and Cambridge. After an impetuous courtship, in 1655 he married a penniless French beauty, Elizabeth St. Michel. Through his able cousin, Sir Edward Montagu, Pepys started a bureaucratic climb in the naval service that brought him to the secretaryship of the Admiralty in 1673. He has often been termed the "savior of the Navy," having rejuvenated it from its lowest depths since the Middle Ages. From 1684 to 1686 he was president of the Royal Society. With the accession of William and Mary in 1689, Pepys was shorn of all his posts. His later years of retirement were partially spent in philanthropy. To his alma mater, Magdalene College, Cambridge, he bequeathed his library of three thousand volumes. In the bequest was a manuscript diary in code that remained neglected until the 19th century.

Diary (published in 1825 in abbreviated form; never fully published because of some lurid passages) was written in the shorthand system of Thomas Shelton's *Tachygraphy* (1639). In its cryptic cypher that was never intended for public perusal, it is the frankest and most revealing diary of all times. Almost daily entries totaling 1,300,000 words cover the period from January 1, 1660, until May 31, 1669, when failing eyesight forced the diarist to break off.

In the opening pages the diary emphasizes the great news of the world, and in the sweep of the work are unique eye-witness accounts of stirring events: General Monk down from Scotland to end the parliamentarian regime, Charles II returning from exile, the horrifying months of the plague, and the holocaust of the Great Fire. Gradually, however, the concerns of Pepys's everyday life command ever-increasing space until he observes with surprise how the news items have become few and far between.

To his secret manuscript Pepys confided the entire truth about himself, making it his complete confessional. Pepys endears himself by his uninhibited self-portrait of human foibles: his hidden anxieties concealed from all others, his indiscretions (for he was a Restoration man), the charming vagaries and inconsistencies of an apparently staid official, the pain that shadows every existence and the stamina that somehow sustains it. Pepys was a frank sensualist. He inordinately delighted in the possession of things and the gratification of the senses, from the sound of music to the fondling of chance female acquaintances. But instead of scorn, the reader expresses sympathy because of Pepys's utter honesty and thorough, connoisseur-like hedonism. Every moment of life was vivid and flavorful for him.

John Evelyn (1620–1706). John Evelyn was born at Wotton, in Sussex, and was educated at Oxford and the Middle Temple. He spent most of the troubled 1640's touring the Continent, accompanied for part of the time by Waller. Back in England, he was a founder of the Royal Society. Where Pepys was a bureaucrat, Evelyn was a courtier and landed gentleman. He served in minor and honorary posts, constantly displaying "public spirit" but modestly refusing high office. Instead of Pepys's concentration upon the life of sensation and emotion, Evelyn's expressed interests are intellectual and cultural.

Diary (published in 1818 in selections, first complete text in 1955) extends from the author's twenty-first year to his eighty-sixth and last. This diary was consciously composed with the idea that others would see it; Evelyn carefully revised past entries. The style is dignified and discreet, with little talk specifically about himself. Nonetheless, Evelyn unintentionally reveals a great deal. Here is a Restoration royalist who disliked both asceticism and debauchery, opposed arbitrary government from either king or parliament, and condemned all religious bigotry while deeply devout himself.

From 1641 to 1652 the diary is chiefly occupied with Evelyn's continental travels. The traveler is a moderate rationalist and humanist, with a propensity for the New Science. The urbanity and mellowness may be the result of alterations and editing by the older man.

Evelyn lived at Sayes Court, Deptford, from 1652 to 1660, and indulged there in the delights of agricultural and scientific experiments, studies ranging from architecture to numismatics, and genteel concern for improvement in everything from London fogs to the English language. Here the "universal man" of the Renaissance still takes all knowledge as his province. From 1660 until his retirement to Wotton in 1694 his diary is our prime source of information about the real conditions of English public and social life of the era, as seen by a judicious observer and participant. Here the diary practically becomes a history of the age. From 1694 until the last entry (one month before his death) the calm delights of his cosy retreat, the unhurried perusal of the London newspapers, and the confident expectancy of the imminent call to the Heavenly City bring the diary to a quiet end. Evelyn's diary is unique in world literature for the long span of years recorded by one man who lived constantly at the focal point of taste and idea of his age.

Dorothy Osborne, Lady Temple (1627–1695). Dorothy Osborne, a remarkable letter-writer, was born at Chicksands, Bedfordshire. During the civil wars she lived a helter-skelter existence with her mother in the Channel Islands while her father headed an epic four-year defense of isolated Castle Cornet, Guernsey. Her family objected to Sir William Temple, with whom she maintained a notable correspondence from their meeting in 1648 until their marriage in 1654.

Her letters were first printed in selections (1836), with complete text in 1888. They reveal the perfect English Lady, impeccable in morals and delicacy. In some respects they are the most charming love letters in English. Dorothy is not the least bit sentimental, but each letter is a delightful vignette of everyday life with an undercurrent of affection. She portrays the round of life for a 17th-century lady of quality: quiet walks in the countryside, visits to and from relatives and friends, reading French heroic romances, parties and dances (only moderately interesting to a cool and sober beauty), and attentive suitors (carefully pushed forward by her family and adroitly pushed away by Dorothy). Swift praised her as "Mild Dorothea, peaceful, wise and great." Her letters reveal an artist of life as well as an adept at epistolary art.

Thomas Sprat (1635–1713). Thomas Sprat was Bishop of Rochester from 1684 and a member of the ecclesiastical commission of James II. He wrote a eulogistic "Life of Cowley" prefacing the poet's collected works (1668) and collaborated on *The Rehearsal* with George Villiers.

The History of the Royal Society (1667) is the great paean to the New Science, demonstrating how even churchmen of the age were abandoning the theological viewpoints of the past in favor of rationalism and science. The mere list of the experiments performed or contemplated by the Royal Society reveals the wide scientific curiosity of the age. Sprat mollifies clergymen by proving that "enthusiasts," or proponents of radical ideas, could not be scientists, and conciliates the literati, such as Butler, by promising them new ideas for their writing. Sprat issues a stirring plea for all English gentry to devote part of their lives to experimental science and for London to become the world center of science. Important from a literary viewpoint is his (and the Royal Society's) insistence upon a clear, simple style to govern all writing. The work is another monument, therefore, in the drive toward a "modern" prose.

Edward Hyde, Earl Of Clarendon (1609–1674). Edward Hyde was born at Dinton, in Wiltshire. After Oxford and Middle Temple training, he associated with Jonson and Waller. In 1643 he became Chancellor of the Exchequer, and in 1645 a guardian of the Prince of Wales (later Charles II). While in hiding with the prince in 1646, he first conceived of his *History,* which was to be written sporadically over a period of thirty years. As Lord Chancellor after the Restoration, his stout royalist principles alienated Parliament, and his stout piety and morality alienated the king's mistresses and fellow roués. His chancellorship of Oxford University from 1660 to 1667 is still memorialized in the Clarendon Press. Dismissed from office and exiled, he completed his *History* before his death at Rouen, France. He was the grandfather of two ruling queens, Mary II and Anne.

History of the Rebellion (1702-04) is the first really important history of contemporary English affairs, and, like Temple's *Memoirs,* carries great weight because it was composed by a focal figure in that history. No previous phase of English history had been so expertly scrutinized by a contemporary. Bias shows in the *History's* threefold defense of Clarendon himself, the concept of constitutional monarchy, and the men heading the governments of Charles I and Charles II; but, nevertheless, Clarendon can respect the integrity of an opponent like John Hampden, a staunch parliamentarian. Considering the civil wars the product of clashing personalities, he produces striking "characters" as studies of the era's great men. Clarendon conceives of his contemporaries as likenesses of the ancient Romans portrayed by the classic historians. A stately prose and a feeling of structure amidst diverse and confusing events impart to the work a truly Roman effect.

Gilbert Burnet (1643–1715). Born in Edinburgh, Scotland, Gilbert Burnet was educated at Marischal College. His denunciations of immoral Restoration life finally caused him to retire to Holland, where he became an adviser to William of Orange. As chaplain he accompanied the king-to-be back to England. In 1689 he was designated Bishop of Salisbury. Burnet was responsible for Rochester's conversion. He represented Whig latitudinarianism in the Established Church.

The History of My Own Times (1724–34) lacks the majestic style and architecture of Clarendon but shows a distinctly modern concept of history writing, not as the struggle of personalities to be examined for its teaching of moral lessons, but as the contest of ideas and principles arising from the total maturation of society. Burnet's liberal (Whig) interpretation of English history has been followed by most succeeding English historians.

Scientific, Philosophic, and Religious Prose

Sir Isaac Newton (1642–1727). Isaac Newton, one of the great scientific geniuses of all time, bore the same name as his father, a small freehold farmer of Woolsthorpe, Lincolnshire. After graduation from Cambridge in 1665, the youth returned to his native community and in the most productive year of any scientist in history determined: (1) the mathematical method of fluxions (differential calculus), the basis for all modern mathematics and modern research in physics; (2)

a theory of the composition of light from which modern optics has developed; (3) the law of universal gravitation. Newton became Lucastrian Professor at Cambridge in 1669 and represented the university in Parliament in 1689 and again in 1701. As master of the Mint in 1699 he reformed English coinage. From 1703 until his death he was president of the Royal Society.

With Newton and Locke, literature and learning definitely part company. Neither of these great minds had the least literary pretense or interest. To Newton, poetry "was a kind of ingenious nonsense." The man of learning henceforth was generally to write technically, appealing solely to rational faculties and a technical audience.

Philosophiae Naturalis Principia Mathematica ("The Mathematical Principles of Natural Philosophy") (1687), known generally as *Principia,* was the last significant work in Latin by an Englishman, thus bringing to an end the tradition of a thousand years. Newton's work is the foundation of modern mathematics, physics, and astronomy. More impressive than its details is its huge over-all concept of mathematical, mechanical law governing the entire physical universe. The old mysteries are discarded, and the universe is seen as a perpetual motion machine of perfect symmetry and order. Newton gave men, not merely a new world picture, but a new way of thinking. Henceforth, although Newton was himself an orthodox Christian, Newtonianism was to mean liberal and rational thought in all aspects of society, freed of superstition or religious prejudices. Newton brought into focus the entire development of rational, secular thought for the modern world. In Shakespeare's world of 1600 a comet was a portent; in Newton's world of 1700 a comet, like everything in the universe, was a phenomenon of mathematical law. Pope caught the era's sense of glorious satisfaction in his epitaph for Newton:

> Nature and Nature's laws lay hid in Night:
> God said, *Let* Newton *be!* and all was Light.

In its influence upon human minds, the *Principia* must be recognized as the most important single work by a member of the English-speaking world.

John Locke (1632–1704). Born at Wrington, Somersetshire, John Locke was educated at Oxford in classics and medicine. In 1667 he became physician to Anthony Cooper (first earl of Shaftesbury, and Dryden's "Zimri") and lived in his house. Since Shaftesbury was one of the proprietors of the American colony Carolina, Locke was commissioned to draw up the colonial constitution. With Shaftesbury's rise to power, Locke moved as high as secretary of the Board of Trade; but with Shaftesbury's fall, Locke's career also fell, and he accompanied Shaftesbury to France in 1675. Returning to England in 1679, he came under suspicion as a radical and took refuge in Holland until 1689. Under William and Mary he was a commissioner of appeals and from 1691 until his death a member of the household of Sir Francis Masham in High Laver, Essex.

Locke was the most outstanding English philosopher in history, if not in originality, certainly in influence. The dominant minds of the era turned to him as earlier men had turned to St. Thomas Aquinas or Plato. Harold Laski terms Locke the first great secular philosopher of Western society. Unlike most philosophers, Locke gained rapid acceptance in his own lifetime and actually witnessed many features of his practical philosophy worked out in English society. He admitted condescendingly that poetry could provide "pleasant pictures and agreeable visions," but his writing neither sought nor displayed literary qualities.

Essay concerning Human Understanding was started in 1671. An abstract in French was published in 1688. The first English edition appeared in 1690, with Locke's final revision in 1706. This is the first significant analysis of the human mind on a purely factual rather than metaphysical basis; it is the foundation of modern psychology. Locke denied the age-old Aristotelian concept of innate ideas. At birth, he asserted, each of us has for a mind a *tabula rasa,* a blank tablet such as the wax-covered boards that schoolboys then used for figuring. The senses bring to the mind data about the outer world, making impressions upon the blank tablet. The most complex and sophisticated ideas of men are ultimately built from combinations of simple sense impressions. Locke assumed that the outer world we sense is a reality, exactly what it appears to be. His observation showed him, however, the differences in individual perception (color-blindness, for example). He therefore postulated primary qualities in objects (e.g. extension, shape, motion, and rest) and secondary qualities (e.g. color and odor), which are not the essential characteristics of objects. Consequently, Locke sees ultimate and complete knowledge as unattainable. In the spirit of English moderation and empiricism, he suggests that we content ourselves with what probable knowledge we can secure and that we recognize that another man's view of the world, though right for him, will differ from ours. This commonsense explanation was the foundation or point of departure for all 18th-century epistemology.

Letters concerning Toleration (I, 1689; II, 1690; III, 1692) are based upon the psychology enunciated above. Since each man is the product of different sense impressions, each man will have a different viewpoint, and for him his viewpoint is right. The letters therefore advocate full religious toleration except to Roman Catholics (deemed subservient to a foreign political power) and atheists (since they are not acceptors of a moral system necessary for social continuity). The same essay, on the same psychological bases, objects to any absolute monarchy as unwarranted power and oppression. Along with *Areopagitica,* this sober and prosaic piece is one of the great 17th-century contributions to the literature of human freedom.

Two Treatises on Government (1690) originated as a reply to Sir Robert Filmer's *Patriarcha: or, The Natural Power of Kings* (written under Charles I but not published until 1680). The first treatise cogently demolishes Filmer's theories of Divine Right of kings and hereditary transmission of national rule; Locke is so expressive of the "modern" view that Filmer and the necessity of answering him seem absurd today. The second treatise, attempting to justify the Revolution of 1688, has been one of the most important and influential political documents of modern times. Locke accepted the social-contract theory of Hobbes but insisted that the contract, voluntary in original agreement by supposedly primitive man, could be abrogated whenever the will of society demanded it.

Locke sees the primary function of any government as the protection of private property. From his psychological bases, he argues for democracy as the best form of government, since one man's view is inherently no better or worse than his fellow's, and the only way to find the general will is a counting of hands. Locke further separates the legislative and executive functions of government and advocates a system of checks and balances to prevent autocracy and overt fighting between governmental units. With an eye to English history, he insists on the primary function of the legislative branch, which must inaugurate legislation and control the purse strings. The American Declaration of Independence and Constitution are firmly based upon Locke's political philosophy, as in fact is virtually all liberal democracy of the past two and a half centuries.

Some Thoughts concerning Education (1693) sees the purpose of education, not as the rote learning of facts, but as the process of mental stimulation and maturation. Good habits and good character, good health and constructive attitudes, should be built by rational and humane treatment of pupils. Whipping of students is "the last Remedy." Sound English works as well as classical models should be studied, and writing exercises in English are as productive as traditional writing assignments in Latin. Locke was a radical educator in his time, but the approximation of modern pedagogical theory to his own demonstrates his probity and to a considerable extent his influence.

The Reasonableness of Christianity (1695) was an attempt to found faith on reason. Locke saw Christianity as the reaffirmation of the eternal, natural, moral code. Its miracles were to assure in the minds of all the certainty of this perfect system of morality. Christianity is essentially simple and does not require the vast paraphernalia of rites, theological subtleties, and complex creeds. Christianity is useful practically, and the hair-splitting of divines pales beneath the "decency, order, and edification" that hallmark the faith. Although Locke was a staunch advocate of Christianity as such, his rational emphasis and search for the common denominator of moral usefulness in religion made his work powerfully influential upon 18th-century deists.

Joseph Glanvill (1636–1680). Joseph Glanvill is remembered chiefly because Matthew Arnold found his scholar-gypsy story in *The Vanity of Dogmatising* (1661). This work as a whole is a clergyman's plea for the open mind in examining all the world's phenomena. Glanvill is delighted with the Royal Society and its prospects of increasing human knowledge. The electric telegraph and Hume's theory of causation, among other things, appear to be predicted in this work. *Plus Ultra* (1668) is a strongly worded plea for the newly maturing idea of progress; Glanvill is a resolute advocate of scientific progress and believes that mankind has greater and greater prospects ahead. And yet in *Sadducismus Triumphatus* (1666), he seriously asserts the efficacy of witchcraft. Here indeed is a strangely transitional figure, an intellectual hovering between two worlds. After Glanvill, the "modern" mind is wholly triumphant among intellectuals.

RELIGIOUS PROSE. The divines of the late 17th century were strongly tinged with the New Science and the new style. Isaac Barrow (1630–77), for instance, taught Newton optics at Cambridge and was an eminent mathematician. He scorned the earlier Jeremy Taylor's style as "sublimities above the apostolic spirit" and favored a "simple and plain way" of preaching. Robert South (1634–1716) was the most popular preacher of his era, his sermons proving so colloquial and racy that Dr. Johnson condemned them for "violence and sometimes coarseness of language." John Tillotson (1630–94), Archbishop of Canterbury from 1691, was, with Dryden, one of the great architects of the new plain style of English prose. The lucid phrasing and "sweet reasonableness" of Tillotson influenced Addison and all the Anglican clergy of the 18th century. The important voices in late 17th-century Anglicanism staunchly favored the national church but tolerated a wide latitude of religious opinion. Scorned were the fanatics—"enthusiasts" such as John Bunyan or George Fox. Questionable to Anglican clerics but not so obnoxious were the genteel voices lifted for deism.

Deism as a theological term has two essentially distinctive meanings: (1) it postulates the idea that the universe, having been created by God and having received its initial laws of existence from Him, thereafter develops without recourse to divine intervention; and (2) it refers more particularly to a movement in religious thought which occurred in the 17th and 18th centuries manifested chiefly in England.

It is the second meaning that concerns us most here. The movement interested itself in the relation between "revealed" theology and "natural" theology, holding that the truths of revealed theology should not be in contradiction with truths arrived at by reason and meditation (natural theology). Thus, while not initially repudiating revealed religion, the deists sought to put religious practices on a firmer universal footing by stating that all necessary theological ideas could be arrived at by man in his capacity as thinker.

English rational deism had its essential origin in Lord Herbert of Cherbury. His appeal to natural theology was perfectly attuned to the intellectuals of the Age of Enlightenment, who had no mysticism in their nature and, because of the tumultuous confusion of the mid-17th century, no great love for theological bickerings and sectarian differences. For the Age of Reason this deism offered a religion of reason, calling upon the tools of human senses and mind to explain all problems of the supernatural, thereby offering a faith for all rational men, everywhere at all times ("All men think alike"). The "Bible of the Deists" (rational variety) was to emerge in 1730 in *Christianity as Old as the Creation, or the Gospel a Republication of the Religion of Nature*, by Matthew Tindal (c. 1656–1733), but a host of deistic voices prepared the way in the late 17th century. Charles Blount (1654–93), in *Anima Mundi* (1679), accepted Lord Herbert's "natural theology," and he sought a universal religion with the common elements of all faiths. John Toland (1670–1722) showed influence of Locke in his *Christianity Not Mysterious* (1696); Toland argues that, taken properly, Christianity has nothing incomprehensible or perplexing about it: no valid part of Christian doctrine is contrary to reason. Anthony Collins (1676–1729), a friend and disciple of Locke, proceeded further in *A Discourse of Free-thinking* (1713), a hostile criticism of the Christian creed.

With the trend of the times, both orthodox Anglicans and rational deists claimed to follow reason. The deists differed largely in their distaste for priesthood and their annoyance at the insistence upon the sole validity of one creed and one ritual. Many clergymen, especially those with a latitudinarian background, leaned toward deism themselves. Throughout most of the 18th century the intellectuals of the English-speaking world were, with a few exceptions like Swift and Dr. Johnson, essentially deists. In the 18th century the strains of deism were to proliferate in wide directions, notably to sentimental deism.

Not a deist but a supporter of natural theology, John Ray (1627–1705) was perhaps England's most distinguished biologist. In his later years he attempted to reconcile Christian faith with the scientific mind. *The Wisdom of God Manifested in the Works of the Creation* (1691) showed a simultaneously pious and scientific spirit seeing the order of the universe and the biological facts as a demonstration of the mind and benevolence of the Christian deity.

Chapter 2

The Age of Pope and Swift (1700–1750)

BACKGROUND INFORMATION

MAJOR HISTORICAL EVENTS. It is an old canard that England's greatest years have been under queens. Although Queen Anne's rule was brief (1702–14), it was glorious for England. In the War of the Spanish Succession (1702–13, called "Queen Anne's War" in America) the Duke of Marlborough, ancestor of Sir Winston Churchill, won a series of great victories—Blenheim, Ramillies, Oudenarde, Malplaquet. During this war the French encouraged James Edward Stuart, son of James II, to land in Scotland in 1708, but he was forced to withdraw to France; one of the terms exacted from Louis XIV in the Treaty of Utrecht (1713) was recognition of the Protestant succession in Great Britain. The peace treaty firmly established the first British empire, entrenched in both America and India. Queen Anne was the last Stuart on the English throne, the last English monarch to "touch" for scrofula (called "the king's evil"; the touch of a royal person was thought to cure the disease), and the last English ruler to veto an act of Parliament. Under her was the first "packing" of the House of Lords in order to secure a desired majority.

From the accession of James I (1603), Scotland and England had one monarch but theoretically remained two separate kingdoms. In 1707 they were formally united under the name of Great Britain. The flags of the two nations were combined (the English cross of St. George and the Scottish cross of St. Andrew) to form the present Union Jack. All subsequent parliaments have been numbered from the first

Parliament of Great Britain in 1707. The Tory ministry that triumphed in 1710 represented the first complete, peaceful transfer of power under the modern English party system.

Touring England during Queen Anne's reign, Defoe labeled it "the most flourishing and opulent country in the world." Commerce and industry accounted for most of this prosperity. Woollen cloth continued to be the staple export, and from the expanding American colonies and the trading posts in the East poured sugar, tobacco, furs, and spices. The monopolies of merchant-adventurer companies (except the Hudson's Bay Company and the East Indian Company) were essentially broken after 1689, and trade was open to all. Vigorous commerce extended to the Baltic, to Turkey, and to Persia. By the Treaty of Utrecht the English held the contract to supply Negro slaves to Spanish America. By the mid-18th century the English were admittedly "entire masters" of trade with Russia. Within England small capitalists were emerging as promoters of workshops, prototypes of the factory system that would boom at the century's end.

For the unfortunate Queen Anne, life was largely a series of stillborn children; none of her seventeen offspring survived her. Her successor in 1714 was George I, great-grandson of James I through the female line. This German House of Hanover was to occupy the English throne until 1901. On the heels of the new monarch came another bid for power by James Edward Stuart in 1715 ("The Fifteen"), but the Jacobite rebels were quickly dispersed. In the next year Parliament, largely because of the possibility of civil war, extended its own life by seven years in the Septennial Act. War with Spain (1717–20) included an abortive 1719 Spanish expedition to Scotland in aid of the "Old Pretender." Fought upon virtually all the continents and oceans, this might properly be termed the "first World War."

With Sir Robert Walpole in 1721, England received its first true prime minister. George I's virtual ignorance of English affairs and his total ignorance of the English language (the king and the prime minister addressed each other in inept Latin) caused Walpole to become the actual ruler of the nation. "I am no Saint, no Spartan, no Reformer," admitted Walpole, and he proceeded to institute one of the most venal political eras of English history. To this prime minister are attributed the famous words "Every man has his price." Although a prosperous nation winked at the peculations of Walpole, the satirists, especially those in the theater, bitterly assailed him. Walpole, by the

Licensing Act of 1737, effectively silenced his playwriting adversaries, notably Henry Fielding who thereafter turned to the novel.

With the death of George I and the accession of George II in 1727, Walpole continued in office. Although the new monarch spoke English (with a heavy German accent), actual government was now firmly in the prime minister's hands. In 1739 England embarked upon the fantastically named "War of Jenkins' Ear," for the nation was roused to ire by the dubious tale of Spanish cruelty to a seafarer, Jenkins (his severed ear was dramatically displayed). English assaults upon the Spanish were generally rather futile, though in the process Commodore Anson performed the memorable feat of a voyage around the world (1740–44). A war-weary nation finally deposed Walpole in 1742, but the war continued and broadened, and from 1740 it was termed the War of the Austrian Succession ("King George's War" in America). England was not remarkably successful abroad and was stunned by the explosion of another Jacobite Rebellion in 1745 ("The Forty-Five"). The "Young Pretender" ("Bonnie Prince Charlie") landed in a tiny boat at Loch Shiel in Scotland, and the Highland clans rallied to his cause. Berserk Highlanders, wildly swinging their claymores, overpowered the "lobsters" (Redcoats) at Prestonpans near Edinburgh. The exultant Scots swept southward with Charles Edward Stuart, reaching Derby, in the English Midlands. Retreating to Scotland for the winter, the Jacobites let the Hanoverians build up the counterattack, and in April 1746 the rebels were crushingly defeated at Culloden near Inverness. "Bonnie Prince Charlie" managed to flee back to France after a number of narrow escapes, thus forever ending the many Stuart bids for return to the British throne. "The Forty-Five" provided the material for Sir Walter Scott's first novels.

The Treaty of Aix-la-Chapelle, ending the long war in 1748, left England practically a defeated nation except in North America. Although politically divided within, England at mid-century possessed in William Pitt the Elder a forceful leader for the days ahead.

At mid-century, too, England was poised on the brink of the Industrial Revolution. The prosperity from Queen Anne's age was gaining momentum, and the population was steadily increasing. The need for fuel and the rapid depletion of available wood caused a "coal rush." But to go deeper for coal was dangerous because of the threat of flooding, and it was Thomas Newcomen who solved the problem in 1712 with the steam pump, thus securing one of Britain's greatest industries, coal mining. As early as 1713 the Darbys of Coalbrookdale were using coke to smelt iron. With the development of fuel and metal industries, England was ready to lead the world in manufacturing. John Kay's flying shuttle (pat. 1733) was the first of the great mechanical inventions that was to transform the weaving industry into one of England's greatest sources of wealth. Although early 18th-century roads were often frightful, transportation was vastly improved by the building of canals and the deepening of rivers; Derby, Leeds, Nottingham, and scores of other inland cities became water-borne before 1750.

The populations of the burgeoning towns and cities were fed by streams of former agriculturists lured in part by greater urban opportunities but most particularly driven from the soil by the mounting pressure of "enclosures." Enclosure consisted of a landowner's consolidation, for his own use, of open fields previously cultivated in common by tenant farmers. At the expense of small rural cultivators, the landed gentry greatly increased in wealth and raised the national output by their efficiency. An Agricultural Revolution was developing with improved techniques of farming. Jethro Tull (1674–1741), with seed selection and especially with the first contrivance to drill grain, and Charles Townshend (1674–1738), with improved turnips and crop rotation, helped establish English agriculture as the world's most scientific and productive.

CULTURAL CONDITIONS. The term the "Enlightenment" is used to characterize the main trend of European thought throughout the 18th century. While identified primarily with the Continent, the ideals of the Enlightenment exerted a very great influence in England and in America also. Basically, the Enlightenment advocated a rationalistic and scientific approach to the religious, social, and economic questions of the time, and a reliance on reason and empiricism rather than on authority and dogma. Leading figures in the movement were such men as: Montesquieu, Voltaire, Rousseau, and Diderot in France; Kant and Herder in Germany; Locke and Hume in England; Franklin and Paine in the United States; and "enlightened" despots like Frederick II in Prussia and Catherine the Great in Russia. However, in most countries the ideas of the Enlightenment gained their strongest support from the rising bourgeoisie, and earned their bitterest opposition from the ranks of the high clergy and the old nobility, both of whom felt their privileged position to be imperiled by the new attitudes—as indeed they were.

However, the bloody upheavals of the latter part of the 18th century (caused in no small part by the Enlightenment ideals) were avoided in England. To understand why this was so, we must examine England at the beginning of the century and discover the conditions that allowed for the acceptance of the new ideas without the consequent destruction of the old institutions.

In England at the beginning of the 18th century, life was hard. Only one child in four survived to adulthood, and the infant mortality rate was almost as high in the luxurious West End mansions as it was in the tenements of London's Cheapside. Almost all work had to be done by the muscles of beasts and men, and the worker commonly toiled twelve to fourteen hours daily. Tuberculosis was "the English disease," killing thousands annually; the lifespan at this time was not greatly advanced beyond that of medieval times. Life was therefore lived with compensating rawness; the well-to-do hunted voraciously, drank vast quantities of wine, and gambled staggering sums at cards, while the poor pummeled each other, drank prodigious amounts of gin, and gambled at bear-baiting or pitch and toss. This seamy world perversely fascinated Ned Ward in *London Spy* (1698–1700) and profoundly repelled Swift. The middle class maintained a pious austerity throughout this age, partly from its Puritan background and partly from its relentless struggle for existence. With no government concern for small business, the middle class found itself pitted against the adversary of social indifference, and therefore had to make its own way by unceasing industry and determination.

The great mass of Englishmen, ranging from the small tradesmen to the peasants, receive scant mention in literature or in Parliament during this age. The all-important concern was with the propertied class, the merchant princes of the cities and the landed gentry in the country. The nation was run by the propertied class for its own benefit. When the Whigs were in power, commercialism and religious dissent were encouraged; when the Tories triumphed, pure landed property and the Anglican Church were put forward. But the intense political rivalry was wholly an intra-class contest. A few dozen great Whig and Tory families, with their eldest sons in the House of Lords and their younger sons in the House of Commons, monopolized political life. Two thirds of the members of Parliament were merely nominated, and the rest were elected by about 160,000 voters, many of whom were wholly controlled. The term "gentleman" specifically referred to a member of the small leisured class who, with no soiling of hands in business, was free to concentrate upon politics. Religious fanaticism was unspeakable vulgarity to this class, and so it transferred all the fanatical elements of its nature into political controversy.

All problems of contemporary life were viewed as parts of the party strife: Whigs loudly praised a poem simply because a Whig wrote it, and Tories vociferously applauded a drama solely because its author was a Tory. Bizarre as it might appear to us, this spirit accompanied the first great modern development of representative government and the party system. The ruling power in England was changing hands, moving from the monarch to the propertied class, and this class felt an enormous exaltation in its newly found prestige.

The comparable class in France rode to bloody destruction in the 18th century, but the English landed gentry maintained their position as England's rulers until the middle-class triumph in the 1830's. The strength of the English propertied class lay in some of its following characteristics:

(1) Its moderate spirit. It continued to maintain essentially the viewpoint of Halifax in the 17th century, a willingness to compromise and tolerate. England's landowners permitted notable freedom of speech and action to Englishmen, so much that French liberals, although overenthusiastically exalting the liberties of England, rather realistically appraised England's surpassing of France as the world's dominant political and cultural power in the 18th century.

(2) Its social flexibility. The French aristocracy was a closed corporation that admitted no newcomers and sought to sustain as idle wasters all those of gentle birth. The younger sons of English gentry were siphoned off into the professions and even into the bourgeoisie. Wealthy tradesmen might never be socially acceptable during their own lifetime, but by purchasing country estates they could usually secure acceptance of their descendants as "gentlemen."

(3) Its sense of responsibility. The English landed gentry generally felt a strong duty to govern effectively and provide for the nation. It was a quip of the age that in France the poor paid the taxes, while in England the rich paid. While the English gentry enjoyed magnificence and luxury, they did not bleed the nation white to supply their pleasures.

(4) Its genuine leadership. The 18th-century English gentry knew itself to be the governors of England, and it produced some of the most remarkable political leaders in history, culminating toward the century's close in the two Pitts, Burke, and Fox. With almost equal strength this class assumed leadership in culture and taste.

Quite a few of the gentry might devote their lives to pursuing foxes (like Squire Western in *Tom Jones*) and others to pursuing women (like Mr. B— in *Pamela*), but a sizable number resembled John Evelyn of the previous century, wide in their scientific and artistic interests. After university residence, the gentry would make the Grand Tour of the Continent, often shipping back tons of art objects. In the winter ("the season") they would live in their London townhouses, participating in the social round and often sitting in Parliament. During the warmer months they might frequent fashionable resorts such as Bath or reside on their country estates, where they often supervised improved scientific agriculture and where they built their mansions, sometimes to their own designs, and furnished them with the exquisite treasures of Europe and later of Asia.

Sensing their closest historical kinship with the rich and powerful nobles (like Agrippa and Maecenas) who surrounded ancient Caesar Augustus, they called themselves the "Augustans" and sought to emulate the enlightenment, refinement, and taste of that distant era. This *neoclassic* spirit was most ubiquitous in architecture and helps to explain the classic appearance of "colonial" American structures and the persistence, from the founding of the republic to our own era, of pseudo-Greek and pseudo-Roman temples for American governmental buildings.

Neoclassicism pervaded most aspects of life for the 18th-century English gentry and manifested itself particularly in literature in the following attitudes:

(1) **Aristocratic courtliness.** In the *Spectator,* Steele asserted that one of the essential qualities of a poet is high breeding and training.

(2) **Restraint and dignity.** The gentry sought an elevated poise consonant with their mighty role. Society was now establishing itself upon secular morals and ethics, and for the sake of national interest and respect, the gentry were usually publicly respectable, not openly engaging in vice, like Restoration rakes.

(3) **Urbanity, sophistication, cosmopolitanism.** Gentlemen sought polish and finish in life and in art as, in the best sense, men of the world. Calm detachment and good nature were preferred to vulgar enthusiasm and exuberance.

(4) **Nonchalant gentility.** "The mere amusements of gentlemen are of more value than the profound researches of pedants," declared Shaftesbury. Pope worked over his verses laboriously but let it be known that he just tossed them off like a gentleman.

(5) **Conversational ease.** The sociable and lively, rather than the

dull or tedious, were courted. Solemn and majestic attitudes therefore seldom appear in this age. Swift clothes even his bitterest pronouncements in an apparent smile. The reader must realize that much of 18th-century writing has a lurking facetiousness about it. If we, like the Romantics, recoil from the "poetic diction" of the age, we must recognize that a great deal of it was at least partly playful. Such a spirit inhibits lyricism but produces excellent *vers de société*.

(6) Preoccupation with the here and the now. Dr. Johnson declared: "All one needs to know he may learn within sound of Bow Bells" (St. Mary-le-bow Church in London). Conscious of their superlative achievement, the English gentry saw no point in ranging through the world and time.

(7) Symmetry and a balance of the useful and the ornamental. We still treasure the beauty of Chippendale and Hepplewhite furniture for its superb 18th-century simple grace and loveliness combined with the eminently comfortable and utilitarian. The purpose of literature, as avowed by a host of men in the age, was to instruct through pleasure, thereby uniting esthetic and didactic purposes.

(8) Artifice. The Romantics have put a curse upon artificiality, but the early 18th century loved it. When James II termed Wren's St. Paul's Cathedral "artificial," he meant that it was "skilfully achieved." The sense of power in man's ability to control the world was one of the dominant impulses of the Enlightenment, and the artful shaping of inchoate nature by man was a great source of pride. The "primitive" paintings of an Henri Rousseau or a Grandma Moses would be scorned by the neoclassicists. They demanded that art be artful, that it appear not "natural" but expertly harmonized and regulated by the controlling hand of the artist.

(9) A taste for broad, general effects. Seeking the common experience of refined gentlemen, the age deprecated the individual and the particular in observation. The greatest virtue in art was a universal significance, rather than that which would touch but a few and give a sense of strangeness and surprise.

(10) Critical and analytical spirit. A self-conscious age, it was deeply interested in technique and method. It wished not to praise emotionally but to weigh judiciously. It is no coincidence that Pope's earliest major work was an *Essay on Criticism*. The second half of the century was to produce in Dr. Johnson probably the greatest of all English critics.

(11) Skepticism. Few of the intellectuals were devoutly pious; and

many would be properly labeled as agnostics, but it was a genteel agnosticism and not the militant form of the 19th century. Such a pervasive attitude among the gentry resulted in a tolerance of any faith, provided it was not a fanatic faith. The same spirit accepted a doctrine of limited objectives in life. It sought to take things pretty much as they were without trying in a wildly enthusiastic or idealistic manner to alter the world.

(12) Rationalism. By "reason" the 18th century meant many things, but generally it meant the commonsense of gentlemen, "sweet reasonableness." Its reason was the calm, balanced judgment of an entrenched and secularly oriented class, and the consequent result of this reason was a hardly surprising proof that the *status quo* in society was exactly right.   *handout ends here*

However, the veneer of static placidity over the "Augustan" age ill-concealed a revolutionary change in the writer's audience. The earlier practice of writing for manuscript circulation by the courtiers and literati had ended; writers now wrote frankly for publication by the printing press. Individual patronage continued but was a declining institution; the patronage system was all but extinct before Dr. Johnson's scathing letter on the subject to Lord Chesterfield in 1755.

Pope worked an adroit variation on patronage by the subscription system, whereby a number of people each contributed a few guineas and had their names printed as sponsors of a literary work. Certainly the 17th-century type of patronage was extinct; writers intended a professional writing career and did not, as Butler or Congreve, pen their writings primarily as a means of obtaining government posts. Even though Wordsworth was to obtain such a sinecure, it was to aid his writing, not to supplant it. However, the writer in the early 18th century, while not contemplating a public career, did usually receive aid from the political party that he backed, and so important was this politically motivated support that most of the writers of this period can be identified as Whigs or Tories. Nevertheless, both parties subscribed to the neoclassic principles of the age, and the works of Pope most nearly represent the ideal of virtually all the authors of the period, whether Whig or Tory.

A wider popular market for books was developing with the growth of population, and especially with an increase in literacy, particularly in the middle class. But the largest market was that for periodical literature: the newspaper, the essay periodical, and the magazine. The most ephemeral type, of course, was the newspaper. The first daily was *The Daily Courant,* established in 1702. In an age when newspapers had not become, as today, a catch-all repository for sports, kitchen recipes, comic strips, gossip, etc., the staple news was political, both national and international. The remaining space was frequently filled with literary pieces: for instance, Dr. Johnson wrote the first leader for *The London Chronicle* upon its founding in 1757. In 1727 a Swiss visitor, De Saussure, noted "All Englishmen are great newsmongers. Workmen habitually begin the day by going to coffee rooms in order to read the daily news."

An 18th-century periodical, unfamiliar to modern writers, was the essay periodical. It was issued at regular intervals (six times a week for *The Spectator*) and was the work of one writer with occasional collaborations or contributions from other authors. Such one-man enterprises were intended for a short life only; they might even be thought of as volumes of essays released in separate installments.

Modern magazines as we know them are usually said to have originated with *The Gentleman's Magazine* in 1731; the term *magazine* in the sense of "storehouse" has been extended from this publication to become a generic term for periodicals. The type represented by *The Gentleman's Magazine* is edited by one person but incorporates a number of pieces by many authors. Although the demand for writing was increasing, the supply of authors increased more rapidly. Hackwork for periodicals barely kept together body and soul for a host of inferior writers. Pope's *Dunciad* pictures in "Grub Street" the misery and starvation of the lesser literary figures of the age.

The Copyright Act of 1709 assured authors their publication rights and gave them superior advantages in bargaining with the booksellers. This era witnessed the first modern book publisher (as distinguished from the earlier bookseller) in Jacob Tonson (d. 1736), who published the works of Dryden, Milton, and Shakespeare (editions by Rowe and Pope).

This is the first era in our culture that we feel can be completely grasped from its surviving writings. If we fail properly to appraise it, the fault is ours; it does not lie in the paucity of source material. The acute self-consciousness and critical temperament of the period offer a canvas of rich variety in subject and personality.

LANGUAGE. Today's universal literacy has insured a general competence in English speech and writing. In the early 18th century the majority of Englishmen were illiterate or barely literate, including many well-to-do women and country gentlemen. The literati of this period, however, took more pride in "correct" English than did any previous English writers, except Dryden. Their pride in their linguistic ability was often expressed as Leonard Welsted did in 1724: "The English Language does at this Day possess all the Advantages and Excellencies, which are many, that its Nature will admit of."

CHARACTERISTICS OF THE ENGLISH LANGUAGE IN THE EIGHTEENTH CENTURY

The ideal English, as the literati saw it, was not that of the scholar or pedant but the refined and elegant language of gentlemen. John Hughes, in *Of Style* (1695), urged the seekers for the best English to substitute for a slavish following of dictionaries and etymologies a "careful Perusal of the most correct Writers." Addison in prose and Pope in verse displayed an almost unprecedented self-consciousness; they knew that they were writing model English. Swift issued three pronouncements upon the proper use of English: (1) a paper in *The Tatler* (※230, September 28, 1710); (2) *A Proposal for Correcting, Improving, and Ascertaining the English Tongue* (1712, the only work to which Swift affixed his name); (3) *A Letter to a Young Gentleman, Lately Entered into Holy Orders* (1720). In each he attacked what he considered carelessness and vulgarity in fashionable English and advocated a language that was familiar without coarseness, elegantly refined without ostentation, and clear and simple without banality or cliché. Addison also showed especial concern with the language: *The Spectator* ※141 for August 11, 1711, objected to the prevalent fashion of shortening and clipping the longer English words, and *The Spectator* ※165 of September 8, 1711, ridiculed the adulteration of English with affected French vocabulary.

In his 1712 *Proposal*, Swift re-echoed Dryden's advocacy of an English Academy to purify and regulate English, but it was schoolmasters and not lofty academicians who were to attempt Swift's program. The 18th century witnessed a notable decline in the Latin-grammar schools and a tremendous rise in charity schools, where English was the language of instruction. In rapid succession schoolmasters issued English grammars analyzing English essentially in the manner of Latin but with a strong eye to current usage. John Brightland published *A Grammar of the English Tongue* and James Greenwood *An Essay towards a Practical English Grammar,* both in 1711. Benjamin Franklin was to teach himself English grammar from these two works.

Michael Mattaire offered a more authoritarian approach in *The English Grammar* (1712). The popularity of these three books elicited an anonymous satire, *Bellum Grammaticale* (1712), which painted a "battle of the grammars" and particularly assailed Greenwood. The same age witnessed numerous other English grammars. Those by Dyche and Dilworth were frequently reprinted into the 19th century, and Noah Webster set out purposefully to supplant Dilworth's *New Guide to the English Tongue*.

In 1721 the great hymn writer Isaac Watts published *The Art of Reading and Writing English*. Watts is invaluable in revealing contemporary London pronunciation. He lists about 238 "Words written very different from their Pronunciation," appending a phonetic rendition of each. Some of these look quite familiar to us: *Cupboard,* "cubburd"; *Psalm,* "saam"; *Yacht,* "yot." Others offer pronunciations now unknown in standard English: *Apothecary,* "potticary"; *Courtesy,* "curchee"; *Jaundice,* "janders"; *Perfect,* "parfet"; *Verdict,* "vardit." This was an age when most Englishmen learned their language by ear and not by eye. The learning of English by subsequent generations through the printed page has caused the pronunciation of many words to abandon age-old practice in favor of following the spelling.

Rimes by contemporary poets also reveal a pronunciation alien to today's standard English. *China* rimed with *rainy, join* with *line, tea* with *obey*. Foreign names continued to receive an Anglicized pronunciation, as they had for centuries. Thus the name of the great 17th-century French dramatist Corneille was pronounced *Cornell*.

Spelling among the literati of this age approximated today's spelling but still permitted more variation than now accepted. Watts listed such variants as: *Accompt, Account; Alarm, Alarum; Balk, Baulk; Biscuit, Bisket*. Most 20th-century words ending in *-ic* were spelled *-ick,* as *musick, publick;* remnants of this spelling still survive in our *picnic, picnickers; traffic, trafficking*. Variant spellings of foreign place names were rife, particularly of foreign places known by ear instead of by the printed page.

As in the age of Dryden, the vocabulary was strangely circumscribed, "correct" authors avoiding old-fashioned, dialectal, and slang terms. Today's readers are surprised to find Sir Thomas Hanmer, in his edition of Shakespeare (1743–44), listing as "obsolete" such expressions as *to bandy, to budge, brooch, dank, a deck of cards*. At the same time there was remarkable resistance to the introduction of new words. Although persons of quality prided themselves upon their knowledge of French and frequently interjected French expressions, they were quite conscious of the foreignness of the words and refused to domesticate such terms with the aplomb of the medieval and Renaissance English. Technical and scientific writing was now using English, but gentlemen and "correct" writers like Pope and Swift, while concerned about the major revelations of the New Science, refused to absorb the technical vocabulary with the speed of today's authors. Quickly adopted, however, were words like *attic, piazza,* and *porch,* associated with the vogue of classical architecture.

A fascinating semantic change has occurred to many English words since the early 18th century, rendering favorable numerous terms that the Age of Reason used unfavorably. To an era consecrating the *status quo, ambition* was a desire to rise above one's appointed station in life and hence a rebellious and dangerous spirit. To a neoclassic period, *Gothic* was synonymous with "crude," "barbarous." *Enthusiasm* was equated with "fanaticism," *imagination* with "wild fancy." To an unromantic age, *romantic* meant "absurd" or "false."

A fashionable practice of this period (deplored by Addison and Swift) was the clipping of words. Some of these shortened forms have become thoroughly familiar in today's English, e.g. *mob* (from Latin *mobile vulgus*) and *wig* (from *periwig*). Others, still retaining their facetious air, have descended from aristocracy to lower-class speakers: *incog* (for *incognito*), *phizz* (for *physiognomy*), *pozz* (for *positively*), *rep* (for *reputation*).

The Universal Etymological English Dictionary (1721), by Nathan Bailey, was the first dictionary ever to attempt a complete listing of all English words. The edition of 1727 was also the first dictionary to indicate the position of accent in words. The great popularity of this work is indicated by Mrs. Western's specific recommendation of Bailey's work in *Tom Jones.* Many other dictionaries were issued in the same era, but none could match that of the great lexicographer of the following age, Dr. Johnson.

Dr. Johnson acknowledged to Boswell his indebtedness in style to Ephraim Chambers, the compiler of *Cyclopaedia, or Universal Dictionary of Arts and Sciences* (1728), the first true encyclopedia in English. Chambers's work was to form the basis of the great French *Encyclopédie,* and to this day the most famed British encyclopedia is still *Chambers's* (*Encyclopaedia Britannica,* of course, is an American publication).

POPE AND HIS WORKS

Alexander Pope (1688–1744). Alexander Pope was a lifelong adherent to Roman Catholicism during a period when such faith was often considered virtual treason. Restrictions against Roman Catholic residence in London forced his family to move around 1700 to Binfield in Windsor Forest. From 1719 until his death he lived at Twickenham, west of London. A severe illness at the age of twelve stunted his growth, so that he was less than five feet tall. He was continuously suffering ("this long disease, my life"), and was forced to wear a corset to keep his tortured spine upright. Although his religion barred him from the universities, he acquired from tutors and friends a wide though possibly superficial classical education. His life was uneventful except for a number of bitter literary-political quarrels. The age universally recognized Pope as its greatest poet. Writers and statesmen, wits and nobility, avidly sought him; Defoe, who was branded a mere hack writer, was acutely pained because he was denied acquaintance with the great man. The one strong affection of Pope's life was for Martha Blount, who was the beneficiary of his will. An epicure, he is reputed to have died from the cumulative effect of warming potted lampreys in a silver dish, but he actually had been ill for several weeks and was thought to have died of "a hundred good reasons."

His deformity, and perhaps his membership in an unpopular religious sect, caused Pope to manifest character traits less than endearing. He was nicknamed "The Wicked Wasp of Twickenham" because of his rancorous satires. His cruelty to political and literary foes, however, did not exceed that of his contemporaries, except that his ability to express himself far exceeded theirs. Partly from egotism and partly in jest, he made a bewildering tangle of his bibliography. He constantly kept revising backward the dates of his composition to make himself a boy wonder. Apparently he purposely encouraged "pirated" editions of his writings, notably his correspondence, so that he could then triumphantly come out with the "correct" edition. Such "compensation," however, can easily be understood in a genius confined to a dwarfish, pain-wracked body. Somewhat more difficult for modern readers to grasp are the following special characteristics of Pope's poetry:

(1) Pope made no pretense of divine inspiration, like Spenser or

Milton. He was frankly a rational man speaking to other rational men.

(2) Poetry has become for us largely a vehicle of private revelation, while the verse of Pope is public utterance. Like his age, Pope turned his back upon profundities and sought to provide consummate polish for the expression of universal social concepts.

(3) The culture Pope exemplifies is almost exclusively literary and secular. Milton, even with his vast erudition, drew upon deep well-springs of human experience that any reader can share. Pope's world is made up entirely of books and his immediate contemporary society.

(4) Virtually all of Pope's verse is "imitation." By imitation Pope meant neither slavish copying nor antiquarian pedantry; he meant the total re-creation of effect in contemporary terms of a work by, say, Horace, Ovid, or Vergil.

(5) Much of Pope's work has the quality of posed portraits and scenes. No other English poet so presents a series of gallery-hung paintings, each consciously balanced and harmonized. The effect is static and, in the most favorable sense, "artificial."

(6) The satisfaction in all of Pope's work is artistic perfection. Donne gives the effect of tremendous power in succeeding against fearful obstacles. Pope deceptively suggests that there are no obstacles and that his verse flows with perfect adjustment of style to content and form. He makes it appear wholly easy and effortless, but he gave much care to each line.

First Period: The Rape of the Lock and Other Early Poems (1709–1717)

Pastorals (1709) consists of four poems, one for each season, which Pope claims were written at the age of sixteen. Essentially Vergilian, they also suggest the English pastoral tradition from Spenser on. They are neoclassic in tone, praising the tranquillity of country life while lacking the satire and social comment of Vergil. The Romantic, ec-static with unspoiled Nature, would consider these unfeeling; but Pope has a genuine love for scenery, which he prefers to observe as a series of set pictures gracefully decorated with mythological figures. Nature's beauty to him is Golden Age tranquillity, inhabited by ideal shepherds. The over-all effect is similar to that of a landscape painting by Nicholas Poussin. Thomas Tickell's praise of the pastorals by Ambrose Philips evoked Pope's ire, delivered with playful maliciousness in ⚡40 of *The Guardian*. *Pastorals* and all subsequent verse of Pope employ the heroic couplet, unless otherwise stated.

Essay on Criticism (1711), one of the most quoted poems in English, was written at the age of twenty-three or younger. Pope claimed a draft of the poem as early as 1706. More noted for trenchant comment and epigrammatical sally than for ordered structure, the poem nonetheless falls roughly into three divisions:

(1) General philosophical position. The plea to "follow Nature" is often considered the keynote of neoclassicism. By "Nature," Pope meant the order and reason in the universe, a reflection of the order in the mind of God.

(2) A concern with esthetic and technical skill. Beauty is generally the result, not of careless rapture, but of precise craftsmanship. Pope shows by example how every effect can be carefully created by the conscious poet.

(3) The proper critical armory. Commonplace advice against narrow prejudices and haste, and a plea for balance and moderation, all of which is superbly phrased.

Pope's immediate model is the work of Boileau which, like the *Essay,* reviewed three broad principles of criticism. Boileau gave the greatest weight to the first of the following three principles, while Pope preferred the last:

(1) Authority, "the rules." Aristotle, in his *Poetics,* conceived of the critic as the scientist of the poetic laws. For Pope's day this principle meant strong reverence for the ancients and careful "imitation" of the classics.

(2) Reason and good sense. In the *Laws,* Plato conceived of the censor of the state as demanding intelligibility and utility in the works of poets. In Pope's day this principle was often invoked by the supporters of the moderns in the "battle of the books," for it opposed reason to authority.

(3) Good taste. Pope essentially favored Horace, who, in *Ars Poetica,* saw the critic as a spokesman for the best audience of his era. The main precepts of Pope's poem advocate a social norm for the critic to employ in aiding good poets and protecting society from inferior poetasters. With an eye to Longinus, Pope notes that genius is a prerequisite and may achieve greatness even in violation of cherished authority.

No one can claim originality for the content of *Essay on Criticism,* but all must admit the incomparable mastery of verse and language.

"Messiah: A Sacred Eclogue" was first printed by Steele in *The Spectator* (#378, May 14, 1712). Pope has made a "harmony" of the Messianic prophecies of Isaiah and Vergil's Eclogue IV. Imitating in the *Pastorals* the middle range of Vergil, Pope here emulates the exalted Vergil, whose high prophetic voice about a coming marvelous boy (probably the son of Pollio, a Roman consul in 40 B.C.) was often interpreted in the Middle Ages as a prediction of Christ. Wordsworth and some other critics have deplored this poem, though parts of it have long been employed as a famous hymn.

Windsor Forest (1713), according to Pope, was first drafted in 1704 with the latter part added in 1710. The finished product is obviously two poems. The first is what Dr. Johnson termed "local poetry," following the lead of Denham's "Cooper's Hill." Although this describes scenery that Pope constantly surveyed, he artfully embroidered it with mythological creatures ("blushing Flora") and elegant epithets ("The bright-ey'd perch with fins of Tyrian dye"). The tacked-on conclusion is Tory praise of the Treaty of Utrecht, which resulted in the Addisonian Whigs breaking with Pope, and Swift's establishing a lasting friendship with him. However, this break and this friendship had been in the works for some time.

"Ode for Music on St. Cecilia's Day" (*1713,* 1717) is an undistinguished tribute to music, quite inferior to Dryden's similar verse. Interestingly, however, this is one of Pope's rare excursions from the heroic couplet, here into the pseudo-Pindaric ode of Cowley.

The Rape of the Lock (two cantos in 1712, enlarged, on Garth's advice, to five cantos in 1714) shows no sign of splicing in its expanded form, as did *Windsor Forest*. From Tassoni's *Sacchia Rapita* ("Raped Bucket," 1622), Pope took only the title suggestion. While the mock-epic genre is an ancient one, the concept of this mock-epic derives immediately from Garth's *Dispensary* and ultimately from Garth's model, Boileau's *Lutrin* (1674–83). Boileau set the pattern for a general, high burlesque poem that would treat of a trivial matter and inconsequential persons in the grand heroic, epic style.

Within the clannish circle of Roman Catholic high society, a considerable rumpus had been aroused because Lord Petre had snipped a lock of hair from the head of Miss Arabella Fermor. John Caryll, a distant relative of Petre, suggested to his friend Pope that he laugh away the contretemps in witty verse. Pope obliged in 1714 with the greatest mock-heroic poem in English:

Summary of The Rape of the Lock

Canto I (Belinda's Toilet). The spoiled society darling Belinda wakes at noon and summons Betty, her maid. Hovering over the girl are the sylphs, in analogy to the supernatural beings attending the figures in epic poetry. Adapted from the satiric *Le Comte de Gabalis* (1670, translated, 1680), by Villars, these sprites of Rosicrucian lore are handled in the spirit of *A Midsummer Night's Dream*. The Rosicrucian sylphs as well as the cosmetic scene that concludes this canto are additions from 1714. The worship of "the Cosmetic pow'rs" satirizes the solemn epic sacrifices to the gods.

Canto II (Sailing up the Thames to Hampton Court). The difficulties of land transportation then favored river-boat rides. Ariel admonishes watchful care by his fellow sylphs, while the Baron meditates the snipping of Belinda's lock. Belinda flirts with all the gentlemen aboard ship, following the code of current fashionable women, a code that sought to incite general masculine interest without committing oneself to any man. The foreboding note imitates the theme of fate in the epic.

Canto III (Card Party at Hampton Court). After gossiping, the party-goers play the fashionable three-handed game of ombre (also an addition of 1714). Pope describes the card-playing in the manner of epic battles, following the lead of Vida's *Game of Chess*. There is no poetic license about the game; in Lamb's "Mrs. Battle's Opinions on Whist," Mrs. Battle plays out this very game to show how completely accurate is Pope's detailing of each turn of the card. As Belinda is pouring coffee, the Baron from behind cuts off a lock of her hair.

Canto IV (The Cave of Spleen). This entire canto is an addition of 1714. Belinda cries in her boudoir for the lost lock, and her friend Thalestris (Mrs. Morley) goads her to hysterical indignation. The passage burlesques the descent to Hades in the *Odyssey* and the *Aeneid*. The foppish Sir Plume (Sir George Brown, brother of Mrs. Morley) unsuccessfully demands that the Baron return the severed lock, in a burlesque of the "word battles" between epic heroes.

Canto V (Battle of the Sexes). Calm remonstrance failing, the ladies decide to take sterner measures against the men. Tossing snuff at the Baron's nose, Belinda causes him to sneeze. At the point of a hair pin he is ordered to return the lock. However, the lock of hair has been carried to the heavens, like Berenice's Locks (the hair of an Egyptian queen transformed into a comet).

Dr. Johnson termed this poem "the most attractive of all ludicrous compositions." Hazlitt dismissed it as the "triumph of insignificance." Pope's point, however, is a social critique of everyday life. The didactic success of the poem is achieved by its colossal gap between the silliness of the episode and the deadly seriousness with which its participants regard it. The mock-heroic style brings the whole quarrel into absurdity. The poem is pure rococo, the one perfect example of this style in English. The delicate, gay manner never sputters but maintains its light quality to the last syllable. A million preachers have railed against the vanity and frivolity of high society, but not one of them could prove as effective and as enjoyable as Pope with his graceful wit and beguiling charm.

"Verses to the Memory of an Unfortunate Lady" (1717) has since substituted "Elegy" for the first word in the original title. In a foreign land a lovely lady of "beauty, titles, wealth, and fame," who "loved too well" and was deserted by her uncle ("false guardian"), stabs herself to death. She lies in unhallowed ground, her grave unmarked except by "rising flowers." Pope suggests strong personal feeling, but in his biography there is no trace of the lady, unless she is a Mrs. Weston mentioned in a 1712 letter. Apparently this is the product of Pope's romantic imagination, for this piece is in the style of the "graveyard school," a type of morbid poetry which we will discuss later in the chapter.

Eloisa to Abelard (1717). The original 12th-century Latin letters exchanged between the philosopher Abelard and his former love, Eloisa, reveal a bitter man and an emotional but restrained woman. In 1687 the Comte de Bussy freely translated Letters II, III, and IV into modern French. The original spirit was here completely altered to the baroque manner of the heroic romances by the Scudérys. Pope read the John Hughes translation (1714) of Bussy and freely versified it without any knowledge of the originals; he even introduces wordings from Abelard's letters. In form Pope imitated the *Heroides,* by Ovid, rhetorical complaints by heroines such as Dido to their former lovers. Pope's central idea is straight from the heroic tragedy of the previous century—the contest of love versus honor. Eloisa is torn between her love for Abelard and her love for God, i.e. carnal versus spiritual love. Largely Pope's own invention is the setting of the poem in a Gothic nunnery amidst dramatic alpine scenery. Pope's technique is baroque heightening, and this may be termed the greatest baroque poem in English.

Second Period: Editing and Translating (1715–1726)

The Iliad of Homer (1715–20 in six volumes) utilized the Greek translating ability of William Broome (1689–1745) and Thomas Parnell (1679–1718), the latter a fellow member of the Scriblerus Club and the author of the long introductory essay prefacing Pope's translation. The work involved a total of nineteen thousand lines, more than all Pope's non-Homeric translations put together. Dr. Richard Bentley, the best Greek scholar of the era, chided the poet: "A pretty poem, Mr. Pope; but you mustn't call it Homer," and in Fielding's *Amelia,* Captain Booth restates the Bentley contention. Pope has not really translated Homer but has imaginatively re-created the *Iliad* in smooth couplets for Augustan England. He scrupulously observed the contemporary standards of "poetic" and "heroic," taking his cue from the *Iliade* (1714) of Hondar de la Motte, which had Homer talk like an 18th-century French neoclassicist. As Dr. Johnson said of Pope, "He has left in his Homer a treasure of poetical elegances to posterity." Until the end of the 19th century this was the standard English translation of Homer, convincing generations of the English-speaking world that Homer was impeccably formal and "correct." The enormous subscription sales and subsequent profits made Pope independently wealthy. A rival Whig translation of the first book of the *Iliad* by Thomas Tickell (1686–1740) was sponsored by Addison and appeared only two days after the publication of Pope's translation in 1715. Addison's support of Tickell and his advice against the alteration of the 1712 version of *The Rape of the Lock* caused Pope's bristling hostility toward the great Whig.

The Odyssey of Homer (fourteen books in 1725, remainder in 1726) was less successful and less Pope. The sheer labor of translation compelled him to enlist aides. Books I, IV, XIX, XX were translated by Elijah Fenton (1683–1730), and Books II, VI, VIII, XI, XII, XVI, XVIII, XXIII were translated by Broome, who also provided all the notes. Pope was accused of underpaying his coadjutors and concealing their large role in the project. Broome admitted, however, that Pope carefully revised every page written by his assistants.

The Works of Shakespear (1725). Nicholas Rowe (whose work will be discussed later in the chapter) was the first true editor of Shakespeare in 1709; Pope was the second. In his preface Pope recognized the excellences of Shakespeare but also noted his defects as they appeared to the Augustan mind. The preface recognized the textual duty of an editor, but the unceasing drudgery of scholarship proved too much for Pope. His knowledge of Elizabethan English was defective and resulted in some grotesque misinterpretations, and the mania for clarity of style produced much unfortunate tinkering with Shakespeare's lines. Pope even "restored" substantial prose passages into blank verse. As an editor of Shakespeare, Pope was poetically perceptive but woefully unscholarly.

Third Period: Satires and Epistles (1728–1744)

The Dunciad is mock-heroic invective satire whose intent is to protect true literature and learning from stultification by pretentious incompetents. Until the edition of 1742 the word *dunce* is used by Pope in the sense of Renaissance humanists, who derived the name from one of the great medieval minds, Duns Scotus, and used it to mean the woeful misapplication of talents by intelligent men. Hence pedantry, abstruse and vacuous erudition, and minute hair-splitting are the targets of the work. With the 1742 edition, however, Pope shifts the meaning of *dunce* to the modern sense of stupidity, and thus the target becomes insipidity and meaninglessness. Throughout, of course, dullness is the universal sin of Pope's dunces. The growth of *The Dunciad* is a tangled flowering, simplified thus:

As early as 1725 Pope was discussing the concept with Swift and Gay. It is impossible, however, to know what constituted this "Ur-Dunciad."

Lewis Theobald (1688–1744) produced in 1726 a two-hundred-page review of Pope's edition of Shakespeare—*Shakespeare Restored: or, A Specimen of the Many Errors as Well Committed, as Unamended, by Mr. Pope*. Much of Theobald is petty, but essentially the criticism of Pope's edition is justified. Theobald therefore made himself liable to Pope's satire. Personal vindictiveness is obvious, but Pope and his circle, with gentlemanly disdain, sneered at what they deemed Theobald's pedantic minutiae.

"Peri Bathous, or The Art of Sinking in Poetry" (March 1728), in the last volume of the Pope-Swift *Miscellanies,* contains grave instructions by "Martinus Scriblerus" (Pope) for the writing of dull verse. (Four volumes of the Pope-Swift *Miscellanies in Prose and Verse* were published from 1727 to 1732.) A host of inferior poets of the era are thinly disguised under initials. For the next two months the journals were seething with abuse of Pope. The trap was ready for springing.

The Dunciad (May 1728) in three books appeared anonymously and under a misleading publisher's name with an equally misleading place of publication, partly to sidestep possible libel actions, but chiefly as a literary spoof.

The Dunciad Variorum with the Prolegomena of Scriblerus (1729) was offered as the "complete" and "perfect" version of the satire. Almost one hundred lines were added to the poem, along with a bulky tongue-in-cheek paraphernalia of Prolegomena, Remarks, and Appendixes. Modeled largely upon Dryden's *Mac Flecknoe,* the satire enshrines Theobald as the King of the Dunces, successor to Elkanah Settle.

Book I pictures Theobald in his library, which is composed of volumes of dull poetry and tomes of antiquarian interest, "Classicks of an Age that heard of none." He is about to burn his own dull writings upon an altar of his ponderous library books when the goddess of Dulness transports him to her abode and crowns him King of Dunces.

Book II consists of games, mock imitations from the *Iliad* and *Aeneid,* attendant upon Theobald's coronation. Here penetrating ingenuity scourges unscrupulous booksellers, authors fawning upon patrons, narrowly political writers, inditers of smut, and dramatists depending upon bombast and stage effects. The concluding game is an endurance contest to see who can stay awake through the reading of Sir Richard Blackmore's endless epics.

Book III has Theobald, asleep from the previous book, dream of "th' Elyzian shade," where Settle (like Anchises to Aeneas) presents a monumental vision of Dulness. Theobald witnesses the past and present triumphs of Dulness and, in a ringing finale, the ultimate victory of the forces of Dulness, when "universal darkness covers all."

The New Dunciad (1742) is a fourth book fulfilling the prophecy at the end of Book III. Dulness, inanity, and perverted taste now rule unchallenged. Chief satire is directed against education in school and college. The epitome of dullness, this education is certain guarantee of the perpetuation of the reign of Dulness to future generations.

In 1730 Colley Cibber, a staunch Whig, had succeeded Laurence Eusden as poet laureate. Though an accomplished actor and successful playwright, Cibber was no poet; Pope understandably considered this appointment the nadir of contemporary letters. In *An Apology for the Life of Mr. Colley Cibber* (1740), the poet laureate good-naturedly objected to Pope's satirizing of him as a minor dunce. In *A Letter from Mr. Cibber to Mr. Pope* (1742), the poet laureate protested more vigorously, and in *Another Occasional Letter* (January 1743), Cibber was wholly enraged and vituperative.

The Dunciad (October 1743) is by Pope's own statement a close parody of the *Aeneid*. The epic action of the *Aeneid* was considered to be the removal of the empire of Troy to Latium; similarly, the epic action of the *Dunciad* is removal of the imperial seat of Dulness from the City (the Merchants' center of London) to the polite world; that is, the merchants and Whigs are taking over the country under Hanoverian rule and the culture is degenerating. The specific parody was of the Dryden translation of the *Aeneid*.

This final 1743 form makes considerable substitutions of dunces, especially in now proclaiming Cibber the King of Dunces instead of Theobald. The essential framework of the four books outlined above is maintained even to the point of ascribing Theobald's type of library quite incongruously to Cibber. The many insignificant writers here granted a dubious immortality should be interpreted as types of inferior literary standards. This was Pope's last work and, according to many critics, his best. Never is the poet's command of the heroic couplet as complete as here, and, perhaps astonishingly, Pope rises on occasion to the truest epic writing of the age.

THE ETHIC EPISTLES. As early as 1729, in a letter to Swift, Pope indicated his intention of writing ethical or didactic verse. Later he conceived of an entire volume of ethic epistles forming one treatise upon all human morality; never completed, the fragments are nonetheless the fullest statement of Augustan principles of ethics. Pope was neither a profound nor a systematic thinker; rather, he purposely ignored metaphysics and theology in striving to create a humanistic structure that would be completely rational and secular.

"Epistle to Richard Boyle, Earl of Burlington, of the Use of Riches" (Moral Essay, IV) (1731). The present order of the *Moral Essays* was established by Warburton, who edited the poems after Pope's death. Pope speaks as Horace to Maecenas (Burlington) in the tone of the genteel Romans. He portrays Timon as the tasteless man of wealth, given to vain pomp and show, while Burlington is celebrated as the ideal man of wealth, responsible aristocrat who builds in good taste for purposes of social utility.

"Epistle to Allen, Lord Bathurst, of the Use of Riches" (Moral Essay, III) (1733). Pope is appalled by the money-mad Walpole era, and he contrasts the extremes among the well-to-do—the miserly skinflint and the reckless extravagant. His ideal is the country gentleman who recognizes that his position and his wealth are public trusts and therefore engages himself in sane and constructive philanthropy. Such men are Lord Bathurst and "The Man of Ross" (John Kyrle), the latter a famed humanitarian of Ross, Hertfordshire.

Essay on Man (three epistles in 1733, fourth epistle in 1734) is inscribed to Henry St. John, Viscount Bolingbroke, from whom Pope may have derived most of the ideas for this poem. Bolingbroke, in turn, is largely indebted to the *Theodicée* (1710) of the German baron Gottfried von Leibniz. The philosophical position of the work is that of optimistic deism (which we discussed in the previous chapter). The poem was widely applauded until the *Examen* (1737) of the Swiss theologian Crousaz condemned it for heresy. However, Crousaz's work was based on the poem's inaccurate translation into French. Pope wished to be considered an orthodox Christian, and when the Anglican bishop William Warburton, in a series of letters in 1738, contended that Pope was orthodox, the poet wrote a letter to the bishop in 1739, lamely stating: "I know I meant just what you explain; but I did not explain my own meaning as well as you." Although influenced, perhaps more than he realized, by contemporary deism, Pope steadfastly maintained his Roman Catholic affiliation, and the priest at his deathbed declared full satisfaction with Pope's last confession.

The poem, like Milton's *Paradise Lost,* seeks to vindicate the ways of God to man, but, typically of Pope's era, it seeks the rational, phenomenological basis of natural theology rather than something similar to Milton's sacred theology. It is not a treatise upon man but rather a survey of the moral order in the universe of which man is part. Providence is vindicated by the assertion that apparent evil arises from human failure to see the total plan of the universe. The resultant position is a "cosmic Toryism" that desires a maintenance of the *status quo.* Actually, Pope declares: "Whatever is, is right," and tinkering with the system is impious. This does not mean that everything is perfect, but rather that there is a reason for whatever appears to be imperfect.

Summary of Essay on Man

Epistle I, "Of the Nature and State of Man, with Respect to the Universe." It is Pope's contention here that man sees but the part; God sees the whole. Our ignorance and weakness are right, fitting us to our place in the "Great Chain of Being," upon which all creatures from microbes to angels are neatly arranged. (To Pope, this chain is rigid and static; in the next century the chain, set in motion, will represent evolution.) The concept of the "Chain of Being" was important at least as far back as medieval and Renaissance thought, and in Pope's age nearly everyone discusses it. To Pope, the apparent confusion of the scheme of things conceals a perfect harmony.

Epistle II, "Of the Nature and State of Man, with Respect to Himself as an Individual." Pope sees man governed by two principles, Self-love and Reason (i.e. selfishness and common sense). Every man is driven by a "ruling Passion," an idea that is a derivation of the "humours" concept. The restraining influence of Reason upon the Passions results in the creative balance and achievement of mankind. In spite of anguished protests to the contrary, the internal nature of man is precisely what it should be.

Epistle III, "Of the Nature and State of Man, with Respect to Society." In society, man's drive for self-fulfillment works perfectly for the good of all. In striving for his own interests, man assures the best interests of his species. God "bade Self-love and Social be the same."

Epistle IV, "Of the Nature and State of Man, with Respect to Happiness." A universe inflicting evil and pain will not conveniently produce the ease, pleasure, and contentment often called happiness. Pope, therefore, defines happiness as virtue, dependent not upon externals but upon the realization of man's inner life. This Stoic virtue, that of the genial Horace rather than of the austere Marcus Aurelius, should be cultivated into a benevolent attitude toward all the world. By recognizing God's holy plan throughout the universe and by re-creating this harmonious balance within himself through self-knowledge, man will truly achieve lasting happiness.

Voltaire termed this "The most beautiful, the most excellent poem ever written in any language." Dr. Johnson differed strenuously: "Never were penury of knowledge and vulgarity of sentiment so happily disguised." Pope was neither a philosopher nor a wholly consistent thinker, and we must realize that the contribution of this work is not to thought but to poetry. Pope's capacity to render abstract concepts in vivid phrases and telling images has made this poem, along with the *Essay on Criticism,* one of the most quoted of the language.

"Epistle to Sir Richard Temple, Lord Cobham, of the Knowledge and Characters of Men" (Moral Essay, I) (1734). Though Pope reaffirms the Ruling Passion as the clue to the understanding of character differences, he recognizes the dark mysteries from which human impulses spring. Pope clearly perceives the impossibility of penetrating to the root of human nature because of the ceaseless changing and shifting spirit of man; therefore he considers all abstract systems to explain man's innermost nature to be doomed to ultimate failure.

"Epistle to a Lady [Martha Blount] of the Characters of Women" (Moral Essay, II) (1735). Pope offers a series of portrait paintings of contemporary society ladies, thinly disguised as Pastora (Countess of Pembroke), Atossa (Duchess of Buckinghamshire), and so on. The elegant outward picturings do not conceal the tangles most of these women have made of their lives, and the poet ironically shakes his head at social hypocrisy and discreet sinning.

THE HORATIAN EPISTLES. Pope's imitations of Horace, written during the same period as the ethic epistles and bearing a close kinship to them, are distinguished by their overt satire and their conscious re-creation of the manner of Horace. No other verses in English have so captured the conversational ease and polished sophistication of that Roman poet. A great deal of the pleasure in this work consists in the literate reader's comparison of the original Latin model with Pope's brilliant application of Horace to the 18th century.

The First Satire of the Second Book of Horace, Imitated (1733) expresses familiar themes of Pope's verse: his compulsion to write, his pride in moral independence, his detestation of folly and dullness, his impatience with pretense and incompetence, and his preference for re-fined friends and a life of elegant retirement. The thinly veiled personal attacks in the work elicited angry counterattacks.

An Epistle to Dr. Arbuthnot (1735) is Pope's apologia, a poetic biography. He portrays himself as the model of moderation and genteel decorum, intent upon high standards for the realm of art. He has attacked specific persons only as they typify violations of good taste and judgment. Especially famous is the portrait of Atticus (Addison), which carefully acknowledges the victim's virtues only to make devastatingly effective the indictment of him as a cold prig. The poem also contains the satiric portrait of Lord Hervey (discussed later) as "Sporus." The value of this poem lies in the matchless grace—even lyricism—of the gentlemanly conversation between Pope and Arbuthnot.

The First Epistle of the Second Book of Horace, to Augustus (1737) is Pope's definitive evaluation of his own Augustan age and its standards of life and art. He reviews what he considers the major 17th-century authors and highly praises the "true Augustans" of his own period, balancing the claims of correctness with poetic fire. The political references are ironic, for George II was notoriously indifferent to the arts, and Pope, as a Tory, thoroughly opposed the current Whig foreign policy.

Epilogue to the Satires (1738) is the now familiar label Warburton gave to two dialogues originally titled "One Thousand Seven Hundred and Thirty Eight." Although more Horatian epistles were to follow, this is an appropriate end to all thirteen of the series. The date in the title indicates the last great bid of the Tories for power in Pope's lifetime. The poet sees in the corrupt Walpole administration and the consequent public apathy the fall of his cherished hopes for an elite culture and literature. Pope's vehemence and his petty animosity do not destroy an essentially apocalyptic vision of a topsy-turvy world: "Not to be corrupted is the Shame."

Pope's Prose Writings

Though lacking the brilliance and incisiveness of Swift's prose, Pope's prose shows much of the same clarity, brevity, and effectiveness that characterized his verse. In addition to the prose pieces mentioned above, Pope wrote several more essays for *The Guardian*. In ⚹61 he displayed what was for his time a strong and unusual opposition toward cruelty to animals. In ⚹173 he indicated his advocacy of the natural garden against the formal gardens on the French model.

One of the least praiseworthy aspects of Pope comes to light in the handling of his personal correspondence. It was not considered proper then for a gentleman to permit the public printing of his private letters; yet in an attempt to display his moral character, Pope schemed to get his letters into print. He engineered an apparently surreptitious printing of some of his letters in 1735 and then seized upon this as an excuse for an "authorized" edition in 1737. He continued to publish other letters through 1741. The printed letters were considerably altered from their original form, even to combining several letters into one and changing the names of the correspondents. In an attempt to strengthen his reputation, Pope, by this piece of trickery, injured his integrity and in the long run lost more than he gained.

THE CIRCLE OF POPE

THE SCRIBLERUS CLUB. Formed by Pope and Swift in 1713 or even earlier, the Scriblerus Club, an informal organization, united the leading Tory wits in an assault upon literary incompetence and social deficiencies. Satire was their major tool in preaching rationalism and polish. Some of the most popular and memorable works of the age, such as *Gulliver's Travels, The Beggar's Opera,* and *The Dunciad,* were struck out from the sparks kindled at the sessions of the Scriblerus Club, even though politics caused the life of the club to be formally terminated in 1714. Other than Pope and Swift, the most notable figures of the club were John Gay and John Arbuthnot.

John Gay (1685–1732). Born at Barnstaple and educated at the Barnstaple Grammar School, John Gay was apprenticed at seventeen to a silk mercer. He abandoned this trade in 1706 in favor of writing. When the Tories were in power, he held minor government posts, but during the Whig administration he had to depend upon the bounty of patrons.

The Shepherd's Week (1714) consists of six "pastorals" in heroic couplets. Intended as a burlesque riposte to the pastorals of Ambrose Philips, these poems present a realistic picture of English rural life which foreshadows the later George Crabbe.

Trivia, or the Art of Walking the Streets of London (1716) is intended as a mockery of the georgic, or country, poem. Its heroic couplets offer the best description in the age of life on the streets of the metropolis. Gay offers excellent advice on avoiding a splash of mud from passing carriages, preventing the depredations of pickpockets, and evading the solicitations of streetwalkers.

Fables (first series, 1727; second series, 1738; total of over sixty editions before 1800) are among the best of this genre in the language, although the form has not proved widely popular among English writers. Johnson accused Gay of confusing allegory, fable, and tale; but such criticism is inappropriate to these blithe bagatelles. Each fable is a brief narrative in octosyllabics ("The Painter Who Pleased No Body and Every Body," "The Elephant and the Bookseller") which carefully points to an obvious and conventional moral.

The Beggar's Opera (1728)—Ballad Opera. With this work, Gay created a form unique to the early 18th century. The basis of the new form was a prose burlesque interspersed with numerous songs sung to popular folk airs. The genre was an extension of the technique, familiar since Elizabethan days, of introducing songs into comic dialogue. The popularity of Italian opera had acclimated the era to musical drama, and the conventions and artificialities of opera and current tragedy proved inviting targets for burlesque. Undoubtedly *The Beggar's Opera* was the most popular state presentation of the century.

Captain Macheath, leader of a gang of highwaymen, is the hero of *The Beggar's Opera*. His wife, Polly Peachum, remains faithful to him, though Macheath makes love to many women, most importantly Lucy Lockit, the Jailer's daughter. Macheath's father-in-law is the apparently respectable Jeremy Peachum, "fence" for the gang and unscrupulous informer to the law when it serves his interests. Peachum betrays Macheath, who is imprisoned in Newgate jail; and his escape, recapture, trial, sentencing to death, and final reprieve form the episodes of the drama. On his release, Macheath promises Polly he will be true to her henceforth.

Swift, who apparently suggested this "Newgate pastoral" to Gay, a fellow Tory and Scriblerian, declared that it "hath knocked down Gulliver." It is the only piece of stagecraft in the period to remain constantly in the English theatrical repertoire down to the present. *The Beggar's Opera* hit three satiric targets in its own era:

(1) The Italian opera, burlesqued in its creaking plot and set arias. The work sets its vulgar low life and English folk tunes against the more pretentious and ornate music of the foreign operas, particularly those of Handel.

(2) The vices of high society. Macheath is as gallant a Don Juan as any contemporary dandy, Polly is as sentimental as any of the heroines of contemporary drama, and the Peachums maintain as decorous an outward respectability as contemporary gentlefolk. Gay makes the point, "that it is difficult to determine whether [in the fashionable vices] the fine gentlemen imitate the Gentlemen of the Road, or the Gentlemen of the Road the fine gentlemen." Gay asks if there is any true difference, except in degree, between the seamy underworld and the shameless upper crust.

(3) Whig politics. The quarrel of Macheath and Peachum is that of Walpole and his brother-in-law and fellow minister, Lord Townshend. The Prime Minister acknowledged his portrait in Macheath by leading the applause on the first night and banning the sequel, *Polly* (1729). The printed text of *Polly* brought Gay twice what he obtained from *The Beggar's Opera*.

Numerous imitations of Gay followed, often categorizing themselves as outlandishly as "Tragi-Comi-Operatic Pastoral Farce," but they were cut essentially from Gay's fabric. By mid-century the exploitation of folk tunes had worn itself out, and the satiric impulse was weakened by the new taste for sentiment.

John Arbuthnot (är-buth′not) (1667–1735). Born at Arbuthnot,

Scotland, John Arbuthnot studied at Oxford and received his medical degree from St. Andrews in 1696. In 1705 he became Physician Extraordinary to Queen Anne. He was a friend of all the literary lights of the age, including Swift, Pope, Congreve, and Lord Chesterfield.

The History of John Bull was the title given in the Pope-Swift *Miscellanies* of 1727 to five collected pamphlets first published by Arbuthnot in 1712 in support of Swift's *Conduct of the Allies*. In allegorical fashion this prose work relates historical events of the immediately previous years; John Bull is England, successive parliaments are his wives, the Established Church is his mother, and the war with France is a wearisome lawsuit. Such a summary might suggest dull Tory propaganda, but it actually is a lusty picaresque account, gaily invective and brilliantly apposite. The style is a robust heartiness. Altogether, Macaulay termed it "the most ingenious and humorous political satire extant in our language." The popularity of the work has fixed in the language the name of John Bull as a reference to the typical Englishman.

The Memoirs of Martinus Scriblerus (1741) was published by Pope, who undoubtedly contributed much, but it was largely the work of Arbuthnot, with some aid from Gay. Cornelius Scriblerus, the pedantic father of Martinus, tries to educate his son in what he thinks was the ancient manner, e.g., he has the Greek alphabet imprinted on his son's gingerbread. Sterne drew upon this work for many of his ideas about Tristram Shandy's eccentric education. Martinus grows up to be a self-assumed analyst of all human problems of mind and soul. He thus is the butt of the club's attacks upon all philosophic system and pedantry. Martinus falls in love with one of a pair of Siamese twins, a happening that entails ludicrous legal complications. Quickly summarized are his voyages to the areas visited by Gulliver. Only the first book of a long projected prose work is printed. *Don Quixote* and *Hudibras* are among the important sources.

OTHER POETRY OF THE AGE

Matthew Prior (1664–1721). Born in East Dorset, Matthew Prior was educated at Westminster School and Cambridge. Under powerful Whig patrons he prepared for public life, in 1699 succeeding Locke as Commissioner of Trade and Plantations and also becoming Undersecretary of State. By 1711, however, he had become a devoted Tory. As ambassador to Paris he was the chief negotiator of the Treaty of Utrecht (1713), which was derisively labeled "Matt's Peace." During the Whig triumph he was in prison (1715–17), where he wrote his most ambitious poem, *Alma: or, The Progress of the Mind* (*1716, 1718*). This poem was a general satire on philosophical systems. After his release he lived quietly at Down Hall, Essex, for most of his remaining years.

Poems on Several Occasions (1709) contains most of what today's anthologies retain from Prior. His serious verse is generally forgotten; it is as a master of light verse that he is now remembered. While politically assailing Prior in the *Whig Examiner,* Addison granted him "a happy talent of doggerel, where he writes on a known subject: where he tells us in plain intelligible language." Prior excelled in gay octosyllabics and epigrams. His amorous verse is graceful, conversational, and unsentimental. Of course, verse to him was a diversion from an active political career, and his work exemplified the Augustan ideal of ease and polish, politeness and good humor. It also demonstrated that the best practicing poet at the century's outset was a world away from the Renaissance power of the 17th century that affected even Dryden. Almost every versifier in the first half of the 18th century was to produce light, Alexandrian poems and *vers de société,* but Prior was the greatest in this genre.

THEMES AND GENRES OF MINOR POETS.

The following discussion lists a number of different kinds of verse written in this age, some of which will seem foreign to our present-day attitudes toward lyric poetry.

SATIRE. As the works of Swift and Pope have demonstrated, the characteristics of the age favored satire, which, in verse, chiefly took the form of the mock-heroic. The neoclassic critical principles asserted that the epic was the greatest form of non-dramatic verse and that imitation of the great epic poets was admirable. For a non-heroic age the epic was inappropriate, though Sir Richard Blackmore (c. 1650–1729), in *The Creation* (1712), laboriously fashioned one of the longest and dullest epic poems in English. More congenial to the era was the burlesque of the epic, perhaps ultimately derived from the ancient *Batrachomyomachia* (translated by Thomas Parnell in 1717), but stemming more recently from Dryden's *Mac Flecknoe,* Boileau's *Lutrin* (translated by John Ozell in 1708), and Tassoni's *Sacchia Rapita* (translated by Ozell in 1713). Educated readers of the time found pleasure in the echoes of Homer, Vergil, and Milton; the burlesque was not to ridicule the models but to berate unheroic contemporaries in pseudo-elevated strains.

The Dispensary (1699, with revisions up to 1714), by Sir Samuel Garth (1661–1719), was occasioned by the 1687 edict of the London College of Physicians requiring its members to dispense free advice and medicaments to the poor. The apothecaries, expecting a reduction in their profits, bitterly opposed the edict. In the poem Sloth induces Envy, who assumes the guise of an apothecary, to stir up animosity, resulting in an epic drug-slinging battle between apothecaries and physicians. The goddess Health appears to shame all into professional behavior and to ministration to the needy. Homeric and Vergilian parodies abound, and the work is in heroic couplets.

"The Splendid Shilling" (1701), by John Philips (1676–1709), is a blank-verse imitation of Milton, mildly lamenting Philips's penniless condition in contemporary London. The parody is vigorous, colorful, and mercifully brief.

"The Spleen" (1701), by Anne Finch, Countess of Winchelsea, burlesques the pseudo-Pindaric ode of Cowley in a social satire of the fashionable fools parading an air of boredom and melancholia.

Namby-Pamby (1725), by Henry Carey (c. 1687–1743), laughingly parodied the nursery pieces of Ambrose Philips in the same year, pieces addressed to the infant girls Charlotte and Margaret Pulteney. The title of Carey's derogatory work has become a permanent fixture in the language. Carey is perhaps most famous for his song "Sally in Our Alley."

A Pipe of Tobacco (1735), by Isaac Hawkins Browne, offered the most famous parodies of the era. His parodies of Thomson and Young are perhaps his best, while the one of Pope is quoted by Jane Austen in *Mansfield Park*. Strangely enough, parody was comparatively rare in the period.

The School-Mistress (1737, expanded 1742), by William Shenstone (1714–63), is a burlesque idyll in Spenserian stanzas of the "dame school." In spite of its bantering tone, it amounts to a respectful tribute to schoolmarms laboring amidst unscholastic atmospheres.

DIDACTIC VERSE. Since the neoclassic age was certain that the role of art was to instruct through pleasure, verse was frequently employed to teach. The period enjoyed the graceful art of phrasing advice melodically. The prime model for the genre was the *Georgics* of Vergil, which beautifully versified the lore of husbandry. The age also believed that Homer had been a source for military science, etiquette, and many other kinds of knowledge to the ancients.

The most famous didactic poem of the age was *Cyder* (1708), by

John Philips. In blank verse, Philips offers excellent advice about grafting, budding, pruning, choosing soils, preparing compost, and battling pests. In the same year William King (1663–1712) produced a most elegant imitation of Horace's *Ars Poetica* entitled *The Art of Cookery.* The diversity of didactic verse may be suggested by two poems of 1729: *The Art of Politics,* by James Bramston (c. 1694–1744), and *The Art of Dancing,* by Soame Jenyns (1704–87).

SCIENTIFIC AND PHILOSOPHICAL VERSE. A favorite specialization in didactic verse, of which Pope's *Essay on Man* is the greatest example, was a poetizing of the investigations of the Enlightenment for the popular reader. Lucretius (translated by Thomas Creech in 1682) was the chief inspirer in verse and Newton in subject matter. Typical was *The Excursion* (1728), by David Mallet (c. 1705–65), which treated of the earth in the first canto and of the solar system and the starry heavens in the second. The voice of Milton is haltingly heard in blank verse, which, however, largely follows Thomson, and afar off can be discerned the later Shelley, for Mallet is stirred by a vision of cosmic grandeur.

The Grumbling Hive; or, Knaves Turn'd Honest (1705) was expanded into *The Fable of the Bees; or, Private Vices, Publick Benefits* (1714, Part 2 in 1729), by Bernard Mandeville (1670–1733). Tumbling octosyllabic couplets, reminiscent of *Hudibras,* propound the expansionist theory of economics: the greater the demand for goods and the circulation of money, the greater the prosperity and general wellbeing. Individual greed and vice therefore promote the general welfare. Like Butler, Mandeville is an opponent of hypocrisy; he is not favoring vice but demanding that men face up to the truths of an acquisitive society. Mandeville follows much of Hobbes in his view of mankind, and, more bluntly than most of his fellows, states the Enlightenment's recognition of human limitations, of the sham of much idealism, and of the reality of selfish human competition.

CONTEMPLATIVE POEMS. Allied tenuously to the didactic poem was the frequently rambling piece of 18th-century poetry that began with the writer's personal observation and reading and then discursively roamed over many subjects. Moralizing, anecdotes, descriptions of city and countryside, graceful tributes to the elegant and the learned, bemoaning of human follies, and admonitory comment on the present state of England could all be worked into this personal contemplation. *The Wanderer* (1729), by Richard Savage (c. 1697–1743), who was made famous in a biography of him by Dr. Johnson, is just such a potpourri in heroic couplets. Such a genre tended away from the neoclassic norm and produced its greatest example in Young's *Night Thoughts.*

PASTORAL POETRY. Behind the 18th-century pastoral verse was the English tradition from Spenser on, but the chief inspiration was from the ancients—Theocritus, Vergil, and Horace. Neoclassic pastoralism was essentially not a faithful copy of the ancients, however, but a rococo art, creating an imaginary Arcadia of limpid sylvan beauty, inhabited by mythological personages. The age made no pretense of realism here but frankly posited an unreal world of charm and quaintness. Bluff Dr. Johnson, a stout neoclassicist, thoroughly disliked this pseudo-pastoralism, and Gay and Swift gleefully burlesqued it.

Pastorals (four in 1708, two more in 1709), by Ambrose Philips (1674–1749), were highly praised by Thomas Tickell. Pope anonymously gave ironic praise to these in *The Guardian* (∦40, April 15, 1713), extolling them for all the wrong reasons—the simplicity of inane lines and crude diction—and denigrated his own pastorals by comparison.

Nereides, or Sea-Eclogues (1712), by William Diaper (1685–1717), struck a new note in English verse. Diaper's heroic couplets display a genuine knowledge about and love of the sea, thus, perhaps surprising for a seafaring people, providing the first poem in English to be highly appreciative of the open ocean.

The Thresher's Labour (1730), by Stephen Duck (1705–56), is an antidote to the pastoral poem. Though in wooden heroic couplets, this verse from a humble farm worker reveals the true miseries of agricultural life and anticipates Crabbe.

"RETIREMENT" POETRY. Beguilingly, Horace sang of the pleasures of his villa in the Sabine Hills, far from the bustle and chicanery of Rome. London of the 18th century was as dirty and disagreeable as ancient Rome and induced similar Horatian effusions, even from confirmed urbanites.

The Choice (1700), in heroic couplets by John Pomfret (1677–1702), set the vogue. In many respects it is the quintessence of neoclassicism, calling for a moderate life by a refined country gentleman surrounded by classically educated friends and by the classics themselves. The dignified calm of Pope's "Ode on Solitude" (1726) and of scores of similar pieces echoed Pomfret.

The Spleen (1737), by Matthew Green (1696–1737), refers in title to the common 18th-century designation for melancholia. In graceful octosyllabic couplets, Green gives remedies for this malady, including society, classic literature, and constructive interests.

THE ESSAYS AND OTHER WORKS OF ADDISON AND STEELE

Joseph Addison (1672–1719). Born at Milston, Wiltshire, Joseph Addison was educated at Charterhouse (where Steele was a school-mate) and Oxford, where he won high praise for his Latin verse. A Latin poem (1697) on the Peace of Ryswick secured for him a £300 pension from the Whig government and fixed him as the great literary voice of Whiggism. Extensive European travel (1699–1703) helped fit him for important government and diplomatic service. He rose through a series of responsible posts to become Secretary of State (1717–18). In 1716 he married the Countess of Warwick.

Macaulay's adulation of Addison has often been superseded by a distaste for the cool priggishness of this superior Whig. Historically Addison is the spokesman for the Whig aristocracy and the first great lay voice to assume the direction of morals in a secular age. Culturally he is a notable social moralist, instilling urbanity and *savoir faire* into a brutal era. Literarily he is a consummate stylist of English prose, numbering Benjamin Franklin and countless others among the students of his style. It was poetry, however, that started his ascent:

"A Letter from Italy" (*1701*, 1703) consists of heroic couplets addressed to his Whig patron, Lord Halifax. The beauty and richness of the Italian landscape are contrasted with the misery of the peasants, which induces the poet to a rhapsody on English freedom. In liveliness and movement it is often deemed his best poetry, as Pope so judged it.

"The Campaign" (1704) was commissioned by Godolphin, Chancel-lor of the Exchequer, at the recommendation of Lord Halifax. The High Church Tories wished to belittle the Duke of Marlborough and his land victory at Blenheim in order to exalt the naval triumphs of Sir George Rooke. The Whigs sided with Marlborough, whom Addison extravagantly praises with facile heroic couplets in baroque heighten-ing appropriate to the conquering hero. This poem won the under-secretaryship of state for Addison in 1706 and started his political star upward. Thackeray quotes extensively from this poem in *Henry Esmond*.

"Ode" ("The Spacious Firmament on high") (first printed in *The*

Spectator, ✗465, August 23, 1712), derived from Psalm XIX, expounds a familiar concept ("The heavens declare the glory of God"), an idea that was granted extra potency by the astronomical observations and theories culminating in Newton. As religious verse this is a signal instance of the rational approach to faith in the era and it also has traces of *deism*.

But verse was not Addison's forte, although, according to Pope, he valued it highest of his work. Addison wrote poetry because in his era it was the established medium for the literary man. His genius lay in the periodical essay, and his opportunity came with:

The Tatler (April 12, 1709–January 2, 1711), published three times weekly by Steele. The first four issues were free; then they cost a penny an issue, and later twopence each. Steele had originally intended a newspaper including foreign and domestic news, but, largely through the influence of Addison, who started contributions with ✗18, the essay soon predominated and journalism was transformed into literature. About sixty of the papers in *The Tatler* were contributed by Addison. Ostensibly the essays originated in the coffeehouses (amusements from White's, literature from Will's, learning from the Grecian, news from St. James's). Steele's purpose was to insinuate moral reforms through pleasurable reading. Each essay was purposely brief to avoid frightening off the reader who worriedly measures length, and the content was couched for a non-erudite audience. For a London much smaller than today, it proved a rather accurate mirror and commentary.

The Spectator (March 1, 1711–December 6, 1712, in six issues weekly; June 18, 1714–December 20, 1714, in three issues weekly) sold about three thousand to four thousand copies of each separate issue until the stamp tax imposed on and after August 1, 1712, reduced sales because of the increased price. Publication in bound volumes was even more successful, for Steele states in the last number of Volume VII that nine thousand copies each of the first four volumes had been sold. Before 1800 *The Spectator* went through over fifty editions. The coffeehouse framework of *The Tatler* was supplanted here by a fictitious club; *The Tatler* developed randomly, but *The Spectator* was carefully planned. It proved to be the supreme representative of a uniquely 18th century type of publication—the single-essay periodical. Addison contributed 274 papers which he identified by one of the four letters C.L.I.O. The revival of *The Spectator* in 1714 was by Addison.

The most memorable figure of *The Spectator*'s fictitious club is Sir

Roger de Coverley, invented by Steele and perfected by Addison. The name is taken from a country dance, similar to the Virginia reel, which Addison claims was invented by the great-grandfather of Sir Roger. This country gentleman is a harmlessly senile Tory, the greatest "humours" portrait or "character" in English literature, developed from the 17th-century example of Jonson, Overbury, and Earle. Sir Roger wears the old-fashioned garb of the previous century, is whimsically prejudiced at all points, and, though a Justice of the Peace, is learned only in the Game Act for hunting, and permits no one but himself to sleep in church. The portrait is a gentle satire of the Tories—old-fashioned and charming, but incompetent to run a government. The rest of the "club" is composed of characters who handle different subjects—amusements by Will Honeycomb, man of fashion; literature by the Templar, professional man; learning by the Templar, the Clergyman, and especially Mr. Spectator. Other characters are Sir Andrew Freeport, commercial magnate, and Captain Sentry, of the military.

The Guardian (March 12–October 1, 1713, in six issues weekly) was originated by Steele. Addison wrote fifty-three of the essays. Claiming impartiality, this publication, like all those by Steele and Addison, was discreetly Whig.

The Freeholder (December 23, 1715–June 29, 1716, twice weekly) was Addison's own publication but added no essentially new material.

Old Whig (two numbers, March and April 1719) was a purely political publication by Addison, supporting the Whig proposal for limitation upon the size of the peerage.

By general acknowledgment, Addison's best work was for *The Spectator,* for which he personally fitted the aloof and omniscient figure of Mr. Spectator. The range of Addison's essays was enormous, but he concentrated chiefly upon two categories—social and "philosophical." The social essays seek to inculcate the Whig principles of tolerance and commerce into a genteel society. Addison might be termed the "first Victorian," for he preaches etiquette, good public morals, and community betterment. He covers the entire realm of social education from the proper types of feminine millinery to the extravagances of Italian opera. His manner here is smiling and gracious, blandly Horatian in satire. Some modern critics may object that it is the surface of life that altogether concerns him, but he undoubtedly exercised a civilizing influence on the age.

The "philosophical" essays were an open popularization of the mighty streams of ideas circulating among the intellectuals of the age. *Spectator* #10 (March 12, 1711) enunciates the avowed purpose of the periodical, "to enliven morality with wit, and to temper wit with morality," and further proceeds to state Addison's desire to bring philosophy "out of closets, and libraries, schools, and colleges, to dwell in clubs and assemblies, at tea-tables and in coffee-houses." Here Addison is serious but never ponderous, lucidly explaining Locke and Descartes, Newton and Burnet, to an interested but unpolished audience. Not himself an original thinker, Addison performed an invaluable service in conveying erudite thought to the lay reader.

Minor in number but highly significant were Addison's papers on literary criticism. The two on the ballad of Chevy Chase (*Spectator* #70, May 21, and #74, May 25, 1711) have usually been heralded as the inauguration of the modern critical taste for the English and Scottish popular ballads. In neoclassic fashion he tried to justify the ballads in analogy to classic literature. The Saturday papers on *Paradise Lost* (starting with *Spectator* #267, January 5, 1712, and running on consecutive Saturdays through #369) are not profound analyses of Milton but represent the first effective critical recommendation of Milton, with justification through Aristotle, Longinus, Vergil, and contemporary French critical theory. "On the Pleasures of the Imagination" was designed as a single extended essay but appeared continuously in *The Spectator* from #411 (June 21, 1712) to #421; Addison is a bit muddled in trying to follow Hobbes and Locke, but when he follows his own inclinations, he anticipates Akenside and the Romantics in seeing Imagination as a creative and illuminating vision. The fundamental critical position of Addison, however, is neoclassic. From #58 (May 7, 1711) through #62 of *The Spectator,* he develops Locke's distinction between wit and judgment into a lengthy criticism of 17th-century metaphysical poetry and all kindred writings firmly supporting "clear and distinct ideas" in rational, unambiguous verse.

Addison's greatest achievement rests in his "middle style" of prose, the neoclassic ideal. His essays are simply but beautifully organized, and the prose flows in clear, perfectly understandable harmony. Dr. Johnson pontificated: "Whoever wishes to attain an English style, familiar but not coarse, and elegant but not ostentatious, must give his days and nights to the volumes of Addison."

Voices in his own age objected to Addison's superior attitude, and today's readers are frequently averse to a writer who is wholly confident that he has all the answers to everything. Addison was completely self-assured, never really at war with his own age and certainly never at war with himself, an attitude our age finds virtually impossible to duplicate.

Cato (c. *1703,* 1713)—Neoclassic Tragedy. Addison wrote the only example of this genre that attracted widespread interest. The play depends upon Plutarch's Life of Cato the Younger for the central story and upon the French dramatists Racine and Corneille for the style.

Favoring Pompey over Julius Caesar, Cato knows he is doomed after Pompey's defeat at Pharsalia. Refusing to submit to a dictatorship and staunchly supporting the lost liberties of Rome, Cato will not compromise with Decius, Caesar's emissary to Cato at Utica. Both sons of Cato, Portius and Marcus, love Lucia, while Cato's daughter Marcia attracts Juba, Prince of Numidia. Marcus is killed fighting mutineers supporting Caesar. Cato commits suicide, in his death speech commending the lovers to each other.

Addison disclaimed political intent, carefully having the prologue written by Pope, a noted Tory, and the epilogue by Garth, a famed Whig; nonetheless, the thunderous acclaim accorded the piece arose largely from political prejudice, the Whigs identifying Cato with the Duke of Marlborough and the Tories identifying Caesar with Marlborough. Both parties loudly cheered the panegyrics on liberty in which Addison obviously alluded to the Bloodless Revolution. Addison desired Cato to represent the epitome of Christian Stoic virtues, but Cato appears an insufferably noble character to modern readers. The lovers are unbelievably cold and wooden. Dr. Johnson said of the play that "it is rather a poem in dialogue than a drama, rather a succession of just sentiments in elegant language than a representation of natural affection, or of any state probable or possible in human life." Voltaire highly praised *Cato* as the first truly classic drama in English, and English contemporaries were lavish in encomiums. The play was translated into Italian, French, German, and Polish, doing more than any other work to raise the esteem of the 18th-century English drama on the Continent.

Sir Richard Steele (1672–1729). Born in Dublin, Ireland, Sir Richard Steele was a schoolmate of Addison at Charterhouse and at Oxford, from which, however, he failed to graduate. Entering the army in 1694 as a trooper, he rose to a captaincy. He fought several duels, and had an illegitimate child by the daughter of Jacob Tonson, the publisher. In contrition he wrote the pious *Christian Hero* (1701), which made him "a disagreeable fellow" to his fellow officers until he wrote a comic drama, *The Funeral* (1702). As a prominent Whig writer, soldier, and man-about-town, Steele held several government posts. Politics caused him to fall out with Swift, who was a Tory, and in 1719 he disagreed with Addison over the plan to limit the size of the peerage. Theatrical writing occupied his later years until he retired to Wales in 1724.

Steele started journalism toward the status of literature, and he was the originator of the periodical essay, a form in which virtually every major writer of the century (Pope, Johnson, Goldsmith, and the rest) was to write much of his best prose. Steele was one of the rare persons who could preach morality without being pompous or dull, and his reckless and extravagant life, plunged first into dissipation and then into remorse, makes him personally far more engaging and human than the eminently proper Addison. Some of the works covered below have their fuller treatment in the earlier discussion on Addison.

The Tatler was preceded by *Mercurius Librarius* (1668 and often termed the first English literary periodical), Defoe's *Review* (1704), and other serials; but with his publication Steele introduced the genuine periodical essay. From Swift's *Predictions for the Ensuing Year 1708* Steele borrowed the pseudonym of "Isaac Bickerstaff" as editor. Increasingly "From My Own Apartment" superseded the coffeehouses as the heading for essays, and the publication concentrated upon one essay per issue instead of several ultra-short items. Steele wrote about 188 of the numbers and collaborated with Addison in perhaps thirty-six others. Steele is the personal, warmly human member of the partnership whose good humor and realistic sense make his Puritan sobriety palatable. Also he is the more specific of the two, handling the news, the theater, and the woman's world.

The Spectator and its famous club were Steele's invention. He wrote 236 of the papers, almost as many as Addison, and his essays are informal and impressionistic, and often careless in organization. Steele urges no specific critical principles other than the common sense and reason which the age applauded, as taste more than classical concepts governed his judgment. His Whig position is not violently put forward, but he does not pretend neutrality, as Addison did, his Whiggism being comprised less of party consciousness than of the desire for progress, and that chiefly in human relations. It is sentiment rather than abstract loyalties that directs Steele.

The Guardian was another of Steele's ventures and is second in excellence only to *The Spectator.* Its diversity matches that of its greater predecessor, although it contains less light-hearted satire and more piety and Whig politics.

Englishman (October 6, 1713–February 15, 1714) revealed Steele as the most vocal and effective Whig propagandist of the day but reveals little else.

Lover (1714) was Steele's attempt to write for the ladies. *The Reader* (1714), *Town Talk* (1715–16), *The Tea Table* (1715–16), and *Chit Chat* (1716) were Steele's solo and minor ventures in the periodical essay. Opposing Addison in *The Plebeian* (1719), Steele as a consequence lost his sinecure as governor of Drury Lane Theatre.

The Epistolary Correspondence of Sir Richard Steele (1787) consists of over four hundred letters to Prue, his second wife. Often sentimental, they are gay, impulsive, and intimately charming; they establish Steele as one of the greatest writers of love letters in English.

The Conscious Lovers (1722)—Sentimental Comedy. This play, the most famous sentimental comedy of the period, was a very free adaptation of Terence's *Andria.* By "conscious," Steele meant "mutually understanding."

Mr. Sealand, a wealthy merchant, wishes his daughter Lucinda to marry Young Bevil, while Mrs. Sealand favors Cimberton, a rustic coxcomb. Lucinda actually loves Myrtle, a friend of Young Bevil. Young Bevil's true love is the orphaned Indiana. Young Bevil dutifully plans to fulfill the parental wishes, but Indiana is revealed as a long-lost daughter of Sealand, and the lovers are properly paired off. The farcical sub-plot has servants Phillis and Tom copying their "conscious" betters.

In this play the contrast between sentimental comedy and Restoration comedy is complete. Here marriage is deemed a matter of love rather than dowries. Young Bevil's love for Indiana is romantically idealistic, not merely physical, and the youth is wholly noble and considerate, willing to sacrifice his own happiness at the command of his elders. The characters are all completely middle class, exemplifying bourgeois morals. In *Joseph Andrews,* Fielding has the worthy if naïve Parson Adams assert that in this play "there are some things almost solemn enough for a sermon."

SWIFT AND HIS WORKS

Jonathan Swift (1667–1745). A native of Dublin, Ireland, Jonathan Swift was a posthumous child educated at Kilkenny Grammar School and at Trinity College, Dublin. In 1689 he became secretary to Sir William Temple, and, after taking clerical orders in 1695 and briefly serving at Kilroot, Ireland, he was again with Temple from 1696 until the latter's death in 1699. In 1700 he was vicar of Laracor near Dublin; he then scorned marriage with the now relenting Jane Waring ("Varina"), who in 1696 had repulsed his proposal. Near Swift at Laracor lived Esther Johnson ("Stella"), possibly a natural daughter of Temple, and it is thought by some that she became Swift's secret wife. A growing literary reputation took Swift to London during virtually every year until 1714. In 1710 he went over from the Whigs to the Tories and proved a major Tory journalist and pamphleteer. With Arbuthnot and Pope he formed the "Scriblerus Club," from which emerged the germs of his greatest writings. In 1713 he was appointed Dean of St. Patrick's Cathedral, Dublin, to which he retired in 1714 after the fall of the Tories. Esther Vanhomrigh ("Vanessa"), who had fallen in love with him in England, followed him to Ireland, living at Celbridge, not far from Dublin. However, no concrete evidence substantiates the tradition that "Stella" was secretly his wife and "Vanessa" his mistress. Starting in 1720, Swift became a vociferous supporter of Irish interests against English exploitation, thus earning the undying esteem of the Irish. A persistent disease of the ear ("that old vertigo in my head") plagued much of his life, and around 1738 his mind failed him, leaving him in a state of apathy or senility until his death.

The greatest satirist in English literature might be explained, superficially, as a sick man to whom, like the sick Carlyle, the whole world had a bad smell. Swift was very much a man of his era in his great desire for earthly recognition; his heart was set upon a bishopric, and he felt as disillusioned and frustrated as any disappointed self-seeker at not getting it. However, the best explanation of the man would seem to lie in the paradoxical idea of his being a practical idealist. Desiring a world of reason and beauty, Swift was anguished by the gross disparity between man's actuality and potential. His scatology is only a furious outcry against the bestiality of a being that he believed was created in God's image. But as a man of reason, a man of the Enlightenment, Swift was not able to take refuge in mysticism. Many equally perceptive men have retained their sanity by turning their hopes to an earthly or heavenly future; and some have merely ignored the world's problems and created a little Augustan sphere of their own. But the tortured sensibilities of Dean Swift, concentrated as they are on the world as it is, goaded him to rip away these complacent hypocrisies with savage indignation. He is not so much a misanthropist as a man yearning for the good life in a wicked world.

Swift has proved for modern readers the most exciting figure of his age, because, instead of the relatively simple nature of most of his contemporaries (like Addison), he displays at least five different facets of his literary personality. While these five aspects of Swift tend to merge at points, they are distinct enough for us to examine his prose writings in relation to them.

Swift's Prose Writings

(1) The first of Swift's five aspects is that of a plain, forthright man of the Enlightenment, a sincere practicing Christian, who, nonetheless, is a thorough rationalist and a hater of pedantry, enthusiasm, and needless ornamentation. Here Swift writes a lean, undecorated prose, clear and simple, and more incisive and aggressive than Addison's.

A Discourse on the Contests and Dissensions between the Nobles and the Commons in Athens and Rome (1701) was written during Swift's Whig period and is credited with turning public opinion against the threatened impeachment of Whig nobles. Swift urges sane moderation and diminution of party vehemence. The pervasive idea of the work is the central idea of the Augustan era: the sense common to all mankind should direct human conduct. *The Conduct of the Allies* (1711), produced after Swift's conversion to Toryism, cogently demands peace with France, demonstrating that the prolongation of the conflict was a severe drain upon England's finances and benefited only the Marlboroughs, the Godolphins, the Whigs, and the Dutch. The work is credited with swaying English opinion to an acceptance of "Matt's Peace."

A Project for the Advancement of Religion and the Reformation of Manners (1709) argues for the Established Church on the basis of its practicality, its current success in function, and its perfect adaptation to English needs. Swift also advocates government proctors to supervise public morals.

A Proposal for the Universal Use of Irish Manufacture (1720) gave to succeeding generations of the Irish a battle cry: "Burn everything from England except its coal." *The Drapier's Letters* (1724) consisted of five letters, supposedly written by "M. B. Drapier," calling for an Irish boycott of the debased copper coinage which the English government had authorized an iron-merchant, William Wood, to issue in Ireland. Swift's attacks killed the coinage project and rendered the author an Irish hero.

(2) The second facet of Swift is his exuberant comic wit. The Bickerstaff Pamphlets consisted of three light-hearted attacks on John Partridge, an astrologer of the age who regularly issued an almanac with bizarre prophecies. Swift's *Predictions for the Ensuing Year 1708* (1708), under the pseudonym of Isaac Bickerstaff, predicted Partridge's death on March 29, 1708. When the vexed prophet retorted that he was very much alive, Swift replied with the circumstantial *Account of Partridge's Death* (1708) and *Vindication of Isaac Bickerstaff, Esq.* (1709). A serious undertone is present, however, because Partridge had opposed the Test Act of 1672, requiring all Crown officials to be communicants of the Established Church. A strong churchman, Swift hyperbolically insisted that the abolition of the Test would be the abolition of Christianity. The waggish Bickerstaff pamphlets delighted London and caused the appropriation of the pseudonym by Steele in *The Tatler*.

(3) A third aspect of Swift is his mastery of light, ironic satire. Here Swift proves the greatest English practitioner (and only Aristophanes and Rabelais are his equals) of traditional "invention," that is, the art of opening up a topic and then exploiting it to its preposterous limit. Remarkable also here is the assimilation of image to idea which was found so striking in the "metaphysical" poets. The intellectual mind is forever bursting forth here, like heat lightning on the horizon.

referred to in his Modest Proposal

Battle of the Books (c. *1697*, 1704) was a mock-heroic prose satire supporting the position of Sir William Temple, Swift's patron, favoring the ancients as against the modern authors. An imaginary battle in St. James Library pits the Ancient books against the Modern books. The Bee, representing the ancients, goes directly to nature and produces "sweetness and light" (used as a title by Matthew Arnold). The Spider, representing the moderns, weaves its web from within itself, producing only "dirt and poison." Swift is here the devastating opponent of pedantry, pretense, and scholasticism (which he found as distasteful in his college days as Milton had in his). The entire work is rich, effective fun, skillful in words and structure.

The Tale of a Tub (c. *1696*, 1704) in title means "a cock and bull story"; specifically it refers to a current sailor's practice of throwing an empty tub into the sea to divert a whale from attacking a ship. In his preface Swift describes the treatise as a jettison to the (Hobbesian) Leviathan of skepticism, to be played with until a scheme can be devised to check the dangerous monster.

Three brothers inherit from their father three suits of clothes (the Christian faith) and a will (the Scriptures) directing their use of the clothes. The eldest brother, Peter (Roman Catholic Church), on the grounds of expediency and tradition, tricks up his garments with confessions, indulgences, holy water, papal bulls, and clerical celibacy (e.g. "flame-coloured satin" is the doctrine of Purgatory). He demands the homage of his younger brothers (i.e. papal supremacy). Rebelling, the younger brothers obtain copies of the will (translations of the Scriptures) and insist on improvement (the Reformation). Martin (Lutheran and Anglican churches) scrupulously removes the false ornaments from his clothes but carefully maintains the wholeness of the fundamental garments. Jack (Calvinism and other Protestant sects) fanatically rips off all ornaments (iconoclasm), thoroughly tattering his clothes. Jack makes a fetish of his father's will, refusing any action not sanctioned by it (bibliolatry), and founds the sect of Aeolists ("wind-makers"), "enthusiasts" who proclaim mystic revelation from God.

One of the most ingenious allegories in literature, it pleads for the elimination of Christianity's superficial trappings and for the unity of all true believers in the fundamentals of the faith. Pious Anglican that he was, Swift apparently failed to see the full implications of his work. The pragmatic reason that he opposes to enthusiasm, fancy, imagination, and vision justifies no faith or sect more than another, except on the basis of its adaptability to current English spirit. The brilliantly elaborated clothes metaphor (cf. the later Carlyle's *Sartor Resartus*) tends to dissolve all spiritual trappings, Martin's as well as Peter's and Jack's, into meaninglessness.

An Argument to Prove that the Abolishing of Christianity in England May, as Things Now Stand, Be Attended with Some Inconveniences (1708) marks Swift's first superb employment of what became his later overpowering device: the false *persona*. The pretended writer is a "man of the world" who blandly assumes a general unanimity favoring the abolition of Christianity. Timorously, in the light of such agreement, he ventures "some inconveniences," for instance that wits and freethinkers would no longer have a convenient butt of ridicule.

The irony seems directed solely against irreligion until the "man of the world" hastens decorously to assure his readers that he is, of course, defending only "nominal Christianity" and would never call upon men to practice "Real Christianity," with all its difficulties and sacrifices. The target of Swift is not only the Deists who would eliminate Christianity as a separate faith but also the great mass of mankind whose allegiance to faith is largely verbal and shallow.

(4) The fourth and most familiar aspect of Swift is that of the master of ironic satire. Here Swift speaks from his anguished heart, producing deep and unforgettable analyses of the human situation.

Travels into Several Remote Nations of the World. By Lemuel Gulliver (1726) was inspired in the Scriblerus Club of 1713–14 as an attack upon pedantry and the fantasies of travelers' tales. Swift mulled over the idea during his exile at the Irish deanery and was actively working upon *Gulliver's Travels* as early as 1721. It was the product both of his greatest maturity and of his deepest personal feelings. The sources of the work are numerous, but the first two books are indebted particularly to Lucian's *True History* (a burlesque of early travelers' tales) and Cyrano de Bergerac's *Comic History of the Moon;* the third book was influenced by *Transactions of the Royal Society* and Pope's concluding chapter to *Memoirs of Martinus Scriblerus;* the last book owes much to More's *Utopia,* Montaigne's *Apology for Raimond Sebond,* and Boileau's *Eighth Satire.*

Summary of Gulliver's Travels

First Voyage (Lilliput). Gulliver, ship's doctor on the *Antelope,* is shipwrecked near Van Diemen's Land (Tasmania) but manages to make shore, where he falls unconscious. Upon awakening, he finds himself a captive of humans only six inches tall (possibly derived from Philostratus's account of the pygmies capturing the sleeping Hercules). After learning the Lilliputian language and obeying the laws of his diminutive captors, Gulliver is permitted to tour the capital city of Mildendo, which he finds a tiny replica of contemporary European cities. Gulliver becomes a nobleman of Lilliput when he single-handedly carries off the entire war fleet of the hostile neighboring kingdom, Blefuscu. The Lilliputian monarch wishes to enslave the defeated Blefuscans, but Gulliver champions a generous peace, which the Lilliputian parliament approves. In disfavor at court because he put out a fire in the queen's palace by urinating on it, Gulliver visits Blefuscu. Here he finds a battered ship's boat cast ashore. With the aid of Blefuscan workers he refurbishes the boat and sails away, to be picked up by an English vessel.

Swift's incredible ingenuity in adapting everything to the six-inch scale of Lilliputians has ironically rendered this adult satire a nursery favorite. Swift calculates exactly how many Lilliputian blankets have to be sewed together for Gulliver, and he even allows for the hemming. Beguiled, the reader hardly realizes that he is being led into satire, but the major intention of this book is to demonstrate the pettiness of human affairs as viewed by a giant from another world. The vehemence of Whig and Tory becomes preposterous in the Lilliputian contention of the low-heelers (Low Church) versus the high-heelers (High Church), and the battling of Catholics and Protestants is satirized in the contention of the Big-Enders versus the Little-Enders (Which end of the egg should be cracked first?). The war between England and France is reduced to the absurd conflict between Lilliput and Blefuscu. Swift also incorporates much specific satire on English politics around 1712–15. Nonetheless, certain passages in Chapter 6, treating of law and education in Lilliput, are essentially utopian, picturing this minute world as the rational ideal.

Second Voyage (Brobdingnag). Wandering away from a landing party of the *Adventure* on the coast of Great Tartary, Gulliver is trapped in a field of giant corn forty feet high. Brobdingnagians themselves are normally sixty feet tall; Gulliver is captured and becomes the pet of a nine-year-old farmer's daughter, not yet over forty feet tall. As a curiosity he is sold to the queen of the kingdom, who lets court physicians and philosophers study Gulliver as a freak. The puny Gulliver has narrow escapes from rats the size of lions, wasps as large as partridges, and hailstones as large as tennis balls. To the tiny fellow the giants of Brobdingnag often appear ugly and ill-favored, but this land knows only peace and simplicity. The monarch is horrified at European politics and disgusted at European warfare. "I cannot but conclude," the giant ruler sadly opines, "the Bulk of your Natives, to be the most pernicious Race of little odious Vermin that Nature ever suffered to crawl upon the Surface of the Earth." At the end of the account a huge bird snatches up the portable box containing Gulliver and drops him into the sea, from whence he is hauled aboard a vessel bound for England.

Swift's ingenuity again is unflagging, with everything in Brobdingnag suitably ten times its normal size as everything in Lilliput was a tenth of the normal size. Gulliver is the prime *naif* (Does the name *Gulliver* come from "gullible"?) wholly committed to the glories of European civilization; however, the more he praises the culture from which he came, the more monstrous it appears in comparison to the rational giants of Brobdingnag. Swift's attack is centered upon human pride, and this book denounces man's vanity concerning his mind, man's pleasure in his own body, and man's unconscionable behavior toward his fellows.

Third Voyage (Laputa and other islands). Marooned by Chinese pirates on a rocky island, Gulliver is astounded to see a flying island descend, and to find the inhabitants of Laputa to be wholly impractical intellectuals, dwelling upon empty abstractions (the ridicule of mathematicians is a slap at Newton). Servants have to flap Laputans' ears with bladders to entice them from their vain speculations back to the matter at hand. Swift is here satirizing all pointless scholarship and impractical philosophy. Laputa's subjugation of islands beneath it is a slap at English oppression of Ireland.

When the floating island hovers over Balnibarbi, Gulliver descends to inspect the Grand Academy of Lagado, a wild burlesque of the Royal Academy. Projectors are softening marble for pillows, sowing chaff, training spiders to supersede silkworms, building houses from the roof down; however, the effectiveness of this satire is lessened for us, since our age has accomplished many of these absurdities, e.g. we extract sunbeams from cucumbers but call it Vitamin C.

By boat Gulliver then proceeds to Glubbdubdrib, the island of sorcerers. By magic the governor of the island summons up the spectres of history's greats: Alexander, Caesar, Sir Thomas More, and others. Gulliver learns that the history books are invariably distorted and false in their accounts. Much of this section is directed at contemporary Whigs and has not the same impact today.

In Luggnagg Gulliver finds the Struldbrugs, the immortals. Long life, however, is a monstrous curse because of their inevitable weakness and deformity (probably suggested by the ancient legend of Tithonus). From Luggnagg Gulliver sails to Japan; from there a Dutch vessel bears him to Amsterdam, and he gets back to England.

This Third Voyage is the most topical and least coherent of all four. The political sallies in Glubbdubdrib are now only moderately interesting, but the fearsome picture of prolonged enfeeblement in the Struldbrugs is literature's most compelling argument for satisfaction with the present life span allotted to man. The chief purpose of the book, exemplified in Laputa and Balnibarbi, is to ridicule the misapplication of man's talents. Swift shared with Pope and most of his age the conviction that "the proper study of mankind is man"—man's relationships to himself, his fellows, and his God. A conservative Tory and an orthodox Christian, Swift sets no store by materialistic progress or the intense curiosity to probe the inexplicable questions of the physical universe. Swift's blinding concentration upon common sense and pragmatic reason makes him very nearly an anti-intellectual.

Fourth Voyage (Land of the Houyhnhnms). Cast adrift by mutinous sailors, Gulliver lands upon the shores of a country governed entirely by intelligent horses, the Houyhnhnms (imitation of horse's whinny). The despised servants of the rational equines are Yahoos (Does *Yahoo* mean "You"?), who are scabrous beasts whom Gulliver gradually comes to realize are virtual human beings. The Houyhnhnms are horrified to learn that in England Yahoo-like creatures use horses as beasts of burden. The Houyhnhnms know nothing of war or courts of law. Love is absent from their hearts, and procreation is solely a civic duty. Their literature is completely didactic, praising rational benevolence and friendship. Gulliver compares irrational England with the land of rational horses and infinitely prefers the latter. When a concupiscent female Yahoo tries to embrace him, Gulliver is thoroughly disgusted. Informed that the Houyhnhnm Grand Assembly has ordered him to be treated as a Yahoo or leave, he hastily departs in a canoe. A Portuguese ship picks him up and deposits him at Lisbon, where he takes ship for England. When his wife rushes to kiss him, Gulliver faints. From that point on he finds the companionship of horses far superior to that of mankind.

In this voyage Swift propounds his deepest analysis of mankind, but it is not misanthropy and it is not theriophily. The Houyhnhnms are not so much an ideal race as a means of criticizing humanity. It is here that Swift obtained the one great tragic vision of his age. Man could be governed by reason and should be governed by reason, but the lower elements of his nature, the very foundations of his existence, have debased what is fine within him. Man's only hope, Swift insists, is to see clearly and without illusion, to recognize the Yahoo in the human. Thus aware of our essential foulness, we may not entirely give in to it. Our own age, unlike the optimistic 19th century, admits to much of the truth of Swift's catalogue of vices: the perverted mind and body of man, his arrogant ignorance and absurd pretensions, and his failures both in himself and in his conduct with his fellow men. But the parable of the Houyhnhnms and the Yahoos is not a nihilistic reviling of humanity; it is a moral, intellectual, and spiritual challenge to achieve genuine human dignity. The true pessimist is Shakespeare's Timon, who utterly abandons his species. But the true benefactor of mankind is someone like Swift, who uncompromisingly compels it to face the truth and accept its challenge. It should be stated here, however, that there is much dispute as to the meanings of the fourth voyage, and probably more verbiage has been expended on this than on any other 18th-century problem.

A Modest Proposal for Preventing the Children of Poor People in Ireland from Being a Burthen to Their Parents, or the Country, and for Making Them Beneficial to the Publick (1729), usually referred to as *A Modest Proposal,* is the greatest piece of irony in literature. Swift, employing his favorite device of fantastic "invention," speaks in the guise of a realistic, unsentimental projector—the cool, benign economist. The very title parallels several contemporary pamphlets that soberly noted the famine of Ireland and that country's overpopulation. Swift therefore proposes that the Irish should fatten their infants to be eaten as table delicacies. The heartless stockyard calculations are a merciless indictment of the English exploitation of the Irish. People were theoretically the riches of a country; but in Ireland this is the only way a population increase can be made profitable. It is a suffering Christian spirit that here protests against the economic conditions to which man had been driven. No other work demonstrates so painfully the sensitive being wracked by man's inhumanity. As Swift wrote in a letter to Pope: "I hate and detest that animal called man, although I heartily love John, Peter, Thomas, and so forth."

(5) The fifth aspect of Swift, and one that is generally unfamiliar, is that of a tender, intimate friend of the individual.

The Journal to Stella (1710–13, 1765) was given this title in 1784 and has ever since been so designated, but Swift apparently had not at the time of writing coined his pet name for Esther Johnson (*Esther* of Hebraic origin equated with the Greek *aster,* "star," and thence the Latin *stella,* "star"). The letters are addressed sometimes to Rebecca Dingley ("Bec"), Esther's duenna, but usually to Esther. They sketch a vivid picture of everyday life in contemporary London and also include much behind-the-scenes politics, but it is the personal relationship to Esther that proves even more interesting to modern readers. Usually considered the epitome of sour masculinity, Swift here reveals a warmhearted domesticity, frequently writing a playful "little language" to Esther. This consists of baby-talk such as "our richar Gangridge" for "our little language," and a private series of abbreviations such as "Ppt" for "Poor pretty thing" (Esther); along, of course, with almost everything else in literature, this "little language" pops up in *Finnegans Wake,* by James Joyce. Writing from London to Esther in Dublin, Swift is particularly affectionate, but the tone is essentially that of a nurse to a loved child. With the exception of "Varina," no woman ever induced Swift to near-normal attitude of a man toward a woman. Swift tended to equate the excretory and genital functions; he was personally over-fastidious in cleanliness, far beyond his contemporaries, and, like Gulliver with the Yahoo girl, hated anyone to touch him physically. Some psychologists suggest that Swift was impotent, and psychoanalysts find great clusters of complexes in him, basically locating in his unstable and almost rootless childhood an anal fixation that caused his later fascination and revulsion toward the entire human body. His resultant attitude bred his devastating satires against mankind, possibly broke the heart of "Vanessa," and molded the submissive "Stella" into a life of unfulfillment.

Swift's Verse

Dryden, a distant relative of Swift, is quoted by Dr. Johnson as saying: "Cousin Swift, you will never be a poet." Although some of Swift's verse is coprophiliac beyond even that of Rochester, much of it has a blunt realism and unpoetic honesty that our age can more readily appreciate than did the 19th century. His best narrative poem is "Baucis and Philemon" (*1706*, 1709), an adaptation from Ovid, fancifully telling of the magical transformation of an honest couple into Parson Philemon and wife, and eventually into two yew trees. The poem shows Swift skillful in the colloquial lilt of octosyllabic couplets. "A Description of the Morning" (1709) and "A Description of a City Shower" (1710) are Hogarthian vignettes of London in heroic couplets. The two birthday poems to Stella, "On Stella's birthday" (*1719*, 1727) and "Stella's Birthday" (1727), both in octosyllabics, are quiet, intimately charming tributes, perfect in their playful, unpretentious grace. Surprisingly, like Thomas Hardy, Swift turned from his middle years, which were largely devoted to prose, to conclude in his later years with his greatest verse.

"Cadenus and Vanessa" (*1713*, 1730), in addition to some fragmentary and inconclusive correspondence, constitutes all the definitive evidence that we have about Swift's relationship with Esther Vanhomrigh. "Cadenus" is an anagram for *Decanus* (Latin, "dean") and "Vanessa" is the *Van* of Vanhomrigh plus *essa* from Esther. In graceful octosyllabics the Goddess of Love recognizes that women are light-headed, frivolous creatures, not truly worth men's regard. Hence she creates in Vanessa a woman with masculine judgment and honor. The Dean is attracted solely by her intelligence and good sense, but she falls in love with him. He leaves the issue dubious but implies that he intends to be no more than a good friend.

"Verses on the Death of Dr. Swift" (*1731,* 1739) imagines what will be said about Swift after his death. The badinage of ladies discussing his death while they play cards and the bookseller's dismissal of Swift as "antiquated stuff" are gaily octosyllabic, but they conceal Swift's gnawing desire for life and fame. He wanted to see himself as a fearless moralist, proclaiming the unvarnished truth in a prophet's zeal for man's betterment.

> His satire points at no defect
> But what all mortals may correct.

If the picture he has drawn is unlovely, the fault is in mankind, but there is no self-pity and no real savagery in this indictment of a hollow society.

"The Beasts' Confession" (*1732,* 1738) starts with hypocritical animals and then turns to hypocritical men who admit no faults but only "virtues carried to excess." Like Samuel Butler, in many respects his poetic predecessor, Swift sees hypocrisy as the crowning human sin.

"On Poetry: A Rhapsody" (1733) is a helter-skelter denunciation in tumbling octosyllabics of poetasters and patrons. In this work Swift equals Pope in cool contempt of mediocrity and sham.

"The Legion Club" (*1736,* 1756), his last known poem, is best characterized as Skeltonic, for virtually nothing since Skelton has matched this brutal invective in rough octosyllabics. Jeffrey had to admit its "demoniacal inspiration" in belaboring the Irish Parliament for its lessened financial support of the Established Church (Anglican) of Ireland.

OTHER PROSE OF THE AGE

The Non-Fiction and Short Fiction of Defoe

Daniel Defoe (c. 1660–1731). Born plain Daniel Foe, Daniel Defoe was a London butcher's son of Flemish ancestry. About 1703 he added the aristocratic French article to his name and usually was styled thereafter as De Foe. He was educated at Morton's Dissenting Academy at Stoke Newington, participated in Monmouth's Rebellion in 1685, and thereafter became a wholesale merchant. He traveled extensively in Great Britain and on the Continent, and for a brief period he was the captive of Algerian pirates. By his wife, Mary Tuffley, whom he married in 1684, he had seven children. His own rashness together with wartime dislocations compelled his bankruptcy for £17,000 (equivalent to hundreds of thousands of dollars today) in 1692. He was a rabid supporter of William III, from whom he received several minor government posts. After William's death the Tories pounced on him, and in July of 1703 he was thrice publicly pilloried, where he was pelted with flowers instead of the usual rotten eggs and vegetables hurled by the populace. His tile business failed the same year, and thereafter he threw himself wholly into a literary career. Though he was a Whig and a dissenter, his pen was available to both political parties. During the War of the Spanish Succession he was a secret-service agent for the government. Defoe was a man of sixty and deeply scarred in the political wars of pamphleteering when in 1719 he began to write the fiction that has largely assured his fame. These contributions to the novel, *Robinson Crusoe, Moll Flanders,* and others, will be discussed later in a chapter dealing solely with the rise of the novel. To his dying day he was haunted by his bankruptcies and died, virtually in hiding, of a "lethargy."

Defoe did not belong to the respectable literary world, which generally derided him scornfully. He was an incredibly fertile journalist, writing in haste and seldom revising. The exact canon of Defoe is far from certain, but he probably composed over four hundred books and tracts, few bearing his own name. His Whiggery lay in bourgeois Dissent, and he made himself the greatest voice of the rising, but struggling, middle class. Throughout his work echo the cries of his class: an intense practicality and eye to business, a sense of isolation in a society not made for the middle class and not sympathetic to it, and an ambitious desire to reform and improve the world. His style is uniformly forceful but unconscious of arts and graces. His emphasis is always upon hard-headed common sense.

ARGUMENTATIVE PAMPHLETS. *An Essay upon Projects* (c. *1694, 1698*) is a singularly "modern" advocacy of many reforms since realized, though often not in the form of Defoe's recommendation. He called for old-age pensions, income tax, a national network of highways, a chain of county banks, humane institutions for the deranged, better treatment of the poor and the bankrupt (from his own sad experience), military academies, and greatly improved education for women. His "Academy for Women" has especially interested later readers. Like most members of a new, rising class, Defoe (barred as a dissenter from the universities) places a sacred value upon education and assumes that it will solve all problems.

The Shortest Way with Dissenters (1702) is the greatest piece of ironic writing in English other than Swift's. Ostensibly the author is a High Church Tory who proposes merciless persecution of nonconformists: their preachers should be hanged, and their sects hounded out of existence by every device. The purpose was to topple over into absurdity the intolerance and injustice of the incumbent Tories. Defoe paid for his audacity by standing in the pillory, for some Tories had at first believed the piece too legitimate, and they were considerably embarrassed and angry when they realized the truth.

ARGUMENTATIVE VERSE. *The True-Born Englishman* (1701) was occasioned by John Tutchin's *The Foreigners* (1700), a versified and disgruntled protest that the ruler of England was the Dutch William III. Of Flemish extraction himself and a staunch supporter of William, Defoe, in doggerel laughter, points out the rich racial mixture of England. Where, then, is your "true-born Englishman"? Defoe moralistically concludes in the bourgeois spirit: " 'Tis personal virtue only makes us great."

Hymn to the Pillory (1703) was hawked about the crowd viewing the pilloried Defoe. This pseudo-Pindaric ode sees glory in the pilloried martyrdom that Prynne and other persecuted Englishmen had endured before Defoe. An annoyed Tory journalist complained that largely in consequence of this work, when Defoe descended "from his Wooden Punishment," the crowd received him "as if he had been a Cicero that had made an excellent oration in it."

ARGUMENTATIVE JOURNALISM. Defoe produced immense quantities of writing for journals and newspapers. Generally he wrote for periodicals run by others, from Dunton's *Athenian Gazette* (1691) to Appleby's *Original Weekly Journal* in 1726. Defoe himself founded the *Mercurius Politicus* (1716–20), but his great journalistic work lay in:

The Review (variously titled but always containing the word *Review*) (February 19, 1704–June 11, 1713, generally three times weekly with minor omissions). Apparently this demanding and enormous task was wholly Defoe's, even though he was employed as a secret agent in Scotland for part of this period. The main concern is

Whig politics and trade, middle-class religion and morals. Its crowded and pragmatic world is a necessary counterbalance to the placid Sir Roger de Coverley atmosphere frequently associated with the age. Just as Addison was the popular literary interpreter to the age of Locke's metaphysics and epistemology, so Defoe was the popular journalistic interpreter to the middle class of the economic and political theories of Locke.

Without literary pretense, the *Review* is an important forerunner of *The Spectator* in "Mercure Scandale; or Advice from the Scandalous Club, being a weekly history of nonsense, impertinence, vice, and debauchery," which ran from the opening number until May 17, 1705. Theoretically, this section was composed of questions from correspondents, with humorous retorts that "censured the actions of men." The popularity of this section was responsible for its appearance as a monthly supplement, "Advice from the Scandalous Club," and a separate periodical, *Little Review; or, An Inquisition of Scandal,* running for twenty-three numbers from June 6, 1705. Brilliantly Defoe does battle with the follies and sins of his era.

NARRATIVE AND DESCRIPTIVE WRITING. *A True Relation of the Apparition of One Mrs. Veal, the Next Day after Her Death, to One Mrs. Bargrave at Canterbury, the 8th of September, 1705* (1706) reveals its theme in its title. It is impossible to separate Defoe's factual journalism from his imaginative journalism. A report of this spectral visitation actually circulated in the era, and the degree of Defoe's elaboration is conjectural. The narrator claims long acquaintance with Mrs. Bargrave, a perfectly normal, "non-psychic" person. Here is Defoe's first demonstration of his astonishing ability to live other people's lives and re-create their experiences with the complete illusion of verisimilitude. Probably no other ghost story has sounded so authentic in its judicious piling up of matter-of-fact details.

A Tour through the Whole Island of Great Britain (three volumes, 1721–26) is our best source for the economic and social life of the islanders during this period. Defoe's is a photographic eye, meticulously detailing the products and behavior of people, the buildings and natural resources of the realm. Material prosperity and middle-class business are his chief concern, while the beauties of scenery are largely ignored.

A Journal of the Plague Year (1722) is ostensibly an eye-witness account by "H. F." of the fearful ravages of the bubonic plague in London, 1664–65. Once deemed bona fide, this is now regarded as perhaps Defoe's greatest imaginative creation—though sources for large sections of it have been discovered in non-fiction writings dating from the actual event—for he was six years old or younger at the time of the plague. The straightforward factual presentation renders vividly memorable some of the most blood-chilling passages in English. "H. F." is supposedly a sober bourgeois tradesman whose unimpassioned report commands belief, especially in his careful discrimination between his own observation and hearsay.

Literary Criticism and Scholarship

The three principles enunciated by Pope in *Essay on Criticism* represented the three significant positions of the age in neoclassic literary criticism.

(1) Authority, "the rules." The only major critic of the era still upholding Rymer's viewpoint was Charles Gildon (1665–1724), whose *Complete Art of Poetry* (1718) insisted upon adherence to the models of the ancients. Shakespeare, claimed Gildon, was great only when he followed "the rules," and his popularity could only be ascribed to the ignorance of audiences. He felt that correct verse had to follow the example of great Greek literature of antiquity, the pronouncements of the *Poetics* by Aristotle, and the formulations of the 17th-century French critics.

(2) Reason and good sense. More typical of the age was Leonard Welsted (1688–1747) in his "Dissertation concerning the Perfection of the English Tongue, the State of Poetry, etc." (1724). All poetry must be reasonable, Welsted contends, but "poetical reason is not the same as mathematical reason." The truth of poetry depends upon imagination, that "bright emanation of reason, painting or throwing light upon ideas." The poet must not violate common sense or deviate into the triviality of private communication, but should be guided by his own genius and should scorn merely slavish imitation.

(3) Good Taste. Though heavy-handed and severely embattled with Pope, John Dennis (1657–1734), the most important professional critic of the period, shared Pope's position. Dennis was fundamentally neoclassic in his assertion that the role of art was to instruct through pleasure and in his belief that art must awake in the perceiver a sense of universal harmony and rational order. Nonetheless, *The Advancement and Reformation of Modern Poetry* (1701), *Large Account of Taste in Poetry* (1702), and *Grounds of Criticism in Poetry* (1704) also display independent thinking. "The poet," Dennis declared, "is

obliged to speak always to the heart"; "all they call wit [clever artifice] is to be banished from true poetry." He defined poetry as "an imitation of Nature by a pathetic [emotional] and numerous [rhythmic] speech." He also felt that because it stirs the emotions, poetry is more effective than philosophy. Dennis noted two types of emotions: "vulgar," which is inspired by objects of actual experience; and "enthusiastic," heightened emotions inspired by "ideas in contemplation." The latter is the province of poetry, and Dennis advocated exalted Christian themes and spirit to exemplify this enthusiasm in religious poetry. His opponents dubbed him "Sir Longinus" for his support of "fine frenzy," a concept put forward by the ancient critic Longinus.

The first critical edition of Spenser (1715) by John Hughes (1677–1720) contained a prefatory essay, "On Allegorical Poetry," in which Hughes justified Spenser's ignoring of "the rules" and the poet's love for "old Gothic chivalry." One of the so-called "School of Pope," Hughes called for recognition of Spenser's individualistic genius, for the adoption of a relativistic taste for writings under conditions alien to the reader, and for an appreciation of medieval materials which this age dismissed as "barbarous."

Richard Bentley (1662–1742). Appointed Master of Trinity College, Cambridge, in 1699, Richard Bentley was one of the greatest classical scholars in English history. He was also an ill-tempered academic tyrant, almost expelled from his post by enraged fellow scholars. As mentioned earlier, Temple had cited as an example of ancient superiority the letters of Phalaris, a Greek king of Agrigentum in Sicily, of the 6th century B.C. Bentley demonstrated by historical, linguistic, and stylistic tests that the *Epistles of Phalaris* were a later forgery. *Dissertation on the Epistles of Phalaris* (1697, rev. 1699) is therefore the first great piece of literary scholarship in English. Bentley's edition of *Paradise Lost* (1732) was an unhappy mistake; assuming that in his blindness Milton had no adequate check upon his published work, Bentley made numerous emendations and alterations in the text.

Philosophical Writings

Rational deism claimed to find full proof of God's existence and moral administration of the universe in "Nature," apprehended solely through the senses and interpreted by human reason. Revelation was therefore discarded as superfluous and irrational. The great English champion of orthodoxy against this deism was Joseph Butler (1692–1752), whose *Analogy of Religion* (1736), in the temper of the age, itself vigorously employed the tools of reason. Butler's thesis is expressed in his quotation from the early Church father Origen: "He who believes the Scripture to have proceeded from him who is the Author of Nature, may well expect to find the same sort of difficulties in it as are found in the constitution of Nature." Butler's analogy attempts to demonstrate that proving God from the observation of Nature presents just as many difficulties as proving God from Revelation. The effect of Butler's work is perhaps pessimistic, possibly even encouraging skepticism, for Revelation appears no more or less trustworthy than Reason. Butler, however, was the outstanding authority cited for almost a century by orthodox English Christians. He certainly sensed, as did few of his age, the awesome mystery of the universe. His prose is undistinguished though cogent.

Locke, on the other hand, offered to the Enlightenment a simple, commonsense epistemology. The outer world was a real and genuine world that, through the senses, conveyed data to the self of each individual. This wholly materialistic philosophy was the standard popular concept throughout the Enlightenment. Upon this basis David Hartley (1705–57) established the "associationism" school of psychology in *Observations on Man, His Frame, His Duty, and His Expectations* (1749). According to the Lockean scheme, Hartley saw every aspect of human thought as ultimately dependent upon sense impressions. A new perception causes memory to associate a previous sense impression with the new perception, and the interplay builds up to concepts of altruism, divine worship, and other abstract ideas. However, other rational philosophers, like Berkeley and Hume, were using the same tool of reason to demolish Locke's theory.

Henry St. John, Viscount Bolingbroke (1678–1751). Secretary of War during the Tory regime from 1704 until 1708, Bolingbroke, with the return of the Tories in 1710, served as Privy Councillor and Secretary of State until his dismissal in 1714. Fleeing to France in the next year, he was briefly Secretary of State to the "Old Pretender." He broke with the Jacobites and was finally pardoned in 1723. His deistic borrowings from von Leibniz formed the basis of Pope's *Essay on Man*. His style was famed for elegance and poise.

The Craftsman (1726–36), Bolingbroke's periodical, sold more copies during its lifetime than did *The Spectator,* according to Goldsmith. It contained the essence of Bolingbroke's political philosophy. Significantly, this Tory spokesman totally rejected the divine right of kings and admitted the premise of the Bloodless Revolution, that the will of the people shall govern the nation. Bolingbroke saw the party system as a "divide and rule" policy. He proposed the elimination of party and the strengthening of a truly representative Parliament through a broad franchise. The nation should be united under a "Patriot King," thereby regaining the solidarity it had not possessed since Elizabeth I. In his proposals for a disinterested survey of history, he has been called the first Englishman truly to sense the continuity of history and to observe contemporary events as workings of fundamental human conflicts paralleling the past and developing out of it.

George Berkeley (bärk'-li) (1685–1753). Of English descent, George Berkeley was born at Dysert Castle, in Kilkenny county, Ireland. After graduation from Trinity College, Dublin, he traveled in England and on the Continent. A clergyman in the Established Church of Ireland (Anglican), he became Dean of Derry in 1724. From 1729 to 1731 he resided in New England, and on the basis of his residence in the New World he wrote "Verses on the Prospect of Planting Arts and Learning in America" (1752), which contains the famous line: "Westward the course of empire takes its way." From 1734 until his retirement in 1752 he was bishop of Cloyne.

Commonplace Book (*1707–09, 1871*), also known as *Philosophical Commentaries,* contains the major part of his philosophy and offers much personal insight into this independent thinker. Acquiescing to no system but seeking his own, Berkeley challenges the reality of Locke's "actual" world. Putting it in its most simplified form, Berkeley posits that all existence is an act of mental will and that we do not perceive any genuine reality in the world of the senses. Matter exists only as we will to perceive it, and the apparent reality is subjective and not objective. According to Berkeley's theory, this book you are now reading has no existence unless someone is reading it and therefore actively conceiving its existence. If you ask how it is that this book has the same apparent reality today as it had yesterday (Did it exist overnight without any perceiver?), Berkeley replies that this book and all other supposedly concrete phenomena are ideas in God's mind, and thus the continuity of apparent reality is in fact an argument for God's existence.

The Enlightenment generally denied Berkeley's theory, some with witty raillery and Dr. Johnson by kicking a stone at Dover and solemnly opining, "Thus I refute Berkeley"; but Dr. Johnson only substituted one sense concept (the touch of his stubbed toe) for another (his sight of the rock) and did not invalidate the bishop's theory. Any good 18th-century gentleman could see for himself that this is a (literally) solid book, but accepted 20th-century scientific theory now states that it is composed ultimately of minute energy units (electrons, protons, etc.) whirling madly in virtual emptiness. Berkeley has never been truly refuted, and a number of current thinkers believe that modern philosophy must start from a consideration of Berkeley's position.

Three Dialogues between Hylas and Philonous (1713) is Berkeley's most literary expounding of his philosophy. In Socratic dialogues, by question and explanations Philonous ("lover of the mind") teaches the Berkeleian metaphysics to Hylas ("of the wood," a boy of Greek legend whom Hercules favored and whom the amorous Naiads carried off.) Hylas is certainly trapped in the Lockean woods and tries desperately but unavailingly to counter his mentor. The prose is clear and straightforward, often humorous, and sometimes exalted. Yeats has called this work "the only philosophical arguments since Plotinus that are works of art, being so well-bred, so sensible." Yeats further extols the dialogues: "Though he could not describe mystery —his age had no fitting language—his suave glittering sentences suggest it; we feel perhaps for the first time that eternity is always at our heels or hidden from our eyes by the thickness of a door."

David Hume (1711–1776). Born in Edinburgh, Scotland, David Hume was educated there at the university. During residence in France, 1734–37, he wrote his first *Treatise*. Back in Scotland, he was companion to the Marquis of Annandale. He accompanied General James St. Clair as judge advocate on embassies to Vienna and Turin in 1748. His skepticism aroused clerical opposition that blocked his appointment in 1752 to a professorship at the University of Glasgow, but for a decade he was the leading figure in the brilliant intellectual circles of Edinburgh. From 1763 to 1766 he was a social success in Paris as secretary of the British embassy, returning to England as escort for the banished French philosopher Rousseau, but the two philosophers finally parted in a famous quarrel. During 1767–68 Hume was England's Undersecretary of State, and later spent his remaining years amid the sparkling minds of Edinburgh in what may be termed that city's Golden Age. His serene death proved a great disappointment to the pious, who expected hell to yawn open for the great skeptic, and his life proved a joy to the 18th-century freethinkers who insisted that morality and virtue could exist independently of religion.

Treatise of Human Nature (1739), though later termed a "juvenile work" by Hume, contains the essence of his thought, later more fully reworked in *Philosophical Essays concerning Human Understanding* (1748). As Berkeley attacked Locke's objective, commonsense outer world, Hume attacked Locke's assumption of a solid inner self. Hume contended that nothing can be stated of mind except "impressions" (sensations) and "ideas," which are but faint copies of previous sense impressions. When we strive to find ourselves, we find only sense data. Pushing still further, Hume attacked the concept of causation. Our idea of cause, he insisted, rests upon nothing more than memory of one phenomenon following another; it is therefore illogical to deduce laws of cause and effect simply from observable sequences or clusters of events. Since his position could be no more logically refuted than Berkeley's, those appalled by his implications either ignored him altogether (William Paley, in *Natural Theology*, 1802, argues from design as if Hume had never existed) or sought a completely altered approach to epistemology, as did Immanuel Kant. Thus, by the tool of reason itself, Berkeley and Hume had demolished the citadel of Lockean reason, the backbone of 18th-century thought. Since philosophy is always somewhat slow in its infiltration of an era (Locke is the most remarkable exception), it was not until the concluding decades of the century that intellectuals, starkly confronted with Hume, plunged into Romanticism because of the Age of Reason's philosophical self-destruction. In many respects Hume represents a watershed of European philosophy. His extreme skepticism was a catalyst to new philosophical attitudes. In metaphysics he cleared the way for positivism; in ethics he prepared for utilitarianism; and in psychology he anticipated behaviorism.

An Enquiry concerning the Principles of Morals (1751) was Hume's own favorite. It denies altogether the necessity of religion as the creator and sustainer of morality. Like "the good," "the moral" is purely a relative term. Morality is solely what has proved useful and agreeable to the individual and to society. Hume thus anticipates the theories of many later sociologists and anthropologists. As always, Hume is not a bitter pessimist in his skepticism but rather a bland optimist, assuming an inherent benevolence in mankind, and confident of human ability to maintain a sane and decent society that is wholly secular and rational. His literary style is eminently clear and straightforward, perhaps the least metaphorical prose in English.

Hume justifiably wished to be honored as a philosopher rather than as a historian, but in his lifetime he was most acclaimed for:

History of England, (I. reigns of James I and Charles I, 1754; II. Commonwealth and Restoration to 1688, 1756; III, IV, the Tudor period, 1759; V, VI, from Julius Caesar to Henry VII, 1761). This was the first significant study to embrace all of English history and the first broad historical survey in English that properly rates as a work of literature. Hume was the first to consider "manners, finances, arms, commerce, arts and sciences" at any length and as often more important than battles and kings. The history diminishes in value the farther back in time Hume goes, and the work displays many errors in fact. Attempting a detached view, Hume is actually strongly Tory and skeptical. The style is elegantly simple, with bland irony playing over all the feverish struggles of men. Detesting fanaticism, Hume confidently feels the Enlightenment to be the zenith of man's achievement. Especially interesting are his suave rationalistic estimates of English authors.

Memoirs and Correspondence

John, Baron Hervey of Ickworth (1696–1743). John Hervey was a Whig intimate of the royal family, especially Queen Caroline. Under Walpole he became Vice Chamberlain in 1729 and Lord Privy Seal in 1737. He is unfortunately remembered too often as "Lord Fanny" and "Sporus," wicked satiric portraits by the Tory Pope.

Memoirs of the Reign of George the Second (1848) covers court life and contemporary politics from the accession of George II in 1727 until the death of Queen Caroline in 1737. No previous work in English so brilliantly records the minutiae of personal relations among the great which history always shrouds with polite generalizations. Hervey takes his readers into the unposed tête-à-têtes of royalty and the private unburdenings of harassed politicians. The last days of Queen Caroline, for example, are presented with vivid realism and astute psychological observation. Hervey is cynical about all his characters except the queen; yet he fully recognizes her failings. In balanced and witty phrases he brings to life a host of interesting personal encounters and, more importantly, shows how ostensibly impersonal government policy is in reality the product of personalities, often petty and lamentably inadequate ones.

Lady Mary Wortley Montagu (née **Pierrepont**) 1689–1762). Lady Mary Montagu was the daughter of the Duke of Kingston. Against her parents' wishes, she eloped in 1712 with Edward Wortley Montagu, English ambassador to Turkey, 1717–18. Upon her return to England, she was at the center of Whig society, but she never achieved the position enjoyed by contemporary French ladies in their *salons* because the masculine coffeehouse dominated English intellectual life in the first half of the century. In 1739, after her daughter's elopement with Lord Bute, she left her husband and went to live on the Continent. When her husband died in 1761, she made her last journey home, where she died of cancer. In her youth, Lady Mary was the reigning beauty of English society (until she was scarred by smallpox in 1715), and even in her later years she played the great lady, a proud scion of Whig aristocracy. In addition, she was a highly intellectual and literate woman in an age when many noblewomen were barely literate. Pope's bitter portrait of her as "Sappho," occasioned certainly by their political differences and, report has it, because of her laughing rejection of his proposal of marriage, has unfairly prejudiced posterity against her.

Letters (1763) rival Pope's correspondence. But whereas his letters were primarily concerned with the state of his mind, Lady Mary's were a scintillating evocation of the taste and occupations of the fashionable world, ranging from shrewd commentary and vivid description to sprightly gossip. Most of the letters up to 1739 are addressed to her sister, Lady Mar; thereafter they are generally to her daughter, Lady Bute. Most interesting of her letters are the Turkish ones, the greatest travel letters of the century, perhaps equaled only by Smollett's. Lady Mary learned Turkish and delved deeply into the feminine areas of Turkish life; afterward she disabused the English mind about the alleged cruelty and sensualism of Turkey. In the East she had her son inoculated against smallpox, and upon her return to England, she vigorously supported this medical innovation. Later letters to Lady Mar are vivacious attempts to rally her sister, who succumbed to mental disorders. The letters to Lady Bute charmingly depict her life in retirement in Italy. Her daughter shipped her huge cases of English fiction, and entire letters are devoted to discussions of these novels.

Writings on History and Travel

HISTORICAL WRITING. *The Compleat History of England* (1707), by Laurence Echard, was the first collective picture of English history ever written. It and its successors during the age are comparatively undistinguished works, though Thomas Carte's *History of England* (1747–55), in its section on Welsh history, by Evan Evans, provided the material for Gray's "Bard."

BIOGRAPHY. The age created singularly little in biography, and nothing of genuine literary quality. *Anecdotes* (1820), by Joseph Spence (1699–1768), is of interest primarily for its record of conversations with Pope at intervals from 1728 until the poet's death. Though he provides some insights into Pope's mind, Spence was no Boswell.

TRAVEL IN BRITAIN. No traveler of this age did much gazing at the scenery. Both the practical Defoe and the engaging Celia Fiennes (1662–1741) were engrossed in human occupations and contacts in *Through England on a Sidesaddle in the Time of William and Mary* (1888). Social historians have found Celia Fiennes's detailed account of everyday life in town and country invaluable. *Hogarth's Peregrinations* (*1732*, 1782) tells of a ramble along the lower Thames by five Londoners, including the distinguished painter William Hogarth, who illustrated part of the tour.

TRAVEL ABROAD. *Voyage Round the World* (1726), by George Shelvocke, an unsavory privateer, is notable only because its account of the shooting of an albatross provided the germ for Coleridge's "Rime of the Ancient Mariner." *A Voyage Round the World in the Years 1740, 1, 2, 3, 4* (1748) was compiled by the ship's chaplain, Richard Walter, from the papers of George, Lord Anson (1697–1762), commanding officer. The circumnavigation of the globe by the *Centurion* is one of the great epics of the sea. The matter-of-fact narrative renders all the more appalling the fearful suffering that brought death to two thirds of the crew. In the horrifying account of a sailor swept overboard off the Straits of Magellan, Cowper found the subject for "The Castaway."

DRAMA IN THE FIRST HALF OF THE EIGHTEENTH CENTURY

During this era London drama was essentially confined to two theaters—Drury Lane and Lincoln's Inn Fields (transferred to Covent Garden in 1732). The Haymarket Theatre, designed by Vanbrugh, was acoustically suitable for opera only. Acting was not truly distinguished until David Garrick took over the management of Drury Lane in 1747. Drama tended to be moral, partly because of the attacks upon Restoration indecency (like Collier's) but especially to secure the patronage of the pious middle class, rising in economic power. Playwrights of the age were no longer the courtiers of the Restoration but professional writers, often hacks, who willingly submitted to revisions by actors and managers. The consuming political quarrels of the period caused the stage to be a vehicle for political satire until Henry Fielding so enraged the Walpole government that it passed the Licensing Act of 1737, which restricted drama to the two theaters and required censorship by the Lord Chamberlain before production. Audiences continued to be unruly and strongly addicted to farce. With a few exceptions, plays of the period proved mediocre.

The most spectacular successes in the English theater of the period were operas. Purely English attempts at this genre, such as Addison's *Rosamund* (1707), failed miserably, but Italian opera became the rage of society in spite of the chorus of disapproval and sarcasm from literary men of the age. Some of the fashionable enthusiasm was akin to later operatic patronage by the upper class, Italian opera being a taste that clearly set apart the elite from the lower strata of society. The towering figure in opera of this epoch was the naturalized German, George Frederick Handel (1685–1759), who directed Italian opera at the Haymarket Theatre, starting in 1720. During his life in London, Handel composed the music for about forty operas, beginning with *Rinaldo* (1711). He wrote the music for *Acis and Galatea* (1731), with a libretto by Gay that included verses from Dryden and Pope.

Comedy

COMEDY OF MANNERS. Prose was the universal vehicle for comedy. The amoral or immoral Restoration comedy of manners was modified to conform to public wishes for at least ostensible morality. The trend of the times manifested itself even before Collier's attack in 1698, as can be seen by the plays of Cibber, Vanbrugh, and Farquhar, discussed in the last chapter.

COMEDY OF HUMOURS. The classical taste and penchant for satire in Ben Jonson continued to render his dramas popular throughout the era. Although there was a moderate amount of imitation, there was no playwright even of Shadwell's stature to continue the active tradition. Of course, the humours technique was applied in many comedies of the era.

COMEDY OF INTRIGUE. The cleverly plotted comedy of Mrs. Behn, with its diversity of escapades and misunderstandings, was best continued by Mrs. Susannah Centlivre (c. 1667–1723). Her *Busie Body* (1709) proved so popular that in 1710 both theaters were performing the play simultaneously. In the hands of many playwrights this type degenerated into farce. As mid-century approached, the comedy of intrigue dwindled as the taste for sentimental comedy took its place.

FARCE. Most dramatists of the era wrote some farces. Arbuthnot, Pope, and Gay collaborated in *Three Hours after Marriage* (1717), a ludicrous sally at the pedants, fathered by the Scriblerus Club. Henry Fielding, in *The Letter-Writers* (1731), produced the best farce of the period, but the entire genre belongs rather to a history of the theater than to a history of literature. Fielding also wrote the most popular non-musical comedy of the period in *The Tragedy of Tragedies,* which will be discussed with the rest of Fielding's works in the later chapter on the novel.

SENTIMENTAL COMEDY. The reaction against the amoral Restoration comedy together with the need to appeal to a respectable middle-class audience prompted the sentimental comedy. One of the major works in this genre, Addison's *Drummer* (1716), offering a moralizing hero and a noble wife faithful to a husband she believes dead, was frequently translated and adapted both in France and in Germany.

Steele is credited with inaugurating the form in the *Funeral* (1704). In the prologue to his last such work, *The Conscious Lovers* (which has already been discussed in the Steele section), Steele states his purpose: "To chasten wit, and moralize the stage." The sentimental comic dramatist is interested in giving instruction in what he considers right conduct and proper character. The play poses a social problem for its characters, who are then presumed to act according to the dictates of general benevolence and inherent goodness, and the audience is expected to see itself in the polite but commonplace dialogue of decent people.

John Dennis assailed this play as grossly violating the classic concept of comedy which held that it should correct human follies through ridicule, but the new vogue won out and lasted throughout the century. The French adapted the English genre into *comédie larmoyante* ("crying comedy"), which became even more pathetic and pseudo-philosophical, and which strongly influenced the late 18th-century drama of England.

Tragedy

Tragedy represented one third or less of the dramatic fare, and the most frequently performed tragedies were those of Shakespeare, usually cut and often "improved." Although critically the age considered the verse epic and poetic tragedy the greatest forms of literary art, it never produced monumental works in either genre. The classic dramatic unities of time, place, and action were universally professed, ex-

cept by such a hesitant dissenter as George Farquhar, in *A Discourse
. . . upon Comedy* (1702); and most dramas of the era show marked
limitations upon the duration of action, shifting of scene, number of
characters, and the employment of sub-plot. Nonetheless, in practice
the dramatists took moderate liberties with the "rules" (such as setting
scenes in different parts of the same village), though never going so
far as Shakespeare did. It was a typical compromise of the age between strict neoclassic tenets and the less restricted taste of the general
populace.

Again neoclassic tragedy was considered the greatest form of drama.
Its subjects were drawn from classic history and legend, its central
figures portrayed statuesque nobility, and its solemn and dignified blank
verse was rhetorical and unemotional. It sought careful following of
the "rules," even to avoidance of violence upon the stage. A comparison with the plays of the great ancient Greek tragic dramatists will
show how stiff and stilted this neoclassic tragedy was: clearly more
"classical" than the classics. Actually, relatively few of such neoclassic
tragedies were written, and only one is noteworthy, Addison's *Cato,*
which has already been discussed in the section on Addison.

Augustan tragedy, which we might call the typical tragic drama of
the era, was an amalgam of elements: neoclassic "rules," echoes of
Shakespeare and Otway, and reminiscences of the 17th-century heroic
drama. Without a really clear formulation, this drama had numerous,
but few notable, progeny. The chief practitioner of this form of tragedy
was Nicholas Rowe.

By general agreement, the prose domestic tragedy, virtually the creation of George Lillo, is the major dramatic contribution of the age.
The English Renaissance had indeed produced this genre, but it expired upon the early Caroline stage. With Lillo, however, bourgeois
tragedy was created in a form that is still being used in the theater
today. Contemporary business people are its characters, its settings are
realistically middle class, and the events are appropriate to a mercantile
society. Its spirit is sentimental and pathetic, and, above all, it preaches
the creed of commerce and bourgeois morals.

Nicholas Rowe (1674–1718). Nicholas Rowe, the most notable
writer of Augustan tragedy, was born at Little Barford, Bedfordshire.
He was educated at Westminster School and the Middle Temple of
Law. He was the first editor of Shakespeare in 1709, and is responsible
for the divisions into acts and scenes, the notations of entrances and
exits, and the prefacing lists of *dramatis personae* still printed in most

collections of Shakespeare's plays. Rowe's introductory "Life of Shakespeare," printed in this edition, is the first formal biography of Shakespeare. In 1715 Rowe succeeded Nahum Tate as poet laureate. His translation of Lucan's *Pharsalia* (1718) is one of the best translations of the century. Among his dramas are *Tamerlane* (1702), Rowe's own favorite, a rather pale version of Marlow's mighty drama, and *The Tragedy of Lady Jane Gray* (1715), a "she-tragedy" (explained below), which depicts the sad figure of England's "Queen for a day," the unfortunate pawn in the power politics about the tubercular Edward VI. Perhaps Rowe's most notable plays are:

The Fair Penitent (1703)—Augustan Tragedy. This play is an adaptation of Massinger's *The Fatal Dowry*.

The noble Sciolto marries his daughter, Calista, to the virtuous Altamount. Before her marriage, Calista had been the paramour of the dashing but faithless Lothario. Horatio, Altamount's friend, discovers that even after her marriage Calista maintains her liaison with Lothario. Sciolto and his daughter both commit suicide.

The "gay Lothario" has become a fixture in our language. The blank-verse dialogue is more poetic than anything else which the century designed for the stage. Most important contributions are: (1) the "she-tragedy"—that is, a tragedy with a heroine as the focal point of the drama, and (2) the essentially domestic tragedy as plot. With the latter, Rowe is literally setting the stage for George Lillo.

The Tragedy of Jane Shore (1714)—Augustan Tragedy. This work is designated by Rowe as an imitation of Shakespeare, and the verse contains many Shakespearean echoes. Essentially it is another "she-tragedy," sentimentally recounting the decline and fall of the mistress of Edward IV. She dies in poverty, penitent in the arms of her husband, a London goldsmith. Pathos rather than tragedy characterizes this essentially domestic plot. The role of Jane Shore was one of the most notable to be enacted by the renowned Sarah Siddons.

George Lillo (1693–1739). George Lillo was a Londoner apparently of Flemish descent, but very little is actually known about his life. He seems to have followed his father's trade as jeweler until induced by Gay's *Beggar's Opera* to write a ballad opera, *Silvia* (1730). His dramatic career lasted less than a decade, his last work, *Arden of Feversham,* an adaptation from the Elizabethan play, being completed by John Hoadly and acted in 1739. Among his plays is *Fatal Curiosity* (1736), a blank-verse domestic tragedy, which is a greater play than the famous *George Barnwell* but which has exerted no comparable influence.

George Barnwell, or The London Merchant (1731)—Domestic Tragedy. This play is based on a street ballad of Elizabethan London, now available in Percy's *Reliques*.

London merchant Thorowgood has two apprentices, the virtuous Trueman and the weak George Barnwell. Maria, Thorowgood's virtuous daughter, is in love with Barnwell, but he falls into the clutches of Millwood, a prostitute, who persuades him to rob his employer. Barnwell is cashiered but not prosecuted by his generous master. The goadings of Millwood cause him to murder his uncle, a well-to-do gentleman who possesses a large estate. The repentant apprentice bids a tearful good-by to Maria and goes to his execution, and the noble Trueman is properly rewarded.

The town came to boo "tragedy" featuring the bourgeoisie instead of emperors, but instead it sentimentally cried its eyes out. Pope praised it, and Queen Caroline read the play approvingly. Along with *Pamela,* this drama marks the powerful emergence of middle-class literature in the era. Its prose seems stilted to us, but it then had a smack of realism unknown to English tragedy for a century. Lillo epitomizes the morality of the Dissenting bourgeois—that is, that wholehearted application to honest business brings happiness and riches, while laziness or capitulation to man's base appetite brings financial disaster and social punishment. For over a century this play was a regular holiday feature, a sort of modern Morality Play for London youth. Rather surprisingly, it produced few immediate English imitations, chiefly because the physically large theaters of the 18th century were better adapted to spectacular pageantry and wild farce. This drama tremendously influenced the continental stage, however, being quickly translated into French, German, and Dutch. Diderot likened the play to the tragedies of Sophocles and Euripides. Lessing imitated Lillo in *Miss Sara Sampson.* Goethe and Schiller hailed the play, and through translations from the German playwright Kotzebue, Lillo's domestic tragedy returned to the English stage at the century's end. Distantly, Ibsen and the modern drama are the offspring of Lillo.

NON-NEOCLASSIC WRITERS OF THE AGE

Although the half-century 1700–50 is often termed "The Triumph of Neoclassicism," this era witnessed breaks in the rational façade which later would develop into Romanticism. The break is somewhat apparent in the drama and novel of the period but most especially in the essentially emotional writers to be discussed here. It should be noted:

(1) Shaftesbury, Thomson, and the other writers here considered were contemporaries of Swift and Pope, offering a crosscurrent at the very flood tide of neoclassicism.

(2) The period detected no horribly alien quality in these writings. Thomson's *Seasons* was popular from the date of publication and proved the poetic bestseller of the century.

(3) These more emotional writers felt no estrangement from their era, until we reach the older William Law. These were not rebels but fellow members of the Enlightenment, sharing many ideas with their neoclassic brethren and offering a welcome variation from the neoclassic norm. The "Augustan" attitudes listed in the early part of this chapter would be approved by most of these authors, although they might differently interpret such key words as "Nature" and "Reason."

Moral Philosophers

The non-neoclassic thinkers of the age were not too far from their rationalistic contemporaries. They all generally shared an essentially non-Christian view of the universe, a denial of the doctrine of original sin, a restrained optimism for humanity and its future, and an aristocratic view of society. Their chief points of difference lay in:

(1) Their turning away from the political and social world of Pope and Swift, the world of aristocratic coffeehouses and volumes of Horace, in favor of the world of external nature;

(2) Their elevation of heart, or at least of subjective taste, over the reasoning mind, and their stressing of creative imagination over the reflective and imitative spirit.

Anthony Ashley Cooper, third **Earl of Shaftesbury** (1671–1713). Shaftesbury was the grandson of Dryden's Achitophel. Born in London, he was educated privately under John Locke and later at Winchester School. After extensive European travels, he was a member of Parliament from 1695 to 1698, succeeding his father to the title in 1700. Briefly he was Vice-Admiral of Dorset, but ill health caused him to prefer a life of study and writing. He spent his last years abroad, and died in Naples, Italy.

Second Characters (c. *1711–13,* 1914) was contemplated by Shaftesbury as his major pronouncement, summing up most of his previous speculation. Shaftesbury rejected both the Hobbesian concept of imagination and the Lockean theory of association. The plastic General Mind, which he defines as original and eternal "Thought," is constantly creating. Man's very existence is part of that Thought, and consequently we are simultaneously participants and spectators. The thinking of every man, and especially that of philosophers and poets, is a finite repetition of the eternal creation, and here Shaftesbury somewhat anticipated the theory of the creative imagination later expounded by Coleridge. Shaftesbury deplored the criticism of art or life by pre-established rules, feeling that man's innate good taste, trained and cultivated, is a better judge. He also felt that this good taste was the true guide to beauty, morality, and faith.

Shaftesbury remained within the Established Church but sought a faith and morality that in his eyes denied both the Hobbesian skepticism-materialism of this world and the Christian punishment-reward hypothesis of an after-life; in short, he favored an approach that may be termed "sentimental deism."

Characteristicks of Men, Manners, Opinions, Times (1711) collects in three volumes a series of Shaftesbury's writings from 1708 to 1710. With the rationalistic deists, Shaftesbury shared the viewpoint of natural theology as opposed to sacred theology, but where rationalistic deism sought faith and morality by man's reasoning from his observation, Shaftesbury found his goal in the universal moral sense of man. "All men think alike," said the rationalistic deists; "All men feel alike," stated Shaftesbury. Shaftesbury saw all men as sharing the same taste for justice, benevolence, and beauty. Men are and should be virtuous from their inherent nature, not because of bargains offered by religion. Especially in *The Moralists* (1709) Shaftesbury waxes enthusiastic about the glories of nature as the teacher of beauty and benevolence. The repulsive in nature and the evil in man he explains away as Pope was to do in the *Essay on Man:* all partial ills and apparent imperfections are part of a universal good. Shaftesbury's idealistic philosophy and his smooth, even prose rhythms caused Montesquieu to term him one of the four greatest poets of the world, and many subsequent English poets, such as Thomson, were to be influenced by him.

Francis Hutcheson (1694–1746). Born in County Down, Ireland, Francis Hutcheson was educated at Glasgow University. As a professor of moral philosophy (1729–46) at the Scottish institution, he taught Adam Smith.

An Inquiry into the Original of Our Ideas of Beauty and Virtue (1725) is strongly indebted to Shaftesbury, but goes further. Hutcheson claims that the perception of beauty is a sense, just like the famous five senses, and, like them, is immediate, not the product of knowledge or reflection. Unlike Shaftesbury, Hutcheson asserts that the esthetic sense is therefore incapable of training or discipline. Spence records Pope as considering Hutcheson a poor writer, but "he has struck out very great lights, and made very considerable discoveries by the way."

Mark Akenside (1721–1770). Mark Akenside was the son of a butcher in Newcastle-upon-Tyne. He studied medicine at Edinburgh (1739) and Leyden (1744); and as a fashionable physician, he rose to become Queen Charlotte's physician in 1761. The latter appointment was possible because of his sudden shift from Whig to Tory at the accession of George III.

The Pleasures of Imagination (three books in 1744, elaborate revision and a fourth book in 1772) brought the author a handsome fee from the publisher, on Pope's advice. This Miltonic blank-verse poem is strongly indebted to Shaftesbury and Hutcheson. Akenside accepts the Shaftesburian harmony of the good, the true, and the beautiful, but raises the imagination to a creative, godlike power. Since the deists saw nature as the evidence of divinity, Akenside concluded:

> Thus the men
> Whom Nature's work can charm with God himself
> Hold converse.

Elaborating the Chain of Being, Akenside suggests that it is not immutable but still evolving new species under the divine hand. In spite of frequent turgidity, the poem does at times rise to exaltation and murky splendor.

Nature Poets

The neoclassic poets frequently loved nature, but their depictions of nature tended to be (1) springboards to human references, or (2) pastoral verse, leaning upon the classics, strewn with mythological references and generalized descriptions much like set paintings. An Arcadian aura hung over their landscapes, and they usually sang only about gentle, benevolent scenes, often "methodized" by man. The poets considered here tended to (1) the specific and individualized nature experience, emotionally perceived, or (2) to the grand and forbidding aspects of nature.

Anne Finch, Countess of Winchelsea (1661–1720). Anne Finch was the daughter of Sir William Kingsmith and the wife of Heneage

Finch, Earl of Winchelsea. Pope celebrated her under the poetic name of Ardelia.

Miscellany Poems by a Lady (1713), in a variety of meters unusual in the age, recounts many of her rural observations after withdrawal from the Court. She sees nature without the intervening neoclassic preconceptions. Wordsworth found in her "Nocturnal Reverie" the sentimental and meditative soliloquy he favored himself, and in the "Essay Supplementary" to the 1815 edition of *Lyrical Ballads,* he extolled her for "new images of external nature." Matthew Arnold and others perhaps overpraised her as the one genuine rural note amidst a host of urbanized songbirds. To Pope and the rest of her contemporaries, Anne Finch seemed simply a female wit with a little facility in versifying. She also wrote "The Spleen," a burlesque Pindaric ode which was discussed earlier under themes and genres of minor poets.

James Thomson (1700–1748). Born at Ednam, Scotland, James Thomson was educated at Edinburgh. In 1725 he moved to London and quickly gained fame as a nature poet. Comfortable income and gracious patrons assured him a pleasant and sheltered existence. "Rule Britannia," from his masque *Alfred* (1740), has ever since been the most famous patriotic song of the British. He wrote five tragedies that were successful on the contemporary stage but that have since been forgotten.

The Seasons proved the most popular verse of the century. For over a hundred years almost every English home had at least three books: the Bible, *Pilgrim's Progress,* and *The Seasons.* When the French Mme. Roland was imprisoned in 1793, she took four books with her: Tacitus, Plutarch, Shaftesbury, and Thomson. In "My First Acquaintance with Poets," Hazlitt tells of Coleridge picking up from the window seat of a country inn a dog-eared copy of *The Seasons* and exclaiming *"That* is true fame." *Winter* appeared first in 1726, *Summer* in 1727, *Spring* in 1728, the collected edition (including initial printing of *Autumn* and the *Hymn*) in 1730. Thomson made several revisions, the final form being printed in 1744.

Winter and *Autumn* are loosely narrative, following the course of each season chronologically. *Summer* depicts a typical day, running from dawn to sunset and thence to consideration of the starry heavens and Serene Philosophy. *Spring* observes the effects of the budding season upon the rising Chain of Being from inanimate objects through vegetation and animals to man. The mass of descriptive details is justified in the poet's mind as philosophical proof of God's goodness revealed in His handiwork.

Thomson's most notable deviation from the neoclassic norm lay in his treatment of nature:

(1) Vast, unbounded prospects in contrast to the well-defined limits and immediate vistas of neoclassicism.

(2) Specific, accurate, sensuous details, though seldom minutely particularized, instead of the generalized neoclassic pictures.

(3) Motion and change instead of static landscapes.

(4) Remote, wild, "Romantic" scenery of the tropics and Lapland, for example, instead of purely local or classical landscapes.

(5) Fascination with the mysterious and the supernatural instead of the purely commonplace.

(6) Exuberance and richness instead of neat balance. He is credited with the contribution of golden, ethereal sunlight, as in the paintings of Claude Lorrain, to English nature verse.

(7) Adoration of Nature and the god of sentimental deism instead of rationalistic arguments. The concluding *Hymn* asserts that the phenomena of nature are the product of a benevolent deity.

(8) A refined sensibility in pensive, moody, ecstatic contemplation of nature instead of the calm aloofness of neoclassicism.

(9) Strong feeling for animals and strong humanitarianism, as seen in his advocacy of prison reform and opposition to slavery, although his humanitarianism, like his patriotism and desire for progress, is Whiggism rather than Romanticism.

A moderate liberal, not a rebel, Thomson displayed many features that assured his contemporary popularity. His verse lacks the disturbing and intensely subjective quality of the Romantics, and frequently proffers moralizing, and deference to the classics and to notable aristocrats of the day.

The Seasons is essentially a baroque poem, specializing in bravura effects and larger-than-life spectacles and movements. The diction is one of the most remarkable in English, striving to carry current "poetic diction" to its utmost in elegance and impressive circumlocution; thus fish are "finny folk" and chickens "household feathery people." When Wordsworth in the "Preface" to *Lyrical Ballads* attacks the inflated language of earlier poets, it is Thomson and his imitators who are the chief targets rather than the main-line neoclassicists.

Thomson was influenced by *Paradise Lost,* but his diction is only the borrowing of that work's superficial features, such as inversion and substitution of one part of speech for another, and hence cannot be termed Miltonic. However, *The Seasons* was the greatest and most influential blank-verse poem between Milton and the Romantics. Thomson's work also stemmed from currently popular reflective and contemplative verse, and hastened the vogue of poems upon solitude, retirement, meditation, and melancholia. Among his contemporaries, Thomson was universally praised except by Swift, who deplored the lack of action in his work. That staunch neoclassicist Dr. Johnson approved: "His descriptions of extended scenes and general effects bring before us the whole magnificence of Nature, whether pleasing or dreadful; . . . our thoughts expand with his imagery, and kindle with his sentiments."

Liberty (five parts in 1735–36) was intended by the poet as his *magnum opus,* but posterity has neglected this long Whig panegyric in blank verse. Thomson traces the development of freedom from ancient Greece to modern Britain. He glorifies an imaginary primitivistic past of simplicity and peace, believing that a renewed dedication to ancient virtues can assure a glorious future ahead. Conventionally lamenting luxury and corruption, he displays considerable optimism for mankind and human achievement. Perhaps no other English poet has been such a eulogist of trade and industry.

The Castle of Indolence (1748) is the first significant non-humorous imitation of Spenser since the Spenserians of the early 17th century. The meager substance of the poem presents an allegory of the wicked magician Indolence luring pilgrims into his castle and the Knight of Art and Industry liberating them. Some portions capture the spell of Spenser superbly well, and, although not enthusiastically received at the time, this work is Thomson's best poetic accomplishment.

John Dyer (c. 1700–1758). Born at Aberglasney, Wales, John Dyer was educated at Westminster School. Intended for the law, he turned instead to art and traveled widely in Italy. Eventually he took clerical orders in 1741, and served various parishes in Leicestershire and Lincolnshire.

"Grongar Hill" (1726) is the one poem for which Dyer is remembered. Three versions exist, and it is assumed that the inferior version in pseudo-Pindaric ode form is the earliest. The notable version employs the octosyllabics of Milton's "L'Allegro" and "Il Penseroso." Although an outgrowth of the neoclassic "loco-descriptive" poem, this verse markedly departs from that genre in its concern with landscape instead of man's creations. It portrays a fresh English countryside subjectively observed complete with picturesque ruins and an air of neoclassic stoicism.

The Graveyard School

The neoclassicists, like Burton, regarded melancholia as an ailment that had to be purged. To find melancholia pleasing was a characteristic of the later Romantic temperament. By the mid-18th century a number of writers were enjoying the gloomy fright that can accompany a dark night's contemplation of charnel houses, burial grounds, and the like. The writers of this group tended to be orthodox Christians with a strong strain of sentimentalism.

Thomas Parnell (1679–1718). A native of Dublin, Ireland, Thomas Parnell was a clergyman of the Established Church of Ireland from 1700. He was a member of the Scriblerus Club, wrote the prefatory essay to Pope's *Iliad*, and contributed to *The Spectator* and *The Guardian*.

"A Night-Piece on Death" (1722), in solemn octosyllabics, goes through all the symbols of death and gloom (ravens, cypress, etc.), to conclude moralistically with promise of heavenly reward for the just. A brooding spirit of pensive melancholia hovers over the entire poem.

Edward Young (1683–1765). Born at Upham, Hampshire, Edward Young was educated at Oxford. From 1730 he was rector at Welwyn, Hertfordshire. Young is a remarkable barometer of the changing taste of the 18th century. His youthful writings follow the Augustan line; *The Universal Passion* (1725) was a heroic-couplet satire that Pope could scarcely surpass. The pieces of Young's middle years indicate the growing taste for emotionalism and sentimentalism. One of his last works, *Conjectures on Original Composition* (1759) is a ringing plea for original genius in literature in general. Although the atmosphere of the period explains much of his transformation, he still remains a remarkable personality in an almost unprecedented shift from conservative neoclassicism in youth to liberal romanticism in advanced years.

The Complaint: or, Night Thoughts on Life, Death, and Immortality (nine Nights, 1742–45) was largely occasioned by the deaths of his stepdaughter ("Narcissa"), his son-in-law ("Philander"), and his own wife ("Lucia") between 1736 and 1741, but it is also a product of his disappointed ambition, his theological preoccupations counter to deism, and the age's mounting appreciation of emotional literature.

Young's central purpose was to inculcate the need for meditation upon Christian truths as recommended by manuals of religious devotion. He saw meditation as "set and deliberate" and as "sudden and occasional." Ethically he interpreted virtue in the conventions of the age as enlightened self-interest. But his contemporary readers were drawn to the poem by two other aspects: first, the epigrammatic quality of his blank verse, which produced quotations comparable to Pope's, e.g. "Procrastination is the Thief of Time"; and, second, the intensely personal and emotional expression set amidst tombs and correspondingly appropriate symbols of melancholia. The pervasive mood is an abandonment of neoclassic interests in favor of solitude, reverie, pensiveness, sentiment, and moody contemplation of death and immortality. *Night Thoughts* vied with *The Seasons* for popularity in England. In Europe the work proved probably the most popular English poem of the century, inducing translations into virtually every major European language, including Portuguese and Magyar.

Conjectures on Original Composition (1759) demands freedom for native genius and an overthrow of the constrictive doctrines of imitation and of "the rules." From the ancients we should grasp vital force, but we must not let the giants of the past hamper our innate imaginative power to create new and different beauties. Dryden, Pope, and Swift he deprecates for lack of imagination, emotional drive, and originality, but Shakespeare and Milton are praised, and, rather unusual for the date, blank verse is highly lauded.

Robert Blair (1699–1746). Robert Blair was the son of a Scottish clergyman in Edinburgh. After studies at the University of Edinburgh and in the Netherlands, he became pastor of Athelstaneford in East Lothian (1731). His wife was the daughter of William Law.

The Grave (1743) contains much of graveyard ghoulishness (coffins and epitaphs, skulls and lichened tombs, worms and winding sheets) but finally settles down to conventionally orthodox morality and religious exhortation. Its blank verse occasionally suggests the cadences of the Elizabethans. The poem proved immensely popular; William Blake prepared the engravings to accompany the 1808 edition.

James Hervey (1714–1758). James Hervey was a native of Hardingstone, near Northampton. He spent his years quietly as a rural Anglican cleric, dying at nearby Weston Favell.

Meditations among the Tombs, in a Letter to a Lady (1746–47) ran through many editions during the century. Morbidity shrouds this prose diapason which dwells upon every conceivable terror of death. Hervey plays upon the twin themes of sensibility and religiosity, always with both eyes upon the "baleful twilight" and "deeper horror" of the sepulchre. Current interest was generated by the many sentimentalized scenes of deathbeds and tearful mourners.

Verse in Scots Vernacular

Since the Age of Chaucer the only dialect seriously to challenge London English as a vehicle for English literature has been Scots. The 15th-century "Makaris" (Scots poets writing in Scots) were at least the equal of their contemporary poets in London English. But the tradition of Scots prose is dead, appearing only as dialogue in, for example, the novels of Scott and the plays of J. M. Barrie. Even in Renaissance times Scotsmen, notably Knox, wrote prose conforming to London English. Scottish poets who sought fame in the great world also elected the dialect of the south, for example, Drummond of Hawthornden in the Renaissance and Thomson in the 18th century. Nonetheless, a persistent and unbroken tradition of verse in Scots vernacular has continued ever since the "Makaris" even to the present day. Such Scots verse has, at least since the Renaissance, been inspired by Scots nationalism. In the concluding decade of the 17th century and the first half of the 18th century Scots nationalism was fostered by Jacobitism (the Stuart family was Scottish in origin, and every bid for power by the "Old Pretender" or the "Young Pretender" focused on Scotland) and by the union of Scotland with England in 1707, frustrating the hopes of Scots separatists.

Scots vernacular verse of this period defiantly opposes the dominant English tendency, i.e. neoclassicism. The poetry in Scots breathes emotional fervor, patriotic ardor, and celebration of Scotland's scenery and common people. The whole tone of such verse is folksy, intimate, and unaffected. Critically during this era the Scots poetry was not regarded even in Scotland as belletristic, and it certainly made no stir in the critical circles of London. At the century's end, however, this tradition of Scots verse was to produce in Burns one of Britain's greatest lyricists.

Allan Ramsay (1686–1758). Allan Ramsay was born at Leadhills, Lanarkshire, Scotland, of humble origin. At the age of fourteen he was apprenticed to an Edinburgh wigmaker but abandoned this trade for that of bookseller. In 1712 he founded the Easy Club, the prototype of literary clubs that later would prove a prominent feature of Edinburgh life. Not a significant poet himself, he stimulated and gave the direction to Scots verse that it would follow for at least a century.

The Gentle Shepherd (1725) was suggested by the *Guardian's* critique of Pope's *Windsor Forest*. Ramsay's pastoral comedy, depicting real Scottish shepherds in their real habitat, has been called "the first genuine pastoral after Theocritus." Though undistinguished poetically, the work was highly popular in its age.

The Ever Green, Being a Collection of Scots Poems, Wrote by the Ingenious before 1600 (1724) is essentially the anthology compiled by George Bannatyne in 1568 and rescued from manuscript by Ramsay. To many Scots it was the resurrection of Henryson, Dunbar, and other of the "Makaris." Ramsay's Preface sounds the patriotic note: "Their poetry is the product of their own country, not pilfered and spoiled in the transportation from abroad." *Ever Green* is a noted precursor of Percy's *Reliques* in its stimulation of interest in medieval and folk poetry.

The Tea-Table Miscellany (I, 1724; II, 1726; III, 1727; IV, 1737) evoked from Scots an even greater enthusiasm than did *Ever Green*. Ramsay here assembled a great host of poems by Scotsmen, mostly in broad Scots dialect, the richest collection of such verse up to its time. The range is enormous in subject and mood, but most are lyrics (music for these pieces was printed 1763–75). This is the outstanding lyric creation of the Age of Reason. Some of the poems are ballads and popular songs, others conscious concoctions by Ramsay and "some ingenious young gentlemen." Ramsay rewrote or edited much of the verse, often unfortunately; but through most rings a racy, realistic idiom foreign to the London English writings of the period. Sometimes there is a wild exuberance and grotesquerie peculiarly Scottish and foreshadowing such Burns works as "The Jolly Beggars." Largely because of Ramsay, the anthologizing of "primitive" and folk poetry burgeoned earlier in Scotland than in England.

Religious Writings

In the 18th century, both deism ("the faith of gentlemen") and the Established Church were reactions against the frenetic religiosity of the previous century. Both were strongly sympathetic to the prevailing temper of the era—neoclassicism. Neither could satisfy many Englishmen's hunger for an intensely personal and emotionally stirring faith. The upper classes leaned toward deism or maintained a discreet adherence to the Established Church. The lower classes often seemed to manifest no religion at all, especially those in the slums, or else they clung to the tradition of the Established Church. The rising middle class, however, was ripe for evangelistic fervor. As a class it continued the Puritan strain, and in a society that ignored the middle class and offered it no security in its struggles for survival, the bourgeois sought a religion of sustaining warmth. Nonconformist churches (i.e. Protestant sects outside of Anglicanism) provided this faith and demonstrated it in literature chiefly through hymns. The 18th century proved the great age of English hymn writing.

Though written in a variety of measures, most hymns appeared in one of these stanzaic forms (arabic numerals indicate number of syllables):

Common meter (C.M.)—a8 b6 a8 b6
Long meter (L.M.)—a8 a8 b8 b8
Short meter (S.M.)—a6 b6 a8 b6

Many tunes existed in each of the three standard measures, and a new hymn could be sung to any tune in its meter.

Isaac Watts (1674–1748). Isaac Watts was born in Southampton and educated at the Stoke Newington Dissenting Academy. In 1700 he became pastor of the London Independent Congregation. From 1712 he resided with Sir Thomas Abney at Abney Hall. Watts was the greatest devotional poet in the first half of the 18th century.

Horae Lyricae (1706) was indited to "the politer part of mankind," and displayed a variety of verse forms unusual for the period. The blank verse was particularly good, and the subjects are all infused with Christian piety.

Hymns and Spiritual Songs (1707), with later additions, was reprinted frequently. Many of these hymns have been sung for over two and a half centuries throughout the English-speaking world: "When I survey the wondrous Cross" (L.M.), "There is a land of pure delight" (C.M.), "Jesus shall reign where'er the sun" (L.M.), and especially "O God, our help in ages past" (C.M.). The outstanding characteristic of Watts's hymns is a lyric intensity that was almost always absent from Augustan verse. Thought, emotion, and image are fused in rhapsodic enthusiasm. In the Preface, Watts states his purpose: "to promote the pious entertainment of souls truly serious, even of the meanest capacity." For many people the Bible and the hymns of Watts and the later Wesleys have constituted the poetry of life.

Divine Songs Attempted in Easy Language for the Use of Children (1720) was written to teach moral and religious lessons to youngsters. The continued popularity of these pieces is demonstrated by Lewis

Carroll's parodies of "How doth the little Busy Bee" and other Watts's children's hymns a century and a half later.

John Wesley (1703–1791) and **Charles Wesley** (1708–1788). John and Charles Wesley were both born in the Anglican parsonage at Epworth, Lincolnshire. At Christ Church, Oxford, John founded the Holy Club with Charles and fourteen others. The pious austerities practiced by this group and their strict regularity in devotions and duties caused them to be derisively labeled "Methodists." The brothers conducted missionary labors in Georgia (1735–36). Contact with the Moravians, a German Protestant sect, profoundly influenced John in his search for an intense, subjective faith. At Aldersgate in 1738 John experienced the deep mystic revelation ("I felt my heart strangely warmed") that impelled him to evangelize England.

From Aldersgate until his death, John Wesley traveled a quarter of a million miles through Great Britain, preaching over forty thousand sermons, an average of fifteen weekly. He wished to remain within Anglicanism, but the cool hostility of the Established Church drove him to outdoor preaching. He brought to the populace a perfervid compulsion to salvation. Sobbing, hysteria, and mass conversions gripped his congregations, even among those who came to jeer or pummel him. Several times he narrowly escaped martyrdom. The first Methodist Conference was held in 1744, and by 1784 a total of 356 Methodist chapels had sprung up throughout the British Isles. The aristocratic and fashionable world of the 18th century looked askance at Methodism, and virtually all literary figures of the century denounced the movement in laughter or in scorn. As the century progressed, the literary opposition mounted in volume and shrillness, a good indication of the sway Wesleyanism was exerting upon commonality.

Wesleyanism or Methodism was Puritanism surcharged with messianic ardor and shorn of political incitation. Exhortation, prayer, and communal confession of sins supplied a much needed emotional release and bound the faithful to piety, morality, and good works. Anti-intellectualism was strong in the movement, along with complete detestation of elegance, opulence, and easygoing gentility. The last words of John Wesley were: "I'll praise, I'll praise."

More than their sermons, the hymns of the Wesleys gripped English hearts. By the early 18th century congregational singing had almost died out in the Anglican Church. Psalms were chanted in metrical versions, often solely by the parish clerk. Through the Moravians,

John became acquainted with the Lutheran hymnology, a potent force in German Protestantism. The *Charleston Hymn Book* (1737) contained pieces by Watts and other English hymn writers and translations by John from the German. Thereafter, until their death, the Wesley brothers jointly published fifty-six hymn books containing their own original lyrics. The major composition fell to Charles, who is estimated to have written the incredible number of 6,500 hymns, most of which, of course, were pedestrian doggerel. The best of Charles's hymns, however, deserve John's praise: "Here are (allow me to say) both the purity, the strength, and the elegance of the English language; and at the same time the utmost simplicity and plainness suited to every capacity." John wrote far fewer hymns than did his brother, but since they published under joint authorship, it is conjectural who wrote such famous pieces as "Hark! the herald Angels sing" (lines of 7 syllables riming in couplets), "Love Divine, all loves excelling" (a8 b7 a8 b7), and "Jesus, Lover of my soul (a7 b7 a7 b7).

The Wesleys are largely responsible for transforming the English people of the late 18th century into the most exuberant choral singers since the Elizabethan period. The better Wesley hymns are marked by vigorous rhythm and exultant emotion, perfect for vigorous singing and the sudden onrush of religious enthusiasm. Visitors to Ireland were astonished to hear even the Roman Catholic youngsters chorusing Methodist hymns. The impulse to lyricism and deep poetic emotion would contribute mightily to the Romantic Movement.

Journal (published in "Extracts" from 1739, first collected in 1808), by John Wesley, consists of daily entries, with frequent gaps, from October 14, 1735, to October 24, 1790. Unlike Fox's *Journal* or Newman's *Apologia,* this is not so much a spiritual autobiography as it is a series of bulletins from the front by one of God's greatest warriors in the Church Militant. Charm and quaintness are missing. This is a straightforward record of one of the most energetic and devoted lives of all times. Only a completely devoted man could have driven himself as relentlessly as did John Wesley. Withal, he had an eye for the everyday business of life, read current literature voraciously, and recorded hosts of anecdotes and revealing personal encounters. Although constantly under attack, he displayed remarkable tolerance and benignity; however, modern readers may perhaps be annoyed at his credulity toward superstition, for he believed in witches and possession by demons. His style is simple but eloquent, an 18th-century prose with strong overtones of the Authorized Version of the Bible. The man who emerges from John Wesley's *Journal* cannot be termed lovable, but his fierce energy must be respected. His work brings to life the 18th-century common man as does no other writing of the period.

William Law (1686–1761). William Law was a native of King's Cliffe, Northamptonshire. He was a fellow of Emmanuel College, Cambridge, when George I ascended the throne in 1714. A staunch believer in the High Church and in Tory principles of hereditary succession, Law refused to swear allegiance to the Hanoverian line, thus losing his fellowship. Thereafter he supported himself as a tutor, tutoring from 1724 until 1740 the father of Edward Gibbon, the historian. John and Charles Wesley were frequent visitors during this period. From 1740 until his death he practiced extensive philanthropy at King's Cliffe. His early writings were rationalistic arguments against Mandeville and against deists such as Tindal.

Like Young, Law presents the remarkable spectacle of a man apparently rooted in conservative neoclassicism during his earlier years, only to turn radically away from it in his later life. Before 1740 Law produced orthodox writings of a commendable but essentially conventional type. After 1740 Law revealed himself as the greatest prose mystic in English since the anonymous Middle English author of *The Cloud of Unknowing*. The incredible nature of Law's diversity is shown in the fact that his earlier works influenced Dr. Johnson and his later works influenced Blake.

A Serious Call to a Devout and Holy Life (1728) appealed to all levels of society, especially the emerging middle class, as Bishop Butler could not. In persuasive, witty, gracefully fluent prose, generally, in short, pithy paragraphs, Law called for a virtuous life of Christian piety. Interspersed are vivid "character sketches" comparable to those in *The Spectator*. A sincere Christian spirit feelingly expounds the difference between Christian precept and practice. Dr. Johnson ascribed his own spiritual awakening at Oxford to this book: "I took up Law's *Serious Call to a Holy Life,* expecting to find it a dull book (as such books generally are). . . . But I found Law quite an over-match for me; and this was the first occasion of my thinking in earnest of religion."

An Appeal to All That Doubt or Disbelieve the Truths of the Gospel (1740) was notably influenced by the writings of the German Protestant mystic Jacob Böhme (variety of spellings) (1575–1624). Law relates that his first reading of Böhme put him in "a perfect sweat." This book and subsequent mystical writings by Law will clarify much of the poetry of William Blake. Böhme and Law assert the fundamental unity of all existence. Nothing exists except as it is given form and concrete shape and as it meets resistance (light is manifest only when reflected by a dark body). Men mistakenly label the warring existences as "good" and "evil," but they are simply God's "power" and "love." All accomplishment in the universe depends upon this contest ("Without contraries is no progression," Blake). The "Fall of Man" was the first assertion of human selfhood and separation from the great unity. What seems evil is only the separation. If the warring elements in each man can reach their apogee, they can be fully formed, balanced, and reunited into the great unity. The process of integration is violently withstood by reason, which meticulously separates and keeps apart, thus protracting the debasement of man and the human feeling of frustration and inadequacy. The rapturous reunion of the total human psyche seems "death" to the reasoner, but it is the fullest life of the mystic. Like all great mystics, therefore, Law denies the validity of an intellectual and intelligential examination of the universe and denies also the material, commonsense world, the only one that possesses full meaning to the rationalistic mind. He casts his lot with the intuitive and inspirational grasp of things. While his contemporaries could tolerate the genteel nature rhapsodies of Thomson and the sentimental deism of Shaftesbury, they branded the later writings of Law as the ravings of premature senility. Even John Wesley broke with Law, bcause Law's mysticism rendered non-essential the atonement of Christ. The prose of Law's mystical writings waxed poetic in exalted imagery and rhythmic cadences.

Chapter 3

The Age of Johnson (1750–1785)

BACKGROUND INFORMATION

MAJOR HISTORICAL EVENTS. In 1752 the English-speaking world brought its dating into line with the rest of Europe by replacing the outmoded Julian calendar with the Gregorian calendar. Eleven days between September 2 and 14 were omitted in spite of popular outcry. Since that time New Style computing of the year's beginning has been uniform, with January 1 the start of each year.

With the purchase of Sir Hans Sloane's huge collection in 1753, the British government founded the British Museum, which in the 19th century was to prove the world's greatest library, to be superseded in the 20th century only by the American Library of Congress.

Boundary disputes in North America touched off the Seven Years' War between England and France (termed the French and Indian War in America) from 1755 to 1763. Initial defeats toppled English ministries and left dubious the entire fate of the empire. Against the opposition of George II, national clamor forced a coalition government, with the major role held by William Pitt the Elder, later the Earl of Chatham. The "Great Commoner" lifted up a defeated people and drove them to spectacular victory, and the Golden Age of English parliamentary oratory was inaugurated by perhaps the most eloquent speaker of English history. Pitt was also a man of action, almost single-handedly directing the war. England rang with shouts of triumph as the "boy-generals," shrewdly hand-picked by Pitt, conquered continents. Clive secured India for the British by sweeping aside the

Franco-Indian army at Plassey (1757). Wolfe, on the night of September 12, 1759, quoted Gray's "Elegy" to his fellow officers and the next morning led his troops up precipitous slopes to confront the astounded French on the Plains of Abraham in front of Quebec; both Wolfe and his equally gallant adversary, Montcalm, perished in the battle, but Canada was thus gained for Britain. An intended French invasion of England was rendered impossible by Boscawen and Hawke, who shattered the French fleet. The Treaty of Paris (1763) established Great Britain at a peak of power previously unapproached in her history.

Much of the Elder Pitt's accomplishment was to be threatened by the new monarch, George III (reigned 1760–1820). The grandson of George II had been imbued with Bolingbroke's concept of the "patriot King" through his mother, so that England was politically rent asunder as George III made the only attempt since James I to rule as well as reign. An able monarch might have succeeded, but George III was blessed with neither tact nor brains. The role of the Elder Pitt was minimized by his illness and his elevation from Commons into the House of Lords as the Earl of Chatham. "The King's Friends" were the new ministers, returning the Tories to power after half a century of uninterrupted Whig dominance.

An unlikely and incongruous champion of English liberties against an arbitrary ruler rose in John Wilkes, personally a dissolute reveler. In #45 (with all the connotations of rebellion against the Hanoverians implicit in "The Forty-Five") of the *North Briton* (April 23, 1763) Wilkes savagely criticized George III, who retorted by imprisoning Wilkes. The London populace showed its support of Wilkes by rioting outside St. James's Palace and throughout the city. In stormy political battles (Wilkes was legally branded an outlaw for several years and took refuge on the Continent) Wilkes eventually proved the means of reaffirming fundamental freedoms: liberty of the press, right of subjects to choose their own representatives, freedom from unwarranted imprisonment or exclusion from rights. Wilkes saw himself fully exonerated in 1782. His magic name even appeared in the new world as part of the Pennsylvania city Wilkes-Barre.

The British colonies along the Atlantic coast from Massachusetts to Georgia petitioned in vain against their exploitation by George III and sought their full rights as Englishmen. Chatham and Burke urged conciliation, but a subservient Parliament proved as intractable as the ruler. Open war between the colonists and Great Britain exploded in

1776. Many Englishmen favored the rebelling colonials, the "New Whigs," under Charles James Fox, borrowing their party colors, buff and blue, from the uniform of the Continental Army. The entrance of European nations—France (1778), Spain (1779), the Netherlands (1780)—against an empire torn by civil war caused a war-weary country to grant independence to the United States in the Treaty of Paris (1783).

The obduracy of George III, the challenge to the rights of Englishmen, and the descent of Great Britain from its pinnacle of glory excited Parliament as perhaps never before. Probably no other cabinets or legislatures have included such brilliant political figures as those in England during the two concluding decades of the 18th century, and in 1783 the popular voice successfully called as Prime Minister, and actual ruler of Great Britain, Chatham's great son, William Pitt the Younger. At the incredibly early age of twenty-four the Younger Pitt assumed what was then the most important political post in the world. Many have considered this Pitt the greatest of all English prime ministers, and certainly the first truly modern prime minister and creator of the office as it still exists. Honest and efficient government, admittedly influenced by Adam Smith's *Wealth of Nations,* rejuvenated a defeated nation and strengthened it for the fearful test of the Napoleonic era to follow. Although both Pitt and Fox detested the American war and the slave trade, and advocated parliamentary reform and conciliation of the Irish Catholics, fate threw them on opposite sides of the floor of Commons. Even the contests between Gladstone and Disraeli in the 19th century could not equal the brilliance of Pitt (Conservative, Tory) and Fox (Liberal, Whig), while ever ready to enter the oratorical lists were one of England's wittiest gentlemen, Richard Brinsley Sheridan, and England's great political theorist Edmund Burke.

However, more momentous even than these dramatic political developments was the Industrial Revolution, which, with rapid technological change, transformed England in the second half of the 18th century. Of course, the roots of this economic change stretch far back. Some historians consider the Age of Chaucer, when the self-sufficiency of feudal manors and individual crafts was being superseded by at least partial dependence upon manufacture and money exchange, the beginning of the Industrial Revolution. Wherever it began, the movement of English society toward modern industrialization is unmistakably clear from 1760 to 1790. Textile manufacture was revolutionized by Hargreave's spinning jenny (1764, patented 1770), Arkwright's water frame (patented 1769), Crompton's spinning mule (invented 1779), and Cartwright's power loom (patented 1785–87). With the invention of the steam engine (patented 1769), Watt inaugurated a new age of power. Factories sprang up, especially in the Midlands, blackening whole counties with coal dust and producing goods at a rate never before known in human history.

From the middle class came the entrepreneurs who established the factories and produced a revolution in man's mode of living. Typical of this new breed was John Wilkinson, the greatest of ironmasters. He created railroads for mines (1767), threw the world's first iron bridge across the Severn (1779), launched the world's first iron boat (1787), cast the water pipes for Paris, built a Wesleyan chapel entirely of iron, and, appropriately, was buried in an iron coffin (1805). By 1774 Manchester had a veritable Chamber of Commerce. By 1777 Wilkinson was assembling the whole iron industry to fix prices and sales practices.

In 1785 Josiah Wedgwood, founder of the pottery industry in Staffordshire, formed the General Chamber of Manufacturers of Great Britain, avowedly created to influence government policy. The middle class also threw its energies into local commissions for paving, lighting, sanitation, and law enforcement, necessitated by the increasing size of the cities and the consequent dislocation of populations. The growth of local authorities was the most important social development of the era, proving instrumental in saving a number of lives, minimizing social confusion and unrest, and preparing for the great reforms of the next century.

Nonetheless, England paid a high price for its supremacy as the world's first industrial country. The laws and customs of a traditionally agricultural society were completely inadequate for handling the problems of the new industrial society. Working conditions were often atrocious, hours were long, wages were close to the starvation level, and child labor was mercilessly exploited. A landless, toolless working class became wage slaves, dependent for sheer survival upon the will of employers. A proletariat rapidly developed, creating a hostile cleavage between capital and labor. Though trade guilds reach far back into medieval times, the beginning of modern trade unions dates from this era.

CULTURAL CONDITIONS. The middle class was so wrapped up in its endeavors to produce goods and make money that it had little concern for art. The interest in music, painting, architecture, and literature was largely that of "gentlemen," who continued largely to stand for the neoclassic attitudes discussed in the previous chapters. Even with the gentry, however, the support of neoclassicism was frequently mere lip service; for, increasingly, feeling and sentiment were beginning to exert their influence against pure rationalism. This transitional age, often termed "The Decline of Neoclassicism," showed that there was a growing discontent with the intellectual concept of art, but such discontent was not yet revolt.

The most remarkable artistic achievement of this age lay in painting. Before the mid-18th century, distinguished painting in England was almost exclusively by imported artists. The late 18th century produced at least two great English painters in Sir Joshua Reynolds (1723–92) and Thomas Gainsborough (1727–88) and at least two near-greats in Allan Ramsay (1713–84) (son of the earlier discussed poet of the same name) and George Romney (1734–1802). Typical of a rich and stable secular society were the portraits by these painters, portraits of confident, realistic, relaxed men and graceful, sophisticated women. The Royal Academy was established in 1768, with Reynolds as its first president. Richard Wilson (1714–82) literally starved because of his determination to paint landscapes, but he proved the founder of the long and notable line of English landscape painters.

English interior decoration maintained the blending of utility and esthetics that still renders 18th-century furniture the epitome of good taste. After the death of Thomas Chippendale in 1779, the great tradition was continued by Thomas Sheraton (1751–1806). The neoclassic ("American Colonial") architecture was still the dominant style of James Gibbs, William Kent, and the Adam brothers, manifesting a chaste simplicity and harmony. The fashionable rage for Chinese, Gothic, and other exotic architectural manners was extensive but did not challenge the significant neoclassic buildings. The Georgian architecture of the second half of the century has been termed the last homogeneous school of architecture in England, the last to spring naturally from the life and temper of the society.

The isolation and provincialism of many English communities were breaking down with the improvement of roads, which were necessitated by booming trade and industry as well as by the growing and more mobile population. Between 1762 and 1774 as many as 452 acts were passed for the construction and repair of highways. With Palmer's mail coaches in 1784, the Golden Age of Coach Driving was inaugurated, to continue until the railroads usurped the carrier's role in the 1830's.

Hazlitt, De Quincey, Cobbett, and a host of other literary men were to be excited by the coaching days, and much of the nostalgia in Dickens is for those bygone days on the road.

An increasing population and widespread literacy spurred extensive journalism. The most famous of all English newspapers, *The Times,* was founded in 1788 as a continuation of the *Daily Universal Register* of 1785. Periodicals continued to proliferate, running the entire gamut from literary magazines to trade and technical journals by the century's end. The *Monthly Review* (1749–1845) is often termed the first literary review, but it consisted essentially of short summaries or abstracts until 1783. Sheridan and Goldsmith were among the numerous contributors to this liberal Whig publication. The rival *Critical Review* (1756–90) was established by Tory and Church patronage to offer more conservative opinion. Smollett was the leading light of the *Critical.* Dr. Johnson, who contributed to this journal, rated it above the *Monthly,* perhaps from loyal Tory sentiment. Though the mounting quantity of printed matter required numerous writers, the supply of authors continued to exceed the demand. Personal patronage was virtually extinct, except as a clerical living might be awarded to a struggling man of letters like Crabbe. "Grub Street" meant severe hardship and deprivation, experienced by Johnson, Goldsmith, and countless lesser figures.

Throughout Western society the greatest cultural achievements of this era were not in art but in science. Though France, especially, produced a number of gifted scientists, England contributed two major figures in Henry Cavendish (1731–1810) and Joseph Priestley (1733–1804). In chemistry, Priestley was the first to isolate oxygen (he called it "dephlogisticated air") in 1774, and Cavendish proceeded to break down water into hydrogen and oxygen. Cavendish, for whom today's important Cavendish Laboratories at Cambridge are named, also isolated argon. In 1766 Priestley discovered the Law of Inverse Squares for the attraction or repulsion of two electrical charges, and Cavendish discovered but did not publicize the concept of potential and specific inductive capacity of electricity. The period displayed an "Electrical Rage," many people, such as John Wesley, ascribing remarkable curative powers to electrical shocks. When Benjamin Franklin invented lightning conductors, George III quickly had them installed upon Buckingham Palace. Though quite dubious in the eyes of those who held a sober scientific view, hypnotism enjoyed a fad in this period (termed "animal magnetism" by its noted practitioner, Mesmer, after whom it was also called "mesmerism").

LANGUAGE (TO 1800). Dryden was perhaps unduly deferential to the royal influence upon the language, but he was more right than wrong. Under the Hanoverians, however, the Court lost all sway over the English tongue. Gentlemen and authors were now the creators of linguistic standards. Gay blades tended to slangy and coarse language, with much vocabulary appropriated from the underworld. *The Connoisseur* in ⚜138 (1756) denounced the half-swearers, "who split, and mince, and fritter their oaths into gad's bud, ad's fish and demme." The jargon of Bob Acres in *The Rivals* seems pure theatricality to modern readers, but it only slightly exaggerated the conversation of dashing young men in Sheridan's age. The standards of refinement had a doughty champion in Lord Chesterfield, who in his letters demanded elegance and precision in speech as well as in all aspects of fashionable life. *The Connoisseur* (⚜42, 1754) describes a club, probably imaginary, determined to "cultivate their mother tongue" and imposing fines upon the members for "modish barbarism" and "cant terms."

However, the greatest incentive to improved language standards was the growing wealth of England. Charity schools were pouring out ever greater numbers of educated students whose courses had featured English instead of the classic languages. Women were given the advantage of education, and while Lady Mary Wortley Montagu seemed a strangely isolated woman intellectual in the early part of the century, the well-educated and intellectual lady was a commonplace toward the century's close. Above all, a firm grasp of English reading and writing was essential to the blossoming middle class of businessmen and administrators.

The period witnessed the first true English dictionary (1755), by Dr. Johnson, discussed under that author. His prefixed "Grammar of the English Language" is perfunctory and conventional. Current modish speech contained many expressions now frowned upon by stylish schools of grammar. From novels of the age—such as those by Smollett and Sterne—it is clear that contemporary good speakers regularly employed such forms as: *you was, he don't,* double negative, *who* as an accusative, adjective or "flat adverb" instead of conventional adverb (*extreme bad terms*), faulty pronoun reference (*everyone . . . their*), indicative in contrary-to-fact statements and accusative after the copulative (*if I was him*), and a host of irregular forms for strong verbs (*he sunk, had broke, had spoke, had wrote, having stole away*).

Later fastidiousness has battled, not always successfully, against these forms.

Joseph Priestley, whose range of thought and writing is truly astounding, in addition to his scientific works issued *Rudiments of English Grammar* (1761), in which he sought uniformity and accuracy. A more epoch-making book was *Short Introduction to English Grammar* (1762), by Robert Lowth, later Bishop of London. Lowth sees grammar as following a universal law precisely as does logic or science; he is largely responsible for the tendency, still strong in many quarters, to apply moral epithets of "good" or "bad" to English constructions and to insist upon absolutism in grammatical rules. Numerous kindred spirits followed Lowth, and the entire culmination of 18th-century grammatical legislation appeared in *Grammar of the English Language* (1795), printed in York and written by the American Lindley Murray (Scots and Americans have been especially diligent in prescribing what is "correct English"). In its original form Murray's book went through fifty editions; its 1816 revision saw over 120 editions in the 19th century. Though neither an innovator nor a true linguist, Murray organized English grammar in a simple and logical pattern and presented it with neat examples and exercises. Whatever their claims to originality, most of the 19th- and 20th-century grammars are Murray's offspring. Probably no other single person has exerted as much influence upon the English language as Murray has.

The most important study of the era specializing in vocabulary was *Philosophy of Rhetoric* (1776), by Dr. George Campbell, Principal of Marischal College, Aberdeen; much of this work was incorporated by Murray. Campbell applies three criteria to judge propriety of usage: (1) national origin (among his disapprovals are *advice* as commercial idiom, and *connoisseur* as a "stray" from French); (2) reputability (*dumbfound* is "disagreeable and unsuitable"; *topsyturvy* and *helterskelter* betray mere "frivolous humour"); and (3) present usage (among "recent introductions" Campbell condemns are *capability, continental, criminality, originality, sentimental;* among words "all writers of any name have now ceased to use" are *fantasy* and *tribulation*). The examples above are chosen, not to discredit Campbell, but to show how a living language picks and chooses as it needs, not as prescribed by theorists. Actually Campbell appears to be the first scholar to make a detailed study of English usage, and most of his pronouncements have stood the test of time.

The formulation of modern punctuation was also made in this era.

Earlier practice had largely followed the rule of thumb: "I put in a comma where I feel a pause." In *De Usu et Ratione Interpungendi: An Essay on the Use of Pointing* (1771), James Barrow moderately advocated the employment of the comma much as it is still used for grammatical rather than rhetorical purposes. Also, English moved to the modern style of capitalization in the second half of the 18th century, using capitals only for proper nouns.

Another liberal of the age, as extraordinary as Priestley in his varied interests, was John Horne Tooke, who, in *Epea Pteroenta, or, The Diversions of Purley* (Part I, 1786; Part II, 1805), virtually inaugurated for English the now zealously pursued study of semantics, "the meaning of meaning" in words.

JOHNSON AND BOSWELL AND THEIR WORKS

"THE CLUB" (LATER THE LITERARY CLUB) OF LONDON. One of the most influential literary societies in English letters was "The Club," which Johnson and Reynolds founded in 1764 with a total of nine members, thus crystallizing a literary and social group that had regularly been meeting since as early as Johnson's Ivy Lane Club of 1749. In all English literature only the Scriblerus Club can compete with "The Club" in the brilliance and creativity of its members. Unlike the short-lived Scriblerus Club, the Johnson-Reynolds organization was to continue its regular sessions throughout the remainder of the century— and to renew itself even down to the present. Though dominated during its lifetime by the "Great Cham," The Club was no mere collection of disciples, but produced such independent and significant writers as Burke and Gibbon. In contrast with the similarly close ties of the 17th-century writers, most of this circle were professional men of letters of middle-class origin. Their support of neoclassic principles followed the established tradition of the genteel public for which they wrote, but their middle-class background made them somewhat susceptible, as Goldsmith was, to the variant tendencies of pre-Romanticism.

Samuel Johnson (1709–1784). Samuel Johnson was the son of a Lichfield bookseller. Scrofula, for which he was "touched" by Queen Anne, caused the loss of the sight of one eye and perhaps the near-sightedness of the other, and also scarred his skin considerably along with a later attack of smallpox. His uncouth appearance and manner militated against him throughout life. While at Oxford he attracted the favorable attention of Pope through a Latin translation of "Messiah," and also while at college he suffered from severe attacks of melancholia that would ever after plague him. He was obliged to leave Oxford for financial reasons, and this was part of the cause of his melancholia. In 1732 he became usher at Market Bosworth school but left this post to marry the widowed Mrs. Porter of Birmingham in 1735. Although she was twenty years older than Johnson, he remained with her until her death in 1752. Among his pupils at the unsuccessful Edial school (near Lichfield) was David Garrick, who accompanied him to London in 1737.

Years of hackwork and physical deprivation ended with the 1755 publication of his dictionary. Through Thomas Warton's intercession, Oxford conferred the master's degree upon Johnson in time for the title to be affixed to his name in the dictionary. Doctor's degrees were conferred upon him by Trinity of Dublin (1765) and Oxford (1775). With the accession of George III in 1760, Johnson, a consecrated Tory, was granted a pension of £300 and thereafter a comfortable income permitted him the elegant amenities of life that soothed his melancholia, along with hosts of adulators who flattered him by their breathless expectancy of wisdom from the learned pundit. His later years were chiefly devoted to society and to superb conversation, divided between "The Club" and the salon of Mrs. Thrale (later Mrs. Piozzi).

Johnson is the first figure in English literature to achieve major stature essentially through scholarship and criticism. His neoclassic drama *Irene,* written in the mid-1730's and not produced till his friend Garrick did it in 1749, was a failure; his political pamphleteering, chiefly *Taxation no Tyranny* (1775), against the rebellious Americans, is undistinguished; and his belletristic prose in periodical essays is highly competent but not startlingly original. His fame as a writer lies particularly in lexicography and literary criticism, and his lasting notoriety springs in large part from his portrait in Boswell's biography, where he emerges as the greatest conversational personality in our language. Boswell's Johnson is *Ursa Major* ("Great Bear," as he was labeled by Lord Auchinleck, Boswell's father), the monumental pronouncer of conservative commonsense against all the world. Good talk was therapeutic to Johnson's troubled mind, and in his verbal domination of all his interlocutors, he found a necessary bolstering of his ego. Our age has sought somewhat to de-Boswellize Johnson, thereby creating a less dogmatic figure than revealed in the famed biography; but the world will probably never shake off the Boswell characterization of the "Great Cham."

Poetic Satires

London: A Poem, in Imitation of the Third Satire of Juvenal (1738) was published on the same day as Pope's epilogue to his collection of satires. In imitating classical satire, Johnson was following a neoclassical tradition. In heroic couplets, Johnson virtually translates much of this diatribe against ancient Rome, here applied, with occasional incongruity, to contemporary London. Eloquently he derides a selfish and acquisitive society only superficially Christian. His references to excise, pensions, and patrons anticipate the scathing definitions in his dictionary. His politics, as always, are stoutly Tory, and the most effective and original parts of the satire are upon the ravages of poverty from his own "Grub Street" existence.

The Vanity of Human Wishes. The Tenth Satire of Juvenal, Imitated (1749) is perhaps the most nobly Roman poem in English. It is less an imitation than an independent heroic couplet poem upon the same topic as Juvenal's satire. For the classic illustrations, Johnson substitutes modern examples of human ambition concentered in power, learning, long life, and beauty, all designed to show how self-seeking in this world is nothing but vain folly. The conclusion of the work is a serene Christian contemplation of the nothingness of this life and the proper reward in after-life for the true believer. Johnson shows an excellent grasp of the pithy compressed power of the couplet and here produces the few verse quotations for which he is still remembered.

Essays and Prose Fiction

The Rambler (twice weekly from March 20, 1750, to March 14, 1752) consisted of 208 periodical essays, all by Johnson except ⚹10, ⚹30, ⚹44, ⚹97 (by Samuel Richardson), and ⚹100. Initial sales averaged five hundred copies per issue, but in bound form this proved the nearest competitor to *The Spectator* during the century and loomed large in Johnson's contemporary reputation. The purpose of the series was "to inculcate wisdom or piety," and the morality he preaches is a practical one, calling upon his readers to cultivate a balanced state of mind and to devote their time and energies to maintaining their individual and communal well-being. The refrain of the vanity of human wishes sounds throughout the work. The imaginary characters he creates (Polyphilus, the purposeless wit; Suspirius, the habitual fault-finder; Venustulus, the effeminate dandy) are "characters" from the Overburian tradition but lacking the sparkle of their prototypes in

Addison and Steele. The literary criticism is vigorously Johnsonian but is really only an inkling of his later and greater critical efforts. This publication established the prose style termed Johnsonian—sonorous, highly Latinate, rhetorically balanced, and magisterial.

The Idler (weekly from April 15, 1758, to April 5, 1760) was a Saturday supplement to *The Universal Chronicle.* All but twelve essays are by Johnson. The papers are shorter and more lively than those in *The Rambler,* possibly because *The Rambler* was written while he was working on the Dictionary, which tended to make his style ponderous. The characters now have English names (Mr. Sober is Johnson himself), and in Dick Minim, the absurdly pretentious critic, Johnson creates his one memorable character. Especially interesting are the essays on style and language, clearly neoclassic in spirit but nonetheless tolerant and undogmatic.

In 1757 Johnson reviewed *Free Enquiry into the Origin and Nature of Evil,* by Soame Jenyns for *The Literary Magazine.* The book under review proposed optimistic deism similar to that of Pope's *Essay on Man.* Jenyns attempted to demonstrate that all human pain and agony are wholly proper within the total scheme of things. "The sufferings of individuals are absolutely necessary to universal happiness," claimed Jenyns, and he suggested that just as men derive pleasure from tormenting inferior creatures, so beings superior to man in the Chain of Being might enjoy tormenting mankind. Grimly and devastatingly, Johnson crushed Jenyns by demonstrating that such reasoning was in fact horrifying pessimism, turning the whole universe into a fiendish torture chamber. Johnson's position was essentially that, although he could not himself account for the presence of evil in the universe, he was not going to endure patiently other people's ridiculous explanations.

Johnson's first printed work was *A Voyage to Abyssinia. By Father Jerome Lobo* (1735), a translation from the French. *The Rambler* contained five "oriental tales" whose purpose was to indoctrinate with moral concepts. These are in a sense forerunners of his only piece of prose fiction, *Rasselas.*

The Prince of Abyssinia. A Tale (1759) was retitled *The History of Rasselas* in the 1787 edition. Ostensibly a novel, this is a prose essay on the vanity of human desires.

Irked by confinement in the Happy Valley, Rasselas flees with his sister Nekayah and the philosopher-poet Imlac. After exploring every way of life, Rasselas decides there is no genuine happiness in any of the pursuits of this world. He and his party turn homeward to reassume their wonted duty.

Voltaire's *Candide* and Johnson's *Rasselas* were published within a few days of each other, and both are attacks upon optimistic deism. *Rasselas,* as perhaps no other work in English, demonstrates the excellence of neoclassic canons of art. In quick generalization, Johnson schematizes most of man's searches for earthly happiness—wealth, power, sensualism, philosophy—and finds that felicity reposes in none. Man's only hope is to practice virtue in his allotted task and await a benevolent deity, who will rectify all errors in the after-life. Imlac, Johnson's alter ego, sees the role of art as inculcating morality through pleasure, and therefore, general and universal truths, not minute instances, are the province of art instruction. The style is completely Johnson's, one that produces massive harmonies and orchestrated grandeurs in contemplation of human destiny. Never elsewhere have hard truths and commonsense wisdom been so impressively stated.

A Journal to the Western Isles of Scotland (1775) was Johnson's version of a journey he was induced to take along with Boswell from August to November 1773. It is less a record of travels than a series of observations upon a different civilization. It is briefer than Boswell's companion work, and far less vivacious. Nonetheless, it is a compelling book for two reasons:

(1) The criticisms, often asperities, upon a culture lacking Johnson's norm of reasoned balance. The longest section discusses "savage virtues," which is what the native customs of Scotland appeared to be to Johnson.

(2) The use of wild landscapes as symbols of the precarious fate of mankind. Scenery and historical associations evoke from Johnson reflections upon the paradox of man's greatness and weakness. The meditation upon the sacred island of Iona is one of Johnson's most impressive passages, approaching almost Miltonic sublimity.

Works of Scholarship and Literary Criticism

The Plan of a Dictionary of the English Language (1747), addressed to Lord Chesterfield for patronage, pointed out the deficiencies of existing dictionaries, offered specimens of Johnson's handling of words, and proposed three years for the undertaking. Fobbing off Johnson with £10, Chesterfield thereafter ignored him until the work neared completion. Late in 1754 Chesterfield sought to gain favor with the lexicographer by his graceful tributes in *The World.* Johnson replied with the famous letter (1755) that, in dignified irony, rejected the whole patronage concept. Though often deemed the death blow to the system of patrons, the letter actually recognized the reality that patronage had already expired.

A Dictionary of the English Language (1755) took eight years and was Johnson's individual effort, aided by six secretaries (chiefly Scots). All subsequent English dictionaries are essentially derivatives from this work, which scored an impressive number of firsts:

(1) It was the first full-fledged dictionary. All predecessors, even Nathan Bailey (1721), produced mere word lists in comparison.

(2) It was the first dictionary to employ illustrative quotations from significant writers. Johnson quoted extensively from authors ranging from Sidney to his own contemporaries. Paradoxically, while accepting the "reform of our numbers" at the end of the 17th century, he saw the High Renaissance writers as "the wells of English undefiled." Dryden is the most quoted; Shakespeare and Pope appear frequently; and among contemporaries, Johnson cited from Richardson, Garrick, and himself. Johnson borrowed books from friends, penciled the passages to be copied by scribes, and returned the defaced volumes. Many quotations (often inaccurate) came from Johnson's own encyclopedic memory.

(3) It was the first genuinely descriptive, rather than proscriptive, dictionary. All previous English lexicographers had been motivated by the passion of "refining" the language. Although Johnson had started with a similar intent, his monumental commonsense turned him to an accurate explanation of how the language is truly employed and thus into the course ever since followed by reputable dictionaries.

(4) It was the first carefully analytical dictionary with workable definitions. *Come* and *go* are each subdivided into more than fifty sections, a spectacular contrast with the lamentable simplifications and omissions of his predecessors. The most frequently quoted definitions from Johnson ignore the multitudes of competent and workmanlike definitions. The rare mistakes (e.g. *pastern* of a horse) are understandable when we realize that Johnson single-handedly did all of the defining, even in areas alien to him. The ponderous, sesquipedalian definitions (e.g. *network, cough*) will not look so ridiculous if we ourselves try to define many commonplace words. The few facetious definitions (e.g. *oats, pension*) should be excused as necessary relaxation during his solitary labors.

Pronunciation is indicated only by accent, and etymological knowledge is meager by modern standards. Nonetheless, this is the true father of all the later English dictionaries by the greatest lexicographer in English. The historian Robertson read Johnson's dictionary from cover to cover twice, and when Browning decided upon a literary career, he read and digested the whole work.

The Plays of William Shakespeare (1765). There were a number of editions of Shakespeare's plays prior to Johnson's. After the 17th-century folios, the editors of Shakespeare were the following: Nicholas Rowe (1709), using the fourth folio ("latest and worst copy," according to Johnson and subsequent scholars); Alexander Pope (1725) ("The little fellow has done wonders," Johnson admitted, in spite of the "refinements" and errors); Lewis Theobald (1733), the "poor, piddling Theobald" of *The Dunciad* (Theobald suggested the famous emendation of "he babbled of green fields" in *Henry V*. He was the best editor before Johnson); Thomas Hanmer (1744) (Johnson sourly commented of his edition: "Its pomp recommends it more than its accuracy"); William Warburton (1747) (Johnson praised the bishop because he had recognized Johnson's ability, but this edition is riddled with gentlemanly and pontifical errors).

In *Miscellaneous Observations on the Tragedy of Macbeth* (1745), Johnson advocated a new and improved edition of Shakespeare. *Proposals for Printing the Dramatick Works of William Shakespeare* (1756) sought subscriptions and indicated 1757 as time of publication. Johnson's editorial principles surpassed those of any previous scholar of English literature. His chief methods for ascertaining correct texts were twofold: first he sought the earliest text (which sometimes led to his unduly exalting the quartos over the folios), and then he steeped himself in the literature that Shakespeare himself read. Johnson was determined to find out to the limits of his ability, not what Shakespeare might have written or what he should have written, but what he *did* write.

Prodded by the barbs of the satirist, Charles Churchill, Johnson finally published his edition in 1765. It was the best edition of Shakespeare until the 19th century, for his successors—Edward Capell (1768), George Steevens (1773), Edmund Malone (1780), Isaac Reed (1785) —largely revised Johnson's edition. The excellence of Johnson's text is miraculous in the light of his limitations: he was a wholehearted neoclassicist; he was bookish and insensitive to music, seldom visiting the theater because of his poor eyesight; his pupil and friend, David Garrick, regularly revised and "improved" Shakespeare to conform to current taste; and he lacked much of the knowledge of Elizabethan life, literature, language, printing, and theater that has been amassed since his era. He was, however, the first editor to delve seriously and extensively into Shakespeare's sources.

Johnson was the most honest of scholars, frankly admitting when he was baffled. His comments and annotations are courageous commonsense and are still used in today's editions; he is more frequently quoted in the modern Variorum Shakespeare than any other editor or critic of Shakespeare.

The Preface to this edition may be the most important single piece of Shakespearean criticism. Johnson points out numerous defects (e.g. puns, bawdry, and structurally loose and melodramatic plots) in the dramatist; some of these "defects" appear only to neoclassic eyes, while others are basically true. Johnson's defense of Shakespeare is not revolutionary (Addison, Pope, and others had held similar positions), but his support is more explicit and more complete. The essence of Johnson's critical stand is an appeal from the neoclassic platform of "the rules" to the neoclassic platform of "imitation." Shakespeare obviously violates the Unities of Time, Place, and Action, and with massive commonsense and logic, Johnson demolishes these Unities, finding in Shakespeare the greater Unities of character and verisimilitude. In attacking the Unities, Johnson appeals to the imaginative basis of literature and expounds the principle of imaginative truth. Chiseled in stone over the entrance to the Folger Shakespearean Library in Washington, D.C., are Johnson's key words about Shakespeare: "His drama is the mirror of life." Also, Johnson finds Shakespeare a great moral teacher, though by accident rather than design. The influence of Johnson's Preface was far-reaching; in the next generation the French Romantics of the theater based their own case against the Unities upon Johnson's work.

The Works of the English Poets. With Prefaces, Biographical and Critical appeared in sixty-eight volumes from 1779 to 1781. In the latter year Johnson's introductions were separately printed in revised form under the familiar title *The Lives of the Most Eminent English Poets.* This is generally regarded as Johnson's masterwork. After his edition of Shakespeare, Johnson did little writing for over a decade, devoting himself mainly to incomparable talk. In 1777 a group of London booksellers, deciding to issue a collection of English poetry in competition with an Edinburgh reprint, engaged Johnson to write the prefaces. Of the fifty-two poets represented, Johnson proposed the addition of only five to the booksellers' original list. The range is from Cowley and

Waller to Gray and Collins, all since the late 17th-century "reform of our numbers," and, except for the metaphysicals and Milton, they are all in the tradition Johnson thoroughly knew, respected, and himself practiced as a poet. The life of Young is largely by Sir Herbert Croft, "Life of Richard Savage" is a reworking of Johnson's earlier appreciation in 1744, and the piece on Roscommon is adapted from Johnson's *Gentleman's Magazine* article in 1748; all the others were undertaken by the literary arbiter at the age of sixty-seven and completed at the age of seventy-two.

Johnson's best treatment is of his favorites—Dryden, Pope, Swift, and Addison. His superb commonsense and rich, rationalistic understanding of human nature, plus a keen recognition of the complexity in the neoclassic greats, result in eminently sound judgment and appreciation. The "Life of Milton" has generally been considered Johnson's least successful study, for the opinionated Tory and devout Anglican could not tolerate Milton's religion or politics, and, in the bargain, detested the pastoral tradition and therefore *Lycidas;* nonetheless, the noble compliments to Milton display a great spirit trying to overcome its prejudices. The "Life of Cowley" contains Johnson's evaluations of the metaphysicals, dismissing them: "their thoughts are often new, but seldom natural; they are not obvious, but neither are they just; and the reader, far from wondering that he missed them, wonders more frequently by what perverseness of industry they were ever found." The lives of minor poets are often perfunctory, but who now recalls Thomas Yalden or James Hammond? Johnson sought to understand the man behind the poetry and therefore welded biography, analysis, and criticism into a meaningful revelation of character and thought. The style is not ponderous Johnson but a lighter, more conversational flow, replete with well-worded comments on humanity and Johnson's own neoclassic dicta about poetry and art.

James Boswell (1740–1795). Born at Edinburgh, James Boswell was the son of Alexander Boswell, Lord Auchinleck, a distinguished Scottish judge. He was educated at the universities of Edinburgh and Glasgow. As early as 1758 he began a journal that was to be maintained throughout most of his life and that would prove the repository from whence came most of his writings. The relatively few works of Boswell published in his own lifetime encouraged Macaulay to call Boswell a foolish toady and sycophant, hovering like a tiny fish behind the huge whale of Johnson—in short, a great biographer by accident.

Unquestionably, Boswell was weak, unstable in temperament, and dissolute.

The most publicized and almost certainly the most important discovery of literary scholarship in the 20th century was the unearthing of the voluminous Boswell manuscripts, believed destroyed for over a century. In the 1920's and 1930's Malahide Castle in Ireland and Fettercairn House in Scotland yielded most of the long-lost journal of Boswell, plus numerous letters and other documents. Since 1950, Yale University, present owner of the collection, has been releasing edited texts of the journal. The revelations have completely changed critical opinion about Boswell, who now stands as a remarkably cultured and intelligent man, almost unequaled in his powers of self-analysis, and richly and widely experienced beyond our previous notions. Boswell's exhibitionism and cultivation of notables apparently arose from the inferiority complex of a son overshadowed by his successful and dour father, and of a Scot conscious of the current secondary position of his native land. The facility of adopting a *persona,* so adroitly exploited in literature by Swift, was exploited by Boswell in life. Practically every original Boswell work, now appearing for the first time in history, reveals another guise —the provincial, the bon vivant, the cosmopolite traveler, the champion of freedom, the devoted husband, and so on. The *persona* of rapt disciple to the overpowering Johnson, the one used for his famous *Life of Samuel Johnson, LL.D.,* is but one facet of a bewilderingly complex personality which artfully lived life and artfully shaped its writings. The recently revealed works of Boswell were partly printed in a limited private edition of eighteen volumes (1928–34), but the summary below will follow the standard annotated editions generally available.

Boswell's London Journal (1762–63, 1950) recounts the experiences of a twenty-two-year-old Scot fleeing from parental authority to try the life of the great metropolis. Boswell's father had insisted that he pass the Scottish civil law examinations, and when he had done that, the youth was permitted, with a small allowance, to seek a commission in the Guards in London. In his nine-month residence, Boswell failed to secure the commission, but he eagerly sought out the personalities of London. The historic meeting with Johnson at Davies's bookshop on May 16, 1763, appears toward the end of the account, and Johnson therefore figures in no more than a tenth of this journal. The extravagance of youth comprises most of the fascination of this book. Boswell plunges into sexual experiences, his liaison with Louisa (Mrs. Lewis), which infected him with venereal disease; but literature, art, and society—

their creators and their patrons—also attracted the young man. He writes with the absolute candor of Pepys but also with remarkably detached self-analysis. He displays a beguiling combination of romantic sensibility and neoclassic principles. Its exuberance, vividness, and variety will probably make this Boswell's most popular work.

Boswell in Holland (*1763–64,* 1952), a substitute for the lost Dutch journal, is composed of miscellaneous papers. Failing to obtain a military commission, Boswell yielded to his father's wishes that he practice law, and set off for a winter of legal study at Utrecht. For ten months in Holland Boswell was studious, chaste, and miserable. The failure of his cherished scheme to get into the Guards, the capitulation to his father, and especially the sense of frustration in a young man anxious to be immediately important, all lend their weight to produce long neurasthenic passages. However, Boswell Reformed and Boswell the Melancholy were transformed into Boswell the Intellectual Lover toward the end of his stay, through his acquaintance with Isabella van Tuyll ("Zélide"). The correspondence between the two continued until 1768 in a series of adroitly fencing, genteelly familiar letters. Perhaps the greatest interest of this book lies in the determined and amusing efforts of Boswell to conform to what both he and his father felt was the proper young man.

Boswell on the Grand Tour: Germany and Switzerland (*1764,* 1953) carries the resilient youth through six months of European travel. Assuming what he considered was the German rank comparable to his Scottish position, "Baron" Boswell traveled from one little rococo German court to another. All the nobility accepted the princely youth except the stern Frederick the Great, who refused to see him. In Switzerland, Boswell assumes a philosophic air, and properly enough, for there he met Voltaire and Rousseau. Only the brash Boswell would have tried to convert the skeptical Voltaire with a paper on the immortality of the soul, but neither of the eminent philosophers scorned the young man. Now twenty-four, Boswell is maturing. Certainly he is wholly ebullient, rejoicing in movement, color, variety, exciting people, and challenging minds. The picture he gives of 18th-century Germany is an excellent descriptive feat in itself.

Boswell on the Grand Tour: Italy, Corsica, and France (*1765–66,* 1955) is a further extension of European travel in spite of Lord Auchinleck's demand that his son return to Scotland. Sex particularly occupied Boswell in Italy. Grand ladies did not prove tractable, and Boswell had to content himself with conquests ranging from "charming girls" to "monsters" until at last capturing the heart of Girolama Piccolomini ("Moma"), wife of a high Sienese official. A bit aghast at her seriousness, Boswell retreated. He also made friends with the dangerous—the exiled John Wilkes and other Jacobites in the pathetic Roman court of the Stuart pretender.

Boswell at this time was actually seeking some cause bigger than himself, a cause to which he might devote his incredible energy. In Corsica, with its impressive leader, General Pasquale de Paoli, Boswell found his cause. This Mediterranean island had been restive under Genoa, which had then brought in French troops to compel order. Letting everyone believe him a British government agent, Boswell conferred with Paoli and obtained the materials for the first published book to bring him fame.

In Paris, Boswell was about to return to Utrecht, but news of his mother's death sent him back to Great Britain after an absence of almost three years. Immediately he called upon Pitt in person in an attempt to aid the Corsican struggle for independence. Boswell the Amorist had been transformed into Boswell the Liberator.

An Account of Corsica, The Journal of a Tour to That Island: and Memoirs of Pascal Paoli (1768) showered national and European plaudits upon Boswell. Characteristic of writers of his era, Boswell was almost oblivious to scenery; he was concerned with people, with the Corsicans in their struggle for independence. Their cause touched him romantically, for here was an island people, replete with "primitive" virtues, courageously seeking freedom. Paoli was a handsome, commanding personality, ideal for the hero-worshiping Boswell. Even more, the general, like Johnson, was a father image to Boswell. Fortunately, calmer heads prevailed, but Boswell's urgent and sympathetic support almost threw England into war with France because of Corsica. When French troops subjugated the little island in 1769, Paoli fled to England, where he was feted by the admiring Boswell, and the little Scotsman made his hero world-renowned.

Boswell in Search of a Wife (*1766–69*, 1956) pictures the author as Boswell of Auchinleck. After a rather irresponsible youth, Boswell settled down in the tradition of his family. The Scots of this period particularly felt the strong ties of the blood line, and therefore Boswell, even against his inclinations, applied himself to legal practice, as his father wished. His chief professional concern during these years was his support of the claims of Archibald Douglas to his grandfather's estate. The old duke died without direct heirs, and the claimant was the son of the duke's sister, born in obscure circumstances in Paris in 1748 when his mother was fifty. Boswell in his advocacy sensed the parallel to himself, for Lord Auchinleck was planning to sequester his estate from James. After unfavorable decisions by lower courts, the House of Lords decided for Douglas. In the Edinburgh riots following the Douglas victory, Boswell led the mob in breaking the judges' windows—including those of his own father.

Casting about for a wife, Boswell tried to interest himself in young ladies of fortune acceptable to his family. He was relieved when Catherine Blair ("the Heiress" or "the Princess") rejected him. He proceeded to Ireland early in 1769 to woo Mary Ann Boyd ("la belle Irlandaise"), accompanied by his impecunious first cousin, Margaret Montgomerie, and by a quirk of fate Boswell fell in love with Margaret and married her in spite of family objections. Witnesses to the marriage contract are Douglas, Johnson, and Paoli.

The entire account shapes itself into a coherent "novel" of converging forces. Boswell reaches his greatest maturity in the acceptance of family and social responsibilities while at the same time following the dictates of his heart. Few novelists have portrayed as effectively as Boswell has the slow unfolding realization that the familiar companion Margaret is actually his prized jewel.

Boswell for the Defence (*1769–74,* 1959) reverses the progress of the preceding volume and carries Boswell from contentment and conjugal virtue to melancholia and dissipation. The first two years of his marriage brought serenity. Two daughters, Veronica and Euphemia, were to provide bright spots in Boswell's life for years to come. Gradually, however, he succumbed to bad habits—heavy drinking, gambling, and, later, wenching. In 1773 he was received into "The Club" and toured the Hebrides with Johnson. Thereafter, during the spring vacation of the Scottish law courts he annually visited London, collecting the conversations of Johnson that would later be incorporated in the biography. Garrick and Goldsmith also shared his attentions.

As a lawyer Boswell made himself a self-appointed public defender, pleading for humble offenders whose cases would bring him neither fees nor reputation amongst his sober colleagues. The climax came with his defense in 1774 of John Reid, a sheep-stealer. Boswell's energetic efforts failed and Reid was hanged. Persuaded not to attempt to revive the corpse, Boswell turned away from the scaffold in shock and dismay. His accounts produce a psychological detective story about the crime and a case study of his own despair.

Subsequent volumes from the journal, such as *Boswell: The Ominous Years, 1774–76* (1963), show some bright moments with his children and the therapeutic value to himself of his writing about Johnson, but, nevertheless, melancholia increasingly fastened itself upon him. Boswell's reputation is now secure, partly as the greatest narcissist of literature and certainly as the greatest autobiographer and biographer.

The Hypochondriack consists of seventy anonymous essays printed monthly in *The London Magazine,* in which Boswell had a financial interest, from November 1777 through August 1783, omitting the number of July 1783. The first paper announces his purpose, "to divert Hypochondriacks of every degree from dwelling on their uneasiness," but from the thirty-ninth essay onward, he is frankly concerned with himself. His essays upon education, tradition, war, luxury, and similar impersonal subjects express conventional views. Personal subjects— love, marriage, death, individual conduct—dwell upon his own defects and advance idealistic proposals which Johnson frequently refuted when Boswell offered them in conversation. The main purpose of the essays, as he hinted in a letter to a friend, was to stimulate in himself the virtuous habits he here recommends to the hypochondriacal.

The Journal of a Tour to the Hebrides, with Samuel Johnson, LL.D. (1785) is much more interesting than the parallel account of this 1773 trip by Johnson. It was quite an accomplishment for Boswell to induce Johnson, the avowed Scot-hater, to brave the forbidding badlands of Scotland at the age of sixty-four, and Boswell alertly recorded the minutest reactions of Johnson to everything the pundit encountered. Where Johnson in writing about the trip is concerned with generalizations concerning mankind, Boswell interests himself in portraying the man Johnson. The publication of the original manuscript in 1936 reveals something of the artist in Boswell. The final version makes Johnson more Johnsonian than the original. While appearing to be only a naïve observer of the great man, Boswell actually carefully shaped the Johnson image.

The Life of Samuel Johnson, LL.D. (1791) is by general consent the world's greatest biography. The detailing of Johnson's experiences before the two met is routine, while most of the work consists of the conversations of Johnson as recorded by Boswell during their years of acquaintance. Boswell thus prefigures modern biography in his preoccupation, not with what his subject did, but with what his subject was. "Warts and all," Johnson appears as the most fully realized figure, the most three-dimensional character, in literature ("I will not make my tiger a cat to please anybody," wrote Boswell). Johnson is irascible, dogmatic, prejudiced, overbearing, and also brilliant and profound. The lost papers of Boswell make eminently clear the twofold art of Boswell. First, he was a consummate impresario, stage-managing the setting and *dramatis personae* amidst which Johnson would glitter, and then providing topics and opinions to elicit the magnificent rejoinders of Johnson. Second, but artistically more important, he selected the exact details of a Johnson encounter (e.g. their meeting at Davies's bookstore or the dinner with Wilkes) which would show his subject in his best light. The man who wrote *Lives of the Poets* and who was also described by other members of his circle is revealed as a more everyday, easygoing, and conventional person than the spectacular giant pictured by Boswell. The genius of the Scotsman can be seen in the fact that while generations held him in little regard, the world is unshakably convinced that the "character" of Johnson which he very largely created is the truest flesh-and-blood man ever to "talk for victory."

LESSER BIOGRAPHIES OF JOHNSON. Sir John Hawkins (1719–89) was one of Johnson's legal executors. He produced the first collected edition of Johnson's works and accompanied this edition with a biography.

The Life of Samuel Johnson, LL.D. (1787) is a conventional biography, lacking the rich personal flavor imparted by Boswell. But Hawkins knew Johnson for twenty years before Boswell; hence his biography is more accurate for those years. Johnson is substantially the Great Cham pictured by Boswell, but the dark side of his personality receives greater emphasis.

A lively record of Johnson appears also in *Anecdotes of the Late Samuel Johnson, LL.D. during the Last Twenty Years of His Life* (1786), by Hester Lynch Piozzi, Johnson's hostess under her previous name of Mrs. Thrale. Boswell's work was actually the sixth biography of the great man.

OTHER MAJOR WRITERS OF THE PERIOD

Members of "The Club"

In addition to Johnson and Boswell, the members of "The Club" who will be discussed here are: Oliver Goldsmith; Edward Gibbon; Edmund Burke; its co-founder, Sir Joshua Reynolds; Henry Temple, Viscount Palmerston; and Sir William Jones.

Oliver Goldsmith (c. 1728–1774). Born near Ballymahon, Ireland, Oliver Goldsmith was the son of an Irish clergyman. After graduating from Trinity College, Dublin, in 1749, he unsuccessfully attempted one career after another: law, medicine, the church, teaching, acting, and clerking in an apothecary's shop. From 1754 to 1756 he was foot-loose and penniless on a walking tour of the Continent. Upon his return, he supplemented his meager income by occasional writings and gradually slipped into "Grub Street" as the prince of hack writers. His indefatigable pen eventually produced a good income, but "Goldy" was always improvident, leaving at his death debts of about £2000. Johnson commented: "Was ever poet so trusted before?" Horace Walpole called him "an Inspired Idiot," and Garrick indited the famous epitaph: "Here lies Poet Goldsmith, for shortness called Noll,/Who wrote like an angel, but talked like Poor Poll."

One of the charter members of "The Club," Goldsmith was easily the most likable because of his geniality, sincerity, and simplicity. His writings were never profound, but their superficiality is redeemed by their grace, ease, and clarity. Although he was a notorious stutterer, his pen never faltered, but rather produced a stylistic innovation in mingling formal and colloquial language. While quite sentimental, Goldsmith supported neoclassic tenets, seeking to evoke not mere sympathy but a spirit of fortitude. His contributions to the drama will be discussed later in this chapter in the section on theater, and his one famous novel, *The Vicar of Wakefield*, will be treated in the next chapter, which is devoted to the 18th-century novel.

PROSE NON-FICTION. *An Enquiry into the Present State of Polite Learning in Europe* (1759) was the first work to earn him reputation, though it is entirely too ambitious a task for one no more profound than Goldsmith. He diagnoses a decline in learning and letters and ascribes the deficiency to the venality of booksellers, the artificiality of writers, and society's failure to recognize and encourage genius. He is closer than he realizes to the truth when he condemns the universities for clinging to outmoded subjects and hair-splitting scholasticism. Goldsmith cogently describes, without actually perceiving, the downfall of the aristocratic world of art, existing, as it was, in a pre-revolutionary society which was in a state of transition between the old order and the dominance of the new middle class.

The Citizen of the World; or, Letters from a Chinese Philosopher, Residing in London, to His Friends in the East (1762) consisted of 123 "Chinese Letters" originally appearing in *The Public Ledger* from

January 24, 1760, to August 14, 1761. The "foreign visitor" genre had been popular in France, particularly in Montesquieu's *Lettres Persanes* (1721), where an imaginary Oriental, the epitome of reason, provided a point of view from which to criticize European society. Goldsmith's is the best English representative of this genre.

Lien Chi Altangi, a Chinese embodiment of simplicity and virtue, pleasantly and without rancor, points out the shortcomings of English society, e.g. oppressive laws and taxation, worship of materialism, hypocrisy, and immorality. Memorable is the character of Beau Tibbs, a pinched and tarnished little dandy, pitifully pretending familiarity with the world of fashion, and whining the refrain "Lend me half-a-crown."

Goldsmith resembles Steele in his moral purpose, his fluent style, and in his stance of a middle-class critic who operates without subtlety or bitterness. The subjective element here is muted, but the author is mildly humorous and witty.

Essays (1765) reprints the best of Goldsmith's periodical essays, including those from his own short-lived serial, *The Bee* (October 3 to November 24, 1759). Goldsmith's dominant concept of man's history is neoclassic; he sees all human events as cyclic, with no genuine progress or retrogression. "Reverie at the Boar's Head Tavern" (*British Magazine,* February, March, April 1760) charmingly muses on Falstaff, Prince Hal, and Dame Quickly from Shakespeare's *Henry IV,* but concludes that it is futile to mourn the degeneracy of the present age, since "every age is the same." "Asem, an Eastern Tale" (*Royal Magazine,* December 1759), in the popular guise of a pseudo-Oriental fable (cf. "The Vision of Mirza," by Addison), demonstrates the cyclic theory within one life; Asem's rash benevolence (like that of Shakespeare's Timon) leads him to misanthropy and thence to regeneration and prudent benevolence. In many respects Goldsmith epitomizes the neoclassic ideal: he explores no new realms and provides no new ideas, but he casts a delightful patina over the familiar, and gracefully adorns the commonplace.

VERSE. *The Traveller, or, A Prospect of Society* (1764) was considered by Johnson the best poem since the works of Pope. In heroic couplets, Goldsmith sweetly and melodiously seeks to justify the different searches for happiness in each nation of Western Europe, and deplores the excesses resulting from each way of life.

The Deserted Village (1770) laments abandoned Auburn, a rural paradise depopulated by the enclosures and by the lure of factory wages in the cities owing to the burgeoning Industrial Revolution. Nostalgia for Lissoy, Ireland, where Goldsmith had lived as a child, is probably influential. Heroic couplets sentimentally limn the village parson and schoolteacher and idealize the life of simplicity and retirement, free from luxury and "trade's unfeeling train." Goldsmith seizes current attitudes and suffuses them with genuine feeling in masterful 18th-century poetry of statement.

The Haunch of Venison, a Poetical Epistle to Lord Clare (*1771, 1776*) shows Goldsmith's facility in light verse. Couplets of anapestic tetrameter acknowledge a gift of venison from Lord Clare and relate how an artful friend bears off the venison for himself. Such a *jeu d'esprit* is really Goldsmith's forte.

Retaliation: A Poem (1774), in the meter of the preceding poem, concocts mock epitaphs for members of "The Club" in rejoinder to Garrick's. Most famous are the epitaphs on Burke, Garrick, and Reynolds. The satire is sparkling and witty, the best of the Horatian type in the century after Pope.

Edward Gibbon (1737–1794). A native of Putney, near London, Edward Gibbon was a sickly youth. Shocked by Edward's conversion to Roman Catholicism while at Oxford, his father sent him to Lausanne, Switzerland, where the youth soon abandoned Roman Catholicism—and, indeed, all faith. Gibbon proved as fluent in French as in English, and in French he wooed Mlle. Curchod, later Madame Necker and mother of Madame de Staël. Threatened with disinheritance, he "sighed as a lover" but "obeyed as a son." Back in England in 1757, he devoted himself chiefly to historical studies, but served sporadically as an officer in the Hampshire Militia. A visit to Rome in 1764 inspired his writing of the great history. In 1774 he joined "The Club" and started a six-year service as Member of Parliament. He served on the Board of Trade and Plantations, 1779–82. From 1783 he resided in Lausanne, dying of a hydrocele during a visit to England.

The History of the Decline and Fall of the Roman Empire (I, 1776; II, III, 1781; IV, V, VI, 1788) covers almost fourteen centuries from Trajan (98) to the fall of Constantinople (1453). Gibbon's thesis claimed that the very forces that brought the triumph of Christianity were responsible for the fall of Rome (a thesis advanced by pagan intellectuals early in the Christian era and strenuously assailed by St. Augustine). Gibbon was the first historian of modern times to examine Christianity as a purely natural phenomenon, arising from social conditions of the times. He was the first English historian to apply a constant cause-and-effect methodology to the examination of history. Gibbon unfolds a colossal tragedy, beginning with Rome of the Antonines (which he considered the peak of human history in tolerance, moderation, and other classic virtues) and following the decline in the West downward to the reign of superstition and brute force. All the more agonizing are the brief upsurges under Diocletian, Constantine, Justinian, and Charlemagne. From a huge number of apparently jumbled events, Gibbon constructed a narrative that imposed an unprecedented order upon history. Although he lacked some sources now available and also displayed inadequate sympathies with the medieval mind, his structure provided the framework for succeeding histories, even those of his bitterest critics.

Gibbon carefully sought an esthetic style in his prose, "the middle tone between a dull chronicle and a rhetorical declamation." After three writings of the first chapter, he hit upon the elevated diction, undulating and cadenced, that would carry him and the reader majestically through fourteen centuries. Balanced phrases, Latinical expressions, oratorical and rhetorical devices of weight and graceful motion often sound like a superb translation from Cicero and sometimes like blank verse. But, more importantly, the style is an image of the rationalistic mind of the Enlightenment, one that contemplates humanity with a suave irony while impeccably maintaining an Olympian calm. Gibbon asks in his will: "Shall I be accused of vanity, if I add that a monument is superfluous?"

Gibbon prepared six drafts of an autobiography. A "harmony" of these was printed by Lord Sheffield in 1796; the original versions of the six sketches were first published in 1896. The Journal of 1761–63 first appeared in 1929, and the entire Lausanne Journal in 1945. Throughout, Gibbon's personal records are urbane and candid, deliberately analyzing his own faults and foibles. The historian disliked fanaticism, romantic love, religious emotion, and political idealism. His one passion was the intellect. He believed in peace, moderation, and charity, and, like Hume, he provided freethinkers with an example of morality and calm assurance.

Edmund Burke (1729–1797). Born in Dublin, Ireland, Edmund Burke was the son of a Protestant attorney. After graduation from Trinity College, Dublin, in 1748 he proceeded to London to study law in the Middle Temple. In 1759 he started writing for the *Annual Register,* a summary of significant events of the previous year, and he was to become the mainstay of this publication for over thirty years. From 1765 until his retirement in 1794, Burke was one of the commanding figures in the House of Commons, but his highest political office was that of Paymaster and Privy Councillor, 1782–83. Most of his political career was spent in the Opposition as the valiant fighter for lost causes. He was one of the original members of "The Club," and a life-long patron of arts and letters. Johnson once asserted the mediocrity of all men, and Boswell countered with Burke. "Yes," admitted the sage, "Burke *is* an extraordinary man." Some have considered him the greatest master of English prose in the 18th century.

ESTHETICS. *A Philosophical Inquiry into the Origin of Our Ideas of the Sublime and Beautiful* (1756) is the first penetrating discussion of "sublimity" in English. Conventionally, Burke saw the "beautiful" as the smooth and symmetrical, appealing to the emotion of love (pleasure). His analysis of the "sublime" (whether or not he realized his own implications) heralded the downfall of Augustan esthetics and anticipated Lessing's *Laocoön*. The "sublime," he explained, is the vast and awesome, appealing to the emotion of terror (pain and peril). Stimulants to the "sublime" are: obscurity, power, privation, infinity, difficulty, and magnificence. Burke explained esthetic moods as emotions generated within the observer instead of qualities in the object observed. While the visual arts are essentially "imitative," poetry is a creative art that communicates "attitudes" rather than purely rationalistic "ideas." Individualism and subjectivity are implicit results of this work, which demonstrates exciting incursions into the physiological and psychological wellsprings of taste.

POLITICS. Our own day has witnessed a disturbing sundering of political theory from political practice. The theory has fallen into the hands of calm professors, immured in their academic retreats; the practice rests with pragmatic and harried officials, generally lacking any deep-searching exposure to theory (while a notable writer, Sir Winston Churchill has but meagerly dwelt upon political science). Burke is the extraordinary combination of a practicing politician and an eminent political theorist. Practically, he was a social psychologist, insisting that government mirror the enlightened mind of the governed. Theoretically, he was a devotee of continuity and was unalterably committed to institutions that had developed through the ages and had stood the test of time. Like Halifax of the previous century, Burke was completely English in accepting change and never calling for a return to previous patterns; but for him the change must be evolution, not revolution. Burke was flexible, experimental, and empirical, considering an idea sound only if it could be justly and reasonably effected. Such characteristics have made memorable many of his pronouncements upon current events that posterity has otherwise forgotten.

Thoughts on the Cause of the Present Discontents (1770) was provoked by the exclusion of Wilkes from Parliament. George III's attempt actually to rule England threatened to destroy the rights of Englishmen in monarchial supremacy if it succeeded. Burke urged the restoration and maintenance of free elections, with the people represented by their choice. Burke's analysis of the relations among ruler, ministers, Parliament, and people was the most thoughtful and balanced study of the complex subject made up to that time. The style matches the subject—setting principles above party or personalities, and choosing calm and dispassionate judgment over excitement.

Speech on American Taxation (1774) called for a removal of the American Tea Duty. The first part urges repeal on the basis of expediency, the necessity of keeping fellow Englishmen together ("the question is not whether their spirit deserves praise or blame—what, in the name of God, shall we do with it?"). The second part reviews the entire field of American taxation for over a century. Burke here expounds careful thinking in strongly emotional language.

Conciliation with America (1775) failed completely (78 to 270) to secure the vote of Parliament, but it ranks with Milton's *Areopagitica* as one of the greatest pieces of classical eloquence in English. From Burke's address alone the modern reader can imagine the grandeur of ancient oratory. After an attention-compelling opening, Burke plunges directly to his contention, which is clearly and forcefully presented. Then he proceeds to unfold and amplify, always in logical order. The conclusion is a ringing peroration, reaching almost lyric intensity.

The first part brilliantly analyzes the American point of view and demonstrates how unalterable forces inherent in colonial life have filled the Americans with a fierce love of liberty. To prosecute this spirit is impossible, and to oppose it will mean only violent resistance. In the second part Burke insists that, like their fellow Englishmen, the Americans are entitled to representative government. After denouncing coercion of the colonists, Burke closes with an exultant tribute to common descent, common institutions, and common sentiment as the strongest ties of empire. Posterity has realized the pre-eminence of Burke's wisdom and oratorical force from this great though futile attempt to avoid what Burke saw would be a catastrophe for England.

A Letter to John Farr and John Harris, Esqrs., Sheriffs of the City of Bristol, on the Affairs of America (1777). Since English legislators need not reside in the community they represent, Burke sat for the city of Bristol, and in this work he explains to his constituents why he absented himself from Parliament whenever it was enacting punitive measures against the Americans. Burke again rises to impassioned pleas for reconciliation and harmony, but hard-headedly and in masterful phrases he also explains what he means by freedom and how the rival claims of liberty and empire should be fused.

Burke's advocacy of justice for Roman Catholics and especially for Irish trade caused the voters of Bristol to renounce him, but he was promptly returned to Parliament by Malton, in Yorkshire. *Speech at the Guildhall, in Bristol, Previous to the Late Election* (1780) is a noble statement of his determination to support what he considers right, regardless of his political career. "The charges against me are . . . that I have pushed the principles of general justice and benevolence too far."

To India, Burke applied the same political principle he had applied to America. The East India Company possessed the legal right to tax, but this right is a trust and should be revoked if it is unfairly employed. In *East India Bill* (1783) and *Speech on the Nabob of Arcot's Private Debts* (1785), Burke touches the sublime himself as he contemplates the color and pageantry and particularly the spaciousness of India. The account in the latter speech of Hyder Ali, the Indian rebel, swooping upon the Carnatic, represents probably the high point of rhetorical splendor in English.

Six volumes of Burke's collected works are occupied with speeches during the trial of Warren Hastings, Governor-General of India. Westminster Hall was the scene of the most dramatic sessions in English political history, with seats selling for as much as £50. Burke was the great accuser, fighting for justice and sound administration. The House of Lords acquitted Hastings in 1795, but it left Burke even nobler in defeat.

Reflections on the Revolution in France (1790) is the classic critique of the French Revolution, and it was *Reflections* more than any other single work that roused England and much of the Continent against the new France. The liberal spirits of the age called Burke a turncoat, asking how he could support the Americans in their revolution and then bitterly oppose the French in theirs. However, it must be realized first that Burke brought to the discussion of France very little of the accurate and encyclopedic knowledge he had possessed about

America, Ireland, or India. Had Burke realized the full plight of the French populace and the sins of the *ancien régime,* it seems fair to assume that the stand of so honest a man would certainly have been different. Second, he did remain intellectually consistent. The Americans were only seeking the time-honored rights of Englishmen. The French Revolution, on the other hand, attempted to wipe clean the slate of the past and institute a new pattern of government, arising from abstract theories. Burke deplored any such abandonment of heritage and detested abstract theories divorced from pragmatic continuity. From anguished depths he asserted: "I do not like to see anything destroyed, any void produced in society, any ruin on the face of the land." The immediate occasion of this piece was a sermon by Richard Price before the Revolution Society (honoring the English Revolution of 1688), congratulating the French upon their overthrow of tyranny. His examination of Price seems overly long to us until we realize that his age, as well as ours, was profoundly worried about "subversives" within; but history had outstripped Burke and had plunged an evolutionary spirit into a revolutionary age.

Sir Joshua Reynolds (1723–1792). Sir Joshua Reynolds was the son of a clergyman-schoolmaster in Plympton Earl, Devonshire. After studying art under Thomas Hudson, he set himself up as a portrait painter in London in 1746. He became the most famed English portrait painter of his age, perhaps of all time, and from 1784 he served as painter to the king. His well-known oil paintings of literary men include Johnson, Garrick, Sterne, and Goldsmith. Reynolds was the first president of the Royal Academy, founded in 1768. Three of the papers in *The Idler* (76, 79, 82) are his contributions.

Discourses consisted of fifteen lectures delivered by the president to the Royal Academy from 1769 to 1790. These were separately printed as presented, and were collected in 1797. Reynolds supports the idealistic tradition of classic art, demanding complete devotion to perfect truth and perfect beauty. The creator of art must start with genius and then pursue a rigid study of technique and taste in order to imitate "nature" (i.e. the Platonic ideal of nature separated from its accidents and deformities). Reynolds felt that the goal of art is to ennoble man. The earlier discourses are relatively specific, emphasizing the four governing principles of painting: invention, expression, coloring, and drapery. The seventh discourse on "The Reality of a Standard of Taste" turns the remaining addresses to the larger consideration of imagination and genius. Particularly the eleventh discourse on "Genius" is a *locus classicus* of the neoclassic concept of the generalizing role of art. The grace, clarity, and distinction of the discourses were immediately recognized. Although some hinted that Johnson and/or Burke had assisted, it seems clear that the work is wholly by Reynolds.

Portraits (1952) consists of miscellaneous pieces by Reynolds found in the Malahide Castle collection of Boswell manuscripts. Boswell assembled such materials for a contemplated Life of Reynolds. Reynolds added word sketches to his paintings of such men as Garrick, Goldsmith, and Johnson, but they do not materially alter our concept of these men. Most interesting is "The Ironical Discourse," written in 1791 and unknown until our generation. With heavy-handed irony, Reynolds pretends to be a Romantic ridiculing all that the *Discourses* had advocated. It is the outraged protest of an aged neoclassicist in a revolutionary era that is toppling his cherished beliefs.

Henry Temple, second **Viscount Palmerston** (1739–1802). Palmerston was born near Romsey, Hampshire. After an undistinguished career at Cambridge, he made the Grand Tour of the Continent. From 1765 until his death he was a Member of Parliament, holding minor posts during Whig administrations, where, since his title was Irish, he was able to serve in the House of Commons. Johnson supported him for membership in "The Club." His son, who succeeded him in the title, was the famous prime minister of Queen Victoria.

Portrait of a Golden Age (first published in 1958) is an editing of about one sixth of Palmerston's manuscripts, which in original form extend from 1758 to 1802 and exceed a million words. As Boswell was the Pepys of the age, Palmerston, like Horace Walpole, was its Evelyn. Most of the great of the era were his close acquaintances—George III, the Prince of Wales, Pitt, Fox, Burke, Johnson, and Sheridan. He bought paintings from Reynolds, heard of the experiences of General Burgoyne and Captain Cook from their own lips, was a guest of Voltaire and a host to Paoli, acted as pallbearer at Garrick's funeral, and viewed the expanding universe through Herschel's telescope. Palmerston carried letters from Fox to the French Constituent Assembly and chatted with Louis XVI and Marie Antoinette only five days before the uprising. Without any profound analysis of this stirring period, Palmerston matter-of-factly creates a vivid and lively world. Without Boswell's powers of self-analysis, he nonetheless reveals the wholly civilized milieu of the Whig aristocracy.

Sir William Jones (1746–1794). Sir William Jones was the namesake of a distinguished mathematician father. Born in London, he was educated at Harrow under Dr. Thomas Thackeray (grandfather of the novelist) and later at Oxford. He early displayed a remarkable facility with languages, eventually fully mastering thirteen and achieving competence in twenty-eight more. His detestation of the American war and of the slave trade lost him a possible seat in Parliament and delayed his advance. In 1773 he was elected to "The Club" at the same time as Garrick. Turning to law for a livelihood, he was appointed judge of the high court at Calcutta, India. In 1784 he founded the Bengal Asiatic Society, and until his death in Calcutta, he proved perhaps the most eminent Orientalist of English history.

Jones revealed to the English-speaking world some of the significant literature of Asia by his translations from Arabic, Persian, Hindustani, and other Oriental tongues. He was the first English scholar to master Sanskrit and the first scholar anywhere to see the kinship of Sanskrit with European languages, thus suggesting the momentous concept of the Indo-European languages as a family group.

The Great Age of Letter Writing

A confluence of forces rendered this the Golden Age of English letter writing. The neoclassic emphasis upon gregariousness and critical analysis caused a meticulous observation of society, and the absence of rapid modern transportation and communication induced the exchange of correspondence. The moderate pace of a leisured class permitted an enormous production of personal letters; Walpole must have averaged close to half a dozen per day during his adult life.

Horace (or **Horatio) Walpole,** fourth **Earl of Orford** (1717–1797). Born in London, Horace Walpole was the son of the Prime Minister Sir Robert Walpole. After training at Eton and King's College, Cambridge, he made the Grand Tour of the Continent along with the poet Thomas Gray. From 1741 until 1768 he sat in Parliament, devoting his energies largely to the furtherance of the political career of his cousin, Henry Conway. In 1747 he secured Strawberry Hill at Twickenham, which from 1749 onward he transformed into a pseudo-Gothic monstrosity. The Strawberry Hill Press, established by Walpole in 1757, is probably the most famous private press in English history, releasing thirty-four books, starting with the Pindaric odes of Gray. To his amusement, Walpole finally succeeded to his father's title in 1791. His contribution to the novel is discussed in the next chapter.

The letters of Walpole were first published in *The Works of Lord Orford* (1798), but each succeeding edition has swollen the total until the monumental *Yale Edition of Horace Walpole's Correspondence* (1937–   ), in over thirty volumes, prints well over six thousand letters. No other author in history has so exhaustively revealed his social milieu. Walpole's world is aristocratic Whigdom, with only the slightest acknowledgment of the existence of lower classes. Every aspect of Walpole's world is minutely scrutinized: politics, personalities, scandal, artistic tastes, and so on. Never profound, Walpole gracefully and colorfully evokes the casual sparkle and the everyday routine of his era. Blasted by Macaulay as a hypocrite, Walpole is better described as a chameleon with no strong principles but rather swayed in his judgments entirely by personal reactions of the moment. His letters are offhand observations of a gentleman, gossipy, urbane, and mildly cynical. Walpole was exceptionally gifted in the vignette—the brief anecdote or thumb-nail characterization that strikes the reader with brilliant clarity. Here, one exclaims, to the very life is the frivolity, gentility, superficiality, and glamour of the age. His immense correspondence conveniently falls into these following periods:

1739–40, which covers the Grand Tour with his companion, Gray, with whom he quarreled en route. These letters are youthfully ebullient, briskly banishing ennui ("The English malady"). Mountain scenery stirred the youth, and especially exciting to him were the color and vivacity of Italy.

1741–60, which covers the most active years of his life. In his best descriptive powers he recounts the political fall and subsequent death of his father and also the famous "Forty-Five." He finds Parliament to be often a bore, but as a rich man's hobby, Strawberry Hill is relentlessly "Gothicized." Visits to his mansion become all the fashionable rage (by application, the quality could receive free admission tickets and Walpole's own descriptive catalogue of his collection of antiques) and they popularized the taste for "Gothic." In his "natural" garden Walpole luxuriates "in the height of its greenth, blueth, gloomth, and honeysuckle-and-seringahood."

1760–85, which is heavily immersed in politics, for tremendous figures—Burke, Fox, the Pitts—are dominating Parliament. Properly Whig, Walpole is horrified at the loss of the American colonies. His visits to Paris are brilliant word pictures, and also quite affecting is his friendship with the blind Mme. du Deffand, of Paris.

1785 to his death, a period that reveals increased melancholia and boredom. As an old man Walpole is aghast at the bloodletting of the

French Revolution, and he dimly senses the doom of the world he had known.

Walpole as a youth had welcomed *The Spleen* (1737), by Matthew Green, and had enjoyed the friendship of Pope; as an aged man he missed reading *The Lyrical Ballads* by a few weeks. Walpole saw Gray as the summit of English poetry, and in 1784 he lamented the irrevocable decay of English verse. Easy grace and simplicity were his criteria in literature. Berkeley and Bishop Butler he found too difficult, and Johnson, he thought, was overly heavy and thought-provoking. Burke he admired, and also Gibbon in spite of a "sedulously enamelled style." While praising Shakespeare, Milton, and Dryden, he felt a true kinship with Terence and Vergil.

Philip Dormer Stanhope, fourth Earl of Chesterfield (1694–1773). A native of London, Chesterfield was a grandson of Halifax. He was a Whig member of the House of Commons from 1715 until his inheritance of his father's title in 1726 placed him in the House of Lords. He served as ambassador to The Hague (1728–32, 1744), Lord High Steward (1730), Lord Lieutenant of Ireland (1745–46), and Secretary of State (1746–48). Losing his political post and suffering from deafness, Chesterfield thereafter devoted himself to reading, writing, and gardening. He was recognized as the most brilliant aristocrat since the Restoration Wits, and his name still lives as a synonym for polished manners and fully assured worldliness. He was as facile in French as in English, corresponding and conversing on equal terms with contemporary French *philosophes;* in fact, he often seems less British than French. His dying words were a polite order for a servant to welcome a visitor: "Give Dayrolles a chair."

The Letters of Lord Chesterfield, published in 1932, contains over 2,600 letters, the majority of which had never before been printed. Chief fame rests upon *Letters to His Son Philip Stanhope* (1774), with lesser acclaim for kindred epistles, *Letters to His Godson* (1890), and *Letters of Lord Chesterfield to Lord Huntingdon* (1923). In all three major collections the noble lord is the mature mentor to youth, the epitome of worldly wisdom and the genteel tradition. The later Romantic emphasis upon "natural" behavior was severely discountenanced by Chesterfield, who demanded studied grace in the most trivial commonplaces of life. Life was an art to Chesterfield, and good manners were to him what charity was to St. Paul. Moralists such as Johnson, Cowper, and Wesley, and the Victorians, were horror-stricken at Chesterfield's sexual morality. To him, what the world says of you was all-important; discreet and undisclosed sinning is politely advised. (Of course, the letters were not themselves ever intended for publication.)

Perhaps no other writings in literature so thoroughly expound the sophisticated code of the world. Chesterfield appeals wholly to self-interest, and his goal is social approval. He counsels the broadest of social experience and wide, but not pedantic, learning. He cautions against vulgar concupiscence, drinking, and gambling. He scorns snobbery; rank is a fact, and an aristocrat carries it gracefully and unostentatiously.

The most famed of the letters are addressed to Chesterfield's illegitimate son, Philip Stanhope, born by Mlle. du Bouchet, the earl's French mistress during his first ambassadorship to The Hague. Chesterfield was intent upon shaping the youth as a diplomat, gentleman, and citizen of the world; the young man died at thirty-three without attaining the social graces or acceptance desired by his father. The godson bore the same name as the earl's illegitimate son, and the letters to him have often been confused with those to the other Philip. Chesterfield's godson inherited the title but remained throughout life an undistinguished country gentleman. Lord Huntingdon called the earl his adopted father but also ended life without notable social distinction. To all three, Chesterfield writes without intimacy or family familiarity, but rather with that reserve so often characteristic in the age between father and son. The style is beautifully suave and succinct, frequently producing still quoted aphorisms. Chesterfield and Walpole masterfully depict the attitudes of an aristocratic society on its unwitting path to dissolution. Surface has completely overwhelmed inner substance, and this class was to succumb to a rising bourgeoisie sure of its worth and confident of its purpose and actions.

Other Neoclassic Prose

Gilbert White (1720–1793). Gilbert White lived most of his quiet life in his native Selbourne, Hampshire. Soon after graduation from Oriel College, Oxford, he became a curate in Selbourne, where he pursued the popular avocation of contemporary clergymen—nature study.

The Natural History of Selbourne (1789) consists of forty-four letters to Thomas Pennant, the naturalist, and sixty-six letters to the Honorable Daines Barrington, written between 1767 and 1787. The work is that rarity, a literary-scientific masterpiece. White is a minutely faithful observer of wild life, revealing the ceaseless rhythms of animals and plants amidst scenic beauty. His literary charm rests upon his unstated but pervasive affection for all living things and a sense of boundless wonder at the mysteries of creation. His simple, unsentimental style cannot obscure a delightful personality and a lover of the English countryside as fervent as Izaak Walton.

Sir Philip Francis (1740–1818). Born in Dublin, Ireland, Sir Philip Francis was the son of an Anglican cleric who tutored Fox. After studies at St. Paul's school, young Francis rose through political posts to become first clerk of the War Office, 1762–72. From 1774 to 1781 he served on the council of four to advise the governor-general of India. From 1784 he was distinguished in Parliament, becoming Knight Commander of the Bath in 1806. Perhaps Byron, in his *Vision of Judgment,* was correct in saying that no one wrote the letters of Junius, but if there was a human author, it was probably Francis.

The Letters of Junius (November 21, 1768, to January 21, 1772, in the *Public Advertiser*) still constitutes one of the prime mysteries of English literature. Their authorship was never acknowledged, though they were attributed to every prominent Whig of the era. Burke, when accused, asserted: "I could not if I would, and I would not if I could." In English political writings, only Burke can match the rhetorical power of these letters, and even he seldom equals the vituperation and invective of Junius. These letters belong to the impassioned and immoderate realm of political harangue, but their facts (often available only to high officials) are almost always accurate and their purpose is basically noble.

George III was attempting to establish a personal rule through catspaws, "the King's friends." Junius attacked these corrupt, subservient, and unrepresentative governments. The fall of the Grafton administration in January 1770 can largely be ascribed to Junius. The enraged monarch desperately sought to apprehend the writer, but the publisher had no idea who Junius was, the letters reaching him by devious routes, which increased in complexity and deception as the royal search was intensified. Junius was never positively identified, but the Francis theory, advanced by John Taylor in 1816, seems the most credible, though denied to the end by Sir Philip.

James Woodforde (1740–1803). Descendant of a long line of Anglican clergymen, James Woodforde was born at Ansford, Somersetshire. After graduation from New College, Oxford, in 1763, he served as curate in various Somerset parishes until he settled down in 1774 as rector in Weston Longeville, Norfolk. Never married, he lived in Weston with his nephew Bill until 1778 and, from 1779 until his death, with his niece Nancy.

The Diary of a Country Parson (1924–31) was a discovery of the 20th century, for the very existence of this diary was unknown until our age. Woodforde maintained his almost daily entries from October 1758, when he began at Oxford, until October 1802, when illness forced him to stop writing. No other work so captures the day-by-day rituals of an English village, the kind of life most Englishmen lived until the Industrial Revolution was in full swing.

This is a far cry from the great world of Walpole and Palmerston; perhaps the only contact Woodforde had with their world was his enforced wait at Hindon in 1787, along with Pitt, for coach horses. The stolid, commonsense parson re-creates the immemorial peace and rhythm of rural life. The only dramas are the inevitable illnesses and mortality of mankind, and the gargantuan meals that would appall today's eaters. External nature does not much interest the parson, but the restrained and undemonstrative cleric is unswerving in his pastoral duties and unceasing in Christian charity. More than any other piece of writing, this diary faithfully depicts the bedrock of English character, and it makes understandable the determination that carried a people through the agony of the Napoleonic Era—and, later, World War II. The unimaginative parson is the epitome of unheroic heroism.

John Byron (1723–1786). Grandfather of the poet, John ("Foul-weather Jack") Byron entered the Royal Navy when he was a boy, serving as a midshipman in 1740 aboard the *Wager,* one of Anson's squadron in the South Atlantic. As Commodore Byron in 1764, he led the *Dolphin* and the *Tamar* on a vast but not particularly revealing exploration of the Southern Hemisphere. From 1769 until 1772 he was governor of Newfoundland. As vice-admiral in 1779 he suffered defeat from the French off Grenada in the West Indies.

Narrative (1768) is a stirring account of the fearful hardships experienced by the shipwrecked mariners of the *Wager* in Patagonia. The unelaborated work by the youthful midshipman actually highlights, by its matter-of-fact attitude, the cold, misery, inhuman cruelty, and great courage of the ordeal. Only the tough and the lucky survived the wild elements and the wilder men. His grandson was to employ much of this material in *Don Juan.*

James Cook (1728–1779). James Cook was the son of a farm laborer in Marton, Yorkshire. He entered the merchant marine in 1755 as an able seaman and rapidly worked upward to become master of H.M.S. *Mercury* in 1759 during the Seven Years' War. His precision and thoroughness in surveying the St. Lawrence riverway and the coasts of Labrador and Newfoundland induced the Admiralty to send him in command of the most dramatic and revealing English voyages since Drake.

First Pacific voyage (1768–71) had a twofold purpose: observation of the transit of Venus and exploration of the South Seas. Sir Joseph Banks, a member of "The Club," also went along to make extensive botanical observations. The greatest achievement of the trip was the six-month circumnavigation of New Zealand (under orders) and the exploration of the east coast of Australia (on Cook's initiative). Cook's own account was first published in 1893. The captain's report is crisp and factual, the businesslike work of a man who lets the facts speak for themselves. Our age would prefer Cook's own sober account, but Cook's contemporaries depended upon the doctored 1773 version of the work by John Hawkesworth. The Hawkesworth account panders to the primitivistic tendencies of the age and twists Cook's straightforward comments into paeans upon dusky beauties and nature's noblemen of the remote Society Islands. Cook indicated to Boswell his distaste for the romanticized picture by Hawkesworth.

Second Pacific voyage (1772–75) sought to delineate the Southern Continent, thus becoming the first serious exploration of Antarctica. Cook also discovered New Caledonia and numerous other Pacific islands. *A Voyage towards the South Pole and Round the World* (1777) is a sea classic, its measured phrases concealing Cook's craggy will and cool courage. The eerie statues of Easter Island, like most of his extraordinary encounters, elicit only a bald, unspeculative description; but in a rare exaltation that was to infect Coleridge, he gazed with awe upon the stupendous icefields and icebergs of Antarctica, though he was also to appreciate them for their "seasonable supplies of fresh water."

Third Pacific voyage (1776–79) sought a sea route from the Pacific into Hudson's Bay. Cook left a comfortable sinecure to volunteer for the task, and France and Spain, though at war with England, ordered their ships to treat Cook as "commander of a neutral and allied power"; and Benjamin Franklin issued American commissions to privateers, specifying the same courtesy.

Cook explored the Pacific coast of North America from California to the ice-clogged straits between Alaska and Siberia, and thence traveled along the frigid coast of northern Asia. Returning to winter in Hawaii before resuming his explorations, Cook was slain by natives. The great navigator had completed the work started by the Renaissance—the definitive outlining of the world map. In massive practicality and calm self-discipline, he was a model of his age. His two-volume account, *A Voyage to the Pacific Ocean* (1784), was rounded out by a third volume from James King.

Thomas Pennant (1726–1798). A native of Downing, Flintshire, Wales, Thomas Pennant wrote extensively as a naturalist and antiquarian, but his reputation rests upon *A Tour in Scotland in 1769* (1771), *Second Tour in Scotland and the Hebrides* (1774), and *Tour in Wales* (1778). Unlike earlier travelers, he elaborately describes scenery, but his full, clear, painstaking descriptions are unimaginative. He is as impersonal in detailing a landscape as in recording the annual haul of fish from Scottish lochs.

John Howard (c. 1726–1790). John Howard, the age's greatest humanitarian, was early apprenticed to a grocer but retired upon inheriting his upholsterer father's estate. In 1773 this quiet widower of forty-seven was appointed High Sheriff of Bedfordshire. Predecessors in the post had nonchalantly ignored their chief duty, the inspection of local prisons, but Howard zealously threw himself into the task, extending his survey thousands of miles throughout the British Isles. Crowned heads of Europe invited him to broaden his examination upon the Continent. At Kherson, in Russia, he contracted typhus while ministering to the sick and died there. His was the first civilian corpse ever to be brought back by warship to England with full military and diplomatic honors. One of the world's leading humanitarians, he bears upon his tomb this inscription: "Whoever thou art, thou standest at the tomb of thy friend."

The State of the Prisons in England and Wales (1777) covers almost every jail in the British Isles. Plain, unemotional language factually re-creates a picture of an incredibly noisome and sordid world. Howard took to riding horseback because the prison stench upon his clothes was unbearable in a closed carriage. The detailed exposé of prison horrors is in itself a profoundly gripping account, but more importantly, this volume, together with *An Account of the Principal Lazarettos in Europe* (1789), awakened the conscience of Western society to its responsibilities toward the imprisoned and diseased. Howard established the pattern ever since followed by intelligent reformers—meticulous investigation, deliberate weighing and sifting of the evidence, comparison with other institutional practices, and reasoned recommendations. His proposals are wholly realistic and practical, so close to the irreducible minimum of sanitation and nutrition as to render even more appalling the penology of his era.

Some Neoclassic Verse

Perhaps the only noteworthy neoclassic verse during this time was satire, which, although below the caliber of Dryden or Pope, far exceeded in sheer volume any previous production of English satire.

Charles Churchill (1731–1764). A native of London, Charles Churchill became a clergyman in 1756 and held various curacies, as well as teaching school. He was a zealous friend of Wilkes but a severe critic of almost everyone else. Called "the meteor of a season," he produced a sizable quantity of satires from 1761 until his death (from a fever, in Boulogne, France), and he briefly reigned as a literary luminary. Cowper, a boyhood schoolmate, remembered him as "the great Churchill." Meditating at the satirist's grave just before his last departure from England, Byron contemplated "the glory and the nothing of a name." Churchill was the most important satirist between Pope and Byron and one of the most virulent Juvenalian satirists in the language.

The Rosciad (1761), its name derived from Roscius, the Roman actor of antiquity, created more of a stir than any satire since *The Dunciad*. Apparently the thespians of the current London stage were terrorized by the stabbing criticism of their every gesture and intonation. Garrick, one of the few singled out for praise, deemed it prudent to conciliate the burly satirist. Few English poets have matched the rugged power of Churchill's heroic couplets, but his lines also display haste and raggedness.

The Ghost (1762), in rambling octosyllabics, lampooned Dr. Johnson as "Pomposo," and with its stinging witticisms it is believed responsible for hastening the publication of Johnson's long-delayed edition of Shakespeare.

Christopher Anstey (1724–1805). A native of Brinkley, Christopher Anstey proved adept at Latin verse in King's College, Cambridge, but was refused the M.A. because of his opposition to regulations. As a country gentleman of means, he contracted gout and went for the cure to the medicinal waters of Bath, from whence arose his famed Horatian satire.

The New Bath Guide (1766) consists of anapestic letters, supposedly from the Blunderhead family, agog at the fashionable elegance and excitement of Bath. The gay badinage about the foibles of the *bon ton,* enlivened with a dash of impropriety, made this one of the most popular poems of the century. The lilting lines caused a vogue of anapests, as in Goldsmith's *Retaliation.* In many respects Tobias Smollett's novel, *Humphry Clinker,* is a prose rendition of Anstey's verse.

EDINBURGH AND THE SCOTTISH WRITERS OF THE PERIOD

"THE SELECT SOCIETY." What many Scots felt was an effective challenge to Johnson's London circle was the brilliant intellectual life of Edinburgh, Scotland. Throughout the second half of the 18th century and until the death of Sir Walter Scott, Edinburgh was celebrated as "The Athens of the North." The most scintillating literary circle in late 18th-century Edinburgh was "The Select Society," founded in 1754 by Allan Ramsay, the painter son of the poet bearing the same name. Scottish contributions in this age to the drama appear later on in this chapter, and their contributions to the novel appear in the next chapter. Robert Fergusson is the only poet represented here, and although the Scots wrote extensive but undistinguished verse in the "Southron" dialect, their impressive achievement lay in scholarly prose. While the following prose writers spoke throughout most of their lives in broad "Lollans" (Lowlands) Scots, they punctiliously avoided "Scotticisms" in their writings. Also, David Hume, a leading light of "The Select Society," has already been discussed in the previous chapter.

William Robertson (1721–1793). Born at Borthwick, Scotland, William Robertson was educated for the Presbyterian clergy. He became royal chaplain in 1761, principal of the University of Edinburgh in 1762, and royal historiographer in 1763. With Hume and Gibbon he formed the "triumvirate" of 18th-century British historians. Like Hume, he was a rationalist (though not a skeptic), but he lacked what Gibbon termed the "careless, inimitable beauties" of Hume's style. Like Hume, too, he failed to see, as Gibbon did, the cause-and-effect pattern of history and the enormous perspective of the centuries.

History of Scotland during the Reigns of Queen Mary and of King James the Sixth (1759) is the first significant history of Scotland. Robertson introduced the practice of presenting a clear, lucid text with notes and documents suffixed. He also explored primary sources more exhaustively than any British historian before Gibbon. He worked so hard to present Mary fairly that many Scots Presbyterians objected.

History of the Reign of the Emperor Charles the Fifth (1769) treats of European events centering about the 16th-century Holy Roman Emperor. It was Robertson's masterpiece, acclaimed in the age by Voltaire and Catherine the Great of Russia, and it still remains a classic. Because of this book, Carlyle was awakened to a consuming interest in history. Robertson masterfully balances the contests of the Emperor and the Papacy. He shows equal fairness to Luther and the Jesuits, though such a rationalist could not fathom the dedicated essence of these men.

The History of America (I, II, 1777; III, 1796) was the first significant attempt in English to examine the history of the New World. Robertson tapped the resources of Great Britain and the Continent for primary material. He was dispassionate about the War for Independence but enthusiastic about the exciting challenge of the Americas. Here appeared his most eloquent writing, approaching almost epical quality in discussing Columbus, Cortez, and Pizarro. His graphic account of Balboa's (the poet's memory faltered, not the historian's) discovery of the Pacific inspired the famous reference by Keats in the sonnet on Chapman's Homer.

Adam Smith (1723–1790). A native of Kirkcaldy, Scotland, Adam Smith was educated at the universities of Glasgow (under Hutcheson, 1737–40) and Oxford (1740–46). In 1751 he held the chair of logic at Glasgow, which he exchanged the next year for that of moral philosophy. From 1764 to 1766 he traveled in Europe and became an intimate friend of the leading French *philosophes* of the Enlightenment. The next ten years were largely devoted to the writing of *The Wealth of Nations* in Kirkcaldy. As commissioner of customs for Scotland, he resided in Edinburgh from 1778 until his death. He belonged to "The Club" in London as well as to "The Select Society" in Edinburgh.

Theory of Moral Sentiments (1759) established his reputation and, unlike his more momentous study to follow, truly belongs to *belles lettres*. It sounds like the spirited classroom lecturing of a good professor, even to humorous sallies and anecdotal digressions. His contention is that each human being should imaginatively put himself in the place of another. Thus sympathy is generated, as is also the concept of human society, and eventually the social amalgam of accepted custom and morality. Smith thus denies the special "moral sense" of Shaftesbury and of his mentor, Hutcheson.

Inquiry into the Nature and Causes of the Wealth of Nations (1776) is one of the seminal works of Western civilization and the virtual inaugurator of the study of economics (which Carlyle was later to label "the dismal science"). Smith intended neither a scholarly treatise nor a textbook; he created a panorama and dissection of the economic world about him as a revelation to every intelligent reader and as a guide to empire.

Smith diagnosed the laws of the market as self-interest and competition. Self-interest drives men to produce goods and services for which society will pay. Competition prevents exorbitant profit and will force the equitable distribution of manufacturing energy and the labor force. In fact, the market is "self-regulating," and Smith therefore advocates *laissez faire*. Government meddling will only muddy the waters, solving nothing; better to let the market adjust itself. Though frequently cited by the rising middle class, Smith had his reservations about manufacturers and wrote with the total population in mind, not favoring any one class. Superbly accurate as his depiction is for late 18th-century England, it could not conceive of the vast economic changes to follow—notably the giant corporation, the giant labor union, and massive intervention by government. It must be remembered that monopoly of any sort was anathema to Smith.

Smith contemplated a dynamism in the economic system, thus mirroring the modern mind, and thus expecting an ascending spiral of production. The Principle of Accumulation (the amassing of capital) will assure constantly increasing production to generate profit for the capitalist. Human greed will therefore benefit mankind. But increased means of production will strain the labor supply and force up wages. Here enters the Principle of Population. Smith sees the laboring population as a commodity; with increased demand, the laboring population will expand (chiefly in his day by lessening the high mortality rate among children) and thus prevent wages from rising to a point where they imperil capitalistic profit. Eventually, however, he foresees a distant era when sizable productive expansion is no longer possible (raw materials and living space on this globe have their limits), and then the capitalist will receive the wages of management and little beyond.

Fox, the Whig leader, ridiculed the book, but Pitt the Younger was more than a mere admirer. With several of his ministers, Pitt rose to greet the aged philosopher at a conference. When Smith urged them to be seated, Pitt refused: "We will stand until you are first seated, for we are all your scholars." It is unlikely that any economist will ever again so thoroughly encompass his age as did Smith. He diagnosed without prejudice, and recounted without rancor. His plane was loftily philosophical, and his ultimate vision was essentially a moderate optimism: he saw all the desperate and inglorious scramble for riches and fame as finally resulting in increased welfare and at least the physical betterment of all mankind.

Henry Home, Lord Kames (1696–1782). Henry Home, Lord Kames was born at Kames, Berwickshire, Scotland. He was a distinguished Scottish judge and writer on legal subjects, a sympathetic friend of Boswell, and in his own day a highly respected literary critic.

Elements of Criticism (1762) denied the principle of authority, so precious to neoclassic criticism, and sought to deduce the fundamentals of the fine arts from human nature, appealing to reason and to universal psychology. Kames coined the term "ideal presence" to account for the impact of imaginative art; the reader's sense of vicarious participation constitutes the power of such art. He also denied the necessity for any rigidity of genre, finding beauty not in the object but in the beholder. The large portion of his work devoted to Shakespeare probably makes him the best Shakespearean critic before the Romantics. He accuses previous critics of undue concern with the "mechanical" aspect of the plays (Unities, historical accuracy, structure, mingling of tragic and comic elements) and minutely details Shakespeare's success in reflecting the thoughts and behavior of humanity. Apparently he was the first to suggest that internal evidence could date Shakespeare's plays, stating that in the later plays Shakespeare "has attained the purity and perfection of dialogue."

Robert Fergusson (1750–1774). A native of Edinburgh, Robert Fergusson studied at St. Andrew's University, and served as an extracting clerk in the Edinburgh office of the commissary clerk until his untimely death in melancholia.

Poems (I, 1773; II, 1779) contains much conventionally neoclassic English verse, but the Scots verse continues the narrative, non-lyric tradition of *The Ever Green*. Burns paid abundant tribute to Fergusson, whom he regarded as his master. The poet utilized many of Fergusson's stanzaic patterns, particularly with the short "bob line." Fergusson is especially a city poet, singing of "Edina" or "Auld Reekie" (Edinburgh). But his verse smacks of robust qualities largely absent from 18th-century English poetry. It contains the Scottish verse tradition of exuberance, rapid motion, wild grotesquerie, and uninhibited spirits. "Braid Claith" is a sample of what Burns would do in native satire of Scottish religious life, and "The Farmer's Ingle" is a forerunner of "The Cotter's Saturday Night."

DRAMA TO 1800

The latter half of the 18th century produced excellent theater but generally inferior drama. The Licensing Act of 1737 confined play production to Drury Lane and Covent Garden, and the patentees zealously hounded rival and illegal companies out of existence. Managers considered it pointless to encourage new playwrights, who would have to be paid, while Shakespeare's plays were free for the taking; also, new dramas ran the risk of being banned or drastically revised by the censor. Blessed with a monopoly, the two London theaters expanded in size until by the century's end they were as large as many of today's sizable auditoriums and opera houses. In such large structures drama was sacrificed to spectacle, comedy degenerating into broad farce and tragedy emphasizing bravura acting. The age produced in David Garrick (1717–79) perhaps the most noted actor of English theatrical history. As a manager Garrick introduced footlights in 1765 and sponsored more realistic stage settings, lighting, and carpentry. Charles Macklin (c. 1697–1797), who was enacting stage roles in his nineties, along with Garrick popularized realism in costume and naturalism in acting techniques.

But with the exception of Goldsmith and Sheridan the era contains meager excitement in the drama itself. They represent the only important drama of the period, and, in fact, the last outstanding drama until virtually the end of the 19th century. Perhaps the most significant aspect of this period's drama, however, was its minimizing of much of the neoclassicism of earlier times, clear evidence of popular movement toward bourgeois attitudes and incipient Romanticism. While all the types of drama discussed in the last chapter, with the exception of ballad opera, continued to be produced, the proportions were changing.

Serious English opera in this age imitated the Italian opera of Metastasio but produced few works and nothing of note. Serious opera was dominated by Italian imports in the original language. The ballad opera from Gay's initiative did not survive into the latter half of the century, but increasingly popular was the comic opera, essentially a stage farce or comedy set to extensive music. Writers cast about for material with all the *éclat* of today's writers of musicals. Isaac Bickerstaffe (an

Irish playwright, not the pseudonym used by Swift) based *The Ward of the Mill* (1765) upon part of Richardson's *Pamela,* and Garrick derived his *Cymon* (1767) from Dryden's poem "Cymon and Iphigenia." Sheridan's *The Duenna* was the most successful work of this type.

Tragedy

No notable neoclassic tragedy followed *Cato,* and the genre petered out to extinction in *England Preserved* (1795), by George Watson, a play dealing with Pembroke's protectorate during the minority of Henry III. There are really only two writers of tragedy of importance in this period: Edward Moore and John Home.

Edward Moore (1712–1757). A native of Abingdon, Berkshire, Edward Moore failed as a London linen draper and turned to writing. From 1753 until his death he was editor of *The World,* a successful newspaper.

The Gamester (1753)—Domestic Tragedy. This play was probably written initially in blank verse, as its prose is a bit too poetic for its realistic portrayals. It is, however, the only significant play of this type, as the emphasis on the drama of spectacle and escapism was chiefly responsible for the ignoring of Lillo's innovation.

A compulsive gambler, Beverley is led astray by Stukely, a pretended friend. Beverley gambles away everything on cards, even his wife's jewels. Stukely's villainy is detected by Lewson, suitor of Beverley's sister. To conceal his crimes, Stukely arranges for Lewson's murder. Accused of the killing, Beverley, in desperate straits, poisons himself. Dying, he is informed of a handsome legacy.

Garrick created the role of Beverley and reputedly wrote part of the drama. Like Lillo's plays, this indicates a note of fate in the lives of commonplace people and also preaches solid middle-class virtues. The play held the boards of the London stage for over a century.

John Home (1722–1808). A native of Leith, near Edinburgh, Scotland, John Home trained for the Kirk of Scotland. He served with Whig troops against the "Forty-Five," was captured by the Jacobites, but later escaped. Home succeeded Robert Blair as pastor of Athelstaneford, but the Presbyterian clergy forced him to resign when he gained prominence in playwrighting. After a few years in London he returned in 1779, to shine amidst the celebrities of the "Select Society" in Edinburgh.

Douglas (1756)—Romantic Tragedy. This work, refused by Garrick, was first presented in Edinburgh to tumultuous patriotic applause. An Englishman was accosted after the first performance by an exultant Scot: "Whaur's yer Wully Shakespeare noo!" Its source is the ballad "Gil Morrice," and it is in blank verse.

Lady Randolph recognizes a stranger as her long-lost son, Douglas. Observing her clandestine meetings with the youth, and inflamed with jealousy by the proddings of the bitter Glenalvon, Lord Randolph has the boy murdered. With a revelation of the truth, Lady Randolph commits suicide.

Home carefully follows the Unities and makes each of the five acts mark a definite forward action in the conflict. Though the historical background is rather vague, Home furnishes an atmosphere of Scottish medievalism. The violent passions and soaring language contrast vividly with the cool Augustan tragedy. Gray in England and Hume in Scotland highly praised the work. It was successful in London performances for years, completely overshadowing Home's other dramatic efforts.

Comedy

Though it is perhaps fair to say that the most popular dramatic genre of the era was farce, and its most successful practitioners were George Colman the Elder (1732–94), David Garrick (1717–79), and Arthur Murphy (1727–1805), it would be equally fair to point out that most of their farcical endeavors belong to the theater rather than to literature. Also, although the tradition of sentimental comedy inaugurated by Steele continued vigorously, Richard Cumberland is the only writer of sentimental comedy to be discussed here. It is to the exceptions to this kind of drama that we really devote our attention, and here we find the two significant dramatists of this period: Oliver Goldsmith and Richard Brinsley Sheridan.

Richard Cumberland (1732–1811). Richard Cumberland was the grandson of Richard Bentley. He sprang from a long line of clergymen, and his father was to rise to the bishopric of Clonfert in Ireland. Cumberland was educated in his native Cambridge and, after a brief career as secretary to the Lord Lieutenant of Ireland, turned to playwrighting. Although he composed over fifty plays, he is remembered for only one.

The West Indian (1771)—Sentimental Comedy. This play takes the neoclassic pattern of comic intrigue leading to marriage and fortune, but sentimentalizes it. In this age sentimental comedy abandons the classic belief in comedy as portrayal of human weakness and sees rather the comic in the not-too-serious misadventures of the virtuous.

Belcour, fresh from the West Indies, plays the rake, importuning Louisa Dudley under the misapprehension that she is the mistress of her brother, Charles. Really a sentimentalist at heart, Belcour quickly reforms under Louisa's guidance. The plot by the Fulmers to defraud the young man of his inheritance is discovered by Major O'Flaherty. Belcour and Louisa are properly united, as are Charles Dudley and his sweetheart, Charlotte Rusport.

Cumberland's huge success with this play firmly established the vogue of sentimental comedy, which to our own day dominates popular comic drama. Of course, modern audiences prefer more pseudo-realism than the late 18th century, and more refining of emotions and sensibilities. At the same time Belcour is parading as a libertine, he is helping the distressed, aged Dudley and proving himself a man of feeling. O'Flaherty is a sentimental Irishman, hot-tempered but pure gold at heart, not the stage Irishman laughed at in *The Beaux' Stratagem* and in a hundred other English comedies.

Oliver Goldsmith (c. 1728–1774). Goldsmith attacked the mawkishness and artificiality of the sentimental comedy in *The Present State of Polite Learning,* which has been discussed earlier in this chapter along with his biographical material. His first attempt at correcting this condition, the play *The Good-Natur'd Man* (1768), states in its preface his positive program to reintroduce "nature" and "humour" in comedy. Goldsmith's assault against the sentimental comedy continued in "An Essay on the Theatre; or, A Comparison between Laughing and Sentimental Comedy," printed in *The Westminster Magazine* (1772).

She Stoops to Conquer, or The Mistakes of a Night (1773)—Comedy of Manners. This work lives up in practice to the author's critical theory. Its indebtedness to *The Beaux' Stratagem* is obvious.

Young Marlow, bashful before well-bred ladies but the very devil with barmaids, hesitantly comes to woo Kate Hardcastle. For a lark, Tony Lumpkin, Mrs. Hardcastle's son by a previous marriage, directs Marlow to "the inn," actually the Hardcastle residence. Kate pretends to be a barmaid, and the wooing is successful. The heiress, Constance Neville, is intended for the bumpkin Lumpkin but is won by Hastings, Marlow's friend.

Goldsmith mocks sentimental comedy continually. Kate defines sensibility as hypocrisy. Lumpkin and his cronies stage a gloriously wild carouse at "The Three Pigeons," and the bear-trainer claims to dance his beast only to the most genteel tunes. Two-faced Marlow is a balance between the sentimental hero and the Restoration rake, and Kate is a dashing, high-spirited girl with more liveliness than most of the stage heroines for several generations. "The Club," led by Johnson, clapped the play to fame on the opening night. "I know of no comedy for many years," said the Great Cham, "that has answered so much the great end of comedy—making an audience merry." Walpole pettishly declared that the play was "set up in opposition to sentimental comedy and is as bad as the worst of them," but he had to admit that it set him laughing. And the world has continued to laugh ever since at this tribute to vivacious youth and bubbling optimism.

Richard Brinsley Butler Sheridan (1751–1816). Born in Dublin, Richard Brinsley Sheridan was the son of Thomas Sheridan, actormanager of the Theatre Royal in Dublin, and Frances Sheridan, author of novels and comedies. Young Sheridan was educated at Harrow. After a romantic courtship he married Elizabeth Linley, a popular concert singer, in 1773. Imitating Anstey, he wrote gay anapestic bits on the gaieties of Bath. *The Rivals* catapulted him into a brilliant theatrical career as playwright and manager at Drury Lane. Entering Parliament in 1780, he forsook the theater for even greater theatricalities in the House of Commons, notably the trial of Warren Hastings. In 1782 he was Undersecretary of State, and in 1783 he was Secretary of the Treasury, but most of his political life was spent in the Whig opposition, where he was the recognized equal of Fox and Burke. Sheridan was an intimate of the Prince of Wales, even composing the love letters dispatched by his royal highness. Three years after his first wife's death in 1792, Sheridan married the daughter of the dean of Winchester. Though he died virtually in poverty, he was buried with pomp in Westminster Abbey. Where Goldsmith sought "nature" and "humour" in comedy, the brilliant Irishman sought and produced wit.

The Rivals (1775)—Comedy of Manners. This work boldly declares for anti-sentimentalism.

Lydia Languish is a sentimental girl who will not consider a tame and acceptable marriage. Hence the wealthy Captain Absolute woos her under the disguise of the dashing but impecunious Ensign Beverley. Lydia's aunt, Mrs. Malaprop, forbids the apparently inappropriate marriage. Bob Acres, suitor for Lydia's hand, is goaded by the fiery Sir Lucius O'Trigger to challenge Beverley to a duel. The cowardly Acres is spared deadly combat when Absolute's identity is revealed. In relief, Acres relinquishes the girl to his rival. In the sub-plot the sensibilities are reversed, with Faulkland, the sentimentalist, paired off with the intelligent Julia.

The characters are derived from long stage tradition, but, as Hazlitt observes, it "appears to have been the peculiar forte and the great praise of our author's genius, that he could imitate with the spirit of an inventor." Mrs. Malaprop (from the French *malapropos*, "badly to the purpose") is derived from Shakespeare's Dogberry and Dame Quickly, but she has immortalized herself with her "nice derangement of epitaphs." The cross-pairing of the four lovers confronts a sentimentalist with an anti-sentimentalist in each instance, and anti-sentimentalism wins in both cases. Lydia is a delightful portrait of the fashionable romantic girl, her head stuffed with the nonsense of giddy love stories. Bob Acres, with his assumed jargon of the gay blades, is one of the most superb low comics of the stage. O'Trigger is a hot-tempered Irishman without a sense of light humor but with a supreme consecration to the code of the duello. Faulkland appears to the modern audience to be a defect in the play, but he is straight out of scores of contemporary sentimental comedies. The play is one of the last significant enunciations of the code of aristocratic neoclassicism; the eccentrics and boors are laughed away, and the ideal is a reasoned serenity of good judgment and good taste.

The School for Scandal (1777)—Comedy of Manners. This play is Sheridan's masterpiece, a comic triumph probably surpassing any other in English drama since Congreve. "It is," suggested Hazlitt, "if not the most original, perhaps the most finished and faultless comedy which we have."

The atmosphere of frivolous London high society binds together three plot elements. Lord Teazle is an old man married to a young and skittish Lady Teazle. Their squabbles leave her open to the advances of Joseph Surface. The Surface brothers are contrasted: Charles is open-hearted but ne'er-do-well; Joseph is a hypocrite who appears to be a humanitarian and a man of feeling. Their uncle, Sir Oliver in disguise, tests both brothers and finds the apparently feckless Charles to be the honest man and the supposedly reliable Joseph a sneaking scoundrel. The two plots come together in the famous screen scene of Act IV, when Charles discovers Lady Teazle at a tryst with Joseph. The scandalmongers—Snake, Lady Sneerwell, Mrs. Candour—represent that part of society which relishes killing a reputation with each word.

Sheridan here launches a twofold attack: upon sentimentalism and upon scandal. Joseph Surface has become proverbial in the language for the ostensible moralist and philanthropist who at heart is a selfish fraud. Charles is a typical English fictional character, like Prince Hal or Tom Jones, who seems to be a wastrel but is innately a splendid fellow. The assault upon the spreaders of scandal is perhaps inspired by *The Rape of the Lock.*

English drama has always been accused of bungling in its manipulation of multiple plots, but this play is an acknowledged masterpiece of tight construction. The actions develop out of the respective character traits without a trace of mechanical shuffling; but Sheridan's crowning feat, and the reason for the play's active stage life down to the present, is the scintillating dialogue. The verbal ingenuity and sparkling prose almost equal the best of Congreve. Where Sheridan falls short of Congreve is in an absence of universalization. *The Way of the World* touches the immemorial pathos of human relationships and the near impossibility of one spirit to communicate itself totally to another. While Sheridan's play cannot be said to touch quite so high a plane, it too concerns itself with the breakdown of communication in a superficially aristocratic society.

The Critic: or, A Tragedy Rehearsed (1779)—Burlesque. Sheridan masterfully followed the tradition of *The Rehearsal* with this play. The *Critic* satirizes the playwrights and critics of the time who favor sentimental comedy and Augustan tragedy.

Puff, a talentless writer, along with Sneer, the critic, views the rehearsal of his historical drama, *The Spanish Armada.* The parodied drama is a wild ferrago of brilliant inanities and tortured "classicism," replete with peripety and stichomythia. Sir Fretful Plagiary is a caricature of Richard Cumberland.

The Green Room and the entire theatrical world of the age come to life in this delightful lampoon. With all the ludicrous characters and hilarious mishaps, the *"theatre"* in all its fascination shines magnificently. Even when its targets are long since forgotten, this pillorying of the woeful author and the benighted (but devastatingly self-assured) critic is still successful in 20th-century revivals.

The Duenna (1775)—Musical Comedy. *The Duenna* enjoyed a remarkable first run of seventy-five performances and was revived often in the 19th century. The plot is an adaptation of Wycherley's *Country Wife.* Though sparkling with Sheridan's whimsical humor and gifted dialogue, the piece is best known for its vivacious and charming lyrics.

THE MOVEMENT AWAY FROM NEOCLASSICISM

Although the non-neoclassic tendencies that we discussed in the last chapter continued and even increased in this age, there was no voice comparable to that of the later William Law in this period, and therefore no hint of the coming of Blake except in the lonely spirit of Christopher Smart. The religious enthusiasm generated by the Wesleyan movement mounted in intensity throughout the later 18th century and proved one of the momentous and dynamic expressions of the age. However, the early 18th-century manifestations of emotional literature and of interest in external nature increased, and especially significant was the rising delight in subject matter foreign to neoclassicism, particularly a growing attention to medievalism. The approach to Romanticism is clear, but still missing is the hallmark of Romanticism—a violent proclamation of rebellion.

The Major Poets of the New Trend

Thomas Gray (1716–1771). A native Londoner, Thomas Gray was the son of a rather harsh money-scrivener. He was the only survivor of twelve children. At Eton, c. 1725, he was a classmate of Horace Walpole and Richard West (whose death he was to mourn in a famous sonnet). In 1734 he entered Peterhouse, Cambridge, as a pensioner but left without securing a degree. With Walpole he started the Grand Tour in 1739 but parted from his friend after a quarrel at Reggio, Italy, in 1741. Gray settled in Cambridge after a brief residence at Stoke Poges with his mother. He received his bachelor's degree in 1744 and was reconciled with Walpole the next year. In 1757 he declined the offer of the poet laureateship. In 1768 he was appointed Professor of Modern History and Languages at Cambridge. During the decade of the sixties he traveled widely through northern England and Scotland. A dutiful son, he was buried by his mother's side at Stoke Poges.

Gray was primarily a scholar, more interested in reading than in writing. He was not a professional poet like Pope or a dedicated poet as Wordsworth and Shelley were to be. Though subsidiary to a life of study, his poems are always competent and effective. He laboriously revised and improved to make them as near perfect as a highly gifted poet can. His literary progress moves with the times, from a decaying neoclassicism toward a growing taste for romantic themes and expression.

EARLY NEOCLASSICISM. "Ode on the Spring" (*1742,* 1748), with familiar personifications (Care, the Proud), moralizes on the transience of man's existence, symbolized in the luxuriant but brief life of springtime. It displays pensive but not deep sorrow in somewhat aloof contemplation. The form of the poem is an elaborate ten-line stanza.

"Hymn to Adversity" (*1742,* 1753) is modeled after Horace's ode to Fortune but rises toward its motto from Aeschylus to proclaim solemnly the dignity of suffering. A stanza of eight lines concludes with an alexandrine. The work was influenced by the death of his beloved friend Richard West. Johnson praised the poem as "at once poetical and rational," and Wordsworth largely followed this poem in his "Ode to Duty."

"Sonnet on the Death of Mr. Richard West" (*1742,* 1775) is the first significant sonnet of the 18th century. In the Italian form, it conventionally proclaims grief. The poet feels that while still beautiful, nature is no longer beautiful to him in his sorrow. In the Preface to the *Lyrical Ballads,* Wordsworth singled out this poem for criticism on the basis of its artificial "poetic diction." Nonetheless, the poem is a sincere outpouring of personal grief, masked in part (like much 18th-century expression) by stylized phrasing but wholly effective in the five lines (6, 7, 8, 13, 14) that Wordsworth praised.

"Ode on a Distant Prospect of Eton College" (*1742,* 1747) was also occasioned by the death of West. The placid, half-jocular opening on the cricket fields of Eton mournfully moves toward the inevitable adult sorrows that supersede the thoughtless joys of youth. Seldom has the platitudinous been phrased so effectively. The work uses the same stanza as "Ode on the Spring." This was Gray's first English poem to be published.

"Ode on the Death of a Favorite Cat, Drowned in a Tub of Gold Fishes" (*1747,* 1748) is probably the best mock-ode in English. It captures the delicacy, mock-seriousness, and playfully wry tone of *The Rape of the Lock* to recount an event in the household of Horace Walpole. The mock-moral advises ladies against deceptive appearances.

MINGLING OF NEOCLASSICISM AND ROMANTICISM. "An Elegy Written in a Country Church Yard" may have been started as early as 1742 during Gray's mourning for West. Walpole's circulation of the manuscript in 1750 forced publication in 1751, but the carefully revised version of 1768 is the one ever since printed. This is perhaps the most frequently quoted short poem in English.

(1) Neoclassic elements. The "heroic quatrain" (a b a b) in iambic

pentameter derives from Dryden's "Heroick Stanzas" to Cromwell and from "Annus Mirabilis." The scene is any churchyard (though Stoke Poges is the probable inspiration), and the elegy is to Man rather than to specific persons. Its universality and its meticulous craftsmanship typify neoclassic art.

(2) Romantic elements. This is the supreme achievement of the "Graveyard School," though, as Gray himself noted, it exudes "white Melancholy" instead of wild ghoulishness. The depiction of the gracious English countryside is a word picture of the canvases of Constable and other English landscape painters.

The poem's enduring success rests upon its consummate artistry in stating the obvious: (1) perfect control of English sounds (e.g. examine the melodious chiming of long vowels and liquid consonants in the first stanza); (2) cadenced and solemnly flowing phrases, making almost every line a famous quotation; (3) vivid imagery that is constantly pictorial and also symbolic.

LATER ROMANTICISM. *Odes by Mr. Gray* (1757), from Walpole's Strawberry Hill Press, may be the most important privately printed book in English. Although Ben Jonson had written true Pindaric odes, the pseudo-Pindaric created by Cowley in 1656 was dominant until Gray produced his odes. In *Discourse on the Pindarique Ode* (1705), Congreve explained the correct ancient form, and in 1749 Gilbert West reaffirmed the pattern that Gray followed. The elaborate public odes by Pindar (c. 522–443 B.C.) consisted of three broad sections. Each section was composed of strophe and antistrophe (stanzas of identical length and meter), followed by an epode that differed in length and meter from the strophe and antistrophe. A new poem started a new series of stanzaic patterns.

"The Progress of Poesy" (*1754*) is a historical lyric, packing numerous centuries within its nine stanzas:

First strophe—the sources of poetry in primitive inspiration from wild nature

First antistrophe—poetry molds and curbs the passions

First epode—poetry sets the ancients to dancing

Second strophe—poetry reassures man of God's just decrees

Second antistrophe—poetry kindles among the remotest people (Chile, Lapland) the love of freedom

Second epode—poetry deserted ancient Greece for Rome and now has proceeded to England

Third strophe—Shakespeare tutored to verse by Warwickshire Nature

Third antistrophe—Milton and Dryden the notables of late 17th-century poetry

Third epode—the poetic mantle to descend upon later English poets.

In sweeping vistas, exultant mood, and sensuous evocation (all essentially romantic), this is probably the best true Pindaric ode in English. Tennyson considered the concluding stanzas among the most liquid in any language. Johnson, understandably, demurred.

"The Bard" derives from the article on Welsh poetry by Lewis Morris in Thomas Carte's *History of England* (1747). Vague Welsh tradition asserted that in conquering Wales (1276–84), Edward I had ordered the slaying of all Welsh bards because their tales of Celtic glory were the chief props of Welsh nationalism.

Amidst romantically wild Welsh scenery a bard, inspired by nature, addresses Edward I from a craggy peak before plunging to his death.

Section I bemoans the low estate of Wales in defeat

Section II predicts dire disasters for Edward I and his successors

Section III prophesies a glorious future for the Tudor line, a Welsh family.

Note that the bard is a seer, intuitively gifted, not the neoclassic product of classical study and aristocratic society. He speaks in grand exaltation and emotional fervor. The scenic backdrop is spectacular and dramatic. In spite of the conscious straining after rhetorical splendors, it is probably the best 18th-century attempt at poetic sublimity.

Poems (1768) contains two short poems on medieval Scandinavian material. These are the first significant English poems since the Norman Conquest to dwell upon the folklore and mythology of the primitive North. So lost to English tradition was knowledge of Thor, Wodin, Valkyries, Valhalla, etc., that Gray had to provide explanatory footnotes.

"The Fatal Sisters. An Ode" (*1761*) is not an ode but a witches' incantation in alternately riming four-line stanzas of iambic tetrameter. Source is a Latin translation of an 11th-century Icelandic poem in Bartholin's *De Causis Contemptae . . . Mortis* (Copenhagen, 1689). The weird sisters (northern equivalent of the Fates in Greek mythology) weave the web of bitter fortune with the battle-grim spirit of Anglo-Saxon verse. The poem's wild, "runic" savagery and primitive mystery reintroduce elements long missing in English literature. Johnson ironically branded it "the Wonderful Wonder of Wonders."

"The Descent of Odin. An Ode" (*1761*), from the same source as its predecessor, is a dialogue in iambic tetrameter couplets between the chief Norse deity, Odin or Wodin, and Hela, goddess of death, at the portals of Niflheimr, the underworld. The goddess predicts the *Götterdämmerung* (Twilight of the Gods), which will involve Balder (Apollo of the North) and Odin himself in destruction. Of this and the previous poem, Johnson declared: "These odes are marked by glittering accumulations of ungraceful ornaments; they strike, rather than please; the images are magnified by affection [i.e. affectation]; the language is laboured into harshness. The mind of the writer seems to work with unnatural violence. *Double, double, toil and trouble*. He has a kind of strutting dignity, and is tall by walking on tiptoe."

Gray's correspondence first appeared in the collected works (1775), edited by William Mason. Mason printed one hundred and thirty letters, many of them considerably altered from the original. Subsequent editions continued to augment the collection, until the Toynbee-Whibley edition of 1935 printed five hundred letters. The letters fall into these broad divisions:

1734–38 (undergraduate days), chiefly to Horace Walpole. These letters display a spirited youthful participation in Cambridge life and a bubbling humor unknown to the poetry. Already, however, Gray evinces the detachment and amused calm of the scholar.

1739–41 (the Grand Tour with Walpole until their quarrel), chiefly to Richard West and his mother. Unlike Walpole's parallel record, these letters reveal a rich mind constantly preoccupied with the literary and historical associations of places. Gray manifests an unprecedented interest in scenery, especially in the journey through the Grande Chartreuse.

1741–52 (the scholar in Cambridge and London), chiefly to Walpole, West (until his death in 1742), and Thomas Warton. This was the most poetically creative period of Gray's life, indicating a slow change from neoclassicism to the mingled harmonies of the "Elegy." Gray's world is not the fashionable whirl of Walpole but the realm of books. Learning and literature, however, are carried lightly, as the age disliked the pedantic bore.

1753–71 (the college don and tourist of Britain), to a widening list of correspondents. Though meager in literary production, these years witness his trend toward Romanticism in verse. A scholar re-creates the placid life of the university world, with increasing antiquarian interest in Welsh and Norse themes. The traveler shows a mounting fascination with landscape. Most famous is the *Journal* to the Lake Country, comprising six letters written to Thomas Warton, whose illness prevented him from accompanying Gray. Although the trip extended only from September 29 to October 15, 1769, the account is quite detailed. It is interesting to note that in the very year before Wordsworth's birth, the beauties of the Lake Country were well discovered and appreciated by an English poet. The sharply observed details, the eye for varied and transient effects, the emotional dwelling upon spectacular scenery, exceed anything in Gray's verse and emphasize a familiar 18th-century parodox: contemporary gentlemen might express themselves rather romantically in private communications while cleaving more closely to neoclassic tenets in public utterance.

William Collins (1721–1759). William Collins was a native of Chichester, Sussex, where his father, a wealthy hatter, was mayor of the city. After studying at Winchester School and Oxford (B.A. 1743), he attempted a literary career in London c. 1744 but encountered financial difficulties. His entire poetic career spanned just one decade from his first published work in 1739, while still a schoolboy, until his permanent mental derangement in 1749.

Odes on Several Descriptive and Allegorical Subjects (1746) contains twelve odes imitative of the Aeolian or Lesbian manner of Alcaeus, Anacreon, and Sappho. Though very close to the pure lyric, they are slightly more formal. Nonetheless, they reveal probably the greatest lyric talent of the century. Thomas Warton declared that these *"Odes* will be remembered while any taste for true poetry remains."

"Ode to Pity" (a4 a4 b3 c4 c4 b3) derives from Aristotle's theory of catharsis, the purgation of pity and terror, to explain the effect of tragedy. Collins praises Euripides and sees Otway as the last great tragic dramatist, but he hopes for subsequent English success in tragedy.

"Ode to Fear" mixes octosyllabic couplets with heroic quatrains in a rough approximation of the true Pindaric ode. Collins recaptures the spirit of Milton's "Il Penseroso" in praising Aeschylus and Sophocles, while also resurrecting the English fairy folk, unknown to the Augustans. He essays a "wild enthusiast heat" in contemplating the beauty of terror.

"Ode to Simplicity" (a3 a3 b5 c3 c3 b5) sounds like the early Keats. It seeks, not the Roman elegance which the Augustans called simplicity, but the Greek stripped outline and purity of tint.

"Ode on the Poetical Character" roughly approximates the true Pindaric ode. The most complex of his odes in thought and imagery, it symbolizes the poet in Spenser and Milton. Unlike the Augustans, Collins sees the poet as an inspired creator and imagination as the prime essential.

"Ode, Written in the Beginning of the Year, 1746" eulogizes in octosyllabic couplets the English soldiers killed in 1745 during the War of the Austrian Succession. Its quiet dignity and restraint of passion are touchingly eloquent and fundamentally classic. It is often called "How sleep the brave," from its opening.

"Ode to Evening" alternates decasyllabic and octosyllabic couplets. Except perhaps for some of Tennyson's pieces in *The Princess,* this is the greatest unrimed lyric in English. Skillful handling of vowels, onomatopoeia, and rhythm are effective even without rime. Instead of the pensive, general landscape of Gray, this is acute and perceptive vision much like that of Keats. Based on Milton's translation of the fifth ode of the first book of Horace, it matches Milton's purity of diction and imagery in a stanza of Milton's invention.

"The Passions, An Ode for Music" is a pseudo-Pindaric ode in the tradition of Dryden's "Alexander's Feast." As in Dryden's pattern, each passion is chanted in a measure fitted to it. Fear, Anger, Despair, and Jealousy each receive a rapid quatrain. Hope is celebrated in limpid lines interrupted by savage Revenge. The ode spreads out upon Melancholy and Joy, with their attendant throngs. The richness of imagery and the appropriate variety of movement have made this the poet's most popular piece.

"An Ode on the Popular Superstitions of the Highlands of Scotland, Considered as the Subject of Poetry" (c. *1749,* 1788), though a fragment at the onset of the poet's insanity, is Collins's longest poem. It is addressed to John Home, the Scots author of *Douglas.* Collins's own invention is the seventeen-line stanza of iambic pentameter ending with an alexandrine. This is the first significant attempt in English literature to tap the romantic elements of Scottish legend and landscape. The poem celebrates imaginative and emotional subjects in opposition to the rational as the proper theme of poetry. This is probably the outstanding 18th-century praise of "hard" primitivism, that is, of severe climatic conditions as breeding a virtuous and able people.

The Minor Poets of the New Trend

Contrary to expectation, the 18th-century English renewal of interest in the medieval period was not primarily the result of increased interest in medieval literature. Antiquarianism was its great impetus, originating in Renaissance figures like Cotton, Stow, and Camden, and strengthened in the age of Pope by many of the "Dunces" he ridiculed. The dominant factor in arousing the age's interest in medievalism was Gothic architecture, superbly represented by the great English cathedrals, and imaginatively evocative in ivy-covered ruins, picturesquely scattered throughout the island. Gothic ruins were a frequent prop in the poems of the "Graveyard School." The chief authors represented in this medieval revival were: Thomas Warton the Younger, William Mason, Richard Hurd, Thomas Percy, James Beattie, Thomas Tyrwhitt, and William Hayley.

The growing fad of medievalism could not be satisfied with the available literature. First, there was as yet comparatively little of English medieval literature in print. Second, the available material lacked the qualities sought for by the faddists—sentiment, "natural" bardic fervor, and rich coloration in tame and prettified form. The demand produced an extraordinary supply of artificial antiques, like the fake "Gothic" ruins constructed in 18th-century gardens. William Henry Ireland concocted forged Shakespearean plays, and Walpole pretended in the first edition that *The Castle of Otranto* was a translation from a medieval manuscript. The most famous hoaxers were the two poets James Macpherson and Thomas Chatterton, both of whose talents could much better have been employed on openly original pieces.

Within the 18th century, English taste performed an incredible and unique journey from the formal garden to untrammeled nature, from nature as a decorative ornament to nature the teacher of truth to the open heart. The pilgrimage was gradual, even imperceptible, in the age itself. Its mounting intensity is manifested in the major poets (Gray and Collins) and in virtually all the verse discussed in this section; however, the most notable of the nature poets of this period is Joseph Warton.

The latter half of the 18th century was the most extensive and impressive age of English hymnologists, dominated by the Wesleys and Cowper. Many lesser hymn writers also contributed, such as Augustus Toplady with "Rock of Ages" (rimed seven-syllable couplets, 1776), and Edward Perronet with "All Hail the Power of Jesus' Name" (C.M., 1780). But the most extraordinary representative of religious "enthusiasm" in the period was Christopher Smart.

Thomas Warton the Younger (1728–1790). Thomas Warton bore the name of his father, an Oxford don, cleric, and poet. He was born at Basingstoke, Hampshire, six years after his brother Joseph. The younger Warton rose to become an Oxford professor of poetry (1757–67) and of history (1785–90). In 1785 he became poet laureate.

"The Pleasures of Melancholy" (*1745,* 1747), in blank verse, enjoys the sensitivity of melancholia while meditating upon "yon ruin'd abbey's moss-grown piles" and "Gothic vaults." It weds "Graveyard School" to a college professor's pensive contemplation of past glories.

Observations on the Faerie Queene of Spenser (1754) first demonstrates the defects of Spenser's work by neoclassic tenets (i.e. ignoring "the rules," and the subordinate role of Arthur), but then urges readers to judge Spenser on a historical basis, accepting relative standards of literary judgment. In carefully demonstrating how Spenser arose from contemporary influences, Warton considerably expanded the dimension of literary appreciation. Seeking to overcome prejudice against medieval romances, Warton insisted that with "fictions and fabling they invigorated the imagination and stored the fancy with those sublime images which true poetry delights to display."

History of English Poetry (I, 1774; II, 1778; III, 1781) is the momentous pioneer in the historical study of English literature. In all English scholarship its single-handed achievement is matched only by Johnson in his dictionary. Warton started with the 13th century and carried through to the 16th. Although he had a number of sources —antiquarians and the like—he was the first to collect and organize all the materials (chronicles, ballads, metrical romances, Goliardic verse, and so on), few of which were known even to the most literarily knowledgeable of the 18th century. He had no predecessors worthy of mention in the actual writing of literary history. Warton presented themes, sources, contemporary influences, and lengthy quotations. Errors are frequent and emphases are strange (Lydgate receives more attention than either Spenser or Shakespeare), but, though now completely superseded, it was the essential ground-breaking work that had to be done.

Poems (1777) contains some of the best sonnets between Milton and Wordsworth and heralds the Sonnet Revival. "Written in a Blank Leaf of Dugdale's Monasticon" is charged with the authentic antiquarian spirit, "Written at Stonehenge" muses solemnly upon the ancient monument, and "To the River Lodon" is a graceful nature tribute.

"The Grave of King Arthur" (1777), in octosyllabic couplets that occasionally suggest the narrative gallop of Scott, tells the legend of Henry II unearthing the remains of Arthur at Glastonbury.

"Verses on Sir Joshua Reynolds's Painted Window at New College, Oxford" (1782) gracefully praises in heroic couplets the work of a fellow member of "The Club." In claiming to renounce his Gothic taste, however, Warton actually reveals his strong emotional attachment to medievalism.

William Mason (1724–1797). Rector at Aston, Yorkshire, from 1754, William Mason is chiefly remembered as Gray's editor and biographer. His *Life and Letters of Gray* (1774) tentatively strove to reveal the poet through his writings and speech, thus providing the cue to Boswell's biography of Johnson. Mason is a counter-current of the times. His earlier works reflect romantic leanings at mid-century. *Caractacus* (1759), dealing with the ancient Britons, was actually staged, although it is more a dramatic poem than a play. In this highly popular patriotic piece, Mason strove to unite "Attic art with Shakespeare's fire." His later works display a return to neoclassic principles. *The English Garden* (1772–81) is typical didacticism. *An Heroic Epistle to Sir William Chambers* (1773), in heroic couplets, is a witty satire against the taste for orientalism.

Richard Hurd (1720–1808). A native of Congreve, Staffordshire, Richard Hurd was educated at Cambridge. Gray and Mason were his good friends; Warburton, Pope's editor, was his patron. Hurd rose through ecclesiastical ranks to become bishop of Lichfield and Coventry, 1775–81; in the latter year he was transferred to Worcester. He acted as preceptor of the Prince of Wales and the Duke of York. Asserted Johnson to Boswell: "Hurd, sir, is a man whose acquaintance is a valuable acquisition," and Gibbon praised "the critical spirit of Hurd" in his autobiography.

Letters on Chivalry and Romance (1762) consists of twelve short letters attempting to restore critical approval of "a world of fine fabling." He compares the society that gave rise to the medieval romances with the ancient Greek society that produced the *Iliad,* and finds great similarities. However, he considers that the medieval themes of chivalry and courtesy and the eclectic supernatural tradition accumulated by the Middle Ages provided a richer background for poetry than Homer's world. No poet of the stature of Homer lived in the Middle Ages, however; the best was Spenser, who lived after the richest poetic materials of the medieval period were outdated. Hurd agrees with Thomas Warton in calling for a judgment of *The Faerie Queene* and "Gothic" pieces upon their own standards rather than upon the critical tenets of the ancients.

Hurd protests that some previous critics had narrowly applied the neoclassic doctrine of imitating Nature to "the known and experienced course of affairs in the world," whereas for a true poet "experience has less to do than consistent imagination." Hurd lent impetus to the broadened study and appreciation of older English literature.

Thomas Percy (1729–1811). Son of a Bridgnorth grocer, Thomas Percy graduated from Christ Church, Oxford, in 1750. He rose in the Anglican Church to be royal chaplain in 1769 and bishop of Dromore, Ireland, from 1782. A minor versifier himself, he was passionately interested in all poetry, providing it was strange and exotic. Percy published translations, at second-hand, from Chinese and Icelandic.

Reliques of Ancient English Poetry (1765) is one of the many landmarks which are thought of as the start of the Romantic Movement. While visiting a friend, Humphrey Pitt of Shifnal, Shropshire, c. 1760 Percy found an early 17th-century folio manuscript "lying dirty on the floor . . . being used by the maids to light the fire." The unknown writer of the manuscript had copied down 192 poems, chiefly popular medieval ballads. Exact reprinting of this "Percy ms." did not occur until 1867–68. The bishop's editing in 1765 actually utilized only about a quarter of the manuscript, though admittedly the most successful ballads, a total of 111 from various sources. Percy's relentless doctoring of the ballads was stigmatized by the scholar Joseph Ritson, who claimed "scarcely one single poem, song, or ballad, fairly or honestly printed."

Percy felt obligated to make extensive (and unacknowledged) alterations in the original text because of: (1) the frequent bawdry; (2) frequent metrical irregularity; (3) the fragmentary character of some ballads; (4) occasional brevity sometimes to the point of obscurity; (5) the roughness and austerity of many ballads. He considered the changes justified because every such editor (e.g. Ramsay) was doing it and because critical opinion (e.g. from his friend Shenstone) approved.

Percy's alterations are sometimes in the authentic ballad style but occasionally appear also in a grotesquely inappropriate rococo decoration. While wholly questionable as a good editor, Percy was wholly right in gauging his era. The current seekers for medieval flavor desired exactly the charming, sentimentalized, and poetically regular pieces that he printed. Percy produced at the right time the "natural" poetry of the people with an air of the marvelous and exciting. The whining contemporary street ballads had caused literary figures to brand ballad poetry as worthless. Now Percy had opened up a fresh and wonderful world. All literateurs of the time (with the exception of Johnson) and of the next generation were profoundly affected by Percy's collection. Even William Cowper, in a letter of 1783, stated of the ballad genre that "if graver matters had not called me another way, I should have addicted myself to it more than to any other." In "Essay Supplemental to the Preface," Wordsworth said of Percy's work: "For our own country its poetry has been absolutely redeemed by it. I do not think that there is an able writer of verse today who would not be proud to acknowledge his obligation to 'The Reliques.'" The contemporary German poets, especially Bürger, were wildly enthusiastic about the work.

James Beattie (1735–1803). James Beattie was born in Laurencekirk, Kincardineshire, Scotland. As a professor of moral philosophy and logic at Marischal College, Aberdeen, he fervently opposed the concepts of Hume. Politically and religiously orthodox, he received the applause of Johnson and a pension from George III.

The Minstrel (I, 1771; II, 1774) was inspired by Percy's characterization of the medieval minstrels in his introduction to the *Reliques*. Beattie's is the first work in English that might properly be titled "The Growth of a Poet's Mind," thus anticipating Wordsworth's *Prelude*. In Book I the young Scottish minstrel, in solitude amidst natural splendors, is educated by the sounds and shapes impressed upon his mind and heart. He is haunted by cloud and forest and waterfall. He sees the fairies, and scans the "Gothic" fables and romances. In Book II the ideas imbibed from the font of nature itself are oratorically inculcated by an aged hermit encountered by the youth in the woods. Dominant is the concept of solitude, the exact opposite of the neoclassic gregariousness. Already in Beattie the idea of solitude induces social, moral, religious, psychological, educational, and political associations that will keynote much of later Romanticism. Implicit is the assumption that man is naturally good, and that evil arises from society's pressures upon the individual. The rhetoric of the second book induced Byron to use the Spenserian stanza in *Childe Harold's Pilgrimage*. Beattie is not as successful in this stanza as Thomson had been, but he gave it considerable renewed vigor.

Thomas Tyrwhitt (tír-it) (1730–1786). A native of London, Thomas Tyrwhitt abandoned his academic career at Oxford to become clerk of the House of Commons in 1762. Resigning his clerkship in

1768, he devoted the rest of his life to literary scholarship, and proved to be the greatest English medievalist of his era.

The essay to his edition of Chaucer's *Canterbury Tales* (1775–78) is probably the most important single piece of scholarship in English. From the beginnings of Modern English in the late 15th century until Tyrwhitt's essay, the versification of Chaucer was wholly misunderstood since pronunciation had radically altered. Dryden had appreciated the vivacity and poetic power of Chaucer but deemed him a writer of crude doggerel verse. Tyrwhitt correctly demonstrated Chaucer's meticulous versifying, for the first time revealing to the modern world the full craftsmanship and sophistication of "the father of English poetry."

William Hayley (1745–1820). A native of Chichester, William Hayley was a country gentleman with a meager talent in verse but an intense desire to cultivate poets. He was the first biographer of Cowper and was also a friend of Southey. Blake worked at engraving and illustration for Hayley at Felpham, fleeing thence after a violent and memorable quarrel.

An Essay on Epic Poetry (1782) contains a *terza rima* translation of the first three cantos of Dante's *Inferno,* the first sizable translation of Dante into English. The first full translation of the *Divina Commedia* into English was Henry Boyd's in 1802. The first notable translation of Dante was by H. F. Cary in 1814.

James Macpherson (1736–1796). While a schoolmaster in his native Ruthven, Inverness-shire, Scotland, James Macpherson showed John Home some alleged Gaelic poems with his translations. The success of Macpherson's "translations" resulted in his appointment as the secretary to the governor of Florida in 1764. In 1779 he became agent to Mohammed Ali, Nabob of Arcot. From 1780 until his death he was a member of Parliament.

Poems of Ossian (1773) was Macpherson's definitive collection of "translations" from the Gaelic published in portions since 1760. The works claim to be translations from the 3rd-century Ossian (or Oisin), an Irish bard whom Macpherson patriotically made a Scot.

Ossian, blind like Homer, is son of the Scottish king Fingal, and father of young Oscar. Fingal successively defeats the Romans, the Vikings, and the Irish. Ossian laments the death of the slain Oscar and numerous other valiant fighters and—eventually—the magnanimous Fingal. Indistinguishable are the crowds of melodiously named warriors, sentimental princesses, and vague supernatural spirits.

The enormous contemporary popularity of the Ossianic pieces arose from:

(1) Cadenced prose, semi-biblical in sound, "primitive," the exciting rhythms of a supposititious antiquity. Nothing could be further in verse from Pope's heroic couplets.

(2) "Northern melancholy," misty and vague.

(3) Exaltation of mood.

(4) Melodious, vowel-haunted names of persons and places.

(5) The "natural" lyric bard, product of solitude and "elemental" emotions.

Modern readers find the Ossianic poems monotonously repetitive. All the characters talk alike, and the meager action is tedious and disconnected. Most of the so-called poems are dithyrambic laments. Modern Celtic scholars have dismissed the vast controversy over the works that burdened late 18th-century presses. No such Gaelic epics as Macpherson claimed are known to have existed, and the genuine extant material quite discredits him. Plagiarism is evident; Macpherson, tongue-in-cheek, actually calls attention to the parallels of the "Address to the Sun" in his *Carthon* to Satan's apostrophe to the sun in *Paradise Lost*. Johnson pooh-poohed *Ossian* by claiming that many men, many women, and many children could have written it. Hume, Gibbon, Gray, and other intellectuals were dubious, especially as no authentic originals could be produced. Macpherson had meager hints from actual Celtic literature, but the Ossianic poems are essentially products of his imagination. Wordsworth rightfully asserted: "The Phantom was begotten by the snug embrace of an impudent Highlander upon a cloud of tradition."

But in overwhelming numbers, England and Europe echoed the adoration of Ossian. In France, Chateaubriand, Lamartine, and Napoleon himself were entranced. In *Werther* (1774), Goethe has his hero loudly proclaim: "Ossian has dispossessed Homer in my heart." Critics still regret the potent influence of Ossian upon Blake. Hazlitt was to list as the four greatest poetic works of all time—Homer, the Bible, Dante, and Ossian.

Thomas Chatterton (1752–1770). Thomas Chatterton from his seventh year pored over the antiquities in his native Bristol. Although openly from his own pen he wrote essentially neoclassic squibs, political essays after Junius, satires, odes, and even a burlesque opera, his medieval forgeries engaged the interest of his age and succeeding generations. Hopeful of a literary career, he came to London in 1770 but fell into dire poverty, even starvation, because of the lack of interest on the part of the literary luminaries. It is thought that he committed suicide by swallowing arsenic in his seventeenth year. Unless we accept Pope's doubtful claims of precocity, no other poet in English ever matched Chatterton's achievement in such tender years, and the Romantics elevated him to heroic martyrdom. He is "the marvellous boy" in Wordsworth's "Resolution and Independence," and, with Keats, he enjoys the company of the immortals in Shelley's *Adonais*.

Poems Supposed to Have Been Written at Bristol by Thomas Rowley and Others in the 15th Century (1777) was declared a forgery by Tyrwhitt, the editor, but some credence in its authenticity lingered until conclusively dispelled by W. W. Skeat in 1871. Chatterton seized upon the genuine historical character William Canynge, a famous mayor of Bristol in the early 15th century. Supposedly patronized by Canynge was the wholly fictitious character Thomas Rowley, the mayor's confessor and gifted poet. Rowley supposedly wrote all types of poetry, in a bewildering variety of stanzas, especially commemorating personages in English and Bristol history from the Battle of Hastings through the age of Canynge.

The qualities that the age sought for in medievalism are well represented—lyricism, external nature, intuitive benevolence, sentiment, the sense of wonder and color, and the absence of the rough or grotesque. The medieval trappings are largely from the atmosphere of St. Mary Redcliffe, with additional flavor from the old documents in the muniment room of that cathedral. The influence of Macpherson and the Percy collection is relatively meager. Spenser is the real master of Chatterton, who obviously modeled his tapestry-like pictures and stanzaic patterns upon *The Faerie Queene*. Apparently Chatterton composed in his own vein and then "antiqued" the poems, partly with Middle English vocabulary from John Kersey's *Dictionarium Anglo-Britannicum* (1708) and Nathan Bailey's *Universal Etymological Dictionary* (1737), and partly with purely imaginative spelling (*its* in "Lyfe and all yttes goode I scorne" was non-existent in the 15th century). Except for an occasional archaic word, the poems can be read as modern English (disregarding the weird spelling), and they display a remarkable lyric talent.

Joseph Warton (1722–1800). Older brother of Thomas Warton the Younger, Joseph Warton was born in Dunsford, Surrey. Entering the church in 1743, he rose to become headmaster of Winchester School (1766–93). He was an active member of "The Club." Warton was a literary Whig rather than revolutionist. He disliked Gothic architecture, frequently wrote in heroic couplets, and employed the conventional forms of satire and elegy. His influence, however, was opposed to many neoclassic principles.

The Enthusiast: or, The Lover of Nature (1744), in blank verse, argues the superiority of wild scenery to all forms of human art. Warton also expounds a soft primitivism, love of the exotic, and the pleasures of melancholy. The title itself defies the neoclassic aversion to "enthusiasm." Such poetry of sensibility would greatly increase in quantity through the rest of the century.

Essay on the Genius and Writings of Pope (I, 1756; II, 1782), though praising Pope, showed his limitations in comparison to other poets Warton felt were superior. Warton asserted that Pope was devoid of the supreme poetic quality, the "glowing imagination" that inspired "sublime and pathetic" (i.e. emotional) utterance capable of transporting the reader. Spenser, Shakespeare, and Milton he elevates as the truly great poets. Warton minimizes the rules, calls for "true and minute representations of Nature," advocates themes from "Druidical times and the traditions of old bards." Like Hurd and his own brother, he calls for relativity of taste and judgment. Significantly, he urges critics to evaluate first the emotional appeal of a poem.

Christopher Smart (1722–1771). Born at Shipbourne, Kent, Christopher Smart was educated at Pembroke Hall, Cambridge. He turned to hack writing but was mentally disturbed by religious mania to the point of insanity. During lucid moments of his confinement (1756–58) he wrote his masterpiece *A Song to David*. His other work is frequently neoclassic in complexion—fables, satires, odes, and a complete translation of Horace (1756).

A Song to David (1763), in six-line stanzas, was omitted from later 18th-century collections of his verse, presumably as the indubitable product of insanity. It was resurrected almost a century later, to be ecstatically hailed by Rossetti and Browning. Its source is 1 and 2 Samuel and 1 Kings. Smart builds a series of tributes: the virtues of David, the bounties of Nature, the seven pillars of the temple, abjurations of moral conduct, adoration of God's goodness, and a culminating "five degrees" from sweetness to glory. Unique to 18th-century literature until Blake (and possibly Ossian) is the ecstatic incantation of bardic fire. Smart chants with growing fervor which sometimes turns to incoherent exultation. The profusion of images and allusions is tied together not so much by logical organization as by emotional intensity.

Jubilate Agno ("Rejoice in the Lamb") (1939) strangely resembles Blake's writings, although no influence can be established. Smart calls upon all creation to unite in the worship of God. With a particularity and exhaustiveness virtually without precedent, he chants of the divine glory as manifested even in the most trivial commonplaces of life (as in the movements of his cat, Jeoffry). The form is free verse, its rhythms following the surging beat felt by the poet and carried for many lines by constant repetition, resembling occasionally the work of Walt Whitman.

New Emphases in the Theory of History

The neoclassic concern lay with the here and the now. In theorizing about history, the neoclassicist accepted human experience as static or perhaps cyclic (as did Goldsmith). Opposing theories moved toward Romanticism. The primitivistic concept sees history as a steady decline from ancient glory. Men of earlier eras are therefore viewed as wiser and nobler than today's humanity, and savages now at a simpler level of culture are considered superior to civilized men. This is an old—even ancient—idea, but it becomes Romantic when it is surcharged with emotion, rebellion against the status quo, and associated with a complex of related ideas such as nature, freedom, simplicity, and anti-intellectualism. Primitivism is expounded in numerous works of the 18th century, especially from Thomson on. A notable proponent of the primitivistic concept discussed here is James Burnett, Lord Monboddo.

Equally opposed to the static or cyclic theory of history is the idea of progress, which interprets history as a steady ascent from the cave man to the civilization of today, with the expectation of continuing development ever upward. This theory is actually very recent, apparently originating in the 17th-century quarrel of the modern versus the ancient writers and never vigorously advocated in our culture until the 18th century. Earlier the primitivistic concept, accentuated by the Christian doctrines of the Fall of Man, original sin, and the necessity of eschewing this world in favor of the next, had dominated. The 18th-century pride in scientific achievement, the age's orderly secular society, and especially the mounting Industrial Revolution created conditions fostering the idea of progress. As the century draws to a close, a rising crescendo of voices will assert this belief. Perhaps the most notable of them was that extraordinary genius Joseph Priestley.

James Burnett, Lord Monboddo (1714–1799). A Scottish judge, Lord Monboddo became sheriff of Kincardineshire in 1764 and an ordinary lord of session in 1767. A pioneer theorist of anthropology, he propounded hypotheses then regarded as highly eccentric, which evoked the disgust of Johnson.

Of the Origin and Progress of Language (six volumes, 1773–92) contemplated the ideal existence of the South Seas, "where the inhabitants live without toil or labor upon the bounty of nature." Monboddo saw civilization as fulfillment of man's social needs and sought to observe in primitive societies the embryonic patterns of higher cultures. He conceived of man as a species of animal and claimed the orangutan as a cousin of man. The derision greeting his theory resulted in the amusing Sir Oran Haut-Ton of the novelist Thomas Peacock.

Joseph Priestley (1733–1804). Son of a cloth-dresser in Fieldhead, Yorkshire, Joseph Priestley was educated at a dissenters' academy in Daventry. As previous references in this chapter indicate, he represented the survival of the universal scholar of the Renaissance into the 18th century. In addition to his distinguished researches in chemistry, he was a Unitarian clergyman and a commentator on an astounding variety of subjects. Bentham lifted from Priestley's *Essay on the First Principles of Government* (1768) the idea of morality seeking "the greatest happiness of the greatest number." In 1785 public authorities ordered the burning of Priestley's *History of the Corruption of Christianity* (1782). His sympathies with the French Revolution (he had been made an honorary citizen of the French Republic) caused a Birmingham mob in 1791 to destroy his house and possessions. Priestley continued his work in America after 1794, dying in Northumberland, Pennsylvania.

Lectures on History (1768) claims that with scientific advancement and the division of labor, "nature, including both its materials and its laws, will be more at our command; men will make their situation in this world abundantly more easy and comfortable; they will probably prolong their existence in it and will grow daily more happy. . . . Thus, whatever was the beginning of this world, the end will be glorious and paradisiacal beyond what our imagination can now conceive." Priestly sees progress made possible even by the Dark Ages, which broke up a dying culture and thereby permitted the greater advances of modern times.

Chapter 4

The Eighteenth-Century Novel (1700–1800)

THE DEVELOPMENT OF THE ENGLISH NOVEL

Although the English novel was really defined in the 18th century, it had its roots in earlier times. The Elizabethans had established prose fiction with the racy popular accounts of Nashe and Deloney, and the aristocratic romances of Lyly and Sidney. Yet both of these English strains died out in the earlier 17th century. The middle class, gripped by Puritanism, ignored practically all fiction—especially pleasurable fiction—and the Jacobean courtiers devoted themselves to drama and masque. With the post-Elizabethan decline, France once again asserted its traditional dominance. In England, especially under Charles I and his French queen, Henrietta, everything French was the rage; in reading matter the popular choice, therefore, was the voluminous French "heroic romance" written by Georges and Madeleine de Scudéry, Calprenède, Gomberville, and many more. These "heroic romances" were vast baroque narratives about thinly disguised contemporaries, always acting nobly and endlessly speaking high-flown sentiment. The settings, in the Orient or in classic antiquity, made no attempt at historical accuracy. Spectacular shipwrecks, disguises, surprise reappearances, and similar bravura effects constituted the plotting. English courtiers snobbishly prided themselves on reading these "heroic romances" in the original French, but many were translated into English for the benefit of would-be snobs deficient in French. It was thus inevitable that original novels in English would copy the French "heroic romances." The earliest known example is the anonymous *Cloria and*

Narcissus or, The Royal Romance (1653), and the indefatigable Roger Boyle, Earl of Orrery, produced *Parthenissa* in the next year. The indebtedness of the already discussed English heroic drama to such heroic romances is obvious.

Paul Scarron, the French novelist and playwright, restored the picaresque novel in *Le Roman Comique* (1651–57); also popular in contemporary Paris were *chroniques scandaleuses,* shockers about reputed immorality in high social circles. Fusing the two was *The English Rogue, Described in the Life of Mariton Lartoon,* by Richard Head; although the work appeared in 1665, well into the reign of the Merry Monarch, the censors banned the book because of its indecencies. Booksellers described the spate of fiction works as "novels" (from the older "novella") to contrast them with the interminable "romances." The most notable of the 17th-century prose fictionists, Mrs. Aphra Behn, has already been discussed in Chapter 1. Also the background information for this chapter has been given in the two preceding chapters.

Prose fiction has three principal points of emphasis, each of which may express itself as a long or a short narrative:

EMPHASIS	LONG NARRATIVE	SHORT NARRATIVE
1. Character	Novel	Short story
2. Plot	Romance	Anecdote
3. Abstract theme	Allegory	Fable or parable

Allegorical works, such as *Pilgrim's Progress* and *Gulliver's Travels* whose primary purpose has been inculcation of propaganda rather than fictional, have been discussed in their appropriate chapters. The romance and the novel will be considered together here, for it is frequently difficult to assign a work unquestionably to one category or the other. The primary interest of the romance lies essentially in spectacular and exciting events designed chiefly to divert and entertain. The novel, on the other hand, arises from a desire to depict and interpret human character, and the reader is not merely entertained but is also aided in a deeper perception of life's problems. Properly speaking, the novel is not a picture of the world we might wish for but a scrutiny of what the honest novelist conceives the true nature of the world to be. Like all artistic literature, then, all fiction is an imagined view of life, selecting only those materials from experience that will most effectively give a structured meaning to human life.

The initial form of extended narrative in Western literature was the poetic epic, and it continued unchallenged roughly from the Fall of Rome until the 12th century. From the 12th century through the Renaissance the long narrative took the form of the medieval romance, at first in verse, later in prose. From the late Renaissance emerged the prose novel, which later in the 18th century took the form that it has fundamentally maintained to the present.

The English novel, one of the most impressive accomplishments of English literature, stands apart from the allegory and romance in its vigorous attempt at verisimilitude, and in English literature the novel has been strongly associated—at least until recent generations—with the middle class, their pragmatism and their morality. During the 18th century the novel went through considerable experimentation largely because it was not yet an accepted literary genre by neoclassic standards. It must be remembered that to the 18th century the great literary forms were the epic and the tragic drama; thus unfettered by established conventions, the 18th-century novel was free to develop much as its authors pleased, and consequently it did so with a degree of raffishness and uncertainty. Characteristic of a yet unformed genre, its practitioners frequently tried to offer it as what it was not in essence: Defoe tried to masquerade fiction as fact, Richardson staked his achievement upon moral preaching, and Sterne cavorted willfully. Part of this uncertain quality of 18th-century novels arose from their incredibly mixed ancestry of form, an examination of which is given below.

(1) The primary impulse of the novel came from the Spanish picaresque tales, apparently originating with *Lazarillo de Tormes* (1554). These stories were initially burlesques of the courtly romance, substituting a low scoundrel for the questing knight. Largely composed of a string of episodes, these accounts were mainly held together by the racy personality of the central figure, and the atmosphere of actual tangible things and genuine earthy experience was pervasive. Also, Cervantes' *Don Quixote,* which was indebted to the picaresque tradition too, exercised great influence on the English novelists.

(2) As mentioned before, through much of the 17th century the fashionable English aristocrats were addicted to the French prose romance from the Scudérys and others. Although inflated and artificial, these romances had contemporary settings and frequently disguised references to well-known persons.

(3) The Italian *novelle* probably started as factual anecdotes but developed through imaginative storytellers into such notable collec-

tions as Boccaccio's *Decameron* (c. 1350). These accounts treated of contemporary life without the grandiose style and idealized plots of medieval romance, but their subjects were generally about aristocratic personages. Such pieces had tremendous influence upon Renaissance English drama, but the English translated more than they imitated these works. However, Gascoigne came close to fathering the English novel in his *Adventures of Master F. J.,* which was influenced by the *novelle.*

(4) The pastoral romance from Hellenistic Greeks such as Apuleius, *Golden Ass* (2nd century), with Italian and Spanish imitations in the Renaissance, stimulated the artificialities of Lyly and Sidney. From other Greeks of that age came the adventure romance, such as the *Ethiopian History* of Heliodorus, and the romance of love, such as *Daphnis and Chloe,* by Longus. Greene and Lodge in the Renaissance were indebted to the above works. Such precursors of the novel at least created an audience for extended prose narrative.

(5) Within the English tradition were the fictions of Malory and Mandeville, generating a taste for recitals of adventurous action. Though often read as factual accounts, they were stimuli to imaginary narratives of comparable scope.

(6) The domestic literature of roguery, in Greene and Dekker of the Renaissance and later in the 17th century from Tom Brown and Ned Ward, strengthened the picaresque influence and provided a bouncy, vivacious narrative of low life.

(7) Thomas Deloney with his bourgeois fictions would probably be termed the originator of the novel if his tradition had been maintained.

(8) Though the sketches of "characters" by Sir Thomas Overbury and John Earle belong with the essay rather than with the novel, their astute appraisals of personalities provide a stimulus for the revelation of character in the later novel.

(9) The English essay, as in the Sir Roger de Coverley papers from *The Spectator,* often provided fictionalized narratives that needed only a plot tightening to approach the short story or novel.

(10) Allegories such as *Pilgrim's Progress* provided fiction with a compelling seriousness it had previously lacked and also offered an imaginative ingenuity and flashes of realism.

(11) Lesser domestic sources of fiction were the jest books and chapbooks of unprofessional literateurs, which perpetuated the story-telling faculties of the people which Chaucer had employed so well, or else vulgarized the tales of chivalric romance. Biographies such as

Walton's *Lives* also offered models for imaginary accounts. The "foreign visitor" genre often came close to becoming a novel.

At the beginning of the 18th century the ingredients were all available for the true novel. All the familiar types had appeared in embryo —love and adventure romances, domestic and bourgeois tales, stories of horror and the underworld. But plots were too often incoherent or improbable, backgrounds were vague or sporadic, and psychological characterization was meager or spotty. To form the true novel, writers would have to produce a unified and plausible plot structure, sharply individualized and believable characters, and especially a pervasive illusion of reality. The social conditions of the 18th century provided the atmosphere, even the compulsion, to achieve these qualities.

(1) The novel provides the literary medium for a bourgeois society. The 18th century saw a vastly increased reading public, chiefly of the middle class. Practical and down-to-earth, this class wanted to read about people it could recognize from its own observations and described in the language it employed. It preferred its stories to end with financial and domestic rewards, its own clear-cut goals in life.

(2) The novel reveals modern social complexity and group relationships. Romances and fairytales still offer escapism, but modern man cannot see in them a picture of the veritable world in which he lives. With the 18th century came an expansion of cities, a greater mobility of population, an increase in trade, and a greater individual and social self-consciousness; hence the average man met more people than ever before and realized as never before the interdependence of society. The novel essentially undertook the task of helping mankind understand the position of the individual in the larger social organism.

(3) The novel is a unified picture of man and society. The 18th century was the great era of intellectual analysis and synthesis, the great age of systematizing. From its 18th-century origin, the novel still maintains today its quality as the solid creation of an authentic world in plot, background, and atmosphere.

(4) The novel is a rationalistic examination of human personality. Bacon, Hobbes, Locke, and other thinkers sought to dissect the nature of man, and the faithful accumulation of details together with the portraying of nuances of action and reaction by the 18th-century novelists make the novel the literary counterpart of the scientific rationalism potent in the age.

(5) The novel is essentially addressed in the second person, to the reader. Lyricism is the first person, and drama is the third person,

with actors enacting roles for spectators in the mass to contemplate. The novel, however, has the conversational, personal appeal that the 18th century politely cultivated. Novelists of today have got over the "dear reader" approach, but they have nonetheless inherited the 18th-century manner of the novel, balanced between the *I* of lyricism and the *he* of drama.

(6) The epic of antiquity and the medieval period recounted essentially collective experience and universally shared concepts. In such ages the individual had minimal decisions to make on the major issues of his belief and conduct. The modern man, however, must be his own hero and bear his own burdens. The novel had begun to emerge in eras of similar stress, such as Hellenistic Greece; and from the Renaissance to the 18th century it was groping for form as society shifted from a "closed" to an "open" condition. Experience in the 18th century clearly indicated that men of the age had to fend for themselves and strive each for his own stability. The novel consequently has been the vehicle for intensely individual encounters with life: one man's search for love and happiness, one man's physical career in a competitive society, one man's pilgrimage of the spirit. The impossibility of creating the one "myth" for 18th-century culture doomed to futility the many attempts in the age to write epics, and so the novel was developed to fill the void. *Beowulf* as an epic quintessentialized the early Anglo-Saxon period, but the reader of the modern narrative must search the English novelists from Samuel Richardson to Elizabeth Bowen, from Henry Fielding to Joyce Cary, from Laurence Sterne to Evelyn Waugh, only to find the essence of modern English life still tantalizingly elusive. There are almost as many great epics as there are epochs of the past. There are as many great modern novels as the novelists can write.

MAJOR EIGHTEENTH-CENTURY NOVELISTS

While the following novelists differ quite radically one from the other, it was their numerous and excellent works that chiefly gave shape and substance to the 18th-century novel. The authors discussed later in this chapter developed special genres of the novel, and hence are treated according to their categories. The major novelists demonstrate, even in all their variety, those qualities considered characteristic of the 18th-century novel.

Daniel Defoe (c. 1659–1731). Daniel Defoe, whose non-fiction was discussed in Chapter 2, may be termed the founder of the modern English novel in his establishment of: (1) a dominant unifying theme with serious thesis; (2) convincing realism by first-person narrative carried to the virtual limit of journalistic reporting; and (3) middle-class viewpoint. There may be some doubt that his fiction was truly novelistic, for the characterization smacks of journalistic over-simplification and displays no genuine development, and much of his fiction is perhaps better classified as romance because of its headlong plunge from one melodramatic situation into another. It is difficult in Defoe to distinguish between fictionalized journalism and journalistic fiction; he presented all his narratives as autobiographical fact and seems to have stumbled by accident in his fifty-ninth year upon the story that would insure his lasting fame.

The Life and Strange Surprising Adventures of Robinson Crusoe, of York, Mariner (1719) was suggested by the four-and-a-half-year marooning (1704–09) of Alexander Selkirk upon Juan Fernández Island from the ship of William Dampier.

Captured at sea by corsairs, Crusoe is wrecked off the South American coast on a desert island. Ingenious and resolute, he builds himself living quarters, cultivates food, and salvages some useful items from the shipwreck. After eighteen lonely years he finds a human footprint in the sand and evidence of cannibal visits. In the twenty-fourth year of his enforced isolation he rescues a victim of the cannibals and names him Friday. The native proves an honest and faithful servant until the two are rescued by an English vessel in the twenty-eighth year of Crusoe's island residence.

The universal appeal of the book springs from the struggle of a lone individual to survive amidst hostile surroundings. Crusoe is the epitome of middle-class English virtues—industrious, practical, pious, and shrewd. Selkirk almost became a savage in four years, but Crusoe is completely triumphant over fate and surroundings for twenty-eight years. This is all rather incredible, and a modern version of the Crusoe story, *The Spear in the Sand* (1946), by Raoul Faure, pictures the breakdown of a civilized man cast completely away from the society of his fellows. Crusoe, however, is the idealization of middle-class solid endurance. Wholly unimaginative, Crusoe stoically applied himself to his immediate problems; he never dreamed, never worried (except at the footprint), and was wholly untroubled by sex. Gorky termed the book "The Bible of the unconquerable." Rousseau considered the work "the finest of treatises on education according to nature."

The impressiveness of the book lies in its detailed realism. Defoe does not merely say that Crusoe fabricated a sieve or a thatched roof; he minutely relates each deliberate step by his patient, self-reliant hero. The reader was indeed induced to believe the prefatory statement: "a just history of fact; neither is there any appearance of fiction in it."

The world has justifiably ignored the sequels by Defoe. *The Farther Adventures of Robinson Crusoe,* rushed into print four months later, bears Crusoe back to his island for a transient call, during which Friday is lost in a canoe battle with natives. Then the hero floats about the East Indies, China, and Siberia. The thrill of the first volume has petered out into a banal yarn of travel episodes. *The Serious Reflections of Robinson Crusoe* (1720) is plotless moralizing that fell flat.

The Memoirs of a Cavalier (1720) sounds so authentic that historians soberly referred to it until it was proved a fiction from Defoe's pen. The book presents Defoe's one gentleman hero.

Colonel Andrew Newport, an English gentleman adventurer, joins the Catholic forces at Vienna in the Thirty Years' War and is present when Tilly storms Magdeburg. Next he serves under the Protestant leader Gustavus Adolphus until the Swedish monarch dies at Lützen in 1632. Back in England, he fights in the Bishops' War against the Scots and in the English Civil War against the parliamentarians at Edgehill and Naseby.

In *The Outline of History,* H. G. Wells states that Defoe's account of the destruction of Magdeburg "will give the reader a far better idea of the warfare of this time than any formal history." The matter-of-fact tone renders especially convincing the colorful scenes of battles and skirmishes. Winston Churchill acknowledges that the method of this work was employed for his lengthy study *The Second World War.*

The Life, Adventures, and Piracies of the Famous Captain Singleton (1720) cleverly achieves verisimilitude by bringing Singleton into association with a real-life pirate, Captain Avery, whose biography Defoe had also written anonymously as *The King of the Pirates* (1719). The fiction falls into two loosely related tales.

In the first half a party of mutineers, abandoned on the east coast of Africa, are led by Singleton across the heart of the Dark Continent to the west coast. So thoroughly had Defoe absorbed the meager

African travel literature of the period that later exploration does not greatly disprove any of his statements. The second half follows Singleton's piratical forays in the Pacific, including a voyage around Australia and meetings with Avery.

Defoe worked a good formula here. The bourgeois reader is regaled with wild tales of wickedness but is soothed by Singleton's concluding and dubious repentance. Quaker William, the pious adviser of the pirates, is one of Defoe's best characterizations, a truly complex character in his attempt to reconcile piracy with his inculcated moral principles.

The History and Remarkable Life of Colonel Jacque, Commonly Call'd Colonel Jack (1722) again pictures real celebrities of the era and again falls into two divisions.

The first part shows the illegitimate Jacque brought up by a baby-farmer and trained as a pickpocket. Defoe knew his London perfectly and here depicts impressively realistic scenes of sordidness and suffering, notably in the urchin pickpockets huddled from the winter night in warm ashes. Less absorbing is the second part, about the adult Jacque. After unrelated experiences as highwayman, deserter, indentured servant, and later overseer in Virginia, he dutifully repents. Thereafter he wins promotion for bravery in the French army and aids the Old Pretender in the uprising of 1715. En route he has been married to five demireps.

With these vignettes of contemporary urban life, Defoe struck a particularly good vein. Jacque is a typical Defoe central character, largely driven by the problem of sheer survival but also relishing the zest of adventure and danger.

The Fortunes and Misfortunes of the Famous Moll Flanders (1722) is probably Defoe's greatest piece of fiction. The gripping authenticity of the account caused contemporaries to identify Moll as Laetitia Atkins of Galway, but the work is probably entirely imaginary.

Born in Newgate Prison, Moll nonetheless seems started on a conventional life as a servant in a kind household. She yearns to be a "lady" and seems on the way with the attentions of the younger son. Seduced by the elder son, she conceals her fall from the younger, whom she weds. Upon his death, she passes from one love affair and marriage to another, living by her wits and playing upon her beauty. One husband is a Virginia planter who proves to be her brother (for her mother had been transported as a felon to Virginia). Fleeing him and returning to England, she sinks lower, marrying an Irish highwayman and becoming a pickpocket. Captured and committed to Newgate, she is reunited with her highwayman. Both repent but retain all their ill-gotten gains. In Virginia they end their lives in prosperous happiness. A box score seems to indicate five husbands and twelve children.

Moll is the most famous female picaroon in English literature. Her episodic adventures are fascinating in themselves but add up to the greater whole of an indictment of a society. There is no melodramatic villain intent upon ruining Moll. Society simply does not care about her. It is the stark and awesome account of a robust character struggling with every weapon at her disposal simply to exist. The sentimental novelists would have wept copious tears over a woman battling alone in a hostile environment and would have made her perennially tearful, but the power of Defoe's account lies in the very absence of this kind of emotion; Moll cannot afford such luxuries. She does what she has to do and never whimpers.

The autobiographical method, while capitalizing on the potency of a True Confessions form, lacks perspective, disclosing no alteration between the seduced servant and the aged veteran of crime. While set supposedly throughout most of the 17th century, there is no hint of that tumultuous era. After some good initial dialogue, Defoe rapidly hastens Moll from one escapade to another, lavishing enough plot material on her for half a dozen works. Moll's repentance is more preposterous than any of her stratagems in thievery, but it is a sop to Defoe's readers, who are assured in the preface of the moral purpose of the work and advised to read it in order to prevent a similar sharper from defrauding them.

Roxana, or the Fortunate Mistress (1724) recounts the adventures of a courtesan amidst the aristocracy, a sort of Moll amongst the upper class. Although she is always interesting, Roxana does not come to life as did her predecessor, for Defoe knew common harlots as he did not know high-placed ladies of easy virtue.

Deserted by a bankrupt husband, Roxana flaunts her charms in several European nations to snare a succession of lovers from aristocrats and wealthy businessmen. In London she moves through court society in the guise of a titled Frenchwoman. A daughter by her first marriage is on the point of unmasking her but conveniently vanishes.

Tension is built up as nowhere else in Defoe (except Crusoe's discovery of the footprint). Motivation and characterization mark a definite advance in Defoe's novelistic art. Roxana sounds much like a "modern woman" in her bold, uninhibited ambition, her desire for independence, her advocacy of free love, her frank admission of feminine passion, and her insistence upon freedom to choose lovers and move from one to another with all the aplomb of males. Virginia Woolf has declared that *Moll Flanders* and *Roxana* "stand among the few English novels which we can call indisputably great."

Samuel Richardson (1689–1761). Samuel Richardson was the son of a pious Derby joiner, or cabinet worker. In 1706 he was apprenticed to the London printer-stationer John Wilde, whose daughter he married. By industrious application he rose to become Master of the Stationer's Company, Printer of the Journals of the House of Commons, and King's Printer. Only three daughters reached adulthood of the twelve children born to him by two wives. Writing was primarily an auxiliary and logical outgrowth of his profession.

As Defoe employed the autobiographical technique exclusively, Richardson used the epistolary form exclusively. As Defoe firmly established the novel or romance of incident, Richardson created the novel of character. Defoe may be challenged as a true novelist, but no one can deny that Richardson wrote genuine novels. Richardson is notable for establishing the following:

(1) The novel of personality. Richardson's works contain the vivid portrayal of a human being struggling for self-realization. While Defoe's characters too often seem to be healthy, determined animals fighting their way out of the traps of circumstance, Richardson's characters appear as the first in English prose fiction that must be acknowledged as complete and complex human beings.

(2) The novel of sensibility. Richardson's criterion of character was quality and intensity of feeling. He brought to the novel the sentimental pattern already tearfully familiar upon the current stage —a story of love and tribulation, whose ordeals would evoke the virtues of chastity, delicacy, piety, generosity, fidelity, and especially prudence and weeping.

(3) The novel of moral conflict in society. Richardson's novels all concern a fearful conflict between a general theoretical principle and a special human situation. Each of Richardson's special cases is an extreme one, and a modern reader is often tempted to pooh-pooh the whole business. However, Richardson's propounding of basically human problems as distinguished from Defoe's basically animalistic problems makes Richardson perhaps a truer father of the English novel.

(4) The novel of concentrated unity. In each of his novels, Richardson selects a crisis in emotional relations affecting only a few individuals, and where Defoe baldly summarizes the conflict in a few pages, Richardson endlessly concerns himself with the potential surges back and forth of emotion. In effect, Richardson carries English fiction from a diffuse series of narrated or described events to a concentrated psychological examination at one leap.

(5) The novel of tragic intensity. Although the 18th century saw the tragic drama as the height of literary achievement, it never produced a really notable dramatic tragedy. In *Clarissa*, Richardson produced a bourgeois tragedy superior to the plays of Lillo and giving to the novel dimensions somewhat approximating those of the world's great tragedies. Richardson's lead was not to be followed for generations, but he firmly established a position for the novel that would later make it an ample vehicle for the presentation of the tragic view of life. If it is argued that pathos rather than tragic grandeur is Richardson's effect, the answer may be that such is the transformation of the tragic in a modern bourgeois society.

As the first genuine creator of fully rounded characters in English prose fiction, Richardson bequeathed to posterity four recurrent figures: the chaste woman, the Protestant martyr (female variety), the impeccable gentleman, and the suave and heartless woman-killer.

Richardson was fifty years old when he was accidentally led into fiction writing. In 1739 two London booksellers, knowing his reputation as an inveterate letter writer, commissioned him to prepare a series of model letters. Such collections were popular throughout the 19th century, and were used to provide well-phrased sample letters which the less educated could imitate and adapt to their problems—paying or requesting payment of a bill, seeking or giving references for a prospective employee, or decorously offering congratulations or condolences. In accepting the commission, Richardson specified that the letters should inculcate morality, and his inventive mind produced some interesting letters, hardly the sort of thing one would frequently indite (one was from a gentleman in London relating a public hanging to a country friend). *Letters Written to and for Particular Friends, on the Most Important Occasions* finally appeared in 1741, but Richardson became intrigued with the story possibilities in Letters CXXXVIII and CXXXIX, the first from "A father to a daughter in service, on hearing of her master's attempting her virtue." "The Daughter's Answer" dutifully bows to the father's advice and promises immediate departure from the lecher's employment. Richardson interrupted his task to compile a lengthy letter series which became a novel.

Pamela; or, Virtue Rewarded (I, 1740; II, 1741). Richardson stated that the story had been reported to him about fifteen years before. Perhaps this avowal was to forestall claims of imitation from *Vie de Marianne* (serialized in France 1731–41, translated into English 1736–41), by Pierre de Marivaux; the French novel, also in letter form, chronicled the rise of its heroine from linen maid to countess. The heroine's name is taken from a character in Sidney's *Arcadia;* the present popularity of this name for girls stems from the success of Richardson's novel.

After the death of Lady B—, her son, Squire B—, attempts the virtue of the maid, Pamela Andrews. She finds no protector, even in the young cleric, Mr. Williams. With his coarse aide, Mrs. Jewkes, Mr. B— unsuccessfully tries to make Pamela his mistress, even offering a contract. She makes ineffectual attempts at escape and suicide. After Mr. B— has imprisoned her, he secures the journal she kept; and in reading it, the hardened rake is transformed into the man of feeling. He gives her freedom, but the two are drawn together by true love. Pamela weds her master.

In the second part Pamela is a model wife for a country gentleman. She even forgives the odious Jewkes. Lady Davers, sister of Mr. B—, insults her humble sister-in-law, but in reading Pamela's journal, the noblewoman's heart is properly melted. While Pamela is pregnant, Mr. B— carries on an affair with a countess but his wife is so forgiving and sweet that Mr. B— repents and promises eternal faithfulness. The reading of Pamela's writings also turns the countess from a shady life. Pamela brings up an illegitimate daughter of Mr. B— along with her son Billy.

Much of the novel's success depends upon the perennial popularity of the Cinderella story. When the townsfolk of Slough learned that Pamela was supposedly wed in their community, they joyfully trooped off to ring the church bells. But this Cinderella does not live in the days of magic slippers and pumpkin coaches. Pamela comes from a lower middle-class family that has slipped to the lower classes but that is ambitious to rise. Her only item of merchandise is her jewel of chastity, and she will barter it for nothing but the top price—an unexpectedly good marriage. Richardson has a genuine human problem: marriage was the only career for a woman, and a bourgeois girl had to play her cards with every finesse at her command to enable her to improve her position in life. Beneath Pamela's fragile exterior is the rocklike English middle-class determination to get ahead in the world. Richardson, however, clouds the issue by surrounding Pamela with a nimbus of religiosity. Of course, the middle class, exactly like Pamela, explained its actions by pious justifications, but a truly prescient novelist should have seen to the root of bourgeois ambition. Pope sat up all night to read this novel and soberly insisted that "it will do more good than a great many of the new sermons." With appropriately but distressingly bourgeois ethics, Richardson awards to every character exactly the amount of earthly riches and felicity he deserved based on his kindness or unkindness to the heroine.

One may reasonably ask, why didn't the girl simply run out on Mr. B—? The answer is twofold. First, it should be remembered that the developing sentimental spirit demanded that a woman be no such virago as the earlier Moll of Defoe; Richardson's readers could not have tolerated such an independent, free-wheeling modern woman, and also important is the power of Mr. B—, a landed gentleman. Current squires were virtual monarchs of their small domains, and where could Pamela turn against the supreme corrupted power of her little world? Richardson is expounding the middle-class protest against the concentration of authority in the landowners. However, in the fashion of his class, Richardson is no leveler; he and Pamela simply want to move upward from servant to master. Second, and most important, is Richardson's desire to make the reader realize that Pamela actually loves her master, and this affection therefore dooms to failure her attempts at escape.

Pamela is the first great character creation of English prose fiction. As much as we may dislike her prudential morality, we must recognize here a complete human being. She scribbles down exactly how she felt only moments after each of her innumerable crises. The manipulations of the letters form a story of their own, even to the device of addressing letters to the wrong party; but especially fascinating is the effect of intimate revelation in reading someone's private correspondence. The minor characters, however, are essentially caricatures. Mr. B— is conceivable only in an age that believed a gush of sentiment could transform a lecher into a man of feeling.

Garrick acted in a dramatic version, and translations of the work into Dutch, German, and French quickly followed.

Clarissa; or The History of a Young Lady (I, II, 1747; III–VII, 1748), four times the length of *Pamela*, is told in 547 letters totaling over a million words. It is probably the longest novel in English. Instead of only one major letter-writer, Richardson here employs multiple correspondents, chiefly Clarissa and her friend Anna Howe, Lovelace and his friend Belford. This many-faceted correspondence permits excellent dramatic irony and reveals the full meaning of an episode by focusing several points of view upon it. Incredibly, though, everyone writes with the same Richardsonian fluency.

A high-spirited but pure and pious nineteen-year-old girl, Clarissa Harlowe, is intended for the rich and repulsive Solmes by her well-to-do family of social climbers. Her family coldly repulses Robert Lovelace, a devilishly handsome rake, who is attracted by her beauty and fortune. Clarissa elopes with Lovelace on his promise of marriage, but he is determined to seduce her as vengeance upon her family. Thwarted in his attempts upon her virtue, Lovelace finally drugs and rapes her. In agonized shame, Clarissa dies of a broken heart. Lovelace's friend Belford repents of his shameful role, while the villain dies at the hands of Clarissa's cousin, Colonel Morden.

Richardson tackles two difficult problems. One is the hero-villain, a libertine of vile propensities who nonetheless would utterly charm the pure, intelligent Clarissa and also the reader. Richardson works hard to understand a man of entirely different nature and social station. Lovelace is genuinely in love with Clarissa and, according to the behavior of his coterie, confidently expects her to marry him after he has seduced her. Socially he despises her family as parvenus, and morally he relishes breaking her Puritanical code and dragging her down to his own level. Lovelace is an earlier model for Byron, a flamboyant poseur even to his last self-dramatizing words, "Let this expiate!"

An even more difficult problem is Richardson's heroine. She is a rebel against parental authority, determined to select her husband herself. But the crux of the entire work is the presentation of a girl who, in losing her innocence, is not degraded but elevated to sainthood. Scott states that Richardson is able to demonstrate "a chastity of the soul which can beam out spotless and unsullied even after that of the person has been violated." Clarissa nobly forgives all who injured her and leaves judgment to heaven. As many words are expended upon her deathbed languishings as many authors would give to an entire novel. Defoe's Moll would have found incomprehensible Clarissa's refusal of a wealthy marriage in favor of a death from shame, for Moll was the epitome of worldliness, while Clarissa epitomizes spiritual idealism. Lovelace is victorious in the flesh, but Clarissa's is the victory of the soul. Her steadfast virtue is symbolic of the conviction of moral and spiritual superiority in her class that in a subsequent generation will economically and politically triumph over an upper class that it considers degenerate.

Moll Flanders covered a lifetime, while *Clarissa* (about six or seven times as long) covers less than a year. One of the great differences lies in character portrayal, for Clarissa is probably the most fully realized woman in all fiction. She is also probably the most believable picture of saintliness in English fiction and the English novel's supreme portrait of tragic grandeur.

Within the vast reaches of this novel, Richardson produced remarkable effects. His completely imaginary (we can be sure) description of the bawdy house in which Lovelace confines Clarissa is the sordid realism more familiar in Fielding and Smollett. To argue that Clarissa might have escaped this imprisonment is to miss the point: her trap is symbolic of the entire physical world in which the heavenly spirit is snared, and escape is possible only to another realm. Anna Howe is a vivacious, sane, and delightful girl whom we should like to find as the heroine of her own novel; here she fulfills much of the role of a Greek chorus. Richardson sketches a superlative picture of the Harlowe household, selfishly ambitious and thoroughly, doggedly stupid.

Contemporaries, such as Fielding and Lady Mary Wortley Montagu, gave their tributes; and even the aloof Lord Chesterfield grudgingly admitted: "The little printer lacks style, but he understands the heart." Thackeray and Macaulay were among the later perfervid English admirers of this novel. European reception was equally enthusiastic; *La Nouvelle Héloise,* by Rousseau, was strongly indebted to Richardson's novel, and Stendhal considered *Clarissa* another *Iliad.*

History of Sir Charles Grandison (1753) was apparently occasioned by the demands of Richardson's female friends for the portrait of a perfect gentleman to counter-balance the caddish Mr. B— and the hero-villain Lovelace. The popularity of Fielding's *Tom Jones* also must have bestirred Richardson to compete against what he deemed the "very bad Tendency" of Fielding's work.

Rescuing Harriet Byron from would-be rape by the wicked Sir Pollexfen, Sir Charles Grandison is attracted to her and she to him. By the code of the day she and society expect him to marry her. However, the estimable Grandison had in Italy saved the son of a noble Italian family; the young man's sister, Clementina della Porretta, wishes to marry Grandison in expression of her family's gratitude. In fact, Clementina is so smitten with Grandison that her reason and life are threatened if he does not marry her. After almost interminable negotiations, the Roman Catholic Clementina parts with the Protestant Grandison because of religious incompatibility. The patiently waiting Harriet is rewarded with the hand of the consummately perfect Grandison.

Jane Austen and George Eliot highly regarded this novel, and Ruskin ranked it with *Don Quixote;* modern readers have generally concurred with Dickens's sneer at the "Grandisonian manner." Although this is technically the tightest of Richardson's constructions, although it foreshadows the novel of manners, and although it displays greater plausibility than his other works, the novel is blighted by a hopelessly priggish hero. Perfectly noble characters are a novelist's greatest stumbling block, and Grandison is impossibly perfect. The perfection of Clarissa is acceptable because of her sufferings, but Grandison seems only an immaculate mink stole awaiting the decision of two contending ladies. Any true affection he possessed is wholly buried in a gentleman's determination to do the right thing by both girls; no vital issue seems at stake. The adulation of every character for Grandison (and even the vicious are quickly transformed into paragons at his exemplary contact) becomes a bit sickening.

Henry Fielding (1707–1754). Henry Fielding was a native of Sharpham Park, Somersetshire. His family prided itself upon aristocratic connections, even claiming relationship to the royal house of Austria. He was educated at Eton, the University of Leiden, and the Middle Temple. In 1740 he was called to the bar and in 1748 was designated justice of the peace for Westminster. His first wife, Charlotte Cradock, was the model for Sophia in *Tom Jones;* they were married in 1734, and Fielding was deeply distressed when she died in 1743. In 1747 he married his first wife's maid. Gout and fever, perhaps induced by the intemperate habits of his class, attacked him in 1749. Nonetheless, he vigorously prosecuted crime from the judge's bench and sought to alleviate the sufferings of others. His worsening condition caused him to travel for health to Lisbon, Portugal, where he died. Forced from theatrical writing by the Licensing Act of 1737, Fielding turned to the novel and thereby produced:

(1) The first avowed novels in English. Defoe had claimed his fictions to be fact, and Richardson had considered his works as moral preachments. Fielding is the first English author unashamedly and forthrightly to write novels—that is, imaginary delineations of char-

acter and circumstances designed primarily for the understanding of the human situation. Upon this basis, some claim that *Tom Jones* was the first and is still the greatest English novel.

(2) The first genuine novelistic portrait of standard English life. Defoe's works pictured the world of romance, the exciting underworld, or the realm of distant adventure. Richardson's are all extreme and rather unlikely cases. In the novels of Fielding, one for the first time in English fiction comes in contact with the solid actuality of English life as most of his age experienced it.

(3) The first novel to depict the panorama of an age. Impressive as Moll is, she operates almost in a vacuum, there being practically no hint of the stirring 17th century in which she supposedly lived; and Richardson's effect is that of a cloistered world. Fielding, on the other hand, creates a convincing backdrop of a rich and multifarious society, a detailed milieu in which his characters have their actions and reactions. *Tom Jones* is the first English novel in which an era truly saw itself almost fully mirrored.

(4) The first critical theory of the novel. Scattered through *Joseph Andrews* and *Tom Jones* are essays constituting the initial English attempt to define and explain the novel as a literary genre.

An Apology for the Life of Mrs. Shamela Andrews (1741) bore the name of Conny Keyber as author, but Fielding probably was the writer of this bagatelle against Dr. Conyers Middleton, Colley Cibber, Richardson, and *Pamela*. These are "the authentic" letters, not those attributed to Miss Andrews by Richardson.

The "true" name of Richardson's heroine was Shamela, and she actually was a scheming demirep carrying on an affair with Parson Williams, a hypocritical, "Methodisticall" cleric. She plays her cards unscrupulously to snare Mr. Booby, which was Fielding's revelation of Lord B—'s name; Richardson left it a dash throughout.

Some of the conversations closely resemble those in *Pamela,* but their purpose is to show that Richardson's heroine was no assailed innocent but a shrewd little baggage gulling Mr. Booby into thinking himself the pursuer. The author sees the pious sermonizings of the heroine as hypocrisy masking an ambitious opportunist.

The History of the Adventures of Joseph Andrews, and of His Friend, Mr. Abraham Adams (1742) lifts the name Booby from *Shamela.* Fielding states on the title page that the novel imitates *Don Quixote.*

Joseph, supposedly the brother and male counterpart of the virtuous

Pamela, is importuned by the widowed Lady Booby, his sister's aunt-in-law. Repulsing her, he is dismissed; he then sets out for home and his sweetheart, Fanny. Fanny in turn sets out to find him. Both are rescued by their clergyman, Parson Adams. After vicissitudes on the road, they discover back in their village that Fanny is the child of the Andrews, and Pamela's sister. The lovers' distress is relieved when Joseph's strawberry birthmark proves him to be the son of a Mr. Wilson, a gentleman.

With this work Fielding abandoned the autobiographical approach of Defoe and the epistolary technique of Richardson in favor of the omniscient author point of view. While perhaps losing some of the sense of identification and verisimilitude, the reader is greatly enriched by the superior insight and analysis of the all-knowing author. The plot is frankly a burlesque of romances, with extraordinary coincidences, startling revelations of identity, and such *outré* devices as the strawberry mark. A picaresque narrative is tied together by the two title characters and the Booby-Andrews families at start and finish. The mass of incidents and human contacts builds from the picaresque novel to be the first English fiction truly depicting the complex interrelationships of modern society and thereby the first English fiction to appeal to intellectuals, as it did to Gray.

The married Pamela is as snobbish as only a poor girl married into the elite can be. Joseph and Fanny are conventional lovers, but Joseph does emerge as a robust though naïve youth instead of the merely fatuous male-Pamela he threatened to be at the outset. He is no Sancho Panza for the Don Quixote, Parson Adams. This burly cleric is the first great and memorable male figure in English novelistic fiction. Chaucer's Parson and Fielding's Parson Adams explain the strength of the English Church in its humble parish clergy and its hold upon the English people in the face of numerous worldly and corrupt ecclesiastics in high places. Even when doused in hogsblood and tumbled into a trough of water, Parson Adams maintains humble dignity and Christian idealism. He is a veritable Don Quixote of righteousness, unselfishness, and altruism—the true Christian spirit shaming a society that proclaims the Christian ethos and lives quite otherwise. Parson Adams is sympathetic because of his sufferings and bunglings, but especially in his simplicity, for the Anglo-American temperament cannot believe in pure goodness unless it is childlike and wholly ignorant of the way of the world.

The History of the Life of the Late Mr. Jonathan Wild the Great

(1743) is one of the greatest pieces of sustained irony in English, a satire worthy of Swift, and a frequently unrecognized masterpiece. Its real-life prototype, bearing the same name, had been hanged in 1725 with the blood of a hundred betrayed accomplices upon his unscrupulous head. Among others, Defoe had recounted the career of Wild.

Wild boasts as lengthy and consistent a genealogy as any romantic hero, but all his forebears were scoundrels. He serves an apprentice-ship in thievery, makes the grand tour of the plantations as a con-vict, and returns to make himself the monarch of London hoodlums. By informing to the authorities, he rids himself of unwanted associates or rivals, while compelling obedience from the rest of his knavish kingdom. He romantically woos and wins Laetitia Snap, daughter of a bordello keeper. Wild brings to lowest misery the honest jeweler Heart-free but is discovered and sent to the gallows. He swings to the Here-after, bearing with him a bottle screw picked from an official's pocket upon the scaffold.

Throughout (except for a moment when contemplating the abused Heartfree) the tone is apparently awed admiration and approval for the genius and accomplishments of Wild. Never has the stupidity of man been so castigated for its confusion of greatness and goodness. By clear inference, a host of the greats (Alexander, Frederick, and the rest) are stigmatized as the scourge of mankind, their greatness lying only in ambition and violence. Fielding's old foe, Sir Robert Walpole, is the ostensible target, but the real opponent is all rulers of mankind who are greedy for power and personal success at the expense of their fellow men. Belonging to the allegory rather than to the novel, this work displays less realism than any other of Fielding's fictions.

The History of Tom Jones, a Foundling (1749) is rated by many as the foremost novel in English. Events in the novel supposedly oc-cur in 1745, year of the Jacobite Rebellion.

Books I–VI, covering twenty years, are set upon the Somersetshire estate of Squire Allworthy. Tom Jones, supposed illegitimate child of a servant girl, is brought up with Blifil, son of Bridget, the squire's sister. Tom is an open-hearted, naturally good young fellow, while Blifil is a sneaking hypocrite. Though loving Sophia, daughter of nearby Squire Western, Tom has an affair with Molly Seagrim, a poacher's daughter. Seeking Sophia for himself, Blifil gets Tom in trouble with Allworthy. Regretfully Allworthy casts Tom adrift. The remaining books cover a period of only thirty-eight days.

Books VII–XII tell of a journey through towns and inns on the road from Glastonbury to London. Tom falls in with a varied assortment of soldiers, gypsies, innkeepers, and travelers. He has an affair with a Mrs. Waters. Sophia, who had run away from home to join him, learns of his amour and hurries off to London, abandoning him. Later it appears that Mrs. Waters was originally Jenny Jones, his supposed mother. Tom is joined by Partridge, an ignorant fellow townsman originally suspected of being Tom's father.

Books XIII–XVIII are set in London, where Sophia has gone to her cousin, the fashionable sophisticate Lady Bellaston, who plans to match Sophia with the dissolute Lord Fellamar. Tom seeks Sophia but is swept into intrigue by Lady Bellaston. Wounding a jealous husband in self-defense, Tom is thrown in prison. At the nadir of his fortunes his good friends and his own honest nature and background work to uncover the truth. He is revealed as the wholly legitimate child of Bridget, Blifil is unmasked and cashiered, Sophia is united with Tom.

As Richardson is the Puritan of the novel, Fielding is the Cavalier. Writing from his elevated class position, Fielding sees the squirarchy as the pillar of social and political stability. Tom's thirty-eight days adrift are painful and confusing; he has lost the sheltering figure of Allworthy and is not again in safe haven until he is back under that gentleman's benevolent protection. Allworthy seems impossibly good, the one wholly abstract idealization of the novel, for he represents the governing and sustaining principle to Fielding. Because Squire Western is viewed by a member of his own class, he is amusing and sympathetic; to any of the poor chaps under Western, he must have seemed an intolerably irascible and arbitrary little tyrant. With the morals of his caste, Fielding has a toleration for robust young manhood impossible in the Puritanical Richardson. Fielding's is frankly the double standard: Sophia is virginly pure, but Tom is sensual, easily succumbing to the lust of the flesh.

Vigorously Anglo-American is Fielding's over-all contention that simple good nature will eventually triumph. While Blifil is premeditated and scheming selfishness, Tom is all innate goodness and unselfishness—often a sinner, never a villain. Intelligence is considered highly suspect and dangerous, while the naif shall inherit the earth. Shrewdly, Fielding makes his central character an uncomplicated extrovert, for otherwise the vast canvas of the novel would be swallowed up in analyses and cerebration. For the first time the novel portrays true character development, as the feckless country boy, Tom, starts the process of maturation.

Sophia is Fielding's version of Clarissa, even to Fellamar's attempted assault. Seeking to avoid a distasteful marriage to Blifil, Sophia runs away like a genuine English girl, high-spirited, independent, intelligent, resourceful, and wholly feminine. Her father is probably the supreme character creation of the novel, a hot-tempered, uninhibited hunter of fox and curser of anything in his way. Western gains the reader's sympathy because he always acts impulsively, always intending good for Sophia no matter how wrong-headed he is. Historians have found Squire Western an excellent representation of the Tory squire of the era, tinged with a dash of Jacobitism.

To control his huge throng of characters, Fielding matches them according to contrast: Tom versus Blifil, Sophia versus Molly and later versus Lady Bellaston, and Allworthy versus Western. Thus also with the minor characters, as the boys' tutors are Square (abstract ethics) versus Thwackum (blind respect for authority). In handling minor figures, Fielding will first designate certain type characteristics (e.g. for inkeepers) and then individualize each personality by emphasis upon one of the typical personality traits (thus one innkeeper is more garrulous or more greedy than the others).

Though skeptical of men, Fielding is strongly optimistic and broadly tolerant and confident about humanity. With an assurance lost to 20th-century novelists, he believes that he can completely understand and delineate his age, and, more importantly, he is certain that with all its inadequacies, his age offers to the active strugglers for life and self-realization—Tom and Sophia—full scope for achievement and happiness.

The neatly articulated plot mirrors this 18th-century faith in the meaningful and essentially right order of its world. Coleridge listed *Tom Jones, Oedipus Rex,* and *The Alchemist* as the three perfect plots in literature. Only at the conclusion does the reader suddenly realize how marvelously everything in the novel falls into place; what seemed superfluous decoration or elaboration is necessary to the full rounding of the story. Fielding's dramatic training influenced the plot, and, as never before in the English novel, he employs concrete visual symbols (such as Sophia's muff) as a dramatist does to focus attention and understanding. His dialogue is dramatically convincing and vivacious.

Fielding's running commentary in this novel constitutes the first full-length critique of the novel in English. Like *Joseph Andrews,* this is termed a "comic epic poem in prose." The legacy of Fielding was to make the English novel fundamentally a study in comedy until the late 19th century. In the epical quality of the novel (occasionally a burlesque like Molly's wild scratching and hair-pulling at the church), Fielding first consciously recognized the role of the novel as the broad epitomizing of an era; he saw the function of the novel as the search for the soul and meaning of an age, and as the modern period's nearest equivalent to the epic. He spoke of the novel as "this historic kind of writing," clearly perceiving that the novel, although a work of the imagination, might better reveal an era than conventional works by professional historians. He also saw that the novel's chief forte is "human nature," plot and background serving mainly to illuminate as well as to evoke human responses. Especially, Fielding felt that verisimilitude was essential to the novel, feeling that it should not be the vehicle for special pleading but a revelation of actual living.

Richardson, Johnson, and Victorian moralists have decried *Tom Jones,* but the chorus of approval far outweighs them. Boswell and the elder Pitt were enthusiastic, and Gibbon grandiloquently asserted that this novel would outlast the Escorial Palace and the imperial eagle of the Hapsburgs. Because of this novel, Byron labeled Fielding "the prose Homer of Human Nature"; Coleridge, Scott, Hazlitt, and Trollope also praised it.

Amelia (1751) came from a man sickened by personal ailments and embittered by the parade of human depravity that he daily witnessed as a magistrate.

Captain Booth, a discharged military officer, fails as a farmer and as a provider for his wife Amelia, who had married him for love. Thrown in prison, Booth consorts with the demirep, Miss Matthews, a former flame. Upon his release, husband and wife cannot exchange confidences. Miss Matthews wants to hold him and threatens exposure. Booth's friend and protector, Colonel James, addresses himself to Amelia, who remains faithful but silent, as she fears the consequences of a breach with Colonel James. A noble lord also seeks her virtue, and she wishes to prevent a duel between her husband and the aristocrat. Again committed to prison, Booth confesses all to his wife. Amelia is suddenly revealed as the heiress to a splendid estate stolen from her by her dishonest sister. All ends happily.

Except for Mrs. Behn's *Oroonoko,* this is the first English novel of social reform, the first novel to depict specific sociological evils with a clear indication of necessary measures for the alleviation of wrongs. Fielding is so heartfully sincere that he frequently descends to preaching and righteous indignation, parallel to his contemporary pamphlets against crime and vice. The breezy world of *Tom Jones* is superseded by a sordid, vicious world where only Amelia shines amidst the lust and selfishness. The scenes of gambling hells, of gin mills, and particularly of prison life reek with a stench of degeneracy that was unmatched until modern "naturalism."

This is the first English novel dealing with the real domestic problems of a married couple. Amelia and her husband are what Sophia and Tom might be if they have no such protector as Squire Allworthy. Booth is a well-intentioned but naïve and improvident youth. Amelia is the perfect wife, utterly devoted to her slack-twisted husband even when all the bases for a worth-while marriage appear hopelessly blasted. She never debates the reasons for her loyalty, for she is the goddess of invincible faith in a man, no matter how unworthy he appears. Even in Tom Jones's darkest hour, the spirit of the entire novel promised a happy outcome, but the shaken reader cannot reconcile the prevailing tragic atmosphere with the strained conclusion. Although Fielding here was staunchly moral in purpose and obviously an orthodox Christian, Richardson still disliked the novel, and posterity has never been able to swallow its bitter dose after the sunny radiance of *Tom Jones*.

As a dramatist, Fielding wrote the most successful non-musical drama of the entire period, *The Tragedy of Tragedies; or, The Life and Death of Tom Thumb the Great. With the Annotations of H. Scriblerus Secundus* (one act in 1730, three acts in 1731). The dramatic portion is a *reductio ad absurdum* of the solemn tragedy of the era and the still represented heroic tragedy of the previous century. Posterity has not forgotten the diminutive hero Tom Thumb, "a little Hero with a great Soul but somewhat violent in his Temper, which is a little abated by his love for *Huncamunca.*" The printed text contains in its tongue-in-cheek annotations telling attacks upon the commentators and critics of the age; the Scriblerus club men were no wittier or more effective in ridiculing Bentley, Dennis, and Theobald. Fielding almost equaled the excellence of the original *Rehearsal* in two plays imitating the Buckingham model: *Pasquin* (1736), with its satire of current poets, pantomimes, and Italian opera; and *The Historical Register, for the Year 1736* (1737), with theatrical, literary, and political satire. The latter play was the direct instigator of the Licensing Act of 1737 because of its barbs against Walpole as

Quidam, and as mentioned earlier, it forced Fielding out of the theater and consequently turned him to writing novels.

Tobias George Smollett (smol'et) (1721–1771). Tobias Smollett was born near Bonhill, Dumbartonshire, Scotland. After training at Glasgow University, he was apprenticed to Glasgow surgeons, but he soon quit to seek his fortune in London. After many vicissitudes, he accepted the post of surgeon's second mate on H.M.S. *Chicester*. In the unsuccessful 1741 naval attack upon the Spanish at Cartegena (in the present-day South American nation of Colombia), he witnessed all the bloody horror of sea warfare. In 1744 he was a Downing Street surgeon in London. His interest in writing turned him from medical treatises to increasingly literary efforts. Much of his writing was literary hackwork, but he was a leading figure in the founding of the *Critical Review,* to which he contributed extensively. His translation of *Don Quixote* (1755) is still reprinted. Personally he was a terror of the literary world, feared for his violent temper and brutal remarks. Even for an unsqueamish age he offered dosages not always palatable. His atrabilious nature was accentuated by illness that finally sent him to Italy, where he died near Leghorn. Although Smollett in many respects appears to have brought about a retrogression of the novel, he made these important contributions to its development:

(1) The novel of the sea. Shipboard life and the nature of seamen were only devices to Defoe for precipitating action.

(2) The "character" or eccentric in the novel. While Fielding acknowledged his debt to Hogarth, Smollett was really the first caricaturist in the novel. Dickens freely admitted his indebtedness to Smollett.

(3) The novel of ideas. Smollett's professional background and his reviews for the *Critical* equipped him to bring to the novel the first sense of the intellectual life of the era, especially in *Humphry Clinker*.

(4) Painstaking observation of the senses, especially the brutal and violent. Smollett's photographic "naturalism" preceded and surpassed Fielding's. Again his medical eye conditioned him to minutely faithful reporting.

(5) Foreshadowing of the Gothic novel. In *Count Fathom,* some episodes show the way to the later Novel of Terror.

The Adventures of Roderick Random (1748) is probably the first truly autobiographical novel in English, although, of course, the material is handled with imaginative freedom.

Disapproving of his son's wife, a Scottish gentleman ignores his needy grandson, Roderick Random. The lad's uncle, Tom Bowling, aids the boy but is frequently absent on long sea voyages. Roderick proceeds with his old schoolmate Strap to London, where the two are fleeced by sharpers and narrowly escape prison. Unable to secure appointment as a naval surgeon's assistant, Roderick is seized by a press gang. He serves in the Cartegena campaign amidst stifling horrors and blundering superiors. Abandoned on a West Indies island, he falls in love with Narcissa but is kidnaped by smugglers. Deposited in France, he teams up with Strap (now Monsieur d'Estrapes) and they appear first in continental wars and then in fashionable London, where he is put into debtor's prison. Bowling rescues him, and he marries Narcissa.

This picaresque novel tumbles the hero through an exciting variety of episodes from the broadest farce to the most terrifying "naturalism." Society emerges as a calloused, brutal grouping of selfish, lusty animals. In the tyrannical Captain Oakum and the dandiacal Captain Whiffle, the masters of a coarse era are savagely indicted. All the characters are caricatures, grotesqueries—in Fielding's phrase, "monsters, not men." However, the English seaman, salty in tongue and roughly good-natured, had entered the English novel. Smollett's vigorous style is pungent and loaded with telling detail but devoid of elegant grace.

The Adventures of Peregrine Pickle (1751) has been deemed the best picaresque novel in English.

At Winchester and Oxford, Peregrine Pickle becomes so addicted to coarse practical jokes and horseplay that even his own mother cannot endure him. He takes refuge in the extraordinary household of retired Commodore Trunnion, with Lieutenant Hatchway and Boatswain Tom Pipes. This eccentric shipboard away from the sea is penetrated by Peregrine's aunt, Mrs. Grizzle, who inveigles the Commodore into marriage. Peregrine then teams up with the cynical Cadwallader Crabtree in a fortunetelling act. By feigning deafness, Crabtree is able to learn many secrets, shrewdly exploited in the act. Peregrine is thrown into debtor's prison but is providentially rescued and marries Emilia, whom he had earlier tried to seduce.

The hero is an unprincipled scamp, tolerable only because of his irrepressible energy and animal spirits. The floundering sea-monsters on land are farcical extravagances, but few passages in any novel can surpass the preposterous wedding procession held up by adverse winds and the mingled pathos and laughter of the Commodore's deathbed. Smollett's incisive and brilliantly descriptive powers successfully carry off the wild absurdities and brutal obscenities. The novel also directs abuse at Garrick and Fielding.

The Adventures of Ferdinand Count Fathom (1753) is a bizarre mixture of the picaresque novel and the criminal biography, romantic adventure and tragic airs, all incredibly ending sentimentally.

The son of a blowsy camp follower is brought up by Count Renaldo, whom he miserably repays. An army deserter, dishonest gambler, and thief, Ferdinand so bestially seeks to seduce the lovely Monimia (left in his care by Renaldo) that she takes refuge in the grave. Her funeral later proves to have been a sham. Ferdinand is united with her, forgiven all the way round, and converted to righteousness.

Instead of the genial picaroon, Ferdinand is a vicious blackguard, committing evil for sheer delight and reveling in the betrayal and injury of his benefactors. The most interesting scenes are the ones in the forest, where Ferdinand escapes from the storm into a murderers' hideout, and one in the church, where the spectral figure turns out to be the living Monimia. These passages exude the atmosphere of terror and shock that was to become the stock-in-trade of the Gothic novel.

The Adventures of Sir Launcelot Greaves, written during the author's imprisonment for libel, is the first English novel to be serialized. It appeared during 1760 and 1761 in successive issues of *The British Magazine.* This imitation of *Don Quixote* pictures an anachronistic knight in armor amidst the contemporary 18th-century landscape. Timothy Crabshaw is the Sancho of Launcelot, and Captain Crowe is an even wilder creation—seaman turned knight-errant as the new Launcelot. They both provide opportunities for satire on political and social chicanery of the times.

The History and Adventures of an Atom (1769) uses a familiar trick of contemporary fiction—a picaresque narrative with the central figure an inanimate object that passes from one experience to another. Smollett seized upon every chance to exploit the scandalous and filthy possibilities of this device. Set in an imaginary Japan (Britain, of course), the work attacks virtually every political figure of the age under weird pseudonyms such as Got-hama-baba (George II). Perhaps this work is much better assigned to allegorical satire than to the novel.

The Expedition of Humphry Clinker (1771) is Smollett's best work. The inspiration for the work came from Anstey's *New Bath Guide,* from which Smollett takes the idea of a diary novel. Unlike Richardson's epistolary method of developing an emotional history, these letters and diary entries play off humours and personalities against each other. The title is a jest, for Humphry is a minor comic character.

The crotchety old bachelor Matthew Bramble, of Brambleton Hall, Wales, bears his household to Bath. They include Tabitha, his narrow-minded old-maid sister, and Winifred Jenkins, their illiterate and ignorant maid. Bramble's schoolgirlish niece, Lydia Melford, is interested in an actor named Wilson, and her dashing brother, Jerry, almost fights a duel with Wilson. The party participates in the festivities of Bath and London, then journeys to Scotland. En route they pick up the Scottish soldier, Lieutenant Lismahago and the indigent Humphry. Wilson turns out to be a gentleman named Dennison, and he marries Lydia. Lismahago and Tabitha make a strange wedding couple. Humphry marries Winifred, briefly rants as a Methodist preacher, and, in a wild burlesque of *Joseph Andrews,* is revealed as Bramble's illegitimate son.

All Richardson's characters wrote with their creator's fluency, but Smollett's letter-writers are genuinely and sharply differentiated. Lydia is quite girlish, Tabitha is a stumbling and crabbed correspondent, Winifred is a ludicrous mangler of the King's English (her fantastic phonetic spellings produce bizarre and wicked ineptitudes such as "grease" for the Methodist "grace"). Humours are delightfully played against each other, as, for example, the festivities of Bath recorded with wide-eyed ecstacy by Lydia and with sour distaste by Bramble. The characters display complexity and personality surpassing those of Smollett's previous works. The brutality is so muted that for the first time Smollett is willing to accept human society, in spite of the fools and sharpers, as essentially a viable civilization. For the first time the English novel becomes a vehicle for the rich stream of intellectual ideas of the age. Economics, architecture, literature, sociology, medicine, and hosts of similar topics are discussed. This material is not really integrated with the plot, but it reveals more than any other single writing of the 18th century the catholicity of taste and interest among the cultured country gentlemen like Bramble. Of course, Bramble is Smollett himself, crusty and shrewd, undeceived by the world but willing to laugh at its incurable follies. Lismahago, a Scottish Don Quixote, is the most remarkable creation of the novel; although a strange eccentric, he gradually unfolds a splendid and commendable character from beneath all his grotesqueries.

Travels through France and Italy (1766) constitutes an unusual travel record. Smollett set out for the Continent with the conviction that most Britishers (like many 20th-century Americans) are unthinking worshipers of European culture and accomplishments. Smollett would not simply concur with the chorus of adulation but was determined to think for himself and say what he truly felt. The result is an engrossingly individualistic judgment, usually disapproving and often scathingly denunciatory. In his *Sentimental Journey,* Sterne brands Smollett as Smelfungus. Smollett blasts the decadence of fashionable Paris and senses the impending doom. He finds Italy dirty and inane. He writes with a hard bite and a sharp eye that render most other travel accounts flat and tame.

Laurence Sterne (1713–1768). Laurence Sterne came from a line of influential Yorkshire clergymen, but his father was a poverty-stricken army ensign (modern second lieutenant) who had married a suttler's daughter to settle his bills with her father. Laurence was born in Clonmel, Ireland, and educated near Halifax, Yorkshire. Soon after graduation from Jesus College, Cambridge, he took holy orders, not from conviction, but to secure an income in several parishes near York. His great pleasure was carousing with boon companions, the "Demoniacks," at Skelton Hall ("Crazy Castle"), residence of John Hall-Stevenson. In 1741 he married Elizabeth Lumley. The success of *Tristram Shandy,* Sterne's only novel, opened all London doors to him, and the income permitted his travels on the Continent, which he undertook partly in search for relief from tuberculosis. During his last winter in London (1767) he carried on an elaborate sentimental romance with Eliza Draper, young wife of an East India Company official.

The Life and Opinions of Tristram Shandy (nine volumes from 1760 to 1767). The word *shandy* is a Yorkshire colloquialism meaning "pixilated." The title seems to burlesque *The Life and Opinions of John Buncle* (1756–66), by Thomas Amory, and, of course, part of the joke is the inconsequential role of Tristram himself. Imbroglios amongst the place-seeking ecclesiastics of York cathedral produced from Sterne *A Political Romance* (1759), later titled *The History of a Good Warm Watch Coat.* This imitation of Swift was the story of a jealously sought-after garment, allegorical for the financial plums contended for by the reverend gentlemen. Although this first piece of Sterne's imaginative writing was suppressed, it was the germ for his lengthy novel. But, to be more accurate, it is well to note that *Tristram*

Shandy is less a novel than a vast improvisation, a picaresque tale of the mind.

Books I–II (1760) are full of local York satire. Tristram, the narrator, begins his account at his own conception. He sketches the principal characters of his family: My Father, Mr. Walter Shandy, a retired merchant obsessed with preposterous theories about everything; My Mother, a nullity; and My Uncle, Toby Shandy, a veteran officer of Marlborough's, invalided by war wounds, who relives his former battles through replicas and toys in which he is aided by another wounded veteran, Corporal Trim. Ecclesiastical lawyers are satirized in the character of Didius, and Roman Catholics and physicians in Dr. Slop.

Books III–IV (1761) are especially risqué. Tristram tells how his nose was crushed at birth by the ineptitude of Dr. Slop. His life hanging in the balance, he was hastily christened by Parson Yorick, who did not call him Trismegistus, as his father desired, but rather Tristram ("sorrow"), a name his father hated. The horrendous curse of Ernulfus, the tale of Phutatorius and the hot chestnuts, and the *double entendre* account of Slawkenbergius and noses are digressions.

Books V–VI (1762) are more domestic and sentimental. Bawdiness continues in Tristram's accidental circumcision and the Chapter on Whiskers. Sentiment is exploited in the death of My Brother, Bobby, and in the death of the retired officer, Le Fever; the latter permits strong emphasis upon the tender heart of My Uncle Toby.

Books VII–VIII (1765). The seventh book is Tristram's account of his continental tour, essentially as told to his friend Eugenius. The eighth book details the amatory interests of the Widow Wadman and My Uncle Toby.

Book IX (1767) was the last, Sterne unfortunately succumbing to death from tuberculosis. The stories of "Poor Maria" and the Negress appeal to the sentimental. Hilariously naughty are the stratagems of the Widow Wadman to ascertain the exact extent of Uncle Toby's groin injuries.

The different characters of the novel are usually identified as follows:

Parson Yorick	Stern himself
dear, dear Jenny	Kitty de Fourmantelle, a Huguenot refugee from France with whom Sterne conducted a sentimental romance
Eugenius	John Hall-Stevenson, friend of the novelist

Didius	Dr. Francis Topham, lay lawyer in the ecclesiastical courts of York and zealous seeker of sinecures
Dr. Slop	Dr. John Burton, Roman Catholic physician in York
My Mother	Sterne's mother, with some suggestions also from his wife
My Uncle	Suggested by Sterne's own father
My Father	Suggested by Sterne's professors at Cambridge

The initial and contemporary popularity was largely occasioned by the eccentricities and naughtiness of the work. Completely blank, black, or marbled pages are inset; chapters are skipped, inserted out of order, ludicrously developed or underdeveloped; crazy diagrams, dashes, asterisks, and other unconventional punctuation are interspersed; and digression and interruption constantly bedevil the reader seeking a straight story line. Sterne carried to the ultimate the comic tendency of the novel of his era. Although he admitted his debt to Rabelais and Cervantes, he more often invokes the suggestiveness of an inherent sentimentalist.

Tristram Shandy fundamentally criticizes humanity on the *Don Quixote* plane of the confrontation of illusion with reality. My Father is the impractical theorist, so devoted to elaborate study, hair-splitting, and insane logic as to bungle completely all the real problems of life. While My Father laboriously considers the proper education of a boy, Tristram grows up without any education. My Uncle is ridden by his "hobby-horse," a character's "ruling passion" in the terminology of the age. His childish war games make him virtually impervious to actual life.

The very willfulness and apparent disorder of *Tristram Shandy* represent a frontal attack upon the concept of life as methodically organized by previous novelists. Life is not the well-plotted Aristotelian scheme of initial exposition, coherent rising action, focal climax, and neat unraveling in the dénouement; life is a bewildered wandering, a daydream continuum, and a bizarre flitting and digression. Sterne anticipates 20th-century experimenters in the novel such as Joyce and Virginia Woolf in his attack on the well-made world of the well-made novel. The prefacing motto from Epictetus, "Not deeds but the teachings of deeds are what concern man," keynotes Sterne's insistence that the proper imaginative reading of life lies not in events but in the psychic aura that each man bears within himself as the cloak of the physical world.

Tristram Shandy may well be termed the first philosophical novel in English or at least the first novel dominated by a conscious psychological theory. From Locke's *Essay on Human Understanding,* Sterne adopts the concepts of relativity of time, association of ideas, and stream of consciousness. Clock time is not the actuality of human experience; subjectively we live an eternity in a few moments, and the scores of pages dealing with My Father and My Uncle in the short period awaiting My birth reflect the actual sense of time felt by an individual. Sterne perceives the past as a genuine truth of the Now; to the individual, time seems not really a series of tidily discrete units, like slices of cucumbers, but rather a nimbus of great clouds of simultaneity. To My Uncle, the battles of the past are not tagged and abandoned lumber but the omnipresent reality of his everyday existence. The comic possibilities implicit in Locke's theory of association of ideas are shrewdly exploited by Sterne, notably in the way Mrs. Shandy's wardrobe flits through the servant girl's mind at the news of Bobby's death; since My Mother will go in mourning, her regular garments will be passed on to the maid. Every person, Locke asserts, has a different series of sense perceptions. As he encounters an experience, his mind will be stimulated to memory of a past sensation somehow similar to the present experience, and then his mind will continue to associate tangential ideas that carry thought far away from the immediate contact. Thus, in the solemnity of proposing marriage to the Widow Wadman, My Uncle opens the Bible, only to find a reference to battle that soon bears him completely away to war and away from his intentions of seeking the hand of the worthy lady.

To portray this process of the mind, Sterne adopts the "stream of consciousness" technique, not again to be truly exploited in the novel before our century. The effect is to depict the vagaries of mental processes and the resulting confusions of speech, misunderstandings, and outwardly incomprehensible changes and break-offs of conversation that mark everyday communication. This, Sterne claims, and not the artificial unity and concentration of most novels, genuinely reveals the pattern of life as it is lived. Beneath the surface jocularity of *Tristram Shandy* is the pathos of human isolation and the impossibility of total communication. The truly exciting and objectively important things of our life are muted by the details of commonplace existence and the constant intrusion of the apparently irrelevant.

Therefore, instead of the neat Aristotelian development of a unified plot, the novel consists essentially of a series of concrete physical sensations about which the individual "streams of consciousness" cluster. No previous English novelist so effectively catches the fleeting human moods, the exact idiom, the minutiae of gesture and facial expression, and the strange wanderings of human thought and statement. The seeming capriciousness of the work actually results in the most accurate novelistic portrayal of everyday life until our century.

All the eccentrics of *Tristram Shandy* have appealed to readers, but My Uncle Toby, the innocent, warm-hearted player with toy soldiers, has been perhaps the most attractive. Hazlitt termed him "one of the finest compliments ever paid to human nature." Leslie Stephen asserted: "There is no single character in Shakespeare whom we see more vividly and love more heartily than Mr. Shandy's uncle." Richardson and Johnson denounced the novel, Victorian moralists decried it, and 20th-century critics praise it highly.

A Sentimental Journey through France and Italy by Mr. Yorick (1768) covers France alone, since Sterne's fatal illness precluded a continuation into Italy. In many respects, as in its very title, this artistic rewrite of the seventh book of *Tristram Shandy* is a riposte to Smollett. Where Smollett's previous travel account is intellectual realism, Sterne's is sentimental impressionism. Each Sternean encounter— the dead ass at Namport, the postilion La Fleur, the *fille de chambre,* the dance with Nanette—is a vivid vignette of color and movement valued not for its objective value but for the quickening of the author's sensibilities. Sterne judges a sensation by how sharply and emotionally it strikes his inner spirit rather than by a reasoned, coherent depiction of phenomena.

Letters from Yorick to Eliza (1775) covers the correspondence to Mrs. Draper while she resided in England, and *Journal to Eliza* (1904) is Sterne's diary about her after she returned to her husband in India. Both are extraordinary documents of sentimentalism arising from Sterne's apparently Platonic passion for this wife of an important official in the East India Company. He addresses her by various affectionate nicknames, particularly "Bramine." He calls himself "Bramin," also "Yorick" and "Tristram." Sterne consciously strives to make this journal rival Swift's to Stella, but the Sternean romance is perhaps too lachrymose and saccharine for today's taste. Theatrically, Sterne dramatizes himself, his self-pity, and his affection for "Bramine." He even pilfers from his early love letters to Elizabeth Lumley to address his last flame.

THE NOVEL OF SENTIMENT

Oliver Goldsmith (1728–1774). Oliver Goldsmith, whose drama and poetry have been discussed in the previous chapter, wrote only one novel, but its popularity in the 18th century was exceeded only by that of *Robinson Crusoe*. In 1845 *Punch* quipped that at the current exhibition of the Royal Academy the most popular subjects were portraits of nobility and the second illustrations to:

The Vicar of Wakefield (*1762*, 1766). According to his famous (though probably apocryphal) account, Johnson found Goldsmith penniless with the bailiff upon him; the Great Cham rummaged among Goldsmith's manuscripts and carried off the novel to sell to a publisher for £60.

The Reverend Dr. Primrose so avidly espouses the doctrine of absolute monogamy that it prevents the marriage of his son George to Arabella Wilmot, whose father is thrice married. An unscrupulous broker has absconded with the clergyman's fortune. Primrose moves to property on Squire Thornhill's estate, where his daughter, Sophia, is rescued from a stream by Mr. Burchell.

Squire Thornhill courts Olivia but is noncommittal. Four days before her scheduled wedding to a Mr. Williams, Olivia runs off with Squire Thornhill and is seduced after an apparently mock marriage. The Primrose house burns down, the cleric quarrels with the squire and is thrown in debtor's prison, his son George is also imprisoned for physical attack upon the squire, and Sophia is kidnaped. But virtue and honesty are rewarded. Mr. Burchell is revealed as Sir William Thornhill; he exposes his nephew's treachery, secures release of the Primrose men, and rescues and marries Sophia. All rejoice when Olivia's marriage to Squire Thornhill proves to be valid. George marries Arabella. The broker is apprehended, and wealth and contentment are now to be the lot of Dr. Primrose and his wife Deborah.

The long-continuing popularity of Goldsmith's novel rests largely upon its novelistic version of a sentimental comedy amidst idyllic surroundings. All the fresh beauties of the English countryside and village (another Auburn) are suggested. The characters are delightful, simple people whimsically delineated, who evoke sympathy because of their predicaments but eventually triumph in a world that brings all things good and fair to the virtuous and the innocent. Every reader recalls charming episodes such as the enormous family painting that proved too large to be carried into the living room and the conning of younger son Moses into trading a colt for a gross of green spectacles. The entire work seems a pleasant rococo sketch of the loving Primrose family, the masterpiece of the middle-class domestic novel.

Dr. Primrose is Goldsmith's great innocent, trailing just a bit behind Chaucer's Parson and Fielding's Parson Adams as the simple but exemplary parish priest, the true pillar of the English Church. The lack of full success with this character arises from Goldsmith's sentimentalism. The naïve cleric, though always treated gently, is earlier the victim of self-deception and of immaturity in the wiles of the world; he emerges in the end as the ideal trinity of priest, father, and husband. The figure of security is Mr. Burchell, who is always right, as Primrose is always wrong. Burchell is Goldsmith's Allworthy, the symbol of the intelligent and powerful squirarchy that will take care of those incapable of solving their own problems.

Squire Thornhill is Goldsmith's depiction of a lecherous landowner, and the reader of today is disturbed by the squire's union with Olivia. The marriage ceremony is proved to be genuine, and all the Primroses rejoice—but why? The squire is still a bounder and roué. Goldsmith is partly asserting the naïveté that a wedding ceremony of indubitable legality somehow transforms a lecher into a respectable husband, but more important to the age is the saving of Olivia's reputation (if Lovelace had only married Clarissa formally before ravishing her, Richardson would certainly have considered his heroine somehow "saved"). Also, it must be noted, the entire 18th century preceding Romanticism took a more practical and less idealistic view of marriage than is now celebrated.

Henry Mackenzie ("The Addison of the North") (1745–1831). A native of Edinburgh, Henry Mackenzie conducted two periodicals, *The Mirror* (1779) and *The Lounger* (1785), in frank imitation of *The Spectator*. Number 97 of *The Lounger* was the first appreciation of Burns. Mackenzie was a close friend of Hume, Adam Smith, and Scott. While in London reading English law for his position in the Exchequer of Edinburgh, he conceived his most famous work.

The Man of Feeling (1771), one of the most successful fictions of the era, is less a novel than a series of loosely related sketches centered about the chief character.

In love with Miss Walton, Young Harley proceeds to London to secure the lease of adjoining property. En route and in London, he meets a wide diversity of people and each experience enables him to display his tender and virtuous sensibilities. Upon his return, he mistakenly believes that Miss Walton loves another. He becomes dreadfully ill and, in spite of her assurance that she loves only him, expires.

Sterne's sentimentalism seems at the root of this work. Every encounter by Harley represents another variety of emotional response. Tears and alms are contributed by the hero to every worthy sufferer, for benevolence and philanthropy are deemed the characteristics of a noble spirit. Harley is not as impossible as he first sounds, for he demonstrates real courage in the face of bullies and finds some characters undeserving of charity. The incidents with swindlers and the press gang are realistic, highlighting the sentiment to follow. Mackenzie assures us that in Harley we have the naturally good man, yielding to his instinctive impulses of benevolence; the deficiencies of our society are artificial warpings of the inherent goodness of mankind.

Henry Brooke (c. 1703–1783). Henry Brooke was born in Rantavan, County Cavan, Ireland. His verse and drama made him the outstanding Irish literary figure of his age, but if he is remembered today, it is for his one novel.

The Fool of Quality (five volumes, 1765–70) is the first pedagogical novel in English, the first of a numerous following introduced by Rousseau's *Émile* (1762).

While his brother is receiving the conventional classical education, young Harry Moreland is neglected. The philosophic Mr. Fenton is therefore free to tutor the youth as he pleases, and the philosopher decides to raise Harry to be what the then current society would term a fool, a man lacking the selfishness and affectation of the times while consecrated to the deeper wisdom of the soul. In the inculcation process, Brooke provides numerous experiences to evoke the natural goodness of Harry, and also incorporates essays on morality and illustrative stories (such as Damon and Pythias, Alexander and Diogenes).

The book rests upon Rousseau's contention that the foundation of education should be the cultivation of instinct; the child should learn "naturally" instead of having facts beaten into him. Not books but the actual contacts with men and nature will instruct him in the truths of life and conduct. Today's reader is annoyed at the sharp discrimination of everything into black or white, at the exalted idealism of

Harry, and at the lavish shedding of tears. John Wesley, however, was so impressed with the work that he edited a condensed edition with the author's approval, and Kingsley enthusiastically recommended the novel in the 19th century.

Thomas Day (1748–1789). A native of London, Thomas Day was educated at Charterhouse and Oxford. He was a friend of Sir William Jones, Erasmus Darwin, and the Edgeworth family. He was widely famed for his philanthropy and humanitarianism. His kindness to animals was in part responsible for his death from an unbroken colt.

The History of Sandford and Merton (three volumes, 1783–89) seems the first novel directed specifically to children.

Harry Sandford, son of a poor farmer, blossoms into perfect strength and courtesy under the Rousseauistic tutelage of Mr. Barlow. When Harry rescues Tommy Merton from a snake, Tommy, the spoiled child of a wealthy Jamaica planter, is entrusted to Mr. Barlow for instruction. Tommy is a good boy, distorted by the improper education of the age. "Natural" education from Mr. Barlow, always arising from real experience (to move a giant snowball, the boys learn the principle of the lever), straightens him out. As in Brooke's novels, numerous illustrative and edifying tales are inserted.

Throughout the 19th century many Englishmen advised growing sons: "Get to *Sandford and Merton*." Here was the popular classic of "natural" and moral education. From real-life experiences, encountered by any small boy, Day drew proper social and moral lessons. Staunchly representative of middle-class attitudes, the work pictures the idle rich as ill-mannered and heartless snobs. All esthetic values are subordinated to practical accomplishment. Perhaps the most dubious aspect of the work is the unceasing depiction of the world as a place where good is always rewarded and wrong is always punished—and promptly.

THE GOTHIC NOVEL

The word "Gothic" has performed a remarkable pilgrimage in English. Originally merely the designation of a tribe of ancient Germans, the word was used in the Enlightenment (which scorned the Middle Ages) as a synonym for "crude," "barbarous." Walpole probably had this meaning in mind when he subtitled *The Castle of Otranto* "A Gothic Story." The vogue of Walpole's novel and of his imitators caused the word to be associated for several generations with "horror" and "fearful suspense." In the writings of the 19th-century author John Ruskin, "Gothic" becomes a synonym for "lofty" and "spiritual."

Horace Walpole (1717–1797). Horace Walpole inaugurated the "Gothic" tale by combining the historical (or pseudo-historical) novel with the tale of terror. The first historical novel in English was probably *Longsword, Earl of Salisbury* (1762), by Thomas Leland. The tale of terror has its roots in primeval folklore, especially in fairy stories; a distant ancestor is the *Babylonica* (2nd century) of Iamblicus, whose atmosphere of tombs, dark caverns, and sinister figures strongly resembles the "Gothic" novel. Walpole's correspondence is discussed in the previous chapter under the age of letter writing.

The Castle of Otranto: A Gothic Story (1764) is the first concoction of pseudo-medievalism and the macabre to form the extensive genre of the "Gothic" novel.

Manfred, the usurping prince of Otranto, is warned by prophecy that he may retain his ill-gotten gains only as long as the castle can hold its rightful owner and Manfred has male heirs. On the eve of his son's wedding to the lovely Isabella, the young man is crushed to death under a huge helmet. Manfred then seeks Isabella for himself, but she flees, aided by Theodore, a most genteel peasant remarkably resembling the dead Alonso, the original and proper owner of the castle. Manfred is about to have Theodore executed when Alonso's ghost, soaring to gigantic stature, splits the castle asunder and reveals Theodore as the genuine heir. Isabella and Theodore are married.

Possibly because the work is ludicrously inappropriate to a debonair Whig aristocrat, Walpole claimed in the first edition that it was a translation by a "William Marshall" from an old Italian manuscript supposedly found in an English house. Walpole thus joined the medieval hoaxers Macpherson and Chatterton. Of course, there is nothing authentically medieval about Walpole's novel; Isabella and Theodore are straight out of the contemporary novel of sensibility. Popular acclaim caused Walpole to acknowledge authorship in the second edition, and it is rather amusing to observe his attempts in the preface to square the romance with the neoclassic "rules," moral teaching, and "nature."

Modern readers are unmoved by the contrived horrors: bleeding statues, portraits that move, and mysterious appearances of disjointed arms and legs. The novel's success apparently arose from an era surfeited with reason and the prosaic, and hence anxious for something wildly different and bizarre. Walpole admitted that in a dream he had experienced the enormous magnification of his pseudo-medieval mansion, Strawberry Hill. The work then obviously stems from the nightmarish dream world which the Age of Reason had tried to stifle. Manfred is the prototype of the hero-villain, and Byron would again employ this name for the central figure of a "Gothic" work. Though later novelists would quite outdo Walpole in the production of horrors, he had provided all the essential ingredients.

Clara Reeve (1729–1807). Clara Reeve was a native of Ipswich, Suffolk. Her *Progress of Romance* (1785) is the first book in English devoted solely to the history of prose fiction.

The Champion of Virtue, a Gothic Tale (1777) is generally known by the title *The Old English Baron,* affixed to the second edition in 1778. Clara Reeve's purpose was to "purify" Walpole's novel. The same fundamental plot structure (the return of the rightful heir) is employed, with Edmund the equivalent of Theodore. The scene is more an 18th-century country mansion than a medieval castle, but Clara Reeve adds a haunted wing. Incredibly, this is a Gothic tale from a thoroughgoing rationalist. She "purifies" the Walpole account by presenting an eerie supernatural effect and then promptly explaining exactly how the effect arose from wholly natural causes. If she had possessed a grain of humor, this novel, like Jane Austen's *Northanger Abbey,* would have emerged as a burlesque of the Gothic novel.

Ann Radcliffe, née **Ward** (1764–1823). Ann Radcliffe was a native Londoner. She traveled widely in England, Germany, and the Netherlands but never visited Italy, the favorite locale of her fiction. Her husband, William Radcliffe, editor and lawyer, was frequently absent from home, and Mrs. Radcliffe seized upon writing to occupy her time. To her own day she was "the Shakespeare of Romance," "the Great Enchantress." Scott was lauded as her successor.

The Mysteries of Udolpho (1794) kept Warton, the poet laureate, up all night to read it. Sheridan, Fox, and many others praised it.

Emily St. Aubert, of aristocratic French origin, is about to marry her sweetheart, Valancourt, when her aunt-guardian marries the sinister Montoni. The Italian forbids Emily's marriage and carries off both women to his Gothic castle, situated among the precipitous crags of the Apennines. Montoni wishes to secure for himself the French properties of both women. The aunt dies from her imprisonment, and Emily signs over her estates to him. Montoni, however, is apprehended by the Venetian authorities. Emily regains her rightful property, and she and Valancourt are married.

Mrs. Radcliffe is the greatest novelist of atmosphere until the 19th century. She creates effects of stupendous mystery and suspense splashed against the most lavish and picturesque backgrounds; but perhaps her greatest contribution lies in the vast imaginative landscapes that she introduces into the English novel. Her castle of Udolpho is the epitome of the Gothic school. Like Clara Reeve, Mrs. Radcliffe explains everything away, but she has the grace to wait for the novel's end before revealing the perfectly logical explanation for all the mysteries. Her heroine is really an 18th-century English girl from the school of sensibility. But perhaps the real key to Mrs. Radcliffe's popularity was her exploration of dream symbolism. Emily's fears are the stuff of nightmares, evocations of the unconscious dreads that the Age of Reason had neglected but that an approaching Romanticism probed with excitement.

The Italian, or the Confessional of the Black Penitent (1797) is Mrs. Radcliffe's masterpiece.

Ellena di Rosalba is loved by Vivaldi, but his high-born mother plots with Schedoni, confessor to the marquess, to get rid of the girl. Schedoni carries Ellena off to a monastery, but she escapes with Vivaldi. Schedoni overtakes the lovers, turns Vivaldi over to the Inquisition, and intends to murder Ellena. About to poniard her, Schedoni recognizes her locket and believes she is actually his daughter. He aids the lovers now, but, in doing so, he himself falls into the clutches of the Inquisition.

Like so many English of the period, Mrs. Radcliffe is not so much anti-Roman Catholic as she is totally ignorant of Roman Catholicism; for instance, the convent of San Stefano is inhabited by both nuns and monks! Mrs. Radcliffe squeezes from her imaginary Italy the last bloody drop of terror and suspense. In the monk Schedoni she achieved her best characterization; he is another prototype of the Byronic hero-villain.

Matthew Gregory Lewis (1775–1818). A native of London, Matthew Gregory Lewis knew Paris and Weimar well, and in 1794 he became an attaché of the British legation at The Hague. From 1796 until 1802 he was a member of the House of Commons. Though opposed to slavery, he inherited a large Jamaica plantation that was staffed by slaves. Returning to England from Jamaica, he died of yellow fever and was buried at sea. He was nicknamed "Monk" Lewis because of the notoriety of:

Ambrosio, or the Monk (1795), subsequently entitled simply *The Monk*.

All Madrid is awed by Ambrosio, abbot of the Capuchins, "The Man of Holiness." Actually his "holiness" is egotism and pride, and he quickly succumbs to the wiles of Matilda, a seductress who steals into his chambers in the guise of a novice. With each succeeding crime, Ambrosio's conscience weakens. He descends to the foulest crimes, including the violation of his sister, Antonia, and the slaying of his mother, Elvira. Ambrosio sells his soul to the devil and expects to evade the compact by Jesuitical casuistry. But His Infernal Majesty bears the monk to a giddy precipice, stabs his talons into the monk's shaven skull, and hurls him to destruction upon the rocks far below.

All previous Gothic novels are Sunday-school literature in comparison to *The Monk*. Much of it shows youthful naïveté (Lewis wrote it when he was twenty), but few readers can peruse the volume without shock, for he has transformed the Gothic novel into an account of audacious lust, treated without any reticence.

Some influences on the work other than the Gothic novel tradition were Marlowe's *Doctor Faustus,* Greene's *Friar Bacon and Friar Bungay,* and Glanville's *Sadducismus Triumphatus;* but most important were German and French accounts, some pornographic, others anti-Roman Catholic. Continental Romanticism displayed extensive interest in sexual perversions, but Lewis and Byron are the only significant English Romantics to follow this trend. Coleridge termed the novel "a fever dream—horrible, without point or terror." Scott admitted that it was "no ordinary exertion of genius." In translation the novel proved highly popular on the Continent and was widely imitated. Sensationalism and extravagance had reached their limits in *The Monk*.

Lewis in his plays concocted the same ghastly paraphernalia of ruined Gothic castles, ghosts, and tingling horrors with which he larded his prose fiction.

The Castle Spectre (1797)—Melodrama. The play is frankly a "thriller," even to its accompanying tense, ominous music.

Her father long buried in Osmond's dank dungeons, Angela is also trapped by the villain. At the last moment the two are rescued by the courageous Percy, aided by the plump and jovial Father Philip.

Contemporary audiences were overwhelmingly gripped with terror at this work and were properly lachrymose at beauty in peril, but the mechanical plotting and bombastic language rendered the play only slightly superior to any conventional "horror" show.

VARIOUS OTHER TYPES OF EIGHTEENTH-CENTURY NOVELS

While some characteristics of these special kinds of novels appeared in the works of authors already mentioned, the following discussion is intended to round out the picture of the 18th-century novel. It is remarkable to note the variety attained by the novel form in this, its first real era of development.

Pornographic Stories. The implicit suggestiveness in Richardson's novels was explicitly exploited by John Cleland in *Fanny Hill, or The Memoirs of a Woman of Pleasure* (1748), using the epistolary technique to recount a harlot's experiences. Its abundant obscenity has made it an under-the-counter favorite of pornographers for over two centuries.

Fantastic Tales. *The Life and Adventures of Peter Wilkins* (1751), by Robert Paltock, was an offshoot of *Gulliver's Travels* and *Robinson Crusoe.* After varied episodes of exciting adventure, Wilkins is cast upon a huge rocky island. While exploring, he is carried in his boat through a cavern opening to the exquisite land of Graundevolet. He finds that the Flying Indian he snares is actually a beautiful woman in flying equipment. The idyll of the pair intrigued Leigh Hunt; Coleridge, Southey, and Scott were also enthusiastic.

Baron Munchausen's Narrative of His Marvellous Travels and Campaigns in Russia (1785) was written by a rather unsavory German, Rudolph Erich Raspe, but he wrote it in English in England. The work constitutes no novel but a series of tall tales. Though essentially intended as pure fun, the book has undertones of satire against absurd traveler's tales and overly imaginative fiction.

The Oriental Tale. Except for Lady Mary Wortley Montagu, very few 18th-century English writers knew much about the East. This did not deter them, however, from concocting pseudo-Oriental fictions, falling into three categories:

(1) Social satire, the "foreign visitor" genre in which a benign and rational Oriental scrutinizes the defects of Western society. Goldsmith's *Citizen of the World* is the outstanding representative of this type. The impetus came from Montesquieu's *Lettres Persanes* (1721).

(2) Philosophical tale, assuming the wisdom of the East and inculcating moral and ethical concepts. Johnson's *Rasselas* is the greatest example of this genre. Inspiration came from extensive literature by European Jesuits who maintained a mission in the Imperial Court at

Peking from 1594 to 1704; associating with the elite and erudite of China on equal terms, the Jesuits painted a glowing picture of intelligent serenity and humane justice among the Chinese.

(3) Fantastic tales, in imitation of the *Arabian Nights*. This collection of Eastern tales (more Persian than Arabic) appeared in Antoine Galland's French version, 1704–17. Rather astoundingly, Pope confessed to Spence that he yearned to write such a wild Oriental tale. The one English masterpiece in this genre was written by William Beckford. It will be discussed below.

The "Tea-Table" School of the Novel. Though many Englishwomen wrote novels in the 18th century, and Mrs. Radcliffe was the most popular of all novelists in the concluding decade of the century, the most "feminine" novels continued to be those by Richardson until Fanny Burney, who will be discussed here, instituted the sort of novel now a commonplace in the women's magazines—a novel by a woman wholly espousing the female viewpoint and addressed primarily to women readers.

The Reform Novel, and the Satiric Tradition. The reform novel is certainly one of the most original of the types of 18th-century novel. The two reform novelists to be discussed are Thomas Holcroft and Robert Bage. William Godwin also wrote an important propaganda novel, but it will be treated in the next chapter along with his other works. The one novelist in the satiric tradition to be treated is Richard Graves.

We will now turn to the authors themselves, beginning with William Beckford.

William Beckford (1759–1844). A native of Fonthill, Wiltshire, William Beckford was probably the wealthiest Englishman of his era. He studied music under Mozart, went to school in Geneva, and toured Europe extensively. In 1783 he married the daughter of the Earl of Aboyne and resided with her in Switzerland until her death three years later. At Lausanne he purchased Gibbon's library. He served in the House of Commons from 1784 to 1794 and again in 1806. His immense fortune permitted him to build a colossal Gothic structure at Fonthill; however, its three-hundred-foot tower soon came crashing down, and today nothing remains of this huge monstrosity. Beckford lavished extravagant sums upon books and works of art; the sale of his collection in 1822 lasted for thirty-seven days.

Vathek: An Arabian Tale was written by Beckford in French during 1781 and 1782. The Reverend Samuel Henley translated the work and published it in 1784 as supposedly from the Arabic. Beckford published the original French text in Paris and Lausanne in 1787.

Vathek, grandson of Haroun al Raschid, is a vain and capricious ruler, sated with pleasures and yearning for more. A mysterious giaour, an East Indian, persuades him to abjure Islam in return for exquisite delights, and Vathek then commits enormities with encouragement from his witch-mother Carathis. He sets out to obtain the treasures of the pre-Adamic Sultans, but en route he dallies with the beautiful Nouroni-har. The pair enter the vast Halls of Eblis, where the damned have all material pleasures but cannot enjoy them, for their hearts are seared with eternal flames.

The work suffers from an alteration of purpose. At the outset Beckford is burlesquing the extravagant Oriental tale, but as he warms to his subject, it becomes a Gothic version of the Faust theme with pseudo-Oriental trappings. The concluding scene in the Halls of Eblis has been termed the most romantic passage in the English novel. There are no true characters, only personifications of vices and passions. Its success lies in its fantastic atmosphere, more redolent of some of the *Arabian Nights* than any other piece of English fiction. This nightmarish, brilliantly colored world of the imagination is more memorable than the conventional plot of a man selling his soul to the devil for earthly enjoyments. More even in tone and quality, though falling below the novel's breath-taking conclusion, is *The Episodes of Vathek*, first printed in the original French and in English translation in 1912. Others doomed to the infernal justice of the Halls of Eblis tell their stories in the best English imitations of Galland.

Fanny Burney (1752–1840). Born Frances Burney at King's Lynn, Norfolk, Fanny Burney was the daughter of a distinguished musician. Her father's house was a gathering place for artists and literati. With her first novel at the age of twenty-six she became a pet of Johnson's circle. In 1786 she was appointed Keeper of the Robes in the Queen's household, thus securing intimate and extensive knowledge of royalty. In 1793 she married General Alexandre d'Arblay, a penniless French refugee. Madame d'Arblay resided with her husband and their son in France from 1802 to 1812. Thereafter she resided in England, outliving her husband, her son, and most of her contemporaries.

Evelina; or, The History of a Young Lady's Entrance into the World (1778) is written in the epistolary manner of *Humphry Clinker* rather than in Richardson's technique. Most of the letters are from Evelina to Mr. Villars.

The dissolute Sir John Belmont deserted his wife and refused to recognize his daughter, Evelina, brought up by her kindly guardian, Mr. Villars; however, an ambitious nurse takes her own daughter to France and tricks Sir John into educating the child as his own. At seventeen Evelina is introduced to London society by Mrs. Mirvan. She falls in love with Lord Orville (another Grandison); is pestered by Sir Clement Willoughby (seeking to be another Lovelace); and suffers humiliation because of her vulgar grandmother, Madame Duval, and the social climbers, the Branghtons. Evelina saves from suicide the young Macartney, natural son of Belmont who is in love with the girl Belmont mistakenly considers his daughter. Everything is straightened out as Sir John, back from France, accepts Evelina as his daughter. She marries Orville, and Macartney marries the nurse's child.

The plot is an old one, deriving ultimately from the fairytale of the unacknowledged prince or princess who finally is recognized, inherits the kingdom, marries royally, and lives happily ever after. But the real virtue of the novel lies in Burney's capturing of the mind of a young girl thrust into London society; she stated herself that her aim was not "to show the world what it actually *is,* but what it *appears* to a young girl of seventeen." Evelina is all wide-eyed ecstasy at her first London ball, and all abject embarrassment at the antics of her vulgar connections. No man could possibly be as perfect as Orville, but he is seen almost exclusively through the eyes of an infatuated girl. Fanny Burney is a meticulous reporter of the transient but vivacious high-society life of the era. She may well be termed the creator of the novel of manners. Johnson, Burke, and Reynolds were enthusiastic about the work.

Cecilia, or Memoirs of an Heiress (1782) is twice the length of *Evelina* and twice as complicated. Its central problem hardly interests today's reader. To secure Cecilia's fortune, her husband is required by terms of the will to take the name Beverley. Love for the heroine and family pride rage through the heart of Mortimer Delville. Again the excellence of the work consists in the depiction of the fops and eccentrics of London society. Cecilia is an older and more sophisticated Evelina. With a wider canvas the machinery creaks a bit, and the innocent spontaneity of *Evelina* is lost. Fanny Burney's two subsequent novels, *Camilla* (1796) and *The Wanderer* (1814), show still further deterioration.

Also of interest are Fanny Burney's diary and correspondence *Diary and Letters of Madame D'Arblay* (I–V, 1842; VI–VII, 1846) begins with 1778 and continues until her death. The *Early Diary,* covering the years 1768 to 1778, was not published until 1889. Posterity has generally agreed that her diary surpasses her fiction, for her real-life account is loaded with sharp vignettes and a faithful reporting of dialogue comparable to Boswell's, and it is unencumbered with a contrived plot. Notable figures of three worlds troop across her pages. In English literary and artistic life she recounts personal contacts with Johnson, Boswell, Burke, and Sheridan. Her role as Keeper of the Robes permitted her to see royalty close up. One of the most touching scenes in English literature is her garden meeting with the insane George III; largely free of sentimentalism, she excellently re-creates the pathos of the encounter. In France Madame d'Arblay gazed upon the pale face of Napoleon and chatted with the tired Louis XVIII. Lesser personages are also photographically delineated.

Thomas Holcroft (1745–1809). Thomas Holcroft was the son of a London shoemaker and peddler. During his youth he passed from one occupation to another: itinerant worker, stable boy, shoemaker's apprentice. Some acting experience induced him to write plays and a wide variety of pieces, chiefly hackwork. In many respects he parallels Paine in career and political philosophy. In 1794 he was indicted for high treason because of his sympathies for the French Revolution; he was discharged without a trial.

Hugh Trevor (1794) starts as a picaresque novel, dilates in proper reform-Jacobin manner against all tyrannies, and skids to a strained conclusion.

Hugh's early misfortunes appear to be Holcroft's own youthful wanderings. After his father's bankruptcy, Hugh moves from one lowly occupation to another. His rich grandfather sends him to Oxford, where he finds the students and staff as wicked and coarse as those in the underworld. As secretary to a politician in London, he discovers a complete absence of principles in his employer. Introduced to a bishop and a dean, he learns what sots and blasphemers they are. His wise friend Turl persuades him not to expose the clerics but to concentrate upon educating the populace toward the better days of democracy lying ahead. A fortuitous fortune enables Hugh to marry his sweetheart, Olivia.

Holcroft apparently wrote himself twice into the novel. Hugh is the younger Holcroft, Turl the mature and wiser Holcroft. Biased on the side of democracy, the work touches on many real inequities of the age in church, state, and school. Holcroft (through the mouth of Turl) advocates no violence. The lower classes must be educated for their gradual assumption of rule; the upper classes must voluntarily relinquish their privileges and power. Corrupt politicians and ecclesiastics are products of an outmoded and grossly unfair system, and instead of castigating these social parasites, Turl advises Hugh to work quietly toward a better society for all humanity, in which the essential goodness of man will insure no more such injustices.

Robert Bage (1728–1801). Robert Bage was the son of a Darley paper-mill proprietor. At twenty-three he married and established himself as a paper manufacturer at Elford in Staffordshire, remaining there for the rest of his life. Bage was a vociferous supporter of women's rights, but his sexual morality distressed Sir Walter Scott, for Bage asserted that a woman violated by force (shades of Clarissa!) could nonetheless be deemed pure and worthy of his heroes' hearts. His first novel was written at the age of fifty-three and his best at the age of sixty-eight:

Hermsprong; or, Man as He Is Not (1796) is really the "foreign visitor" genre in novel form.

Brought up among American Indians, Hermsprong is a paragon of virtue, simplicity, and fearless truth-telling. He measures all English institutions and all Englishmen with the yardstick of justice and goodness. Hermsprong and the daughter of Lord Grondale are in love, but her father bitterly hates the forthright, critical Hermsprong. Grondale conveniently dies and Hermsprong, now revealed as the nobleman's distant long-lost heir, marries the girl.

Bage shows himself as the typical English liberal of the era. His hero dissects a wide range of social ills and inequities, but never is there the call to revolt. He preaches no radical alteration of society but trusts to the innate sense of justice in Englishmen to evolve society toward a fairer day. Bage is often quite good in dialogue—witty, aphoristic and idiomatic.

Richard Graves (1715–1804). Born at Mickleton, Gloucestershire, Richard Graves was a classmate at Cambridge of George Whitefield, later a famous Wesleyan clergyman. As rector of Claverton, Graves was a famous figure in nearby Bath.

The Spiritual Quixote (1772) almost matches in the satiric tradition the exuberance of Fielding without matching the structure. The novel is somewhat akin to *Joseph Andrews*.

Geoffrey Wildgoose a young Gloucestershire squire, is so enraptured by the reports of Whitefield's preaching that he sets off with the cobbler

Jerry Tugwell (his Sancho Panza) to meet the great man. En route he harangues audiences in Whitefield fashion, only to be pummeled and ridiculed. Finding Whitefield in sybaritic luxury, Wildgoose is disillusioned. The estimable Dr. Greville reconverts him to orthodoxy, and Wildgoose returns home to marry Julia Townsend.

The central purpose of the book is an attack on Methodism, and most clever indeed is this caricature of Whitefield sent in search of the actual Whitefield. Wildgoose is a mixture of Don Quixote and Hudibras. Graves astutely works theological and other arguments against Whitefield into the story, e.g. in Wildgoose's justification of Mrs. Placket's bawdy house because she is so careful of the hearts and the faith of her girls. Real people enter the story in the persons of Shenstone the poet, the Man of Ross (famous from Pope's reference), and John Wesley (treated with respect). Jostling these real characters are figures from other fictions—a member of the Grandison family and Mrs. Booby (to whom Wildgoose is another Joseph Andrews).

Part Two

THE REVOLUTIONARY ERA
AND THE ROMANTIC MOVEMENT

Chapter 5

Pre-Romanticism and the
Age of Blake (1785–1800)

BACKGROUND INFORMATION

MAJOR HISTORICAL EVENTS. The First Ministry of the younger Pitt (1783–1801) was perhaps the most remarkable ministry in English history. Although unsuccessful in his plans for parliamentary reform and abolition of the slave trade Pitt laid the foundation for the great 19th-century reforms. He took control of a nation enfeebled by the loss of the American colonies and burdened with outmoded governmental machinery, and within a decade he restored prosperity and national confidence, paid off a substantial part of the national debt, increased public revenues by more than one third, and was still able to rebuild the fleet and strengthen the army. Pitt's India Act of 1784 placed the East India Company under crown control and remained the basis of English policy in that vast sub-continent of Asia until 1858. Pitt's Canada Act of 1791 started that Anglo-French domain toward true self-government, and embodied the idea of respect for cultural and religious differences. Diplomatically cut off from the rest of Europe at Pitt's appointment in 1783, England was joined in a triple alliance with Prussia and Holland by its prime minister's efforts in 1788.

In 1788 also, George III suffered his first seizure of insanity. Recurrent attacks rendered him almost useless in government affairs, and from 1811 until his death in 1820 he was hopelessly deranged.

Pitt's program of peaceful reconstruction was destroyed by events occurring across the Channel. In July 1789 the French Revolution was inaugurated with the Fall of the Bastille. Fox declared it the "greatest and best event that has happened in the world." When the French National Assembly, in the name of the rights of man, swept away feudal rights, disestablished the Roman Catholic Church, and proclaimed the rule of democracy, ardent liberals welcomed the new age of justice and freedom. Many Englishmen, especially in the new industrial communities, formed societies extolling France and demanding comparable programs in Britain. But the violence of Parisian mobs, the looting of the *châteaux,* the persecution of pious French Christians, and the stream of refugee French nobility alarmed religious and conservative Englishmen. Burke's *Reflections on the French Revolution* (1790) elicited cries of liberal protest, especially Thomas Paine's *Rights of Man.* In 1791 the controversy exploded in violence, the Birmingham mob wrecking Joseph Priestley's home. In the next year a shoemaker, Thomas Hardy, founded the London Corresponding Society, advocating numerous reforms, especially universal suffrage, and the Society established branches throughout the island. The French Revolution assumed horribly threatening proportions with its 1792 decrees offering assistance to all peoples everywhere in their desire to overthrow tyranny. On January 21, 1793, Louis XVI was executed, and ten days later, in the words of Danton, flinging down to the kings of Europe the head of a king in gage of battle, the French Revolutionary Convention declared war on Holland and Britain.

As the first British expeditionary troops embarked for Holland in 1793, no one realized that England was committed to a savage conflict that would rage for virtually a quarter of a century, that would test English stamina almost to the breaking point, and that for a brief period would pit England alone against a bristling and hostile Europe.

Anxious for peace, Pitt had battle thrust upon him. Fired with revolutionary fervor and led by military geniuses, the French swept the Continent clear of British troops and allies, and late in 1796 they were poised for invasion of Great Britain. In the hour of severest national peril, Pitt's official proclamation was the verbatim message of Elizabeth I to an earlier England awaiting the Armada. Again another providential storm and intrepid English seamen, this time under Lord Nelson, saved England in 1797. Later in the same year the naval squadron at Spithead mutinied, for seamen's pay had remained the same since the Restoration, and even this pittance was withheld until a ship was paid off. Through the intervention of Admiral Howe, the sailors' demands were met and the squadron returned to duty, but mutiny spread to ships at the Nore, and for a few ghastly days the entire eastern coast was open to enemy invasion until the mutineers were put down by force.

The Nore mutineers issued manifestoes proclaiming the Age of Reason and brotherhood. Shocked English conservatives as deeply feared revolutionaries within their midst as they feared the French across the way. As early as 1793 the British government took measures against domestic agitators in the Traitorous Correspondence Bill, and in 1794 the right of Habeas Corpus was suspended. Thomas Hardy, Horn Tooke, and other avowed liberals were tried for high treason in 1794 but were eventually exonerated.

Seapower was the measure of English resistance. The British grand strategy was to sustain as many European enemies of France as possible, but especially by blockade to contain the French upon the Continent. Napoleon Bonaparte, the able general of the French Republic, tried to open the entire East to France by evading the British fleet and invading Egypt in 1798. At the Battle of the Nile, however, Nelson smashed the French fleet, and Napoleon, abandoning his troops in Egypt, managed to get home to be proclaimed Consul. With the resounding land victories of Marengo and Hohenlinden in 1800, Napoleon gained mastery of Europe west of the Vistula; Russia brooded in irritation at the continental blockade by the British, and England held on in dark concern.

Longing to throw off English sovereignty, in 1791 the Irish organized the United Irishmen, who rose in rebellion at the French threat of invasion in 1796. The insurrection was finally defeated at Vinegar Hill in 1798. A result was the legislative union of Great Britain (England, Scotland, and Wales) with Ireland in 1801 to form the United Kingdom. Pitt sought unsuccessfully for concessions to Irish Roman Catholics and, failing, resigned on February 3, 1801.

CULTURAL CONDITIONS. During those wild last fifteen years of the 18th century, Englishmen suddenly sensed, as never before or since, that they lived amidst profound revolutions. Even during the civil wars of the 17th century many had succeeded in maintaining the even tenor of their ways, but that was not true in this revolutionary age.

The Industrial Revolution had by this time sent its reverberations into the quietest villages of the countryside. The age-old self-sufficiency of the individual farmstead was forever broken, and everyone depended to some degree upon manufacturing. Rural and urban populations had arrived at a virtual balance, to be tipped in favor of urbanization early in the next century. The great industrial cities of the Midlands had suddenly exploded to giant size, the nation experiencing, not merely a sizable increase in population, but also a drastic relocation of population. Dwarfed by later technological advances, the age nonetheless felt awed at some of its spectacular developments: canals that formed an intricate lattice-work pattern upon the map of England, even climbing the Pennine hills; the coaches that cut to twenty-eight hours the London-Manchester run, a four-and-a-half-day trip as late as the 1770's; the China clippers that plowed the fifteen thousand miles from Canton to England in 109 days. For the first time in human history, individual men had witnessed vast material alterations and improvements in a brief span of years. We take such changes as a matter of course, but for Englishmen about 1800 there was the unprecedented thrill of change, and excitement brand new to the world, a psychic expectancy of momentous movement that certainly seemed to be progress.

A far-reaching social upheaval was also underway. The Whig-Tory quarrels of the 18th century were intra-class conflicts, with both factions subscribing to the principle of rule by hereditary landed aristocracy. For over a thousand years, through various transformations from a warrior elite to the refined 18th-century "gentleman," this upper class had dominated social, political, and economic life all the way from international levels down to the humble peasant. Now the emerging middle class was an effective challenge, assuring the later 19th-century triumph of middle-class rule. The concluding decades of the 18th century witnessed the amassing of gigantic fortunes by middle-class entrepreneurs, as wages were low, an outmoded tax structure barely touched the unprecedented industrial development, and markets for goods were expanding with incredible rapidity.

With the sublime confidence of opportunity and success, the middle-class businessmen and industrialists pursued whatever course gave them power. John Wilkinson, the great ironmaster, coined his own money and printed his own guinea notes. The Boultons, the Peels, the Horrocks, and other industrial magnates, armed with newly accumulated finance capital in vast quantities, were literally creating economic empires. The destinies of the factory workers were now in the hands of industrialists as earlier the fate of agriculturists had been determined by the landed gentry. Sensing the realities of the age, Pitt started the creation of middle-class peers, a prevailing practice of the next century.

In addition to the leaders of industry and finance, thousands of middle-class enterprisers were gaining wealth and moderate power in production and trade, superseding the small landowners in importance as the great industrialists were superseding the aristocrats. The landed gentry might look askance at these "vulgar upstarts," as Jane Austen does at the Tupman family in *Emma,* but their economic position permitted the middle class to marry into the established upper class. The change-over was gradual and bloodless, but the successful middle-class rise to power represented one of the most significant social revolutions in English history.

The most obvious and disturbing revolutionary spirit was the French Revolution. The past century and a half have mellowed our feelings toward this fearful upsurge, but in its own day it rocked the English people to their depths. Essentially, three groups of Englishmen were strong sympathizers with the French cause:

(1) Young Whig aristocrats of the type later represented by Byron who saw the Revolution as a fulfillment of their rationalistic hopes for freedom and justice. Their leader was Charles James Fox, personally an impressive and sincere liberal. Fox publicly wore the *sans-culottes* (modern trousers) of the *Révolutionnaires* to show his support of them, and at the expense of his own political career and the endangering of his party, he constantly urged peace with France. For toasting the "sovereignty of the people" at a public banquet, Fox was removed from the Privy Council. However, the social eminence of such revolutionaries saved them from persecution.

(2) Intellectual radicals seized the Revolutionary cries to call for an end to all the shackles of the past. Members of the circle of William Godwin sinned against conventional morality as a matter of principle. They inaugurated for the English the now familiar cliché that the true artist and thinker must be hostile to contemporary society, and that he must live counter to the established and hallowed mores of ordinary beings. While watchful, the Pitt government tolerated such Revolutionists, because their very antipathy to the mass mind rendered their influence negligible.

(3) The third group seriously worried the government and was extensively prosecuted. Men like Thomas Hardy, Thomas Paine, Richard Price sought to inflame the populace with appeals in language it understood to correct the ills it daily experienced. The ensuing legislation panic culminated in the Combination laws of 1799, which branded as conspiracy the combination of workers into groups seeking improved working conditions and wages.

Classifying the men who rose to literary maturity in this period is wholly dangerous. The currents and cross-currents of thought tended to extremism or confusion in many minds, resulting in violent shifts of viewpoint and often a baffling inconsistency. Also, no longer did there exist the clear-cut reading public to which earlier writers had appealed, i.e. either the now dead system of individual patron or the genteel aristocratic peruser of books. The increase in general literacy and the emergence of the middle class blurred any image a writer might have of his readers. Consequently, a writer now wrote for himself to an anonymous and undefinable audience. The costs of book production were still quite low, and a publisher was willing to take a chance on a wide diversity of works, betting that somewhere were enough readers to cover the moderate expenses. From this era on, the writer is independent, and it becomes increasingly risky to interpret an age from any writer. The author is now a spokesman for himself and only in a strictly qualified sense a spokesman for society or even a sizable segment of society.

With this era the professional writer had arrived. Previously only a towering literary giant, a Pope or a Johnson, could reasonably expect to make a living solely from literature, but the market for writings was now sufficient to end the starving existence of Grub Street. The middle-class authors, as most writers were, no longer depend upon clerical, governmental, or aristocratic patronage, or, indeed, on any other employment than writing. Almost all the significant writers of this age and succeeding ages were cut off from direct working ties with the great world and instead formed a definite literary class. This isolation from other tasks greatly encouraged the subjectivity and self-scrutiny of the literary artist.

COWPER, CRABBE, AND LESSER POETS OF THE PERIOD

An Introspective and a Realistic Poet

William Cowper is discussed here because in his introspective and often darkened verse he prefigures Blake; George Crabbe, on the other hand, is a great realistic poet, very much a part of the social consciousness of the age.

William Cowper (kou'per) (1731–1800). William Cowper descended on his mother's side from the family of John Donne. His father was parson of Great Berkhamstead, in Hertfordshire. Sickly and sensitive, he was distressed by the rigid discipline at Westminster School

(1741–48). In 1749 he was articled to a solicitor to study law, and in that same year he fell in love with his cousin Theodora Cowper, the "Delia" of his poems. His legal training at the Middle Temple secured him a Commissionership of Bankrupts (1759). When Theodora's father forbade marriage, Cowper fell into melancholia that led to insanity in 1763, when he was perturbed about an examination for Clerk of the Journals of the House of Lords. Three attempts at suicide caused his confinement in a private St. Albans sanitarium from 1763 until 1765, during which time he experienced a powerful religious conversion.

Later Cowper resided at Huntingdon with the Reverend Morley Unwin and Mrs. Unwin ("Mary" of the poems) until Unwin's death in 1767. Moving with the Unwin family to Olney, he collaborated with the Calvinist preacher John Newton in hymn writing. Betrothal to the widowed Mrs. Unwin (it was probably an engagement suggested by convention) was broken off by another spell of insanity in 1772, resulting in another suicide attempt during the next year. A fearful nightmare convinced him that he was eternally damned, and it clouded all the rest of his life. He spent his remaining years in the household of Mrs. Unwin, his gloom partially brightened by Lady Austen and the Throckmorton family. It was chiefly with the help of his friends the Throckmortons that he completed his translation of Homer (1791). After moving to Weston, Norfolk, in 1786, he suffered another period of insanity in the next year and again in 1794. He died in East Dereham, Norfolk.

Cowper's earlier works follow the neoclassic tradition, his first separately published volume in 1782 containing satiric and didactic poems. Much of his total work consists of translations from the Greek or Latin or from English into Latin. Throughout his career he was never to lose the sense of craftsmanship, epigrammatical force, and the conversational style; he remains one of the masters of English light verse. "Romantic" themes gradually rose to dominate his verse, largely in the area of religion and humanitarianism. Cowper was the first significant English poet, outside of the hymnologists, to sound the religious enthusiasm of the Methodists. These were the days of Jean-Jacques Rousseau and his message of love and brotherhood, and Cowper supported all current humanitarian ideas, opposing slavery, mistreatment of natives in the colonies, and institutional neglect. But the most "Romantic" quality in Cowper's writing is his tendency to be confessional. No poet in English before the Romantics so purposely revealed himself in his writings. Much of his poetry is frankly self-therapeutic, its topics assigned by

Mrs. Unwin or Lady Austen to dispel his melancholia. It reveals a gentle soul ("a stricken deer") too weak for the buffets of the great world but exquisitely sensitive and humane.

Olney Hymns (1779) was a joint publication of Cowper and Newton (whose most famous contribution was "How sweet the name of Jesus sounds"). Of the 348 hymns in this collection, about sixty-eight (signed "C.") are by Cowper. Cowper's hymns were written before 1773 and therefore reflect hopeful fervor instead of his later profound pessimism. Their dominant quality is direct lyrical sincerity. Few other English hymn writers have equaled Cowper in the number of long popular pieces, such as "O! for a closer walk with God," "There is a fountain fill'd with blood," and "God moves in a mysterious way" (all in Common Meter).

Poems (1782) consists chiefly of heroic-couplet moralizing in long poems with abstract titles (such as "Expostulation," "Charity," "Retirement"), proposed by Mrs. Unwin. Perhaps best are the following two:

"The Shrubbery, Written in a Time of Affliction," in delicate and suggestive lyricism, regrets that beautiful scenery cannot soothe his tortured spirit.

"Verses Supposed to be Written by Alexander Selkirk, during His Solitary Abode in the Island of Juan Fernandez" shows how Cowper can transform the anapest from Anstey's chitter-chatter to solemn meditation. The relation between the lost, isolated Selkirk and the tortured poet is obvious.

First published in *Public Advertiser* (1782), "The Diverting History of John Gilpin" has proved the most popular verse by Cowper. The sprightly Lady Austen told Cowper of the misadventures of a Mr. Beyer of London's Paternoster Row, and Cowper fashioned the ballad-stanza narrative about a linen draper whose horse runs away with him at his twentieth wedding anniversary celebration. This is the most cheerful piece written by Cowper, a masterpiece of its sort in rollicking good humor, its artful sketches of scene and character being concealed by its deceptive simplicity.

The Task and Other Poems (1785). More worldly-wise than Mrs. Unwin, Lady Austen off-handedly gave Cowper the task of writing an extensive poem in blank verse upon a sofa (introduced into England in mid-17th century and therefore comparatively new). The subject of *The Task* was certainly a better gloom-chaser than the lengthy poems upon abstractions. After a playful opening upon various kinds of seats, Cowper gracefully moves from the sofa out to nature and spends the rest of six books amidst rural life. An outgrowth of the loco-descriptive and reflective neoclassic verse, *The Task* makes the poet himself the actual subject. The "we" of *The Task* are the poet and the reader together exploring the natural beauties of the Ouse Valley. All perceptions of nature are channeled through the sensorium of Cowper, and the only order of the poem is the easy movement of the author from one scene to another. The virtual absence of "poetic diction" and the presence of first-hand observation help make this the most important nature poem between Thomson and the Romantics. Cowper's treatment of nature is marked by:

(1) Placid and cultivated landscapes, instead of Thomson's baroque vistas. This is true partly because this gentle loveliness was character-istic of Cowper's section of England and partly because his dark inner world sought relief in the milder aspects of external nature.

(2) Affection, tenderness, and intimacy unprecedented in English nature poetry. The author is not a public voice addressing mankind but a close friend sharing his emotional sensitivity with the individual reader.

(3) Rare sharpness and minuteness in nature perception. Cowper detects the manifold shades of greenery and the delicate tints of many wild flowers, even the most inconspicuous.

(4) Hence a remarkable realism in portrayal of country life, such as hay-carting, the woodman and his dog, the postman, and the wagoner. Cowper views these rural characters sympathetically and simply, with-out the condescending smile or the arch "refinement" of many neoclas-sic poets.

(5) Nature as a moral teacher, though as yet without Wordsworthian exaltation. Madness forced Cowper to flee from the city, and he views rural life as the harmonious balance of man and nature. Amidst such natural beauties, man is cleansed of base and selfish passions, and is lifted in mind and spirit.

The blank verse of *The Task* is eminently successful. After the mock-heroic opening like that of hosts of 18th-century facetious imi-tators of Milton, Cowper settles down to a line that is supple and mellifluous, simple and graceful.

"*To Mary*" (*1793,* 1803), addressed to Mrs. Unwin by a sensitive, tortured spirit, mourns age and feebleness. Highly effective is the triple-riming stanza of octosyllabics with the anguished refrain, "My Mary."

"On the Receipt of My Mother's Picture" (1798) is an almost painful confession of filial love, intensely personal. The heroic couplet has here been transformed from the early 18th-century formality to fervid subjectivity.

"The Castaway" (*1799*, 1803) was apparently Cowper's last poem. It derives from the account in Anson's Voyage of a seaman swept overboard in the wild seas off Cape Horn. The poet sees the episode as symbolic of his own bitter loneliness and predestined damnation. It is a poem of despair, written in the dark of madness and approaching death. In Virginia Woolf's *To the Lighthouse,* Mr. Ramsay frequently quotes this poem in his own sense of dreadful isolation.

The Letters of William Cowper first appeared in 1809 but are still being added to. Southey called him "the best of English letter-writers." His letters span almost half a century from 1758 until his death. Cowper's place of residence and mode of life are as quiet and uneventful as those experienced by Parson Woodforde, but in contrast, the poet's letters are remarkably "feminine"—mostly light, intimate playfulness about his tea parties and his digestion, about noisy robins and chatterbox visitors. The letters are warmly intimate, exploring every nuance of personal vagaries; only on occasion do Cowper's grim bouts with gloom and insanity darken them.

George Crabbe (1754–1832). Failing as a surgeon in his native Aldeburgh, Suffolk, George Crabbe proceeded to London, where he experienced severe poverty. Rescued by Burke, he started his reputation with *The Library* (1781). After serving as chaplain for the Duke of Rutland, he became rector of Muston and Allington in 1789. After various clerical livings, he served in Trowbridge from 1814 until his death.

Crabbe is almost certainly the greatest realistic poet in English. Although he treated extensively of the lower classes, he preferred the "middling classes" as subjects, because in them "more originality, more variety of fortune, will be met with." Johnson read him "with great delight"; Burke and Scott praised him; Byron termed him "nature's sternest painter, yet the best"; and Wordsworth asserted that his works "will last, from their combined merits as Poetry and Truth." Crabbe's verse suffered in reputation during the 19th century partly because it lacked lyric excitement and partly because of his addiction to the heroic couplet. In many respects his work seems to belong more to narrative fiction than to current poetic practice, and later readers have preferred their short stories in prose. Crabbe is as fascinated as the Romantics with the strange aberrations and perversities of man, but his searching examination of such tendencies is firmly based in the 18th-century demand for balance and good sense.

The Village (1783) was a retort to Goldsmith's *Deserted Village*. It has the atmosphere of Jonson's comedies in contrast to the aura of Shakespeare's romantic comedies. Devoid of sentimentalism, Crabbe pictures his native Aldeburgh as he saw it, empty of pastoral glamour, replete with coarseness, penury, suffering, callousness, and squalor. The leading lights of the community are not Auburn's picturesque schoolmaster and noble cleric but a brutal quack doctor and a heartless "sporting parson." The nearest previous approach to such stark photography of rural life was Gay's *Shepherd's Week*.

Poems (1807) appeared after Crabbe's long silence since *The News-Paper* (1785). Its major piece, *The Parish Register,* established Crabbe as a realistic teller of tales. The heyday of the Romantics had not affected his style one jot, but these and all later verses move from the epigrammatic quality of *The Village* to a vigorous narrative swing that sweeps across a still end-stopped heroic couplet. Leafing through his registers, a country parson reflects upon the people noted in the divisions of "Baptisms, Marriages, and Burials." There are some fortunate people, but Crabbe's emphasis is upon the burdens and disappointments of life. Best known is the account of Phoebe Dawson, the rustic beauty, whose husband proved "a captious tyrant or a noisy sot"; Fox was especially impressed with this account.

"Sir Eustace Grey" may have been induced by opium, prescribed for Crabbe by a physician. Octosyllabic stanzas (a b a b b c b c) recount a madhouse scene in which a patient, once happily rich, tells a physician and a visitor of his downfall after the murder of his wife's paramour and of the wild dreams of his madness. A "Methodistic call" to conversion soothes the madman. With remarkable force, a realist plumbs the agonies of insanity.

The Borough (1810) consists of twenty-four heroic-couplet letters to a country friend, minutely examining every phase of a town's life (clearly the life of Aldeburgh) from the professions to the almshouse, from amusements to schools. The work brilliantly dissects a community by perceiving motives and revealing character. In spite of frequent dull passages, it contains some of the poet's best writing, especially in the highwayman's dream of his youth as his execution nears. The story of Peter Grimes, a sadistic fisherman who kills his apprentices with overwork and dies insane, served as the basis for an opera by Benjamin Britten in 1945.

Tales in Verse (1812) offers twenty-one stories, each following the same pattern of initial happiness eventually converted into misery, sometimes by fortuitous circumstances, but more usually by character defects. Skillful variety of treatment avoids monotony. Middle-class personalities predominate. Strange for Crabbe, several of the tales reveal remarkable humor, though usually a grim humor reminiscent of Anglo-Saxon warriors. "The Parting Hour" may have influenced Tennyson's "Enoch Arden."

Tales of the Hall (1819) displays in its twenty-two accounts perhaps the most careless verse and the most penetrating character analyses in Crabbe. The framework is the meeting of half-brothers, George and Richard, after a long separation. As they exchange tales of their encounters, their own relationship grows ever more intimate. These tales demonstrate less brutality than earlier works and more subtle fingering of temperament and mind. The most powerful, however, is "Smugglers and Poachers," in which Rachel marries a gamekeeper to save his poacher brother, her lover. When the two men kill each other in the dark wood, Rachel discovers that she actually loved her husband.

Genteel Romanticism and Late Neoclassic Verse

The Sonnet Revival, instituted by Thomas Warton in *Poems* (1777), was stimulated by a group of minor versifiers, less important intrinsically than for their repopularizing of the form for later poets. Charlotte Smith (1749–1806) was encouraged by the enthusiastic reception of her sixteen pensively melancholy *Elegiac Sonnets* (1784) to constant additions, eventually totaling ninety-two in the tenth edition (1811). William Lisle Bowles (1762–1850), with *Fourteen Sonnets Written Chiefly on Picturesque Spots during a Journey* (1789), deeply affected Coleridge, then a schoolboy at Christ's Hospital; by the eighth edition (1802) Bowles had increased his sonnets to thirty. A famous "Pope Controversy" was started by Bowles in 1806 with deprecation of Pope in an edition of the Augustan's verse. Bryon vigorously championed Pope's cause. However, the only genteel Romantic poet of note was William Gilpin, whose works we will discuss.

Of course, the great voice of conservatism in this era was Edmund Burke, although a host of minor voices in the same period less adequately but ever more voluminously championed the cause of a decaying neoclassicism. Widespread popular distaste for the French Revolution and for English radicals insured a numerical superiority of reactionary writings, though the major literary figures of the age, except for Burke, had abandoned the old ways. Erasmus Darwin, the Rolliad Writers, and others will figure in our discussion of late neoclassic verse.

William Gilpin (1724–1804). A Hampshire parson, William Gilpin proved to be the high priest of the Picturesque. He objected to Burke's insistence on smoothness as essential to beauty. "Regularity and Exactness," Gilpin asserted, "excite no manner of Pleasure in the Imagination." The decline of neoclassic principles fostered a growing taste for that deviation from the symmetrical and smooth which is called picturesque. Between 1782 and 1809 there appeared a series of Gilpin's travels throughout England, Scotland, and Wales in the determined pursuit of the picturesque. No previous traveler had been so completely enthralled by natural scenery to the exclusion of all else. Wherever he went, Gilpin sought the "unspoiled" beauties of nature, which he minutely and rapturously recorded. A delightful parody of Gilpin was William Combe's *Tour of Dr. Syntax in Search of the Picturesque* (I, 1812; II, 1820; III, 1821).

Erasmus Darwin (1731–1802). Grandfather of two famous scientists, Charles Darwin and Francis Galton, Erasmus Darwin was born at Elston, Nottinghamshire, and educated at the universities of Edinburgh and Cambridge. He was an acquaintance of many of the literary and intellectual figures of his time. His work is listed here because he followed the 18th-century tendency, now out of favor, to write textbook material in verse form.

The Botanic Garden (1803). Part II (*The Loves of the Plants*) appeared in 1789, Part I (*The Economy of Vegetation*) in 1792; there were seven editions by 1825. Biological inheritance and selection, the subjects to preoccupy his grandson, interested Erasmus also, and, surprisingly, he anticipates much of Charles Darwin. But, in his own words, Erasmus sought to "enlist imagination under the banner of science." The result is the rather preposterous combination of a botany textbook with *The Rape of the Lock*. With the machinery of Rosicrucian sylphs, Erasmus turns out endless heroic couplets about "swains" (male plants) and "belles" (female plants). Cowper and Hayley were enthusiastic about this poem, and Walpole found here "the most sublime passages in any author or in any of the few languages with which I am acquainted." With this monstrosity, serious neoclassic verse might be said to have committed suicide.

The Rolliad Writers. The Rolliad Writers were comprised of a band of witty Whigs; George Ellis was chief among them, but they included

General John Burgoyne and other devotees of Fox in the Esto Perpetua Club. Disgruntled by the Tory triumph in 1784 under Pitt, this
group produced irregular satiric pieces in *The Morning Herald*.
Their notable accomplishments were: vivacious satire instead of the
traditional Juvenalian solemnities of Churchill and other political sati-·
rists, and, more importantly, the first significant liberal satire in English,
for until that time satire had been almost exclusively the province of
conservatism.

An M.P. from Devonshire, John Rolle, had arrogantly assailed Fox
on the floor of Parliament. The Esto Perpetua clubmen seized upon
him as the epitome of Toryism and produced a mock-epic, *The Rolliad,* a burlesque version of *The Aeneid,* tracing Rolle's ancestry to
Rollo, a Norman lord. Unfortunately, the work, for all its delightful
laughter, rests not so much upon political principles as upon the man-
nerisms and private lives of distinguished Tories.

Thomas Warton succeeded to the poet laureateship in 1785 upon the
death of William Whitehead, and the Rolliad group leaped to the occasion with the gloriously absurd *Probationary Odes.* Supposedly these
were candidating poems submitted to the lord chamberlain by would-be
poets laureate. The burlesque Ossianic ode is priceless, but there are
almost equally good parodies of Mason and the two Wartons. Non-
literary writers, clerics and politicians, were also alleged submitters
of ludicrous odes.

John Wolcot (1738–1819). Born near Kingsbridge, Devonshire,
John Wolcot practiced medicine and rose to be physician general of
Jamaica. Ordained in 1760, he nonetheless continued to pursue a medi-
cal career in Cornwall until he discovered the painting talent of
John Opie in 1781. After moving to London with Opie, he took to
satiric verse under many pseudonyms, chiefly Peter Pindar. It is a bit
pitiful to see the high esteem that Burns held for this minor poetizer.
Wolcot's later years were spent in blindness.

Wolcot's was a sleazy muse, but he is perhaps the greatest caricaturist in English verse. Perhaps most interesting to our day are his
satires on Boswell ("pilot of our literary whale") in *A Poetical and
Congratulatory Epistle to James Boswell, Esq., on His Journal of a
Tour to the Hebrides* (1786) and on both Boswell and Mrs. Piozzi,
formerly Mrs. Thrale, in *Bozzy and Piozzi, or the British Biogra-
phers* (1786). Wolcot's chief butt was the monarch; and private accounts, such as those of Fanny Burney, all too well confirm Wolcot's up-
roarious and unflattering portraits of George III.

William Gifford (1756–1826). William Gifford was a native of Ashburton, Devonshire. The success of his satires made him editor of *The Anti-Jacobin* (1797–98) and first editor of *The Quarterly Review* from 1809 to 1824. Perhaps his best work was his translation of Juvenal in 1802.

The Baviad (1794), imitating the first satire of Persius, and *The Maeviad* (1795), imitating the tenth satire of the first book of Horace, are savage Juvenalian satires directed against Robert Merry and the "Della Cruscan" school of treacly sentimentalists then writing insipid but highly pretentious verse. Sir Walter Scott avowed that these satires "squabashed at one blow a set of coxcombs, who might have humbugged the world long enough." But in truth the gnats were unworthy of such heavy blows.

The Anti-Jacobin Writers. The Anti-Jacobin Writers produced the most brilliant political satires in verse since Dryden. Leading spirit was George Canning, later Prime Minister of England. His chief accomplice was John Hookham Frere, who, with *Prospectus and Specimen* (1817), introduced the Italian burlesque epic to English and provided Byron with the model for *Don Juan*. Gifford was editor, and also prominent was Ellis, converted from Whiggism to the Tory cause. Even the current Prime Minister, Pitt, contributed a few lines here and there to the potpourri. From *The Rolliad* this group of solid Tories seized the idea of bantering laughter as more effective than solemn diatribes. The effectiveness of these pieces consists in the exaggerated and perhaps all-too-logical carrying-out of revolutionary political credos to their ultimate conclusions.

"The Friend of Humanity and the Knife Grinder," by Canning and Frere, burlesques an inept attempt by Southey to imitate classic Sapphic meter in a humanitarian poem, "The Widow." The grotesque twisting of accent is purposeful, superbly ridiculing Southey's poetic clumsiness. Effectively lampooned is the Revolutionists' theoretical love of mankind but intolerant behavior toward an actual individual of the downtrodden mass.

"The Progress of Man," in heroic couplets, is a burlesque of *Progress of Civil Society* (1796), by Richard Payne Knight. Canning and Frere attack the Romantic concepts of primitivism, amorality, and anarchy as an insane abandonment of a proved society for wild and dubious theories.

"The Loves of the Triangles" is Canning's marvelous parody of Erasmus Darwin's *Loves of the Plants*. Following the naturalist's lead, the satirist sings in heroic couplets of "blest Isosceles" and "fair Parabola." If even the name of Darwin's work has survived, it is because of this delightful take-off.

"The Rovers; or, The Double Arrangement" is a burlesque German drama. The group of Tories perceived a vital connection between the extravagance of current German Romanticism and the subversive concepts of the Jacobins. Rogero is a properly noble-minded young Romantic imprisoned by nasty tyrants. The noted "Song by Rogero," from Canning's pen, is a comic masterpiece of dislocated rime and impassioned Romantic cries for freedom.

"New Morality," in heroic couplets composed largely by Canning but with aid from the entire group, including Pitt, was the last poem in the series and the one intensely serious piece. The poem summarizes the group's conservative political principles and its basis for attacks upon its revolutionary victims. Its sincerity and power make it the chief poetic statement of current conservatism, as Burke was the towering conservative figure in prose. The sweeping condemnations of the poem extend to Godwin, Paine, Priestley, Southey, Coleridge, and even Lamb.

THE POETRY OF BURNS

Robert Burns (1759–1796). Robert Burns was born at Alloway, Ayrshire, Scotland, in a cottage built by his father. Educated by his father and by the local schoolmaster, Burns was nonetheless working full time on the farm at an early age, becoming a skilled plowman by the age of fifteen. At sixteen he wrote his first song and embarked upon his first love affair. Although hard-working, his father was meagerly successful, dying of tuberculosis in 1784; Robert and his brother Gilbert salvaged what they could to buy the farm of Mossgiel, near Mauchline. A liaison with Jean Armour produced a child, but their separation at her family's instigation caused Burns to feel free to turn to Mary Campbell. Seeking funds for emigration with her to Jamaica, he printed the "Kilmarnock Poems" in 1786. Mary died, and the appreciation of literary Edinburgh dissuaded Burns from leaving Scotland. Burns acknowledged Jean as his wife and tried farming at Ellisland, near Dumfries. In 1791, failing at this farm, he became a gauger, or exciseman. Heavy drinking may have induced the endocarditis that proved fatal to him.

Most of Burns's verse appears in *Poems, Chiefly in the Scottish Dialect* (Kilmarnock, 1786), with expanded Edinburgh editions in 1787 and 1793. James Johnson secured 184 songs from Burns for inclusion in *The Scots Musical Museum* (1787), and *A Select Collection of Original Scottish Airs for the Voice* (1793–1803) received about seventy Burns songs.

The later 18th century, seeking the "natural bard," unearthed such curiosities as "The Thresher Poet," "The Poetical Milkwoman," and "The Poetical Cobbler." In Burns, "The Ploughman Poet," the age found not merely a remarkable "natural" poet but one of the world's supreme lyricists. Broadly, the poetry of Burns falls into three divisions: poems in the English tradition, the native tradition of Scots vernacular verse, and the innate lyricism of Burns.

POEMS IN THE ENGLISH TRADITION. A sizable amount of Burns's verse employs "Southron" dialect. Many today quote: "Man's inhumanity to man/Makes countless thousands mourn!" without realizing that it comes from "Man Was Made to Mourn," by Burns. Probably this is the one non-Scots poem by Burns that has survived. His other "English" poems generally resemble the conventional work of pre-Romantic poets such as Shenstone, whom Burns greatly admired. "The Lament," occasioned by the separation from Jean, is genteelly lovelorn, and "Despondency" is genteelly melancholic. (First) "Epistle to Robert Graham" has heroic couplets reminiscent of Pope, as this reference to Nature: "Her eye intent on all the mazy plan/She form'd of various parts the various man." "Epistle from Esopus to Maria" contains lines like "A wit in folly, and a fool in wit," lines that could have come from a host of neoclassic satirists.

THE NATIVE TRADITION OF SCOTS VERNACULAR VERSE. Much of what has been termed "romantic" in Burns is not traceable to current Romantic tendencies in England but to the exuberant, earthy, and grotesque force in the "Makaris" and in the work of Ramsay and Fergusson. Burns's rabid advocacy of the French Revolution is not the product of Paine or Godwin appeals but an outgrowth of Scottish nationalistic fervor and Jacobitism. The Romantics' resemblance to much of Burns arises from their conscious revolt against neoclassicism, and their harking-back to characteristics that were never lost in the stream of Scots vernacular verse. While the Romantics were largely symptomatic of a rising middle class, Burns is the authentic proletarian voice, previously heard in Langland, Bunyan, and the early balladeers but never with such energy and sheer melody.

(a) Democratic hostility toward the aristocracy.

"The Twa Dogs, A Tale," in octosyllabic couplets, describes a conversation between Caesar, a gentleman's Newfoundland dog, and Luath, a poor man's mongrel. The vivacious mock-heroic animal tale springs distantly from the medieval beast fable and more recently from the comic *Fables* of Robert Henryson. The sting comes in the attack on the heedless rich, who will callously "Stake on a chance a farmer's stackyard" at cards.

"The Jolly Beggars. A Cantata" was not published until 1799, after Burns's death. The poet had actually witnessed a bacchanal of beggars in the low alehouse of "Poosie Nansie," in Mauchline. The work consists of wild bravado songs linked together by brief descriptions. Lustful, sordid beggary has never been so extravagantly depicted, nor has such camaraderie, sturdy independence, and courageous defiance of fate. Both Carlyle and Matthew Arnold considered this the most remarkable creation by Burns.

"For A' That and A' That" sounds the libertarian cry of the French Revolution, looking to the days when class and discrimination will end and all men will be brothers, recognizing inherent worth and character. It has been termed the Democratic Anthem of the World.

(b) Glorification of the simple and humble life.

"Scotch Drink," in the "Standard Habbie" stanza (3a 3a 3a 2b 3a 2b) invented by Robert Sempill (c. 1595–c. 1668), moves from bacchanalian revelry to the praise of native Scots domestic simplicity and happiness.

"The Cotter's Saturday Night" is self-consciously directed to a genteel audience and therefore suffers most especially from the current taste for sentimentalism. The posturing is obvious in the drawn-out pictures of simplicity and naïveté, homey virtues and solid character, and patriotism and rusticity. Following the pre-Romantic fad, this praise of unaffected peasant life incredibly appears in Spenserian stanzas. The most quoted line, "An honest man's the noblest work of God," is actually from Pope's *Essay on Man*.

"To a Louse, on Seeing One on a Lady's Bonnet at Church," in "Standard Habbie" stanza, confronts high-flown airs with the vulgar louse crawling over the finery. Pretense and hypocrisy should yield to true recognition of what we are.

(First) "Epistle to J. Lapraik," in the same stanza, is a defiant poetic credo. Though exaggerating his lack of learning and minimizing his artfulness, the poem contains Burns's insistence upon the poetry of the heart rather than the academic exercises imitating Anacreon or Catullus with sprinkled classical allusions. In vehemently affirming his indebtedness to the native Scots tradition, Burns lashes out at the entire English genteel tradition with a democratic passion.

"Second Epistle to J. Lapraik," in the same stanza, asserts the poet's resolution in spite of troubles and poverty.

(c) Man's interdependence with the rhythms of nature.

"To a Mouse," in "Standard Habbie" stanza, bridges the gap between man's world and that of the mouse in the similar unexpected misfortune visited upon both. The renowned lines on "The best-laid schemes o' Mice an' Men" display Burns's facility in phrasing commonplace thought in the inevitable fall of a folk proverb.

"To a Mountain-Daisy," in the same stanza, attempts the same apostrophe to a flower. His crushing of the blossom with his plow is symbolic of man's own fate. Burns reveals himself as a "man of feeling," and, appropriately, Mackenzie praised the work.

"The Auld Farmer's New-Year Morning Salutation to His Auld Mare, Maggie," in the same stanza, recounts a farmer's musing as he provides the traditional extra food to his beast at the start of a new year. The deep sense of the shared labor of animal and man is realistic and unsentimental ("Monie a sair daurk we twa hae wrought"). It is the veritable binding of man with lower creation that no bourgeois Romantic could so honestly express.

(d) The essential goodness of life. While pre-Romantic sentiment is strong, Burns speaks really from an innate zest for living.

"Epistle to James Smith," in "Standard Habbie" stanza, expounds a simple hedonism. Burns finds that if he can have good health, homey but adequate fare, and the gift of versifying, he envies none of the wealthy and titled.

"Epistle to a Young Friend" (apparently Andrew Aiken, son of the Robert Aiken in "The Cotter's Saturday Night"), in eight-line octosyllabic stanzas, considers mankind to be weak and selfish but seldom inherently wicked. Burns offers familiar advice on conduct and wryly admits that he too frequently ignores his own good advice.

(e) Satire on Scottish religious life. Burns is not so much an 18th-century anti-clerical as he is a shrewd peasant, cynically mocking hypocrites and the "unco guid."

"The Holy Fair" describes a summer Kirk of Scotland convocation at Mauchline. Incessant preaching in the open air is supplemented by relays of communicants taking the Sacrament in the nearby church. Incongruously, heavy drinking and amorous intrigue accompany the piety. Burns is keenly aware of the inconsistent mixture of the vulgarly secular and the strait-laced religious, suggesting that richly vigorous nature will assert itself against the most rigid theology. This boisterous, rollicking piece strongly resembles Fergusson's "Leith Races," composed of an eight-line stanza with added bob-line, called "Christis Kirk" stave.

"Address to the Deil" reduces Milton's Satan to the folklore devil in an attack upon the hell-fire Calvinism of current Scottish divines.

"Address to the Unco Guid" attacks self-righteousness, urging a tolerant attitude instead of puritanism. In abstractions and moral preaching the poem resembles 18th-century didactic English poems.

"Holy Willie's Prayer," in "Standard Habbie" stanza, is a dramatic monologue, probably the best of all, Browning notwithstanding. Willie, a parish elder at Mauchline, is overheard at prayers. Willie is an antinomian, i.e. a believer in faith without works. He is convinced that he is one of God's elect, and that his eternal salvation is assured regardless of his moral conduct. In solemn, biblical cadences Willie bares his filthy, hypocritical soul. A sinner has effectively damned himself and his doctrine without the slightest awareness of his deed.

(f) Folk narrative.

"Tam o' Shanter," first published in *Edinburgh Magazine* (1791), is probably the best short narrative poem in the language.

Against his Kate's advice, Tam drinks prodigiously and lengthily before riding home from Ayr. Passing ruined Kirk Alloway, his horrified gaze sees a witches' dance amidst flames in the structure. One of the attractive witches, whirling to the devil's hellish tunes, wears a short skirt. Involuntarily shouting "Weel done, Cutty-sark," Tam is set upon by the witches. His horse Meg reaches the middle of Brig o' Doon, where, since it is well known that demons cannot pursue one beyond the middle of running water, a witch snatches off the horse's tail. Meg and her master otherwise escape the infernal powers.

Only Burns among poets in English could tell this tale, for he had a sympathy for rustic superstitions. If you wish so to explain it, Tam was gloriously drunk, but it is also possible that he was not. The tone is perfect—comic but suspenseful, realistic and macabre, pulsating with gusto and vivid coloration. The central figure is the narrator, Burns himself, who, over a tankard of ale, regales the listener with his own lusty and powerful personality. The octosyllabic couplet and the verse paragraph are more skillfully handled by Burns than by Matthew Prior, the "Southron" master of octosyllabic narrative.

THE INNATE LYRICISM OF BURNS. His later poetic career was increasingly devoted to songs, and no other single poet in any literature has produced so many lyrics that compulsively sing themselves. Their charm lies in their utter simplicity and deeply emotional sincerity. Only a few can be cited here from such abundance.

(a) Bawdy songs. *The Merry Muses of Caledonia* (c. 1800), surreptitiously printed, contained many of Burns's obscene verses. These spring partly from the strong popular Scots tradition of lyrical obscenity and partly from the hearty masculine grossness of Burns. Some of the ribaldry (e.g. "Wha'll mow me now") approaches that of Chaucer, other (e.g. "An Ode to Spring on an Original Plan") that of smutty collegians; but none has the sophisticated nastiness of Rochester or Swift.

(b) Love lyrics. Burns is possibly the world's supreme love lyricist. "Green Grow the Rashes," on the exuberant joys of courting, was Burns's first significant lyric. This is the lyric of happy and requited love, as in "I Love My Jean" and "Of a' the Airts the Wind Can Blow," on Jean Armour, the incomparable "Afton Water" (in "Southron" dialect), the ecstatic "A Red, Red Rose," and the lilting "Coming through the Rye."

The sad song, the lyric of blasted romance, appears in "Ae Fond Kiss" (which, in its celebration of Mrs. M'Lehose, quintessentialized according to Scott a thousand unhappy love affairs), the sentimental "Banks o' Doon," and the parallel "Ye Flowery Banks." "Mary Morison" was probably inspired by Alison Begbie, who rejected Burns's proposal of marriage. Humorous treatment of unsuccessful marriages dominates "Whistle o'er the Lave o't" and "Merry Hae I Been Teethin' a Hackle."

"To Mary in Heaven" is a moving eulogy upon the death of Mary Campbell and the cry of all bereft lovers at the passing of the beloved.

Burns seized upon existing lyrics and completely revamped them. "John Anderson My Jo" is a touching piece of loyalty in aged husband and wife, but its folk original was wholly filthy. His last notable lyric, "Address to a Lady" (Jessy Lewars, nurse during his fatal illness), was suggested by a mere tag of an old tune.

(c) Patriotic and political lyrics. "My Heart's in the Highlands" (in "Southron" dialect) is a Scot's intense love of his native hills, though Burns was "Lallans." "Scots Wha Hae" has been called the national anthem of Scotland. The distant inspirer of the work is Blind Harry's *Wallace* on the Scottish victory over the English at Bannockburn, but the actual impulse is Burns's rabid support of the French Revolution and hostility to current reactionaries. Burns ended his poem with a prose pronunciamento: "So may God defend the cause of Truth and Liberty, as he did that day!" "Charlie, he's my darling" and "It Was a' for Our Rightfu' King," on the Stuart Pretender, Bonnie Prince Charlie, are sentimental Jacobitism.

(d) Conviviality. "Willie Brew'd a Peck o' Maut" has been the favorite drinking song, the "Sweet Adeline," of the British Isles since the days of Burns. It is the apotheosis of harmless befuddlement and alcoholic exultation, a far cry from the Christmas-card good spirits of "Southron" drinking songs. "Auld Lang Syne" has become the reunion and parting song of the entire English-speaking world, the peculiarly Burnsian amalgam of simple but inevitable melody with homey nostalgia for friendship.

THE POETRY OF BLAKE

William Blake (1757–1827). William Blake was the son of a London hosier whose antecedents are unknown. After studying at Pars's Drawing School and receiving little conventional education, he was apprenticed in 1771 to James Basire, an engraver, who set him to drawings of Gothic monuments. For a time Blake studied in the antique school of the Royal Academy and then set himself up as an independent engraver. In 1782 he married Catherine Boucher (or Bouchier), whom he taught to read and write, and although it was a childless marriage, it was apparently a happy one. From 1792 until 1800 the Blakes lived in Lambeth, on the south bank of the Thames. Blake moved to Felpham in 1800 to do art work for William Hayley but quarreled with his benefactor in 1804 and returned to London. He made his living by engraving, much of it hackwork. His works, starting with the *Songs of Innocence,* are among the most remarkable books ever issued; Blake wrote the verse, drew the illustrations, prepared the engraved plates, and hand-colored the printed volumes with his wife.

After *Songs of Innocence and Experience,* the literary world of his own age completely dismissed Blake as a competent engraver with a penchant for fantastically eccentric, if not downright insane, verse. William M. Rossetti and William Butler Yeats highly praised Blake but admitted that much of his work was enigmatic. Writers of our century, notably James Joyce, have increasingly traversed the highways explored by Blake; and at last he has gained wide recognition. However, much of the enthusiasm for Blake has been a trifle faddist, and when, if ever, he becomes wholly clear, many of his admirers may troop off to the banners of another esoteric writer. Eminent modern interpreters agree upon only one point concerning Blake—his greatness; except for Shakespeare, he is the most discussed English poet in the 20th century, and Blake studies today are bewildering both in their mass and in their variety of approaches. Greatly oversimplified and with the expectation of definitive analyses of Blake yet to come, the following suggestions are offered as partial helps in comprehending this difficult poet.

Blake's verse must be considered in conjunction with his illustrations. He was simultaneously a pictorial and a literary artist whose drawings and poetry form an indissoluble unit, each clarifying and reinforcing the other. In his major works every page is his own engraving of intertwined verse and picture.

Poetical Sketches (1783), his first work, consisting of poems written between the ages of twelve and twenty, is largely imitative, the product of a poet who has yet to find his own voice. "My Silks and Fine Array" resembles "Come away, come away, death" from *Twelfth Night.* "Fair Elenor" belongs essentially to the Graveyard School. "Gwin, King of Norway" follows the Scandinavian verse of Gray. "To the Evening Star" sounds rather like Collins. "To the Muses" is neoclassic simplicity and beauty, perhaps the last masterpiece of its type. "Mad Song" is what Chatterton might have done had he lived.

Thereafter, from *Songs of Innocence* to his last prophetic book, Blake is wholly himself, seeking his own vision of life. All of these mature writings constitute one unit. Blake intensifies and widens his search, but none of his alterations of viewpoint negate his previous works. Distantly the germ of his later *Milton* and *Jerusalem* appears in the *Songs of Innocence and Experience.* The earlier poems clarify the later works, and the last poems bring depth to the earlier.

In "An Imitation of Spenser" in *Poetical Sketches,* Blake refers to Apollo, Mercury, Minerva, and Pan, i.e. the mythological figures dear to Western poets ever since the 13th century at least, and celebrated endlessly in neoclassic verse. Had his later poetry continued to recount these familiar beings, he might have been clearer to his own age and to ours (e.g. Los resembles Apollo, Urizen resembles Jupiter). But Blake begins *The Marriage of Heaven and Hell* with the strange Rintrah and proceeds in his later works to lard his text with such puzzling characters as Ololon, Palamabron, Bromion, and Theotormon. This private mythology apparently arose in part from: (a) his lack of formal classical education; (b) the triteness of these shop-worn classical figures; (c) the close association of classical mythology with neo-classicism which Blake detested; and (d) Blake's own violent independence and innate power of myth-making.

Unrestrained by conventional education, Blake zealously immersed himself in readings and study of esoteric literature such as the Hebrew Cabbala, and alchemical and astrological writings. He therefore frequently represents a tradition of great antiquity and continuity that nonetheless is alien to the cultured reader of his own day and of ours. His own 18th century provided numerous, and now forgotten, highly imaginative works of speculative mythology before K. O. Müller early in the 19th century inaugurated the modern scientific examination of mythology. As early as *Stonehenge* (1740), William Stukeley asserted the now discredited theory that the primitive monument was a worship place for Druids who had emigrated from Phoenicia; Druid Stonehenge figures prominently in the later works of Blake. In India a protégé of Sir William Jones, Francis Wilford, mistakenly believed that East Indian myths of a White Island referred to Albion. Around the turn of the 19th century English periodicals reprinted from *Asiatic Researches* (1788) Wilford's grandiose contention that England was the site of all antediluvian history and the original point from which all myths had developed. At any rate, Blake's Albion became the prototype of all mythology and all mankind, and when Richard Brothers declared in 1798 that the ancient Britons were the lost tribes of Israel, Blake apparently agreed, at least symbolically.

From a numerous host of such speculative mythologists, Blake derived and amplified several contentions:

(a) All myth has a common origin. With great imagination Blake perceived what modern psychologists agree to—that myth has arisen because all men share kindred attitudes of mind.

(b) Myth arose among distant primitives who were given direct symbols from God, but man has since perverted and confused the original truth. The speculative mythologists saw Jupiter as cognate with Seva of India, Pan as a corruption of Jehovah, and so on. Blake felt that man's present ill estate had resulted from a failure to follow the guidance of God, and he felt that myth held the key to God's pristine revelation.

(c) Myth was the symbol of innate human drives and purposes. Some of these speculative mythologists scandalously interpreted virtually all myth as sex symbolism. Blake saw all myth as projection from the universal unconscious of mankind.

The distinguished psychologist Carl Jung (1875–1961) would probably have described Blake as an intuition introvert. Such a being is dominated by imagination and spins his imaginative picture of reality from his own psyche. Perhaps the fundamental key to Blake is a realization that he is never really talking about the outer world of the senses which preoccupies most of us; all his vast mythology is talking exclusively, as he plainly states, about the tumultuous forces warring within the individual human being. The world-shattering figures of the prophetic books are the personifications of impulses within Blake himself. Although he apparently recognized that his vision was conditioned by his own nature, to make all men understand themselves, he made an unprecedented exploration of his own psyche. Blake's process of self-analysis in his mature verse falls into three broad divisions:

1. FIRST PERIOD (1789–93). The conflict within his own psyche is diagnosed as the duel between Inspiration and Reason. Associated concepts such as humanitarianism, personal and political freedom, emotion, and creative activity cluster about Inspiration. Opposing attitudes such as callousness, political and individual restraint, cold calculation, and static rigidity cluster about Reason. The symbolism of this verse cannot be fully comprehended except in the light of his subsequent writing, but it is sufficiently conventional to appear understandable and relatively familiar to readers of the standard English poetic tradition.

2. SECOND PERIOD (1793–97). The conflict continues as the previous duel, but the symbolism emerges as Blake's personal mythology. Although the strange figures initially puzzle the reader, the vividness of imagery, the masterful phrasing, and the bardic intensity grip the reader and carry him over occasional bewilderment.

3. THIRD PERIOD (1797–1820). Here the conflict broadens to become fourfold with four personified elements—[1]Inspiration,[2]Reason,[3]Emotion, and[4]Senses—all warring each with each other. Instead of the earlier relative simplicity of two main struggles, the later works then offer a total of twelve major struggles (however, all of these are not equally expounded). The complexity now becomes astounding, and the average reader is often left confused.

At the turn of this century Jung, without indebtedness to Blake (whose international reputation has arisen only within the last few decades), made a charting of the psyche which bears a remarkable resemblance to Blake's final definitive analysis. Jung posits the Self as the goal of individual life, and this self is composed of the harmonious balance of all elements within a being's nature. The Self is dream-symbolized as a sleeping giant as yet unaroused to vibrant living (for all of us to some degree lack the perfect psychic balance). Blake's sleeping giant is Albion. Jung also says that within every male the latent feminine qualities are personified as the "Anima," and the masculine element in the female is the "Animus." Blake gives the name "Jerusalem" to the Jungian Anima. Jung sees the fulfillment of personal balance in the union of the Anima with the sleeping giant, who is now aroused to full creativity, and just such awakening at the end of Blake's *Jerusalem* is occasioned by the union of Jerusalem with Albion.

Jung observes four functions in each human being—Intuition, Thought, Feeling, and Sensation. In dreams each of these is frequently personified by men as four male figures. The four functions in the order above are personified by Blake as Los (probably an anagram for *Sol,* the sun), Urizen ("your reason"), Luvah ("lover"), and Tharmas (from Tama, Tamas, or Tamasee, "darkness" in the East Indian *Bhagavad-Gita*). "Four Mighty Ones are in every Man," Blake asserts. Jung states that people, at least in European culture, tend to equate the dominant function with the North compass point. For a man dominated by Intuition (as Blake was), his Jungian psychic compass would look thus:

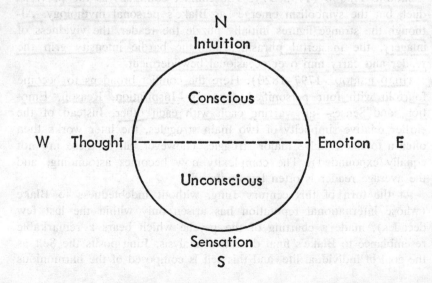

Blake himself proposes a fascinatingly similar arrangement:

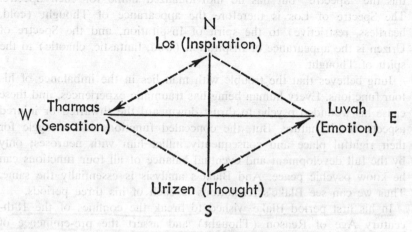

The Jungian scheme may actually explain more of Blake than Blake would realize, for Tharmas (Sensation) is obviously the most vague and repressed function in Blake; Tharmas is the last of the four to emerge, and his creator goes far afield to find a name for him.

Blake pursues his analysis of his own psyche so far that he produces an anima (Blake terms it an "Emanation") for each of his four functions:

BLAKE'S TERM FOR FUNCTION	SYMBOL	EMANATION	INTERPRETATION
Los	Inspiration	Enitharmon	Sensation regarded by Inspiration
Urizen	Thought	Ahania	Emotion regarded by Thought
Luvah	Emotion	Vala	Thought regarded by Emotion
Tharmas	Sensation	Enion	Inspiration regarded by Sensation

As the Blake chart above indicates, the Emanations can best be understood by following the arrows of the broken lines (for example, Enitharmon is the way Inspiration looks out from its vantage point and interprets Sensation).

Jung further suggests that each of the functions has a "Shadow," that is, an image of what its opposing function seems to be. Blake calls this the "Spectre" but has no individualized name for each Spectre. The Spectre of Los is therefore the appearance of Thought (cold, heartless, restrictive) to the spirit of Inspiration, and the Spectre of Urizen is the appearance of Inspiration (wild, fantastic, chaotic) to the spirit of Thought.

Jung believes that the trouble with man lies in the imbalance of his four functions. Every human being has traumatic experiences, and these cause his wounded psyche to thrust downward the thwarted or injured aspects of his nature. But, the concealed functions will struggle for their rightful place and consequently inflict him with neuroses; only by the full development and eventual balance of all four functions can he know psychic peace. And Blake's analysis is essentially the same. Thus we can see Blake's resolutions in each of his three periods.

1.) In his first period Blake wished to break the confines of the 18th-century Age of Reason (Thought) and assert the pre-eminence of Inspiration. He sensed, however, that the easy dichotomy (Thought-Inspiration, Evil-Good, Bondage-Freedom) is an oversimplification and that the problem is not solved simply by brushing away all that seems opposed.

2.) In his second period Blake realized that the opposites must be reconciled, that Thought and Inspiration must be harmoniously balanced. Since the Age of Reason had overwhelmingly stated its position, Blake as vehemently supported Inspiration in order to correct the balance.

3.) In his third period Blake, so far as his own dominance by Inspiration would permit, attempted to see all four functions through to complete development and eventual harmony.

"The whole of Freud's teaching may be found in *The Marriage of Heaven and Hell,*" asserts W. H. Auden. Sigmund Freud (1856–1939) bases much of his psychological theory upon the danger of repression. In a highly complex and interdependent society, the individual is constantly compelled to repress certain elements of his nature: overt sexuality, violent disagreement, and so on. These repressions cause a maiming of the psyche for which most civilized people must supply compensations: hobbies, competitive sports, and the like. Many human beings, however, are warped or even destroyed by the inner upheaval of repressed elements, and even the most "normal" are frequently troubled. Blake senses the same trouble and advocates a release of these inhibitions. Paradoxically he asserts: "The road of excess leads to the palace of wisdom." To him restraint is deformation, while the unchained spirit, carrying every aspect of its nature to its apogee, will surprisingly achieve true balance and creative harmony.

It must not be assumed from his advocacy of complete freedom and unrepressed expression that Blake was a wild-eyed anarchist. He was actually the mildest of mortals for the most part (even the quarrel with Hayley is more in his verse than it was in the flesh), and the warfare he chronicles in such detail is inward and not outward. By what Freud would call "sublimation," Blake works out his struggle in art, not in attacking the physical world about him.

The dream world, so elaborately explored by Freud, was previously scrutinized exhaustively by Blake. The upper part of this realm of the unconscious is "Beulah," which Blake frankly declares was "created for those who Sleep." This is the area of sweet dream-nymphs, the Arcadian abode of idyllic slumber. Below lies "Ulro," a nightmarish wasteland, and here the repressed functions erupt in hideous horrors, the terrifying dream-ghosts. Blake sees the psychic life of man upon a great wheel that descends through Beulah, Generation (the physical world in which we live), and Ulro to surge upward to Eden, which is the state of imaginative power and balanced harmony. Again anticipating Freud, Blake sees the way to psychic salvation, not in ignoring the unconscious life, but in plumbing to its depths, releasing and developing the repressed elements, and thus achieving the purified and symmetrical psyche.

Some recent Blake scholars, anxious to rescue the poet from the fervent lovers of esoterica, have denied that Blake was a mystic. Perhaps one should better suggest that there are mystics and mystics. Blake certainly seems in the direct tradition of Jakob Böhme (1575–1624) and William Law. The Böhmist contemplation of the *Urgrund* (the ultimate cosmic principle) within the human spirit reaches these proportions in *Jerusalem:*

> in your own Bosom you bear your Heaven
> And Earth; & all you behold, tho' it appears Without, it is Within
> In your Imagination, of which this World of Mortality is but a Shadow.

Blake is asserting here that the psychic or spiritual world is the true world and that God is not a cosmic monarch on a distant throne but the omnipresent dweller within each receptive human soul. Blake's profound probings of his own psyche convince him of what kindred mystics proclaim—that the moral governance of the universe is beyond good and evil. Sensation and Thought have too often led men to a dualism (God versus Satan, right versus wrong, light versus darkness). Mystics like Blake intuit a unified universe wherein the apparently warring elements are actually different aspects of a divine fitness. What is frequently termed evil is really power and energy, mistakenly condemned by the unimaginative and the unilluminated.

From Böhme and from a long line of mystics also came the "double vision" developed by Blake. Every experience and perception of life is actually a symbol to those gifted with imagination. As Joyce was later to see "epiphanies" in supposedly the most trivial episodes, so Blake saw the world in a grain of sand and cosmic perturbations in his domestic life with Catherine.

Blake's father had been associated with the Church of the New Jerusalem in London, an offshoot of an 18th-century sect founded by the Swedish scientist-mystic Emanuel Swedenborg (1688–1772). Blake was deeply affected by Swedenborg's prediction that a new dispensation for mankind was starting in 1757, the year of the poet's birth. Swedenborg also advocated a symbolic interpretation of every experience and especially of the Bible. At great length the scientist recounted "Memorable Relations," in which he personally made spirit calls in Heaven upon the angels and ancient Hebrew prophets, receiving elucidation for difficult passages in scripture. Impressed in his earlier years, Blake later revolted against what he deemed rather conventional theological interpretations discovered by Swedenborg in his heavenly visitations, and he propounded "visionary" mysticism in a retort to the Swedish thinker's frequently "rational" mysticism.

Blake was no doubt aware that his writings had aspects of genius. The reader must therefore approach him with the "visionary" imaginative mind.

Governed by the foregoing ideas, the interpretations that follow will attempt as conservative and uncultish a viewpoint as possible.

Poems of the First Period (1789–1793)

Songs of Innocence (1789) represents the later "Beulah" of Blake. This is an imaginative picture of the state of innocence derived from the Bible, pastoral tradition, and the growing Romantic fascination with childhood and a supposed primitive condition of human perfection in innocence. A. E. Housman says of these apparently naïve pieces: "The meaning is a poor foolish disappointing thing in comparison with the verses themselves."

"Introduction" is in effect a brief essay on poetry. It indicates a divine command to sing, the subject of innocent bliss, the fitting of melody to words, and the writing from unstained imagination.

"The Echoing Green" reminds one of portions of Goldsmith's *Deserted Village,* but its idyllic nostalgia is much more artfully artless.

"The Lamb" sees kindred innocence in the child, the lamb, and the Christ. The goodness of God's innocent gifts elicits heart-felt praise of the rightness of creation.

"Infant Joy" gives the name Joy to an infant two days old and viewed as the epitome of unsullied innocence.

"The Little Black Boy" is peaceful celebration of the shared innocence of all children, but it is obviously inspired by the current anti-slavery agitation. It was a favorite of Coleridge's.

"Laughing Song" strikes a note of simplicity and nature rhapsody virtually unknown since the Renaissance Elizabethans.

"A Cradle Song" is a mother's crooning over her infant, seeing in it the parallel to the Christ child. This was probably influenced by Watts's "Cradle Hymn."

"Nurse's Song" is the happiness of uninhibited childhood, freely romping and playing.

"Holy Thursday" recounts the procession of charity youngsters on the holy day to St. Paul's Cathedral for a service of joyful song. Blake here speaks in his own voice.

"The Chimney-Sweeper," from an urchin's mouth, tells of a dream of release from the drudgery and dirt of chimney sweeping, a dream that steels the children to continue their job. Lamb particularly admired this poem, which was occasioned by agitation to outlaw employment of children as chimney sweepers.

"The Divine Image" is man who in purity mirrors the fourfold divine creed of brotherhood—Mercy, Pity, Peace, Love. This poem especially delighted Coleridge. It was composed in the London Church of the New Jerusalem.

"Night" brings pleasant dreams, assuring a Golden Age in the Hereafter, when the lion will lie down with the lamb.

"On Another's Sorrow" asserts that compassion is integral to man's imaginative nature, and through such emotion he can transform existence.

Songs of Experience (1794) are the poems of "Generation," the actual world of suffering mankind. They are sufficient cause to force man into the nightmarish horrors of "Ulro," when he contemplates the inhumanity and injustice attendant upon fallen man. Blake already perceived, however, that this apparently evil descent is necessary in the wheel of destiny. By following the complete cycle, the soul may pass through the apparent horrors into a fuller, more active life in the Creative Imagination. Analyses of these poems seem nastily textbookish, for Blake's concepts are powerfully poetized by concrete, evocative symbols; and their sheer lyricism has sung itself to many who care little for the theoretical content or who might be slightly horrified if they fully grasped the implications. Many of these poems are deliberate ripostes to pieces in *Songs of Innocence*.

"Introduction," spoken by the Bard (later "Los"), calls upon Earth (later "Vala," Material Nature) to proceed to its cycle, which will include the bitterness of experience, for this physical world (later "Mundane Shell") will be superseded by the visionary age (later "Eden").

"Earth's Answer" despairs initially at the imprisonment of mankind in fear and jealousy (by the later "Urizen") but calls for the release of men's spirits from bondage and repression.

"Nurse's Song" counters the identically titled poem in *Songs of Innocence*. Thinking of her own withered life, the nurse rues that the innocence of childhood is followed by the hypocrisy and inhibitions of adulthood.

"The Fly" reminds one of Gray's "Ode on the Spring," but where Gray saw the fly as a symbol of man's brevity and inconsequence, Blake sees the fly as symbolic of the universal importance of life. Every living thing is a work of God and has God within it.

"The Tyger" counters "The Lamb," asking the same questions about its role in the universe. The tiger symbolizes the fierce forces in the soul which are necessary to break the bonds of experience. From the later works, it appears that "When the stars threw down their spears" is Reason capitulating before wrathful energy. Blake, like Böhme, senses that the apparent evil and malevolence in the tiger are simply another manifestation of the unity of God, here showing His power and energy. Limited minds appreciate the lamb but are aghast at the tiger element in the universe. Power and energy are not to be scorned but to be revered and carried to their apogee of fulfillment. Charles Lamb said of this book: "There is one to a tiger . . . which is glorious." Its impressive stroking in octosyllabics makes it one of the most technically successful lyrics in English.

"The Clod and the Pebble" contrasts self-sacrificial love in the clod with selfish, acquisitive love in the pebble. Throughout the later verse of Blake the plastic symbols, such as clay or organic life, are deemed ^(bending) capable of change and improvement, while the rigid symbols, such as rocks or the complaisant neoclassic mentality, are associated with eternal, spiritual death.

"Holy Thursday" counters the similarly titled poem in *Songs of Innocence*. Blake attacks traditional, organized charity by which elders frighten and repress children. In England, then reputedly the world's wealthiest nation, how could so many youngsters be mistreated and denied necessities?

"A Poison Tree" recounts the dangers of repression. Wrath that is vented will clear itself. Concealed wrath breeds pestilence and destruction. Blake suggests that the evil fruit of the Tree of Knowledge in the Garden of Eden was actually the fruit of restraint.

"The Angel" is an old woman's bitter lamentation for her wasted life. Strait-jacketed by the code of maidenly forbearance, she could not freely accept love, as she likewise could not resist it. Love (Eros of the ancients, later "Luvah" to Blake) departed, and now she lives only with her regrets.

"The Sick Rose" portrays the destruction of love by selfishness and restraint in the figure of the cankerworm upon the flower of love.

"To Tirzah" has every appearance of being a later poem. Although Tirzah is merely part of a list in Numbers 27:7, Blake in *Milton* labels her "Natural Religion," i.e. the rationalistic, pragmatic mind of the Enlightenment. She is the cold, chaste woman who ensnares men to the delusion of mortal bodies by her hypocrisy and selfishness. To Blake, the true body is spiritual.

"My Pretty Rose-Tree" seems to symbolize sexual indulgence in the rose tree. When the initial spontaneity of impulse or of act is hindered, it turns to calculation, and jealousy is born.

"Ah! Sun-Flower," in the flower that turns its head to follow the sun's course and yet is rooted in the earth, provides Blake with a symbol for all human beings whose lives are dominated and frustrated by a longing they can never expect to satisfy. Despite their desire to escape to a freer sphere of full psychic expression, they are chained to earth by their own limitations.

"The Garden of Love" counters the entire spirit of the previous volume, perhaps most especially "The Echoing Green." Organized religion, stigmatized as the great forbidder ("Thou shalt not"), is the frozen state of repression. Like most liberals of the era, Blake as an opponent of the political and social order is also an assailant of the Established Church, which is dedicated to the maintenance of the *status quo*. He sees jealousy, cruelty, hyprocrisy, and repression denying the natural play of the affections, turning potential joy into real misery.

"London" is the most powerfully effective indictment of the period. What Paine, Godwin, Mary Wollstonecraft, and numerous other liberals among his contemporaries scourge in countless pages, Blake excoriates in sixteen lines. What man has made of man is the horror. Daring imagery renders appalling the era's deformations, demonstrated in child labor, militarism, and harlotry. Instead of the complaisant self-portrait of the age as prosperous and free, Blake with a few strokes depicts a blighted world of slavery.

"The Chimney-Sweeper" counters the similarly titled poem in *Songs of Innocence*. Parental tyranny and the determination of Church and State to impose a repressive social and economic system result in the enslavement of childhood and all humanity.

"The Human Abstract" counters "The Divine Image." The hypocrite who speaks is the plausible supporter of Hobbes and Mandeville, with their explanation of human behavior as "self-interest." Blake sees the result as a system of hypocrisy rigidly binding mankind to a false and oppressive tyranny.

The Rossetti Manuscript, sometimes termed "The Manuscript Book," was a notebook maintained c. 1793–c. 1818 by Blake. It is filled with sketches and verses, some of which he incorporated in his printed works; others were unknown until printed by William M. Rossetti. The first section of the manuscript, c. 1793, consists of poems apparently rejected from *Songs of Innocence and Experience*. These are exquisite lyrics recapitulating Blake's attitudes during this period.

Poems of the Second Period (1793–1797)

Title-page dates during Blake's lifetime do not necessarily signify the exact year of release. They may, as in *Milton,* indicate the year when Blake commenced the work or, as seems likely for *Ahania,* when in retrospect Blake felt that the germ of the piece was first in his mind. The following arrangement tries to show the developing concepts of Blake.

APPLICATION OF BLAKE'S MYTHOLOGY TO EVENTS OF HIS DAY. *Tiriel* (c. *1789,* 1874) was apparently the first of the prophetic books, though it remained in manuscript until printed by Rossetti. Because, almost uniquely in Blake, it has a full, clear story line, many would deny that it belongs among the prophetic writings. The poem is Blake's proclamation that an old age is dying and a new one is coming to birth. Tiriel (he never reappears after this work, Urizen largely taking his place) is an enfeebled religion, or, at least, a way of thought whose children are usurping his tyrannous rule. With the death of his wife Myratana (his inspiration), he wanders aimlessly in the Vales of Har (degenerate poetry of the neoclassic variety). His mad brother Ijim (representing the common people) tries to restore Tiriel to his kingdom, as the mass mind clings to old traditions. Disillusioned, Ijim wanders off into sterile repetition of formulas. Tiriel blights everything, especially Hela (Sex), and finally, conscious of his futility, he expires. The old error is at last dead and a new spirit may rise. With this work Blake first produced the long rhetorical line employed throughout most of the prophetic books. This septenary in loping heptameter frequently fails to scan conventionally. It is the deep emotional conviction of Blake that gives power and cadence to the line.

The Book of Thel (1789) opens with the famous motto that asks whether the opposites can be reconciled—"Love in a golden bowl?" (the human brain case). Thel's answer is no, but Blake insists that they can be and must be harmonized. With this work Blake first presents the theme that will dominate all his subsequent works: the soul is eternal but must pass through the wheel of Destiny, through Generation, and ultimately to Eden. Thel is an unborn soul, fearfully hesitant about entering life. Blake rigorously carries through his metaphor that to a "Beulah" spirit like Thel the human earthly existence seems death. Coming from the Vales of Har and therefore suffering from an unrealistic idealism, Thel cannot face the prospect of the brevity and pain of terrestrial life. Deficient in imaginative power, she refuses the challenge of human existence and flees back into the Vales of Har. Projected in more commonplace terms, Blake suggests that the artificial neoclassic picture of life, apparently so calm and neat, cannot comprehend the full, uninhibited participation in life that is needed to break the narrow circle and expand to the richest, completest experience. Thel's name seems to come from the Greek *thelos* ("will" or "desire"), and the poem details the tragedy of inadequate will to live. The lucid simplicity and relative paucity of bizarre names have caused this poem often to be excluded from the prophetic books.

The Marriage of Heaven and Hell is undated but was printed by Blake probably c. 1790–93. It is a satiric retort to Swedenborg's *De Caelo et Inferno* ("Concerning Heaven and Hell"). While Swedenborg espouses the conventional view that evil is to be eliminated and good exalted. Blake, as his title indicates, regards "good" and "evil" as misnomers for "passivity" and "energy," both of which must be fully developed to achieve the full life. Since this is satire and since conservatism had long been in the ascendancy, Blake purposely overstates the case for "energy."

The opening Argument may be the first consciously free verse in English. Blake enunciates his version of the descent of man from primal simplicity to the current era of moral repression. The opening and closing lines state his belief that a new age of the liberated spirit is now marshaling its revolutionary spirit.

"The voice of the Devil" is Blake's own voice, exalting Energy (the Freudian Pleasure Principle) over Reason (the Freudian Reality Principle). Self-restraint is considered not strength of will but weakness of desire. Applying his concept to *Paradise Lost,* Blake sees Milton's Messiah as Urizen, the great forbidder, and Milton's Satan as Los, energy and inspiration. Blake's memorable wording is greatly responsible for the dubious Romantic assertion that Satan is the hero of *Paradise Lost.* In *Milton,* Blake will more exhaustively "correct" the earlier poet.

The first "Memorable Fancy" satirizes the "Memorable Relations" of Swedenborg, in which the Swede recounted his own intimate conversations with celestial beings to reveal orthodox theology and morality. Blake allows Inspiration to give him the vision that the supposed objective world is really an inner concept projected as a world outside man's consciousness because of his subservience to the senses. He maintains that the great reality is the human Imagination.

"Proverbs of Hell" offers perhaps the most astounding collection of original aphorisms in the language. Their dominant themes are an attack upon any form of psychic repression, an advocacy of impulsive and energetic action, and a glorification of imagination. Although at this period Blake still sees the inner conflict as essentially a duel, note the constant recurrence of fours throughout this section.

Following the proverbs is an untitled page in which Blake asserts his and modern psychology's general belief that the figures of mythology are not modeled upon outer sense perception but are projections of unconscious symbolism.

In the second "Memorable Fancy," Isaiah and Ezekiel praise energy and inspiration as the pole stars of life.

The third "Memorable Fancy" first allegorizes the creativity of art as the product of Genius (Eagle) and Revolutionary Imagination

(Lions), with some aid from Reason (Viper). It concludes with renewed insistence upon the necessary warring of Reason and Imagination from which true creativity will emerge.

The fourth "Memorable Fancy" has a wholly conventional person (the Angel) conduct Blake through the abysses of the human mind. Believing in the depravity of the natural man, the Angel can see only evil within man—a contest between physical passion and bloodless abstractions. Leviathan (from Hobbes) causes Orthodox reasoners to be drowned in the Sea of Time and Space. Believing in the essential goodness of man, Blake, on the contrary, finds in the human mind imaginative powers that release and ennoble the human spirit.

The fifth "Memorable Fancy" anticipates his later "Everlasting Gospel," with its interpretation of Christ as energy and inspiration, vigorously countering the traditional piety of passivity and reason.

Visions of the Daughters of Albion (1793), using the septenary, insists that everyone is entitled to the most ideal union he or she can secure. Marriage should be no restriction; in fact, any restriction is wrong. Perfect unions are frequently prevented by the jealousy of lovers, hypocrisy in those loved, and the rigid persecution of an authoritarian society. These deficiencies, not the sex impulse, are the genuine crimes and the true cause of human suffering. Oothoon, the female spirit yearning for unfettered love, sounds like a poetized Mary Wollstonecraft, and indebtedness to Macpherson can easily be seen:

Ossian names: Oithona, Tonthormod, Brumo, Lutha
Blake names: Oothoon, Theotormon, Bromion, Leutha

A Song of Liberty (c. 1793) considers the current unrest throughout Western Europe the prelude to the overthrow of all repression by the flaming powers of innate energy. Although not so named in this work, Orc (spirit of rebellion) will overpower Urizen (conventional rationalism). Urthona (cf. Urthono in Ossian) is named; he is the regent of the world of spirit and appears in this world as Los.

America (1793) looks like an elaboration of *A Song of Liberty*, now in the septenary form. The American Revolution is seen by Blake as the wild upsurge of Orc (in men like Washington, Franklin, and Paine) against Albion's Angel (sarcastic for the repressive George III). Not political freedom alone, but complete liberation of the human spirit from all restrictions is foreshadowed. Orc is a time name of Luvah, as Los is of Urthona; possibly Orc is an anagram for *cor* (Latin, "heart"). The association of Orc with flames and ruddy flesh suggests the ancient Eros, a powerful god of love's violence, not that saccharine cherub, the infant Cupid. Certainly Orc is Blake's Prometheus and Adonis.

Europe (1794) envisions Orc now as the spirit of the French Revolution, freeing himself from Asia (repression as symbolized in the Mosaic code). The North in Blake's symbolism is properly the realm of inspiration, but Urizen has usurped control. Albion's Angel and his ministers improperly counter the revolutionary spirit with reactionary oppression, but Los is roused to summon mankind to freedom. The septenary is here varied with a number of three- and four-beat lines.

THE BEGINNING OF THE COSMIC MYTH. *The Book of Urizen* (1794) is Blake's first attempt at an over-all explanation of man's total psychic problems. The arena of struggle is simultaneously within the individual soul and within the entire spirit of mankind throughout earthly existence. Characteristic of this second period, Blake sees the struggle as twofold: between Urizen and Los. Reason is not evil in itself, but the domination of Reason is evil. In usurping the role of Inspiration, Reason acts sincerely, but Urizen's lack of imaginative power results in terrible errors. Urizen resembles Jehovah or Uranus as he fabricates the material world, from which Eternity is barred. Superstition and restraint are imposed upon the created world to maintain Urizen's dominance. Los, realizing that fullness of form must be achieved in order to reach the goal of harmonious balance, establishes an evolutionary cycle which, through Revolt (here personified as Fuzon), will eventually bring the new age of perfection. Most of the poem is written in lines essentially of four beats.

The Book of Ahania (dated 1789, engraved 1795) continues the Fuzon myth from *Urizen* and has therefore been termed by Swinburne and others "The Second Book of Urizen." Fuzon (who does not subsequently appear in Blake's writings) seems identical with Orc. Like Kronos (Saturn), he is his father's last-born and the leader of revolt against his father Urizen. In his assault upon his father Ahania is born from his loins, much as Aphrodite sprang from the genitals of Uranus. Ahania is Passion or Pleasure, cast out by Urizen in his search for "joy without pain." Fuzon is crucified upon the "Tree of Mystery," as youthful energy is fettered by the restrictive powers of Urizen's law. The concluding fifth chapter is Ahania's exquisitely beautiful lamentation for Urizen's fall from pristine freedom and beauty. The poem employs the same line as *Urizen*.

The Book of Los (1795) recounts much of the story of *The Book of*

Urizen but now from Los's viewpoint. Los resembles Apollo, as he is the god of light amidst the dark world of Urizen. To Urizen, Los's inspiration and energy seem evil, but whatever faults Los displays arise from repression, which results in inadequate expression. Los, the spirit of poetry, starts the process of building and forming that will eventually carry man on the wheel of destiny to perfection. The work is in the same line as *Urizen.*

The Song of Los (1795) mixes the septenary with the four-beat line. The poem consists of two parts:

"Africa" is a Blake symbol of Beulah, the realm of primitive innocence and freedom. The rule of Urizen blights this paradise. Honestly —but mistakenly—trying by reason to establish a state of wisdom and happiness, Urizen enunciates philosophies through "Brama," Moses, Trismegistus, Pythagoras, Socrates, and Plato. The final result is 18th-century deism, a rationalistic faith roundly condemned by Blake. But a new spirit is in the air, and, significantly, the last line of "Africa" is the first line of *America.*

"Asia" as throughout the prophetic books is a symbol of error, the equivalent of Ulro. The Kings of Asia call for tyrannical control of man, but Orc is rising against Urizen. Blake concludes with ecstatic contemplation of the revolutionary explosion portending the new era of freedom.

With *America* and *Europe,* these two poems form a Blakean tetralogy upon the four continents.

Poems of the Third Period (1797–1820)

Short Lyrics. The second portion of the Rossetti manuscript contains verses written c. 1800–10.

"My Spectre round me night & day" represents the inner conflict of fallen man. It may be Blake's first use of the terms *Spectre* and *Emanation.* The Spectre is the conscious logic of man, while the Emanation is his outcast imaginative nature which has been relegated to the unconscious. Intellect discards pleasure and brands her as "sin." Only the proper union and harmony of the two can produce a genuine happiness and accomplishment.

"Mock on, mock on, Voltaire, Rousseau" scorns 18th-century rationalism and sees the imaginative mind creating a new and more valid interpretation of life and the world in the very teeth of the reasoners.

"I saw a Monk of Charlemaine" portrays the persecuted pacifist who realizes that war and repression breed only more war and repression. He preaches non-resistance, although it ruins his physical life. Blake is nonetheless confident that returning good for evil will insure the eventual triumph of good.

"The Everlasting Gospel" consists of eight sections scattered throughout the Rossetti Manuscript, the divisions indicated by successive letters of the Greek alphabet. Date of composition is 1810 or slightly later. The poem is Blake's own interpretation of Christ, a savage rebuttal to the "Gentle Jesus" of the sentimentalists. It violently asserts: the true God is within Man; Jesus was the Ideal Man; Jesus was all energy and inspiration; Jesus denied the Urizen-Jehovah deity and considered the Creation to be the actual Fall; and Jesus was a violator of the Decalogue, an advocate of true freedom and creative individualism.

The Pickering Manuscript contains poems written c. 1801–03. "The Mental Traveller" obviously depicts a cyclic spiritual recurrence, but interpretations are almost as numerous as interpreters. One contends that the work is a recounting of the mystic experience; another is Rossetti's suggestion that the poem symbolizes the career of any great idea or intellectual movement: (a) birth; (b) adversity and persecution; (c) triumph in maturity; (d) decadence through over-ripeness; (e) gradual transformation into renovated idea and a start upon a new cycle. It clearly resembles the Orc myth of Blake and also Vala, the Shadowy Female, who attempts to divert idealism into purely materialistic channels.

"Auguries of Innocence" may as a title apply properly only to the initial lines of this series of octosyllabic couplets. It appears to be jottings by Blake that were never made into a finished poem. Some of his most striking and exquisite lines are evidently intended to inculcate Blake's assertions that the spiritual world of inspiration is the only true world, that the cruelty in the outer world is really the externalization of our inner weakness, that every sorrow is a spiritual birth, and that God veritably dwells in the righteous heart.

THE CROWNING PROPHETIC BOOKS. *The Four Zoas, The Torments of Love & Jealousy in the Death and Judgement of Albion the Ancient Man* was originally titled *Vala*. Probably written between 1797 and 1804, the poem was extensively revised, and modern editors have not agreed upon a definitive text. The work remained in manuscript form until Yeats printed a doctored version in 1893. Apparently Blake realized that *The Four Zoas* was a somewhat confused mélange, best left unpublished. He incorporated sizable portions of this work in the concluding prophetic books. *The Four Zoas* is highly important in an understanding of the later books, for some of his completed myth is not elsewhere discussed. This work contains some poetry of coruscating splendor unmatched by other verse of Blake and almost without equal in any English verse.

The Four Zoas consists of nine Nights, corresponding to the nine Nights in Edward Young's *Night Thoughts,* for which Blake prepared the illustrations in a 1797 edition. Blake's last Night, like Young's, is apocalyptic. The term *zoa* is Greek for "living creatures"; the Authorized Version translates the word as "beasts" in the Book of Revelation.

For the first time, Blake here fully perceives the internal struggle as fourfold. Luvah had previously been quite minor. Tharmas is named for the first time. The complexity and difficulty of this work are owing to Blake's greatly expanded conflict in which each zoa is locked in fearful battle with each of the other three. The total personality first appears in this work as Albion, the sleeper. Also new are the theories of Spectre and Emanation (unless "My Spectre round me night & day" predated this poem).

The arena of this work is truly vast, for Blake is recounting the psychic struggle of every human being (though he fundamentally plots his functions according to the Jungian compass for an imagination-dominated personality); but even further, this conflict is also the entire destiny of mankind throughout history. As in Joyce's *Finnegans Wake,* the Fall is every fall—that of Nebuchadnezzar, Rome, the *ancien régime* of France, and so on. Perhaps most important of all is Blake's metaphysics. Hartley had carried Locke's concepts to the logical conclusion. Current rebels like Paine and Godwin were equally materialistic. Blake, examining his own psyche, wholeheartedly believed in the supreme reality of the noumenal world. The all-important governors of human life are not, as Locke believed, to be found in the phenomenal world outside (cutting impressions upon the *tabula rasa*), but rather, Blake insists, they are the unconscious forces within us.

As *Finnegans Wake* is essentially the dream of HCE, so *The Four Zoas* is essentially the dream of Albion. Its theme is: the Fall of Man in the fearful contest of each function for dominance; the completion of the cycle, resulting in the Redemption of Man through Christ, the Perfect Man; and Man's final reintegration in a ringing apocalypse.

Night I relates the fall of Tharmas and the end of the Golden Age.

Night II relates the fall of Luvah and the end of the Silver Age. Enion's lament for lost innocence at the end of this section is a biblical chant in majestic harmonies.

Night III relates the fall of Urizen and the end of the Bronze Age. This section makes excellent use of contrasting images of darkness and light.

Night IV begins the present Iron Age. Los, as in *The Book of Urizen,* forges order out of chaos, setting a limit of Opacity (Satan) and a Limit of Contraction (Adam) below which man cannot fall.

Night V retells the Orc cycle. Although Orc is chained to the Rock of the Decalogue, his spirit remains free. Blake reaches eloquent heights in extolling the transforming power of the revolutionary spirit.

Night VI is reminiscent of Satan's exploration of chaos in *Paradise Lost,* as Urizen journeys through his caves as far as the creation of the Web of Religion.

Night VII is the psychological crisis of the poem, presenting a two-fold consolidation. Truth is strengthened by Los in the building of Golgonooza, the City of Art, through contact with Urthona. Error is made fuller by the creation of the Shadowy Female, the epitome of secrecy, deceit, and repression. Blake wrote two versions of this Night. The second version, c. 1800, particularly excoriates the Industrial Revolution (obviously a product of Urizen) and current institutions of fixed ritual and moral repressiveness.

Night VIII outwardly looks tragic. Christ descends in the robes of Luvah to be crucified on the Tree of Mystery. Urizen starts to "stonify," freezing institutions that enslave mankind. But Los is deeply moved by Christ's sacrifice, and the complete defining of Urizen's horrors is actually the initial step toward the overpowering of his error. Albion is beginning to stir as Enion chants a rhapsodic song of hope.

Night IX is subtitled "The Last Judgment" and may be read by itself as one of the most ecstatic and powerful of all apocalyptic visions. Kings and tyrants are hurled from their thrones, the Tree of Mystery is consumed in flames, and the Last Judgment metes out long-delayed justice. The Four Zoas assume their rightful positions and responsibilities, and Albion and the universe surge with mighty vitality and creativity.

Milton bears the title-page date of 1804 but was first released in 1808 (the only three copies known are on paper water-marked 1808). In the same year Blake released his handsome illustrations for *Paradise Lost.* Apparently planned as a work of twelve books, paralleling *Paradise Lost,* Blake's poem was compressed into two: Milton, in Eternity, realizes his error and descends into the person of Blake to assert the truth.

Blake's minor symbolism is here considerably expanded beyond *The Four Zoas;* the work includes Bowlahoola and Allamanda (respectively the digestive and nervous systems), and frequently bewildering personal allusions to London and English geography. The most important innovation, however, is Blake's discussion of Selfhood, which resembles the *persona* of modern psychology. This Selfhood is what we believe ourselves to be, even what we persuade the entire world to believe we are. Blake interprets the mystic plea for "self-annihilation," "losing oneself to find oneself," as meaning the destruction of the *persona* in order to probe the genuine nature of the unconscious and reveal the genuine personality previously concealed and repressed.

The dedicatory hymn, "And did those feet in ancient times," is a vision of Christ associated with the primitive pastoral past and the liberated future. It is a revolutionary cry for "mental fight" that will end materialistic tyranny and assert the new era of perfection. The one portion of Blake's prophetic books to become popular, this hymn was used to break the General Strike in England in 1926, and it was sung in the streets by London crowds after the Labourite victory of 1945.

Book I portrays Milton in Eternity, guilty of the errors of all Puritans. He actually worshiped Jehovah-Urizen (Reason and Repression) instead of Christ (Impulse and Inspiration). He is separated from his "Sixfold Emanation" (his three wives and three daughters). To achieve the right, he must sacrifice his Selfhood.

The song of the Bard at the tables of Eternity convinces Milton of his error. After the familiar account of Albion's slumber and Urizen's usurpation of authority, the Bard elaborately relates the Satan-Palamabron struggle. Satan fell, not from pride and ambition, as Milton had stated, but from hypocrisy, rigid moral judgment, and rationalism. Palamabron, a son of Los, is Blake himself in struggle with Satan (apparently William Hayley). It is the ceaseless contest that exists between the artist and the well-intentioned supporter of conventional morality who seeks to control the artist's expression "for his own good." In Blake's own wording, Hayley was a "Corporeal Friend" but a "Spiritual Enemy."

Now realizing that he had misinterpreted Satan altogether, Milton descends into the person of Blake, where he struggles with Urizen and overpowers him. Rintrah and Palamabron are opposed to Milton's entry into the City of Art, and they bitterly detail the growth of materialism from Milton's earthly days until 1800. Los, however, reveals the regenerated Milton. As Milton enters the City of Art, the sleeping giant Albion begins to waken. The first book may properly be considered Blake's revised version of the vision Michael shows to Adam at the conclusion of *Paradise Lost.*

Book II begins with Blake's fullest statement of Beulah and some of the most exquisite nature lyrics in the language. From this idyllic realm, Ololon (Milton's "Sixfold Emanation") makes the descent that Thel would not. Milton casts off Selfhood and is joyfully reunited with Ololon. Milton's pronunciamento is perhaps the greatest Romantic plea for the Imagination:

> To cast off Bacon, Locke, & Newton from Albion's covering,
> To take off his filthy garments & clothe him with Imagination;
> To cast aside from Poetry all that is not Inspiration.

The Four Zoas now appear in proper harmony to herald the Apocalypse.

Jerusalem, the Emanation of the Giant Albion is Blake's masterpiece, offering the richest and most coherent revelation of his dazzling vision. Like *Milton,* it bears the title-page date of 1804, but the earliest extant copies appear on paper water-marked 1818. Its one hundred engraved plates were probably prepared over more than a decade.

Here Blake's symbolism and his specialized technical terms (Non Entity, Minute Particulars) reach staggering proportions. Perhaps the most important additions are the Sons and Daughters of Albion. The twelve Sons are divided into the fourfold Accuser, the fourfold Judge, and the fourfold Executioner. These characters have their origin in Blake's personal peril in August 1803, when he expelled an impertinent soldier, John Scofield, from Hayley's garden at Felpham. Scofield and his trooper friend Cock swore before a nearby justice that Blake had uttered foul treasonable language during the eviction, and Blake went on trial at Chichester in January 1804 for sedition. Although he was cleared, with Hayley's intervention, he was so deeply affected that Scofield and Kox (both in various spellings) appear as accusers among the Sons of Albion. Among the judges in *Jerusalem* are Gwantok and Peachey, obviously John Quantock and John Peachey, justices at Blake's trial. Hyle, the inferior artist of Puritan leanings, resembles Hayley. As a whole, the Sons of Albion represent Man's Cruelty to Man. The twelve Daughters of Albion, "emanations" of the Sons, represent Woman's Cruelty to Man.

The theme of *Jerusalem* is the Fall of Man and his regeneration.

Salvation comes through becoming "wholly One in Jesus." Christ is identified with Los, and the following of Inspiration, therefore, is the means of completing the cycle of destiny to perfect harmony in Eternity. The entire work is a rhapsodic tribute to the Romantic Imagination for its ability to form a new and perfect world of the spirit from the wreck of fallen man.

Chapter I is the descent from Eternity, horrible to the fallen, but still essentially Beulah. Los builds Golgonooza, the City of Art. The world without is the desolate dead world as perceived by Science. The Sons of Albion in the desolate world worship nature (Vala) and scorn freedom (Jerusalem). Albion is dismayed at his own sundered character.

Chapter II continues the Fall, now into Generation. The appearance of matter produces the Tree of Mystery, repressive religion and morality, and all the bonds of materialistic philosophy. Divine vision establishes the limits of Opacity and Contraction below which Man cannot fall. Los struggles to bring Albion back to Eternity, but the fallen man rejects Inspiration. Albion tries to banish passions and cling wholly to reason and materialism.

Chapter III descends into the depths of Ulro with the crucifixion of Christ and the subsequent distortion of his purpose. Freedom (Jerusalem) is branded a harlot. The liberating Christ is forgotten and his message is perverted by tyrants and mystigogues. The Sons of Albion are triumphant in achieving all the objects of Blake's hatred: war; the Industrial Revolution; religion of reason; materialistic philosophy; Puritanical morality; and other forms of man's cruelty to his fellow man. But at the very depths, when the Daughters of Albion have created kings, Los creates prophets.

Chapter IV swings the cycle to Eden and concludes in Eternity with the Apocalypse. At the outset, Freedom (Jerusalem) is an outcast in utter despair. Los seems to have succumbed to his Spectre, the anti-Christ. But from this deep abyss the only way is up. Los arises to proclaim the inspired truth of Eternity. Albion destroys his Selfhood, but instead of being annihilated, the giant rises to towering glory. Like Shelley in *Prometheus Unbound,* Blake insists that all man's weakness and baseness are self-delusion. If hate and selfishness are discarded, it will become evident that evil was only an illusion. If the skeptical onlooker thinks that evil seems too easily overpowered, Blake and the Romantics would insist that since man's nature is essentially good, he has only to assert the fullness of his true nature to achieve the millennium. The concluding lines are ecstatic choral praise to the perfect man in great chiming fourfolds. The four zoas or four functions are properly positioned in the human psyche, fulfilling their roles in absolute harmony and colossal productivity.

PROSE WRITERS OF THE PERIOD

Realists

The term "realism" is often applied to the gusto of Chaucer or Fielding, but the word here will be used in the fashion of the 19th century, when modern "realism" was firmly established. Such realism is essentially a picture of a bourgeois-dominated world, largely defined by the standards of the bourgeoisie, and its settings, characters, and events are chiefly those associated with the middle class or its effects. Predominant is the sense of fact, the demand for the authenticity of accurate observation, and the feeling that here is life as it is really lived. The emergence of this viewpoint coincides with the middle class's rise to power. The poet Crabbe, whom we have already discussed, displays just this very sense of realism in his work.

Jeremy Bentham (ben'them) (1748–1832). A Londoner by birth, Jeremy Bentham received a B.A. (1763) and an M.A. (1766) from Oxford. After a brief practice of law, he devoted the rest of his life to reform and to the theoretical bases upon which that reform should be founded. His writings were completed long before their publication, for Bentham turned his manuscripts over to zealous disciples (some of the most distinguished thinkers of the age both in England and on the Continent) who saw the works through to publication. His triumph came years after his death, until by 1875 English statutory law and general practice bore remarkable resemblance to his proposals. In his later years, especially through the influence of the brilliant James Mill, Bentham discarded his conservatism. With Mill he established *The Westminster Review* in 1823 as an organ for the "philosophical radicals."

An Introduction to the Principles of Morals and Legislation (*1776–80*, 1789) coined the word *international,* but this, his acknowledged masterwork, is chiefly famed for its enunciation of the concept of utilitarianism. Here Bentham attempts to treat of human morality and social organization with the precision of the physical sciences. Man, he says, is an animal who seeks to gain pleasure and avoid pain. Pleasure and pain for the individual can be quantitatively computed according to intensity, duration, certainty, propinquity, fecundity (its chances of being followed by subsequent similar experiences), and purity (its chances of not being followed by opposite experiences). This scheme has been termed "the hedonic calculus." The total social aims are subsistence, security, abundance, and equality, with emphasis and importance in descending order. Society and its legislation should be based upon the achievement of the maximum of satisfaction for the individual and for all mankind. The regulating principle, therefore, is "the greatest happiness for the greatest number." The forces compelling men to conform to the utilitarian principles are: physical (hangovers follow dissipation); political (the cell block and the execution block for the recalcitrant); moral (society shows its ill will to the unconventional); and religious (Bentham relies upon this compulsion only as it is actually a means of social pressure). Men's energies and the material wealth of the world should be concentrated positively to fulfill the "hedonic calculus" and the total social aims. Bentham observes that man secures pleasure from poetry and from beer, but since obviously more human beings gain pleasure from beer than from poetry, the productive powers of mankind are certainly better employed in making beer than in making poetry. With a perfectly straight face, Bentham gave the following definition: "Prose is when all the lines except the last go on to the margin; poetry is when some of them fall short of it."

Thomas Robert Malthus (mal'thus) (1766–1834). Thomas Malthus was born near Guildford in Surrey. In 1788 he graduated from Cambridge and in 1793 became a fellow of Jesus College. Taking holy orders, he started as a curate in Albury, Surrey. His fame as a writer was responsible for his appointment as professor of history and political economy at Haileybury in 1805. Politically a Whig, he supported Catholic Emancipation and the First Reform Bill.

An Essay on the Principle of Population as It Affects the Future Improvement of Society (1798) expounded the famous Malthusian doctrine: population increases in a geometrical ratio while the means of subsistence only increase in an arithmetical ratio (thus 2:2; 4:4; 8:6; 16:8; 32:10; etc.). In response to Godwin's optimism, Malthus paints a grim picture of an expanding population outstripping the means of livelihood and dooming millions to deprivation and death. The checks upon population increase are war and disease, vice and crime. The revised edition of 1803, prepared after Malthus had traveled widely, offers fuller evidence for his contention and adds another check upon population: "moral restraint," i.e. voluntary refusal to procreate. The popular distaste for Malthusianism is demonstrated by Cobbett's scoffings at "parson Malthus," and later 19th-century observers felt that the tremendous population increase and prosperity of the era effectively refuted Malthus. Nonetheless, Darwin started his thinking about the struggle for existence while reading Malthus; and the 20th century, apprehensive over the "population explosion," is even less quick to laugh at Malthus.

Arthur Young (1741–1820). Arthur Young, from Suffolk, was noted for his writings on travel and farming. In 1793 he was appointed secretary of the Board of Agriculture.

Travels in France (1792; enlarged, 1794) is still one of the prime sources for an understanding of France at the time of the Revolution. Although stoutly English, Young stamps upon each page the authenticity of a factual study, blending a specialist's over-all scrutiny of trade and soils with his colorful and revealing personal encounters. He scans women's garments, vintage wines, table manners, *chateaux,* and revolutionary assemblies all with the determination to be unprejudiced and to note things as they truly are. Devoid of literary pretension, he writes with a laconic precision that is effective and impressive.

Rebels

Thomas Paine (1737–1809). Son of a Quaker corset-maker in Thetford, Norfolk, Thomas Paine "repressed" his "tendency to poetry" at school. During his early years he witnessed the ceaseless movement —from his father's trade to sailor, tobacconist, schoolteacher, and excise officer—that was to end only with his death. His first wife died a year after their marriage, and shortly after his second marriage, he and his wife separated. Bearing a letter of introduction from Benjamin Franklin, he went to Philadelphia in 1774, where he edited the *Pennsylvania Magazine.* His *Common Sense* (1776), demanding secession from England, and *The Crisis* (1776–83), bolstering American morale in dark days, belong to American literature. After official visits to France, he was back in England, associating with London radicals and attacking Burke. Under indictment for high treason, he narrowly escaped to France, where in 1792 he was elected a member of the National Assembly. Opposing the execution of Louis XVI, he was cast into prison and escaped the guillotine only through the intercession of

James Monroe. His last years were spent in New York, where he died poor and obscure.

Paine's credo ran: "My country is the world, and my religion is to do good." He was a professional revolutionist, a consummate pamphleteer with a superlative ability for coining phrases, and a courageous and uncomplicated fighter. But he was a man possessed by an ideology: the revolutionary shibboleths of natural rights, equality of mankind, the pure state of nature, and the social compact of Rousseau. Paine displayed the closed, one-track mind of the avid controversialist; he was incapable of comprehending the subtleties and complexities perceived by Burke. Tradition was nonsense to him: "the claim of one generation to govern beyond the grave is of all tyrannies the most insolent."

The Rights of Man (I, 1791; II, 1792), a riposte to Burke's *Reflections,* sold hundreds of thousands of copies. Paine reproached Burke for his love of royal pageantry: "He pities the plumage and forgets the dying bird." Such striking phrases made this work the bible of republicans. Paine offered no new ideas in advocating universal suffrage, the sovereignty of the people, the abolition of monarchy and aristocracy as outmoded anachronisms, the right and indeed the necessity of revolution to establish equality, free universal education, government subsidies for the maternity costs and the children of the poor, government housing, old-age pensions, and a progressive income tax. What he did offer was an unequivocal statement in a stirring cry for direct action.

The Age of Reason (1794–96) is the basis for Theodore Roosevelt's branding of Paine as "that dirty little atheist." However, Paine was not an atheist but a deist. Typical of the Revolutionary Era is Paine's vehement and emotional advocacy of what had been a genteel aristocratic concept of the 18th century. The head-on assault against orthodox faith by the French Revolution has been blunted by the years, but the union of Church and State in those days meant that a political revolutionist must perforce also attack the Church. It is this spirit that causes Paine to dogmatize: "The Christian theory is little else than the idolatry of the ancient mythologists accommodated to the purposes of power and revenue." Paine looked to the God revealed by external nature and his own conscience, a God that was both a scientist and a philanthropist. With virtually no concept of the awesome or the esthetic, Paine propounded a deity in his own image.

Mary Wollstonecraft (wŭl'stun-krãft) (1759–1797). A native of

London, Mary Wollstonecraft early made a living by teaching and by working for a book publisher. In 1792 she went to Paris and lived with Gilbert Imlay, an American captain during the War for Independence. Although she bore his daughter, Fanny, she found him increasingly cool. In 1796 she tried to commit suicide and finally broke with Imlay; later that year she and Godwin began living together and were married during her second pregnancy. She died in giving birth to Mary Godwin, later Shelley's second wife.

Vindication of the Rights of Women (1792) is the first and still the most important expression of feminism in English. The "rights" Mary pleads for are those to be women rather than "ladies." She does not want her sex to be men in skirts; she wants women "duly prepared by education to be the companions of men" and "free to strengthen their reason till they comprehend their duty." She denies "a sex to mind" and calls for co-education, with women permitted to take whatever learning they are capable of absorbing. Published before her meeting with Imlay, the work passes over love as a momentary excitation calmly subsiding into friendship after marriage. Mary is severe in attacking the masculine ideal of the "clinging-vine" female, and in her fervent sincerity she is devoid of humor. Reading this work, the annoyed Walpole called her a "hyena in petticoats."

William Godwin (1756–1836). Born at Wisbech, Cambridgeshire, William Godwin studied for his father's calling, the ministry, at Hoxton Presbyterian Academy. After various pastorates, he abandoned the clergy in 1782 to preach social radicalism in London. By 1787 he was an avowed atheist. His first wife, Mary Wollstonecraft, died in childbirth, and in 1801 he remarried. His second wife, Mrs. Clairmont, had a daughter by a previous marriage—Clara Mary Jane Clairmont, who was subsequently a mistress of Byron. The small publishing business he established in 1805 went bankrupt in 1822. Increasingly conservative in his later years, Godwin was supported by the sinecure post of Yeoman Usher of the Exchequer (1833).

The Inquiry concerning Political Justice and Its Influence on General Virtue and Happiness (1793) is the supreme monument of purely philosophical radicalism in English political literature. The "dangerous teachings" of the book were brought to Pitt's attention, but, learning that it cost sixty-three shillings, the shrewd prime minister refused to suppress it, nonchalantly avowing that "a three-guinea book could never do much harm among those who had not three shillings to spare." Godwin's work rests upon the two following fundamental theses:

(1) Character is shaped by environment. Godwin is a determinist, denying free will; thus tracing evil to ignorance and outmoded institutions, he asserts the essential goodness of man. He also maintains that all men are morally equal and are entitled to the same opportunities in life, and that the highest pleasure of life is the pursuit of goodness.

(2) Reason should govern men wholly. A perfectibilitarian (a believer in man's limitless powers to improve), Godwin urges rational argument without violence of any sort to secure an eventual reign of philosophic anarchy. This final perfection will permit the fullest human expression of individuality unfettered by any restriction. He foresees an era without war, corporal punishment, private property, marriage, patriotism, organized religion, or any societal restraints upon the free human spirit. Kings and tyrants will have vanished, and an hour or two of daily work will be man's only burden. Enlightened public opinion will be sufficient to forestall and reform a potential evil-doer.

No other English writer has been so intoxicated with reason as to abandon common sense altogether. Godwin did not realize that what impersonal logic might denounce can be psychologically valid. His relentless insistence upon logic came to absurdity: for instance, in demanding the full and honest realization of one's individualism, he would extirpate the theater, since an actor is warping his own nature in projecting the character of another. Revisions in 1796 and 1798 showed some humanization of Godwin's ideas but left the central structure of the work fully intact.

Though largely a curiosity to our age, and in its own era without an appreciable appeal to the mass mind, *Political Justice* held in thrall many of the young intellectuals of the time. Godwin's Utopia opened to them vistas of constant and rapid betterment of mankind, and promised heaven on earth. Wordsworth, Coleridge, Southey, and especially Shelley were at least momentarily rapturous followers of Godwin.

Godwin followed *Political Justice* in the next year with his most remarkable novel.

The Adventures of Caleb Williams (1794) is perhaps the most effective propaganda novel in English and the first psychological "thriller."

As secretary to the wealthy recluse Falkland, Caleb Williams gradually realizes that his employer was the murderer of Tyrrel and that he compounded his crime by letting two innocent laborers hang for the killing. When he confronts his employer with his knowledge, Falkland threatens him with death should he reveal this information. Caleb flees but is apprehended and jailed as a thief, because Falkland's jewels have been planted in his belongings. Falkland pursues Williams relentlessly, branding him as a criminal and completely ruining him, but finally he breaks down in court under Caleb's accusations and admits his guilt. Falkland's death brings genuine remorse to Caleb, who now recognizes his great affection for the man.

The novel is remarkable for the following reasons:

(1) Technical mastery in creating suspense. Here the honest accuser is the pursued and the criminal is the pursuer.

(2) Psychological intensity. Though neither Falkland nor Williams is truly a flesh-and-blood character, the psychological problems of criminal and accuser had never before been so dissected in the English novel. The more Falkland tries to silence the accusing voice of Williams, the more an inner voice demands that he confess. The more Caleb is oppressed by Falkland, the more he realizes that he is actually the inner voice of Falkland demanding to be heard; the more, therefore, he feels binding ties with his murderous employer. Caleb is the objectivized conscience of Falkland.

(3) Indictment of a society. Falkland's persecution of Williams is not typical of social oppression, but it superbly makes the point that the poor man stands little chance of justice against a rich adversary. Wiser here than many fiction writers, Godwin does not preach but lets the story speak for itself.

Byron, Shelley, and Keats were all fascinated by this novel, and George Colman's dramatization of it as *The Iron Chest* was triumphantly presented in England, on the Continent, and in America. The first American novelist, Charles Brockton Brown, was strongly influenced by Godwin's novels. *Caleb Williams* also foreshadows the later detective novel.

Romance of Distant Travel

The first two works that follow recapture for English travel literature the sense of giddy excitement and awed surprise virtually missing since the accounts of Hakluyt and Purchas. Both Bruce and Park deeply felt the raw darkness of primitive Africa and the thrill of gazing upon sights never before seen by Europeans, at least in modern times.

James Bruce (1730–1794). James Bruce was a native of Kinnaird, Scotland. Between 1768 and 1773 he explored Syria, the Nile valley, and Ethiopia.

Travels to Discover the Source of the Nile in the Years 1768, 1769, 1770, 1771, 1772, and 1773 (1790) was often discounted and ridiculed in the period for its dramatic and spectacular account of the Scotsman's exploration of the Blue Nile. Written some years after his actual travels, the five volumes certainly idealize and perhaps exaggerate the exotic and the bizarre. Nonetheless, later explorers essentially confirm the wonders that Bruce reported. His style is colorful and emotional, especially appealing to Coleridge. Garnett has said of Bruce: "He will always remain the poet and, his work the epic, of African travel."

Mungo Park (1771–c. 1806). A native of Selkirkshire, Scotland, Mungo Park was the first European to explore the Niger river in Africa. His wish to die while exploring the unknown was granted, and he vanished in the Dark Continent in 1806.

Travels into the Interior Districts of Africa (1799) is sober in comparison with Bruce's work but even more effective in its graceful flow and underplayed splendors. One of the most moving passages in travel literature is Park's arrival, after painful and hazardous search, at his goal: "the long-sought-for, majestic Niger, glittering in the morning sun."

William Bligh (blī) (1754–1817). A native of Tyntan, Cornwall, William Bligh was commander of the H. M. S. *Bounty* upon a South Seas expedition starting in 1787. His Spartan discipline caused a famous mutiny from which he escaped with his life only because of his incredible courage and seamanship. He later became governor of New South Wales, Australia, and died a vice-admiral in London.

Narrative of the Mutiny on Board the Bounty (1790) is an unvarnished account, much like the plain prose of Captain Cook. Without literary pretensions, the lieutenant matter-of-factly relates ordeals that would have annihilated a lesser or more imaginative soul. This real-life account renders credible the fantastic fictional endurance of Robinson Crusoe. From the Nordhoff and Hall fictionalization the world knows the story of the mutiny, but it too often forgets the unbelievable voyage of Bligh and his eighteen companions, cast off by the mutineers in an open boat, over almost four thousand miles of wild Pacific.

Chapter 6

The First Generation of
Romantic Poets (1800–1814)

BACKGROUND INFORMATION

MAJOR HISTORICAL EVENTS. At the beginning of the century, England and France were locked in mortal conflict. England's concern here was not as in medieval times, the port of Calais or a slice of Picardy but rather the hegemony of Europe, and the future and perhaps even the national existence of England itself. The vast conscripted armies of Napoleon were the masters of Western Europe. England held the seas. Hoping to break England economically, Napoleon instituted the Continental System, forbidding the importation of English products or colonial raw materials. The English countered with a continental blockade, seeking to confine the French. The neutrals were understandably restive under the British blockade and formed the threatening Northern Convention in 1800. England desperately needed the naval stores of the Baltic to maintain its fleet, and to top it off, without allies as she was, she added a new enemy in the previously neutral Denmark. Again the intrepid Nelson proved to be England's savior; at the Battle of Copenhagen, in 1801, he reopened the Baltic to England. With the accession of the Russian Czar Alexander I, the Northern Convention was dissolved. The Treaty of Amiens, in 1802, brought momentary peace or, more accurately, an armed truce, for the savage struggle resumed with greater intensity the next year.

In 1804 Pitt returned as Prime Minister. In the same year the French Consul proclaimed himself Napoleon I, Emperor of France. Vast concentrations of men and matériel spread along the coast of France, Belgium, and the Netherlands, waiting to invade England. The English government called for volunteer militiamen, built Martello towers (circular masonry forts) and other coastal defenses in feverish haste, and planned to evacuate government offices to the Midlands and the North. Doggedly the British fleet maintained the blockade; Nelson was off Toulon for twenty-two months without a moment ashore.

The French fleet sallied forth to do battle, meeting Nelson at Trafalgar on October 21, 1805. With tactical audacity, Nelson drove his ships in two parallel spear thrusts through the combined French and Spanish fleets. The courage of the French could not match the superior seamanship and determination of the English, and more than half the French ships were destroyed or captured. England paid a heavy price, for in the moment of triumph, Nelson died of wounds aboard the *Victory,* his flagship.

On the Continent, however, Napoleon's armies continued victorious. The Battle of Austerlitz, just six weeks after Trafalgar, was one of Napoleon's most resounding successes, the news of which hastened Pitt's death. The new British cabinet in 1806 belatedly included the great statesman Charles James Fox, who also died before the year was out.

The seizure of Spain by France in 1808 caused the Spaniards to rise in revolt, and they called upon the English for aid. In the same year Sir Arthur Wellesley, later Duke of Wellington, led British troops into Portugal, thus inaugurating the long Peninsular War. The stern "Iron Duke" proved to be England's most successful general since the Duke of Marlborough. Through years of bloody fighting, he pushed the French backward until in 1814, after the disastrous French invasion of Russia and Napoleon's defeat at Leipzig, Wellington's troops poured across the Pyrenees, invading France. Napoleon abdicated in April, retiring to Elba.

With peace in Europe, contingents of Wellington's Peninsula veterans were sent to the "side-show" war against the United States, occasioned by British claim of right to inspect neutral ships in the blockade of Europe. British troops burned the capitol in Washington, but England was satisfied to see the American War of 1812 end late in 1814 with a mere restoration of the *status quo ante.* It was just in time, for on March 1, 1815, Napoleon secretly left Elba and landed in France. Even the Bourbonist soldiers sent to oppose him rapturously rallied to his banners. Triumphantly he entered Paris to begin the fateful "Hundred Days."

Austria, England, Prussia, and Russia hastily concluded a new alliance against Napoleon. The Duke of Wellington was designated supreme commander with over one million allied fighting men available against Napoleon. To prevent the conjunction of allied forces, Bonaparte threw the full weight of the *Grande Armée* upon the English at Waterloo, Belgium, on June 18, 1815. After a day of ceaseless assault, the British still held their position, albeit, tenuously. The arrival of Prussian troops at nightfall decided the issue, and the Allies started their pursuit of the defeated French. Napoleon abdicated a second time, just four days later, and went into permanent exile at St. Helena until his death in 1821. English arms had probably reached the apogee of their prestige in European history.

After twenty years of warfare, in 1815 Great Britain stood as the richest and most powerful nation in the world. War had accelerated her industrialization and had greatly increased her merchant marine. She alone had been Napoleon's continuous opponent and had engineered his downfall at sea and on land. She alone among the significant European nations had never experienced the physical devastation of her soil by war. In international affairs, England had emerged as the architect of the unfolding century, the amasser of new territory and the arbiter of nations. Yet inwardly she appeared in frightful travail. The Continental System and the wartime dislocation had seriously aggravated the confusions and hardships of incredibly rapid industrial change. The demobilization of four hundred thousand soldiers and the end of huge government contracts meant widespread unemployment and commercial disaster. From 1811 through 1816 workers in the Midlands, incited to the Luddite riots, smashed the new machinery, which they blamed for their poverty.

The administration (1812–27) of Lord Liverpool was long but hardly distinguished. Government measures sought to protect vested interests and repress radicals and reform. The Corn Law of 1815 virtually excluded foreign grain and protected native agriculture at the expense of costly bread for the workers. Agitators demanded parliamentary reform, and a frightened government responded to the riots at the Spa Fields, London, reform meeting of 1816 with the repressive Coercion Acts of 1817, which suspended the Habeas Corpus Act and severely penalized seditious assembly. Popular clamor rose higher, and about sixty thousand people flocked to St. Peter's Fields, Manchester, in 1819 to hear a radical orator; there soldiers charged the gathering, killing eleven persons and wounding about four hundred in what was to be called "The Peterloo Massacre." Liberals like Shelley, along with the populace, were enraged at the tyrannous action, while the government intensified its repression with the Six Acts of 1819. Feeling rose so high that extremists plotted the Cato Street conspiracy in 1820; they were apprehended just before they attempted to blow up the entire cabinet at dinner and seize the Bank of England.

English royalty in this era reached the nadir of its reputation. Hopelessly insane, George III died in 1820 and was succeeded by his son, the Regent, George IV. One of the new monarch's first actions was to institute divorce proceedings against Queen Caroline on a charge of adultery. Branding the king a debauchee, Englishmen loudly acclaimed the queen; the divorce measure narrowly passed the House of Lords but was dropped by the cabinet in the face of certain defeat by Commons.

With the death of Castlereagh in 1822, more liberal Tories infiltrated the cabinet—Huskisson and two later prime ministers, Canning and Peel. Huskisson effected the first breach in the protectionist mercantile system by reducing duties on many significant imports, such as iron, sugar, and cotton. The repeal of the Combination Acts in 1824 permitted a brief but spectacular growth of trade unionism which a worried government quickly countered the next year with new Combination Acts.

Great hopes were aroused by the elevation of the national hero, the Duke of Wellington, to the post of Prime Minister in 1828, but the old warrior sided with the reactionaries. The tide was flowing the other way, however, and grudgingly, in 1828, the Iron Duke supported a modification of the Corn Law and the repeal of the Test Act, which had barred Roman Catholics and Protestant Dissenters from public offices. The Catholic Emancipation Bill of 1829 extended full suffrage to Roman Catholics and made them eligible for any English office except that of lord chancellor in return for an oath denying papal interference in British domestic affairs, recognizing the Protestant succession, and repudiating any intent to overthrow the Established Church.

With the death of George IV in 1830, his younger brother ascended the throne as William IV. The accession forced a new election (this requirement was eliminated in 1867), and the reforming Whigs secured the majority in Commons. Wellington's forced resignation ended a continuous Tory rule of half a century (except for the brief Whig cabinet with Fox in 1806).

Civil war and national breakdown were prevented by the reform period inaugurated with Earl Gray's cabinet in 1830. The English genius for compromise and the recognition of realities permitted evolution instead of revolution. The reforms were the culmination of the liberal demands for necessary improvement, and with the liberal cause triumphant, the Romantic spirit of the age mollifies into the milder romanticism of the Victorian Age. In essence, the reform period represents the capitulation of English landed gentry to the middle class. The July Monarchy in France, starting in 1830, signified the same bourgeois political triumph across the Channel, but what had meant bloody turmoil and repeated revolutions in France was accomplished bloodlessly in Great Britain. In typical English fashion the old forms were retained without outward alteration, but their inward substance was transformed. After a millennium and a half of aristocratic rule, England's political destinies were now committed to the bourgeoisie. This process was symbolized in 1832 by the Third Reform Bill (the House of Lords, appalled that the traditions of centuries were crashing down, killed the first two bills). On the eve of reform no more than one third of Commons was freely chosen. In pocket boroughs a patron exercised exclusive right to designate the representative. In rotten boroughs the selection was pre-ordained by influence, even bribery. Allocation of seats followed medieval patterns of population, so that some tiny hamlets sent two members to Parliament, while the new industrial and commercial giant of Manchester was unrepresented. The reform bill disfranchised fifty-six pocket and rotten boroughs (returning 111 members) and reduced thirty-two small boroughs from two to one member; the resulting 143 seats were redistributed. Moderate financial qualifications for voting were now the sole criterion for adult male citizens, superseding the previous potpourri of regulations. While the middle class was now generally enfranchised, the bulk of the population (including, of course, all women) was voteless, and the secret ballot was not accepted.

Other reforms followed. In 1833 slavery was abolished in all colonies and in all territory controlled by Great Britain. This measure culminated the labors of the abolitionists, led by William Wilberforce. The Factory Act of the same year, passed over vociferous objections, clearly indicates in its provisions the horrors that the Industrial Revolution had brought to child laborers. By the provisions of the Act, children under nine were not permitted to work, those between nine and thirteen were limited to forty-eight hours a week or nine hours in a

single day, those between thirteen and eighteen to sixty-nine hours a
week or twelve hours in a single day. Two hours of daily schooling
were required for children under thirteen. The measure applied only to
the textile trade and was distressingly inadequate even there, but it
was the forerunner of later remedial legislation. The Grand National
Consolidated Trades Union swelled to over half a million members
within weeks of its founding in 1834, but after a few sputtering
strikes, it fell into apathy. The New Poor Law of the same year
ended the vicious system of supplementing low wages with the dole,
limited the dole to aged and sick paupers, and provided extensive
workhouses for the able-bodied indigent. In 1835 the Municipal Cor-
porations Bill (excepting London and a few other communities) specified a uniform plan of government for all cities and boroughs. Further
reforms in 1836 legalized civil marriages, equalized some ecclesiastical
incomes, and extended more rights to prisoners.

The labels *Liberal* and *Conservative* were now supplanting the
earlier *Whig* and *Tory*. Lord Melbourne headed the Liberal administration that extended from the reign of William IV several years into
that of his niece, who in 1837, at the age of eighteen, ascended the
throne as Queen Victoria. The subsequent era was to be termed, after
her, the Victorian Age.

For all its terrifying problems, the England of the first third of the
century had embarked upon an exciting adventure: before any other
nation, England was entering into our contemporary world. The idea
of progress gripped the minds of Englishmen, especially the bourgeoisie,
the new rulers of society. Moreover, it had already begun to stir the
working class, so that a conscious proletariat had begun to draw the
battle line against its master, the middle class. The tempestuous Revolutionary Era that closed the 18th century had bequeathed these three
significant schools of thought:

(1) Conservatism, primarily derived from Burke. The old stand-
patters of 18th-century tradition were gone or coolly mute. The vocal
group was chiefly composed of converted revolutionaries such as Wordsworth and Southey, or of solid middle-class personalities such as
Peel and Scott. They repudiated the claims of reason and revolution
and based their case upon sentiment and emotion, conscience and
custom. They wished to maintain the "old England" unaltered, or reluctantly to give as little ground as possible to the new age.

(2) Revolutionism, relying chiefly on the ideas of Paine and Godwin.
A now triumphant middle class was turning a deaf ear to their pleas,

but the lower classes were displaying interest. Hazlitt, Shelley, and Cobbett (with all their personal differences) were spokesmen for this group, which demanded the end of tradition and the creation of a truly egalitarian society.

(3) Utilitarianism, following Bentham. Accepting the middle-class society, championing the principles of practicality and usefulness, seeking necessary change and improvement without revolutionary overthrow, the utilitarians offered the most satisfactory "third force" to the age. Much of 19th-century England was to follow their dictates, brought forward by James Mill and Henry Brougham.

While the institutions and practices of early 19th-century England rested fundamentally upon an older, agricultural society ruled by the squirarchy, the State, the Church, the economy, and the whole temperament of the nation were dramatically adapting themselves in the 1830's to the new utilitarian age of the middle class.

LANGUAGE. The 18th-century rage for order had almost completely triumphed in the written language. The regularization of English spelling, grammar, and punctuation had been so thoroughly effected that only minor changes have occurred since. The popularity of the grammar by the American Lindley Murray continued unabated in spite of rivals. The grammar by Samuel Kirkham in 1825 sold sixty thousand copies in one year and achieved ninety-four editions by mid-century. Correctness was the concern of even so unpedantic an author as William Cobbett, who published *Grammar of the English Language* (1818) in the form of letters to his fourteen-year-old son, James. Like the more academic grammarians, Cobbett sought to impose logic and analogous structures upon English, often in defiance of everyday usage. The anonymous *Vulgarities of Speech Corrected* (1826) printed long lists of words and expressions stigmatized by the author as provincial, lower class, criminal, or otherwise inappropriate. Oaths were deprecated, only *by Jove* receiving the author's approval; indeed, Victorianism is close upon us.

In spite of the purists, some new constructions were winning out. *Had rather* and *had better* were singled out for attack by Dr. Johnson as inexcusable substitutes for *would* or *will better/rather*, but in the early 19th century they became general. Perhaps the major new form to be adopted was the progressive passive, e.g. *the book was being written*. The earliest recorded use of the construction dates from 1769, and no English grammar notes it before 1802. Although avoided by some (such as Macaulay) and often bitterly denounced by formal grammarians, the form appears in a host of writings by Southey, Coleridge, Lamb, Shelley, and even the purist Landor.

English pronunciation in the 18th century is not wholly clear, for writers of the era are ambiguous in their statement. Some authorities now assert that the familiar broad *a* of today's British English (*bäth* instead of the standard American *bath*) originated at the very end of the 18th century. Concomitant perhaps was the loss of the final *r* (*far* is generally pronounced *fä* in British English). Increased literacy and demand for elegant conformity by the start of the 19th century caused the full -*ing* pronunciation instead of -*in,* though in substandard British and American English *runnin, singin,* etc., are still frequently heard. In the "Ode on Intimations of Immortality," Wordsworth rimes *sullen* and *culling.* The interior *w* in such words as *backward* and *athwart* was now being pronounced, though the older practice still survived in place names (*wor'ik* for *Warwick*) and in the inelegant *innards.* By 1800 the diphthong *oi* had also come essentially to today's pronunciation (Pope rimed *join* with *line*), though *choir* still maintains the earlier pronunciation. After 1800 the dictionaries drop older pronunciations such as *bile* (boil), *creater* (creature), *feller* (fellow), *figger* (figure), even though such pronunciations are not unknown today. Authorities such as Jesperson and Wyld believe that the very end of the 18th century originated the Cockney employment of the aspirate which was inserted before vowels for emphasis and omitted before unemphatic vowels ("Them lucky uns *hought* to be 'appy!"). Every reader of *Pickwick Papers* is acquainted with the Cockney confusion of *v* and *w* (Sam Weller is *Veller*); this practice appears to have originated about the turn of the century and now seems extinct.

Of course, some of the 18th-century pronunciations survived well into the 19th century among older and more conservative people of culture. In his *Autobiography* (1850), Leigh Hunt objects to the pronunciations of John Philip Kemble, the distinguished actor who died in 1823; Hunt cites against Kemble such forms as *varchue* (virtue), *furse* (fierce), *ojus* (odious), *maircy* (mercy). The before-mentioned *Vulgarities of Speech Corrected* objected to the growing practice of trying to pronounce foreign words in their native fashion. This new method of pronouncing foreign names was just gathering strength (Byron still insisted on riming *Juan* and *ruin*) and represented the most significant change necessary to bring early 19th-century pronunciation in essential conformity with today's British English.

But the most important development in English of the early 19th century was the vastly altered vocabulary, resulting partly from historical developments and partly from Romantic literature. Modern warfare brought in new terms, but even more contributory to the expansion of English vocabulary was England's new world position. The Continental System had forced the British to look beyond Europe to the rest of the globe, and had intensified English contacts with exotic landscapes and products. New words poured in: Polish *mazurka* (1818); Russian *vodka* (1802); *samovar* (1830); Hungarian *shako* (1815); Turkish *bosh* (1834); Japanese *soy bean* (1802); Australian *boomerang* (1827); and especially East Indian terms such as *raj* (1800), *dinghy* (1810), *thug* (1810), and *suttee* (1813 in sense of "immolation").

Almost equally important was the shift of meaning in long-familiar words. Technological change caused terms to be used in new ways: *train, car,* and *coach,* originally applied to horse-drawn vehicles, came to denote different things when used in connection with railroads. The growth of Romantic attitudes caused a revision of the meanings of more abstract words. The shift in the meaning of *Gothic* was discussed in the previous chapter. The term *romantic* itself, once a term of abuse ("romantic nonsense"=wild, extravagant), came to connote delightful stimulation and excitement, though it was largely applied to scenery and became a general label for the age only around mid-century. *Enthusiasm,* which in the 18th century meant "fanaticism" or "lack of self-discipline," came to be used in today's favorable sense. *Imagination,* synonymous with "fancy" or "fantasy" to the neoclassicists, came to be exalted by Wordsworth and Coleridge to denote the supreme faculty of artistic creation.

CULTURAL CONDITIONS. Most of the populace and critics of the day were dubious of or downright hostile to the artists we call Romantics. Though Sir Walter Scott gained a popular following for Romanticism, his success was partly owing to his *omission* of many features found in other Romantics. Moreover, Crabbe, perhaps England's greatest realistic poet, and Landor, one of the finest classic poets in our language, wrote in the so-called Romantic Period, and some of the Romantic writers themselves—Wordsworth in "Laodamia," Byron in his satires—produced works that can hardly be called romantic. Nevertheless, the term seems justified as essentially true for the predominant temper of the literature of the period.

THE ROMANTIC MOVEMENT IN LITERATURE

Hostile critics of early 19th-century Romanticism saw it as an attempt to escape from the realities of the age. Indeed, the Romantic took refuge in a supposedly glorious past (medieval times, ancient Greece, and even the remotely primitive), a utopian future (as in Shelley's *Prometheus Unbound*), a distant and exotic present (orientalism and the noble savage), or, perhaps as a last resort, an oasis away from the general world of men (with Wordsworth's "dalesmen" or Byron's own magnificent, isolated self).

On the other hand, a neutral estimate might see the Romantics as asserting the fundamentally valid position of irrational man. Modern psychoanalysis, greatly indebted to the Romantic spirit, insists that man lives essentially by his unconscious and subconscious nature, not by facts or reason. In plumbing their own psychic depths, the Romantics evidenced an interest in the true source of human motivation and purpose. Blake, as already noted, astonishingly anticipates a sizable amount of Carl Jung, and Hazlitt, in his essay "On Dreams," anticipates much that Freud will later say about dreams. Though it may be unwise to apply the now fashionable psychoanalytic approach too vigorously to older literature, the Romantics demand it in their extensive probing of the inner life of symbology.

The enthusiastic supporter of the Romantics sees them in their own self-appointed roles as liberators and creators. Common to all the Romantics was an idealism that sought for the individual and for society the fullest of freedom and expression. Joined to the Romantic task of liberation was the equally important task of imaginatively creating a new and right world. Not escapism but the exploring of genuine human potentials and the formulation of the truest world for the human spirit comprise the Romantic quest in the eyes of its advocates. They see the Romantics as the first contemporary men, the first architects of an ideal democratic society.

Some of the causes of early 19th-century Romanticism must certainly include the following:

ECONOMIC. Romanticism appears to be largely a middle-class movement. Most of the Romantic authors, minor as well as major, were bourgeois in origin. Keats had the humblest origin, his father starting as a laborer in a hostler's stable and marrying his employer's daughter to gain the business, and certainly Keats's early training for a medical career has all the characteristics of a family seeking firm bourgeois status from an obscure beginning. Byron was a noble lord, but his formative years (until the inheritance of title and property) were essentially bourgeois, and Byron's reading public was essentially middle class. Shelley, though of aristocratic origin, was a thoroughgoing rebel, denouncing the entire position of his father and his class.

The middle class during the Romantic period was making its momentous bid for social power and status. It could not base its claims upon tradition but upon the inherent worth of the individual—and that position is the core of Romanticism. Democracy, ambition, selfhood, and self-reliance are the combined ideals of bourgeois and Romantic, though, admittedly, these goals were generally vulgarized by the non-intellectual middle class.

Also, the increased luxury and leisure of the middle class induced a desire for the unusual and different which was exploited by the Romantics. The crowded cities and the growth of unsightly, dirty, noisy industrialism stimulated the wish for release and escape. We are accustomed to the Industrial Age and to an extent have mitigated some of its most distressing features, but the Romantics were just experiencing its first onrush and were therefore understandably aghast.

RELIGIOUS. From the 18th century on, the English middle class has been associated with religious nonconformity—the Presbyterian, Congregationalist, Baptist, and especially Methodist sects. Some of the Romantics arose from nonconformist backgrounds; Hazlitt was the son of a Unitarian cleric, and no Romantic writer during his genuine Romanticism (except Scott, a faithful follower of the Kirk of Scotland) was at all orthodox.

The religious enthusiasm of Wesleyanism unquestionably fed the Romantic spirit, as it had powerfully influenced Cowper, though no significant Romantics espoused this denomination. The "inner light," the transport, the powerful individual appeal of evangelicalism preceded the Romantics and certainly passed many features to them. The Established Church, on the other hand, breathed an air of elegant calm, as manifested in many of Jane Austen's clerics. The need for an emotional faith caused many to rebel against the dignified, uninspiring edifice of the Church of England. United with the State, the Established Church was jocularly termed "The praying branch of the Tory party."

POLITICAL. During the reigns of the four Georges, the prestige of the

English monarchy steadily declined, reaching a low water mark in the first third of the 19th century. Used to the impeccable and wholly non-political English rulers from Victoria on, we find it difficult to realize how abysmally low was the reputation of the Georges among thinking Englishmen. Burke respected kingship but he could not revere the king. In their flush of Romanticism, all the Romantics (except Scott) were republicans, perhaps largely from a personal distaste for the Hanoverian kings.

Strongest, of course, were the principles of political democracy. These stemmed from the native atmosphere, notably from Locke, but especially from the vogue of the French *philosophes* who were avidly read throughout Western society. The French *Encyclopédie* (1751–72) was an avowed revolutionary work, and *Encyclopedist* became a label for an intellectual rebel. But more important than the theory was the world-shaking excitement of the American and French revolutions. The Age of Reason had produced the idea of democracy, but the revolutions and the Romantics surcharged the concept with emotional fervor.

Today's anthologies often minimize the political writings of the Romantics, since these (like Wordsworth's *Convention of Cintra* and Shelley's *Oedipus Tyrannus*) are often not their most successful works of art. It may be claimed, however, that the democratic crusade was of great moment to all the great Romantics (again excepting Scott). Wordsworth stated that in his earlier years he devoted two hours to politics for every hour he gave to poetry.

PSYCHOLOGICAL. Perhaps also strongly conditioned by the revolutions (industrial as well as political) was the Romantic theory of human history. Tentatively, cautiously, the 18th-century rationalists had suggested the idea of progress; but the Western world saw human history as fundamentally static until the Romantics. It is chiefly they who have bequeathed a view of mankind's destiny as dynamic and evolutionary.

The Age of Reason and the march of science provided another powerful irritant against which the Romantics revolted. In these days of cautious scientists, who realize that every advance they make only opens bigger mysteries, we can hardly imagine the dogmatism and the absolute confidence of the 18th-century scientists (then termed "natural philosophers") who, intoxicated with their epochal discoveries, were too frequently proclaiming that they knew all—or would in a year or two. The general Romantic reaction to scientific dogmatism was a horrified recoil which pointed to the vast gulfs of human experience still defying the scientific approach. Many scientists were materialists and determinists, producing works like La Mettrie's *The Human Machine* (1748). Scientific impersonality and virtual inhumanity led the Romantics, like Wordsworth, in "A Poet's Epitaph," to lash out at a scientist as ". . . a fingering slave,/One that would peep and botanize/ Upon his mother's grave!"

PHILOSOPHICAL. As the passages on Berkeley and Hume have indicated, the rational mind of the 18th century eventually destroyed Locke's commonsense, materialistic explanation of the nature of man. In the 1780's, just in time to influence the rising Romanticism, the German philosopher Immanuel Kant proposed that our perception of the idea of a thing (a table, a nation), which exists in the Lockean scheme only as a disjointed succession of sense data, arises from a God-given innate power to intuit the oneness of objects. It was upon this suggestion that Coleridge constructed the theory of Primary and Secondary Imagination, the cornerstone of whatever philosophy was to guide the Romantics.

SOCIAL. Perhaps with the Romantic Period we are entering the logical development of an "open" society. Earlier "closed" societies spelled out virtually every response and attitude expected from a member of the society; the individual had very few decisions placed solely upon his shoulders. In the "open" society the individual must make all his decisions and assume all his responsibilities. Full consciousness of the meaning of an "open" society seems first to have been grasped by the Romantics. Their soaring ecstasy springs from this realization of freedom, but accompanying this sense of release is a powerful reaction of pessimism. The monstrous burden of their freedom can plunge them into despair, though "Romantic pessimism" is not as prevalent in English Romanticism as it was upon the Continent. In spite of his posturings, Byron, more worldly than his fellow Romantics, senses and expresses this problem best of all; in life and in the art of *Don Juan,* where he most fully explored the challenge of an "open" society and tasted most deeply of its freedom and its pain.

It will be seen from the following list of Romantic elements that the Romantics seized upon and frequently enlarged to gigantic proportions the tendencies already begun by the pre-Romantics discussed in the preceding chapters on the 18th century. Although certainly no one

Romantic exemplified all the characteristics discussed below, they are all in one way or another manifestations of the Romantic attitude.

(1) Medievalism. The Romantics developed a fascination with the glamour of the Middle Ages, and it is chiefly they who must be thanked for our contemporary delight in and curiosity about the historic past. Medievalism was the largest Romantic element in Scott.

(2) Orientalism. This was sought less for the wisdom assigned to the Orient by the 18th century than for the exotic and richly colored. Wordsworth is seldom touched by this motif, but all the other Romantics dabble in it, especially Byron. Eroticism was also prominent in this area of interest.

(3) Primitivism. This was the conviction that a less advanced stage of culture, even a savage condition, breeds greater happiness and character than complex modern society. Rebellion and escapism loom large in the primitivists, and every Romantic expressed at least some primitive leanings. Byron's unrestrained masculinity may be a reaction against a world where self-discipline becomes increasingly necessary— and irksome. The medievalism of this period is better understood when one realizes that for the Romantics, medieval society was a primitive society.

(4) The idea of progress. This entailed the belief that man is now progressing ever forward to a more glorious tomorrow. The revolutions, especially political and industrial, suggested as never before in human history that life might show continuous improvement. Incongruously, many Romantics espoused both primitivism and progress; however, some reconciliation was possible in the desire to brush aside the unsatisfactory accretions of civilization and proceed rapidly forward from a fresh start. Perhaps the strongest Romantic avowal of the idea of progress appears in *Hyperion,* by Keats.

(5) Anti-intellectualism. This expressed the basic Anglo-American distrust of the completely logical and rational. Through much of English and American literature runs the connection of goodness with naïveté and evil with shrewd intelligence. Paradoxically, Coleridge and Shelley, for instance, were well read and scholarly; nonetheless, like Wordsworth, they counsel a following of the heart rather than the intellect. This Romantic attitude springs largely from the belief in the innate goodness of human nature.

(6) Sentimentalism. This is here employed in the sense of enjoying emotion for its own sake. The sentimentalist revels in the sensitivity of his soul, delighting in the moods that sweep over him. Lamb is

especially sentimental but not nearly as extreme as some of the minor Romantics.

(7) Humanitarianism. Today's humanitarianism in Western society stems fundamentally, not from the Christian tradition of almsgiving, but from the Romantic insistence that we are indeed our brother's helper and are duty bound to provide the minimum of physical necessities and the maximum of human opportunities to all men. Humanitarianism chiefly arises from the Romantic belief in the equality and inherent worth of every man.

(8) Democracy. Except for Scott, all the major Romantics went through a republican period. Their urging came partly from a theoretical conviction of human equality bequeathed by the Age of Reason. This belief was strengthened emotionally by the Romantics in their hostility to monarchical authority and established institutions.

(9) Originality. Our own age has been so profoundly influenced by the Romantic demand for originality that we cannot realize the novelty of this doctrine. Only one Shakespearean play is without known source, and medieval men so scrupulously disliked originality as to be willing to accept new ideas only when they were falsely ascribed to the ancients or to the patristic writers. The jealous Romantic reverence of individualism has bred the demand for originality to the extent that "imitative" is now considered a pejorative term. Also, it must be understood that the new reading public of this age was not educated to the classical tradition, could not recognize an allusion, and therefore naturally preferred "original composition."

(10) Diversitarianism. Indicative of the loss of cultural centrality and of the cult of individualism is the demand for every conceivable or inconceivable viewpoint and expression. As children of the Romantics, we of today often share the same attitude, welcoming and even demanding every approach to every problem. Today's art is a continuation of the Romantic impulse, and perhaps many of today's extraordinary artistic experiments can claim justification solely under the doctrine of diversity.

(11) Confessionalism. Dr. Johnson considered it wholly improper to present his personal problems in his publc writings. However, since his chief or even only subject is himself, the Romantic individualist relates all. It is painful to read Hazlitt's *Liber Amoris,* in which he fully discloses how completely he made a fool of himself over a frivolous servant girl; but this same personal revelation from the Romantics

was responsible for the lyric outburst of the age, surpassing any other lyricism in English literature except that of the Renaissance.

(12) Belief in the purgative purpose of art. Aristotle said that the purpose of tragic drama was the purgation, through pity and terror, of the audience. The Romantics reversed the contention to see art as the necessary relief of the artist. They are responsible for the cliché that the artist must suffer and pour out his tortured soul. Though it would be injudicious to claim that non-Romantic art develops under these circumstances, for the Romantic artist the assertion is essentially correct.

(13) Fundamental antipathy of the artist to his times. Unlike Shakespeare (in Ben Jonson's words, "the soul of the age") and other earlier writers who epitomized the ideals of their eras, the Romantic writer goes his own way against the conventions of his time, generally registering protest and discontent.

(14) Love of the wild and the picturesque in external and human nature. Perhaps only at this point in human history could such a taste develop, for the Age of Reason had removed the superstitious dread from natural phenomena and the Industrial Revolution threatened to tame their savagery. The wild inner and outer Nature were opposite sides of the same coin, as in Byron's work, which so obviously sought the devastating spectacles of Nature that would mirror his own turbulent spirit.

The attitudes and expressions we term Romantic were shared in the era by all Western society from Poland to the Americas. Russia's participation was less extensive but included the notable poet Pushkin. All aspects of modern life were profoundly affected, with the exception of the scientific. Western art since the early 19th century has been fundamentally Romantic, forcing the separation of modern intellectuals into what C. P. Snow has called the "two worlds"—the artistic and the scientific—with relatively little mutual understanding or sympathy.

This chapter will devote itself to the first generation of Romantic writers, chiefly the poets Wordsworth and Coleridge, and the poetry of Sir Walter Scott. The next chapter will deal with the second generation of Romantic writers, principally Byron, Shelley, and Keats, and lesser writers. Most of the prose of this period will be discussed in the two succeeding chapters, on the early 19th-century novel and on the essays and non-literary prose of the period respectively. Thus it must be kept in mind that all the writers of this and the succeeding three chapters were roughly contemporary and many were personal friends.

THE POETRY OF WORDSWORTH

William Wordsworth (1770–1850). Following is a list of the more important events in William Wordsworth's life.

1770: Born April 7 at Cockermouth, Cumberland, second son of John Wordsworth, solicitor for the Earl of Lonsdale. Grew up with sister Dorothy and brothers Richard, John, and Christopher. At Anne Birkett's school, Penrith, his future wife, Mary Hutchinson, was a classmate.

1779–87: Attended Hawkshead school after his mother's death. Although school days were long, he was free after classes to roam the countryside. These periods with Nature were probably the happiest of his life. Father died in 1783.

1787–91: Entered St. John's, Cambridge, through aid of his uncle-guardian. Found independent study and ramblings near Cambridge more appealing than classwork.

1788: First summer vacation at Hawkshead.

1789: Second summer vacation at Penrith with Dorothy and Mary Hutchinson.

1790: Third summer vacation spent in walking tour with Robert Jones through France, Switzerland, and Italy. Alpine scenery chiefly impressed him, but his interest was greatly aroused by the first anniversary of the French Republic.

1791: Graduated from Cambridge in January, resided in London until May, went on walking tour of North Wales with Jones until September. Left London in November for Orléans, France, on pretext of studying to be a language tutor.

1792: At Orléans he fell in love with Annette Vallon, four years his senior, who bore him an illegitimate daughter, Caroline. At Blois he was influenced by Captain Michel Beaupuy to enthusiastic support of French republicanism. Summoned home in December.

1793: First published works, *An Evening Walk* and *Descriptive Sketches.* Blocked from return to France by war. His republicanism distressed his relatives. Summer hiking tour with William Calvert through south of England and Wales. Associated with Godwin's radical circle and converted to Godwinism.

1795: Settled with Dorothy at Racedown, Dorsetshire.

1797: Fruitful association with Coleridge caused move to Alfoxden, Somersetshire, where William, Dorothy, and Samuel conceived the plan for *Lyrical Ballads*. Coleridge interested him in the associationism of Hartley.

1798: Revisited Wye River with Dorothy. *Lyrical Ballads* published in September. Accompanied Dorothy and Coleridge to Germany.

1799: Productive writing in Germany until May. Walking tour of Lake Country with Coleridge. Settled with Dorothy at Dove Cottage, Grasmere.

1800: Prolific writing. Second edition of *Lyrical Ballads*.

1801: Visit to Scotland.

1802: Spent month in Calais with Dorothy visiting Annette and Caroline. Married Mary Hutchinson in October.

1803: Birth of their first child, John. Visited Scotland with Dorothy and Coleridge, staying with Scott for a week.

1805: Brother John drowned in wreck of *Abergavenny*. Finished first version of *The Prelude*.

1810: Estranged from Coleridge.

1812: Reconciled with Coleridge. Deaths of two of his children, Catherine and Thomas.

1813: Appointed to sinecure as Distributor of Stamps for Westmorland. Moved to Rydal Mount, his permanent home until his death.

1820: Toured Continent with wife and sister. Dorothy's *Journal* describes trip.

1842: Published last work, *Poems Chiefly of Early and Late Years*. Relinquished sinecure and received pension.

1843: Succeeded Southey as Poet Laureate. Dictated notes on his verse to Miss Fenwick. These comments are illuminative of the aged man's mind, but are often misleading when applied to his youthful poetry.

1850: Died April 23 at Rydal Mount. *The Prelude* posthumously published.

Wordsworth, like Milton, felt himself a dedicated spirit and wished to be regarded as a prophet and teacher rather than as a skilled versifier. His primary message in his early greatness was a reassertion of man's sharing of life with all organic things and with the cosmos. The Age of Reason had rendered man an alien in the universe, an observer of phenomena. Wordsworth insisted: "We are part of all that we behold." He was not a Nature poet in extensive description of scenery, like Cowper, but a commonplace flower or a mountain view could stir him to a rapt mood of transcendent ecstasy in which Nature would speak to him of the "mystery of infinitude, of Powers, Spirits,

Presences." He saw as one and the same thing the divinity in Nature and the divinity within himself. A 20th-century critic like Aldous Huxley may sneer that a taste for Wordsworth is a sign of "academic frigidity," and in the post-Darwinian world, Wordsworth's concept of the gentle, loving hand of Mother Nature may appear preposterous, but our own age often recognizes the fundamental point of his conviction that man must be one with the universe in which he is placed, obedient to its powers and participating in its plan. Though the later Wordsworth often seems less attractive than the earlier (the years brought him to conservatism and orthodoxy, in which he continued to compose verse with diminishing fire), nonetheless, the older poet is skillful, and today's critics are less willing to echo his own bemoanings of lost ability. In fact, many critics feel that he is the greatest English poet since Milton.

He is the strongest link between the 18th century and the Romantics. He is essentially a reflective poet, more deeply emotional than his predecessors but rather like them in experiencing a sensation or feeling and then building a figure of speech or a symbol to convey his meaning. With the exception of the Lucy poems, he wrote virtually no love poetry. His reticence concealed his affair with Annette from his contemporaries, and it was not publicly discovered until 1913. His later orthodoxy is less the apostasy stigmatized by the younger Romantics than the emergence of an innate conservatism.

Early Period

IMITATION OF 18TH-CENTURY POETRY. *An Evening Walk (1787–89, 1793)* is typical pre-Romantic Nature verse in heroic couplets. Addressed to Dorothy, the poem describes the Lake Country from noon through night scenes, interspersing passages of sentimentalism and quaint superstition.

Descriptive Sketches (1791–92, 1793) was written in France along the Loire. Its heroic couplets describe continental landscapes with more bravura than found in *An Evening Walk*. Written in the flush of democratic fervor, the poem vigorously espouses the cause of the French Revolution and idealizes Swiss republicanism. The effect, however, is essentially rhetorical and disconnected, the product of an excited young man imitating contemporary models and feeling his way uncertainly. The style is awkward and toward the end indulges in conventional neoclassic personifications of abstract ideas. Its chief literary source is Ramond de Carbonnières's remarks included in his French translation (1781) of Coxe's *Tour in Switzerland*.

THE INFLUENCE OF GODWIN AND RATIONALISM. "Guilt and Sorrow, or Incidents upon Salisbury Plain" (*1791–94*, 1842), in Spenserian stanzas, portrays the bitter sufferings forced upon the poor by war.

On Salisbury Plain two travelers fall together. One is a destitute war widow. The other is a sailor who had been shanghaied by a press gang and later cheated of his pay by "slaves of office." In desperation he robbed and murdered a wayfarer. He is barely able to meet his wife and secure her forgiveness before she dies. He surrenders to authorities and is hanged.

Following Godwin's contentions, Wordsworth sees man as "mild and good" in the person of the sailor. Circumstances, the cruelty of government and society, not man's innate nature, have made him a criminal. Man's inhumanity to man arouses the youth to dark, angry protests and desire for social reform. This is Wordsworth's most pessimistic piece. It is his first strong enunciation of his insistence upon the dignity of poor, untutored people. Suffering is portrayed in sentimental and almost Gothic detail. Part of the work was published in 1798 as "The Female Vagrant."

The Borderers (*1795–97*, pub. 1842) was Wordsworth's only play, a closet drama never acted. It is his only significant incursion into medievalism. Although Redpath's *History of the Borders* provided some atmosphere and hints, the plot is apparently original. Other influences are Shakespeare (*Lear* and *Othello*) and Mrs. Radcliffe. Oswald owes much to Robespierre, Marat, and other tyrants of the Reign of Terror. Marmaduke resembles Wordsworth himself.

During the reign of Henry III (1216–72), the border with Scotland was wild territory paying no heed to the King's law. Oswald's life had been saved by Marmaduke, but the wily, vindictive Oswald hated being under any obligation. He corrupts Marmaduke until the youth slays the blind Herbert, father of Idonea, Marmaduke's beloved. Oswald is stabbed by Wallace, one of the borderers, and Marmaduke sentences himself to repentant exile.

Written essentially in reaction to Godwin, the drama ignores social ills to examine a phase of criminal psychology. Oswald, according to Wordsworth's prefatory essay (first printed in 1934), is "a young man of great intellectual powers yet without any solid principles of general benevolence." The tragedy is that of intelligence and reason devoid of human sympathy and acting in ruthless self-interest. Nature is true benevolence, as Marmaduke perceives. The atmosphere of the work is reminiscent of the Gothic novel, and its blank verse is generally inferior but kindles occasionally, as in Oswald's bold urging of Marmaduke to action rather than thought.

THE INFLUENCE OF HARTLEY AND ASSOCIATIONISM. The most fruitful poetic partnership in English literature was that of Wordsworth and Coleridge. After the mediocrity of his early verse, Wordsworth started upon a ten-year period (1797–1807) of remarkable productivity and achievement. During 1797–98 Coleridge stimulated Wordsworth with the psychology of Samuel Hartley, which had been ultimately developed from Locke. Denying innate ideas and diagnosing all mental life as the product of sense perception and subsequent association of ideas, Wordsworth proceeded almost like a scientific researcher "to explore the primary laws of our nature." He purposely selected as his subjects uncomplicated persons, even mental defectives, since in them he felt that he could more easily trace the principles of associationism.

The Lyrical Ballads

Coleridge (then twenty-six) and Wordsworth (then twenty-eight) planned to produce co-operatively a book of poetry revealing a sense of lasting joy in Nature and in human experiences common to all men. They intended to drop pleas for political and social reform, and to avoid entirely traditional practices in verse style, in order to offer forceful sincerity and elemental human emotions. Folk ballads, as "natural" poetry, were to be their models. A fuller exposition of their intent will be given in the Coleridge discussion under *Biographia Literaria,* and Coleridge's contribution to their joint volume will also be discussed under that author. However, in quantity, Wordsworth far exceeded Coleridge in the resultant work.

Lyrical Ballads (1798; enlarged edition with preface, 1800; definitive edition, 1802; reprinted, 1805) stated in the advertisement to the first edition that it sought "to ascertain how far the language of conversation in the middle and lower classes of society is adapted to the purposes of poetic pleasure" (the "middle classes" vanished in the 1800 edition in favor of "low and rustic life"). The book was frankly a special experiment, and both Wordsworth and Coleridge were writing other types of poetry during the same period. This work is often termed the inaugurator of the Romantic Period.

"Preface" (1800, revised in 1802) is the pronunciamento of the New Poetry. Wordsworth states that it was written at the request of friends to explain his poetics, but also motivating him were pique at the cool reception of the first edition and a youthful desire to proclaim a new doctrine to the world. This "Preface" constitutes one of the most famous pieces of literary criticism in English.

Wordsworth's primary purpose was to reform poetry by deposing an artificial literary tradition and substituting in its stead a new poetics, more in keeping with normal contemporary speech patterns. This is an oft-repeated cry in English; Donne, in contrast with Spenser, saw his verse as reproducing true spoken English, and Dryden revolted against metaphysical verse. The neoclassic tradition in turn was moribund in Wordsworth's youth, and it is notable that the one poem he specifically attacks in the "Preface" is by Gray, and the faults he pillories are far more applicable to William Shenstone or Erasmus Darwin than to Pope. Wordsworth objects to the decaying 18th-century "poetic diction" (or prescribed vocabulary and phraseology for verse) which rejected as "unpoetic" many common words and phrases. The artificialities of expression which Wordsworth opposed included ponderous words and phrases, personifications of abstractions, inversions and other elaborate rhetorical patterns, mere listings and catalogs, stereotyped allusions and elegant wordings, and inflated figures of speech.

Against these, Wordsworth supports "a selection of language really used by men." In practice the verse of Wordsworth does not reproduce the dialect or illiterate jargon of his humble characters, but it does employ a vocabulary and phrasing much closer to standard English speech than the preceding "poetic diction."

The death knell of aristocratic art was sounded in Wordsworth's insistence upon "humble and rustic life" as his chosen subject matter; to neoclassic art, such characters and settings were proper only for low comedy. Wordsworth justified his choice largely upon the intimate ties between country dwellers and Nature. With such simple people, Wordsworth believed it relatively easy to trace Hartley's doctrines in "the primary laws of our nature." When the pre-Romantics celebrated the humble and the lowly, they were rather patronizing and condescending; with Wordsworth, the humblest are exalted to the highest dignity and worth.

Wordsworth's theory of poetry justified his hostility to "poetic diction." He saw poetry, not as a different rendition of the conventional, but as a different level of human sensitivity. Poetry, he declared, is "the spontaneous overflow of powerful feelings." The excellence of poetry therefore lies, not in the "action and situation," but in the poet's intensely subjective feeling toward his experience. Wordsworth's neoclassic predecessors would have agreed with him that the object of poetry "is truth, not individual and local, but general, and operative," but they would not have gone so far as his insistence that this truth be "carried alive into the heart by passion." So potent was the influence of Wordsworth and his fellow Romantics that to many of today's readers this daring definition of poetry seems a truism.

Although advocating the language of prose for poetry, Wordsworth still wished to retain meter. He maintained that the regularity of meter tends to "tempering and restraining the passion" and is able to transform a distaste for excited expression into a feeling of pleasure.

Wordsworth saw the poet as the possessor of superior sensitivity and also gifted with imaginative and creative powers; but it is Coleridge to whom we owe the Romantic concept of the Secondary Imagination. While the essential 18th-century attitude saw the poet as the skillful ornamenter and neat phraseologist, Wordsworth, on the other hand, believed that the poet seizes "the breath and finer spirit of all knowledge," speaking oracularly to all men and surpassing all other voices in causing mankind better to understand the totality of life.

Most of Wordsworth's poetic contributions to the first edition of *Lyrical Ballads* emulate ballad meters from Percy's *Reliques,* follow the Hartley psychology, and exemplify the contentions of the "Preface." All poems were written in 1798.

"The Idiot Boy" was always one of Wordsworth's favorites, though posterity has not favored it and Byron scathingly denounced it in *English Bards and Scotch Reviewers.*

Betty Foy sends her idiot son on horseback to fetch the physician for an ailing neighbor. When no one appears late at night, she runs to town herself and wakes the physician, but finds no sign of Johnny. She finally locates him idly regarding the March moonlight. The neighbor recovers without medical assistance.

The subject had not formerly been judged worthy of poetry. Wordsworth, always deficient in humor, tried to treat much of the story with heavy-handed pleasantry. The chief points of the poem are: (1) Betty's consuming affection for her child, idiot that he is, and (2) Nature's powerful appeal even to the simplest mind.

"The Thorn" was stimulated by the poet's sight of a thorn tree on Quantock ridge in a hailstorm. The narrator is supposedly a retired sea captain. The story shows how Nature protects her own, especially those who have been abandoned by society and who are persecuted by their fellows.

Jilted by her lover, Martha Ray gives birth to a child who vanishes. Townsfolk believe that she buried the infant under a thorn tree where she frequently sat in wild despair. Attempts to dig for the body are thwarted by unaccountable movements of the earth.

"Simon Lee, the Old Huntsman" praises the virtue of gratitude. Godwin denied gratitude as a virtue, stigmatizing it as cringing to wealth and power. The poet, unearthing the root of a tree for the weak old man, denies Godwin and exalts the feeble elder's spirit of gratitude as natural, praiseworthy behavior.

"Goody Blake and Harry Gill" portrays the lamentable passions generated by poverty and the vicious treatment of the underprivileged. The story comes from Erasmus Darwin.

Desperately seeking some faggots to keep herself warm, Goody (applied to an old woman of the lower classes) Blake pulls some sticks from Harry Gill's hedge at night. From his secret vantage point, he leaps upon her. Goody Blake prays God never to let Harry be warm thereafter. Chills thereupon leave Harry in ceaseless misery. This belongs to the "curse cycle" of Wordsworth and Coleridge verse, the most famous example of which is "The Rime of the Ancient Mariner."

"We Are Seven" is based upon an actual conversation with a little girl at Goodrich Castle in 1793. Although sister Jane and brother John are both dead, the child insists that there are still seven children in the family. Wordsworth's purpose is to demonstrate "the perplexity and obscurity which in childhood attend our notion of death, or rather our utter inability to admit that notion" (quotation from the "Preface").

"Her Eyes Were Wild" and "The Complaint of a Forsaken Indian Woman" both treat of deserted women. The subject perhaps preyed upon Wordsworth's mind because of his abandonment of Annette.

Ten Years of Great Productivity

By general consent, the best of Wordsworth's poems in *Lyrical Ballads* do not follow his doctrinaire position in the "Preface" but speak in his own authentic voice:

"Lines Written in Early Spring" is the first eloquent plea for the poet's new ethics. While the contemplation of man's treatment of his fellow men often brings pessimism and despair, a study of Nature's teachings will bring true serenity and joy. "Nature's holy plan" offers sensitivity and delight to every organic being.

"To My Sister" calls upon Dorothy to abandon books and accompany him on a March walk near Alfoxden. Sustaining joy for the years to come is offered by the renewing spring, and they shall sense behind Nature's beauty a universal benevolent spirit that justifies optimism.

"Expostulation and Reply" arises from conversation with Hazlitt, who visited Alfoxden in 1798. Wordsworth is reacting against current books on moral philosophy, works that he regards as arid, mechanical rationalism. The poet instead exalts the "primary passions" of affection, kindness, gratitude, and pity, and maintains that intellectual sources are insufficient to generate and sustain these passions. Eschewing the searching rational mind of the 18th century, Wordsworth calls upon his friend to submit himself passively to Nature's teaching, from whence will come the eternal verities.

"The Tables Turned," a companion poem, insists that Nature as a teacher surpasses all the "sages" in the instruction of elemental truths. A fundamental Romantic contention is the superiority of the synthetic process (putting all things together) over the analytic (breaking-down) process of the 18th century. Again the poet urges the receptive, passive soul rather than the active, grasping mind.

"Lines Composed a Few Miles above Tintern Abbey, on Revisiting the Banks of the Wye during a Tour" was occasioned by Wordsworth's return, now with Dorothy, to a scene he had first enjoyed in 1793. They took along Gilpin's *Tour of the Wye* (1771), which influenced the opening lines of the poem. This is a thanksgiving hymn, the first great work of many the poet was to enjoy in this ten-year period of richest achievement. The work is often termed *"The Prelude* in miniature,"* for, like the longer poem, it is primarily concerned with the poet's own development through the ministry of Nature.

The poet here diagnoses three stages in his appreciation of Nature:

(1) Childhood (11. 73–74), composed of essentially animalistic sensation, unheeding but unconsciously influenced for good by the lovely Lakeland countryside.

(2) Adolescence (11. 66–72, 75–83), composed of sensuous rapture as a growing mind and spirit revel consciously in beauties of Nature

and are therein satisfied. He considers himself in this stage during the 1793 visit to the Wye.

(3) Early maturity (84 ff.), which lacks the élan of the younger Wordsworth but is enriched by transcendentalism in which Nature reveals an eternal principle of rightness behind the transient phenomena. The sense of the eternal abiding amidst the fleeting caused Tennyson to consider 11. 94–102 among the grandest utterances in English.

The memory of the beautiful Wye vistas from 1793 is credited with three benefits during the intervening years:

(1) Healing emotions (11. 22–30). Although expressed with haunting lyricism, this passage seems really to suggest the almost universal pleasure those pent up in cities take in memory of green fields and natural scenes.

(2) Development of moral character (11. 30–35). Wordsworth follows Hartley here in the doctrine of associationism. While some might believe that our conduct and character are largely, if not solely, the product of human relationships, Wordsworth attributes his development not to society but to Natural powers addressed to him.

(3) Mystic union with the spirit of the universe (11. 35–49, 88–102). Wordsworth here proclaims a benefit that cannot be explained by Hartley's associationism or by any other rationalistic, materialistic concept. Although Coleridge, his associate, was well read in mysticism, Wordsworth does not appear to realize that his ecstatic moods duplicate, or at least parallel, the experience of many of the world's great mystics. He indicates the wearing away of any sense of the world into a trancelike state in which the soul is warmed by a feeling of absolute peace and a conviction of the unity of the entire cosmos. The poet's soul senses a "presence" that pervades all things. Properly this is termed "pan-psychism" (one supernatural spirit appears in all things but is not, as in pantheism, identical with all things). Wordsworth, as generally in his verse, touches upon such exalted moments without further clarification; the mystic experience is ineffable, and human vocabulary can relate only "how he felt and not what he felt."

Wordsworth's apologetic attitude toward such moods (e.g. 11. 49–50) makes him appear to be a quasi-mystic, for genuine mystics have blinding certitude about their visions. Of course, like the 18th century and the general tenor of Western culture, he feels hesitant about a dogmatic assertion of the mystic path; such hesitation, coupled with descriptions of "mystic" touches that many persons experience in normal life and find here expressed in perhaps as cogent and understandable language as mysticism can offer to the layman, insured the vogue of Wordsworth beyond that which Blake could ever assume for the mass of readers.

Consequently a "worshiper of Nature" (in later years he termed this "a passionate expression uttered incautiously"), he expresses the hope that Nature will continue to shower him with such blessings and will similarly affect his sister.

The second edition of *Lyrical Ballads* printed additional Wordsworth poems, in 1800 notably the ones discussed below.

"The Old Cumberland Beggar" (*1798*) arises in large part from the poet's hostility to "workhouses" for the indigent, which increased greatly as a result of the act of 1722. Wordsworth always preferred human associations to the institutionalism advocated by the Utilitarians. The old beggar of the poem is a free man, at one with the Nature amidst which he wanders. The subject is consistent with the poet's preference for the social misfits and aliens whom he felt had a communion with eternal Nature. The work truly exemplifies the contentions of the "Preface."

"Nutting" (*1799*), written in Germany, was originally intended for *The Prelude,* but, rather unaccountably, was "struck out as not being wanted there." In the poem, an innocent boy penetrates to a secret covert, is momentarily carried away by thoughts of "faery" beauty, and then pulls down branches to get hazel nuts. He feels pain at his ravishing of unspoiled natural beauty.

Wordsworth's major assertion in *The Prelude* is his covenant with Nature, but this poem records a dark aspect of the sexual myth as the boy momentarily experiences the sense of harmony with Nature and then proceeds to violate it. He then yearns for a restoration of the virginal perfection he had destroyed.

The "Lucy" poems (*1799*), written in Germany, consist of five exquisite short lyrics, constituting practically the only love poetry Wordsworth wrote. "Lucy" may refer to Margaret Hutchinson, sister of his future wife, who died in 1796. Mary Hutchinson and Dorothy have also been suggested; but "Lucy" may be an unknown love of the poet or else wholly imaginary. The simplicity and tender emotion of the poems are remarkable, but it is also notable that the concluding poem ("A slumber did my spirit seal") displays the "Tintern Abbey" sleep of the senses in which the soul and imagination perceive the absorption into the Eternal One.

"Lucy Gray, or, Solitude" (*1799*), written while Wordsworth was snow-bound in Germany, recounts an incident from Dorothy's childhood at Halifax. A little girl is sent through the snows to light her mother home. Her footprints reach the middle of the bridge and there vanish. In this, his most haunting ballad of childhood, Wordsworth suggests the surviving spirit of the child as part of the Nature that claimed her.

"Ruth" (*1799*), written in Germany, is ascribed by the poet to a Somersetshire account. "A Youth from Georgia's shore" deserts Ruth to return to the Cherokees in America. Ruth wanders in madness.

"Michael. A Pastoral Poem" (*1800*) fuses two accounts current around Grasmere, where the poem was composed. The prototype of Luke had years before lived in the very home occupied by Wordsworth. Michael derives from an old shepherd who spent seven years building a stone sheepfold in an isolated valley.

Luke is the only child of the aging shepherd, Michael, and the sole hope for the continuation of the grazing property in the family. The family is financially hurt by the bankruptcy of Michael's nephew, whose note Michael had signed. Luke, at his father's wish, begins to build a sheepfold before he leaves for the city to make his fortune. In the city, Luke is corrupted and flees abroad. Michael's life is empty, and the sheepfold remains incomplete at his death.

The subtitle defies the tradition of English pastoral poetry derived from Theocritus, Vergil, and other ancients. Though a living form as late as Milton, the pastoral poem was turned into a rococo confection by the 18th century. Instead of this artificiality, Wordsworth here depicts real sheepherders with the genuine smack of earth about them. In a letter to a friend, the poet designated the two dominating themes as "parental affection and the love of property." Old Michael had a covenant with Nature, but the covenant with his son was broken by the world of man (cities are most generally evil to Wordsworth). Yet Michael is not pathetic but rather tragically grand, an Old Testament patriarch. Never before had English literature cast such a humble, commonplace man in such a role of grandeur, at least not since *Piers Plowman*. The poetics of the "Preface" are here ringingly justified in "And never lifted up a single stone," a prosaic enough statement which in context perfectly and poetically symbolizes Michael's futility after his son has broken the covenant.

The Longer Poems

As early as March 11, 1798, Wordsworth had written substantial portions of a contemplated vast philosophical poem to be entitled *The Recluse, or, Views on Man, Nature, and Society,* which would detail the sensations and opinions of a poet living in retirement. His preface to *The Excursion* in 1814 makes clear that certainly by that date he had planned the following structure:

(I) Introduction, studying the growth of the poet's mind and showing thereby his qualifications for writing the lengthy and all-embracing work to follow. In the poet's own figure of speech, this would be the ante-chapel to a Gothic church.

(II) First part, surviving only as a fragment. Book I was first published in 1888 with the title *The Recluse*. No further portions are known.

(III) Second part, nine books published as *The Excursion* (1814).

(IV) Third part, never organized but almost certainly considered fulfilled by Wordsworth in a number of short poems. Continuing his metaphor, he suggested that the minor poems in proper arrangement would display "such connexion with the main Work as may give them claim to be likened to the little cells, oratories, and sepulchral recesses, ordinarily included in those edifices" (Gothic churches).

The Prelude; or, Growth of a Poet's Mind. An Autobiographical Poem is Wordsworth's completion of (I). The title was given by his widow. The first draft of this poem, addressed to Coleridge, was begun in 1799 and was completed by 1805 in thirteen books. This 1805 text was first printed in 1926, and some scholars consider it the definitive version as it was done by the youthful poet during his most creative period. However, from 1805 until his death, Wordsworth continued to revise the work into the form printed posthumously in 1850. The following discussion will examine the 1850 version, the more familiar text, and, on the whole, the better poetically. It contains fourteen books.

The Prelude is the greatest verse autobiography in English, but it is not a conventional autobiography. It omits many factual details and transposes or telescopes many experiences. Its purpose is to explore the psychology of a poet, determining what forces molded him to poetic utterance. Excerpts were printed during Wordsworth's lifetime as separate poems, but these are here considered within the total work. The over-all scheme of the poem pictures the initial Paradise of Nature in childhood, Paradise Lost in the poet's wrong turn to the persuasive lures of the French Revolution, and Paradise Regained in the return to the undiluted intercourse with Nature. Its central purpose is to portray the development of the Romantic Imagination.

Book I, Childhood and School-time, recounts contacts with Nature from early childhood to Hawkshead schooling (c. 1775–87). Here human associations are negligible in comparison to the ministry of Nature, which teaches both by fear and by love. The Eternal Spirit has revealed itself in Nature and provides affinities in the mind of childhood. Wordsworth sees much of his development in the Lake Country as explicable by Hartley associationism, but his realization of oneness in the universe mystically transcends this materialistic psychology. Whitehead has termed this book "Wordsworth's greatest poem."

Book II, School-time, tells of Hawkshead experiences. Line 198 marks the transition to adolescence, a transition from the earlier animal spirits which were essentially passive and heedless to an active, sensuous mind. A "plastic power," the poetic imagination, takes possession of Wordsworth; he sees this inner resource as an intuitive force, divinely granted and corresponding in man to the creative agency of God in the universe.

Book III, Residence at Cambridge. Wordsworth ignores or minimizes his own conscious intellectual efforts. Separation, for the first time, from his native Lakeland heightens his appreciation of Nature. Continuous close observation saves him from the vagueness and unreality to which his mystic, visionary side might have taken him. The finest passage, on the statue of Newton, is a product of his later years.

Book IV, Summer Vacation (in 1788), recounts the covenant made between the poet and Nature. Henceforth he is a "dedicated spirit." As in "Tintern Abbey," he indicates the fading away of sense impressions and the feel of the naked soul passing through the veil of the material world to stand in the presence of the One.

Book V, Books, is an interruptive section attempting to evaluate the influence of books upon the poet's growing mind. He sees their benefit as reinforcing the teachings of Nature. He implies the Platonic and Kantian remaking of the world through the mind. Romantic stories stimulated his imagination, and even "Gothic" tales acted apparently in Aristotelian purgation of pity and terror. W. H. Auden has discerned significant Romantic symbology in the dream sequence of this section, which was inspired by Don Quixote. The sea and the desert have become fascinating symbols of vastness and expansion of the modern ego. The stone is inorganic, cold rationalism; the sea shell is organic, producing living music. Romantics often see themselves as the idealistic Don Quixote and/or as Ishmael, the solitary outcast.

Book VI, Cambridge and the Alps, covers the period from October 1788 through October 1790. In the journey through the Alps from France to Italy, Wordsworth encounters scenic grandeur surpassing any of his previous sensations. Here he reaches the climax of his youthful Nature experience. The sublime and awesome in the mountains stir his imagination to a realization of the Infinite One toward whom individual destiny moves. The forms of the sensible world are analogous to and inextricably tied to his inner spirit. Again, as with the mystics, Wordsworth perceives in such beatific visions that the One is beyond good and evil, that all the confusing opposites that seem to exist in the sensed world are reconciled in the supreme One without contradiction.

Book VII, Residence in London, chiefly details London residence for three and a half months after graduation in 1791, but also incorporates stays in 1793, 1795, and 1802. The metropolis proves colorful but not truly stimulating to the poet of Nature. He is deeply moved, however, by the alienated and the lonely in the big city, and especially by a blind beggar. He feels that the discipline of Nature enables him, even amidst urban confusion, to sense the permanent in the transitory. An eloquent tribute to Burke is obviously the addition of the older poet.

Book VIII, Retrospect—Love of Nature Leading to Love of Man, is a re-survey of Wordsworth's developing interest in man, an interest that he attributes to Nature. Countrymen were ennobled by their association with things of Nature, and real shepherds proved more stimulating to his imagination than did any book characters. Here he records his sole "mystic" experience in a crowd amid "mean" surroundings, and in the Gardens of Jehol his only excursion into lush orientalism.

Book IX, Residence in France, covers his stay at Orléans and Blois from December 1791 to July 1792. Instead of the dignity of great events a young liberal would expect from the French Revolution, he encountered passion, bickering, and pettiness. A young French officer, Michel Beaupuy, showing the concrete evils against which the republicans were contending, convinced Wordsworth as the theorists could not.

Omitted from the 1850 version is the "Vaudracour and Julia" episode, obliquely referring to the Annette experience.

Book X, Residence in France, covers the period from October 1792 until the death of Robespierre in August 1794. The youth is shaken as never before when his native England opposes France, and he is torn between deep-seated loyalty to his homeland and perfervid loyalty to the revolutionary principles of France.

Book XI, France, runs from August 1794 to September 1795. The poet reaches the height of youthful enthusiasm as the glorious expectations of the French Revolution promise the end of centuries-old tyranny and the creation of an ideal society. No other passage in literature so epitomizes the exultant optimism of young liberals. Wordsworth then believed himself a rationalist of Godwinian persuasion, but English bigotry and French perfidy dashed his splendid hopes and left him despairing and desolate.

Book XII, Imagination and Taste, How Impaired and Restored, begins the road back—the reassembly of stability based upon the spirit instead of reason, upon abiding Nature rather than man's revolutionary principles. Returning to the impressions of his earlier years and to the sustaining English countryside about him, Wordsworth begins to regain composure and psychic strength.

Book XIII, Imagination and Taste, How Impaired and Restored, ignoring any inherent alteration in Nature, emphasizes the permanent and unchanging. He turns from man's vagaries to the prop of steadfast Nature. Dorothy was important in reorienting him and convincing him of a poet's need to see his enduring and inspiring foundation in the elemental things of life and Nature.

Book XIV, Conclusion, is a paean to the Romantic Imagination, which to Wordsworth was the mystic experience. Rational 18th-century Nature is discarded for an intuitive Nature. The climactic vision is taken from his walking tour of Wales in 1791 with Robert Jones. In moonlight, from atop Mount Snowden, Wordsworth beholds a gigantic spectacle of sky, mountains, and ocean that to him is "the emblem of a mind/That feeds upon Infinity." This ecstatic experience is vouchsafed by the Almighty as symbol of Its Imagination, and within Wordsworth's spirit is the divinely implanted Imagination that thus can intuit the abiding in the flux and can create universal truths. With this gift within his grasp, the poet is one with the cosmos, fully prepared for all of life and eternity.

The Recluse (c. 1800, 1888) is apparently all that Wordsworth completed in one book toward (II) above. It is somewhat disappointing after the high level of *The Prelude*. Wordsworth describes Grasmere, his early appreciation of its beauties, and his present satisfaction in settling there. He had long conjectured that he was destined to write an impressive epic poem, but he now realizes that simple subjects, treated with a contemplative and prophetic spirit, are his poetic destiny and might indeed prove more profound and significant than heroic verse.

The Excursion, Being a Portion of The Recluse (*1795–1814,* 1814), in nine books, was intended as the fulfillment of (III) above. The work is diffuse and seldom rises to exciting poetry. Broadly, the first five books attempt to establish a philosophical position, and the remaining books offer numerous accounts of specific human experiences to illustrate the philosophy.

The poet accidentally meets the Wanderer, an aged Scottish peddler who grimly joys in the failure of the Age of Reason and dogmatically asserts Christian optimism. The two visit Solitary, a man whose faith in man and God has been so horribly shaken as to send him into exile in lonely Langdale Pass. The trio descend to Grasmere church, where the Pastor recounts the lives of many now lying in the churchyard. Within the parsonage the four men criticize science, the Industrial Revolution, and the decline of agriculture, while upholding state schools and compulsory education. Solitary leaves, deeply affected by the optimistic faith of his three companions.

The philosophical contentions of the poem are:

(1) The universe is governed by a conscious, benevolent Spirit, willing happiness for mortals.

(2) Human life is essentially good and man's nature is essentially good. An exultant after-life awaits the virtuous.

(3) The human soul is a minuscule counterpart of the Great Soul. Communion between the two is effected by Nature, the visible symbol of omnipotent goodness. All men may experience this communion, the majority perhaps unconsciously, the gifted few in imaginative perception and creativity.

The Excursion is a third stage in the intellectual contest between optimism and doubt. The rational optimistic deism of Leibniz, mirrored in Pope's *Essay on Man,* had crumbled under the skeptical assaults of such thinkers as Hume and Voltaire, leaving many in the impasse of Solitary. Wordsworth shifts the optimistic position to the spiritual and intuitive. His examples from humble life attempt to demonstrate compensations that the rational eye overlooks: defeat can produce humility, suffering can teach patience, the struggle of life can elicit surprising resources, and the materially underprivileged can be richly rewarded with imponderable but soul-sustaining joys.

The Shorter Poems of the Middle Period

Poems, in Two Volumes (1807) printed some of the poet's best short pieces:

"My Heart Leaps up When I Behold" (*1802*) lyrically expounds the familiar Wordsworthian reliance upon impressionable and unspoiled childhood to perceive Nature's truths intuitively and thereby minister to later years with bolstering faith. These truths are also inculcated by the response to a number of growing things in "To the Daisy" (two different 1802 poems bearing identical titles), "The Green Linnet" (*1803*), "Yew Trees" (*1803*), and especially in "I Wandered Lonely as a Cloud" (*1804*), often mistitled "The Daffodils."

"Resolution and Independence" (*1802*) brings the poet to a lonely pool on a sunny morning after great rains. Especially he muses upon the unhappiness of poets, notably Chatterton and Burns. An aged leech-gatherer fires his imagination as the poet senses in the old man the immemorial bond between humanity and Nature.

With the sonnets (Italian form) of this collection, Wordsworth established himself as the first great English sonneteer since Milton. "London, 1802" calls upon the spirit of the mighty Puritan to reinvigorate a dispirited England. Other eloquent expressions of patriotism in an embattled age appear in "Composed by the Sea-Side near Calais, August 1802," "Great Men Have Been among Us" (*1802*), and "It Is Not to Be Thought of " (c. *1803*). "Thought of a Briton on the Subjugation of Switzerland" (*1807*) laments the Napoleonic conquest of the Helvetian Republic in 1802 and sees England as the last hope of freedom (appropriately Nature symbolizes freedom in the Swiss mountains and in the oceans about Britain). Not until this century was it realized that the poet was referring to his French daughter, Caroline, in "It Is a Beauteous Evening, Calm and Free" (*1802*). "On the Extinction of the Venetian Republic" (*1802*) grandly commemorates the vanished republican glories of Venice, annexed by Napoleon in 1797. "To Toussaint L'Ouverture" (*1802*) assures the ex-slave liberator of Haiti that even in prison he has the allies of freedom-loving men and the free forces of Nature. "Nuns Fret Not at Their Convent's Narrow Room" (*1806*) is one of the memorable sonnets upon the sonnet, and it may well be that Wordsworth's greatest poetic artistry lies in the sonnet form, which compels a discipline not required in his favorite blank verse. "Composed upon Westminster Bridge, 3 September 1802" seems extraordinary from a poet of Nature; however, his delight in the quiet city at dawn romantically arises not from the bustle of London but from the tremendous potential of energy in the slumbering metropolis. Most famous of all is "The World Is Too Much with Us" (c. *1802*), which calls for men to renounce the modern mania for materialism and money, and to regain the spirit of Natural Man amidst the earth's ministering beauty.

"At the Grave of Burns, 1803" was one of the poetic results of Wordsworth's tour of Scotland with Dorothy and Coleridge. Wordsworth employs Burns's favorite stanza, the "Standard Habbie." The tribute is summed up in: "How Verse may build a princely throne/On humble truth."

"The Solitary Reaper" (*1803*) celebrates a Highland girl singing in Erse as she works cutting grain. The poet speculates upon her subject— troubles of distant eras or perhaps homey griefs. The Romantic fascination with the unknown makes the mysterious music haunt his memory.

"She Was a Phantom of Delight" (*1804*), concerning his wife, Mary Hutchinson, is not a love poem. It celebrates her social qualities while, as usual in Wordsworth, sensing the grandeur of simple beings intimate with Nature.

"Character of the Happy Warrior" (*1806*), by the poet's admission, is based upon the personalities of Lord Nelson and his drowned brother, John Wordsworth. Probably Beaupuy was also in the poet's mind. The poem has become the acknowledged definitive statement of the ideal military man. Unusual for the later Wordsworth, this poem employs the heroic couplet.

In 1804 and 1805 Wordsworth arrived at a crisis in his imaginative career. His Nature myth was fading from him, perhaps because of his advancing maturity, perhaps because of a growing family that claimed increasing attention. The process was strongly accelerated by his brother John's death on February 5, 1805. This crisis can be seen in the following works in the 1807 volume.

"Ode. Intimations of Immortality from Recollections of Early Childhood" (*1802–04*) is probably the most famed pseudo-Pindaric ode in English. The memorable fifth stanza is the germ of the poem. It supports the infusionistic theory of the soul, claiming that the soul is eternal, coming from Heaven to dwell momentarily in the flesh for a certain time and then returning to eternity. The innocent rapture of childhood is the reaction of an eternal spirit which has only recently come into the world from the Eternal. With maturing years the "vision splendid" gradually vanishes and the adult is left in the drab world of the commonplace. In the eighth stanza the poet protests the change, but in the concluding stanzas, he seeks to find adequate compensation in maturity. His mature Imagination recognizes the truth of immortality as it senses childhood's disbelief in death and its own ability to conceive of that unknowing. He embraces the commonplace, simple things of life; though "splendour in the grass" has departed, he is sustained by the "sober colouring" of an adult acceptance of adult responsibilities.

"Ode to Duty" (*1804*) is modeled upon Gray's "Ode to Adversity," which in turn follows Horace's "Ode to Fortune." Obedience here is considered more important in the universe than joy. The former freedom-loving young Romantic abrogates the self-willed imagination and consecrates himself no longer to "Nature's law" but to social experience. Though rhetorically splendid, this ode is a reversal of the earlier Wordsworth, who accepted no direction but what his own nature and, supposedly, external Nature dictated to him.

"Elegiac Stanzas Suggested by a Picture of Peele Castle in a Storm, Painted by Sir George Beaumont" (*1805*), usually called "Peele Castle," is occasioned, not by the excellence of this amateur canvas from his patron, but rather by the subject, a castle upon a cliff overlooking a stormy sea. Now Wordsworth realizes that the benevolence he had ascribed to Nature was a delusion. His vision "never was," except as a dream fiction. His great poetic productivity was the result of blindness to the truth. Though "Nature" is now recognized as a betrayer, he still loves her and seeks in human sympathies to find the continued sustainer of his spirit. The deciding factor in this shift of mind was almost certainly the death of his brother John.

Poems (1815) was the first collected edition of Wordsworth's verse, omitting only *The Excursion*. The poet arranged these pieces under such categories as "Childhood" and "Affections," probably intending them to form (IV) above, i.e. the third part of *The Recluse*. Perhaps the best poem to appear here in first printing is:

"Laodamia" (*1814*), which was suggested by the poet's preparation of his eldest son for the University. He encountered the story while reading with John in Homer, Ovid, and most notably in Vergil's *Aeneid* (Book 6).

The recently married Protesilaus, knowing of the prediction that the first side to lose a man in battle would win the war, willingly sacrifices himself to the Trojans. In Greece, his bereft wife, Laodamia, pleads with the gods to permit her to see her husband again. For three hours his spectre revisits her but must then depart by divine edict. Laodamia dies of a broken heart. Trees grow from his tomb in Asia Minor and from hers in opposite Greece; when their tops are high enough to descry each other, they wither.

One may consider Wordsworth's great cycle of Nature poems as sublimated sexuality, for here he depicts overt sex passion for the only time, and condemns it. The spectre's lecture to the amorous Laodamia superbly declaims the classic reverence for harmony and decorum, but in Protesilaus's "self-devoted" sacrifice, he wholly ignores the claims of his wife. All other considerations must give way to his pleasure in martyrdom and the certainty that he will enjoy immortal fame in the memory of men. The physical drives that Earth creates are destroyed by Earth, and the after-life will not recognize them. The ending gave Wordsworth considerable trouble, and he devised several versions before the present conclusion. Though its sentimentalism is inappropriate to the preceding classicism, the end balances the sexual problem, for denied sexuality springs from the tomb as natural growth symbolically blighted by repudiation.

The White Doe of Rylstone, or, The Fate of the Nortons (1807, 1815) is based upon the ballad "The Rising of the North," in Percy's *Reliques*. The conservative Roman Catholic north of England briefly rebelled against Protestant Elizabeth I in 1569–70. Wordsworth chooses a form generally unfamiliar to him, octosyllabics rimed in couplets, and occasionally *a b a b*. An obvious influence on the work is the narrative verse of Scott.

The historical figure Norton, master of Rylstone Hall, with eight sons joins Percy and Neville in revolt. His Protestant children, Francis and Emily, remain neutral. In trying to save the Banner of the Five Wounds (symbol of the uprising), which Emily had sewed and his father and brothers had died for, Francis is killed. Emily finds consolation amidst her ruined family mansion from a doe formerly her playmate.

Though ostensibly historical and objective, the poem is Wordsworth's parting from his poetic youth. Like the Nortons, Wordsworth fought for a lost cause and here conveys a deep sense of the futility of action. Salvation comes from suffering, not from deeds. Francis chooses the best course—pacifism. From the natural companionship and love of the beast, Emily derives sustaining and healing powers.

Peter Bell, a Tale in Verse (*1798,* 1819) was so sorely smitten before and behind as never to have a chance. A few days before Wordsworth's poem was published, John Hamilton Reynolds printed *Peter Bell, a Lyrical Ballad,* a wicked burlesque upon Wordsworth's egoism and his "moral thunder from buttercups"; his Peter Bell proses over the tombstones of Betty Foy, Goody Blake, Martha Ray, the Ancient Mariner, and even "W. W." Shelley's *Peter Bell the Third* (1839) has probably completed for most readers the interment of the second (Wordsworth's) Peter Bell.

Peter Bell is a selfish, brutal, insensitive countryman who loses his way. Finding an unattended ass, he tries to steal the animal. In struggling with the refractory beast, Peter discovers the drowned owner of the ass. His redemption begins when he mounts the animal and lets it take him as it will. The animal bears him and his dead master back home. Peter is moved by the singing and call to repentance of isolated Methodists.

This is a Wordsworthian Ancient Mariner, a similarly coarse-grained common man arrested and touched by Nature through one of her suffering beasts. The plan for the *Lyrical Ballads* is carefully followed: as Coleridge in his poem sought to make plausible the weirdly supernatural, Wordsworth here sought to evoke supernatural awe through entirely natural effects. When Peter rides upon the ass carrying the drowned man, a fierce struggle ensues between his unregenerate nature and the new spirit of benevolence within him. Salvation strikes him with his hearing of the Wesleyans, an orthodox Christian appeal indicative of Wordsworth's alterations of the original before publication. The poem is marred by dull and prosaic passages, and the horrible playfulness of the Prologue should never have been attempted by a humorless man.

The Later Poems

Much of Wordsworth's poetic gift departed after 1807, with the end of his radicalism, but "Laodamia" (*1814*) is a notable work, and much of the sound revision of *The Prelude* was accomplished in his later years. The significant verse of this latter period is largely in sonnet form.

The River Duddon, a Series of Sonnets (1820) consists of thirty-four Italian-type sonnets following the Lake Country river from its rise at

Wrynose Fell until it empties into the Irish Sea. It is an area singularly lacking in folklore; so Wordsworth concentrates in chaste, felicitously worded lines upon the poetic evocation of lonely farmsteads, grassy paths, and small white churches. The concluding sonnet, "I Thought of Thee," is one of his best, sensing in the timeless river the role of the individual human life in the eternal stream of life. The same volume included a prose travel guide to the Lake Country that proved highly successful, going through five editions by 1835.

Ecclesiastical Sonnets (1822) contained one hundred and two sonnets to which thirty more were added in subsequent editions. Apparently original was Wordsworth's idea of a sonnet series tracing the history and spirit of the Church of England chiefly through prominent figures and noteworthy events, though the aging Wordsworth was more a pillar of the invisible church than a meticulously regular attendant at church services. When he essayed doctrine as in "Baptism" (※30), he performed only meagerly; but in awed reverence of man's hope and faith, he could produce the magnificence of "Inside of King's College Chapel, Cambridge" (※43). "Places of Worship" (※17) superbly evokes the calm ministry of rural churches, bringing solace to commonplace men in their daily lives. Some claim among the foremost of all sonnets in English "Mutability" (※34), with its hushed contemplation of the relentless process of dissolution.

Subsequent collected editions of his verse added other excellent sonnets, especially the following. "Scorn Not the Sonnet" (1827) is one of the great sonnets upon the subject of the sonnet, paying tribute to noted practitioners of the form from Petrarch through Wordsworth's own model, Milton. "Most Sweet It Is with Unuplifted Eyes" (1835) celebrates the inner power to make the world of individual "Thought and Love" richly satisfying. "A Poet—He Hath Put His Heart to School" (1842) scorns poetic systems and demands that verse be written from the "divine vitality" of the heart.

THE POETRY AND PROSE OF COLERIDGE

Samuel Taylor Coleridge (kōl'rij) (1772–1834). Following is a list of the more important events in the life of Samuel Taylor Coleridge.

1772: Born October 21 at Ottery St. Mary, Devonshire, youngest of the fourteen children of the Reverend John Coleridge. Avoided the society of other children for absorption in imaginative literature.

1782–91: At Christ's Hospital, London, after father's death. Established lifelong friendship with schoolmate Charles Lamb. Led to poetry by the sonnets of William Bowles. Permanently injured health by swimming the New River fully clothed and letting garments dry upon him.

1791–93: Academically brilliant as a scholarship student at Jesus College, Cambridge. Prominent among young radicals, a convert to Unitarianism and democracy through the influence of William Frend. Hopelessly in love with Mary Evans and deep in debt, he enlisted in the King's Light Dragoons under the fantastic alias of Silas Tomkyn Comberbacke.

1794: Returned to Cambridge after his brothers secured his release from the army. With Southey, he became imbued with Pantisocracy, a utopian community to be established in Pennsylvania on the banks of the Susquehanna. Engaged to Sara Fricker, sister of Southey's fiancée. Left Cambridge without a degree.

1795: Started lecture career. Broke with Southey. First met Wordsworth. Married Sara and resided at Bristol.

1796: Started the short-lived *Watchman* and published first poems. As relief from neuralgia, began the practice of taking opium.

1797: Sheridan rejected his play, *Osorio*. Fruitful association with Wordsworth which produced *Lyrical Ballads* the next year.

1798: Briefly a Unitarian preacher. Accompanied Wordsworth and Dorothy to Germany to imbibe current German intellectualism.

1799: Fell in love with Sarah Hutchinson, sister of Wordsworth's future wife.

1800: Settled at Greta Hall, Keswick, near Wordsworth at Grasmere. Took refuge from his unhappy married life in metaphysical studies.

1803: Accompanied Wordsworth and Dorothy on tour of Scotland as far as Loch Lomond.

1804–06: Mediterranean residence in search of health. Briefly secretary to military governor of Malta. Resided in Naples and Rome. Returned in poor health, completely addicted to narcotics.

1807: Separated from wife.

1808: Lectured on literature at the Royal Institution. Lived with the Wordsworths at Grasmere.

1810: Quarreled with Wordsworth because of William's criticisms of his habits.

1811–16: Financial distress and literary hackwork. Reconciled with Wordsworth in 1812, but their "glad morning friendship" of youth was forever gone.

1816: Placed himself under the care of Dr. Gillman, at Highgate, spending the rest of his life there.

1819: Concluded lecture career.

1819–30: As "The Oracle of Highgate," drew about him eager young disciples.

1834: Died July 25.

"He was the only *wonderful* man I ever met," claimed Wordsworth. Unquestionably Coleridge possessed one of the most brilliant minds of his era. However, a natural lassitude abetted by dope addiction nullified much of his great gift, and he frittered away a great amount of his time in contemplation of vast works that generally aborted. But even the fragments of a stupendous potential notably produced:

(1) Three poems ("Rime of the Ancient Mariner," "Christabel," "Kubla Khan") of incomparable Romantic effect. No other English poet claims so high a rank upon such few verses, especially remarkable when only the first, by the poet's admission, is complete. All of the Coleridge poetry commonly printed in modern anthologies amounts to far fewer lines than *The Prelude*. If Watts-Dunton is correct in labeling Romanticism as "The Renascence of Wonder," Coleridge is then the key figure in Romantic poetry.

(2) Seminal thought in politics, metaphysics, religion, and particularly in critical theory. Coleridge provided the philosophic basis for Romanticism and proved to be probably the most penetrating analyst of the Romantic accomplishment. Modern scholars such as I. A. Richards and James V. Baker utterly deny the traditional belief that Coleridge feel into impotence after the "wonderful year" from June 1797 to September 1798.

The Poetry

Poems on Various Subjects (1796) consists of verses composed before his fruitful collaboration with Wordsworth. While most of these pieces are in the vein of pre-Romantic poetry current in the era, they suggest some of the vivid imagery and sensuous mysticism in which Coleridge was to excel.

"The Eolian Harp" (*1795*) is the best example in the volume of the "conversational poem," a specialty of Coleridge's that he passed on to Wordsworth. The blank verse derives from Cowper's modification of Milton. It moves from a minor key of commonplace affection to climactic apostrophes to Nature. The poem indicates an internal struggle within the poet. He is inspired by the Eolian harp, a favorite Romantic symbol, a loose-stringed instrument upon which the wind plays "Natural" music. He suggests that "one intellectual breeze" that sweeps through all Nature is the universal soul, which identifies God, Nature, and man as one. Fearing a descent into pagan worship of Nature, the poet meekly collapses into a concluding acceptance of conventional orthodoxy. Coleridge feared to let his Romantic imagination steer him completely.

"Religious Musings" (*1794–96*), also in blank verse, was the most ambitious effort of the volume. The young radical idealistically supports the French Revolution and the cherished dream of Pantisocracy. While acknowledging his earlier support of Hartley associationism, Coleridge now emerges through Berkeley into an intuitive faith instead of a rational one. He expects to find union with a loving God from poetic contact with Nature.

The second edition (1797) of his first volume omitted almost a third of the previous poems and substituted about an equal amount. Perhaps of chief interest is:

"Ode to the Departing Year" (*1796*), which attempts to follow the Pindaric ode form but results in a mélange that is actually pseudo-Pindaric. Like Cassandra, quoted from Aeschylus's *Agamemnon* in the prefacing Greek, Coleridge gloomily predicts the downfall of England as the result of its opposition to the French Revolution.

First published in *Annual Anthology* (1800), "This Lime-Tree Bower My Prison" (*1797*) offers the first real touches of the "authentic" Coleridge. His three guests, Wordsworth, Dorothy, and Lamb (to whom the poem is addressed), have gone upon a walk, leaving him beneath the lime tree. He postulates that sharp, incisive observation of and contact with nature will mean mystic communion with the deity: "Nature ne'er deserts the wise and pure."

Lyrical Ballads (1798) was intended as a joint effort by Coleridge and Wordsworth (whose contributions to this volume have already been discussed). Coleridge provided much needed stimulus for the older poet, who sometimes has been termed "Coleridge's greatest work." In turn, Wordsworth galvanized Coleridge to the "wonderful year" (June 1797 to September 1798) during which most of Coleridge's memorable verse was written.

"The Nightingale" (*1798*), another "conversation poem," is a statement about the poetic imagination in the presence of Nature. Coleridge carries his infant son, who has been crying, into the moonlight. The loveliness and harmony of Nature are communicated to the infant, and he stops crying. At the same time the interchange of light between the moon and the infant's eyes represents a sending-forth of imaginative power already present in the infant. Such poetry indicates how strongly Wordsworth was indebted to Coleridge for theories of Nature and the Imagination.

"The Rime of the Ancyent Marinere" (*1797*) dropped many of the archaic spellings in the 1800 edition ("Ancient Mariner" thereafter) and some stanzas of lugubrious Gothic horror. The marginal glosses were first printed in *Sibylline Leaves* (1817), and this discussion follows the final version. A neighbor, John Cruikshank, related to Coleridge his dream of "a skeleton ship, with figures in it." The two poets originally intended to write the poem co-operatively, and thus Wordsworth supplied the albatross theme from Shelvocke's *Voyages* and wrote 11. 13–16, 226–27, "and four or five lines more in different parts of the poem, which I could not now point out." Most of the poem, of course, is Coleridge's, who had never been to sea at the time of the poem's composition. He was indebted to innumerable accounts of voyages which he had absorbed in his omnivorous reading. This is the most famous "art ballad" (or imitation by a modern poet of the early English and Scottish popular ballads) in English. Coleridge employed the standard four-line ballad stanza but varied it by stanzas extending up to nine lines. Since popular ballads upon the supernatural represent a small minority of the medieval folk verse, Coleridge achieves awesome effects quite opposite from the often homey touches of supernaturalism in the popular ballads.

Part I. A gallant going to a wedding is persuaded, indeed hypnotized, into hearing the story of an aged seaman. The narrator tells how his medieval ship sailed south from England to the cold Antarctic and how he had killed an albatross that had followed the vessel for scraps of food.

Part II. Doubling the Cape, the ship proceeds northward through the Pacific to the horse latitudes. Exasperated by the prolonged calm and blaming it on the slaying of the "good-luck" bird, the crew hang the albatross around the ancient mariner's neck.

Part III. A skeleton ship approaches across a windless sea, disclosing the figures of Death and Life-in-Death. In a dice game Death wins the crew, and Life-in-Death wins the ancient mariner.

Part IV. Now the sole living being aboard the ship, the ancient mariner looks upon the slimy things of the deep and intuitively blesses them, whereupon the albatross falls from his neck into the sea.

Part V. Wind and rain return, and the ship is conveyed by angelic spirits back to the Atlantic as far as the equator.

Part VI. The curse finally expiated, the ship is miraculously brought to the very harbor from which it had first sailed.

Part VII. The ship suddenly sinks, but the ancient mariner is saved by the pilot's boat, wherein he is shrieved by the hermit of the wood. Thereafter he must wander through the world relating his experience for the benefit of anyone needing this lesson. The wedding guest departs "a sadder and a wiser man."

Coleridge modifies the traditional tale of the Jewish tradesman who refused Christ a pause for rest on the *via dolorosa* and was condemned to life-in-death, during which he must recount his sin until Christ's second coming. Nature has been denied by the ancient mariner, who receives similar penance. The Wandering Jew theme was popular with the Romantics, appearing in Shelley's accounts of Ahasuerus in *Queen Mab* and in his *Revolt of Islam*.

The albatross is a symbol of Nature's ministry which has been slain in pure caprice. The ancient mariner has not merely violated the laws of hospitality and gratitude; he is all thoughtless humanity wilfully destroying the life impulse and the ties with Nature. Killing a human being would have brought human retribution, but the mariner's deed compels Nature's retaliation. His crew implicate themselves, for they condone the slaying; heedlessly they make momentary convenience their sole measure of judgment. Likewise, they fail to realize that their continued progress is the deceptive momentum of a life cut off from the deeper impulses of the spirit. The becalming of the ship and the hideous threats from creatures of the sea symbolize a life sundered from all sympathetic powers of Nature by a paralyzing guilt. Death for the crew is the lesser punishment, for Life-in-Death is the consciousness of utter abandonment and hopelessness. In this motionless state the mariner envies the steady progress of the moon and stars. The turning point comes with his intuitive blessing of all living things. The innate goodness of man and his psychic bond with the life force save him as no rational process could. The preceding sterility has been symbolized by drought and the absence of a breeze; now the life-giving rains descend and the winds of breath and inspiration start up. The definitive statement of the sacramental vision of the "one life" theme appears in the famous lines "He prayeth best who loveth best/All things both great and small." The entire poem exemplifies the rebirth myth, paralleling Wordsworth's experience in *The Prelude* and, of course, innumerable other literary and religious works.

Wordsworth instigated the "curse" theme possibly from his sense of guilt about Annette. Coleridge apparently found the theme congenial because of his warring temperament, as indicated in "The Eolian Harp." He seems to be trying to stifle his concern with orthodoxy by vehement insistence upon the Romantic cult of Nature. Pervasive is the sense of fearful loneliness, the curse of the solitary quest. Probably no other Romantic work so grippingly portrays the burden of the individual search for self-realization.

Perhaps as Coleridge himself stated, there is too much moral to the poem. This work is Coleridge's supreme fulfillment of his own critical theories. From reading, acute perception of Nature, and the stuff of dreams, his "shaping spirit of Imagination" has transfigured and unified a powerful vision. His role in the assembly of *Lyrical Ballads* is eminently achieved in securing the "willing suspension of disbelief" for a supernatural subject in the trappings of realism. Technically this achievement stems largely from sharp observation of Nature (note how the aching memories of landscapes intensify with the prolonged absence from land) and also from the wedding-party framework in which the narrative is imbedded. Probably no other piece of literature is so fantastic and yet does not overstrain our credulity. Generations of readers of this poem have been awed by its sense of the world's mystery and surprise. Technically this effect is largely achieved by the suddenness with which ice floes, the sunrise, etc., appear, and by a deft shift of conventional symbolism; this latter is especially notable in the treatment of color, emerald-green icebergs, leprous-white Life-in-Death, etc.

The fragmentary "Christabel" was first printed in 1816. Part I was composed in 1797, Part II in 1800. The classical ideas about the lamia (a man-eating monster with the head and breast of a woman joined to a serpent's body) and the medieval concepts of the vampire worked in Coleridge's brain along with his readings in Percy's *Reliques* and tales of Gothic horror. Many of the Nature references remarkably parallel current entries in Dorothy Wordsworth's journals. Coleridge thought that he had invented the line (four stresses with any varied number of unstressed syllables), but it is essentially the ancient Anglo-Saxon line that survives even to today in some nursery rimes.

Part I, a product of the "wonderful year," is in the magic vein of "The Rime" and "Kubla Khan." Christabel is the lone child of Sir Leoline, whose wife died in childbirth. One day in the woods the maiden finds a beautiful woman under an oak tree. It is Geraldine, who explains her presence by an unlikely account of kidnapping. Mysterious portents accompany Christabel's leading of Geraldine to her private quarters. The warning spirit of Christabel's mother is chased away by the newcomer. Geraldine joins Christabel in bed and hypnotizes her into accepting the bizarre happenings.

Part II incorporates Lake Country scenery and frequent echoes from Scott's narrative verse. Geraldine informs Sir Leoline that she is the daughter of his enemy, Lord Roland de Vaux of Tryermaine. Christabel urges her father to remove Geraldine, but the newcomer charms Sir Leoline. He sends bard Bracy to announce Geraldine's safety to Lord Roland.

Gillman relates Coleridge's proposed ending. In the absence of the bard, Geraldine gains power over Sir Leoline and plays upon his emotions. With Bracy's return, Geraldine assumes the form of Christabel's absent lover. The ensuing courtship distresses Christabel, but she reluctantly agrees to marriage. As the pair approach the altar, Christabel's real lover appears, producing the betrothal ring. Geraldine vanishes, the dead mother's joyful voice is heard, the proper marriage proceeds, and Sir Leoline is reconciled with his daughter. In 1800 Coleridge stated that the poem would extend from its present 677 lines to 1400 lines, and in 1815 he declared that it would consist of five books.

The extant "Christabel" is too incomplete for definitive analysis. Upon first printing, the poem was greeted with charges of obscenity, which, along with the poet's own conventional morality, may, instead of laziness or flagging imagination, be the genuine reason for its incompleteness. Coleridge's imagination had taken him into dark shadows of sex symbolism, and the poet's later diminished imagination probably resulted from his distrust of and distaste for what he dredged up. The poet carefully distinguished between the "supernatural" in "The Rime" and the "preternatural" in "Christabel." The poem's subject obviously is witchcraft. Geraldine is the folklore witch, seemingly fair but cursed with withered parts (in manuscript Coleridge wrote 1. 253, "Are lean and old and foul of hue"). By superstition, she must establish physical contact with innocent youth to secure rejuvenation. Lines 379–80 emphatically demonstrate that Geraldine has obtained heightened femininity from contact with Christabel. Certainly the most interesting character of the work is Geraldine, whose spine-tingling evil is apparent from her initial appearance under the Druidical mistletoe and oak to her triumphant alienation of Sir Leoline from his daughter as the poem breaks off.

As Geraldine is the embodiment of evil, so Christabel is the symbol of purity. Coleridge stated that while writing the poem he had in mind Crashaw's "Hymn to Saint Teresa." This suggests that he intended at least a partial martyrdom for Christabel. It looks as though (note 11. 227–32) Christabel might be willingly offering herself to Geraldine to save her absent lover from some bondage of evil into which he has fallen. In the process, while Geraldine obtains rejuvenation from Christabel, the hapless maiden herself takes on increasingly the aspects of the lamia. Here external Nature is the abode of demoniacal forces, not the benevolent Nature of the Romantic Wordsworth or the usual Coleridge, and the castle is not a sanctuary of good; Sir Leoline is trapped in morbidity and misguided temper, while Christabel is actually aiding Geraldine's evil spirit in avoiding such protective elements as the Virgin and the spirit of her dead mother. The Gillman account indicates a romantic "rescue" and a happy ending, but in the completed portion, Coleridge had worked himself into an impasse of evil from which he could hardly extricate himself. As in "The Rime," the theme of loneliness dominates the poem, but it is a horrifying isolation of Christabel without the promise of a road back through Nature.

"Kubla Khan," first printed in 1816, was written, according to the poet, in 1797. His dating may be correct, though from other Coleridge references many scholars believe that he meant 1798. In the well-known prefatory lines, Coleridge stated that he had taken opium before dreaming the poem. Hastily scribbling the verse when awake, he was interrupted by his tailor demanding payment. When Coleridge returned to the manuscript, he could recall no more of the dream, though he believed it to extend to two or three hundred lines, instead of the mere fifty-four extant. Coleridge's admission that before slumber he had been reading from the Renaissance travel writer Samuel Purchas induced John Livingstone Lowes, a modern critic, to a detailed study of the poet's reading that resulted in *The Road to Xanadu* (1927), one of the most famous 20th-century scholarly studies of English literature. Lowes conclusively demonstrates that Coleridge lifted every phrase, even every word, from the many works of travel and imagination that he read so tirelessly.

"Kubla Khan" is a poem about the Secondary Imagination and simultaneously a perfect demonstration of the workings of that Imagination. (This subject will be more fully discussed later). Lowes's revelations, far from discrediting the poem, substantiate the poetic faculty, which "dissolves, diffuses, dissipates, in order to re-create." From a bewildering variety of samples of the Primary Imagination, Coleridge's power of the Secondary Imagination forms a new and unique unity.

The "sacred river" is the Secondary Imagination, a deep intuitive welling from unconscious reservoirs of Nature. It is not amenable to rational discipline but goes where it will. Kubla Khan has attempted in his "pleasure-dome" to create the conscious and secure world of art. Disdainful of such Age of Reason attempts, the "sacred river" leaps upward from subterranean sources, follows its natural unchanneled course, and drops again into the unconscious from whence it came. In its career it reveals the opposites of warmth and ice which the rational mind cannot cope with. Inspired by the muse of Nature ("An Abyssinian maid"), Coleridge intends imaginatively to create the true picture of reality that will reconcile the opposites and reveal the totality of human experience. With such gifts from the deep stores of Nature, the poet is himself a sacred being, a prophet endowed with transcendent powers of revelation.

Subordinate but obvious is the association of the "sacred river" with the life force and sexuality. In spite of Coleridge's statement (dreams have the delusive semblance of endless continuity), the poem appears to be a complete and finished pronouncement. Opium, as with De Quincey, may have heightened the ecstatic sensuous imagery of the dream, but, lacking the innate poetry of Coleridge, many addicts have consumed opium without producing anything remotely resembling "Kubla Khan." Kipling has considered 11. 14–16 three of the five lines of pure poetry in English. The poem may well be termed the supreme achievement in Romantic poetry and theory.

"Frost at Midnight" (1798) was first published in a quarto pamphlet in the year of its composition. It is Coleridge's masterpiece among the "conversation poems" and demonstrates how Coleridge transmitted to Wordsworth the myth of Nature memory as a means of salvation. In concept and style, the "Tintern Abbey" poem seems to derive from this work. Coleridge writes in this poem of a solitary vigil by the fireplace near his sleeping infant son Hartley on a cold night. The soundless ministry of frost corresponds to the silent ministry of memory, both binding together in unity what seem irreconcilable phenomena. Operating by apparently whimsical but actually momentous associations, memory links the child Coleridge with the mature poet, thereby offering him confidence in the essential goodness of the universe. Coleridge wishes for his son a deeper impression from Nature than that which his childhood gave him.

"Fears in Solitude" (*1798*) was published along with "Frost at Midnight." Coleridge affirms his own patriotism in the face of the imminent French invasion of England. He promises spiritual peace to the humble man who will let Nature speak to him of its joys and "religious meanings."

"France: An Ode" (*1798*) was first printed in *The Morning Post* in 1798. Coleridge here spells out the downfall of liberal expectations of the French Revolution, a distress of mind somewhat vaguely treated by Wordsworth in Book XI of *The Prelude*. Like Wordsworth, Coleridge states that he was led to the cause of freedom by Nature and believed that cause incarnated in the French Revolution. Liberals discounted the reports of the Reign of Terror as counter-revolutionary propaganda, feeling that some violence might accompany the birth of the new democratic era. But now in 1798 the French invasion of the Swiss Republic showed that the Revolution had gone sour and that the French were the enslavers rather than the liberators of mankind. As in the concluding books of *The Prelude,* this poem concludes by recognizing freedom, not as a social goal, but as a personal goal. The last ringing lines sound Byronic as the poet, standing on a cliff, is swept by the winds of freedom and feels the expansion of his soul to the infinite in individual creativity and power. Shelley told Byron that this was the greatest modern ode, and imitated it in "Ode to the West Wind."

"Dejection: An Ode" (*1802*) first appeared in *The Morning Post* on Wordsworth's wedding day, October 4, 1802. Interpretation here is somewhat difficult, owing to extensive manuscript revisions. The earliest version (first published in 1937), over twice the length of the printed text, clearly states that the poet's depression arose from his hopeless love for Sarah Hutchinson. The standard text bemoans the loss of his "shaping spirit of Imagination" and thereby parallels Wordsworth's "Peele Castle" poem three years later. Coleridge denies the Nature cult he had earlier revered and largely communicated to Wordsworth. Even the most spectacular displays of Nature no longer move him, as he realizes that what he thought was revealed in Nature was actually a product solely of his own mind. The loss of imaginative power and his subsequent distress are explained, but he does not explain the reason for the loss. In his correspondence, Coleridge sees the loss as arising from his devotion to "abstruse researches," and also hints that his unhappy private life is likewise responsible. Another explanation suggests that Wordsworth's marriage was obviously going to curtail the association of the two poets, and Coleridge therefore is casting out the Wordsworth within himself. Perhaps, like Wordsworth, he simply experienced "the light of common day" with his maturing years. Quite likely is the religious problem that is implicit in the tensions of earlier poems; Nature and the Romantic Imagination are shed like Pantisocracy and the French Revolution in the need for orthodox conformity.

"Hymn before Sun-rise, in the Vale of Chamouni" (*1802*) was first printed in *The Morning Post* in 1802. Coleridge never visited this valley with its prospect of Mont Blanc. His poem is considerable amplification of the German "Ode to Chamouny," by Frederika Brun. The great mountain is celebrated as the symbol of God's omnipotent power and glory in blank verse reminiscent of Thomson. Nature is no longer the fostering mother but a symbol for a Jehovah-like deity.

"To William Wordsworth" (*1807*), first published in *Sibylline Leaves* (1817), is a "conversation poem" written immediately after hearing the full reading of the 1805 version of *The Prelude*. It is a glowing but mixed tribute to Wordsworth's poem. Coleridge praises the power of Wordsworth but insinuates, as in the "Dejection" ode, that Wordsworth is mistaken in ascribing to Nature the power that actually lies within himself. The early version of *The Prelude* left the soul of the poet untrammeled, but in his summary, Coleridge revises the end in the fashion of "Ode to Duty": "Of Duty, chosen Laws controlling choice,/ Action and joy!"

"Youth and Age" was initially published in its present form in 1834. The first forty-three lines were written in 1823, the concluding six lines in 1832 as an afterthought. It is Coleridge's first poem of old age. Few lyrics so achingly convey the sense of lost youth and the poet's unwillingness to accept its passing.

"Work without Hope" (*1825*) was first printed in the *Bijou* (1828). The very protest of poetic incapability is lyrically impressive. Nature no longer moves him, and advancing years separate him from the hopes and actions of abounding life.

"The Gardens of Boccaccio" (*1828*), first published in *The Keepsake* (1829), is a remarkable resurgence. Coleridge celebrates the gay, irresponsible *joie de vivre* which he found in the *Decameron* with facile couplets that tunefully depart from the clicking 18th-century versification without going as far as Keats does in *Endymion*.

DRAMATIC WRITINGS. Coleridge worked upon four plays. To *The Fall of Robespierre* (*1794*) he contributed the first act, while Southey wrote the two remaining acts. Coleridge's portion, modeled after *Julius Caesar,* depicts the conniving of the plotters against Robespierre. *Wallenstein* (*1799–1800*) is a competent translation from Schiller. The drama's vision of heroism, ambition, and destiny far exceeded that of current English tragedy and probably stimulated the dramatic attempts of Byron and Shelley. *Osorio* (c. *1797*) was revised and produced as *Remorse* at Drury Lane Theatre in 1813 through Byron's influence. Osorio unsuccessfully tries to kill his elder brother, Alvar. Alvar reappears in disguise to work upon Osorio's feelings. As in Wordsworth's *Borderers,* a man who has yielded to base motives is stirred to innate impulses of benevolence. The plot and treatment derive from *The Brothers* (1769), by Cumberland, and *Die Räuber,* by Schiller. *Zapolya* (*1817*) imitates *Winter's Tale* with romantic flourishes of spectacular palaces and mazy caverns, but is chiefly remembered for a few songs that recapture some of the ethereal magic of the earlier poet.

The Prose Writings

POLITICAL WRITINGS. *The Watchman* consisted of ten desultory numbers from March 1 to May 13, 1796. Coleridge supported the principles of the French Revolution but regretted the misguided course France later took.

Constitution of Church and State (1829) is Coleridge's definitive statement of his political convictions, influencing Green and many subsequent English historians and political theorists. Coleridge counters the utilitarian approach by conceiving of the "social contract," not as an actual agreement in the sense of Rousseau, but as a Platonic "idea" truly though not consciously operative in all Englishmen. The harmonious balance of English rule rises from the proper balance of this unexpressed understanding with the specified laws and regulations. Thus he tries to combine the conservative (organic) theory of institutions with the liberal (mechanical) theory. Consequently, both the Liberal Gladstone and the Conservative Disraeli were influenced by Coleridge's political philosophy. The Platonic "idea" of man's political status is not fixed but is changing and is increasingly revealing itself.

PHILOSOPHICAL WRITINGS. *The Friend* consisted of twenty-seven numbers over an eight-month period in 1809 and 1810. Prose and verse by Wordsworth and others are included. Coleridge recast many of his contributions for book publication in 1818. Many of the essays are scattered over personal and esthetic interests, but those papers most influential treated of philosophy. These latter are heralded as a turning point in English philosophical and literary thinking. Coleridge attacked the philosophical basis of 18th-century English and French thought, and advanced the new German philosophy, especially that of Kant. An intuitive apprehension of truth (as derived from Kant) provides the Romantics with a basis for their artistic credo.

Much of Coleridge's philosophical material consisted of lectures, powerfully stimulating to his listeners but now either lost or still buried in manuscript form. The 1818–19 series of *Philosophical Lectures* was first published in 1949. The scope of his contribution has not yet been fully assayed. English-speaking philosophers tend to exalt Coleridge for brilliant originality; Muirhead terms him the founder and still chief representative of "the voluntaristic form of idealistic philosophy." European and especially German scholars minimize his originality, pointing out his many borrowings of ideas and even unacknowledged translations from Kant, Schlegel, Schelling, Jacobi, and other German thinkers.

RELIGIOUS WRITINGS. *Aids to Reflection* (1825) proved to be Coleridge's most popular prose work. In a series of aphorisms with commentary, Coleridge, completely abandoning his earlier unitarianism, accepts wholly orthodox tenets: trinitarianism, original sin, vicarious atonement, etc. His approach, however, is neo-Platonic, strongly influenced by the Cambridge Platonists. As throughout his philosophy, he sought the realization of a spiritual unity, here the Divine Idea of Plato. The physical world manifests the Idea in concrete form, the mind of man reflects the Idea in reason, the soul of man ecstatically contemplates the Idea in religion. In the broad church tradition he identifies true faith with reliance upon conscience.

LITERARY THEORY AND CRITICISM. Articles in *The Morning Chronicle* (1793–95), *The Morning Post* (1798–1802), and *The Courier* (1807–12), as well as in his own periodicals, *The Watchman* and *The Friend*, treated in somewhat desultory fashion the problems of literary criticism and theory. The only volume on criticism and the only work of genuine critical importance published during Coleridge's lifetime was:

Biographia Literaria; or, Biographical Sketches of My Literary Life and Opinions (two volumes, 1817). Though occasionally obscure or difficult in meaning, this is one of the world's most significant treatises on the nature of poetry and the poet.

Coleridge relates the origin of *Lyrical Ballads* in the Somersetshire conversations of the two young poets. Conceiving the power of poetry to be twofold—that is, it can arouse reader sympathy by "faithful adherence to the truth of nature" and by "giving the interest of novelty by the modifying colors of imagination"—Wordsworth was to assume the first task by rendering the familiar marvelous and beautiful, while Coleridge was to accept the second task of making the unfamiliar credible. Coleridge's role is explained in one of the most memorable of all critical phrases: "to produce that willing suspension of disbelief for the moment which constitutes poetic faith."

To Coleridge, the essence of poetry is its unifying, synthesizing power. In a famous phrase, poetry "brings the whole soul of man into activity, with the subordination of its faculties to each other, according to their relative worth and dignity." He subscribes fundamentally to the ancient concept of beauty as harmony. The creator of poetry therefore sums up all within him: the conscious and the unconscious, the constructive and the emotional, the philosophical and the childlike, the pleasant and the truthful. "Finally, Good Sense is the Body of poetic genius, Fancy its Drapery, Motion its Life, and Imagination the Soul that is everywhere, and in each; and forms all into one graceful and intelligent whole."

The most important, and most extensively discussed, of Coleridge's contributions lies in his theory of the Imagination. He dismisses Fancy as the mere shuffling of sense data and memory by talent, producing castles in Spain and unicorns. Imagination he conceives of according to the Kantian distinction between the *Verstand* (understanding of familiar perceptions and concepts) and the *Vernunft* (direct apprehension of universal truths); both words are frequently translated as "understanding." The *Verstand* faculty is possessed by every human being, who intuitively realizes the oneness of an object (automobile, house) or a concept (New York City, General Motors). The *Vernunft* faculty is a superior intuitive power that conceives of the oneness of universals (truth, the deity). Corresponding to the *Verstand* is the Primary Imagination, and to the *Vernunft,* the Secondary Imagination. This Secondary Imagination is the creative gift possessed by poetic genius. From the Greek, Coleridge coins the word "esemplastic" to refer to this Imagination which can balance or reconcile the apparent opposites in experience, transforming the "essence into existence," "the potential into the actual." The Secondary Imagination breaks down the familiar perceptions of the Primary Imagination and then constructs a new creative unity, the poet's unique vision of truth. What "Kubla Khan" does poetically, the *Biographia Literaria* attempts to do philosophically, producing a critical basis for the Romantic Imagination.

Coleridge highly praises Wordsworth as the supreme contemporary manifestation of the Imagination and, in lengthy analysis, further points to Wordsworth's poetic virtues: weight and wholesomeness of thought and feeling, purity and appropriateness of language, strength and felicity of expression, originality and sensitivity, and adherence to the truth of nature. Wordsworth's defects are politely but firmly noted: verbosity, unevenness, strange inconsistency between some of his subjects and his treatment of them, and a sometimes deadly matter-of-factness. Coleridge regrets Wordsworth's disparagement of meter, which the younger critic sees as contributing a necessary heightening and "continued excitement of surprise," elevating poetry above prose. He considers most of the Wordsworth poems in *Lyrical Ballads* a special experiment; Wordsworth was better when he ignored his theory and let his Imagination produce poetry. Probably no other literary critic has proved as fair and just to a friend whom he knew intimately and with whom he worked.

Besides the *Biographia Literaria,* Coleridge left a vast treasure house of unpublished critical material falling roughly into:

(1) Private conversations recorded by his nephew and literary executor, Henry N. Coleridge, and published as *Specimens of the Table Talk of Samuel Taylor Coleridge* (1835).

(2) Notes he scribbled in the margins and blank spaces in the numerous books he read. This material appeared in *The Literary Remains* (1836–39), also edited by his nephew. Though not as bold and startling as Blake's annotations, they are the sparks from a fascinating and profound critic.

(3) Notebook jottings selected by his grandson, Ernest H. Coleridge, and printed as *Anima Poetae* (1895). A fertile mind cannot adequately apply itself to work, but it can throw off enough momentous ideas and illuminating analyses to provide here the germ for dozens of critical volumes.

(4) The lectures (ranging from 1795 to 1818), which constituted his chief reputation in London literary circles of the early 19th century. All the English artistic world flocked to hear him, even the sneering Byron—"We are going in a party to hear the new Art of Poetry by the reformed schismatic." All listeners testified to the entrancing flow of speech and impressive stimulation of thought and literary appreciation. Unfortunately, Coleridge left no complete texts of these lectures. Some were virtually extemporaneous; only sketchy notes survive for others. In compiling *The Literary Remains,* H. N. Coleridge sought for transcripts of the lectures wherever he could find them. The reported

texts are therefore sometimes questionable, notably those supplied by John Payne Collier, a forger. Enough authentic material remains to establish Coleridge as the most important English figure in Romantic criticism. Coleridge, perhaps more than any other one person, interested the English-speaking peoples in classic Greek drama, Dante, and Cervantes.

Especially, Coleridge gave to the entire 19th century a bent in Shakespearean criticism that still survives strongly in the popular mind, though 20th-century scholars are trying to counterbalance his influence. Coleridge ignored or minimized Shakespeare's plays as plays, and virtually divorced the dramatist from his age. His criticism of the playwright is primarily character analysis. Believing Shakespeare to be a pre-eminent psychologist, Coleridge frequently read more into Shakespeare's characters than was justified. He speculated upon their existence and actions before and after their appearances on the stage. Although his interpretations are often penetrating and subtle, his fluent, persuasive powers instilled such questionable concepts as the extreme vacillation of Hamlet and the "motiveless malignity" of Iago. Following the German critics, Coleridge considered Shakespeare a great philosophical writer, insisting that the dramas were a spiritual as well as an esthetic experience. More important to Coleridge than the outer form of the dramas was the supposed inner reality; Shakespeare emerges from Coleridge's scrutiny not as a playwright but as a profound Platonist.

THE POETRY OF SCOTT

Sir Walter Scott (1771–1832). Following is a list of the more important events in Sir Walter Scott's life.

1771: Born August 15 in Edinburgh, son of Walter Scott, lawyer.

1773: Afflicted with the first fully authenticated case of infantile paralysis in medical history. His childhood was consequently sickly, and he remained permanently lame. Sent for his health to his grandfather's farm at Sandyknowe, in the Border country. Here he first became fascinated with the accounts of by-gone times.

1778–92: Educated at Edinburgh, graduated from the University, and was admitted to the bar.

1796: First publication, verse translated from the German.

1797: Married Charlotte Carpentier, daughter of a French emigré from Lyons. Previous unsuccessful love affairs with Williamina Stuart and Margaret Belches may account for the reticence and superficiality of his treatment of love.

1799: As sheriff-deputy of Selkirkshire, he conducted his "Border raids" largely to amass antiquarian lore.

1805: First public triumph with *The Lay of the Last Minstrel.* Secret partner in the publishing house of James Ballantyne.

1806: Appointed permanent Clerk of Session at Edinburgh.

1809: Instrumental in founding of *Quarterly Review.* In this publication, Scott, tongue in cheek, was later to review his own novels.

1812: Started the construction of a baronial mansion at Abbotsford.

1813: Declined poet laureateship in favor of Southey.

1814: Published first novel, *Waverley.*

1815: Travels in England and on the Continent, enjoying wide acclaim.

1820: Was created a baronet.

1826: Following depression of 1825 and collapse of Ballantyne publishing firm, Scott refused bankruptcy and labored indefatigably to repay huge deficit ("spinning gold from his entrails," said Thomas Moore). Death of wife and increasing ill health.

1827: In *Chronicles of the Canongate,* first acknowledged authorship of the novels.

1831: Declining health caused sea voyage through Mediterranean upon government vessel placed at his disposal.

1832: Died September 21 at Abbotsford.

Historians of English literature frequently cite *Lyrical Ballads* in 1798 as the start of the Romantic Movement, but, truth to tell, this noted volume made a relatively small impact on its contemporary English readers. A sizable following for Romantic writings was first created by Scott, beginning with his *Lay of the Last Minstrel* in 1805. The very characteristics that in his own lifetime insured him popularity far beyond that of any other Romantic except Byron have militated against his subsequent reputation. Scot's works incorporated most of the exciting elements of Romanticism we have already discussed, but wholly absent are the features that made the other Romantics disturbing to their age. Scott was not rebellious; he was always a Tory in politics and a loyal Presbyterian in faith. He plumbed no dangerous gulfs; passion, mystic awe, and the deep well of the unconscious never really interested him. Psychoanalysts have avoided Scott as zealously as they have seized upon his contemporary Romantics. He probably belongs in large part to the 18th century, though especially on the basis of the *Journal*, some critics consider deceptive his appearance as simple, straightforward, and uncomplicated. Scott was a middle-class figure fully accepting the stratified and fixed society of his own era. His one qualm about his time can be seen in his turning backward to find in an imaginary past the heroic and adventuresome qualities denied to his period and to his own lamed body. Shining throughout virtually all his works is a wholesomeness, and a confidence that life is (or can be) a thrilling challenge that should be met with courage. In his life and writings he exemplified the true gentleman. Serious critics have suggested that the code of the ante-bellum American South, as well as that of many other portions of the 19th-century English-speaking world, was an attempt in the flesh to achieve the noble gentility conceived by Scott. All his writings can be divided into three groups: apprenticeship and imitation (1795–1805), original poetry (1805–14), and novel-writing (1814–32); this last will be discussed in Chapter 8, which will be devoted entirely to the early 19th-century novel.

TRANSLATING AND EDITING. Before the Edinburgh Royal Society, in April 1788, Henry Mackenzie delivered a paper on current German literature which began a tremendous craze in the "Athens of the North." One upshot of the resulting interest was Scott's first publication of "William and Helen" and "The Wild Huntsman" in 1796, translations respectively of Bürger's "Lenore" and "Der Wilde Jäger." German horror poetry is here somewhat influenced by the English Gothic novel, then at its fever pitch of popularity. A translation of Goethe's lyric "Erlkönig" and Veit Weber's drama *Der Heilige Vehme* (*The House of Aspen*) followed in 1797. Scott later used his translation of Goethe's play, *Goetz von Berlichingen* (1799), for the close of *Marmion* and scenes in *Ivanhoe* and *Anne of Geierstein*.

Minstrelsy of the Scottish Border (I, II, 1802: III, 1803) is the second of the three major collections of popular ballads in English; Percy's *Reliques* (1765) preceded, and the Child collection (1857–58) followed. Scott's compilation developed from his recording of the oral tradition in the Scottish counties bordering England. The collection contains sixty-two true folk ballads and thirty-eight folk lyrics. Many of these folk poems and many versions of them were first printed by Scott, e.g. "Clerk Saunders" and "The Wife of Usher's Well." In the preface to the work, he admits taking some liberties (as Percy had) with the texts. Since he omitted critical apparatus and did not print the verbatim texts, it is impossible fully to assess his changes except where an occasional manuscript scrap from which he worked has survived. Although the preface asserts that the poems "carry with them the most indisputable marks of their authenticity," it is clear that many were doctored by Scott. Since he was a better poet than Percy and more imbued with the genuine ballad spirit, his refurbishings are much less apparent. For instance, he added to "Sir Patrick Spens" a stanza that any ballad lover would dearly yearn to find in the original. Whatever his manipulations, he preserved a number of folk pieces otherwise lost, and he vigorously stimulated interest in the ballads. So potent was his influence that many in the 19th century thought of the popular ballad as essentially a product of the Anglo-Scottish border, though the ballad impulse of late medieval times seems to have been about evenly distributed throughout the British Isles.

In addition to the folk ballads are twenty-seven signed "modern imitations," five by Scott and the rest by his friends. These are decidedly inferior, Scott yielding here to the baleful influence of German horror poems and contemporary British copies of the ballad. One ballad, "Kinmont Willie," for which Scott is the unique source, has been challenged by some scholars; if Scott actually concocted this by himself, he produced the only "art ballad" that has the ring of an original. The whole bent of Scott's later imaginative writings, both in verse and prose, was governed by this ballad spirit. Probably this work was Scott's greatest contribution to poetry.

The Works of Dryden (eighteen volumes, 1808) prints an excellent "Life." As later revised by George Saintsbury, this is still considered the best edition of Dryden's writings.

The Works of Swift (nineteen volumes, 1814) has a less satisfactory biographical study, for the intricacies of Swift's mind are beyond the range of the genial Scott; but this edition remained the best until superseded by the Davis edition in the 20th century.

The Poems

The Lay of the Last Minstrel (*1802–04*, 1805) was originally intended as a "modern imitation" for the *Minstrelsy* collection but grew too long. The ballad stanza proving too constrictive for a long account, Scott adopted essentially the four-beat line from "Christabel" (read to him from manuscript) with variations in occasional three-beat lines. A favorite Scott device was to carry the rime through three or even four of the four-beat lines, then to fall away with a three-beat line. The whole effect is one of rapid dash and scurrying adventure—

horseman's verse. "Lay" is the appropriate designation for his narrative poems, though he was striving toward an epic quality. The inspiration for the work came from a Border legend about Gilpin Horner, a mysterious goblin.

Although set about 1560, the atmosphere suggests earlier centuries. Lady Buccleuch of Branksome Hall sends Sir William of Deloraine to Melrose Abbey to secure the prophetic book of Michael Scott from the magician's tomb. Returning, Deloraine is overpowered by Baron Henry of Cranstoun, secret wooer of Margaret, Lady Buccleuch's daughter. While the goblin-page of Cranstoun assumes various shapes, Cranstoun, in the armor of Deloraine, slays Richard Musgrave, champion of the invading English. Reconciled with his erstwhile enemy, Cranstoun gains Margaret's hand.

No previous verse in English literature excited so much popularity and such large sales. Scott was immediately the most successful and most acclaimed writer of the day. Both Fox and Pitt praised the work, the latter astutely observing that it had achieved pictorial qualities he had thought beyond poetry. The medievalism of the work lends glamorous colors and the piquancy of the wondrous and superstitious. While often rambling, the poem rushes excitingly in the ride of Deloraine and the onrush of the English raiding party. It is the freshest, most entrancing of Scott's verse narratives. Perhaps best as poetry are the interspersed lyrics, "It Was an English Ladye Bright," "The Lovely Rosabelle," "Dies Irae." The phenomenal success of the poem determined Scott's further writing career.

Marmion (1808) turned Scott from a Border poet into the national poet of Scotland.

On the eve of Flodden Field (1513), the English knight Marmion jilts Constance de Beverley, a perjured nun, and seeks Lady Clare, wife of Sir Ralph de Wilton. By a forged letter, Marmion charges De Wilton with treason and, on the resultant field of honor, leaves him for dead. Constance is punished by being walled up alive, and the revived De Wilton is forced to disguise himself as a palmer. Marmion dies in battle, and Clare and the exonerated De Wilton are reunited.

Scott here effected his nearest approach to the epic; Thomas Hardy termed it the most Homeric poem in our language. The account of Flodden Field is perhaps the most stirring battle piece in English literature, and also famous is the description of Marmion's view of Edinburgh over Blackford Hill. For the first time Scott attempts a character portrayal, the "hero-villain" in Marmion. While false in court and courtship, Marmion is valorous and unswerving in battle. Like many of Scott's characters, he talks less like men of his own age than like an 18th-century man of feeling. Intended as a portrait of the medieval robber baron, Marmion is the prototype of Byron's hero-villains. The "Christabel" metrics are here abandoned for conventional octosyllabics (with occasional six-syllable lines), though all with the special Scott gallop. Short pieces include "Where shall the lover rest" and the renowned "Lochinvar." Noble too are the tributes to recently deceased Pitt and Fox. Although the critics expressed annoyance at more of Scott's medieval paraphernalia, a people wracked with war avidly devoured it.

The Lady of the Lake (1810) is also set in the early 16th century during the reign of James V of Scotland, father of Mary Queen of Scots. The gorgeous description of Nature quickly made Loch Katrine and the Trossachs a tourist mecca.

Separated from his hunting party, the disguised James V (calling himself James Fitz-James) comes upon the lovely Ellen, who lives in hiding with her outlawed father, the Douglas. Her favored suitor is Malcolm Graeme, but also seeking her hand is Roderick Dhu, a fiery and picturesque chieftain of Clan Alpine, who rallies his clansmen at the rumor of the king's approach. The king overpowers Roderick Dhu in single combat, forgives the Douglas, and honors the union of Ellen and Malcolm.

Within eight months over twenty-five thousand copies were sold, surpassing Scott's previous triumphs and all previous sales of English poetry. Scott had reached the apogee of his poetic fame with a felicitous blend of medieval glamour, swashbuckling adventure, thrilling hints of superstition and Highland customs, and spectacular touches such as the surprising appearance and disappearance of the clansmen in the hillside. With the perceptivity of the later novels, Scott, in the mouth of Roderick Dhu, eloquently summarizes the case of the Celtic Highlander against the Anglo-Saxon Lowland monarchy of Scotland. For a populace locked in battle with the French, Scott offered comforting accolades to monarchy and harsh words for the "democratic" mob. In sustained idyllic and Romantic atmosphere, together with a well-controlled plot, this is probably Scott's best narrative poem. Again the best poetry appears in the lyrics, led by the haunting melancholy of "Coronach." Also famed are "Harp of the North," appealing to the Romantic muse of balladry and medievalism; "Soldier, rest! thy warfare o'er"; "Hail to the Chief," traditionally played to greet the President of the United States; and "Lay of the Imprisoned Huntsman."

Rokeby (1813) is a transitional step to the novels. The scene shifts to Yorkshire, England, after the battle of Marston Moor (1644) during the English civil wars. The civil wars never quite come to life, but in Matilda the author limns his most convincing heroine of the poetic narratives, in Redmond the one hero who is more than a male ingenue, and in Bertram of Risingham (highly regarded by Swinburne) his best version of the hero-villain. The excellence of this piece lies primarily in the Yorkshire landscapes, the melodic roll of Yorkshire names, and the still more attractive lyrics: "Brignall Banks," "A weary lot is thine, fair maid," "Allen-a-Dale," "The Cavalier." Never greatly esteeming his own verse, Scott was flagging in enthusiasm. Moore, in *Twopenny Post-Bag,* quipped that Scott was working his way south in a metrical guide to gentlemen's estates. Also, a new poetic star, Byron, was ascending to claim the Romantic readers of poetry created by "The Wizard of the North."

The Bridal of Triermain (1813) was published anonymously a few weeks after *Rokeby,* partly for the fun of deceiving the critics and partly to prevent an over-saturation of Scott verse. It is Scott's one incursion into Arthurian material, recounting the breaking of the spell cast upon Merlin by Gyneth, daughter of Arthur and the fairy Guendolen. The magic of the tale is not for Scott, though he tried to imitate "Christabel." Chief source of the work is Geoffrey of Monmouth.

The Lord of the Isles (1815) was Scott's last real attempt in narrative verse. Some have termed it the first Scott novel, for it possesses more good plotting than any of the other poems and introduces more historical personages. Scenes worthy of the later novels include the quarrel in Lorn's hall when his enemy the Bruce doffs his disguise, and the meeting of the Bruce and Ronald (Lord of the Isles) with pirates; these show the stuff of sheer adventure and incisive human conflict for which Scott's novels would be famed. Set in the year 1307, this narrative poem chronicles Robert the Bruce's return from exile in his successful re-bid for the Scottish throne. Scott's treatment of the battle of Bannockburn, concentrating on Scottish patriotism and masculine prowess, carries none of Burns's revolutionary fervor in poetizing the same event. Chief source is Barbour's *Brus.* With the inferior *Harold the Dauntless* (1817), recounting the Christianization of a Danish prince in the Danelagh of Anglo-Saxon times, Scott ceased writing narrative verse.

Any sustained reputation of Scott as a poet must rest not upon his narrative poems but upon his lyrics. He was actually the greatest lyricist of his generation, for the talents of Wordsworth and Coleridge were fundamentally in contemplative or narrative verse. As indicated above, the best portions of Scott's narrative poems consisted of the interspersed lyrics. Collections published in 1806, 1820, and 1830 added lyrics and ballad-type accounts in verse. Perhaps the richest source of poetry lies within the novels. Some of Scott's very best lyrics are incorporated within the prose fiction as Meg Merrilies spins a gypsy charm ("Twist ye, twine ye!") over a newborn infant in *Guy Mannering*, and Madge Wildfire in *The Heart of Midlothian* chants a number of superb lyrics, especially "Proud Maisie," which in sixteen lines says all that can be said of the death of proud girlhood in probably the best single poem by Scott. Most chapters in his novels were preceded by appropriate poetic mottoes, and where Scott did not find a quotation readily at hand, he concocted his own, puckishly ascribing his lines to imaginary works, "Old Play," or the convenient "Anonymous."

THE JOURNAL. *The Journal of Sir Walter Scott,* though available to his biographer Lockhart, was not printed until 1890. The famous life of Scott by his son-in-law has impressed upon the English-speaking world, perhaps ineradicably, the concept of the gentlemanly Scott, reinforcing the picture of his works but on the whole suggesting a rather superficial extrovert. The *Journal* reveals in the man depths and breadths elsewhere absent from his writings. It consists of almost daily entries from 1825 to 1832, covering the crisis years of his finances, illness, and family tragedies. Never intended for public viewing, the *Journal* is perhaps Scott's greatest work, for it fully reveals a noble and honest spirit, much bigger than that suggested in any of the "public" works. The style is straightforward, never blundering with the frequent diffuseness or turgidity of some of his novel passages. To the *Journal* he confided fears and contemplations, spiritual and psychic problems, and even a healthy strain of coarseness only hinted at in his other writings.

LESSER ROMANTIC POETS OF THE PERIOD

The reputations of one era are notoriously subject to revision by later times. In *Gradus ad Parnassum* (1813), Byron rated his contemporary poets in this descending order: Scott, Rogers, Moore, Campbell, Southey, Wordsworth, and Coleridge. Of course, Byron was prejudiced against the "Lake Poets" (Wordsworth, Coleridge, and Southey) and he was not a noted critic, anyway; nonetheless, the reading public of the period consistently valued Rogers, Moore, and Campbell, for instance, almost as much as their great contemporaries.

Robert Southey (su'þi or sou'þi) (1774–1834). Born August 12, 1774, son of a Bristol linen-draper, Robert Southey was expelled from Westminster School in 1792 for an essay objecting to flogging. He was barred from Christ Church, Oxford, because of the essay but was admitted to Balliol. With Coleridge, in 1794, he projected the utopian scheme of "Pantisocracy." In the next year he married Edith Fricker, sister of Coleridge's wife. After 1809, Southey supported both families for a time. He visited Portugal in 1795–96 and again in 1800–01. After a half-hearted attempt at law, he settled at Greta Hall, Keswick, for the rest of his life, devoting all his time to writing. When Scott refused the poet laureateship in 1813, Southey accepted. He later refused the offer of a baronetcy. After two years of insanity, his wife died in 1837. In 1839 he married Caroline Bowles, for long a correspondent with him and a minor writer in her own right. He died March 21, 1843, reputedly of a brain fatigue.

Few English writers have labored so indefatigably and voluminously as Southey. Never collected, his total writings would probably fill about a hundred volumes. He and his age shared the conviction that he was a great poet, but posterity has steadily lowered his poetic reputation to the vanishing point. No other English poet has suffered such a signal eclipse. Because of his prominence, younger Romantics vehemently berated him as a deserter from liberalism to reaction, though in Tory orthodoxy he generally proved more amenable to reform than did contemporaries Wordsworth and Coleridge. A slight upsurge of 20th-century interest in Southey has been induced largely by his prose. As his brother-in-law, Coleridge, said, Southey possessed talent but not genius.

VERSE. Southey's better poetry was written before 1810. While a rabid republican at Balliol in 1794, Southey wrote *Wat Tyler;* in his conservative later years he was quite embarrassed by the pirated printing of the work in 1817. During the *Lyrical Ballads* period, Southey was imitating Wordsworthian ballads and short narrative poems in simplicity and language, and so successful was he that many of these were indistinguishable from a curbstone conversation. "The Battle of Blenheim" (1798), on Marlborough's famous victory in 1704, is a good attempt at portraying the futility of war. "God's Judgment on a Wicked

Bishop" (1799), recounting the legendary eating of a 10th-century German bishop by rats, is a grim horror narrative of the Gothic sort that Southey could do well. "The Old Man's Comforts" (1799) is the Southey banality that laid him open to wicked parody, delicious in *Alice in Wonderland*. In the dying years of the 18th century the *Anti-Jacobin* made rare sport of the radicalism that Southey professed.

In 1801 Southey started a pretentious series of epics ranging from India to the Aztecs with *Thalaba the Destroyer*. These manifested the Romantic urge to find grandeur and glamour in distant places and remote eras, but Byron was undoubtedly correct in declaring that the epics of Southey "will be read when Homer and Vergil are forgotten —but not until then." Probably the best Southey epic is *The Curse of Kehama* (1810), a Hindu tale which occasionally rises to Oriental magnificence and romantic enchantment. Solemnly clutching the wreath upon his brow as poet laureate, Southey, in *A Vision of Judgment* (1821), lengthily strove to preach into heaven the dead, insane George III. The laureate's stab in the preface at "The Satanic School" of poetry was obviously intended for Byron, who retorted with a much more famous *Vision of Judgment*.

Southey's real poetic ability, had he properly appreciated it, lay in shorter and less ambitious pieces. "My Days among the Dead Are Past" (*1818,* 1823) evokes the calm love of books amidst a good library. "The Cataract of Lodore" (*1820,* 1823) is one of the best onomatopoetic poems in English, though admittedly designed for the nursery.

PROSE. The forty volumes of Southey's collected prose represent perhaps half his total output. Most of this vast storehouse of miscellaneous writings is now hopelessly buried in dust.

Letters from England by Don Manuel Espriella (1807) is perhaps the first of Southey's prose to survive until today. Following the worn tradition of the "foreign visitor" genre originated by Montesquieu, Southey sketches in slightly satiric fashion the everyday life of contemporary England. Like all his better prose, it is shrewdly observant and workmanlike, though not deeply penetrating or memorably phrased.

Life of Nelson (1813) was written before full materials for a biography were available or properly scrutinized, and Southey was not an expert in naval warfare; nonetheless, this is one of the classic biographies in English. Southey sensed the greatness and power in Nelson as a man and as a leader. History and biography are skillfully interwoven, and the character of the illustrious seaman memorably unfolded. Designed as a manual "for the young sailor," the study is simply and forcefully written.

Life of Wesley and the Rise and Progress of Methodism (1820) is inferior to the biography of Nelson, largely because the now strict Anglican has imperfect sympathy for evangelicalism. Southey tries, however, to analyze the Wesleyan credo and manages to convey a vivid sense of the sincerity and magnetism of the great religious figure. Thumb-nail biographies of Whitfield and other Methodist "saints" are astutely inserted.

Sir Thomas More: or, Colloquies on the Progress and Prospects of Society (1829) consists of conversations between the spirit of the Renaissance humanist More and Montesinos, representing Southey himself. In calling up the author of *Utopia* to examine the course of modern society, Southey writes his most important and most influential work (it has been termed the founder of the Young England movement and one of the dominant molders of later conservatism). The manufacturing system had tended to concentrate wealth in the hands of capitalists while reducing many workers to the status of machines. Southey objects to the orthodox political economy of Bentham, Ricardo, and James Mill as ignoring moral and human considerations. "The moral improvement of the people . . . [is the] first great duty" of government. In opposition to the *laissez-faire* concept of the political economists, Southey demands that a nation's legislators seek first the general health of society. He then details reform proposals for benevolent law and order, increased national education, planned emigration, universal instruction in religion, national savings banks, and planned communities for residence and manufacture. Southey sees an especially important role for literature in humanizing and elevating all members of society.

The Doctor (seven volumes, 1837–47) is a *Tristram Shandy* type of book. Ostensibly a history of Dr. Daniel Dove of Doncaster and his horse Nobs, the work is a vast improvisation lugging in Southey's enormous and varied reading. Its sure claim to immortality is the first known telling of the nursery story of the three bears.

Samuel Rogers (1763–1855). A native of Newington Green, London, Samuel Rogers entered his father's bank after studying at the local Nonconformist academy. His home became a noted literary center, and for more than half a century he was practically a literary dictator as friend and patron to many men of letters. In 1850 he refused the poet laureateship because of advanced age and recommended Tennyson instead.

Rogers was a poet of "taste," pleasant, glossy, always competent, and never inspired. He never really departed from the quality of his first printed poem, *The Pleasures of Memory* (1792), which strongly resembles Goldsmith. His collected *Poems* (1838) displays similar soft, elegant verse which is thoroughly "literary" in the discreet 19th-century parlance, but unfortunately no more.

Recollections of the Table Talk of Samuel Rogers (1856), edited by his friend Alexander Dyce, shows, rather surprisingly, that Rogers was a brilliant and witty conversationalist. Prose might have been a better medium for him, since his comments show an incisiveness and penetration lacking in his verse.

Recollections by Samuel Rogers (1859) is a posthumously printed "Pleasures of Memory" in prose. Unfortunately the product of a valetudinarian in his anecdotage, these memories survey a huge segment of London life from the Gordon Riots of 1780 to the mid-19th century without delving beneath the surface or truly grasping the momentous forces at work. But here was a man who talked on equal terms with Burke and Tennyson, Adam Smith and Carlyle, and many more. His memories are interesting though hardly memorable.

Thomas Campbell (1777–1844). Born in Glasgow, Thomas Campbell rose to be lord rector of the University of Glasgow (1826–29). In 1825 he proposed the establishment of the University of London. After his death in Boulogne, France, his body was brought back for burial in the Poet's Corner of Westminster Abbey. Even for Scottish subjects he wrote in London dialect.

VERSE. Campbell's reputation was first secured by *The Pleasures of Hope* (1799), one of the last didactic poems in heroic couplets, reminiscent of Mark Akenside; the proverbial quotation "distance lends enchantment" still survives from this poem. His contemporary fame rested largely upon stirring patriotic verse, "Ye Mariners of England" (1801) and "Battle of the Baltic" (1809), praising British naval valor. *Gertrude of Wyoming* (1809) also proved popular in its recounting of a Pennsylvania Indian massacre in Spenserian stanzas; Campbell fed the Romantic appetite for exotic material treated sentimentally. His one still frequently reprinted poem is the imitation ballad "Lord Ullin's Daughter" (1809); its account of the drowning of a Scottish noblewoman fleeing with her lover from a pursuing father is simple and only moderately sentimental. Like Wordsworth, Campbell wrote most of his best verse before 1806.

PROSE. Campbell sided with Byron in supporting the poetic reputation of Pope against the disparagements of Bowles. As a critic he praised the neoclassicists and revealed incomplete sympathies with the Romantics. His critical summaries of English poets from Chaucer to Burns, printed in *Specimens of the British Poets* (1819), covered a wider range than Warton, Johnson, or any previous critic but without notable insight.

Thomas Moore (1779–1852). Born in Dublin, Ireland, Thomas Moore was educated at Trinity College, Dublin. He entered Middle Temple, London, in 1799, and in 1803–04 traveled in America. He established friendship with Byron in 1811 and in the same year married an actress, Bessie Dyke. As literary executor he chose to destroy Byron's autobiography, writing his own *Life of Byron* (1830).

The most ingratiating of Irishmen, Moore was socially the rage of London, while his verse lifted him to metropolitan popularity second only to Byron. Yet even in his own time critics gradually branded him as a "mere melodious trifler." His lighter work was generally written under the pseudonyms of Thomas Little or Thomas Brown the Younger. His verse falls largely into three divisions:

(1) Political satire. This was immensely successful in its age but is now dated, for its wit and insouciance (rivaling John Wolcot) never plumb below the surface of personalities and events. Best known of this type was *The Twopenny Post Bag* (1813), largely directed against the Prince Regent.

(2) Oriental romances. These were occasioned by the vogue of Byron's exotic narratives. Sight unseen, Longmans agreed to pay £3000 for *Lalla Rookh* (1817), a series of four Eastern tales supposedly related to Lalla Rookh, an East Indian princess, journeying to her betrothed. Like all his verse, this reads easily and pleasantly, but its rococo "literary" flavor is no longer beguiling.

(3) "Irish" Lyrics. These caused Shelley in *Adonais* to term Moore "The sweetest lyricist of her [Ireland's] saddest wrong." These appeared, both words and music, in the ten folio numbers of *Irish Melodies* between 1808 and 1834. Almost all of these lyrics practically sing themselves, and all have a blend of sentimental nostalgia appealing to Moore's contemporaries and to the later 19th century. "Oh, Breathe Not His Name" commemorates Robert Emmet, a Trinity schoolmate of Moore's, who was executed in 1803 for leading a Dublin

revolt against English rule. "The Harp That Once through Tara's Halls" recalls the days of legendary grandeur when Ireland consisted of five kingdoms with a "high king" at Tara. "The Minstrel Boy," favorite of countless Irish tenors, suggests the tragic end of an Irish minstrel, witnessed often in uprisings against England. While singing in Romantic Irish fashion of freedom, Moore was not really so much the bard of Ireland as was his contemporary James Clarence Mangan (see next chapter). Perhaps Moore's greatest impact was in wistful lyrics like "Believe Me, If All Those Endearing Young Charms" or "The Last Rose of Summer" and the playful pieces like "The Time I've Lost in Wooing." The expression of the visionary and mysterious quality in the Irish soul had to await the later Celtic Renaissance.

James Hogg ("The Ettrick Shepherd") (1770–1835). Born at Ettrick, Selkirkshire, Scotland, James Hogg was largely self-educated, and he tells of hearing a "half daft man" recite "Tam o' Shanter" in 1797; then and there, he said, "I resolved to be a poet, and to follow in the steps of Burns." Like his master, but more conservative, Hogg is a proletarian writer risen from the masses.

VERSE. *Mountain Bard* (1807) arose from Hogg's dissatisfaction with Scott's *Border Minstrelsy*. Scott encouraged him to print these ballad imitations which seek to avoid the artiness of the literary imitators. Hogg's pieces often catch the artlessness and spare vigor of the original folk ballads, but they are frequently marred by mawkishness from the street ballads of the 17th and 18th centuries. Probably his best is "The Liddel Bower," relating the Douglas's abduction of Liddel's widow after he slew Liddel.

The Forest Minstrel (1810) consists largely of Hogg's Scots lyrics. The range is impressive, placing Hogg as second only to Burns in this genre. The influence of Scott appears in many pieces, such as "Lock the door, Lariston." "The Village of Balmaquhapple" almost matches the homey satire of Burns, and "When Maggy gangs awa'" reminds one of the love lyrics of Burns.

The Queen's Wake (1813) established Hogg's reputation, suggesting that he was a rival of Scott and Byron in narrative verse. For three nights Mary Queen of Scots keeps "wake" in Holyrood, listening to seventeen bards recounting poetic tales in competition. The queen considers Rizzio, her favorite, as best, but the audience prefers Gardyn, a Highlander. Critics have set both aside in favor of "The Witch of Fife," a wild Scots grotesquerie that the "Makaris" would have relished, or "Kilmeny," a fairy-land tale of a mortal who returns from the

Elysian realm only to vanish again from the grossness of earth to "the land of thochte." Though the tales vary in quality, this is Hogg's greatest verse product, and although he attempted further narrative poems, he never equaled this.

PROSE FICTION. *The Private Memoirs and Confessions of a Justified Sinner* (1824) has been somewhat overenthusiastically hailed by André Gide as the greatest novel in English, but unquestionably it is one of the neglected masterpieces of English fiction. What Burns treats satirically in "Holy Willie's Prayer" is serious, unnerving psychological drama in Hogg. The setting is Scotland about 1700.

The story is told in two parts. In the first, the supposed editor gives a factual account of the murder of the gay and good George Colwan by his "unco' pious" brother, Robert Wringham. Brought up by a rigidly righteous cleric named Wringham, the younger brother has adopted the name of his guardian. The murder is to obtain the family estate. Suspicion falls upon an innocent man, and when the truth is finally revealed, Robert has completely disappeared. The second part is Robert's own record, recounting the first part from his viewpoint, that of a psychopath. Hiding under a false identity, the murderer eventually commits suicide.

Robert has been schooled by the Reverend Mr. Wringham in antinomianism, the belief that faith is all-important and good works are immaterial in salvation; the elected of God are predestined for grace regardless of their behavior. Actually covetous of his brother's property, Robert convinces himself that fratricide is a pious act. He is egged on to his foul deeds by a being he belatedly realizes is the devil in disguise. The characterization of the fiend is an eerie masterpiece, appearing sometimes in the guise of Robert's Doppelgänger, sometimes in the guise of the slain George or the innocent suspect. The examination of a warped and perverted mind is elsewhere unmatched in the English novel. The chilling horror lies, not in the superficial trappings of the Gothic novel, but in the interior world of a cunning but deranged mentality. Virtually ignored in its own day, this work is now often considered to be the supreme example of the Romantic novel.

DIARIES AND MEMOIRS OF THE PERIOD

Dorothy Wordsworth (1771–1855). Only sister of the poet, Dorothy Wordsworth was one year his junior. Following her mother's death in 1777, she lived with relatives until taking up residence with William at Racedown, Dorsetshire, in 1795. For the rest of her life she subordinated herself to her distinguished brother, never marrying. As he recounts in *The Prelude,* it was her sympathy that sustained him in the dark days of his distress over the French Revolution (and Annette), and it was her gentle prodding that rekindled his interest in Nature. Even after his marriage she continued her ministry, accompanying William to Scotland and to the Continent. In 1829 she suffered a breakdown and from 1836 until her death she never possessed full mental faculties. Dorothy never published and never pretended to be a writer. Her *Journals* were first printed in part in 1897. Since the almost complete De Selincourt edition of 1941 she has often been acclaimed, not merely as a catalyst for both Wordsworth and Coleridge, but as a notable author in her own right.

Alfoxden Journal consists of brief, almost daily entries from January 20 to May 22, 1798, during a wonderfully productive period for both her brother and Coleridge. Subjects, Nature perceptions, and entire phrases appearing in the verses of the two poets are noted in her journal, some items before, some after, the known date of their poetic composition. It is impossible to assess her contribution, for many of her references predating their poems may nonetheless first have arisen from William or from Coleridge. Undoubtedly she shared poetic impulses with the two poets and provided them with much-needed sympathy and stimulation.

Grasmere Journal offers daily entries from May 14, 1800, to January 11, 1803 (manuscripts covering nine months in 1802 are missing). This is probably Dorothy's best work, an intensely revealing document intended solely for herself and William. It moves on two completely different levels, mingled as one would expect in a continuous diary. Homey details of family living and contacts with Grasmere neighbors uniquely evoke the everyday routine of rural life at the turn of the 19th century. At far greater length than in the *Alfoxden Journal* are sensitive responses to Nature that cast invaluable light upon William's current milieu, but, even more, induce some critics to say that Dorothy was innately as much of a poet as her brother.

Recollections of a Tour Made in Scotland was composed in 1803 shortly after her return from the trip with William and Coleridge. Instead of a purely personal diary it is intended for "the sake of a few friends." Written as a unit instead of daily entries, it presents her finest finished construction. It is her most readable piece and one of the most delightful of all travel accounts. The reader is charmed by a delicate and highly perceptive guide who vividly creates the freshness and joy the author experienced in novel sights and sounds. Whether buying a thimble in Dumfries, listening in awe to the torrents of the Hidden Vale of Glenfalloch, or hearing Scott recite *The Lay of the Last Minstrel,* Dorothy makes the reader intimately share her pleasures and welcome her as a vivacious companion. Fluent and unaffected, this is probably the best Romantic travel piece on the British Isles.

Journal of a Tour on the Continent details the Wordsworths' trip through France, Belgium, Germany, Switzerland, and Italy from July to October 1820. This work is almost as long as all her other writings put together. It has tedious spots, unlike the sparkling *Recollections,* and Dorothy is occasionally less perceptive amidst alien culture and languages. Nonetheless, it contains invaluable impressions of post-Napoleonic Europe from an observant and sensitive Englishwoman. Here as in her other journals she proved one of the best of English descriptive writers.

Henry Crabb Robinson (1775–1867). A native of Bury St. Edmunds, and son of a tanner, Henry Crabb Robinson entered a solicitor's office in 1796. From 1800 to 1805 he traveled on the Continent, studying for three years at the University of Jena and meeting Goethe and Schiller. During the Peninsular War he was foreign correspondent and later foreign editor for *The Times* in Spain. From 1813 to 1828 he practiced law, and in the latter year he was one of the founders of London University. Thereafter he concentrated upon travel and reading. A vigorous and social bachelor, he sought out all the literary men of his time, becoming a close friend of Wordsworth, Coleridge, Lamb, Rogers, Southey, and many more.

Diary, Reminiscences, and Correspondence (1869) is a sampling from over one hundred manuscript volumes, covering eighty-five years of literary memorabilia. The heart of the materials is the diary running from 1811 until his death. Robinson tells of memorizing Cowper's "Gilpin's Ride" upon its appearance in 1782, and his last entry, five days before his death, notes Matthew Arnold's "Function of Criticism." Robinson read virtually every significant English and German writing over this long period. While he was neither profound nor original, he was truly receptive and well demonstrated the impact of literature upon intelligent readers of the era. Even though he could not understand Blake, his interview with the poet remains about the fairest contemporary estimate now extant. He is our best source for information about Coleridge's lectures. His fondness for German and his wide acquaintance in literary circles made him immensely influential in the development of English interest in German literature. Robinson had a genuine gift for thumb-nail characterization, and his style is simple and unpretentious.

William Hickey (1749–c. 1830). Son of a London lawyer, William Hickey studied for the law, and disported himself as "last of the 18th-century rakes." His despairing father sent him to the Orient with the East India Company, where he practiced law. His travels also included the West Indies and much of the world. Returning from India to England in 1808, Hickey settled at Beaconsfield to write his life story.

Memoirs (c. *1809*–c. *1813*, 1913–25) looks back across a richly variegated and colorful life from the vantage point of sixty years. Legal contacts in England made him an acquaintance of Burke, and in India he knew Sir William Jones well. The memory of Hickey seems incredible, but at all significant points he has been proved accurate. He possessed virtually a novelist's eye to pick out the concrete factual pictures that bring his era to life without the boring chatter of garrulous old age. The style is eminently readable, straightforward, photographic. Hickey shares with Boswell the ability to thumb-nail character in an anecdote. This is our best source for everyday British life in late 18th-century India.

Thomas Creevey (1768–1838). Son of a Liverpool merchant, Thomas Creevey studied at Cambridge and the Inner Temple, entering Parliament in 1802. His marriage to the wealthy widow Mrs. Ord took care of him comfortably until her death in 1818. A Whig much in the manner of Fox, Creevey received minor office during the brief Whig ministry in 1806 and again in 1830.

Creevey Papers (1903) refurbished a memory lost for almost a century. This collection is so meager a selection from Creevey's voluminous remains that *Creevey's Life and Times* (1934) carefully avoids printing any of the earlier selections and still leaves most of the Creevey manuscripts unprinted. Unverified rumors that Creevey was actually the illegitimate offspring of the Earl of Sefton may account for his rise into the aristocratic Whig circles. More likely is Creevey's ebullient and charming manner. Students of literature have neglected him mainly because he had little interest in *belles lettres,* but he is as beguiling and revealing as Horace Walpole in, first, his depiction of the political life about the turn of the century and, second, especially in the correspondence of his last fifteen years, in which he describes the social scene of fashionable London. Croker's manuscripts tell the Tory side less divertingly (see last chapter). Few correspondents are as vivacious as Creevey, and he walked with the great, blithely nicknaming them "Prinny" (The Regent, later George IV), "The Beau" (Duke of Wellington), "Viccy" (Victoria). Vividly alive and joyously naughty are these aristocrats in the last age of privilege before the bourgeoisie took over. Historians find Creevey a prime source for contemporary life, and all readers are delighted by his frank and lively correspondence.

NON-ROMANTIC AND SATIRIC POETRY

Certainly the best non-Romantic poet of the period was Walter Savage Landor (1775–1864). Indeed, Landor stands alongside the truly great and truly classical English poets Robert Herrick and Ben Jonson. However, as he said himself, "Poetry was always my amusement, prose my study and business." His prose far exceeded his verse in quantity and remains the chief basis for his continuing reputation, and so we will discuss Landor's poetry along with his prose in Chapter 9, which will be devoted to the essays and non-literary prose of the Romantic period.

While the "New Poetry" was dominating the major poets of the time, the majority of critics and readers (at least until Scott's vogue became general) still preferred the neoclassic verse. Many works in this older style were still produced, though none of them proved notable. Crabbe wrote probably the greatest realistic verse in English during the two openings decades of the 19th century, and, as mentioned above, Landor wrote purely classical verse throughout the entire period. Most frequently ignored, however, is the mass of verse satire that from 1800 to 1820 actually achieved the largest sheer volume of satiric production in all English literature. Afterward, the end of the Queen Caroline scandals and the mounting Reform spirit apparently caused a decline in satire. Thomas Moore's satire has already been noted; at least one other satiric effort has somewhat survived from that mountain of criticism.

Horace (or **Horatio) Smith** (1779–1849) and **James Smith** (1775–1839). Horace and James Smith were brothers and native Londoners who took the literary world by storm with:

Rejected Addresses, or The New Theatrum Poetarum (1812, eighteen editions by 1833). The committee for the reopening of the Drury

Lane Theatre in 1812 asked authors to compete in writing an address for delivery at the first performance. The Smith brothers offered in their volume a series of supposedly unsuccessful entries, actually parodies upon contemporary authors. In contrast to the *Anti-Jacobin* parodies, the Smith parodies were intended as amusement, not as hostile correction of the victims. These pieces delightfully mimic the style and subject matter of noted authors without stinging deeply. Best in this volume are the burlesques of Wordsworth, Crabbe, and Byron by James and the heroic lay of Marmion-Higginbottom, parodying Scott, by Horace. The serious addresses submitted to Drury Lane were unintentionally more ludicrous than the Smith productions. Byron was called upon to compose the address that was actually delivered.

Chapter 7

The Second Generation of Romantic Poets (1815–1837)

The background information for this chapter has been covered in the previous chapter. Also, while the writers discussed here are generally considered the second-generation Romantics, it must be kept in mind that there is considerable overlapping with the writers discussed in the previous chapter.

THE POETRY OF BYRON

George Gordon Noel Byron, sixth **Baron Byron of Rochdale** (1788–1824). Following is a list of the most important known events in Lord Byron's life.

1788: Born January 22 in London, only son of Captain John ("Mad Jack") Byron, a fiery guardsman whose ancestry stretched back to the Norman lords accompanying William the Conqueror. The poet's grandfather was Admiral John ("Foulweather") Byron, and his grand-uncle was William ("The Wicked Lord") Byron, fifth Baron Byron, who had killed his neighbor in a duel. Through his mother, Catherine Gordon, Byron could trace his line to James I of Scotland.

1794–98: Attended grammar school at Aberdeen, Scotland, and was strongly influenced by his nurse, May Gray, a staunch Calvinist. His temperamental mother spent large sums on unsuccessful treatments of his "twisted" foot. In anger she labeled him a "lame brat."

1798: Inherited family title and estates upon death of granduncle.

1799–1801: Attended Dr. Glennie's academy in Dulwich.

1801–05: Attended Harrow, where the boys laughed at his gait until Byron won five out of six fights. Excellent swimmer, boxer, and cricketeer.

1803: Fell in love with Mary Chaworth, grandniece of the man slain by Byron's granduncle. Desolate at her marriage in 1805.

1805: Entered Trinity College, Cambridge, where he squandered his large allowance.

1807: First published work, *Hours of Idleness.*

1809: Graduated from Cambridge and, reaching majority, took seat in House of Lords. Entertained wildly at Newstead Abbey, Nottinghamshire. Left Falmouth in July for tour of Mediterranean.

1810: Residence in Athens and travels in Near East.

1811: Returned to London in July. Met Thomas Moore and established lifelong friendship.

1812: Maiden speech in Parliament defending Nottingham laborers against Frame-work Bill, which called for the death penalty for saboteurs of machinery. With first two cantos of *Childe Harold,* was lion of society. Liaisons with Caroline Lamb and Lady Oxford.

1813–14: Mounting literary and social triumphs.

1815: Married Anne Isabella Milbanke, about the only society woman not pursuing him. Established friendship with Sir Walter Scott. Prominent in management of Drury Lane Theatre. Birth of only legitimate child, Augusta Ada.

1816: Separated from Lady Byron under cloud of his alleged incestuous relations with his half-sister, Augusta Leigh. Sailed from Dover never to return. Toured Western Europe and became close friend of Shelley. Liaison with Jane "Claire" Clairmont, stepsister of Mrs. Shelley.

1817–18: Established residence in Italy, where police believed him closely associated with the revolutionary Carbonari. His child Allegra born to "Claire."

1819–22: Extensive literary work while living with Teresa Guiccioli, wife of an aged Italian count.

1823: Threw his fortune, prestige, and person into the cause of Greek freedom, arriving in Greece in August of that year.

1824: Died of fever at Missolonghi, Greece. Body brought to England for interment at Hucknall Torkard, near Newstead. The young

Tennyson wept at the news of Byron's death, and the aging Scott declared, "It is as if the sun had gone out."

Byron is the most flamboyant and spectacular personality in all literature. Goethe called him "a personality of eminence such as has never been and is not likely to come again." To his contemporaries, Byron was first and foremost a fascinating person. He was inordinately handsome, and irresistibly dashing in the Albanian costume that he wore in society as a souvenir of his Mediterranean tour. He led the youngbloods of his era in athletic prowess, boxing with the champion "Gentleman" Jackson and swimming the turbulent waters of the Hellespont. For a while he seemed the leading Whig politician of the day, and as a nobleman of remarkably ancient lineage he was the cynosure of all eyes in a period when aristocracy was more widely discussed than it is today. And, withal, he was a poet.

Byron was the showman of Romanticism. All the untamed vigor and masculinity of Romanticism were displayed in his demands for freedom, for liberalism, and for unrestrained individualism. In his *History of Western Philosophy,* Bertrand Russell devotes an entire chapter to Byron, not because he was intellectually profound, but because he gripped the soul of Western society as no other literary man ever has and because he stamped upon the entire 19th century his own image as the idol and embodiment of Romanticism. Some Europeans still consider Byron the foremost poet in English after Shakespeare.

Though almost inexhaustible and never boring, for this entrancing figure there was essentially one subject—himself. Such exhibitionism, perfectly timed for the self-revelation of Romanticism, seems explicable mainly as compensation for his physical affliction. The opposites that made him so puzzling and disturbing as a man and so various and contradictory as an author probably sprang from his internal conflict. Cruelty and benevolence, sincerity and posturing, seriousness and flippancy, rationalism and Romantic illusion, conformity and revolt, courage and self-pity, faith and cynicism—these were the opposites that helped to make him appear immensely complicated. The following chronological discussion of his works uses suffixing letters to indicate the dominant quality of each piece. It must be remembered that Byron's different facets are not periods of his career but conflicting elements in his nature present throughout his life. There is, of course, some overlapping in the moods of Byron, but he usually maintained a remarkably split personality such that he could write the conventional *Island* at the same time he was working on the sophisticated *Don Juan.* Explained below are the letters that will be used to indicate the dominant qualities of each of his works.

(A) EXUBERANT ROMANTICISM. This aspect of Byron first won his enormous popularity and probably still remains our chief impression of the poet. The outstanding quality here is abounding youthful energy and manhood.

(B) ROMANTIC PESSIMISM. Byron provides the most notable expression in all literature of *Weltschmerz* ("World Grief"). One Byronic hero succeeds another in this series; all are titans wrestling desperately with a cruel world of men but torn more deeply by an unnamed inner taint that galls terribly beyond the buffetings of the world. Europeans have been so enraptured with this element of Byron as to employ the word *Byronism* (in various spellings and pronunciations) in virtually every continental language and to equate Byronism with *Weltschmerz*. The causes of this "World Grief" seem to be: (1) The international chaos of the Napoleonic period, disrupting all European society; (2) England's transformation from a traditional aristocratic world of rural agriculture to a bourgeois society of urban industrialization; (3) the convention of Romantic (especially continental) writing, which interested itself in the themes of sin, struggle, and remorse; (4) a personal pose, as Byron was happy only when basking in the light of publicity and constant gossip; (5) possibly his purported relations with Augusta, although it must be remembered that Byron was expressing his *Weltschmerz* before this event; (6) Byron's own peculiar background, which included his violent and dissolute ancestry, his sense of sin and damnation from an early indoctrination in Scottish Calvinism, his unsatisfactory relations with his mother, and, of course, his resentment and guilt over his physical defect.

(C) THE 18TH-CENTURY SATIRIST IN HEROIC COUPLETS. Byron's initial fame sprang from *English Bards and Scotch Reviewers,* and throughout his meteoric career he continued to produce similar satire. Had he written nothing else, literary history would have regarded him as a surprisingly late imitator of the satires of Dryden and Pope, only a notch below his great models. Critically Byron considered Dryden and Pope the true poetic geniuses, quite superior to the Romantic scribblers of his own times. Too often ignored, Byron's heroic couplet satires are probably the works closest to his true critical bent.

(D) THE URBANE SOPHISTICATE. Byron's lasting literary reputation, as discriminated from his personality, will probably rest chiefly upon *Don Juan*. In this and in a few kindred works Byron drops the pose of

"Byronism" and speaks directly to the reader as a fully experienced man-of-the-world who has really been everywhere and done everything.

Early Poems (1806–1809)

Hours of Idleness (1807) (A) was his first circulated volume, the earlier *Fugitive Pieces* (1806) being suppressed. His maiden works, as normally in a beginning poet, are imitations, ranging from Gray to Ossian, and translations of Vergil and Anacreon. Their sentimentality and mawkishness evoked from *The Edinburgh Review* a not wholly unjustified deprecation, probably by Lord Brougham. In retaliation Byron produced:

English Bards and Scotch Reviewers (1809) (C). This work was inspired by Pope's *Dunciad* and frequently matches its model in wit and epigrammatic lash. Also influential were Charles Churchill and William Gifford. Only those poets like Thomas Campbell and Samuel Rogers who deferred to Pope and sought even distantly to emulate him are praised. The neoclassic critical principles are invoked to decry the morality of Moore, the diffuseness of "ballad-monger Southey," the "stale romance" of Scott (accused of writing solely for money), and especially the new poetry of Wordsworth and Coleridge. The chief reviewer attacked is Francis Jeffrey, who probably did not write the offending review. Byron calls upon Gifford to scourge the fools and poetasters. By 1811 four editions had been sold, and Byron was widely recognized as a poetic power. He later regretted some of his waspish sallies, particularly those against Moore.

The Man of London Society (1812–1816)

Childe Harold's Pilgrimage. A Romaunt (*1810–12*, 1812), eleven editions by 1819) (A) called its hero "Childe Burun" (archaic Norman spelling of the name Byron) in manuscript, but the poet resolutely insisted that he was not identical with the central figure. The opening stanzas employ the Spenserian stanza with pseudo-medieval vocabulary ("whilom," "ne"), but Byron soon tired of this pretense and in his own voice produced a swirling stanza quite different in effect from Spenser's sweetness. No previous poem in English literature enjoyed such immediate triumph, and, as Byron stated, "I awoke one morning and found myself famous."

Ernest Coleridge termed these two cantos "a rhythmical diorama," for they are essentially the versifying of Byron's Mediterranean tour.

Probably no other poet can equal the rhetorical drive of Byron in the bravura splendor of an exotic landscape (Portugal or Turkey) or wild scenes of action (a Spanish bullfight or the Albanian clans surging forth in bloody feud). Byron epitomized the Romantic desire of the age for an escape to a life of color and energy. The theme of the work is the quest for self-realization by removal from the commonplace into a dream world of powerful emotional release. Publishers persuaded Byron to omit the most shocking stanzas (particularly those denying immortality), but enough was left to picture a modern dissolute youth fleeing debauched Regency society to revel in an existence of pure sensuous delight and melodramatic deeds.

"Maid of Athens, Ere We Part" (*1810,* 1812) (A) was one of the short poems published along with *Childe Harold's Pilgrimage.* It is a wild, impassioned love lyric addressed to Teresa Macri, eldest daughter of Byron's Athens landlady, widow of an English consular officer.

Hints from Horace (*1811,* 1831) (C), a free adaptation of Horace's *De Arte Poetica,* also shows indebtedness to Pope and Gifford. In ostensible advice to aspiring authors, Byron raps contemporary poetry and drama while praising Dryden, Pope, Swift, and Samuel Butler. It is an inferior sequel to *English Bards and Scotch Reviewers.*

The Curse of Minerva (*1811,* 1815) (C) savagely attacked Lord Elgin, British ambassador to the Sublime Porte, for his bearing off of the friezes of the Parthenon to their present resting place in the British Museum. Taking the side of the Greeks, Byron likened the Scots lord to Alaric, and had the ancient goddess of wisdom, voice of the plundered land, place a curse "on him and all his seed." Byron later regretted his intemperate attack but never condoned the removal of the art objects.

The Waltz (*1812,* 1813) (C) attacks the lascivious new dance that was superseding the minuet. Strangely enough, confirmed rakes like Byron are often the staunchest defenders of public morality and the most vociferous opponents of innovation. As a German importation the waltz provided the satirist with opportunities to strike at the Germanic monarchs of England. Possibly the poet's physical handicap also influenced his antipathy to the new dance.

The Giaour (1813, twelve editions in eighteen months) (A) was the first of Byron's Eastern narrative poems. Scott had created the market for Romantic tales in verse, but Scott was elbowed aside by readers eager for the exotic and erotic fare offered by Byron. In this and the following verse tales Byron unleashes a handsome, hot-blooded, noble Byronic hero amid Islamic fanaticism and melodrama. The giaour ("non-Moslem") avenges the death of Leila by slaying Hassan. The inspiration probably arose from Byron's personal rescue of a girl in Athens sentenced to drowning for illicit love.

The Bride of Abydos (1813, six thousand copies sold in the first month) (A), Byron's second Turkish tale in octosyllabics, relates Selim's abduction of Zuleika from the harem. In the first draft the pair were brother and sister, but they were changed to cousins for publication. Selim is a dashing leader of brigands-for-freedom. He is slain spectacularly, and Zuleika dies of a broken heart. The conclusion is lushly sentimental, and the love scenes boast such lines as: "For, Allah! sure thy lips are flame."

The Corsair (1814) (A) sold ten thousand copies on publication day and twenty-five thousand copies in the first month, far outstripping Scott's successes and indeed any previous sale of verse in English history. Turning to heroic couplets, Byron sends his pirate-hero Conrad (probably modeled after the American Jean Lafitte) ranging through "the dark blue sea" of the isles of Greece in a series of feverish adventures, eventually to disappear mysteriously. Conrad seems to be more definitely Byron than any of the poet's previous creations, especially in his desperate craving for boundless freedom and impassioned adventure.

"Ode to Napoleon Buonaparte" (1814) (A), written in one day, is a blistering denunciation of the abdicated emperor. Byron had mixed feelings toward Napoleon: although he saw himself in the brilliant strategist and dynamic soldier and condemned the English Tories for warring against him by the side of corrupt and tyrannical allies, Byron was shocked at Napoleon's brutal conquest of the Iberian Peninsula and his perversion of liberal ideals. When Napoleon meekly abdicated after Waterloo instead of Byronically sweeping to his death, Byron was simply disgusted.

Lara (1814) (B) is a clearly autobiographical heroic-couplet narrative. The hero of *The Corsair,* now called Lara, returns to the feudal castle (obviously Newstead Abbey) he had left in youth. He dies in the arms of the page Kaled, actually the lovely Gulnare in disguise (perhaps modeled on Lady Caroline Lamb, who often pursued Byron in page-boy costume). The absurd melodrama is unimportant beside the first fully realized presentation of the conscience-ridden hero-villain who was to become the embodiment of "Byronism." Byron told his wife that *Lara* was "the most metaphysical" of his works, but he probably meant "psychological." Certainly Byron accurately diagnosed himself in ascribing Lara's nature and behavior to:

> some strange perversity of thought
> That swayed him onward with a secret pride
> To do what few or none would do beside.

Hebrew Melodies (1815) (A) sold ten thousand copies within the year in spite of the high price, a guinea, for a thin folio. There is nothing truly religious about these short poems, their ancient Jewish setting providing simply another backdrop for Byronic orientalism. Most famous is "The Destruction of Sennacherib" (based upon 2 Kings 18–19 and 2 Chronicles 32), technically remarkable for Byron's ability to write highly emotional verse even in anapests. The opening poem, "She Walks in Beauty," is wholly irrelevant to the volume's title. It celebrates the appearance of Lady Wilmot Horton, Byron's cousin by marriage, in mourning at an evening party but with spangles upon her gown. It is one of the loveliest Romantic lyrics, suggesting that Byron might better have devoted his poetic talents to such delicate works instead of his gaudy narratives.

The Siege of Corinth (1816) (A) recounts in octosyllabics the bloody capture of Corinth by the Turks from the Venetians in 1715. With resistance hopeless, the governor of Corinth explodes the powder magazine, sending both defender and attacker to death. All the accustomed Byron vigor is present, but the versification is often slovenly and mere doggerel. Byron publicly maintained the pose of the aristocratic author, but actually he usually worked rather carefully. However, during the writing of this piece he was so sorely beset with financial and marital difficulties that his muse was woefully slipshod. Byron acknowledged that "Christabel" had been running through his mind at the time of composition, even to the inclusion of several Coleridge phrases.

Parisina (1816) (A) appeared in the same volume as the previous work but stands in astonishing contrast to it. It is the best of Byron's narrative tales in construction and characterization. Its source is Gibbon's *Antiquities of the House of Brunswick*. During the reign (1438–41) of Nicholas III, Duke of Ferrara, the Marquis of Este (Azo) was persuaded of an incestuous love affair between his wife Parisina and his illegitimate son Hugo. By order of the Marquis, the accused pair were executed. In this work Byron imaginatively enters the emotional wellsprings of his characters as he seldom does elsewhere, and Hugo's defense before his father is eloquent and moving. The octosyllabics frequently achieve an almost hushed effect, rare in Byron.

Poems on His Own Domestic Circumstances (1816, fifteen editions within the year) (B) displays to the world, in Arnold's phrase, "the pageant of a bleeding heart." Byron cannot here be accused of restraint or gentlemanly behavior. "Fare thee well," addressed to Lady Byron, reeks of the sentimental pathos of a play actor, and is rather embarrassing to read and ineffectual in its stagey plea for reconciliation. "A Sketch from Private Life," Byron's most bitter verse, is a savage attack on Mrs. Clermont (a friend of his wife, not "Claire" Clairmont), whom he considered influential in causing the rift between him and his wife. Never before had a significant English writer made such a public display of his private life.

Major Creativity in Self-Imposed Exile (1816–1824)

Childe Harold's Pilgrimage. Canto the Third (1816) (B) was written in Switzerland from "the lava of the imagination." Instead of a continuation of the two cantos from 1812, this is a completely different poem. This, together with *Manfred,* comprises the definitive statement of the *Weltschmerz* of Byronism. Its framework is a travelogue of Byron's journey from Dover to the battlefield of Waterloo, and thence down the Rhine into Switzerland. The grandiloquent rhetoric of the Waterloo passage (beginning "There was a sound of revelry by night") has made it a standard declamation piece for over a century.

Byron (all pretense that Harold is not the poet has been dropped) darkly refers to a burnt-out youth tasting of all the cups of good and evil of all the world. Although grossly mistreated and misunderstood by "vain man," he is most deeply seared by a mysterious inner taint burning at his vitals. He asserts that his love for his half-sister, Augusta, was pure. To the world he presents a front of impenetrable aloofness, disdainfully exiling himself from the polluted herd and, in devil-may-care fashion, defying the world and plunging into wild adventure. Byron sees poetry as a purgation for himself, a necessary release of the hurricane forces within him. He considers the great geniuses of the world as driven like himself into a hostility toward mankind and rising to glory at the expense of lesser beings. Napoleon, Voltaire, and Gibbon are therefore interpreted in the Byronic image. In this poem Byron comes closest to the Nature worship of Wordsworth, but he seeks the most grandly desolate of Alpine scenery, not to lead him to man or to mystic communion, as in Wordsworth, but rather to escape from man into a mirroring of his own magnificent and tumultuous nature.

Pose and rhetoric it might be, but hardly any other work in literature possesses the same titanic power and grand flourish. Awestruck in reading this third canto, Shelley exclaimed to Byron, "What are you not further capable of effecting?"

The Prisoner of Chillon (1816) (A), also written in Switzerland, imaginatively recounts in octosyllabics the imprisonment of François Bonnivard (1493–1570), leader in Geneva's revolt against Charles III, Duke of Savoy. The actual Bonnivard was a somewhat quarrelsome and unattractive personality, but Byron here makes of him a Promethean figure, the embodiment of the "chainless mind," defying tyranny and resolutely suffering for noble principles. The account is told in a dramatic monologue with Bonnivard speaking. Remarkable for the tempestuous Byron is the re-creation of calm meditation and quiet endurance. It is one of the few character portrayals by Byron at least partially to escape the Byronic image. The accompanying "Sonnet on Chillon," treating the same subject, is a paean to the spirit of freedom and an indication that Byron could work effectively in the narrow compass of the sonnet.

"The Dream" (1816) (A) is a highly sentimentalized series of recollections of Mary Chaworth, who is seen platonically as the ideal of beauty and purity. Byron summarizes his own course from idealistic youth through sickening disillusionment to melancholia and sorrowful resignation.

"Darkness" (1816) (B) is a nightmarish picture of our dying planet in a frigid universe. In the insane struggle for survival, civilization utterly collapses, and men become no better than predatory beasts. The last shred of unselfishness is displayed by a dog who guards his master's body until his own death. The alarming eschatology of much 20th-century science fiction seems to spring from such Romantic nightmares.

"Prometheus" (1816) (B) is a short ode in octosyllabics. Byron sees the archetype of himself in the Titan who brought fire from heaven to man. In the first strophe, Prometheus, like Byron's concept of himself, suffers in solitude while viewing the agony of humanity with clear eyes. In the second strophe, the poet attributes to Prometheus his own inner conflict: sympathetic participation in mankind's suffering versus his defiance of fate in seeking to alleviate human suffering. In the concluding strophe, Byron sees man's perverse state as half-god, half-dust. The mingled elements make for the torture of human life but also for its capacity of self-sufficient endurance. Byron views himself throughout his mature career as either the defiant Prometheus or the defiant Don Juan. In this poem he achieves perhaps his most intense and effective lyricism.

Manfred, a Dramatic Poem (1817) (B) consists of two acts composed in Switzerland and the concluding act written in Venice. The title character seems to come from Walpole's *Castle of Otranto*. Sources include Marlowe's *Dr. Faustus* and Goethe's *Faust,* though Byron preferred to acknowledge indebtedness to *Prometheus Bound,* by Aeschylus.

Tortured by inner conflict, Manfred conjures up spirits from whom he seeks "Forgetfulness." When they cannot grant his request, he travels up a mountain and contemplates suicide but is saved by a chamois hunter. Boldly entering the hall of the Spirit of Darkness, Arimanes (from the Zoroastrian myth of ancient Persia), Manfred refuses to bow to any spirit. He conjures Nemesis to summon the phantom of his true love, Astarte (ancient Phoenician goddess of love), but she departs after informing him of his approaching death. Consolation from an abbot unavailing, Manfred dies.

Southey and many others saw the "Satanic School" in this production. Remorse for an inexpiable crime, apparently forbidden love with Astarte, reveals the brand of Cain upon Manfred. Many read Astarte as Augusta and assumed an admission of incest, though Astarte may also be interpreted as Mary Chaworth. Equally horrifying to the orthodox was the Byronic brushing-aside of all conventional religion. Byron's towering Romantic ego saw heaven and hell as purely internal states. After death the immortal mind can be rewarded or punished solely by its own knowledge of its goodness or evil. Manfred revels in the Promethean confidence of asserting the supremacy of his will over all natural or supernatural forces confronting him. The bravura rhetoric of this piece and its surcharging of Alpine grandeur with melodramatic Gothicism lent themselves to musical interpretations; Robert Schuman provided one version. Goethe praised the poem, especially the revised interpretation made to his *Faust* theme.

The Lament of Tasso (1817) (A) is an impassioned dramatic soliloquy supposedly uttered by Torquato Tasso, author of *Jerusalem Delivered,* after his imprisonment for love of Leonora d'Este. This is the first of Byron's so-called "Italian" poems inspired by the color and history of the new land of his residence.

Childe Harold's Pilgrimage. Canto the Fourth (*1817*, 1818) (B), though continuing somewhat after the manner of the third canto, is sufficiently different to be considered as a separate poem. In form it is a spirited travelogue of Italy, with Byron conducting the reader from Venice through Arqua (associated with Petrarch) and Ferrara (Tasso's city) to Florence and thence, for the longest part of the poem, to Rome. Like Scott, Byron has an osmotic feel for the atmosphere of places, and senses the dramatic history of a storied community as vivid colors and tingling action. For generations of the English-speaking people, Bryon's grandiloquence formed the concept of Italy and provided set declamations ("I stood in Venice on the Bridge of Sighs," "Oh Rome! My country! City of the Soul"). But his overlying theme is that of a burnt-out culture. Italy, land of ancient Roman splendor and Renaissance magnificence, is the symbol of all Western society—a glorious past now fallen into decay and futility. The Pilgrim of Eternity (Shelley's phrase for Byron-Childe Harold) finds solace from Western culture only partly in the timelessness of art and beauty; chiefly the modern Prometheus finds meaning only in the expression itself of his irreconcilable inner tumults set against the backdrop of disease, death, and bondage of modern life. Behind the swelling rhetoric is the painful sense of modern man's isolation, of his having been cut adrift from the cultural tradition and forced to rely solely upon his own resources.

Beppo (*1817*, 1818) (D) was Byron's first poem in *ottava rima* (iambic pentameter riming a b a b a b c c), an Italian stanza employed by Tasso, Ariosto, and especially by Luigi Pulci (1432–84) in *Il Morgante Maggiore,* translated by Byron in 1820. Pulci utilized the stanza for comic improvisation, and although *ottava rima* was occasionally employed in English Renaissance verse, it was forgotten until revived by William Tennant in *Anster Fair* (1812). Pulci's breezy improvisation was first attempted in English by John Hookham Frere in *Monks and Giants* (1817), which inspired Byron to the writing of *Beppo.*

Though inconsequential, Byron's first imitation of the Italian "medley-poem" let the poet experiment with the vehicle that would prove most congenial to him. The story is based upon a Venetian anecdote related to Byron by the husband of one of his Venetian mistresses. Beppo (nickname for Giuseppe, equivalent to the English Joe), a Venetian merchant, has long been missing on business in the East.

His wife Laura waits a decent period and then takes a count as "protector." At a carnival ball, a costumed Turk proves to be the long-absent Beppo. The three pleasantly discuss the amatory triangle, the count and Beppo becoming friends. Here Byron doffs the mantle of the Pilgrim of Eternity to saunter along the streets of Venice chatting about Venetian belles, the gay carnival trappings, authors, and Moslem sexual practices. The central theme, of course, is lost innocence; but instead of the brow-beating, soul-ravaged Byron, there appears the ironic observer of life as it is, advising the polite acceptance of man's fallen state.

Mazeppa (*1818,* 1819) (D) is based upon an episode in Voltaire's *Histoire de Charles XII,* the Swedish king defeated by the Russians at Poltava (1709). In the retreating Swedish forces was the real-life Ivan Stepanovitch Mazeppa, here the supposed teller of this octosyllabic narrative. To divert the downhearted monarch, Mazeppa relates his early experience as a page in love with Theresa, beautiful daughter of a Polish count. Apprehended, the young Mazeppa is bound naked to a wild horse which is lashed to a mad gallop. After a terrifying ride, the young man is released and nursed back to health by Cossacks. None of Scott's racing narratives can match the headlong pace of this work, and Romantic as it is, it is an old campaigner's yarn, certainly exaggerated and perhaps a fabrication. It is spun to conceal grave cares, and it succeeds, for Charles XII proves to have been sleeping for most of the account.

Don Juan (I–II, 1819; III–V, 1821, VI–XIV, 1823; XV–XVI, 1824; fragmentary canto XVII of 14 stanzas, 1903) (D) was begun in September 1818 and was left incomplete at the poet's death. Since its separate cantos form essentially one coherent unit, unlike *Childe Harold's Pilgrimage,* it is here considered in toto.

The hero is not the Don Juan of legend, best known in Mozart's opera *Don Giovanni,* but an imaginary Spanish contemporary, a thinly disguised Byron pictured before his maturity. Byron resolved to recount nothing in Juan's adventures beyond actual facts. The work falls into seven major episodes:

Canto I. Liaison with Donna Julia. Don Juan, a sixteen-year-old native of Seville, has received a prim education from his puritanical mother, Donna Inez (Byron's wife). His mother's friend, Donna Julia, married to the middle-aged Don Alfonso, seduces the handsome lad. Upon discovery, Donna Julia is committed to a nunnery, and

Don Juan is shipped on a vessel bound for Leghorn, Italy. Byron ascribed the episode to an Italian acquaintance, Parolini.

Canto II (to stanza 112). Storm and Shipwreck. The *Trinidada* is wrecked in a fearful storm, and survivors are left clinging to an overcrowded and ill-provisioned ship's boat. Suffering and deprivation reduce the castaways to cannibalism. Juan alone escapes, collapsing upon the shore of an island in the Greek Cyclades. This most realistic and gripping account of shipwreck in English literature is based upon reading, for Byron was not knowledgeable in seamanship. Its chief sources are Byron's grandfather's book, Dalzell's *Shipwrecks and Disasters at Sea* (1812), and William Falconer's poem *The Shipwreck* (1762).

Canto II (stanza 113)–IV (to stanza 74). The Haidée Idyll. Juan is nursed back to health by a beautiful Greek girl, Haidée, in the absence of her pirate father, Lambro. The two young people fall in love. Lambro returns, wounds Juan, and sells him into slavery. Haidée dies of a broken heart. Haidée (meaning "a caress" or "the caressed one") appears in contemporary Greek songs, cruelly treated by her relatives for loving a stranger. The lush Oriental love theme is at least as old as Hellenistic Greek prose romances of antiquity. The passage displays strong resemblances to Christoph Martin Wieland's *Oberon*. Lambro was a historic character, not associated with this love story.

Canto IV (stanza 75)–VI. The Harem Episode. Juan is purchased in Istanbul by a veiled woman who proves to be Gulbeyaz, the love-starved sultana. She disguises the youth in female garb as Juana and conceals him in the seraglio. Repulsed because Juan honors the memory of Haidée and suspecting him of loving the harem girl Dudù, Gulbeyaz orders Baba to slay Juan. Escaping, Juan makes his way to the Russian lines. The theme of the Moslem lady and the Christian slave has been a familiar Mediterranean tale since medieval times. In *La Provençale,* by Jean-François Regnard, the account is declared a "true story." Byron also utilized versions by Cervantes (*The Liberal Lover*) and Wieland (*Oberon*).

Canto VII–VIII. Siege of Ismail. Juan serves with the Russians under Suvaroff (later famous in Napoleonic battles) against the Turkish city of Ismail, a genuine historical event of 1790. Amidst frightful slaughter, Juan distinguishes himself and saves the life of a little girl, Leila. Slightly wounded, he is sent with despatches to St. Petersburg. Chief source is Castelnau's *Essai sur l'Histoire ancienne et moderne de la Nouvelle Russie* (1820).

Canto IX–X (to stanza 64). The Court of Catherine the Great. Handsome Juan is made the latest favorite of the Russian empress but becomes sick, for "in royalty's vast arms he sigh'd for beauty." Reluctantly Catherine agrees to send the youth, accompanied by Leila, on a diplomatic errand to the milder climate of England. Source is the *ottava rima* mock epic *Poema Tartaro* (1797), by Giambattista Casti.

Canto X (stanza 65) to breaking-off point. England. In the secure land of England, Juan is first held up by a highwayman, whom he shoots. His handsome person makes him the darling of London high society, even like his creator. He is a guest at Norman Abbey (obviously Newstead Abbey), Gothic mansion of the politician Lord Henry Amundeville. Here Byron sketches many English aristocrats of his own circle. Juan attracts three predatory females: Adeline, volatile wife of his host; Aurora Raby, a young heiress; and the Duchess of Fitz-Fulke, a female Casanova. The sixteenth canto offers a spectre who turns out to be the Duchess disguised as the local ghost, the Black Friar; she is also intent upon a liaison with the good-looking Juan. Here Byron drew largely upon his personal knowledge, though such material was also widely available in articles, journals, memoirs.

Literary men of the time lavishly praised *Don Juan*. Goethe termed it "a work of boundless genius." Shelley considered it "something wholly new and relative to the age, and yet surpassingly beautiful." Gifford asserted that with this poem Byron had elevated himself head and shoulders above all other English poets except Shakespeare and Milton. Outraged bourgeois moralists, however, loudly cried for suppression of the poem; and the subsequent Victorians largely ignored *Don Juan,* frequently omitting it from collections of Byron's verse and dismissing it with moral condemnation in discussions of his work. Swinburne's extravagant praise of the poem stemmed largely from his bitter hostility to Victorian mores. Since World War I the reputation of *Don Juan* has steadily mounted until some enthusiastic critics might concur with Gifford's judgment. The pervading notes of disillusionment and cynicism accord well with the spirit of the later 20th century.

Don Juan is the greatest English verse epic since *Paradise Lost,* or at least the nearest approach to the poetic epic achieved in recent times (some term it the greatest picaresque novel in verse). The theme is the odyssey of modern man in search of his soul in an "open society." Juan has no real moral principles or code of life. Opportunistically he takes what comes, exploring the full range of passion and action without ever achieving fixed principles. Even if death had not silenced the poet, genuine development of Juan's character seems unlikely. Juan had not achieved maturity or stability and shows no clear signs of approaching maturation. Nonetheless, the skeptical Byron repeatedly affirmed his belief in God, in truth, and in right as demonstrated by the human mind and will. *Don Juan* might therefore be taken as the protest of a perfectionist against the fallen state of man. It is the modern *Paradise Lost* without Providence remaining as a guide. Juan is the epitome of the modern innocent completely deprived of innocence and the modern passive being compelled to activity. The sole program Byron envisaged for the modern hero was courageous moral action in the cause of human freedom. Whether or not intended for Juan, Byron's hero never so acted. Byron in the flesh so acted at Missolonghi.

Byron found the perfect instrument for his themes and his attitudes in *ottava rima*. In his hands this proved the most facile and varied verse form in English, capable of every conceivable effect. Especially it made possible the vast improvisation that is *Don Juan*. Much of the effect is that of the complete man-of-the-world. The *Weltschmerz* pose is dropped. In his ripest maturity a man who has lived numerous lives in a few decades and has known in the flesh most of the fundamental experiences of modern humanity shares with his listener the fantastic scope of his observation. Comedy is the dominant approach, for life is a comedy to those who think (as it had been a tragedy to the Byron who felt in *Manfred*). Incredible rimes, hilarious pranks, insolent anticlimaxes, sarcastic parentheses embedded in sentiment, and sudden collapses from romantic exaltation to realistic matter-of-factness deflate the pretenses and hypocrisies of modern life. In this fallen and utterly chaotic modern world, what, asks Byron, is sacred?

Devotees of classification try despairingly to label *Don Juan* as satire. But satire, like that written by Pope and by the 18th-century satirist in Byron, requires a fixed standard of judgment. The whole point of *Don Juan* lies in "mobility" (a favorite word for Byron). Byron calls for the individual in modern life to accept our world and human nature for what they are, displaying agile "mobility" in following the world's fashion while still seeking genuine satisfaction in self-realization. In a world sure to play us false, he urges us to be true simply to ourselves.

Bizarre indeed is the spectacle of many of the works of Byron discussed below; Byron was continually at work on *Don Juan* while also writing these pieces often strangely inconsistent with the spirit and tone of his masterpiece.

The Prophecy of Dante (1821) (A) is a dramatic soliloquy in *terza rima* supposedly spoken by Dante between the completion of the *Commedia* and his death. The poet forcefully predicts the eventual liberation and unification of Italy.

"Stanzas to the Po" (*1819,* 1824) (A) was composed while Byron was sailing on the river Po from Venice to Ravenna, where he was to join the Countess Guiccioli. In some of his purest lyric diction the poet relates his hesitation at the liaison. He thought himself depleted of love by the misadventures of his past. To his own surprise, his heart has been moved again, and he finds he must yield to his nature and destiny, although he senses destruction ahead.

Marino Faliero, Doge of Venice (*1820,* 1821) (A) was Byron's first attempt at playwrighting since *Manfred,* and the first in a series of romantic tragic dramas. While some Byron adherents find virtues in them, these plays have never proved successful either in their occasional theatrical representation or in closet reading (*Cain* is a possible exception). *Marino Faliero* was inspired by Venice, about whom Byron states in his preface, "Her aspect is like a dream, and her history is a romance." The plot is that of Otway's *Venice Preserv'd* but suffers from stock characterization, slow movement, and overly punctilious fidelity to the classic unities. Byron himself stated the theme to be the unfortunate consequences of the passion of outraged pride, as the chagrined doge plots treachery against his own city. Autobiographically the drama shows Byron's resentment at the ostracizing he had received from his own caste. The work was also encouraging contemporary Venice to throw off Austrian rule.

The Vision of Judgment (*1821,* 1822) (D) in *ottava rima* is a satiric parody on Southey's poem of the same name written upon the death of George III. The poet laureate's interminable ode is the height of pretentious banality, stirring the exiled Whig aristocrat to retort in what many consider one of the best satires in English. Anyone repelled by Byron's irreverence should peruse Southey's inflated, sanctimonious verse, against which Byron rebelled, and Southey's savage prefatory remarks about the "Satanic School" (Byron, Shelley).

Parodying Southey's solemn recital of the funeral cortege of George III, Byron sees the elaborate rites not as fitting ceremonies but as mockery for a dead madman who, in his right senses, had been an upholder of despotism instead of freedom. Further burlesquing Southey,

Byron brings the dead monarch's soul to St. Peter's Gate, where Satan comes to claim it. St. Peter is ready to relinquish George III because of the king's hostility to Roman Catholicism, but the Archangel Michael demands witnesses against George III. From the host summoned by Satan, Wilkes and Junius testify against the king. An angel brings Southey from the Lake Country, and a little reading of Southey's *Vision of Judgment* causes the vast throng of spirits to flee. In the confusion, George III slips into heaven.

Byron's preface is angry prose denunciation, but in verse he artistically controls his rage, producing an essentially genial judgment which history would probably substantiate. The final treatment of his butts, Southey and George III, caused Lamb to term this the "one good-natured thing" written by Byron. The depiction of Satan was called "sublime" by Goethe, for, remarkably, this burlesque poem is the only poem in English somewhat to match Miltonic grandeur. Milton's heaven is sublime; Byron's is sublimely funny. After equaling Milton on his own ground, Byron strikes out at Milton's hold upon him and the English world. The result is the only piece by Byron in which he truly reconciles his warring elements by the elimination of the sense of sin. The poem therefore approximates much of the modern mind in its denial or mere ignoring of "original sin"; any eternal judgment is to be relativistic, based solely upon an individual's actions, for which circumstances, rather than ourselves, are to be blamed. The world may belong to the Devil, but Satan is a disinterested gentleman. In sheer wit, fertile invention, and buoyant fluency, this work at least equals any satire in the language.

The Blues (*1821,* 1823) (C) is an anapestic satire, reminiscent of Christopher Anstey's *New Bath Guide*. Byron lightly ridicules the frivolous taste of current London literary coteries in two "eclogues" in the form of dialogue. Wordsworth and Southey are mildly satirized.

Sardanapalus (1821) (B), dedicated to Goethe, is another tragic drama. Its hero is the ancient Assyrian monarch described by Diodorus and Ctesias as a slothful debauchee. Byron transforms the character into a contemplator of human folly, who hates violence and scorns man's lust for power. The king's indulgence in sensual delights is fundamentally a way of escaping from the world and avoiding even baser passions. The suicide of Sardanapalus is the final gesture of renunciation of a sordid world. Writing an apologia for his own conduct, Byron achieves some passages of exciting poetry, notably in the ruler's diatribe against war.

The Two Foscari (1821) (A), like *Marino Faliero,* is a tragic drama closely following events in Venetian history. The 15th-century Francis Foscari, doge of Venice, in his official capacity, must sentence his own son Jacopo to death. Byron conceives of the elder Foscari as a noble Roman, loyal to the state and to his own honor regardless of the cost and regardless of the unworthiness of many of his fellow citizens. Although the intended theme is the necessity of social responsibilities, the elder Foscari seems a Byronesque figure, who rejoices in the grand gesture.

Cain: A Mystery (1821) (B) is a closet drama widely departing from the fourth chapter of Genesis. It evoked the loudest protests of moralists against any piece of English literature before Joyce and Lawrence. Byron was quite literally correct in telling Moore that "the parsons preached at it from Kentish Town to Pisa." Reports circulated that at least one man had promptly committed suicide after reading the work. Although even the king, George IV, denounced the poem, Goethe and Scott (to whom the work was dedicated) praised it extravagantly, while Shelley insisted: *"Cain* is apocalyptic—a revelation not before communicated to man."

Cain is portrayed as the first skeptic, a compound of 18th-century rationalism and Romantic Prometheanism. Lucifer, identified with knowledge rather than with evil, conducts Cain through the abyss of space, reducing to nothing Cain's sense of self-importance. When both Cain and Abel make offerings to the incomprehensible Maker, Abel's pious counterings to Cain's questionings cause Cain impulsively to strike Abel, inadvertently killing him. Cursed by Eve, Cain, more wracked inwardly than burnt by the mark placed upon his brow, goes his way in sad contrition with his sister-wife Adah.

The theme is again: Man in the Fallen World. Byron, claiming that by scriptural reading the temptation came from the serpent and not (as assumed by Judeo-Christian tradition) from Lucifer, sees the Fall of Man as purely a human decision, unaffected by any supernatural intervention. Byron rages against the doctrine of original sin, Cain shouting about his parents, "They sinn'd, then let them die!" The vicarious atonement of Christ seems to Byron a ghastly joke, that the innocent should suffer for the guilty. This cannot be termed a drama, for Lucifer is simply an alter ego of Cain (and Byron); essentially it is a lyric complaint about the world and life. The world cannot supply happiness and fulfillment to a Romantic soul seeking the freedom of spirit possessed by deity. Further, Byron suggests gloomily that since not even all knowledge can produce happiness, even divine beings may not enjoy happiness. In some respects this is the ultimate, if naïvely conceived, Romantic and rationalistic protest. Cain and Byron want eternity without death, knowledge without pain, complete happiness without sacrifice. All that is left for Byron is a sort of desperate stoicism based upon his unconquerable will and his acceptance of the futility of aspiration. Most shocking to his readers was the presentation of the first murderer as an honest and righteous questioner, more to be sympathized with than the blindly accepting family of Adam and Eve. Equally distressing was the incest theme, the mating of brothers and sisters. Byron had actually reached beyond his grasp, and the ambitious theme is treated more pretentiously than majestically. The poem is also marred by "gentleman's grammar" and some slovenly versifying. Nonetheless, it touches moments of bitter human pathos, and with great power superbly expresses the genuine anguish that a completely non-mystical soul experiences in confronting the baffling cosmos.

Heaven and Earth (*1821,* 1823) (A), another "mystery" in dramatic form, was intended to have none of the shocking effect of *Cain.* Goethe said of this work, perhaps satirically, that it could have been written by a bishop. Source is Genesis 6:2: "And it came to pass . . . that the sons of God saw the daughters of men that they were fair; and they took them wives of all which they choose." Though apparently intended as biblically serious, the liaisons of angels with mortal women seem unintentionally ludicrous. Japhet is "a man of feeling" like Cain in finding Jehovah's decisions distasteful: why are innocent children, for instance, drowned in the great flood and only Noah and his family spared? Facing destruction from the cruel, wrathful Jehovah, mortals display proud stoicism instead of Byron's earlier ranting or gloom. Occasionally the poetry touches Miltonic majesty as Byron could not elsewhere except in a part of his *Vision of Judgment.*

The Deformed Transformed (*1822,* 1824) (B), a closet drama, was condemned by Shelley as a bad imitation of *Faust.* The lame hero, Arnold, becomes a Manfred-Byron figure but is uninteresting except in the opening scene, which is poignantly reminiscent of the poet's stormy early years with his emotional and unsympathetic mother.

The Age of Bronze; or, Carmen Seculare et Annus Haud Mirabilis (1823) (C) pays tribute to Napoleon (died 1821), rhapsodizes upon Greece and America and freedom, and especially scorns the reactionary Congress of Verona (1822). One of the most effective slashing satiric passages in English verse is the attack upon the "uncountry gentlemen" who profiteered during the Napoleonic wars; seven times in a row comes the word "rent," with mounting disdain of the "Warbucks."

The Island; or, Christian and His Comrades (1823) (A) relates in heroic couplets the famous story from Captain Bligh's *Narrative of the Mutiny of the Bounty,* with some indebtedness to the descriptions in Mariner's *Account of the Tonga Islands.* The astonished reader wonders what Byron had learned in his poetic career, for this seems the early Byron beguiled by headlong action and exotic sex (Neuha is blessed "With faith and feelings, naked as her form"). It is incredible to find this Romantic naïveté being penned simultaneously with *The Age of Bronze* (finished on exactly the same day) and the later cantos of *Don Juan.*

"On This Day I Complete My Thirty-Sixth Year" (1824) (A), written in Greece, is the poet's dedication to the cause of Greek liberation as he assumes command of the expedition carrying supplies and reinforcements to the Greek rebels against Turkish rule. Though the posturing Byron is present, as always, it is a noble consecration and affirmation of the principles of freedom. He plans to expiate a bungled life by dying for a glorious cause.

Byron's Letters

As literary executor, Moore published portions of Byron's correspondence and jottings in 1830, but still the definitive edition is the six-volume collection (1898–1901) by Rowland E. Prothero (later Lord Ernle), extending from 1799 to the poet's death. The correspondence falls into six major categories:

(1) Family and early associates. Byron here is intimate, bantering, more a normal domestic creature than elsewhere.

(2) Publishers and literary friends. To these men of the world, Byron speaks as a fellow sophisticate. To them he wrote some of his most slashing and energetic letters.

(3) Women in his life. Byron is a surprisingly proper correspondent to his numerous inamoratas. His polite reserve makes him no writer of ecstatic love letters, but such restraint seems to have heightened his attractiveness to women. He prefers to write to the wise Lady Melbourne, venting his sarcasm upon fashionable foibles.

(4) The Shelley group. The intensity and artiness of the Shelley circle make Byron a bit uncomfortable. Byron greatly admires Shelley but does not quite understand him. These letters seem a bit guarded, fencing, except when denouncing common opponents.

(5) The Venice group. With Teresa Guiccioli and surrounding Italians, Byron is the noble Whig lord, nonchalant, chatty, tolerant.

(6) The Greek adventure. Byron is quite realistic and hard-headed in the cause of freedom. He advances practical plans, not idealistic rhetoric. He recognizes the real difficulties and the human failings of the freedom fighters.

Among all English letter writers, only D. H. Lawrence approaches the vigor and movement in Byron's letters, a compelling rhythmic prose that sweeps and punches. The man becomes blazingly alive in these incisive and driving letters. During the very period of his wild Oriental tales and ostensible *Weltschmerz*, his correspondence reveals the witty, cynical Byron of *Don Juan*. The robust honesty and vitality of the letters make him more attractive and human than does any of his flamboyant verse.

In *Astarte* (1905) the poet's grandson, Lord Lovelace, sought to blacken his grandfather's memory by reassertion of the alleged incest between Byron and Augusta. The revised edition of this work in 1921 printed thirty-four of Byron's hitherto unpublished letters (thirty-one to Augusta), but this innocent correspondence could not substantiate the accusation. In 1922 the issuance of the Lady Dorchester collection of Byron's correspondence (she was the daughter of Hobhouse, Byron's closest friend) revealed extensive letters, previously unpublished, falling into three groups:

(1) Early residence in Greece (1809–11), of minor interest.

(2) "Years of notoriety" as a Regency dandy (1811–16), chiefly to Lady Melbourne. Many critics believe that these letters fully confirm the accusation of incest.

(3) Years in Venice (1816–19). These include some of his most brilliant letters.

Byron: The Last Attachment (1949), by the Marchesa Iris Origo, published 156 letters written by Byron to the Countess Guiccioli. This new collection revealed or much more fully emphasized than ever before: (1) Byron's fervent interest in Italian patriots conspiring for national liberation and unification; (2) Byron as a writer of love letters, more rapturously gay and insouciant than ever to his English loves.

Byron has proved probably the most popular figure in English literature as a subject for biography, usually to the subordination of his poetry. The best possible picture of the man (his literary executor, Moore, destroyed the autobiography) Byron has himself presented in his incomparable letters.

THE POETRY OF SHELLEY

Percy Bysshe Shelley (1792–1822). Following is a list of the more important known events in the life of Percy Bysshe Shelley.

1792: Born August 4 at Field Place near Horsham, Sussex. Father, Timothy, was a Whig squire; his mother, Elizabeth, was an imaginative and emotional woman. With his four younger sisters, Shelley played at highly imaginative games.

1802–04: At Syon House Academy, near Brentford, cultivated simultaneously scientific interests and fascination with horror literature. Here dedicated himself to a life of elevated idealism.

1804–10: At Eton rebelled against system of fagging. To continued enthusiasm for scientific experiments and Gothic reading matter, Shelley added intense radicalism in politics and religion. Was writing extensively in 1810. First love affair, with Harriet Grove, was terminated by her family because of opposition to Shelley's radical views.

1810: Entered University College, Oxford, where he plunged into wide reading of skeptics, materialists, and determinists, especially Godwin.

1811: Expelled from Oxford as co-author of *The Necessity of Atheism.* Correspondence with schoolteacher, Elizabeth Hitchener. Married Harriet Westbrook to save her from parental tyranny. Hasty marriage to lower middle-class girl plus his radicalism alienated him from his father.

1812: Campaigned ineffectually for radicalism in Ireland. Disciple of Godwin, advancing money to the philosopher.

1813: Birth of daughter Ianthe. Practiced vegetarianism.

1814: Incipient love affair with Cornelia Turner broken up by her mother, Mrs. Boinville. Eloped to France with Godwin's daughter, Mary, accompanied by Jane ("Claire") Clairmont (later Byron's mistress). Returned to England, found finances almost ruined and acquaintances hostile. Harriet's second child, Charles Bysshe, born.

1815: Death of grandfather, Sir Bysshe, left poet independently wealthy for life. Settled fifth of his income upon Harriet. Mary's first child dead soon after birth.

1816: Birth of Mary's second child, William. Accompanied by "Claire" Clairmont and Mary, Shelley proceeded to Switzerland, where he established friendship with Byron. After Harriet's suicide, married Mary.

1817: Back in England, was refused custody of Harriet's children by decision of Lord Chancellor Eldon. Birth of daughter Clara.

1818: With Byron in Italy, never to return to England. Daughter Clara died. Adopted a daughter, Elena Adelaide Shelley.

1819: Death of son William and birth of son Percy Florence Shelley.

1820: Met Emilia Viviani. Intimate with colony of British expatriates at Pisa.

1821: Planned with Byron to found *The Liberal,* inviting Leigh Hunt to Italy as editor. Admiration for Jane Williams.

1822: Drowned in the bay of Spezzia, July 8, along with Edward Williams. Body cremated on the beach in the presence of Byron, Hunt, and Trelawny. Ashes buried in the Protestant Cemetery, Rome, near the grave of Keats.

Shelley was a radical reformer suffused with poetic lyricism and philosophic idealism. Following his own impulses, he made a horrible bungle of his private life, inflicting grave mental anguish upon himself and others. His amatory entanglements arose from an idealistic quest for perfect love and beauty in a woman, and since women are human beings, Shelley's quest was doomed to pathetic failure. His verse has often been coupled in failure with his personal life; even the astute Matthew Arnold said of him in a memorable phrase, "In poetry, no less than in life, he is a beautiful and ineffectual angel, beating his luminous wings in vain." True as this estimate may be of the young Shelley, it ignores the remarkable maturation of the poet. In the verse of *Prometheus Unbound* and in the prose of *A Philosophical View of Reform,* Shelley achieves perhaps the most accurate and viable position possible for the spirit of idealistic reform. He thence emerges as an almost unique character, a philosopher-poet. Probably Lucretius of ancient Rome is the only truly comparable figure, a poet passionately and imaginatively stirred by philosophy and science, for Shelley, considering his years, was probably as well read as any man in history. His lasting fame, however, may well rest upon his lyricism, unmatched elsewhere in English verse in its ethereal, ideal beauty.

Shelley has seldom been judged solely upon the totality of his literary contribution. His contemporary critics were indignant at his personal conduct and enraged by his radicalism. Current reviews virtually ignored his poetry *qua* poetry, and Victorians relishing his soaring lyricism frequently sought to justify the man as a hopelessly impractical artist. The disillusioned and cynical 20th century is so impatient with idealism that Shelley is now often scornfully dismissed as a muddlehead by sophisticated critics and even omitted from collections of "major" English writers. Few authors, however, have ever possessed such a gift of sheer poetry, and a resurgence of interest in Shelley seems clearly in the offing.

All the following pieces are verse unless they are followed by (P), indicating prose, or (D), designating dramas. Interpretation of Shelley's works is often highly controversial. The following comments seek a moderate position, holding as far as possible to clear textual intentions.

The Materialistic Reformer (1810–1814)

The early Shelley was tremendously influenced by the skeptical and materialistic thinkers of the 18th century, notably French *philosophes* such as Condorcet, Helvetius, d'Holbach, La Mettrie, and Voltaire. But the most potent influence came from Godwin, whose *Political Justice* implanted in the youth's mind a number of ideas, among which were: a conviction of man's innate goodness, the essential corruption of institutions, reason as the sole arbiter of morals and conduct, the doctrine of necessitarianism (determinism), and a belief in the perfectability of mankind. Especially important was Shelley's agreement with Godwin at this stage that alteration must come, not from individual education and improvement, but rather from a complete revamping of the entire political structure. The immature Shelley insisted that nothing could be considered true unless it was verifiable by the senses or logically deducible therefrom. Hence, all religion is false, and Christianity, hypocritically professing love, had set up a god that would maintain the status quo of tyranny and cruelty. "The only true religion," Shelley then asserted, "is the religion of Philanthropy." In opposition to corrupt Christianity, Shelley advocated the pre-eminence of reason. With reason prevailing, the brutalizing institutions of Church, State, and marriage would be scrapped along with their attendant hate, repression, and selfishness. Omnipotent Necessity would operate to create the utopian world of peace, happiness, universal freedom, and love. Necessity is the law behind human history, guaranteeing progress ever forward.

The Necessity of Atheism (1811) (P) seems to have been written jointly by Shelley and his friend Thomas Jefferson Hogg. Correspondence within three weeks of publication demonstrates that Shelley was a deist, but Hogg's vehement atheism apparently convinced Shelley, who was responsible for publication. The tract argues that knowledge of God arises purely from three sources—senses, reason, testimony—

and that none of these produces genuine proof of the existence of God. The foregoing appears to be largely Hogg's contribution, while Shelley apparently wrote the following denunciation of the Christian intolerance that condemned to damnation all mankind not accepting Christianity. Shelley's own position seems less truly atheistic than agnostically antagonistic to the tyranny of Church and State. This pamphlet, one of the earliest writings in English openly to support atheism, caused the expulsion of both young men from college.

Irish pamphlets (P). In 1812 in Ireland, as a champion of the oppressed, Shelley issued three short works: *An Address to the Irish People, Proposals for an Association,* and *Declaration of Rights.* All three sought Catholic emancipation (i.e. giving Roman Catholics the right to vote) and repeal of the Union Act that incorporated Ireland under English rule. Especially the latter pamphlet advocated a republic for Ireland. Like Godwin, Shelley opposed violent means of change; unlike Godwin, he urged an organization actively to strive for liberation.

A Letter to Lord Ellenborough (1812) (P) is Shelley's first significant writing. Lord Ellenborough had been the thoroughly biased judge in the trial of Daniel Isaac Eaton, a radical journalist sentenced to prison in May 1812 for publishing anti-Christian literature. In the first part of the pamphlet Shelley argued for the freedom of belief and disbelief. Against the prosecution's contention that an attack upon orthodox faith would injure public morality, Shelley asserted that morality is purely a social product, bearing no inherent relationship to religious belief or disbelief. In the second part of the letter Shelley insisted that Eaton was railroaded for expressing doubts about Christianity, as though orthodox faith was exempt from questioning. Shelley maintained that since religious concepts are not verifiable by scientific demonstration, they are therefore wholly disputable. The persecution of Eaton arose essentially, Shelley insisted, from the churchmen's fear of attacks upon their livelihoods and the government's fear that a weakening of the Church would imperil the entrenched oligarchy. Shelley called for complete freedom of expression on any subject and complete toleration of every belief or lack of belief. He looked to a day of universal brotherhood, when every man would have an unshakable right to his own personal convictions. For the first time Shelley rose above violent present issues to well-stated general principles. His pamphlet has several times been reprinted during more recent English and American controversies over the rights of freethinkers.

Vegetarian pamphlets (P). *A Vindication of Natural Diet* (1813) and

On the Vegetable System of Diet (c. *1813,* 1929) strongly object to the eating of flesh and the drinking of alcoholic beverages. Considering the eating of meat and the drinking of spirits as "unnatural," Shelley traces to man's carnivorous and alcoholic habits both physical ailments and the coarsening of moral fiber. Shelley later recognized human ills as traceable to causes other than diet, but throughout his life he was extraordinarily sparing in his eating of meat and drinking of liquor.

Queen Mab (*1812–13,* 1813) was Shelley's first major belletristic writing. Earlier he had written two immature Gothic novels, *Zastrozzi* (1810) and *St. Irvyne; or, The Rosicrucian* (1811); "terror" poems such as "The Wandering Jew"; and some sentimental verse in *Original Poetry* (1810), "by Victor and Cazire" (pseudonyms for himself and his sister Elizabeth). However, *Queen Mab* epitomizes the first radical stage of Shelley's thought; yet even while completing it, he was modifying his earlier ideas. In later years he deprecated the poem, terming it "villainous trash."

Introduction. Canto I and Canto II (to 1. 96) create the machinery. Queen Mab, ruler of the fairies, descends in a magic car to a sleeping girl, Ianthe, whose spirit is transported by the fairy monarch through space to perceive a vision of the world's development.

The past. Canto II (from 1. 97) sweeps across the whole past of civilizations, dismissing them as inadequate because of their non-scientific, superstitious viewpoints and their cruel exploitation of mankind.

The present. Canto III castigates monarchy and aristocracy as the causes of bloody wars abroad and heartless oppression at home. In a republican fervor, Shelley calls any system of class or privilege "unnatural." Canto IV denounces political tyranny as not merely governing by force but as inculcating militarism and brutality in mankind from the cradle. Religion here is a tool of the dynasts to keep the people from asserting their just rights. Canto V decries economic corruption in perhaps the most ringing indictment of the age. Shelley sees all human woes, from war to prostitution and thievery, as springing from the gross maldistribution of goods, services, and property. Canto VI is perhaps the best philosophical poetry in English after Pope's *Essay on Man*. The paean to Necessity, derived ideologically from d'Holbach rather than Godwin, denies creation but sees Necessity as the spiritual form pervading matter. Shelley here proves a dualist (recognizing both spirit and matter) and not a strict materialist. His Necessity is blind and impersonal, but it drives through all things toward perfection. Canto VII is a diatribe against Christianity. Christ is seen as a "parish demagogue," the Christian church is a consecrator of oppression and tyranny, and the most heinous atrocities are sanctified and encouraged by the priesthood. In the perspective of an infinite and eternal universe, Shelley finds that the claims of Christianity dwindle to absurdity.

The future. Canto VIII pictures the final Godwinian egalitarian society in which mind has asserted "omnipotence" over matter, and mankind is immortal. With prophetic zeal Shelley beholds science transforming the world; chemistry and especially electricity (only recently discovered) will perform miracles. Canto IX surveys the process of transformation into the new society. From Shelley's own blighted era, men will surge forward driven by Necessity to the Age of Perfection, though the process will be gradual. Reason and emotion will blend harmoniously as repressions and injustices vanish. The conclusion befits a revolutionary propaganda piece rather than an idyllic picture of utopianism.

Queen Mab is an anguished protest by a sensitive and idealistic youth against a corrupt and brutal age. Shelley was following many current liberals in the vehemence and in the objects of his attack, and in this work he produced the most thoroughgoing revolutionary document of the period. *Queen Mab* is derivative in its verse form (Southey's *Thalaba*), and many of its ideas come from Shelley's reading: framework for the poem from Volney; science from Erasmus Darwin and Cuvier; political theory from Paine, Godwin, Condorcet; and metaphysics from Hume and d'Holbach. Yet with all its indebtedness it achieves a synthesized originality. George Bernard Shaw declared: "*Queen Mab* is a perfectly original poem on a great subject. Throughout the whole poem Shelley shows a remarkable grasp of facts, anticipating the modern view that sociological problems are being slowly worked out independently of the conscious interference of man." Shelley's notes to *Queen Mab,* as inflammatory as the verse and more specific and direct in their accusations, were effectively cited against the poet in his 1817 suit for custody of Harriet's children.

A Refutation of Deism (*1813,* 1814) (P) closes out Shelley's early period as a highly incendiary radical. In a Socratic Dialogue, first the deist Theosophus attacks Christianity; then the Christian Eusebes refutes deism. The first part imitates the witty anti-clerical literature of the 18th century in denouncing original sin and the vicarious atonement (cf. Byron's *Cain*), in challenging a divine origin for the Christian church and its teachings, in castigating Christianity for its support of wars and political repression, in denouncing Christian emphasis upon asceticism and elevation of conformity above "natural" conduct, and in ridiculing miracles and prophecies. The second part is a closely and seriously reasoned assault upon the major arguments of deism. First, using the skeptical empiricism of Hume, Shelley assails the argument of design to prove the existence of God. Second, he charges that the universal belief in a creator springs from the perception of individual human beings, while in truth the universe is eternal rather than created. Third, to the argument of motion as presupposing a deity, Shelley counters with a surprisingly modern concept (essentially d'Holbach's) that motion is not imparted to matter but is the fundamental nature of matter.

Shelley's purpose is to cancel out both Christian and deistic contentions, and thus conclude with agnosticism or atheism. The work is one of the outstanding writings in English free thought, but it is only a stepping stone to Shelley's later and considerably altered viewpoints.

Transition from Skepticism to Idealism (1814–1817)

Maturation and experience slowly, almost imperceptibly, changed Shelley. His reading became more belletristic, including Wordsworth and Coleridge, and more inclined to the idealistic philosophers—Plato, Spinoza, and Berkeley. Leigh Hunt and Thomas Peacock encouraged his shift from a scientific and materialistic bent to literary and humanistic interests. His Alpine tour in 1816 stirred in him feelings akin to Wordsworth's Nature myth. Perhaps most of all, his first real encounters with misfortune and grief modified the youth's earlier loud avowal of pure reason and materialism.

Shelley began to recognize the reality of mystic experience and the genuine existence of mental and psychological phenomena that cannot be entirely dismissed as merely physical. His sweeping condemnations of religious faith cease; he is respectful to Christ, though profoundly distressed at how Christians have distorted or ignored the teachings of Christ. He conceives of a spirit of Nature similar to Wordsworth's "Presence." While still an unswerving opponent of priestcraft and kingship, he now realizes that the utopian age not only awaits the freedom of man and human reason, but also requires a thoroughgoing renovation of the human spirit.

Alastor, or, The Spirit of Solitude (*1815,* 1816) is a blank verse quest-romance, its title meaning "avenging demon" in Greek. Peacock suggested the fancy title, which seems only partially appropriate.

Leaving an alienated home behind him, the young, unnamed poet sets out to explore "Nature's most secret steps" to their ultimate sources. Oblivious to the Arab maiden in love with him, the poet experiences a vision of a veiled girl whose voice seems that of his own soul. Awaking, he seeks his ideal in vain, pursued by the avenging demon of his self-elected solitude. Prematurely aged, the poet is driven along in a boat until he dies on the threshold of a green recess.

This obviously autobiographical poem begins the formulation of Shelley's doctrine of love, which then gradually supersedes the doctrine of Necessity. It is a dream allegory of the poet's fate in the world. His scientific and philosophical studies have left him with a sense of isolation. In later Shelleyan terms, the poet's psyche imagines its ideal (epipsyche) and then yearns to possess the epipsyche; in Blakean terms, the girl of his dreams is his Emanation. The poet's roamings through the world in search of his epipsyche are in vain, because the vision, a voice from his own soul, can never be embodied. Shelley accurately diagnoses the ecstasy and inevitable tragedy of his own and all Romantic love: the lover rapturously conceives of the ideal beloved and ceaselessly searches the world for her, only to find that no real woman can long exemplify the perfection of his dream. The extensive nature descriptions here first display the typically Shelleyan characteristics, not of sensuous imagery, but of symbols of mental and emotional states.

"Hymn to Intellectual Beauty" (*1816*, 1817), finished just a few months after *Alastor,* indicates an emotional conversion to Platonic or neo-Platonic idealism, exorcising the *alastor* of despair. "Intellectual" in the title means "spiritual," "beyond the senses." Greatest indebtedness of the poem is to the Diotima of Mantinea passage in Plato's *Symposium.*

Stanza 1. Maintains that beauty is not in the object (early Wordsworth) or in the beholder (later Coleridge) but in the Platonic idea of beauty, a spiritual essence which momentarily touches the physical world and kindles it to loveliness.

Stanza 2. Poses the question why man is not granted the eternal presence of this unalloyed beauty; why instead he suffers from the oppressive dualities of "love and hate, despondency and hope." In life we perceive beauty always with "accidents" (philosophically, characteristics extraneous to the essence of an object).

Stanza 3. States that attempts by superstition and religion to explain the puzzling dichotomies of life universally fail. In the ensuing confusion, only the evanescent visits of Platonic beauty give "grace and truth" to appearances and solace man in his despair.

Stanza 4. The heart of the poem argues the philosophical logic of transitory beauty. If man lived eternally with the pure Ideal, he would be an immortal god with nothing to strive for. The point of life is the struggle for self-realization, with the glimpse of beauty offering to man the stimulus of "Love, Hope, and Self-esteem." The esteem is for the Creative Imagination, which is capable of forming the good and the true within every man.

Stanza 5. In boyhood the poet had sought ghostly revelations and had employed the familiar Christian exhortations, without avail. One spring, however, while "musing deeply on the lot/Of life," he had experienced the impact of the Platonic idea of beauty with all the force of a spiritual awakening.

Stanza 6. Henceforth the poet dedicates himself to this ideal spirit.

Stanza 7. States that this essential Spirit of Beauty will provide the dedicated poet with reverential awe for the Imagination ("to fear himself") and universal benevolence ("love all human kind").

"Mont Blanc" (1816, 1817) is the poet's attempt to convince himself philosophically of the Platonism emotionally espoused in the "Hymn." Materialistic Necessity still exercises its mental fascination upon him, but he is seeking an idealistic philosophy. The momentous queries of the poem consider the rule of the universe, the moral nature of the cosmos, and the interrelations between mind and the universe.

ll. 1–48 compare the flow of thought through the human mind to the flow of the Arve river through its ravine. As the river reflects the ravine but also adds splendor to it, so the mind receives impressions but also lends its own coloring to those impressions.

ll. 49–83 state that the lesson of the great mountain is that we are free to employ natural power as we will, for the power of good or evil resides solely within us. We may utilize the power for the freeing of man (like Byron) or for deep feeling of benevolence (like Wordsworth).

ll. 84–126 insist upon the impersonality of the secret power of the universe. Nature and the human imagination offer the potentials of both creation and destruction.

Lines 127 to conclusion provide the key for the later *Prometheus Unbound* and Shelley's vision of Nature. Denying Byron's egotistical imposition of his will upon Nature or the earlier Wordsworth's confidence in the ministry of Nature, Shelley sees the interaction between the phenomenal and the noumenal. The power of the universe offers both good and evil, but the free and creative mind of man can imaginatively operate to trigger the inevitable working-out of good.

A Proposal for Putting Reform to the Vote (1817) (P) suggests that the question of parliamentary reform be submitted to a plebiscite. If the majority of the populace supports reform, every effort should be made for its quick realization. If the majority disapproves, the reformers should accept the decision and work peacefully at education of the people. Shelley, now twenty-five, displays rapid maturation. Without renouncing his radical opinions, he has come to realize the slow process of improvement and the danger of chaos in sudden change. Most men, he recognizes, have been kept long in political infancy and must be carefully led to political maturity. Shelley envisages a republic, but here says nothing about the anarchism of *Queen Mab*.

An Address to the People on the Death of the Princess Charlotte (1817) (P) was occasioned by the simultaneous announcement in the newspapers of the death of the royal princess in childbirth and the execution of three weavers in Derby on a charge of insurrection. The killing of the three laborers was a blot upon the government, for they had been stirred up to protest by a government *agent provocateur*, who promptly informed upon them. Shelley calls upon his countrymen to mourn Charlotte's death but also to mourn the loss of English liberties. He denounces a society existing for the benefit of a few aristocrats at the price of unremitting poverty for most of the people. Particularly he deplores the "new aristocracy" with "its basis in funds" (i.e. investments in government bonds to carry the huge national debt). The first step to a just society is "a free representation of the people" in Parliament. Outside of *The Defense of Poetry,* this is Shelley's most eloquent prose.

Laon and Cythna; or, The Revolution of the Golden City (1817) was revised and reissued as *The Revolt of Islam* (1818). Chief source was an unpublished poem by Peacock, *Ahrimanes (1813–15),* also in Spenserian stanzas. In the preface Shelley insists that the poem "is narrative, not didactic"; its purpose is to arouse the reader to emulation of virtuous fighters for freedom. The verse dedication "To Mary" tells how his experience of schoolroom tyranny made him a spirit dedicated to human liberty; he had found a cold and brutal world almost too much to endure until Mary, "beautiful and calm and free," gave him her sympathy and understanding.

Canto I, as Shelley stated, is virtually a complete poem in itself.

"From visions of despair" the narrator witnesses an aerial struggle between an eagle and a serpent. The wounded serpent falls into the sea, to be rescued and cherished by a lovely woman. She bears serpent and narrator across the ocean to a temple of the Departed Great in which one throne is vacant. Both lady and serpent are transformed into a handsome man occupying the formerly vacant throne. The man then begins the tale of his divided existence (as Laon and Cythna) on earth as a martyred reformer.

Shelley evidently thinks of the universal moral struggle as Manichean (good versus evil). Like Blake, he reverses commonplace imagery to suggest that the serpent (also a familiar sexual symbol) is good, while the eagle is actually evil masquerading in the modern world as hallowed tradition and authority. The rescuing lady may be variously interpreted as the spirit of beauty, hope, or love. She bears the narrator (mankind in process of idealistic instruction) across the ocean of universal being to a spiritualized, intellectualized Valhalla. This hall of the immortals appears in Zoroastrianism (as the abode of Ahura-Mazda), in neo-Platonism, in Theosophy, and in other mystical writings. The man, the result of the fusing of the lady and the serpent, is a symbol from the unconscious, a fusion of male and female, as in Blake's Albion-Jerusalem, which will form the one human entity.

Canto II through stanza seventeen of Canto XII relate the adventures of Laon and Cythna in the struggle for human freedom. Laon and Cythna are sibling lovers, planning to advance with a great multitude upon the Golden City to institute reform. The tyrant Othman carries Cythna off to his harem and has Laon chained in a cage atop a high column. A hermit finally releases Laon, informing him that Cythna, by the power of noble words alone, had charmed Othman into freeing her, and then that her teachings of freedom, love, and equality had won all to her except for a small retinue about Othman. Laon hastens to join her, and both restrain the populace from destroying Othman. Appealing for foreign assistance, Othman leads a counterattack of alien soldiers which captures Cythna. Laon offers himself in Cythna's place on condition she be permitted to emigrate to America. However, she refuses to go, and joins him in martyrdom.

Canto XII from stanza eighteen to conclusion has the martyred pair reawaken to an after-life on a river bank from whence they embark upon the river to reach the Temple of the Spirit that appears at the beginning of the poem.

Cythna is the poem's real prop in both words and action. Laon's one deed is his sacrifice of himself for her, displaying a martyr complex, like his creator. Allegorically Cythna seems to represent Justice; Laon, Truth; Othman, Tyranny. The child of Laon and Cythna (dying of the plague and in spirit conducting their boat to the temple) apparently is Freedom. In this poem Shelley first develops the symbolism so pervasive in his later verse. Some suggested interpretations are:

Tower—outward-looking mind, receptive to sensations, working for benefit of others

Cave—inward-looking mind, contemplative, wrapped in self

Cloud and dew—fertility, enlightenment of mind and spirit

Fountain—creative power of the human mind to liberate and fertilize

Ocean—universal life, the great impulse of all living things

Human love—joining of the human soul with the eternal beauty of the Platonic One

Spring—sure prophecy of the new age of freedom and creativity

"Ozymandias" (1817, 1818) uses the Greek form of the name of the Egyptian pharaoh Rameses II, who, according to the ancient historian Diodorus Siculus, commanded the largest statue in Egypt to be carved in his image. Shelley's poem asserts the emptiness of tyranny and mere pomp. Though despots may revel in their power and their glory, these inevitably fade away. Although in fourteen lines with an octave and sestet pattern thematically, the poem employs a bizarre rime scheme (a b a b a c d c e d e f e f) quite alien to the conventional sonnet.

Platonic Idealism (1818–1821)

Shelley's reputation rests chiefly upon the writings of approximately three years in Italy, a productive effort almost without parallel in literature. Contemporary and subsequent critics have often tended, erroneously, to read into the works of this period the ideas and attitudes that Shelley had by this time abandoned. He must be judged by the intrinsic value of these mature writings. His interests have now turned wholly away from a materialistic determinism to a belief in human free will and the power of regenerated imagination to transform the world. Most important, of course, is his increased maturity as Shelley enters his late twenties. While still a fervent believer in man's progress toward a glorious future, he now sees social and political change as wholly gradual. Though seeking greater economic justice, in these later years he is no longer a socialist or a communist, and while zealously praising Periclean Athens for its superb cultural achievement, he nonetheless recognizes that Christian ideals have advanced civilization. Impatient still with priesthood and institutionalized religion, Shelley greatly admires Christ and proclaims the Bible the world's greatest piece of literature. Although he does not profess a belief in a Christian deity, he proclaims a Universal Spirit revealed as natural beauty and human love.

The Banquet (*1818*, 1840) (P), a translation of Plato's *Symposium*, occupied the early weeks of Shelley's residence in Italy. Though occasionally challengeable from a scholarly viewpoint, this is the most readable and appealing translation of the *Symposium* in English. Graceful, easy, and fluent, it sounds like an original. In the preface, Shelley's elevation of intuition over reason marks perhaps the most significant event in the poet's intellectual development. The poet also translated the *Ion* and portions of other Platonic dialogues.

"Lines Written among the Euganean Hills" (*1818*, 1819) has the writer standing high in the hills gazing upon distant Venice and the plain of Lombardy. The poem contrasts natural splendor with human degradation. Society, liberty, creativity, learning, and philosophy will not compensate for the sense of human pain and misery. Momentarily he falls back upon a Platonic sense of union with the all-encompassing spirit of the universe. Such union, however, he grasps intellectually, not emotionally, for the absence of love and friendship make him prophesy his own fate. In its fusion of precise observation, felicitous phrasing and word choice, depth of emotion and reflection, the real and the ideal, this work has been termed the first product of the poet's artistic maturity.

"Stanzas Written in Dejection, Near Naples" (*1818*, 1824) contrasts the sunny beauty of Nature with the poet's self-pitying despondency induced by ill health and low reputation.

"Sonnet: 'Lift not the painted veil'" (*1818*, 1824) is one of Shelley's best sonnets, though it uses an unconventional rime scheme (a b a b a b c d c d d e d e) and a thematic effect of an initial sestet followed by two quatrains. Likening life to a painted veil is a favorite Platonic image to Shelley. The pessimistic note sounds in his unsuccessful search for love and truth among men.

Julian and Maddalo (*1818*, 1824) purportedly records Shelley's association (Julian) with Byron (Maddalo). In spite of some magnificent poetry, much about the piece remains cryptic.

Julian and Maddalo ride on horseback along the Venetian sands at sunset and return after dark by gondola. The sight of a madhouse on an island and the clanging of its bell induce Maddalo to pessimistic statements about life, to which Julian vigorously replies with optimism. Maddalo conducts Julian to the madhouse to hear the ravings of a man deserted by his beloved.

Maddalo gloomily proclaims the futility of life, while Julian insists that the soul is free and creative. If we are underlings, "it is our will/ That thus enchains us." All evils besetting mankind exist only because we permit them to exist. The soliloquy of love-madness by the maniac is the most anguished of its type in English poetry and must certainly refer to a deep personal sense of desertion by the poet.

Prometheus Unbound (1818–19, 1820) (D) was the title poem of Shelley's 1820 volume, which, with its appended shorter poems, comprised the poet's greatest single volume and most of the poetry upon which his popular reputation is based. Shelley's own favorite work, this poem is generally regarded as his masterwork. It ranks with Milton's *Samson Agonistes* and Hardy's *Dynasts* as one of the greatest closet dramas in English.

Shelley was supplying for the modern world the lost play by Aeschylus that would follow *Prometheus Bound.* From ancient allusions it appears that the Athenian dramatist intended that Prometheus, chained to the Caucasus mountains for his impiety in bringing divine fire to mortals, would secure his release from Zeus-Jupiter by revealing the secret known only to Prometheus: the sea nymph Thetis would bear a son greater than his father. In his preface Shelley asserts: "I was averse from a catastrophe so feeble as that of reconciling the champion with the oppressor of mankind." As in the prophetic books of Blake, the reader striving for comprehension of *Prometheus Unbound* must realize that the entire dramatic action is completely internal, here within the mind and soul of collective mankind.

Act I begins with the setting that concludes Aeschylus's *Prometheus Bound,* but Shelley thinks of his drama as set today or tomorrow in the era of man's desire for freedom and love. Prometheus (free, creative human mind) recounts to Panthea (faith) and Ione (hope) his sufferings at the hands of Jupiter (tyranny) and his knowledge of the hour when the tyrant will fall. From any dramatic viewpoint, the climax has already occurred, because Prometheus through suffering has already lost hate; he now merely pities Jupiter. Prometheus summons the Phantasm of Jupiter to repeat the earlier curse of Prometheus against the tyrant. Prometheus now renounces the curse, and Earth (the limited commonplace viewpoint) believes incorrectly that its defender has thus capitulated. Mercury, messenger of Jupiter, appears with the Furies to demand from Prometheus the hour of Jupiter's dethronement. The Furies strive to break the titan's spirit by picturing the miseries of mankind (including the crucifixion of Christ and the debacle of the French Revolution) and by offering the ultimate disillusionment to an idealist in forcing him to witness the distortion of ideals to base ends. But the spirits of consolation suggest that evil is merely the occasion for greater efforts toward good. Prometheus endures without hate, and as dawn closes the act, Panthea goes to summon Asia (love) to join Prometheus.

Act II, Scene I, occurs in an Indian vale, where Asia, as the active principle of love, receives from Panthea the news of the titan's purging of hate from his heart. As the cradle of civilization, Asia represents pristine culture, uncontaminated by hate. Panthea accompanies Asia toward the cave of Demogorgon.

Act II, Scene II, in its forest scenery represents ordinary human experience, and the fawns represent simple naïve men who need leadership toward the higher life. Asia's passage here is through the sensuous world to the higher realm of Platonic beauty and truth.

Act II, Scene III, brings Asia to mountain heights representing exalted thought. She and Panthea are on the verge of confronting Demogorgon. The concluding song of the spirits has been termed the greatest Platonic lyric in English.

Act II, Scene IV, bears Asia to Demogorgon (Necessity) at the ultimate sources of existence. Demogorgon (the name is a medieval scribal error for Plato's *demiurgon,* "primal cause") is awakened to action by the power of love. Shelley here maintains that man is master of his own fate. When he wills to universal love, he triggers the action of Necessity, which will thereby bring the inevitable victory over evil and error. In a passage of notable poetic majesty, Demogorgon selects the hour at which Jupiter will fall.

Act II, Scene V, carries Asia toward union with Prometheus. Through the scene she becomes increasingly radiant, recognizable as Intellectual Beauty, the Life of Life.

Act III, Scene I, begins with Jupiter at his height of power and pride, confident of complete mastery over Prometheus through Demogorgon, his child by Thetis. Demogorgon, however, precipitately casts Jupiter down to destruction. Readers may be distressed at the apparently easy and hasty overpowering of the tyrant, but Shelley insists that the real ruler of the world is man, and whenever man collectively purges evil from his heart, evil immediately ceases to exist.

Act III, Scene II, presents the vision of Ocean (the universal life force) seeing the benefits to mankind in the overthrow of Jupiter.

Act III, Scene III, witnesses the liberation of Prometheus by Hercules (power). In union with Asia (love), Prometheus (free, creative human mind) starts the new Promethean age of perfection.

Act III, Scene IV, was originally intended as the conclusion of the drama. Tyranny is now incomprehensible, and free mankind inhabits a glorious world of peace and brotherhood. Love rules the heart of mankind altogether.

Act IV was an afterthought, a continued celebration of the Promethean age and man's right employment of his own faculties and the opportunities of the world. This act contains some of Shelley's most melodious and soaring lyricism.

ll. 1–183. Lyric prelude of Hours and Spirits, recounting the passing of the dead Hours, in which wretchedness prevailed, and heralding the wondrous achievement of future Hours.

ll. 184–318. Elaborate mechanisms bring in the Spirit of the Moon and the Spirit of the Earth. A ray of light from the forehead of Earth represents the new spirit of inquiry, revealing scientific truth instead of old superstitious error.

ll. 319–509. Earth and Moon ecstatically sing the interpenetration of the whole universe by love, which cures and vitalizes everything.

Lines 510 to end. Ascendancy of Demogorgon. Man's will has freed the world and determined its future course of love and beauty. The age of perfection does not mean an age of passivity but a continued dynamism of "Gentleness, Virtue, Wisdom, and Endurance" to insure the preservation of man's victory and to prevent any backsliding.

The central contention of *Prometheus Unbound* is that man is able to will his own destiny. The palladium of our rights and privileges reposes, not in documents or in organizations, but in the hearts of men. If men groan beneath tyranny, it is because mankind wills the acceptance of tyranny. The way to end evil is not by countering with violence but by suffusing the collective spirit of humanity with love. Although Shelley would never accept the Christian claim of man's helplessness save through the Redeemer, he states the Christian ethics with unparalleled eloquence and poetry. He denies the glib Romantic contention of "man's natural goodness"; man always possesses the potential to evil, but by an active assertion of love he can guide human destiny to righteousness.

Shelley conveys this theme by myth. The Promethean legend is seen as the contest of good versus evil. The solution lies in the sacrificial love motif of *The Revolt of Islam,* here carried to cosmic proportions, and the reunion of Prometheus and Asia likewise develops the Psyche-Epipsyche concept of *Alastor* to universal stature. The two themes are joined by Demogorgon, suggested not by any ancient mythology but by Boccaccio's fanciful *Genealogies of the Gods.* As in "Mont Blanc," Necessity is amoral but at the behest of creative, imaginative mankind.

The poetic effects of *Prometheus Unbound* that evoke a "spiritual" response from sensitive readers arise largely from the use of sensuous imagery as symbolic of mental processes. The poem's claim to lasting fame will rest upon the soaring, idealistic lyricism, especially in the stanzaic tributes to the free, creative spirit of man. Shelley employs a wide variety of stanzas with easy grace.

Included in the same volume with *Prometheus Unbound* are the following lyrics, among which are some of Shelley's most famous short poems.

"Ode to the West Wind" (*1819*) along with the two following poems represents Shelley's search in the physical world for reassuring analogies to substantiate his belief that regeneration follows destruction, that alteration does not mean obliteration, and that mankind should heed the prophetic voice of poets. Wind, cloud, and skylark are Shelleyan symbols for spirit freed from the clogs of the material. All three are appropriately light, ethereal, mobile, ready for a poet's animistic imagination.

In this poem Shelley employs *terza rima* to form a series of four tercets, concluding with a couplet; although the result is a stanza of fourteen lines, the effect is unlike any conventional sonnet. The five stanzas consider:

1. The wind carrying autumnal leaves and seeds, the promise of rebirth.

2. The effect of the wind upon cloud formation. Winter rains are a promise of fertility to return with the spring.

3. The effect of wind upon water. All life, in the sea as well as on the land, is touched with wintry torpor.

4. Union of all varied aspects of the wind, and desire that the poet might be lifted from "the thorns of life" as the wind lifts leaves.

5. A plea that with the strength of the wind the poet's prophecy of

reawakened earth and man's conquest of evil will be broadcast to mankind.

"The Cloud" (*1820*) employs accurate scientific observation to insist upon the essential unity amidst the seeming variety of the cloud, and the poem maintains also the eternality of the concept of the cloud. Behind the changing Many is the constant One, and behind the delusive appearance of the material is the eternal reality of the ideal. In succeeding stanzas Shelley considers: rain in summer, snow in winter, daytime clouds, nighttime clouds, unity of all cloud aspects, and the eternal Platonic idea of the cloud. The twelve-line stanza alternately rimes the even-numbered lines, while the odd-numbered lines use internal rime. Although some critics object to the resultant effect as monotonously repetitive, Shelley purposely employs this scheme to convey the ceaseless rhythm that binds together disparate events.

"To a Skylark" (*1820*) is appropriate to Shelley's symbolism, for the skylark is one of the few birds to sing in flight. This is probably Shelley's most popular poem.

Stanzas 1–3 describe the rapturous song heard from the unseen bird.

Stanzas 4–12 compare the disembodied beauty of the birdsong with many other natural and human examples of concealed loveliness.

Stanzas 13 to conclusion conceive of the lark as abstract beauty possessing the vision sublime denied to earthbound men but suggestively communicated to us by the lark. The poet seeks inspiration from this vision to reveal the ideal truth to mankind.

A famous anti-idealistic retort to this poem is stated by Rampion (D. H. Lawrence) in Aldous Huxley's *Point Counterpoint*. Shelley's poem uses a five-line stanza (a b a b b) of four trimeters with a concluding hexameter; the long concluding line effectively utters a sweeping lyric statement after the light tripping effect of the preceding lines.

"The Sensitive Plant" (*1820*) may properly be thought of as portraying the separation of Asia (love) from Prometheus (free, creative human mind) before Shelley's drama depicts their reunion. Even in their separation, however, the Platonic ideal assures their return together.

Part I somewhat resembles Erasmus Darwin's *Loves of the Plants*. In a garden, an "undefiled Paradise," exist numerous beautiful flowers. The Sensitive Plant possesses no beauty of its own, but it is intensely receptive to beauty and love.

Part II is devoted to the Lady of the garden. She bears off "into the rough woods far aloof" any intrusive ugliness or injury, and thus maintains the garden undefiled. When the Lady dies, weeds and noxious insects invade the garden, destroying the beautiful flowers and also the Sensitive Plant. The poem's conclusion reiterates Shelley's conviction that beauty cannot be destroyed, for beauty is an eternal idea unaffected by the change and destruction of material things.

The Lady obviously is love, and the Sensitive Plant a poet (the death of Keats a few months later must have seemed confirmation of Shelley's interpretation). Shelley sees sensitive people as doomed in a loveless world where only the tough and insensitive beings ("mandrakes, and toadstools, and docks, and darnels"), feeding solely on materialism, can survive.

"Ode to Liberty" (*1820*) is the best of Shelley's political poems. It was occasioned by the Spanish revolt in January 1820 under Colonel Rafael de Riego, who proclaimed the liberal constitution of 1812. Following Hobbes instead of Rousseau and the Romantics, Shelley sees the primitive "natural state" of man as brutish and bloody. Then he goes through a short history of the struggle between liberty and tyranny, touching on ancient Athens, and a few other precursors of liberty like Martin Luther and Milton. Finally, Shelley restates the cardinal points of *Prometheus Unbound;* man is the slave only of his own weakness; he can will to freedom and love, thereby uniting himself to the One, the ultimate cosmic power.

While preparing the poems for his 1820 volume, Shelley wrote several pieces aimed specifically at the current English political situation:

"The Masque of Anarchy" (*1819,* 1832) was occasioned by the "Peterloo Massacre" at Manchester. Although intended as popular verse for the masses, this work was not published until after the passage of the Reform Bill. These impassioned but hardly poetic tetrameter quatrains propose passive resistance by a united popular front. The first thirty-six stanzas picture a revised Four Horsemen of the Apocalypse—Murder, Fraud, Hypocrisy, and Anarchy. These depredators seek to enslave the people by masquerading as tradition and constituted authority. On the point of complete triumph they are confronted by Hope defended by Liberty. Revealed in their true hideousness, the villains beat a hasty retreat, and the remainder of the work calls for another Peterloo, where the united people will declare their independence and shame the forces of oppression into acceptance of the new era of freedom and brotherhood.

"Song to the Men of England" (*1819,* 1839), in the same stanza as the "Masque," vehemently calls for a boycott by the workers against the parasitic aristocrats. Although inferior poetry, it has a simple chanting quality that could have made it effective proletarian propaganda.

"England in 1819" (*1819*, 1839), ostensibly a sonnet, offers a bizarre rime scheme (a b a b a b c d c d e e f f). The first twelve lines angrily denounce current English conditions: a mad George III and a debauched regent (George IV in the next year), an oppressed people, an army used as a tool of tyranny, and a corrupt church and legislature. In the concluding couplet, Shelley prophesies the new and righteous era that should arise from this horror.

"Peter Bell the Third" (*1819*, 1837) attacks Wordsworth literarily, politically, and morally. Shelley himself dismissed the work as a "party squib."

Peter's self-reform was short-lived, and at his death he becomes a footman in Hell, "a city much like London." Among the infernal guests is a "subtle-souled psychologist" (Coleridge) whose example moves Peter to become a poet. Peter vociferously praises the Peterloo Massacre and all forms of Tory repression, but is so dull that he bores a sizable portion of the universe.

This is Shelley's *Vision of Judgment,* displaying surprising humor for the generally un-funny poet, but falling far short of Byron's satiric mastery. Peter Bell is Wordsworth himself, the former liberal now succumbed to the blandishments of reactionary patronage. Shelley genuinely admires the earlier Wordsworth, offering judicious praise, but he wickedly equates Wordsworth's diminution of power and effectiveness with his conversion to conservatism. He criticizes Wordsworth as lacking the imaginative self-projection necessary to a true poet, but his cruelest attack lies in his contention that Wordsworth actively supported the bloody acts of repression by the Tory government.

Oedipus Tyrannus, or Swell-foot the Tyrant (1820) (D) was suppressed after the sale of only seven copies. This mock drama, with ingenious analogies to the classic drama of Sophocles and with other ancient allusions, was a response to the unedifying spectacle of George IV seeking a divorce from Queen Caroline on the charge of adultery.

The obese Oedipus (George IV) refuses Whig pleas to feed the swinish multitude and orders mass castration. The situation appears dire to his ministers Purganax (Castlereagh) and Mammon (Liverpool) because of the prediction that Queen Iona Taurina will hunt down Oedipus with the assistance of her lean hogs. To prevent the Queen's action, the ministers call in the Leech, the Rat, and the Gadfly to concoct a poisonous brew in the Green Bag (the Gadfly is the Milan Commission, which, at the instigation of George IV, had assembled evidence about the Queen's adventures on the Continent and offered at the trial a mass of documents in a Green Bag). Just as the Green Bag is to dump its nauseous contents upon the Queen's head, the Spirit of Liberty snatches it from Purganax and spews it over Oedipus and his court, who are thereby transformed into wild animals. The lean hogs, devouring the food intended for Oedipus and his cronies, join the Queen in a hunt after the wild animals. The prophecy is fulfilled.

Although Queen Caroline was herself far from admirable, liberals of the time rallied to her cause against the despised George IV and his Tory administration. Shelley's obvious parable suggests that the starving masses will rise to take what is rightfully theirs and overthrow the tyranny oppressing them. As in all his political satires, Shelley is too terribly serious to be really amusing, and most critics have written this piece off as an unfortunate failure. Much of the imagery is extraordinarily clever, though it is lost upon those lacking a background in classical literature.

A Philosophical View of Reform (c. *1819,* 1920) (P) surprisingly displays a balanced and moderate attitude in contrast to the impassioned political verse of the same period.

Chapter I first traces the development of despotism in Church and State after the fall of Rome, and then the gradual rise of freedom. Shelley sees the Reformation and the Renaissance as providing the atmosphere for great English literature. By the Revolution of 1688 "The will of the People to change their government is an acknowledged right in the Constitution of England." Shelley maintains that philosophers and poets must create the stream of ideas to vitalize a people to progressive improvement.

Chapter II diagnoses the contemporary ills of English society as the imposition upon the working classes of two parasitic groups—the landed aristocracy and the new class of bondholders (both national debt and private investments). Both deprive the worker of his just sustenance, though Shelley is less caustic about the landed gentry. Specific reforms to be sought are: abolition of the national debt, elimination of a standing army, ending of titles and sinecures, inexpensive and rapid justice, equality of all religions, capital levies upon the well-to-do, and a more equitable distribution of the national wealth.

Chapter III posits an ultimate goal of universal freedom and equality, but Shelley proposes remarkably moderate steps immediately toward that goal. The disfranchisement of rotten boroughs is the first step, to be followed by gradual increase in suffrage; quite unlike the earlier flaming radical, Shelley now considers woman suffrage and universal suffrage as desirable measures but steps best postponed until the people are more politically mature. Thoroughly detesting war and any violence, Shelley seeks an education of the masses toward the day of their self-rule; he urges energetic use of all legal means to end reactionary oppression, and urges passive resistance to any display of force.

In many respects this is a prose *Prometheus Unbound,* sober, unpoetic, and practical. Shelley continues to base his proposal upon the freedom of man's will to elect the good and bring it to pass. The ideal society is a society of free men, each of whom has willed for right. Shelley thus reconciles his Romantic individualism with his mystic concept of the all-embracing One of the cosmos.

The Cenci (*1819,* 1820; first acted in 1886) (D) is life as it is instead of, as in *Prometheus Unbound,* life as it should be. As *Prometheus Unbound* was a study of moral reform, this is a study of moral deformity. Unlike *Prometheus Unbound,* this blank-verse play was definitely intended for public stage performance, and Shelley purposely tried to write dialogue that was at least theatrically realistic.

He wrote a tragedy, not a history, and therefore he took considerable liberties with the real-life Italian scandal of the 16th century on which the play is based. The dissolute Francesco Cenci was frequently fined by the Pope for his escapades in murder and sodomy. In 1595 he locked up his second wife, Lucretia, and his eighteen-year-old daughter, Beatrice (by his previous marriage), in the remote castle of Petrella. Chafing at her captivity, Beatrice wrote for help to friends in Rome, but she received nothing for her pains but a flogging from her father. Beatrice's lover, Olympio Calvetti, seneschal of the castle, killed the elder Cenci in 1598 with the connivance of Beatrice, her brother Giacomo, and her stepmother and flung his body from a balcony, simulating an accident. Marzio was his fellow murderer At the trial Beatrice's counsel accused the elder Cenci of incest. Olympio was murdered before he could be brought to justice, and at the order of the Pope, Beatrice, Lucretia, and Giacomo were executed in 1599

In Shelley's dramatic version, Count Cenci is a sadistic pervert who

gaily celebrates the death of two of his sons and makes improper advances to his pure and gentle daughter, Beatrice. She appeals in vain
for protection against her father; but the worldly prelate Orsino com-
plicates the problem by wanting her for himself. Miserably treated by
his father, Giacomo plots with Orsino to slay Cenci. Cenci rapes his
own daughter, who then hysterically plans her father's murder. Beatrice and Lucretia listen below as the hired killers, Olympio and
Marzio, kill Cenci. The papal legate Savella, bearing a warrant for
Cenci's arrest, discovers Beatrice paying off the killers. At the trial the
conspirators confess under torture, but Beatrice does not, for she considers herself innocent. Cardinal Camillo seeks clemency, but Pope
Clement VIII orders all involved to be executed, and Beatrice resolutely
goes to her death.

This has been termed the greatest verse drama in English since
Shakespeare. The influence of Shakespeare, Webster, and Middleton
is apparent, along with minor indebtedness to Calderón. Wordsworth
labeled Shelley's play "the greatest tragedy of the age," but the reviewers scorned it because it was by Shelley and treated of incest.
Victorian critics (except, of course, the most prudish) praised the
drama, but contemporary mores rendered the subject inappropriate for
performance until a private staging by the Shelley Society in 1886.
The later theater, shaped by Ibsen and Shaw, has generally shifted
popular taste from the Romantic and poetic drama; but there have been
several notable performances of *The Cenci* in this century, and even a
radio presentation in 1947 by the BBC.

Cenci is certainly one of the prime villains of drama, but unlike
most of the Elizabethans, Shelley carefully motivates his villain's enormities. The count is congenitally a sex pervert, reveling in sadistic
torture of others and finding most exquisite delight in afflicting supreme mental agony upon his victims. His insatiable appetites cost
money and drain him even further in the fines levied by the attentive
agents of the Pope; avariciously the count rejoices at the death of
his two sons, who will therefore make no further inroads on his fortune,
steals from his son Giacomo by trickery, and wishes to prevent Beatrice
from marrying, to avoid a dowry payment. In attacking Beatrice, he
also seeks vengeance against her dead mother; from experience with his
first wife, Cenci assumes that the most effective way to hurt a woman
and cow her is to overpower her sexually. Psychoanalysts have interpreted Cenci as Shelley's extreme father-hatred against Sir Timothy.

The role of Beatrice is one of the longest and greatest acting parts in

English for an actress. Her spiritual career is the exact antithesis of Prometheus in *Prometheus Unbound*. She begins in a state of saintly innocence and explores every avenue of defense against her father, and seeks also to evoke a righteous response within him, but the prolonged mental agony climaxed by the hideous assault transforms her into a vehicle of Vengeance. She is a victim of a society that is heedless of the pure of heart. Ironically, Cenci's stroke to assert final mastery over her is the very means of precipitating his downfall. Critics have taken exception to Beatrice's lies in the final act and her self-possession when fully confronted with her deeds. Shelley's purpose here was not so much to condone Beatrice as to demonstrate the inevitable corruption of purity by the repeated cruelty of social circumstances and unmitigated tyranny. Psychoanalysts suggest that Beatrice is unconsciously a self-portrait of the poet, another victim of cruel society.

Minor characters are less significant, but in Cardinal Camillo, the playwright sympathetically pictured the embodiment of judicial mercy, acting as a Greek chorus. Orsino is a shrewd touch thematically to complete the picture of the heartless, selfish world in which Beatrice is a pawn. Because he seeks Cenci's life for selfish gain and not as an escape from persecution, he is permitted to flee the country, not sharing in the somewhat clouded martyrdom of Beatrice and her family.

The Witch of Atlas (*1820,* 1824) has often puzzled Shelley's readers, who perhaps seek for too deep and solemn a purpose in a piece quickly dashed off in a light and mischievous spirit. The name apparently arises from the brief reference to "a priestess of the Massylian race" by Dido in the fourth book of Vergil's *Aeneid*. The tone derives from the pseudo-Homeric "Hymn to Mercury," which Shelley had translated into English *ottava rima* (the stanza of *The Witch*) just five weeks before; the Greek poem is merry and fantastic in recounting the cleverness of Hermes in stealing the cattle of Apollo and avoiding the punishment of Zeus.

Born of the Sun and one of the Atlantides (note Shelley's familiar symbolism of light and the water of universal life), the witch lives in a cave amidst the Atlas mountains. Lovely, gentle, and powerful, she attracts gods, men, and beasts to her marvelous storehouse of treasures. The Naiads, Hamadryads, and Oreads (spirits in natural objects such as streams and trees) would be her familiars, but she is immortal and each of them will eventually die. In a magic boat that can sail on air or water, the witch is conducted everywhere by a hermaphroditic pilot. Watching sleeping mortals, she sends helpful or imaginative dreams. At other times she plays merry pranks.

Among the longer poems by Shelley, this displays perhaps the richest and most graceful of consistent imagery and lyricism. Keats thought the witch was Beauty; others have interpreted her as Creative Imagination, Venus Genetrix, and even as the spirit of electricity. She seems definitely to be spiritualized love, eternal but lending beauty to mortals and the objects of time. She is certainly the utmost compound of grace and beauty, sympathy and wisdom. Perhaps the witch might be thought of as Asia before she meets Prometheus; she is the ideal of Love before it is personified in human flesh. Sexless herself, the witch creates in the hermaphrodite the perfect union of male and female. In this frank escapism to a dream world and dream symbolism, Shelley sought a respite from the real world that was increasingly pressing upon him.

Epipsychidion (*1821,* 1822) in title is a coined Greek wording to mean "this soul out of my soul," carrying on the psyche-epipsyche theme from *Alastor.* With the *Defence of Poetry* and *Adonais,* both completed soon thereafter, it forms a triad contemplating the process of creativity in the poet, the forces contributing to his achievement, and the forces corrupting and negating him.

This heroic-couplet poem arose from Shelley's profound sympathy for Teresa (known to the Shelleys as Emilia or Emily) Viviani, daughter of the governor of Pisa. Her stingy father had virtually imprisoned her at the convent of St. Anna in Pisa while seeking for her a husband who would ask no dowry. A beautiful nineteen-year-old brunette with some facility in writing poetry, she powerfully appealed to Shelley as the victim of parental tyranny. She extravagantly praised Shelley and fascinated him throughout the writing of *Epipsychidion,* but even before the publication of the poem, she disillusioned Shelley by meekly submitting to her father's choice of a husband. Shelley stated to the publisher that it was "a production of a portion of me already dead," and later he mused: "The person whom it celebrates was a cloud instead of a Juno."

ll. 1–245 celebrate the seraph-Emily as a "poor captive bird" behind "unfeeling bars." In mounting tribute Shelley sees her as "a Splendour leaving the third sphere pilotless" (i.e. she is the spirit of Venus, the *terzo ciel* of Dante). She is the incarnation of Intellectual Beauty which he had long sought.

ll. 246–387 begin with the cave image from Plato's *Republic.* The "shadows" glimpsed on the inner wall are usually interpreted: "true one"—Harriet Grove; Moon—Mary; Sun—Emilia; Comet—"Claire"

Clairmont. This section seems to start with strong autobiographical references, to proceed to Platonic implications and then to dwell especially upon astronomical conjectures. The Platonism seems based upon a threefold division of soul enunciated in Plato's *Phaedrus, Republic,* and *Timaeus:*

(1) Immortal spirit to which Shelley aspires. Emilia is the *anima* or epipsyche embodying this highest realm of the soul.

(2) Higher rational or mortal soul, which Shelley believes represented by Mary.

(3) Lower appetitive soul, apparently symbolized by "Claire."

ll. 388 to conclusion call upon Emilia to fly with the poet to a dream island in the Aegean, where "We shall be one spirit within two frames." This is generally accepted as a plea for a physical elopement, but some have considered it a metaphor for the communion of souls.

Epipsychidion is Shelley's *Vita Nuova,* like Dante's work celebrating the perfection of spiritual love and truth made manifest in a lovely Italian girl. Shelley sees Emilia as that portion of his inmost soul which forms part of the great world-soul. Like Dante's Beatrice, Emilia is as sexless as an angel, Love carried completely beyond the erotic to a purely spiritual and intellectual plane. This poem is an odyssey of the poetic soul, like *Alastor,* but here the dream girl (epipsyche, *anima*) has been found; spirtual love will provide the togetherness long sought by the poet; and poetic imagination is fired to full creativity.

A Defence of Poetry (*1820,* 1840) (P) was a retort to Thomas Love Peacock's *The Four Ages of Poetry* (see next chapter). Shelley planned the work in three parts. The first part, all that was written, considers general principles. The second and third parts were to apply these principles to a specific defense of contemporary poetry against hostile critics. From Plato's *Ion* and *Phaedrus* Shelley took the major contention that poets are possessed of a divine madness in which they are inspired prophets of eternal beauty and truth. From Sidney's *Apology for Poetry* he adopted the argument that poetry, by its esthetic and emotional appeal, is a far better moral teacher than the prosaic preacher or philosopher.

Shelley discriminates between reason, which analyzes and enumerates known things, and imagination, which acts upon known things to create a new synthesis. Poetic imagination breaks through the veil of the customary to reveal the infinite and eternal One. Poetry must give pleasure, but poetry need not be solely in the guise of verse. Poetry is the best moral teacher because it enlarges the mind and invests the commonplace with a spiritual aura.

Almost half the essay examines the course of Western literature in order to refute Peacock's claim of a consistent degeneration in letters. Shelley is a confident believer in progress. For a confirmed individualist, he remarkably interprets literature as a mirror of the taste and standards of an era. Although he ranks Homer as one of the world's greatest poets, he sees in the Homeric poems the glorification of many human actions that a more advanced age will deem vices. The poetry of Christian doctrine survived the dark ages to flower in the greater freedom and righteousness that produced Dante, and still further progress is shown in the spirit of Milton. Shelley contends that periods of liberalism and energy produce significant literature; thus periods deficient in great poetry should not criticize poets and poetry but rather look to their own total social improvement in order to provide the stimulating milieu for creative minds.

Poets should not yield to the prosaic reasoners, as Peacock contends. Man needs not only the factual contributions of the scientists but also "the poetry of life" to integrate all forms of knowledge and experience. Poetry produces "light and fire from those eternal regions where the owl-winged faculty of calculation dare not ever soar." The poet is the vehicle of an inspiration beyond his own control, and in an impassioned peroration Shelley concludes: "Poets are the unacknowledged legislators of the world."

Shelley's pronunciamento became the dominant 19th-century concept of the role of poetry, and Yeats in 1900 termed this "the profoundest essay on the foundation of poetry in English." The inevitable 20th-century reaction has patronized the purple passages of Shelley's rhetoric, and ridiculed the sentimentalism of his plea for love and benevolence, the absolute reliance upon the *furor poeticus* of inspiration, and especially his messianic complex about the prophet-poet.

However, Shelley has a telling explanation of poetry: "It compels us to feel that which we perceive, and to imagine that which we know." Perhaps his greatest realization, beyond that of his fellow Romantics, was the essential role of poetry in the total fabric of society; instead of the 18th-century artful polisher of phrases, the poet is an epitomizer of the age, its fullest, truest self-expression.

Adonais (1821), in Spenserian stanzas, ranks with Milton's *Lycidas* and Arnold's *Thyrsis* as one of the greatest pastoral elegies in English. Shelley modestly stated that this was "perhaps the least imperfect" of his compositions. The occasion was Keats's death from tuberculosis in Rome, February 23, 1821. The reader may logically assume from the poem that the two young men were close friends, but such an assumption would be erroneous. Shelley praised Keats as the "rival who will far surpass me," but he was judiciously critical of the younger poet's writings. Keats was cool in return, writing in somewhat condescending pity: "Poor Shelley, I think he has his Quota of good qualities." Shelley's monumental tribute arose from the sad contemplation of the death of youthful genius (Shelley, like Milton, also thought strongly about his own fate) and especially from the spectacle of a persecuted poet, for any victim of oppression received Shelley's vociferous support.

Analysis of Adonais

MYTHOLOGICAL BACKGROUND. The Aphrodite-Adonis legend, derived by the ancient Near East from the Mesopotamian Ishtar-Tammuz myth, is the underlying myth of the poem. The basic outline of the myth is: the immortal goddess of love, Aphrodite, is enamored with a mortal shepherd, the handsome Adonis. Fearing the jealously of her belligerent suitor, Ares (Mars), the goddess urges caution upon the youth as she is summoned away to the rites of some of her worshipers. The heedless youth goes hunting, only to be fatally wounded by a wild boar which has been set upon him by Ares. The goddess hastens back, in time only for a last kiss from her beloved Adonis. Mourners, chiefly fellow shepherds, arrive, and sub-deities offer their gentle ministrations. Aphrodite yearns for the resurrection of Adonis, one of the possibilities being metamorphosis into the anemone flower (ancient Greeks construed the markings upon this flower as the Greek letters for "woe"). Proserpine, goddess of the underworld ("the amorous Deep"), falls in love with Adonis and permits his reunion with Aphrodite on the earth's surface for only six months of the year (hence the application of the myth to the cycle of the seasons). All of these episodes appear in the elegy in modified form. Shelley alters the account to make the goddess, not the physical love of Cyprian (or Pandemic) Aphrodite, but, as permissible by ancient speculation, the spiritual love of Uranian (i.e. astronomical or heavenly) Aphrodite. Further to transcend the erotic element, Shelley makes Urania the mother rather than the sweetheart of the fallen youth. Milton, in Book VII of *Paradise Lost,* invoked Urania to guide him to the highest poetic effort. The name *Adonais* is a modification of *Adonis* perhaps for the long-drawn-out vocalic quality but also to assimilate the Hebrew *Adonai* ("Lord").

CONVENTIONS OF THE PASTORAL ELEGY. Shelly followed the structure made familiar in Bion's *Lament for Adonis* and Moschus's *Epitaph on Bion* (both in the *Greek Anthology*). The first thirty-seven stanzas are the lamentation for the dead youth, signified by the recurrent "Weep for Adonais." The last four lines of the twentieth stanza momentarily suggest consolation; although quickly muted, they provide a hint for the poem's conclusion. The change comes with stanza thirty-eight, and thereafter, in the pattern of the pastoral elegy, the poem sounds the note of joyous triumph over death: "He lives, he wakes."

CONTEMPORARY APPLICATION. Tribute is paid to Milton (another child of Urania) in stanza four, but most references are to circumstances surrounding the death of Keats:

(a) In the conventions of the pastoral elegy, as Moschus first applied them to Bion, the dead poet is referred to as a shepherd and his poems are therefore his flocks. The opening of stanza seventeen clearly refers to Keats's "Ode to a Nightingale." Stanza seven specifies Keats's death in Rome, and stanzas forty-nine and fifty indicate Keats's burial place in the Protestant Cemetery near the pyramidal tombstone of Caius Cestius.

(b) As Adonis was slain by the wild boar, Keats, as Shelley sees it, was slain by hostile reviewers. In a bitter parody of "Cock robin," Byron demanded "Who killed John Keats?" and pointed to the *Quarterly,* "So savage and Tartarly." In *Adonais,* Shelley searches for every vituperative epithet for the reviewers: cowardly bowman, blasting frost, envenomed serpent, "unpastured dragon," wolf, hound, raven, vulture, carrion kite. The angry accusations of Byron and Shelley popularized for the 19th century the erroneous sentimental belief that Keats died of chagrin from the adverse reviews; truthfully, although Keats was understandably irritated by hostile criticism, he died actually of tuberculosis. Shelley was much more sensitive to disapproval than was Keats. Shelley's tirades against the critics are wholly valid in the figurative sense that the hostility to genius and true art is a death principle in society.

(c) The "one" mentioned in stanza two cannot be identified but may be Henry Kirke White (1785–1806). The mourners for Adonais include Leigh Hunt, whom Shelley disliked but whom he generously praises highly for intimate friendship with and assistance to Keats. All the others are liberals also, but they are not close friends of the dead poet. The first mourner, Byron, here dramatically called "The Pilgrim of Eternity," actually uttered quite scornful remarks about Keats. In the same stanza appears Thomas Moore, whose fame was then high and whom Shelley honored as a supporter of the Irish against English tyranny. Like Byron, Moore never pretended the feelings ascribed to him.

ASSURANCE OF IMMORTALITY. After the lamentations opening the pastoral elegy, the conventional turn and conclusion insist: "He is not dead, he doth not sleep." From the Renaissance revival of the pastoral elegy onward, Western poets traditionally (as in Milton's *Lycidas*) based the consolation upon the Christian promise of immortality. Shelley is equally confident but ignores the orthodox Christian approach in favor of a series of hypotheses:

(a) The end of stanza twenty proposes a logical argument: since there is no death of the perception, there is no death of the perceiver. Shelley bases this contention upon the Newtonian law of the indestructibility of matter. The mind ("sword") is the one power to apprehend matter ("sheath"); if the physical is eternal, then the spirit in man which alone perceives that eternality must itself be eternal.

(b) The major doctrinal positions appear in four different claims of immortality. These move in successive stanzas from pagan myth through Platonic philosophy and pre-exilic Jewish concepts to essentially the Christian belief in personal immortality:

Stanza 42—Pantheistic absorption into the cycle of Nature. This theory is closest to the original Aphrodite-Adonis myth. The poetry of Keats is the music of reanimated Nature, and will continue to manifest itself in all things beautiful.

Stanza 43—Platonic absorption into the unitary essence of creative power. Keats is now part of the One, the spiritual reality which, impinging upon the world as stated in "Hymn to Intellectual Beauty," will continue to mold physical things into lovely forms.

Stanza 44—Immortality by contribution to the race. Apparently this was the ancient Jewish belief before the Babylonian captivity evoked the idea of personal immortality. The noble human spirit, though dead in the body, continues to quicken the living.

Stanzas 45–46—Individual immortality. Though without any appeal to Christian consolation, Shelley here suggests the survival of Keats as a personal entity in eternity along with other youthful poets (Chatterton, Sidney, Lucan), opponents of tyranny, who died prematurely.

(c) Perhaps the most famous expression of Platonism in English opens stanza fifty-two. The reference is to the cave image in Plato's *Republic*. Shelley ecstatically contemplates the union of Keats's soul with the

Essence of Absolute Beauty and Truth. The death of the poet is not extinction but a welcome escape from the clogs of earth to the everlasting glory of the One. So rapturously does Shelley celebrate the liberation of the poet's soul that life seems a paltry thing in comparison, and the last stanza of the poem breathes a death wish in the prophetic vision of Shelley's own death by drowning. Ironically, a volume of Keats's poems was upon Shelley's recovered body.

MAJOR SYMBOLISM. Shelley's chief assertion in *Adonais* is that poets are the bearers of light to the men of earth. In life Keats was an instrument of light; in death he becomes the agent of light. The first stanza ends with the labeling of Adonais as a light; the concluding stanza designates him as a star. Binding together this complex and richly textured poem is the star symbol, aided throughout the first thirty-seven stanzas by Urania (muse of astronomy) and allusions to fire and light (tapers, sun, lightning, etc.). In the victorious finale the soul of Adonais is an intense spiritual essence merged into the world-soul to be the guiding star for all mankind to come.

Hellas (*1821*, 1822) (D) was the last work of Shelley to be published during his lifetime. Though written as a drama, it is really an ode to liberty. By the poet's own admission, this is based upon the *Persae* of Aeschylus, but where the ancient dramatist gloried in notable Greek victories, Shelley, inspired by the Greek rebellion, looks to future victory.

In a fragmentary prologue, before the invisible One (God), Satan, Christ, and Mahomet contend for control of Greece. Sympathetically portrayed, Christ seeks a free and creative nation. In the drama proper the Turkish pasha, Mahmud, receives news of a "moral victory" of insurgent Greeks at the so-called "battle of Bucharest" and a limited Greek success in a small naval encounter at Nauplia. Ahasuerus ("Wandering Jew") substantiates the bad dreams of the pasha with visions of the downfall of Turkish tyranny. Reports, however, rejoice in the crushing of Greek resistance. The concluding semichoruses see the day of liberation as certain but far off.

Shelley prophesies the failure of the contemporary bid for Greek independence (he would have been exultant at the later disproof of his gloomy prediction), but he envisages the triumph of freedom at some distant time. Most famed from this work are the lyrics interspersed in the blank verse and concluding the drama; they rate among his most impassioned tributes to the free, creative mind.

Shelley's purpose in this work was threefold: (1) politically, to prop-agandize for the cause of Greek rebellion against the Turks; (2) ethically, to celebrate ancient Athens as a summit of human civilization and as a model for a new Athens of brotherhood and freedom; and (3) philosophically, to proclaim that the sole reality is thought, and that all else is a shadow of reality.

The Final Years (1821–1822)

The concluding months of Shelley's career hastened a process of disillusionment and despair about life already foreshadowed in the earlier poems of 1821. Approaching the age of thirty, the poet felt trapped and beaten. His personal affairs were tangled and unhappy, and the world had chosen to ignore or despise his attempts at social improvement. He was experiencing the imaginative crisis earlier suffered by Wordsworth and Coleridge, and he was losing the "vision splendid" of the Romantic Imagination. Gradually, like his predecessors, he realized that his reading of the world and of life had been purely a projection of himself, perhaps even a vain delusion. His mature reaction was no Byronic breast-beating but a sense of both profound regret and calm resolution. Browning was convinced that Shelley was on his way to full acceptance of Christianity, but sudden death ended his further development.

Short lyrics of exquisite beauty and pathos in the last few weeks of 1821 mark the departure of his transcendent faith. "Mutability" shows the unhappiness of awaking from dreams to the reality of life. "A Lament" upon the vanishing of imaginative joys has been termed by Lafcadio Hearn the most perfect lyricism in English verse. "Lines" (*1822*) significantly takes from Plato's *Phaedo* the skeptical argument by Simmias against the immortality of the human soul. "A Dirge" (*1822*) briefly but poignantly urges "Wail, for the world's wrong."

The last completed works by Shelley consist of love lyrics in 1822 to Jane Williams, wife of Edward Williams, with whom Shelley was soon to drown. Jane's effect on him was soothing and familiar, and these lyrics are Shelley's only verse in which he could deal with a sexual motif in level, even conversational tones. The best known is the charming "With a Guitar: To Jane," and probably the most finished is "Lines Written in the Bay of Lerici," in which Shelley tries, without complete success, to accept ordinary life as it is and to seek no dreams beyond. "The Magnetic Lady to Her Patient" pleasantly celebrates Jane's experiments in hypnotism ("animal magnetism").

The Triumph of Life (*1822,* 1824), 544 lines in *terza rima,* breaks off at the poet's death. Complete, this might well have proved to be

Shelley's greatest work, for it displays a detachment of manner, a sureness of phraseology, and an unexcited clarity never previously achieved in his verse. It is impossible to say exactly how Shelley intended to round out this fragment. It is even uncertain what his title means. Does *Triumph* mean "procession" (the etymological meaning) or "victory"? If "victory," then is it of the spiritual over the material, or of physical life over the imaginative hopes of man? Perhaps the extant portion is, like Act I of *Prometheus Unbound,* a rather gloomy preliminary to liberation and joy. However, coming after the disillusioned lyrics, the work is probably to be interpreted pessimistically.

The poet observes a nightmarish procession dominated by a coldly glaring chariot of worldly life. The deformed charioteer displays four faces, all blindfolded. Chained to the chariot are the great and the powerful. Youths and maidens dance ahead of the chariot, momentarily escaping worldly taint but eventually falling back under the chariot. Behind is a pathetic throng of oldsters straining after the chariot, which rapidly outdistances them. The specter of Rousseau points out notables in this parade of life ranging from Plato to Napoleon. Questioned by the poet, Rousseau recounts his own spiritual biography, concluding with the fading-away into the commonplace by his "Shape all light." Rousseau explains that the phantom procession consists of shadows of humankind made visible by the "creative ray" of the chariot. "Then what is life? I cried" as the poem is broken off.

The poem's title and the idea of the procession are derived from Petrarch's *Trionfo.* Meter is from Dante, and, in fact, this is Shelley's *Inferno* (perhaps also *Purgatorio,* since he would not accept the Catholic division of the after-world into three parts). The vision parodies the chariot of Ezekiel, but the chariot of life significantly has no beasts pulling it, for it moves solely by its internal force. The blindfolded cherubim negate the many-eyed figure of biblical origin, for the chariot's movement is without direction or purpose. Rousseau fulfills for Shelley the role of Vergil in Dante's *Commedia,* but the modern guide is a horrible example of the world's slow strain. The greatest despair sounds in the passage on Napoleon, where it is manifest that the Creator "made irreconcilable/Good and the means of good." Apparently the only proper responses to life are quietism or suicide. Life triumphs over Nature, even as Nature triumphs over the Romantic Imagination.

Perhaps a *Paradiso* was intended to swing the cycle to idealism and creativity, but like Coleridge in "Christabel," Shelley seems to have fallen into a despair from which no skylark or anything else could lift him.

Shelley's Letters

Mary Shelley's 1840 edition printed a large number of Shelley's letters, but many others appeared in scattered works during the later 19th century until the notable assembly in 1909 by Roger Ingpen. The Ingpen-Peck edition of 1926–30 seemed definitive, but additional letters were first printed in Shelley's *Lost Letters to Harriet* (1930) and *New Shelley Letters* (1948).

The greatest interest in Shelley's correspondence lies not so much in their intrinsic merit as letters but in their autobiographical value, for these letters are a strong and salutary correction to the average reader's concept of Shelley. The letters are cool and careful, seldom showing emotion. Rarely does Shelley deeply intrude himself, and when he discusses himself, he is surprisingly impersonal and unpretentious. The letters often display a jocularity and off-handedness for which the readers of his poetry are unprepared. In the letters to Ollier, his publisher, Shelley reveals a surprising businesslike manner. The letters from Italy to friends in England are replete with vivid descriptions of art treasures, and it is surprising to find that Shelley's artistic criticism is quite conventional. Smollett, of the preceding century, had demonstrated a far more independent approach to continental art and culture than does this "arch-Romantic." The lucidity and precision of Shelley's letters caused Matthew Arnold to say of them and of Shelley's essays that they might "finally come to stand higher than his poetry."

THE POETRY OF KEATS

John Keats (kēts) (1795–1821). Following is a list of the more important events in the life of John Keats.

1795: Born October 29 or 31 at Finsbury Pavement, Moorfields, London, eldest child of Thomas Keats, head ostler of John Jennings.

1803–11: Studied at the John Clarke school, Enfield. Avid reader. Formed lifelong friendship with his schoolmaster's son, Charles Cowden Clarke.

1810: Mother died of tuberculosis.

1811–15: Apprenticed to apothecary-surgeon Thomas Hammond, Edmonton. Introduced to the works of Spenser by Clarke and thereby inspired to poetry.

1815: Quarreled with Hammond; entered Guy's and St. Thomas's Hospital, London.

1816: First published poem, "Solitude," in Leigh Hunt's *Examiner*. Received certificate from Guy's and St. Thomas's Hospital, but abandoned medicine for poetry. Encouraged by Hunt and met Benjamin Robert Haydon, Hazlitt, Lamb, and Shelley.

1817: First volume of poetry coolly received. Moved about southern England writing extensively. In December participated at Haydon's residence in the "Immortal Dinner" with Lamb, Wordsworth, and others.

1818: Second volume of poetry denounced as "Cockney School of Poetry" by reviewers. During extensive walking tour of England, Scotland, and Ireland, displayed the first symptoms of tuberculosis. Brother Tom died of tuberculosis in December. Deeply in love with Fanny Brawne at end of year.

1819: Year started with despondency over family tragedy, personal ill health, financial difficulties, hopeless love for Fanny, and chagrin over reviews. Quarreled with Fanny, who played the coquette with his acquaintances. From April to September of this year he expended the greatest known six-month poetic effort in literature.

1820: Third volume of poetry received moderate success. Ordered by physicians to suspend work. Sailed with friend Severn in September for Italy in an attempt to regain health.

1821: Died from tuberculosis in Rome, February 23. Buried in Protestant Cemetery, Rome, near the marker of Caius Cestius. His own requested tombstone inscription reads: "Here lies one whose name was writ in water."

Although his name is frequently linked with that of Shelley and his remains are buried near the latter poet's grave, Keats in life went his independent way. He was touched with the liberal sentiments of the era but was never a Shelleyan rebel, never over-involved with metaphysics. Principally he was the poet of sensuous beauty. The problem that dominated his brief poetic career was a search for a reconciliation of the world's loveliness with its evanescence, its pain with its pleasure, its vulgarity with its delight. The result seems to many to be "pure poetry," and the entire later movement of "art for art's sake" may be traced to him. Keats often seems to be the first man to have looked upon the world's beauty, and certainly appears to be the first to experience it without preconceived notions, and as unalloyed esthetic experience may intuitively produce a spiritual consummation, Keats moves from a sensuous rapture to an undogmatic idealism. Of all the

Romantics, he has worn best, so that he now enjoys a higher reputation than any of his contemporary fellow Romantics.

First Volume of Poems

Poems, by John Keats (1817) is filled with youthful enthusiasm for various discoveries, chiefly Spenser's poetry, classic Greece, as seen through Renaissance enchantment, and Nature's beauty. Many of the poems use the "poetic diction" of the pre-Romantics.

"Imitation of Spenser" (*1812–13*), in Spenserian stanzas, is the earliest known poem by Keats. Source probably is the Bower of Bliss in Book II of *The Faerie Queene,* although the over-luxuriant phrasing is more reminiscent of the Spenserians (such as William Browne and the Fletchers) than of Spenser himself. It is certainly a commendable effort for a lad of seventeen.

"To One Who Has Been Long in City Pent" (*1816*) is the first notable sonnet by Keats, who was to prove one of the greatest sonneteers in English matched in his own age only by Wordsworth. He favored the Italian form, as he was influenced by Milton (the opening line here is lifted from *Paradise Lost* with only one word altered). The sonnet recounts the delight of a townsman in the lovely "Home Counties" about London. The "gentle tale" mentioned in the work is probably *Rimini,* by his friend Hunt.

"On First Looking into Chapman's Homer" (*1816*), another Italian sonnet, is the poet's first indisputably great poem. C. C. Clarke and Keats read George Chapman's Renaissance translation through an entire October night, and Keats produced the poem at breakfast (hence, perhaps, his excusable lapse of memory about Balboa from Robertson's history). Keats, who could not read Greek, had previously known the works of Homer only through the genteel Pope translation, and he was amazed at Chapman's virile rendering. In the first quatrain of his sonnet he indicates his wide reading of Western literature, and in the second quatrain he states how he accepted Homer's reputation solely on faith until stirred by Chapman's translation. The concluding sestet evokes the wonder of awesome discovery through powerful symbols: Herschel's telescope first finding Uranus, Balboa (not Cortez) expecting "big water" but not the stupendous spectacle of the planet's greatest ocean.

"Addressed to Haydon" (*1816*), an Italian sonnet, sees three men as the great spirits building a new age: Wordsworth is treated in the first quatrain, Hunt and Haydon in the second. Typical of Keats is his open-hearted praise of others and a minimizing of himself. The next-to-last line attempts a daring piece of metrics; the reader is expected to pause for enough silent beats to complete the iambic pentameter.

"Keen, Fitful Gusts" (*1816*), also an Italian sonnet, contrasts the autumnal cold with the warmth of friendship and literary ramblings (Milton and Petrarch) at Hunt's Hampstead cottage.

"I Stood Tip-Toe" (*1816*), in heroic couplets, is the record of an exciting country experience to a city youth. Frequent echoes of Hunt and boyishly sentimental references to Greek mythology cannot obliterate the pervasive sense of lovely stillness in what is often memorable phrasing. Keats feels that natural loveliness renders the poet oblivious of present reality, and in contemplation his imagination becomes free to soar in further creation of beauty.

"Sleep and Poetry" (*1816*), in heroic couplets, is Keats's first important poem beyond sonnet length. After a stimulating evening of literary discussion, he spent the night on a sofa in Hunt's cottage. Too excited to sleep, Keats determined to write a poem upon poetry. The pseudo-Chaucerian poem *The Floure and the Lefe* (which provided the motto) generally suggested the scheme of the work.

ll. 1–18 set the joys of sleep above many other delightful things, but

ll. 19–121 offer the even more glorious realm of poetry. Poetry can provide a powerfully erotic state of innocence and delight without any discordant note.

ll. 122–162 picture the poet as a virile young charioteer descending from the previous idyllic state of untrammeled imagination to the world of experience: "agonies, the strife/Of human hearts." The poet's achievement is here twofold: increasing the vivid sense of reality and experience, and also forcing a realization of the "muddy stream" of the everyday.

ll. 163–247 state the poetics of Keats. He ridicules Pope's poetry with its "rules," and maintains that poetry arises from Nature and the unconscious, and by imaginative power transcends normal human limitations to display the Apocalypse. Disinterested and undogmatic, poetry is the true revelation and consolation of life.

ll. 248 to conclusion state his dedication to poetry. Modestly he recognizes the enormity of the challenge, but he is consecrated to an expression that, beyond all else, embraces the full truth of man and life.

The poem as a whole is Keats's "Tintern Abbey," for in it he considers the nature of poetry and the imaginative development of the poet.

"On the Grasshopper and Cricket" (*1816*) was written in friendly sonnet competition with Leigh Hunt on December 30. His mentor's sonnet on the same subject is quite inferior to Keats's, which sees the grasshopper in summer and the cricket in winter as a pledge that "The poetry of earth is never dead."

"On Seeing the Elgin Marbles" (*1817*), an Italian sonnet, was occasioned by Keats's visit to the British Museum along with Haydon to see the Parthenon friezes which the British Ambassador Lord Elgin had recently shipped from Athens. In the consummate loveliness of the Elgin marbles the poet perceives the role of art in the identity of truth and beauty. Momentarily the observer of this art glimpses infinitude, the whole cycle of man and the cosmos, the meaning of existence.

Second Volume of Poems

Endymion: A Poetical Romance (*1817*, 1818) is the only completed long poem by Keats. It is an extended parable of the strivings of the soul for full communion with the essence of Beauty. The myth derives from the ancient Greek account of the nightly visits of the moon goddess Seléné to kiss her lover Endymion, the shepherd prince wrapped in everlasting sleep and everlasting youth upon Mt. Latmos under the spell of Zeus. Keats follows the idyllic mood of a Spenserian pastoral romance, but in distinctly Romantic fashion he makes the quest essentially internal. The chief influences on the work seem to be *The Faithful Shepherdess,* by John Fletcher, and *Man in the Moone,* by Michael Drayton.

Book I (The incitement to the quest for Beauty). During the Pan festival, Endymion, suffering from an unaccountable soul-sickness, falls into a trance from which he is revived by his sister Peona. In a dream vision he has soared with a female apparition of incomparable loveliness, and his heart is irremediably set upon eternal communion with her.

Book II (The quest of love surpassing all other human actions). Lost in an underground labyrinth, Endymion prays to Cynthia, not realizing that the moon goddess was his dream girl. He stumbles upon the Gardens of Adonis and witnesses Aphrodite's awakening of Adonis from his six-month slumber. Back in his own bower, Endymion sleeps in the arms of the unknown goddess. Again awake, he observes the plight of Arethusa, beloved of the pursuing Alpheus, and prays to Cynthia to give Arethusa her lover. For the first time he sympathizes with another's pangs.

Book III (The alchemy of fellowship and brotherhood). Bewitched by Circe, Glaucus under the waves is the custodian of all drowned lovers. Endymion releases Glaucus from his spell by the bond of friendship and revives the drowned lovers. Endymion swoons during a spectacular submarine pageant and is transported by the goddess back to his native Caria.

Book IV (The consummation in poetic truth). Endymion falls in love with an Indian maid taken from her native soil by a Bacchic procession. He now is tormented by a "triple soul," loving the earthly maiden, the unknown apparition in his dreams, and Cynthia. The contraries create in him the state of "negative capability" which Keats felt was the characteristic of the poet (that is, the ability to reconcile seeming opposites by perceiving them objectively). The Cave of Quietude into which Endymion plunges seems deathly isolation, but in reality it proves to be the abode of reconciliation of the opposites of life. All three of his loves prove to be the same. Had he only realized it, his earthly love, born of desire and nurtured with human pity and fellowship, was identical with his poetic aspiration and quest for Beauty. Poetry is thus the reconciliation of the real and the ideal, the material and the spiritual.

Endymion is Keats's *Alastor* brought to triumphant success. Through Nature and sensuous beauty the poet learns the love of man, but loving the reality of human life does not destroy the "vision splendid" and does not result in split confusion; rather, all the poet's drives and all humanity's purposes become fused and unified in the poetic vision. Though in rimed couplets, the poem daringly runs over lines completely, destroying the end-stop effect of heroic couplets. This rushing effect derives in part from Drayton's *Man in the Moone* and William Browne's *Britannia's Pastorals,* but chiefly from Hunt's influence. Beyond question, there is a great deal of sentimentalism, even mawkishness, in the poem, but these can be found along with passages of exquisite beauty. John Wilson Croker's blistering attacks in the *Quarterly Review* and probably Lockhart's in *Blackwood's* are the "herded wolves" excoriated by Shelley in *Adonais.*

Third Volume of Poems

Lamia, Isabella, The Eve of St. Agnes, and Other Poems (1820) is generally considered the greatest volume of poetry by any English poet, with the single exception of Shakespeare's sonnets. Except for a few sonnets, this volume contains virtually all the poetry upon which

Keats's reputation is based. So far as possible, the contents of this volume are treated in the order of their composition.

"Lines on the Mermaid Tavern" and "Robin Hood," both written early in 1818 in the seven-syllable line of John Fletcher and Ben Jonson, are graceful, spirited, and wholly English in sentiment. So likewise are heptasyllabic "Bards of Passion and of Mirth" and "Fancy," written in 1819. All, in the Elizabethan manner, evoke a charming nostalgia for the picturesque by-gone England.

"The Human Seasons" (*1818*) shows Keats's mastery of the English or Shakespearean sonnet. Each of the three quatrains considers a time of human life—spring, summer, autumn—to end impressively in the concluding couplet with life's winter.

"Isabella; or the Pot of Basil" (*1818*) in *ottava rima,* romantically embroiders a tale from Boccaccio, transferring the scene from the original Messina to Florence.

Secretly Isabella loves Lorenzo, one of the clerks of her greedy merchant-brothers. Learning of the blot on the family escutcheon, the brothers lure Lorenzo into the forest, where they kill and bury him. His ghost visits Isabella in a dream, revealing his fate and burial place. She exhumes the head of her dead lover, which she waters with her tears in a pot of basil until her brothers discover it. With the removal of the pot of basil, Isabella pines away to death.

Chaucer's *Troilus and Criseyde* furnished the techniques for telling the story, which include short digressions, apostrophes to the reader, and invocations to Love and the Muses. Following the ideas brought out in *Endymion,* Keats shows the triumph of love over horror, and makes into a thing of beauty what could have been a ghoulish Gothic tale. Stanzas fourteen to sixteen represent one of the few diatribes of Keats against mercantile exploiters of their fellow men. He regretted the sentimentalism of the love treatment and later called the poem "mawkish."

Hyperion (*1818–19*) is a blank-verse fragment of a projected epic. Keats broke off this poem early in 1819; late in the same year he tried again with *The Fall of Hyperion,* a shorter fragment remaining in manuscript form until 1856. Though owing a great deal to Dante, *Hyperion* is essentially Miltonic.

Book I begins with mighty Saturn in defeat and Hyperion's wife, Thea, seated at his feet. The two painfully move to the covert where the other titans languish after their downfall at the hands of Zeus and the new Olympian deities. Meanwhile, Hyperion, god of the sun, the only titan to continue his rule, feels ominous forebodings and descends to aid Saturn.

Book II parallels the second book of *Paradise Lost* in the debate of the fallen titans. Saturn wishes to resume war with the Olympians but does not know how. Oceanus preaches serene acceptance of their lot, and Clymene reports a new music from Apollo, destined to be the last of the new generation of gods. Enceladus calls for war, and the downhearted titans seek some encouragement from Hyperion's arrival.

Book III brings Mnemosyne as preceptress to Apollo. The fragment breaks off as Apollo undergoes the pangs of dying into godhood. Richard Woodhouse, friend of Keats, later stated that the poet intended to continue with the dethronement of Hyperion and the unsuccessful assault of the titans upon the entrenched Olympians, but it is possible to think that Keats had shaped virtually a complete poem at the breaking-off point.

The poem recounts the superseding of a good way of life by a better. The titans represent an older and cruder culture based upon Nature and natural powers. The Olympians represent a newer, superior culture enlightened by art and ethics. In complete independence of Shelley, Keats conceived of this paean to progress, the evolution of man's spirit from brute strength and imperfect knowledge to imaginative wisdom. Keats believed that perfect knowledge consisted of: (1) intuitive comprehension through disciplined imagination; and (2) contemplative calm, reconciling the contraries of life and rising above passions. With all his majesty and pathos, Saturn wholly lacks these prerequisites. Oceanus (who in Book II is spokesman for Keats in the poem's key passage) and Clymene have attained much of this wisdom but are incapable of applying it productively. Hyperion is the least deficient of the titans, and he is to be dethroned, not by greater physical beauty, but by superior Apollonian imaginative knowledge. Apollo possesses the intense yearning and the intuitive grasp missing in Hyperion. The birth of imaginative, divine wisdom in Apollo is agonizing, for such heights of perceptivity are reached only through suffering. Keats may well have broken off his poem because he felt that he had actually completed this statement of the Romantic poetics.

Shelley declared: "If the *Hyperion* be not grand poetry, none has been produced by our contemporaries." The poem may well be considered Keats's greatest achievement. He had succeeded in objectivizing an internal struggle—a rare achievement for a Romantic poet, and for himself. His characters display a human majesty different from the cosmic grandeur of Milton, but his titans are so magnificent that it would indeed be difficult for him to outdo them by subsequent pictures of Olympians. The blank verse is mature and powerful, with a consistent stately march probably unequaled since his time. Perhaps above all, the poem in its massive weight and calmness best exemplifies Keats's own insistence upon detachment ("negative capability") in the poet.

"The Eve of St. Agnes" (*1819*) is perhaps the most enchanting tale of romance in English verse. The story is derived from Boccaccio's *Il Filocolo,* and the legend about St. Agnes appears in one of Keats's favorite books, *The Anatomy of Melancholy,* by Burton. At the age of thirteen St. Agnes was condemned to be debauched and burned at the stake on January 21, 304, for her Christian beliefs and her refusal to marry a pagan Roman. Miraculously, her honor was preserved, although she suffered martyrdom. The saint thus became the patron of young girls and virgins. On the saint's eve, maidens who wished a dream vision of their future husbands were supposed to go to bed supperless and sleep supine. Traditionally, St. Agnes's Eve (January 20) was the coldest day of the year.

Stanzas 1–4 portray the bitter cold of St. Agnes's Eve, during which an aged beadsman says his prayers in the frigid medieval chapel and then goes to await death.

Stanzas 5–41 start with Madeline (Magdalen in manuscript) withdrawing from the wild revelry of the castle to sleep in expectation of her lover appearing in a vision. Porphyro (the name means "purple") stealthily enters the castle of his enemies and is secretly conducted to Madeline's chamber by the enfeebled Angela. He sets rare dainties before the maiden, and she awakes to see her lover in the flesh. Furtively they slip out of the castle.

Stanza 42 sends the lovers out into the storm, leaving Angela and the beadsman dead, while nightmarish dreams trouble the drunken slumber of the revelers.

The poem's outer frame is the chill of death and icy faith. The inner frame is the vulgar roistering and stupor of the castle rulers. At the poem's center, vividly contrasted with the frames of cold night and bestial excitement, is the warm, ecstatic beauty of young love. As in *Endymion,* the spiritual ideal of beauty is fused with physical reality, but here, because of the poet's recent and rapturous love for Fanny Brawne, it is fused with the sensual and sensuous triumph. In the presence of the sleeping Madeline, Porphyro grows faint, partly because of the courtly love convention, but particularly because of her symbolic spirituality, "so free from mortal taint." Awakening her, he vows that she is heaven to him and he is her hermit, a nice contrast with the heaven yearned for by the beadsman. She awakes from a dream of the ideal Porphyro to be confronted with the actual man, "how pallid, chill, and drear!" In the confrontation of the imagined and the real, her love is tested by this "painful change," but she embraces the actual ("Into her dream he melted").

Every reader has been enthralled by the rich, exotic foods that Porphyro sets before Madeline, but some critics surprisingly label the passage as interruptive or irrelevant. The whole point is the association of Eastern objects with eroticism and the lover's gift plus shared food as the lover's proffering of the physical and sexual world.

Not even Spenser himself could surpass the melodious phrasing and sensuous loveliness of these Spenserian stanzas. However, while Spenser's verse is chiefly addressed to sight, Keats directs his imagery fundamentally to touch (a sense significantly equated with sex by Blake). With the animistic power of a poet, Keats endows with life even the corbels supporting the roof of the banquet hall. Without a false or vulgar note, Keats achieves the apotheosis of the sensuous and the physical.

"La Belle Dame sans Merci" in its first version (*1819*) was not printed until 1888; this is usually the version now preferred. A second version (*1820*) appears in the third volume by Keats. In "The Eve of St. Agnes," Porphyro sang a piece bearing this title in stanza thirty-three, presumably the song by Alain Chartier, an early 15th-century French poet, translated supposedly by Chaucer. The Keats poem challenges Coleridge's "Rime of the Ancient Mariner" for rank as the greatest art ballad in English. The central concept springs from "Thomas the Rhymer" in the Scott collection. Medieval peasants believed that the eating of "fairy food" was to be snatched away from the land of the living, only to be returned after seven years with a profound distaste for the physical world. James Hogg's "Kilmeny" (1813) had emphasized the yearning desire of the bewitched creature to return to the lost fairy land. The Keats poem emphasizes the shock of the "Knight at Arms" upon return to earth after beguilement by "La belle dame." Stanzas five, six, and seven ascend Keats's ladder of glory in mounting succession: Nature, poetic song, love. In the "elfin grot" the knight momentarily achieved the vision splendid, but the cruel Lady does not sustain the vision, and he falls back to the troubled everyday world.

The fearful disillusionment after ecstatic joy certainly appears to have been influenced by Keats's feelings toward the coquettish Fanny Brawne. The poem follows the conventional five steps of medieval courtly love through (1) Le regard, (2) Le parler, (3) L'attouchement, or touch, (4) Le baiser, or kiss, but stops short of (5) Le don de merci. The poem may also be interpreted as the aching sense of deprivation and the descent to the commonplace after the joys of poetry, beauty, and romance. The magic quality of the verse is partly achieved by the hushed shortening of the last line of each ballad stanza from four to two accents. The pre-Raphaelite poets were especially enamored of this poem.

"Ode to Psyche" (*1819*) is the first of the great odes by Keats. Although stanzas are not uniform, they vary much less than those in the pseudo-Pindaric ode. Psyche (the soul) was a mortal transformed into a deity at the request of her divine lover, Eros. Since her deification was in late classic times, there were no temples specifically in her honor; therefore, as Keats stated, "I am more orthodox than to let a heathen goddess be so neglected." This goddess, the human-soul-in-love, may well dispense with the outward worship ironically deprecated in 11. 24–35; thereafter Keats promises the inner worship of the imagination. The poet is a priest of Psyche, creating an imaginary world as a sanctuary for the human soul. T. S. Eliot deems this the greatest ode by Keats.

"Ode on Melancholy" (*1819*) uses a stanza of iambic pentameter riming a b a b c d e c d e.

The first stanza scorns the conventional Gothic insignia of sorrow as too sentimental and cloying.

The second stanza suggests the paradox that the most exquisitely beautiful things of life are the truest source of melancholy because of their brevity.

The third stanza states the tragic vision of the contraries of experience. The greatest happiness inevitably carries with it the deepest of sorrow. To gain the fullest of humanity's joy, we must vigorously and fully plunge into life, at the same time accepting as a necessary consequence the completest pain.

Such resolute acceptance by Keats of the paradox of human life has made his spirit far more palatable than the anguished cries of the Byronic hero for pleasure without pain, joy without sorrow.

"Ode to a Nightingale" (*1819*) is probably the most famous ode in English. The stanzaic form is that of the "Ode on Melancholy" except for the substitution of a trimeter in the third line from the end of each stanza. The poem was occasioned by a nightingale singing near the Hampstead home of the poet's friend, Charles Brown, early on a May morning. The exquisite birdsong elicits the mingling of the two familiar contraries of Keats much like Tchaikovsky's romantic Sixth Symphony.

Stanza 1 pictures the poet, sick with tuberculosis and saddened by family tragedy, obsessed with the painful beauty of mortality, the mood of the "Ode on Melancholy."

Stanza 2 surges with the impulse to sensuous life, a counterpoint to the previous stanza.

Stanza 3 restates the sorrowful mood, re-emphasizing the mutability and pain of life.

Stanza 4 lifts higher and, at "Already with thee," enters the state of charged imaginative vision.

Stanza 5 is Keats's poetic paradise, where, sight denied, the poetic imagination creates, heightens, and vivifies the sensuous beauty of the world. The poet is identified with the bird, a supercharged participant in and maker of all things beautiful.

Stanza 6 reverts to the death wish. The birdsong is so painfully joyous (such paradoxical statements are typically Keatsian) that he wishes physical death at the moment rather than the falling-back into the life-in-death of the commonplace.

Stanza 7 soars to the lyric climax. The birdsong is immortal, the very universe of the poetic vision. But indissolubly linked to the rapture of this beauty is his own curse of mortality. Keats's relation to the world's beauty is like that of a mystic to the divine vision: the vision is achingly glorious because it transcends the everyday, and because the mystic and the poet are denied their wished-for fusion with the vision and are dropped back into the everyday world. Kipling has termed the two concluding lines of this stanza two of the five lines of pure poetic magic in literature (the other three, he asserted, are in Coleridge's "Kubla Khan").

Stanza 8 picks up the word "forlorn" ending the previous stanza to keynote the poet's return to the mundane. Keats is left musing still over contraries: is the poetic imagination an exaltation of experience or an evasion?

Allen Tate has declared that the ode "at least tries to say everything that poetry can say." The first three stanzas and the concluding stanza take place in the daylight of the material world, while the intervening stanzas seek to penetrate into the dark mystery (symbolized by both forest and night) of being. The torment of mortality is assuaged by the immortal ideal of beauty represented by the singing bird, but the mystery remains.

"Ode on a Grecian Urn" (*1819*) vies with the previous poem for the title of the most famous ode in English. No known urn of Greek antiquity contains the two scenes (marriage ritual and sacrificial procession) of the urn in the poem; in fact, it is rare for an ancient urn to contain more than one scene. Keats imagined his contrasting scenes from several sources: the Sosibios vase (there exists in his own hand a tracing of the print of this vase from the *Musée Napoléon,* a French art volume) with a ceremonial procession; the painting "Sacrifice to Apollo," by Claude Lorrain; the sacrificial procession in the Parthenon friezes; several Bacchanal paintings by Nicolas Poussin; and various British Museum vases, especially the Townley Vase. The stanzaic form is that of the "Ode on Melancholy."

The first three stanzas apparently picture the ritual of bridal pursuit in ancient Greek wedding ceremonies. This practice is a relic of the primitive marriage-by-capture, still retained vestigially after marriage-by-consent became general. "Heard melodies are sweet, but those unheard/Are sweeter" epitomizes the Romantic Imagination, to which fulfillment betrays the glorious potential. In its unchanging and immortal perfection, the art of the urn asserts its infinite superiority over the transient mortality of Nature.

The fourth stanza contrasts with the previous orgiastic scene a completely serene picture of an ancient religious procession proceeding to an altar of sacrifice. The comments on the hypothetical emptied village from which the worshipers came consider the limits of art. The sole reality of art rests in the eternal present. Art is a selective process, the creation not of all things but of the essences of all things. Matthew Arnold says of this stanza: . . . "as Greek as a thing from Homer or Theocritus; it is compared with the eye on the object, a radiancy and light clearness being added."

The concluding stanza triumphantly ends with one of the most famous and most misinterpreted lines in English poetry: "Beauty is truth, truth beauty." In the poem's frame of reference Keats is here talking about the power of imaginative art to seize the eternal essence of human experience. Such artistic imagination produces essential beauty and essential truth, which are the same. Through art the poet here is reconciled to the human situation as he is not in the other odes. He fully accepts the Romantic Imagination as producing all the vital answers man is capable of securing and all that he really finds necessary: "that is all/Ye know on earth, and all ye need to know."

"Ode on Indolence" (*1819*) employs the stanza of "Ode on Melancholy." The poet allegorizes Love, Ambition, and Poesy as three figures which he dismisses in favor of Indolence. The statement is ironic, as demonstrated by the concluding lines. He is dismissing what the popular mind means by love, ambition, and, especially, poetry. He is eschewing a sentimental, fallaciously embroidered poetry (perhaps that of Southey and Hunt) for the deep visions of truth and beauty. What the unperceptive deems indolence is true poetic meditation from whence shall emerge "the finer tone" (probably he was planning *The Fall of Hyperion,* composed a few weeks later).

"Lamia" (*1819*) in form is modeled after Dryden's *Fables* in technique and pace (heroic couplets diversified by triplets, alexandrines, and rounded paragraphs). The atmosphere derives from the charming Elizabethan concept of the ancient Greek world. The narrative follows the account in Burton's *Anatomy of Melancholy,* derived ultimately from the ancient Philostratus.

Claiming to be a bewitched woman, a snake (Lamia) persuades Apollo to transform her back into a woman. In love with the handsome Lycius, she bears him to her supposed palace in Corinth. At their wedding feast the young man's philosopher-tutor, Apollonius, appears and his clear eyes and analytical mind reveal all as an illusion. Lamia therefore vanishes and Lycius falls dead.

Lamia is a contrast of two views of life, the imaginative and the scientific (Apollonius is termed a "philosopher" because the word *scientist* had not yet been created). Lamia is an illusion dissipated by the coldly factual mind of Apollonius. She thus appears to be the personification of imagined beauty or poetry. Keats appeals to the reader to take sides with the imagined view of life against the scientific.

Unquestionably, Fanny Brawne is the chief model for Lamia. The poet was as passionately committed to Fanny as Lycius was to Lamia. Perhaps it is best to interpret the protest against science as really Keats's protest against his own rational judgment about Fanny. The poet knows in his inmost spirit that she is a frivolous coquette toying with his affections, but he bitterly refuses to face the truth and pleads for a continuation of his dream.

Less convincing is the interpretation of Apollonius as representing the reviewers, whose calculating and factual eyes would destroy the imaginative product of poetry.

Lycius seems to be Keats himself, especially in the dilemma of the outcome. Does Lycius die of grief because he now realizes the true identity of Lamia, or does he die simply because she is torn from him? It is bitterly ironic that Apollonius, in his well-intentioned efforts to help Lycius, is responsible for the youth's death. The poet's conclusion seems a pessimistic belief that imagination and stark reality can never be reconciled, and human tragedy inevitably accompanies their conflict.

"To Autumn" (1819) employs a slight modification of the stanza used in the great odes, iambic pentameter lines riming a b a b c d e c d d e. It has frequently been termed the most nearly perfect short poem in English. Some of this praise undoubtedly arises from the resolution of tensions and the beatific resignation of the poem.

The first stanza is opulent Spenserian sensuousness celebrating the pre-harvest ripeness.

The second stanza personifies autumn as a woman amidst the realized harvest. She is all languorous repose, full without satiety, calmly joyous in repletion.

The third stanza is post-harvest beauty awaiting winter without qualms. Unlike Shelley, ("Can spring be far behind?") Keats accepts the life of man exactly for what it is. The be-all and end-all of life is the living of it. Brief as he clearly knew his own lifespan to be, Keats saw his course not as a broken arc but as complete fulfillment, running its course to proper conclusion.

Poems Published Posthumously

First printed in *Life, Letters, and Literary Remains of John Keats* (1848), edited by R. Monckton Milnes (later Lord Houghton):

"When I have fears" (1818), perhaps his first employment of the Shakespearean sonnet, seems prophetic of Keats's early death. Poetry, imagination, and love seem his goals, but the concluding couplet bears him to that "negative capability" which will produce the greatest art. Note resemblance to "Ode on Indolence."

"Fragment of an Ode to Maia, Written on May Day, 1818," addressed to the mother of Hermes by Zeus, is in Keats the equivalent of William Collins's plea: "Revive the just designs of Greece." Classic scholars such as Matthew Arnold have noted that this cockney youth, untutored in Greek, sensed far more of the true classic spirit than many who were erudite in that language.

"The Eve of St. Mark" (*1819*), a fragmentary piece in octosyllabic couplets (his only attempt in this narrative form), does not follow the contemporary practice of Scott, Byron, or Coleridge, but looks backward to the style of Chaucer. By the time it breaks off in line 119, the fragment has pictured the maiden Bertha on a quiet Sunday evening reading from a wondrous (though hopelessly jumbled) medieval illuminated manuscript. Rossetti coupled this poem with "La Belle Dame sans Merci" as "the chastest and choicest example of Keats's maturing manner," and the work was markedly influential upon the entire pre-Raphaelite movement because of its simple yet evocative concrete imagery and medieval atmosphere (though Keats probably thought of Bertha as a contemporary of his).

"Bright Star" (*1819*), a Shakespearean sonnet, was long—but erroneously—considered his last sonnet. The first line is a prayer to possess eternity. The octave admires the eternally detached observation of life, but the sestet insists upon the poet's preference for an eternal commitment to life. Satisfied with the sensuous reality and asking no more, he yearns to fix and hold it forever. Though passionately expressed, the sonnet is not an outcry against the contraries of life but a lyric resolution of the "undescribable feud."

"Two Sonnets on Fame" (*1819*) calms the earlier ambition of Keats. He suggests that the poet should dedicate himself to art and to life, letting fame come if it will. The first sonnet is Shakespearean; the second has a Shakespearean effect but employs an Italian-type sestet rime scheme.

The Fanny poems consist of three pieces written in 1819: "Lines to Fanny," "Ode to Fanny," and "To Fanny." They are among the most agonized love poems in English. The poet is wracked by intense, perfervid love that he achingly realizes is hopeless because of his fatal illness and her coquetry.

Keats wrote three poetic dramas in 1819. The only complete one is *Otho the Great,* a five-act play replete with Shakespearean echoes, dealing with the revolt against the 10th-century Holy Roman Emperor, Otto I ("the Great"), by his son Ludolf and Duke Conrad of Lorraine. Keats's friend Charles Brown prepared the scenario, and the poet provided romantic blank verse; the characters, however, never quite come alive. *King Stephen,* subsequently undertaken by Keats on his own, is considerably more impressive, even in its mere three and a half scenes of the first act. The unfortunate 12th-century English monarch sounds like a real king in real difficulties. *The Cap and Bells, or The Jealousies* incredibly attempts to use the Spenserian stanza for a drama, a light, fragmentary *jeu d'esprit* about an Indian "faery" emperor, Elfinan, who is in love with an English girl, Bertha Pearl, but who is forced by political considerations to seek "faery" princess Bellanaine, who actually loves an English lad named Hubert. The purpose seems to be satire on the marital quarrels of the Prince Regent. Keats tries partly to copy *Don Juan,* but he is no Byron.

First printed by Milnes in *Bibliographical and Historical Miscellanies* (1856):

The Fall of Hyperion. A Dream (*1819*), a blank verse fragment of 529 lines, was long thought to have been a preliminary draft of *Hyperion,* but it is now accepted as a later revision. Not a mere rewrite, this is a completely different poem, concerned with the true functions of a poet and his proper attitude toward mankind. Apparently Keats is reinterpreting the deification of Apollo to see it as the maturing of the poetic spirit within himself.

The poet begins in the sumptuous garden of youthful sensuous delight, where he drinks the enchanted draught of poetry. He passes through the temple of knowledge, art, and philosophy, which appeals to the intellect, and approaches the altar of true poetry. Here the goddess Moneta (actually a Roman epithet of Juno, meaning "Warner" or "Adviser") reveals the secret of true poetry—sympathy and solace for human suffering. Keats unnecessarily condemns himself as having been previously a mere self-indulgent lover of the sensuous, and he pictures the fearful agonies of the truly consecrated poet. After this prelude, Moneta presents the vision of the fall of Hyperion, beautiful in power, before Apollo, beautiful in enlightened participation in and love for all human experience.

Dante is the greatest poetic influence upon this version. If complete, this might have proved to be Keats's *Prelude*. It details the successive steps in the development of the poet, and, by implication, the process of maturation in every person. Keats sees all the old faiths and myths as inadequate, and poetic imagination as the basis for a new faith (as Matthew Arnold was later to suggest). The new faith to be built by poetry is based fully and solely upon the actuality of life. The key passage consists of ll. 256–271 in Canto I, in which the countenance of Moneta, eternity beyond all the contraries perplexing Keats, calmly reconciles the poet to all existence and all non-existence.

Keats's Letters

Milnes's 1848 publication was the first to carry Keats's correspondence. The elder and younger Forman spent two lifetimes largely upon the editing of Keats's letters, beginning with the edition of 1895 and offering additions and revisions up to the present, to achieve one of the most complete and carefully edited collections of correspondence by any figure in literary history. The letters reveal far beyond the poems a warm family relationship, a strong political interest, and an engaging sense of humor. Of greatest interest is their depiction of: Keats in his love for Fanny Brawne, and, more importantly, Keats as critic.

The love letters to Fanny Brawne are perhaps the most passionate in all literature. Arnold regretted them as "the abandonment of all reticence and dignity, of the merely sensuous man, of the man 'who is passion's slave.'" Others consider them the frankest and most impressive opening of a lover's heart in all writing.

In letters to his friends and publishers, Keats expounded his poetics as he never did in any formal prose treatise (of course, much of his verse is concerned with the nature and role of poetry). Keats leaned heavily upon the ideas of Wordsworth and Hazlitt, but his expressions are powerfully original. He denied both the earlier 18th-century concept of intellectual and didactic purpose in poetry, and later 19th-century "art for art's sake." Poetry, he asserted, must come as "naturally as the leaves of a tree." To Keats, poetry was self-expression, the revelation not of moral precepts or abstract ideas but of personal feeling. The "genius of poetry must work out its own salvation in a man: it cannot be matured by law and precept, but by sensation and watchfulness in itself. That which is creative must create itself."

The most impressive and most important statements in Keats's letters concern "negative capability," his insistence upon impersonality in the poet. The poetic character "has no self—it is everything and nothing." In contrast with most of his fellow Romantics, Keats was therefore the avowed champion of "pure poetry" by the completely uncommitted poet. He conceived of "negative capability" as the state of "being in uncertainties, mysteries, doubts, without any irritable reaching after fact and reason." Shakespeare, he felt, best exemplified this poetic role and thereby achieved the supreme position as a poet. "Shakespeare was the only lonely and perfectly happy creature God ever formed."

Imaginative intensity is his criterion for the effect of great poetry.

Rarely in his letters does he express Platonism, but memorable is his early statement (November 22, 1817) that "what the Imagination seizes as Beauty must be Truth," anticipating the concluding lines of the "Ode on a Grecian Urn."

LESSER ROMANTIC POETS OF THE PERIOD

Leigh Hunt (real name **James Henry Leigh Hunt**) (1784–1859). Born at Southgate, Middlesex, of a West Indian cleric father and a Philadelphia Quaker mother, Leigh Hunt was educated at Christ's Hospital. In 1808 he and his brother John established *The Examiner,* a radical weekly newspaper that gained a wide audience. His attacks in this publication on the licentious Prince Regent caused his imprisonment for two years (1813–15). He was widely hailed as a martyr by young liberals, though his incarceration was not uncomfortable. After his release, he was the notable encourager of Keats. In 1821 he went to Italy to edit the short-lived *Liberal* with the support of Shelley and Byron. Back in England in 1825, he published *Lord Byron and Some of His Contemporaries* (1828), which alienated many of his acquaintances because of its lack of propriety and its recriminations against Byron. Hunt is caricatured by Dickens in *Bleak House* as Harold Skimpole, a selfish, sentimental esthete. Hunt wrote voluminously, always with talent, never with genius.

POETRY. *The Story of Rimini* (1816), written during his imprisonment, is his best sustained effort in verse. The account elaborately details the Paolo and Francesca love affair, hauntingly recounted in the fifth canto of Dante's *Inferno.* Hunt proved one of the most vigorous supporters of Italian literature in England. Though often deficient in taste and sometimes horribly banal, this poem is full of Romantic beauty. It influenced the greater narrative poetry of Keats in subject, tone, and especially in the run-over of lines in rimed couplets.

Actually Hunt's poetic ability appears best in short pieces. "The Nile" (1818), a sonnet written in competition with Keats, surpasses in its majestic contemplation the sonnet on the same subject written by the younger poet. The charming "Rondeau" (1838) is ascribed to a kiss given Hunt by Jane Carlyle when Hunt announced a publisher for Carlyle's *Frederick the Great.* Generations have recited "Abou Ben Adhem" (1838), based upon an anecdote in D'Herbelot's *Bibliothèque Orientale* (1697); upon Hunt's tombstone is inscribed a line from this poem: "Write me as one that loves his fellow man."

PROSE. As an essayist Hunt is somewhat reminiscent of Steele but without the thoroughly engaging personality of his predecessor. His subjects are haphazard: shaking hands, the Italian poet Pulci, dolphins, Lady Godiva, etc. The style is loose, without incisiveness or the true excitement of discovery.

As a critic Hunt was notable in his day, especially in his scrutiny of contemporary drama, and he was one of the first to recognize the genius of Shelley and Keats.

Autobiography (1850) is the one significant book by Hunt. Although never deeply perceptive, it offers extensive and revealing pictures of the English literary world in the first half of the century, mellowed by the author's advancing years. Even the atrabilious Carlyle was highly impressed by this work.

Charles Wolfe (1791–1823). Educated at Trinity College in his native Dublin, Charles Wolfe served as curate in Down for the Church of Ireland (Protestant) until his death after prolonged illness. He is remembered essentially for but one poem:

"The Burial of Sir John Moore at Corunna" (*1816,* 1817) was derived from Southey's prose account of the 1809 burying of the British commander against the French in Spain. In a *tour de force* Wolfe achieves a remarkably solemn and meditative quality in anapests (4a 3b 4a 3b).

Ebenezer Elliott (1781–1849). A native of Masborough, Yorkshire, Elliott failed in the iron business of Rotherham in 1815–16. Ascribing all political and economic ills to the Corn Laws (which placed high tariffs on grain imports for the protection of domestic agriculture), he vehemently supported Free Trade. *Corn-Law Rhymes* (1830) impressed Wordsworth, Bulwer-Lytton, and Carlyle. Elliott was labeled "The Corn-Law Rhymer" and equated with Crabbe and Burns. These verses display all the emotional intensity and radical enthusiasm associated with Romanticism, but, lacking art, they died with their cause in the repeal of the Corn Laws (1846).

Allan Cunningham (1784–1842). Born at Keir, Dumfriesshire, Scotland, Cunningham was apprenticed to a stone mason but quit this work in 1810 to be a London reporter for the *Literary Gazette.* From 1814 until his death he was secretary to the sculptor Sir Francis Chantrey. He wrote extensively, bringing out plays, novels, and biographies. His verse appears in Scots dialect as well as in standard English, and his notable poetry is almost entirely a product of the Romantic fascination with balladry. Today he is remembered for one poem, "A Wet Sheet and a Flowing Sea," published in *The Songs of Scotland, Ancient and Modern* (1825). This is perhaps as stirring and dashing as any sea verse in English.

John Clare (1793–1864). Son of a Helpston, Northamptonshire, farm laborer, John Clare drifted from one menial job to another: herder, gardener, lime burner, militiaman, hobo, and farmhand. Frail in body and sensitive in nature, Clare took refuge from a harsh environment in insanity. During his confinement in a Northampton asylum from 1837 until his death, he continued to write poetry in the intervals between his madness. Much of his verse still remains in manuscript, and the real scope of his work has been realized only in this century.

Before his madness Clare published four volumes of poetry. The first, *Poems Descriptive of Rural Life and Scenery* (1820), quickly went through three editions, established him as "the Northamptonshire peasant poet," and carried him to London to meet Coleridge, Darley, De Quincey, and Lamb. The failure of succeeding volumes caused his name to be forgotten. These early poems delight with Romantic description of Nature—simple, unpretentious, full of sharp observation and tellingly appropriate dialectal terms. It seems the sort of poetry Wordsworth wanted to write but did not. In "The Eternity of Nature" (1835), Clare says of the living things about him: "Nature is their soul, to whom all clings/Of fair or beautiful in lasting things." Poetry, recording this truth, offers a vital therapy: "to all minds it gives the dower/Of self-creating joy" ("Pastoral Poesy," c. *1825*).

Much of Clare's verse was first published in this century in the years 1920, 1924, and 1935. Startling to the public were the previously unknown poems written during his madness. These revealed a hitherto unsuspected lyricism in the poet, apparently released by his derangement. Clare was haunted by the memory of Mary Joyce, a childhood sweetheart long since dead, and scores of simple, delicate lyrics sing of his yearning for a lost and unattainable love. Perhaps as beautiful and compelling as any verse by the Romantics are three poems, c. *1844*, upon the Romantic Imagination: "An Invite to Eternity," "I Am," and "A Vision." From the latter, the lines "Till loveliness and I did grow/The bard of immortality" tell of the triumphant escape from Nature and everything material to a realm of unsullied creative imagination.

George Darley (1795–1846). A Dubliner by birth, Darley was for a long time on the staff of the *London Magazine*. In the 1820's, when poetry was languishing, many saw him as the new luminary; but although Darley always seemed on the verge of greatness, exasperatingly he never attained it. On one hand he harks back to the Elizabethans in cadence and feeling, while on the other he anticipates the later symbolists in his use of specific symbols to suggest abstract ideas. In 1906 Robert Bridges attempted a resurrection of Darley's reputation, chiefly on the basis of:

Nepenthe (1839) is a tormented dream in octosyllabics, with interspersed lyrics. In the first canto the poet witnesses the rebirth of the phoenix and begins a quest for nepenthe, the elixir of life and poetry. He soars to ecstatic bliss but is plunged into a deep sea grave. The second canto is dark with wild terrors until the poet encounters the unicorn of purgation, to end calmly upon the shores of the wide sea of life. The poem may be interpreted as a manic-depressive cycle or, not contradictorily, the poetic quest of *Alastor* and *Endymion* by the Romantic.

Hartley Coleridge (1796–1849). The eldest son of Samuel Taylor Coleridge, Hartley Coleridge was born at Clevedon. He was expelled from Oxford for intemperance. Unsuccessful in teaching and writing, he wandered about the Lake Country until his death at Grasmere. This is the child for whom the elder Coleridge held high hopes, but by Hartley's own admission, "I am one of the small poets." Nonetheless, he achieved distinction in the sonnet, ranking as the best in this genre between Wordsworth and Rossetti. Typical is the sonnet "Hast Thou Not Seen an Aged Rifted Tower" (1851), plaintively ruing his premature aging in a background of Romantic symbols of Nature and Gothic ruins.

William Motherwell (1797–1835). A Glasgow native, William Motherwell worked competently in contemporary themes in Scots verse and in medieval Scandinavian themes in standard English. He is remembered chiefly for one poem, "Jeanie Morrison" (1832), a tribute in Scots to a childhood sweetheart. Like Cunningham, he demonstrates how Scots poets after Hogg generally abandoned the tradition of native verse and emulated the English Romantics even when they were writing the broadest Lollans.

Thomas Hood (1799–1845). A native Londoner, trained as an engraver, Thomas Hood turned to writing because of ill health. As editor for several magazines, he became the friend of many writers, including Hazlitt, De Quincey, and Lamb. To make a living, Hood largely expended his poetic effort upon comic verse, most of which later generations have neglected as mere facetiousness. Much of his serious verse (e.g. "Fair Ines" and "I Remember, I Remember") is cloyingly sentimental, vastly appealing to much of the 19th century but ignored now.

Hood wanted to base his reputation upon poems of social protest. "The Song of the Shirt," on evils of labor conditions, first appeared in the Christmas 1843 issue of *Punch* (then a crusading publication) and quickly trebled the magazine's circulation. By his own wish, Hood's monument bears the inscription: "He sang the 'Song of the Shirt.'" Such verse, however, has largely gone the way of Ebenezer Elliott's.

If Hood is remembered, it will probably be for several narrative poems strongly resembling those of Keats and the Elizabethan Ovidians. Best of these is *Hero and Leander* (1827), in iambic pentameter riming a b a b c c, which relates the famous story of Leander drowning while swimming the Hellespont to his beloved, but adds Hood's own variation of Scylla, a sea nymph, bearing off the drowned youth. Although he never lived up to his promise, he and Beddoes may well be termed the best English poets between the early Romantics and Tennyson.

Thomas Lovell Beddoes (1803–1849). Born at Clifton, son of an eminent physician (counting Wordsworth, Coleridge, and Southey among his patients) and a mother who was the sister of Maria Edgeworth, Thomas Lovell Beddoes proved to be a boy genius, publishing remarkable works, *The Improvisatore* and *The Bride's Tragedy,* while still an Oxford undergraduate. In 1825 he went to Germany to study medicine but frequently associated himself with liberal agitators. Except for brief visits to England, he resided on the Continent until his suicide in Basel, Switzerland. After his literary triumphs in college, Beddoes published practically nothing for the rest of his life.

Darley acclaimed Beddoes as "a scion worthy of the stock from which Shakespeare and Marlow sprung," and Lytton Strachey was later to exalt him as "last of the Elizabethans." Perhaps no other significant English poet except Donne has been so preoccupied with death. Perhaps Beddoes's scientific training made him perceive further that the whole world is a charnel house with momentary life feeding upon virtually an eternity of death. However, in true Romantic fashion, he believed in a supreme spirit of man that could not be extinguished. To Beddoes, suicide was an act of faith which freed him from the morbid fetters of the physical. In his work, he constantly revised and discarded, and the results are some titanic fragments of long works and a few short lyrics that rate with the best in the language. "Poor Old Pilgrim Misery" (1822), "How Many Times Do I Love Thee, Dear"

(1851), and "Dream-Pedlary" (1851) display the exquisite dream world of the most delicate Romanticism, while consummate in their metrical skill.

Death's Jest-Book, or The Fool's Tragedy, begun in 1825, was worked upon for the rest of the poet's life but still remained unfinished in its 1850 publication. The work in form is a Jacobean revenge tragedy resembling the plays of Webster and Tourneur. It is set in an imaginary 13th-century court of the German Duke of Münsterberg. Some of the blank verse has a biting power almost unknown since the Renaissance tragedy. Most notable are the interspersed lyrics, ranging from the hauntingly beautiful ("If Thou Wilt Ease Thine Heart") to the disturbingly macabre ("Old Adam, the Carrion Crow"). This is perhaps the most heady witch's brew ever concocted by English Romanticism. Landor declared: "Nearly two centuries have elapsed since a work of the same wealth of genius as *Death's Jest-Book* was given to the world."

Richard Henry (or **Hengist**) **Horne** (1803–1884). A native Londoner, Richard Henry Horne lived a varied and adventurous life that Scott would have envied. As a boy he reputedly threw snowballs at Keats. He fought and won a life-and-death struggle with a shark off the coast of Mexico. He explored wild areas of the United States and Australia, serving in the latter country as commissioner for crown lands, 1852–69. He collaborated with Elizabeth Browning (then Miss Barrett) in essay-writing. During his later years he suffered from dire poverty.

Of his several dramas, *The Death of Marlowe* (1837) is remarkable for some blank-verse speeches that sound like the genuine Elizabethan playwright (Marlowe's reputation had been resurrected by the Romantics after generations of virtual oblivion). Horne momentarily succeeded where most writers have failed—in placing believable lines in the mouth of departed genius. Although Horne's epic *Orion* (1843), cavalierly offered for sale by the poet for one farthing, is now forgotten, it has left a few quotations embedded in the language: "The roar of Time's great wings," "'Tis always morning somewhere in the world."

Robert Stephen Hawker (1803–1875). A native of Stoke Demerel, Devonshire, and an Oxford graduate, Robert Stephen Hawker became an Anglican clergyman in Cornwall. He achieved fame as an antiquarian and poet upon the storied land of Cornwall. When he published "The Song of the Western Men" (1826), on Bishop Trelawny's opposition to James II, Scott and others accepted it as an authentic 17th-century ballad. Missing the eldritch quality of Celtic folklore, Hawker effectively projected its drama and glamour.

James Clarence Mangan (mang'gen) (1803–1849). Son of a Dublin grocer, James Mangan received only a smattering of education. While working as a copying clerk and legal clerk from 1818 to 1828, he largely educated himself. Friends secured him a job in the Trinity College library, but his addiction to alcohol and opium ruined him for steady employment. He supported himself irregularly by hackwork for Irish periodicals until his death. He was called "the Irish Poe" because of the similarity of their lives.

Previous poets of Irish birth (those considered earlier in this text) were fundamentally in the English tradition. Even Moore was actually an English poet frequently employing Irish references. Mangan is the first significant poet in the English language to be truly Irish. Roman Catholic Ireland sounds in many of his eight hundred or so poems, notably in "St. Patrick's Hymn before Tara" (1848). His most famous piece, "Dark Rosaleen" (1846), breathes the passionate ardor of the Irish for their emerald isle. The poem is a free re-creation of an anonymous Gaelic poem of the 16th century. In the tradition of the native bards, the poet personifies Ireland as Roisin Dubh, "dark-haired little Rose." In humorous verse Mangan could capture the wild incongruity of the Gaelic spirit that baffles the sober Sassenach (Englishman). "The Woman of Three Cows" (1848) simultaneously and incredibly portrays the grandeur of Irish nationalism and the ludicrous tongue-lashing of peasants.

Although his knowledge of Gaelic was meager, Mangan sensitively absorbed the lilt and cadence of native verse. Some of his best poems, such as "O'Hussey's Ode to the Maguire," pulse with the bardic intensity that Gray and the English Romantics greatly admired but never could quite reproduce. From the Gaelic, too, Mangan adapted metrical innovations of strongly stressed initial syllables, a sweeping line, and a melodic falling-away at the end. He displayed remarkable virtuosity in all metrics; no two of the score or so of his generally anthologized pieces employ the same stanzaic pattern.

In Romantic fashion Mangan wrote quite a few poems upon Oriental subjects. Although unversed in Eastern languages, he has a truer ring here than his contemporary Romantics, especially when the subject suggests oppression like that of Ireland's, as it does in "The Time of the Barmecides" (1839).

NON-ROMANTIC POETRY OF THE PERIOD

Throughout this period Landor continued to produce his polished classical verse, and Winthrop Praed, although his life was unfortunately brief, proved himself a master of *vers de société* unequaled since Matthew Prior.

Winthrop Mackworth Praed (prād) (1802–1839). Winthrop Mackworth Praed was born in London; on his mother's side he was related to the New England Winthrops. He early started the writing of verse and drama, and in 1820 at Eton he edited the *Etonian,* which, although it lasted only ten months, has been considered the most brilliant schoolboy magazine in English. At Cambridge he outstripped his fellow student Macaulay, carrying off most of the prizes for poetry, both English and Latin. He was a conservative member of Parliament but campaigned actively for improved education. Great things were expected of Praed, but he was suddenly brought to death by tuberculosis.

Collected Poems (1864) and *Political and Occasional Poems* (1888) encompass most of Praed's work. He is the soul of English gentry, free to view ironically and wittily the upper class, of which he was an integral part. Nurtured upon Horace, he approximates his model. He explores the politics and social life of high society, and, though never profound, he is a brilliant reporter of the surface of life and a delightful commentator on his world. Praed proved adept at a wide variety of stanzas and meters, helping to widen appreciably the forms of English verse. The host of subsequent light-versifiers in English down to the present might well be termed "the sons of Praed."

AUTOBIOGRAPHY, MEMOIRS, AND TRAVEL ACCOUNTS OF THE PERIOD

Benjamin Robert Haydon (1786–1846). A native of Plymouth, Benjamin Robert Haydon became a painter in spite of slightly defective eyesight. Determined and hot-tempered, he insisted upon being a historical painter when portraits were all the rage, and for years he conducted a feud with the Royal Academy. Typical of his irascible failures were two fiascos in 1841: he sabotaged his own lifelong pleas for government subsidy for art by attacking German paintings when Prince Albert, a German, was head of the Royal Commission considering subsidies; and when his private exhibition was unattended while

Barnum next door was making a fortune exhibiting Tom Thumb, Haydon ran an advertisement in the newspapers excoriating English taste. His most famous painting, "Christ's Entry into Jerusalem," contains portraits of Wordsworth and Keats among the onlookers.

Autobiography and Journals (1853) consists of memoirs covering the painter's life from 1786 to 1820; journal entries thereafter extend to June 22, 1846, only a few minutes before the artist's suicide. Haydon's account of his hates and his loves, his friends and his many self-created enemies, is enthralling and completely frank, though never scandalous. The reader can intensely realize the robust and sparkling personality that so impressed Keats. The most famous passage treats of the "immortal dinner" that Haydon arranged in his lodgings on December 28, 1817, for Keats, Lamb, and Wordsworth. Haydon proved more of an artist with the pen than with the brush.

Edward John Trelawny (1792–1881). Though the London-born son of an army officer, Edward John Trelawny was of Cornish stock through both parents. Apparently to escape a tyrannical father, he took service on H. M. S. *Superb* in 1805, arriving at Trafalgar too late for the battle. His experiences thereafter until 1820 are known solely through his highly dubious autobiography. In 1820 he appeared in Switzerland and became attached to the Shelley-Byron group. In looks and behavior, Trelawny fascinated the Romantics, for he seemed the embodiment of impetuous adventure. Mary Shelley described him as "a kind of half-Arab Englishman, whose life has been as changeful as that of Anastasius, and who recounts the adventures of his youth as eloquently and well as the imagined Greek" (referring to a novel by Thomas Hope, who will be discussed in the next chapter). Byron was a bit startled to find his Corsair in the flesh.

In 1823 Trelawny accompanied Byron to Greece, where, impatient at delays, he joined the insurgent chief Odysseus and married his daughter, Tersitza. Severely wounded, Trelawny at last recovered and returned to England in 1828. From 1833 to 1835 he resided in America, where he was famed for swimming the Niagara river between the rapids and the falls. His handsome appearance and Romantic air made him famed for decades, and it has been said that Trelawny's greatest contribution to the Romantic Movement was himself.

The Adventures of a Younger Son (1831) is fictionalized fact, for in spite of Trelawny's insistence upon its truth, it does not jibe with historical records at the few points where it can be checked. However

accurate, it far outstrips the romances of Stevenson. Trelawny claims
that after service on the *Superb* he sailed in a naval warship to
India, where, because of the cruelty of the ship's captain, he jumped
ship. In Bombay he met a pirate leader, De Ruyter, under whom he
ranged as a freebooter all the way from Zanzibar to the East Indies.
Because of his swarthy Cornish complexion, he frequently passed
himself off as an oriental. He states that he married the lovely primitive Arab girl Zela, a being straight out of a wildly Romantic narrative
poem. Hair-breadth escapes and stormy passions are spectacularly
enacted against a lush tropical background (these spirited descriptions of the Eastern isles seem generally authentic). The feverish
narrative concludes with the pathetic death of Zela and the melodramatic death of De Ruyter.

Recollections of the Last Days of Shelley and Byron (1858) may
well be termed the most Romantic prose work in English. Byron is
rather deprecated, for Trelawny was himself a Byronic figure and
could well understand "The Pilgrim of Eternity." Shelley was an enigma
to Trelawny and is admiringly portrayed. Perhaps the most emotionally stirring passage in English literature—and it is substantially
accurate—is the pagan magnificence of the cremation of Shelley's remains on the beach of the Bay of Spezzia in the presence of Byron,
Hunt, and Trelawny. Unobserved, Trelawny plucked Shelley's flaming
heart from the crematory.

Trelawny's account is too often suspect, especially in the light of his
revision of this work as *Records of Shelley, Byron and the Author*
(1878). In the earlier version Trelawny tells of his clandestine examination of Byron's corpse at Missolonghi: "Both his feet were clubbed, and
his legs withered to the knee—the form and features of an Apollo,
with the feet and legs of a sylvan satyr." This splendiferous wording is
superseded in the later version by the mundane statement: "It was
caused by the contraction of the back sinews, which the doctors call
'Tendon Achilles,' that prevented his heels resting on the ground, and
compelled him to walk on the fore part of his feet; except this defect,
his feet were perfect."

Sir John Franklin (1786–1847). A native of Spilsby, Lincolnshire,
Sir John Franklin was intended for the church, but the lure of the sea
took him aboard H. M. S. *Polyphemus* into the midst of the battle of
Copenhagen. He served on H. M. S. *Bellerophon* during the battle
of Trafalgar, and on H. M. S. *Bedford* during the engagement at

New Orleans. His arctic exploration began in 1818. The notable expedition of 1819–22 is described in his famous book. His honors were numerous, including the lieutenant-governorship of Van Diemen's Land (Tasmania), 1837–42. Although fifty-nine years old, Franklin claimed the command of the *Erebus* and the *Terror* upon their search for the Northwest Passage. The ships left England in 1845 and were last seen off the far northern coast of Canada in July. The most intensive search in history up to that time filled in much of the blank map of the arctic, but not until 1859 were substantial traces of the expedition uncovered. On the basis of the recovered log, Franklin is credited with actual discovery and negotiation of the Northwest Passage, and the date of his death is given. All members of the expedition perished.

Narrative of a Journey to the Shores of the Polar Sea in the Years 1819–22 (1823) is one of the classic tales of exploration. Franklin recounts a journey, mostly overland, of approximately five thousand, five hundred miles through the wastes of northern Canada. Though factually stated, the work evokes the pathos of frightful suffering and the unshakable resolution of intrepid men. Brooding over all is the somber and appalling magnitude of vast space and an intractable landscape of desolation.

Charles Waterton (1782–1865). The proud Waterton family of Walton Hall, Yorkshire, mentioned in Shakespeare's *Richard II,* had distinguished themselves at Agincourt and Marston Moor, and Charles Waterton, like his ancestors, proudly insisted upon remaining a Roman Catholic. Family property took him to British Guiana, where he resided from 1804 to 1813. He conducted three more explorations in this region by 1825. For the remainder of his long life he was a distinguished naturalist, writing and carrying on extended but amiable controversies with Audubon and other scientists.

Wanderings in South America, the North-west of the United States, and the Antilles in the Years 1812, 1816, 1820, and 1824 (1825) is the masterpiece of Romantic travel accounts. In spite of Waterton's clear and accurate descriptions of wild life and scenery in South America, naturalists eagerly relinquish the work to literature. First, the outstanding effect is that of a delightful eccentric. Waterton's personality shines through the entire work in his eager observation, adventuresome spirit, and flippant manner. Who else among naturalists would ride an alligator? Second, the account frequently sounds like a rewriting of *Tristram Shandy* and *The Anatomy of Melancholy.* Waterton skips from one topic to another, lugs in irrelevant allusions from a wide world of reading, indulges in Latin puns, and jumbles chronology in a flurry of verbal exuberance. Nonetheless, the book has never lost its hold upon readers, and Theodore Roosevelt, for one, praised it.

Chapter 8

The Early Nineteenth-Century Novel
(1800–1837)

NOVELS CONTINUING THE EIGHTEENTH-CENTURY TRADITION

Although Scott was a published novelist before half of Jane Austen's novels had been printed, there is no meeting ground for the two writers. Jane Austen was not influenced by the Romantic Movement and deprecated such Romantic tendencies as sentimentalism and medievalism. She has been termed a "feminine Augustan," and might well be considered the last great novelist of the Enlightenment.

Jane Austen (1775–1817). Jane Austen was the seventh of eight children of the Reverend George Austen, rector of Steventon, Hampshire. She never married but accompanied her family in successive moves to Bath (1801), Southampton (1805), Chawton (1809), and Winchester (1817), dying in the latter city and receiving burial in the cathedral. She never associated with the literati of the era, and gained belated recognition when the Prince Regent (later George IV) praised her work.

By her own statement, Jane Austen is a miniaturist, working upon "small, square, two inches of ivory." She has no interest in broad social problems or public affairs; the mighty roar of the French Revolution and the Napoleonic era is reduced to a whisper in her provincial communities. She has no concern for the masses, and the few middle-class figures appearing in her novels are viewed with polite distaste. Her characters are unaffected by abstract thinking or disturbing doctrines of the era, and they scarcely ever bother their heads about human destiny or spiritual turmoil.

Regarded as the greatest English novelist of manners, she restricts herself to the narrow circle of the landed gentry. First and foremost her characters are English ladies and gentlemen; her clergymen are too genteel to be infected with religiosity, and her true heroines can face the shipwreck of their fondest hopes with calm resolution. The total of sixteen kisses recorded in her novels contains not one lover's kiss, but the absence of passion in her works is not hypocrisy but the product of many generations of genteel upbringing. In the circumscribed world of landed gentry the central problems are maintaining social prestige, marrying acceptably, and inheriting property. Jane Austen confines her scrutiny so thoroughly to the feminine viewpoint that she never portrays male figures without a woman being present. With no sense of repetition, her six novels deal with the same fundamental theme: her heroine is confronted with several apparently eligible young men and must thoughtfully discard the less desirable choices in favor of the right man. Each of her heroines begins with misconceptions that she must overcome to achieve success and maturity. Her works are here considered in order of composition.

Love and Freindship [sic] (c. *1790–93, 1922*) consists of letters from Laura to Marianne, in travesty of current fiction. Mrs. Radcliffe is the only novelist still remembered among Jane Austen's victims.

Volume the First (c. *1790–93,* 1933) consists of short pieces gaily satirizing the silly novels in the circulating libraries.

Lady Susan (c. *1792–96,* 1871) is her one portrait of a completely bad person, Lady Susan, who seeks to sell her sixteen-year-old daughter, Frederica, to a wealthy roué. While carrying on with a married man, Lady Susan attempts to trap for herself a young man attracted to Frederica. Lady Susan is a cold villainess, calmly analyzing herself in a series of letters. Jane Austen seems to have cut the work short, as alien to her temperament.

Sense and Sensibility was started as the epistolary *Elinor and Marianne* (c. *1795*), now lost, and was several times revised before publication in 1811 as the novelist's first printed work.

Mrs. Henry Dashwood has two daughters: Elinor, who possesses sense, and Marianne, who cultivates sensibility. The family moneys have gone to a half-brother, John. Elinor loves Edward Ferrars, while Marianne is enamored of an attractive rogue, John Willoughby. Willoughby drops Marianne to wed a woman of considerable wealth, and

Edward, who has been engaged for four years to the selfish Lucy Steele, considers it dishonorable to break his engagement. Learning about Lucy, Edward's mother disinherits him in favor of his younger brother, Robert. Lucy promptly discards Edward in favor of Robert, enabling Elinor and Edward to marry. Marianne realizes her immaturity and accepts the proposal of the staid, reliable Colonel Brandon.

Elinor wisely prefers a man of honor and character, while Marianne, giddy from sentimental novels, throws herself into an infatuation with an unworthy man. Tearfully Marianne comes to realize that Elinor has stoically endured even greater trials, and she awakens to the solid worth of Brandon, getting far better than her girlish sensibility might have justified. Elinor is Jane Austen's first depiction of the English Lady, the best in literature to its date. Although the sole career of a lady is marriage, with money, if possible (the only alternative being an arid, ignored spinsterhood), the author nonetheless decries marriages of convenience. A lady must be guided by the logic of her position to select the proper man and then fix her affections upon him. Under such a code, a woman weighs every word and glance of a man, judging what it indicates of his attitude toward her. Meanwhile, she maintains impeccable dignity, betraying neither concern nor intensity.

Although not Jane Austen's best work, *Sense and Sensibility* contains some excellent things, notably the portrait of the selfish older Dashwoods, who reason themselves into doing nothing for the two girls. Willoughby is not too successfully modeled after Richardson's Lovelace. Edward is shadowy, one of her least interesting heroes.

Pride and Prejudice was initially conceived c. 1796–97 as *First Impressions* (now lost), was written c. 1812, and was first published in 1813. It has proved to be one of the most consistently popular novels in the English language.

Since the property of Mr. and Mrs. Bennet will pass by entail to a male cousin, William Collins, it is imperative for them to marry off all five of their daughters. Charles Bingley falls in love with Jane, the eldest. His friend, Fitzwilliam Darcy, nephew of the haughty Lady Catherine de Bourgh, is attracted to the second daughter, Elizabeth, but she thinks him proud and condescending. She is further prejudiced by an unfavorable report of him from George Wickham, a young officer. Misunderstandings separate both pairs of lovers, and Elizabeth rejects Darcy's haughty proposal. But when Elizabeth's younger sister Lydia runs off with Wickham, Darcy persuades him to marry her, and he also reconciles Jane and Bingley. Elizabeth refuses to promise Lady Catherine that she will not marry Darcy, and when Darcy hears this from his indignant aunt, he proposes again and is accepted. Along with the main theme of the Bennet family, there is also the marriage of the pompous Mr. Collins, after Elizabeth refuses him, to her friend, Charlotte Lucas.

The theme and title of this book—in which Darcy's pride and Elizabeth's prejudice are eventually replaced by tender understanding— were suggested by Fanny Burney's *Cecilia*. The superbly constructed plot deals with four romances (or at least husband-capturing themes) —Jane-Bingley, Elizabeth-Darcy, Lydia-Wickham, and Charlotte Lucas-Collins—all of which are determined by the romance of the central character, Elizabeth. Unlike the sentimental women novelists of her day and before, Jane Austen tells her story straightforwardly, revealing character through dramatic dialogue and behavior.

This is the first significant novel dealing with an entire family. Each of the Bennets is beautifully delineated: imperturbable Mr. Bennet, skittish Mrs. Bennet, sweet Jane, vivacious Elizabeth, reckless Lydia, catarrhal Kitty, and sententious Mary. Elizabeth, wholly lady-like, is also lively, witty, and resourceful. Darcy is perhaps the best novelistic representative of a familiar type of Englishman; seemingly stiff and supercilious, he is actually a shy, well-intentioned gentleman encased in the shell of a reserved, inadequately communicating aristocrat. Only some of Dickens's novels have equaled this book in the number of memorable characters in one work of fiction.

Irony suffuses this novel, as the characters labor under their misapprehensions, but it is a gentle irony, and even Wickham is rather a victim of weakness than a vehicle of evil. Life is viewed as a high comedy, certain to work out satisfactorily for decent men and women of good will.

Northanger Abbey, begun c. 1797–98 as *Susan* (now lost), was extensively revised and enlarged in 1816, and was first published in 1818. Its primary impulse was a burlesque of the sentimental Gothic novel.

Catherine Morland, daughter of a prosperous clergyman, has read too many of Mrs. Radcliffe's Gothic novels. Taken to Bath by the wealthy Allens, she and Henry Tilney fall in love. His father, General Tilney, believes that she is wealthy, like her friends, the Allens, and cordially invites her to his medieval residence, Northanger Abbey. There Catherine's wild Gothic imagination runs riot. She imagines the

General a murderer and takes for an incriminating document what turns out to be a laundry list. Informed that Catherine is penniless, the General summarily casts her out. Henry, however, follows her and persuades her to marry him. The General is appeased by learning Catherine's true circumstances and by the marriage of his daughter Eleanor to a peer. In the minor plot Catherine's brother, James, is engaged to the selfish Isabella Thorpe. Believing that Captain Tilney, Henry's elder brother, is interested in her, Isabella breaks the engagement, only to discover that the Captain was simply amusing himself.

Though never ranked with her four great novels, this is Jane Austen's most delightful and amusing one. Catherine is first viewed satirically, as her creator parodies *The Mysteries of Udolpho* and ridicules a youthful mind beguiled by Radcliffian fancies, but then Catherine is transformed into another Evelina and sympathetically delineated. To contrast Gothic delusions with sound sense, Jane Austen purposely makes her heroine a commonplace girl, perhaps too drab but an interesting novelistic challenge anticipating Charlotte Brontë's *Jane Eyre*. Henry is a more believable Lord Orville. He is the anti-hero, providing a running ironic commentary on the errors of social and literary conventions. The Thorpes are another version of the Branghtons. The finest characterization is that of General Tilney, the pretentious hypocrite. Catherine is absurdly mistaken in believing the General to be a murderer, but her instinct correctly detects his falseness. Though completely feminine, Jane Austen is unswerving in her insistence upon character and honor above Tilney's goals of "fortune" and "consequence." James Morland is a distressingly pale character, existing only to be deceived by Isabella. Eleanor Tilney is another thin characterization, typical of a beginning and yet unsure novelist. The self-conscious intrusion of the novelist, as well as the author's obvious spokesman in Henry, shows the writer not yet in the true vein of her great works.

The Watsons (c. *1803,* 1871) is a first draft, a fragment breaking off at about one fifth the usual length of her novels. It is Jane Austen's one try at shabby-genteel realism in the later fashion of the French realists. Maria Edgeworth's influence seems clear.

Emma Watson has been returned penniless to her family after being raised by an aunt. Her father is an invalid. Her sisters, Elizabeth, Penelope, and Margaret, are painfully, desperately eager to marry and escape the near-poverty of their family. At a dance Emma receives the attentions of Lord Osborne, the nobleman's worthy chaplain-tutor Mr. Howard, and the flirtatious Tom Musgrove. Jane Austen confided to her sister that she proposed to end the novel with Emma's refusal of the noble lord and acceptance of Mr. Howard.

Emma rises above the rest of her family, and certainly it is rather painful reading to observe the fearful urgency of her sisters. Jane Austen is unflinching in her realistic portrayal of harried people. Though too unfinished to judge, the work does show sound and gripping characterization. Although never again treating such a subject, Jane Austen from this point on manifests a graver, less light-hearted tone.

Mansfield Park (c. *1811–13, 1814*) is Miss Austen's most complex and least dramatic novel.

The residents of Mansfield Park are the kind baronet Sir Thomas Bertram, his selfish wife, sons Tom and Edmund, and daughters Maria and Julia. Lady Bertram's sister, Mrs. Price, wife of a poor marine officer, has so many children that Fanny is sent to live at Mansfield Park, where Edmund proves her only real friend. While Sir Thomas and Tom are away in the West Indies, Maria flirts with newcomer Henry Crawford although she is engaged to the vapid Rushworth. Not realizing that Fanny loves him, Edmund is interested in Henry's frivolous sister Mary. All the young people except Fanny participate in amateur theatricals that are interrupted by the return of Sir Thomas. Fanny rejects Henry's proposal. Maria marries Rushworth but shortly thereafter runs off with Henry. Julia elopes with the fashionable but questionable Mr. Yates. When Mary Crawford treats her brother's behavior cavalierly, Edmund at last recognizes Fanny's true worth.

This is Jane Austen's most didactic novel, preaching the importance of proper education of children. Sir Thomas loves his offspring but exercises inadequate control over them. Raised in luxury and idleness, they are all—except Edmund—flighty and unreliable. Both daughters run off with bounders, and the slack-twisted Crawfords are likewise the product of injudicious upbringing. Edmund's problem is therefore one of "recognition." He makes a confidante of Fanny, telling her of his interest in other women, never realizing until almost too late that she is the right one for him. Incidentally, he is Jane Austen's lone serious cleric, not "unco guid" or pious, but soberly conscious of his responsibilities. Fanny is her one "perfect" heroine and the one completely "feminine" embodiment of timidity and passivity. She is quiet, rather than sprightly like Elizabeth Bennet. She suffers agonies concealing her love for Edmund and observing his infatuation with Mary Crawford before her excellence is properly noted. Although the writer always operates on the conscious realistic level, Fanny seems more archetypal than her other heroines. Fanny is a Cinderella entrapped within Mansfield Park, unappreciated by the handsome prince. Her perfection is tolerable because she suffers greatly and meets every reverse with fortitude.

Modern readers often wonder at Jane Austen's objections to the amateur theatricals. The play is *Lover's Vows*, a translation by Mrs. Elizabeth Inchbald from the German of Kotzebue. Miss Austen is not squeamish, but she sees impropriety in unsupervised theatricals involving a tale of illegitimacy and seduction performed by impressionable young people. Mansfield Park is typical of contemporary rural decorum, a far cry from the libidinous freedom of Regency London, while the Crawfords come from the urban society that Byron knew. Both Henry and Mary are Byronic lovers, not so much villains as disturbing aliens to the staid morality of English country gentlefolk. Mary's nonchalance about her brother's adultery is inappropriate to the ethical standards of Edmund and his social group. Henry's interest in Fanny is well considered, for, like Byron with Lady Byron, Henry had been ceaselessly pursued by women and found a fascinating challenge in a good woman who was totally unattracted to him.

This is Jane Austen's most complicated plotting, tracing at least six stories (those of Fanny and Edmund, the two Crawfords, and the two Bertram sisters). The production of the play is one of several means of carrying many threads without missing any stitches. Minor characters are good, especially the nagging Mrs. Norris, who resolutely keeps Fanny in the position of a poor relative. The squalid Price household in Portsmouth introduces more realism than any other of the published novels and is part of the greater variety this novel offers over the others.

Emma (c. *1814–15,* 1816) is Jane Austen's only novel concentrated almost wholly upon one character. All but one chapter is told solely from Emma's viewpoint. Technically its construction is her best. It was the last work published during the novelist's lifetime.

With the marriage of her companion and former governess, Miss Taylor, to Mr. Weston, Emma Woodhouse is complete mistress of Hartfield estate, for her father is a hopeless valetudinarian. Setting herself up as a matchmaker, Emma induces Harriet Smith (a seventeen-year-old ingenue of illegitimate birth) to reject the proposal of Robert Martin, a young farmer, and to concentrate on the vicar, Mr. Elton. The vicar misinterprets Emma's maneuvers and proposes to her. He then settles for an ill-mannered bride from a community other than Highbury. Emma steers Harriet toward Frank Churchill, son of Mr. Weston by a previous marriage; but Frank is secretly engaged to Jane Fairfax, niece of the chatterbox, Miss Bates. Harriet falls in love with the estimable Mr. Knightley, and Emma wakes to her horrible blundering. Emma's heart has itself actually been destined for this man whom she took for granted as an old and trusted friend. The wise Knightley proposes to Emma, and Harriet accepts young Martin.

Perhaps the greatest comedy of manners in the English novel, this work is much in the spirit of Molière. In the mirror held up to life, a self-deluded woman learns her errors and submits. "I am going to take a heroine whom no one but myself will much like," stated Jane Austen of Emma. The woman who would play God eventually realizes that she has misunderstood the purposes and best interests of all her would-be puppets (six times spinning a web of delusion) and even the inclination of her own heart. Because Emma is well-intentioned and humbly, graciously admits her mistakes, she is properly rewarded and the reader reconciled to her. Emma must accept Mr. Knightley's philosophy, the practical one of what constitutes proper social decorum. Environment molds the manners and even the impulses of these beings; Emma, a busybody by any standards, has erred in trying to adapt and direct the course of social forces instead of rightfully heeding and following them.

Mr. Knightley (the name is significant) is a much improved Grandison. He is a woman's man, cast in the role of the great stabilizing figure, the sturdy rock to which even the strong-minded Emma must cling. He is a father image, close to forty, as Emma is twenty-one, and Mr. Woodhouse exudes not the slightest trace of the father figure. Knightley is always right, as Emma is always wrong. He can be tolerated because he is never smugly self-righteous and because in his jealousy of Churchill he displays one human foible. Two of the greatest comic creations of English literature are the two characters Miss Bates and Mr. Woodhouse. Emma's father is an amusing caricature of a preposterous invalid, oblivious to everything but health and diet. Miss Bates possesses "total recall," gabbing on harmlessly, magnificent in her sheer plethora of words. The class lines are neatly drawn, as Mrs. Elton represents the rising middle class, to whom social position is solely governed by money. Miss Austen's delicate touch is apparent here, for the reader is convinced of Mrs. Elton's uncouthness, whereas to a masculine novelist, the cleric's wife would be a genuine "lady." The author significantly gives her own Christian name to Jane Fairfax, an attractive and capable girl whose poverty makes marriage essential;

otherwise her bleak prospects are those of a governess, a high-grade servant. Churchill is not worthy of her; he is a mild sadist, making Jane writhe inwardly as he gaily moves from one flirtation to another while secretly engaged to her. He is the one plot-ridden character of the novel.

The novel somewhat resembles a series of Chinese boxes, one within the other. Although the story hinges upon mystification and misunderstanding, it moves smoothly. The novelist's supreme ability is displayed in the perfect insertion of everything; only upon completion does the reader suddenly realize how indispensable was even the most casual conversation or reference. Many critics have pointed out the picnic scene at Box Hill as one of the best focusings of plot thread and character revelation in fiction. Especially in the 20th century have many students of the novel rated this as Jane Austen's greatest work.

Persuasion (1815–16, 1818) bears a title given by Miss Austen's brother Henry, who published this work along with *Northanger Abbey* after her death.

Eight years before, at the age of nineteen, Anne Elliot broke her engagement to the young naval officer Frederick Wentworth, persuaded by Lady Russell that he was poor and without certain prospects. Now at twenty-six Anne is resigned to spinsterhood. The extravagances of her father, Sir Walter Elliot, compel him to lease Kellynch Hall to Admiral and Mrs. Croft. Captain Wentworth, brother of Mrs. Croft, is now well off, chiefly from prize money secured during the Napoleonic wars. He is thrown in with Anne, to whom he is polite but cool, and with Louisa and Henrietta Musgrove, lively young sisters-in-law of Anne's younger sister, Mary, and they catch his eye. Louisa, however, becomes engaged to Captain Benwick. At Bath, Anne is courted by the devious William Elliot, heir to Sir Walter and cousin of Anne. Simultaneously William is secretly consorting with Mrs. Clay to prevent her from marrying Sir Walter. Learning of the intrigue, Anne breaks with William and accepts Federick's proposal.

An autumnal mellowness pervades this novel, astutely keynoted by the fall season, a more fully presented natural background than any-where else in Jane Austen's printed novels. Anne is a quiet, pensive girl like Fanny Price, but more mature. Like Fanny, she has difficulty in concealing her continued affection for Frederick. Anne's mistake occurred some time before the start of the novel, and she is perfection itself while patiently awaiting the renewal of true love. Hers is the plight of a sensitive girl in an acquisitive society, in which love is subordinated to economics. This is Jane Austen's most intimate love story and her most moving one. Perhaps only she could make so poignant and warming the reconciliation of the two lovers in Mrs. Musgrove's crowded sitting room, a meeting of hearts without crescendo, without even a kiss.

Through her sailor brothers, Jane Austen knew naval officers, and Wentworth is an unspectacular but solid figure, especially well conceived in his loyalty to his shipmates. Frederick does not realize that his coolness toward Anne conceals an undiminished affection for her, but William's interest in her arouses his jealousy and triggers him to action. Class-consciousness is strong, as always, in the portrait of the vulgar aspirant for Kellynch Hall, Mrs. Clay (note the name). Daughter of Sir Walter's agent, she is typical of the middle-class risers striving to inch into the landed gentry. William is a scoundrel for plot purposes but not as fully realized as, say, Frank Churchill. An excellent touch is Anne's intuition that he is too agreeable, too suave.

Construction is again excellent, the only real flaw lying in Mrs. Smith, who exists solely to aid Anne in seeing through William. A small but devoted corps of Jane Austen's admirers consider this her greatest novel. With its calm and gentle atmosphere, its maturing heroine, its quiet farewell to the world-shattering Napoleonic times, and its pervasive charm, it is a fit coda for the novelist and for the 18th century.

Sanditon (*1817*, 1925) bears the title by which it was known to the Austen family. It is a fragment of twelve chapters written during the novelist's illness and left incomplete at her death.

Mr. Parker is a "projector," a real-estate speculator, intent upon making his seacoast property at old Sanditon a resort community. His daughter, Diana, is equally eager and officious in making the place boom. The Parker's visitor, Charlotte Heywood, is evidently one of the novel's two heroines. The other is Clara Brereton, youthful companion of aged Lady Denham, Mr. Parker's financial associate. The noblewoman's nephew, young Sir Edward Denham, imitating Lovelace, has determined to seduce Clara.

This last work of Jane Austen does not follow a spirit of increasing mellowness but is highly comic. Sir Edward, with his botched quotations from Scott and others, and his absurdly pretentious sentimental wooing, is pure farce. Mr. Parker is the closest she ever got to the modern businessman. Also farcical is the confusion about the Camberwell boarding school and the party of the West Indian heiress, which turn out to be the same group—the determined Mrs. Griffiths and three young ladies, who positively will not be a market for Lady Denham's asses' milk. This wildest comedy seems promised, with even stronger jibes at the sentimentalists of current fiction. No other Austen piece is so replete with natural scenery and atmosphere, though such is of course demanded by the plot.

Maria Edgeworth (1767–1849). A native of Black Bourton, Oxfordshire, Maria Edgeworth was taken at the age of sixteen to Irish estates of her family. She was the aunt of Thomas Lovell Beddoes and a friend of Sir Walter Scott, who, in his preface to *Waverley,* acknowledged his debt to her Irish novels. In fact, even the Russian novelist Turgenev was influenced by her, for she is almost certainly the most important and influential of all English novelists below the top rank. She created the provincial, or "local color," novel; she created the family, or dynasty, novel carried through several successive generations; and she introduced the narrative viewpoint, later so extensively employed by Henry James, of telling the story through a minor character.

Castle Rackrent (1800) manifests all three of Maria Edgeworth's notable innovations. The title means "destructive rentals."

Thady Quirk, devoted servant, unintentionally reveals his succession of masters as greedy oppressors of their Irish tenants, reckless and extravagant masters who ruined themselves. Sir Patrick Rackrent drank himself to death. Sir Murtagh Rackrent was a demon for litigation. Sir Kit Rackrent married a Jewish heiress for her money and imprisoned her in her room for seven years because she refused to hand over her diamonds to him. Sir Condy Rackrent brings final financial disaster to the family and dies in a drinking bout. The property falls into the hands of Attorney Quirk, Thady's canny son.

Quietly and without moralizing, she demonstrates how environment and heredity carry the ill-fated Rackrents slowly but surely down to oblivion. In Thady, the Irish peasant is immortalized, not as a comic character, but as a simple, loyal figure, unquestioning in his acceptance of his lowly status. His son, whom he cannot understand or agree with, is symbolic of the rising bourgeoisie, shrewd and opportunistic, which is gradually usurping the domain of the entrenched gentry.

John Galt (1779–1839). Born at Irvine, Ayrshire, Scotland, John Galt died at Greenoch, near Glasgow. He published about sixty works, most of them displaying a Zola-like fidelity to current Scottish life.

The Annals of the Parish (1821) is a sort of prose *Parish Register* (Crabbe).

The Reverend Micah Balwhidder chronicles the events in his parish of Dalmailing during the first fifty years of the reign of George III.

International events are noted cheek by jowl with trivial events such as the birth of twin calves. The onward rush of the Industrial Revolution brings a cotton mill to Dalmailing, with changes that are bewildering and disturbing to the clergyman. Not truly a novel, though full of dramatic themes, the work superbly evokes the feel of everyday life in a Scottish community of the late 18th century.

Memorable is the personality of the narrator, a shrewdly simple pastor of his flock, an essentially mundane but wholly virtuous cleric. Surrounding him are believable and interesting, though commonplace, townspeople. The atmosphere is realistic: sometimes humorous, sometimes tragic, but always without Romantic glamour. The treatment is gentler than most of Galt's works, and the piece is a Scottish classic, widely read throughout the 19th century.

THE ROMANTIC NOVEL OF THE PERIOD

Sir Walter Scott (1771–1832). Sir Walter Scott's biography and a discussion of his poetry are found in the previous chapter. The authorship of Scott's novels, though widely known, was not openly acknowledged until 1827. Scott started novel publication anonymously because, having already achieved a reputation as a poet, he feared that his public would think him debased for turning to a genre frequently stigmatized as frivolous even by its avid readers. He continued the pose largely as a gentlemanly whim. His immense success (he was the first figure in English literature to earn a sizable fortune by his pen) established the popularity of the novel as a literary form, not only in England, but throughout Western society.

However, the very wholesomeness and apparent simplicity that secured a large 19th-century reading public for Scott have prejudiced 20th-century readers against his works. His contemporaries enthusiastically ranked him with Shakespeare, and Wilkie Collins was to term him "the God Almighty of novelists." Not only English and American writers but an impressive roll of European novelists also could truly be designated the "Sons of Scott."

From the rise of the novel of the intelligentsia with George Eliot until well into the 20th century the stock of "The Wizard of the North" steadily declined. Critics scornfully pointed to his hasty writing; his often ill-contrived and clumsily manipulated plots; the frequently wooden and self-conscious style; the errors in historical interpretation; and the heroes and heroines who are generally shallow, sometimes insipid, and often sexually neuter. Many called his works "romances" rather than "novels," and relegated them largely to the nursery. However, with the contemporary bent toward conservatism, Scott is regaining some stature, while all the rest of the Romantics, except Keats, are frequently being challenged. Modern studies of Scott's novels emphasize his realistic character portrayals (usually of lower-class personalities) and his imaginative (if not always wholly accurate) grasp of social and political forces.

In this regard his novels of 17th- and 18th-century Scotland are now considered his best, since here (even when the setting is generations in the past) Scott tells of the people he best understood and appreciated. Scott's greatest achievement lies not in his medieval pageantry of knights, as popular legend often states, but in his bringing to life the sights and sounds of Scotland's recent past. He accomplished what few writers have done for their native land: Scotland since his time has largely conceived of itself in the image Scott created. More than any other person or force, Scott is responsible for uniting formerly hostile Celtic Highlander and Anglo-Saxon Lowlander into a common Scotland.

Even with this new emphasis, the works of Medieval and Renaissance Britain, among them *Ivanhoe,* are still the most widely popular of Scott's novels; and with them are included also a few novels of 17th-century England. *Quentin Durward* and *The Talisman,* while still popular, are felt by modern critics to contain material most remote from Scott and therefore to be his poorest works. Certainly Scott more than anyone else, including the professional historians, developed through his works the historical perspective of the English-speaking peoples.

Scott's novels are here treated in chronological order, but for grouping by type they are followed by an identifying letter:

(A) The novels of 17th- and 18th-century Scotland.
(B) The two novels of Scotland in Scott's own day.
(C) Novels of Medieval and Renaissance Britain.
(D) Historical novels in foreign settings.

Waverley, or 'Tis Sixty Years Since (1814) (A). The first seven chapters were written in 1805 and found by Scott in 1810 while he was searching for his fishing tackle. Scott completed the novel in 1813 and published it anonymously. Most of his subsequent novels were listed as "by the author of *Waverley.*"

Edward Waverley, captain of English dragoons, is sent on leave of absence by his uncle, Sir Everard, to the Scots baron Bradwardine.

When some of the baron's cattle are stolen by Highlanders, Waverley goes to intercede with the clan head, Fergus Mac Ivor, only to fall in love with Flora Mac Ivor, the chieftain's daughter. Wounded by a stag, Waverley is recuperating as Bonnie Prince Charlie, the Stuart Pretender, lands in Scotland to precipitate "The Forty-Five." Branded a deserter, Waverley tries to clear himself with the English army, only to be arrested for treason and then rescued by Highlanders. Chagrined, he serves with the Jacobites, capturing and saving Colonel Talbot, a family friend come to help him. After Waverley obtains Talbot's release, the Jacobite rebellion collapses. Talbot clears Waverley, who marries Rose Bradwardine, daughter of the Scots baron. Fergus is executed, and Flora takes refuge in a Benedictine convent in Paris.

Though the Gothic novel had a pseudo-medieval background, and Thomas Leland had attempted the historical romance in *Longsword* (1765), in the following particulars *Waverley* may be said to have established the pattern for the modern historical novel:

(1) The historical background is authentic, the product of Scott's personal knowledge (in his childhood he had known veterans of Prestonpans, where Waverley fought) and his extensive reading. Behind the melodramatic plot is an attempt to grasp the meaning of broad movements in history.

(2) Minor characters are portrayed realistically to provide a backdrop of actual living conditions.

(3) The central character, treated romantically, is fictitious. Scott varied successfully from this formula only when he chose a historically dim person like Amy Robsart in *Kenilworth*. Famous persons are seen by the central character, but no attempt is made to enter their minds.

(4) The central character is uncomplicated. Shrewder than many of his critics realize, Scott sensed the right method for the historical novel, for, although a searching fictionalized study of a past mind can produce the splendid *Memoirs of Hadrian* (1955), by Marguerite Yourcenar, the result is a novel of a man, not of history.

(5) The central character is also essentially a man of the author's own times dressed in period costume. Although Waverley, a "Man of Feeling," is appropriate for the book because his sort of spirit was indeed developing by 1745, a similar sort of character, Osbaldistone, is an anachronism in *Rob Roy*. This convention was to become the bane of the 19th-century historical novel, with the possible exception of Thackeray's *Henry Esmond*. Though it gained him the sympathy of

his readers, this incongruity is the most glaring flaw in Scott's conception of the historical novel.

The first readers of *Waverley* were therefore thrilled by the new and heady concoction, luxuriating, as critical reviews of the day indicate, in the spectacular actions enlivened by dashing figures and colorful descriptions. Only uncertainly did they realize that Scott was employing his imaginary beings to project an interpretation of history. "The Forty-Five" was not merely a romantic episode in British history; it was the last overt attempt by Scots to assert their equality within the United Kingdom. More specifically, it was the last uprising of feudalism (represented by the Highland clans) against modern, urban, commercialized society. Fergus Mac Ivor typifies the old code of barbaric honor. Although Scott has often been considered a lover of lost causes, he here judiciously balances the attractive claims of two different worlds. The spirit that will triumph, the wave of the future, is symbolized most by Talbot, but also by Waverley himself; this spirit contains the ideas of public responsibility, justice, acceptance of the realities of modern times, and "the greatest happiness of the greatest number." The execution of Fergus is the end of a way of life, and Waverley's choice of Rose instead of Flora is symbolic of the new order for Scotland.

Except for the 1805 chapters, this first novel is as good as almost any subsequent Scott novel. Suspicious scholars therefore challenge the entire chronology of the novels, believing Lockhart, in the famous biography of his father-in-law, to be incorrectly picturing the lightning rapidity of Scott's fiction writing. Perhaps Scott worked upon his novels at a much earlier date than their publication, and the order of appearance may not correspond with the order of composition.

Guy Mannering, or The Astrologer (1815) (A), supposedly a work completed in six weeks, is set approximately one generation after *Waverley*. No historical events are involved.

Godfrey Bertram, Laird of Ellangowan, finding that his English guest, Guy Mannering, is an amateur astrologer, asks for a horoscope upon his son Harry Bertram, born that night. To his distress, Mannering finds disaster for the boy at the age of five. Five years later the child vanishes, and not long afterward his sister Lucy becomes a poor orphan in the care of the impecunious Dominie Sampson. Returning after many years of distinguished military service in India, Mannering learns of her plight and brings Lucy and Sampson to live with him and his daughter Julia. While in India, Julia had fallen in love with Captain Vanbeest Brown. He follows her to England and proves to be the long-lost Harry

Bertram. Instrumental in his kidnaping at the age of five was the six-foot-tall gypsy, Meg Merrilies, who later saves the grown Bertram from murdering renegades.

Rather than a historical novel, this was frankly intended as an adventure yarn, set in the previous century. The *Waverley* theme of contrasting an old way of life with the new is carried through the economic decay of the Bertram family. However, as is usual with Scott, he began without any full idea of how the work would develop; he was prone to allow the novel's characters to take over and mold the account to themselves. Mannering is largely a self-portrait of Scott, emphasizing the somewhat stiff and conventional elements of the novelist's nature, but fundamentally revealing the successful, generous man of action that Scott yearned to be.

Really dominating the work are the personalities of Dandie Dinmont and Meg Merrilies, two of the most remarkable character creations in the English novel. They represent the polarities of Scott's vision of life. Dandie Dinmont is a superbly realistic Border farmer, simple and limited in intelligence, but a faithful and courageous being of the earth. Whenever he appears, the reader is firmly convinced of the actuality and the essential goodness of mankind. At the other pole is Meg Merrilies, the first great imaginative character portrayal of the Romantic novel, something previously unknown to English fiction. Where Dandie is all sane, healthy normality, and the embodiment of the comic view of life, Meg is all Romantic poetry, a larger-than-life depiction of the tragic intensity of life. She is a grandly wild creature, and she speaks and sings in her own bardic fashion, in a language and concept representing some of the best truly Romantic poetry of Scott.

The Antiquary (1816) (B) was Scott's own favorite. The one historical link is the French threat of 1805.

Major Neville is refused the hand of Isabella Wardour because her father, a fanatical devotee of genealogy, believes the young man to be illegitimate. Disguised as Lovel, the officer follows Isabella to Scotland, where he makes friends with Jonathan Oldbuck, a learned antiquary. Lovel saves the life and fortune of Sir Arthur Wardour and is revealed as the son and heir of the Earl of Glenallan. He thus wins the hand of Isabella.

The love affair is insipid, and the plotting is careless. But Scott can blunder into a dramatic scene and weave it to greatness. Oldbuck is a delightful comic picture of the antiquarian, but when Saunders Mucklebackit in grief refuses to touch his son's coffin, Oldbuck steps to the head of the bier and assumes his exalted role as Laird of Monkbarns. Mucklebackit, the fisherman, is a figure out of the Norse sagas—stark, dour, and elemental. His mother, Elspeth, haunted in the fisherman's hovel by memories of Glenallan majesty and dark evil, is a Romantic witch who in her madness chants "Red Harlow," probably Scott's best imitation of the ballad. The most remarkable character, and a unique Scott creation, Eddie Ochiltrec, is a richly comic old beggar who rises to epic grandeur as he stoically faces death from drowning. He has been termed the most Shakespearean character outside of Shakespeare's plays. Although never a democrat, as were most Romantics of his generation, Scott perceived the potential dignity and majesty in the humblest of people.

The Black Dwarf (1816) (A) was a failure which Scott quickly cut short. Set in the Jacobite days early in the 18th century during the reign of Queen Anne, the novel applies the label "black dwarf" (a malicious troll-like creature blamed by peasants for injury to herds) to the deformed Scottish recluse called Elshender or Canny Elshie. The misshapen creature saves Grace Armstrong when she is abducted from her beloved, and helps Isabella Vere thwart her father's plan to marry her to the repulsive Sir Frederick Langley. The dwarf is finally revealed as Sir Edward Mauley, once in love with Isabella's mother. The dwarf speaks an impossibly affected jargon, but, as the one redeeming virtue of the novel, the Scots peasants speak a tangy Scots dialect.

Old Mortality (1816) (A) was printed with *The Black Dwarf* under the broad heading *Tales of My Landlord,* supposedly written by Jedediah Cleishbotham. For the first time Scott moves earlier than the 18th century in a work exclusively the product of his reading and not of folk tradition or of hearsay. The title is misleading, for it is the sobriquet of Robert Paterson, a late 18th-century Scot who devoted his life to restoring the tombstones of the 17th-century Scottish Covenanters.

A moderate Presbyterian, Henry Morton, seeks a balance between the Troy bishops and the Covenanters in the Scottish rising of 1679. He also rivals the royalist Lord Evandale for Edith Bellenden's hand. Because he helps the Covenanter leader John Balfour to escape, Henry is condemned to death by Colonel Grahame of Claverhouse, the Tory leader. Saved by Evandale, Henry rides with the Covenanters and saves Evandale, who is captured by the Covenanters. With the defeat of the Covenanter forces at Bothwell Bridge, Henry is exiled in Holland until the accession of William and Mary. Returning, he finds Edith about to marry Evandale. Henry gallantly tries to save his rival from murderers, but Evandale is mortally wounded, and he gives Edith to Henry as he dies.

Henry and Evandale are anachronisms, enlightened and moderate men in an era of bitter fanaticism. The melodramatic adventures of the two rival suitors constitute a conventional romance. However, the novel's claim to excellence (and it is often considered Scott's best) lies in its historical canvas. This is the first English novel to approach the proportions of a serious epic. Momentous national issues are embodied in the contest of the curt, determined Claverhouse with the impassioned Covenanters.

Although Scott deplores the hysteria of the Covenanters, only his Romantic imagination could so fire them with life. Novelists of the 18th century could conceive of Kettledrummle and Poundtext, humorous readings of the rabble-rousing preachers, but only Scott could measure out the vast dimensions of the zealot Macbriar, the maniacal Balfour, and the towering Habbakuk Mucklewrath. There is a wild splendor about these men that renders credible and magnificent the 17th-century religious fighters. These Covenanters of Scott are the creations of Romantic genius and proof of the unique power of the historical novel to make us believe and understand the fantastic events of the past. With this work, Scott opened to the novel breathless vistas of imaginative re-creation of history.

The Heart of Midlothian (1818) (A) constituted the second series of *Tales of My Landlord*. The character Jeanie Deans is founded upon a real-life Helen Walker who refused to perjure herself for her sister but obtained a pardon for the infanticide by traveling on foot to London and securing the intercession of the Duke of Argyle. "Heart of Midlothian" was a nickname for Edinburgh's Tolbooth jail; its demolition in 1817 suggested the novel.

During the Porteous riots of 1736, Scots led by Robertson seize Porteous, the detested captain of the City Guard, and lynch him. Robertson (whose real name is Staunton) uses this action as a ruse to offer escape to Effie Deans, charged with murdering the child she had by him. Effie refuses to escape, and is tried and convicted for murder because her sister Jeanie refuses to perjure herself to save Effie. Jeanie walks all the way to London to secure her sister's pardon from Queen Caroline. Jeanie marries Reuben Butler, a clergyman, and Effie marries Staunton, a nobleman's son. Years later it is discovered that the missing child is not dead; the boy was kidnaped by the crazed Madge

Wildfire and given to bandits. In seeking his son, Staunton is killed by his own child.

Fascinated by the heroic past of Scotland, Scott searches for the role of heroism in the modern world. Staunton, the jaded nobleman, finds release for his energies in illegal violence along with a band of marauders. An unsatisfactory response for the modern world, his choice eventually results in his death ironically from the hands of his own son. The right response is that of Jeanie Deans, who finds the heroic in the commonplace, the legal, and the moral. Sprung from Covenanter stock, her character is so rigid that she will not lie even to save Effie's life. While her epic journey to plead for her sister's life epitomizes heroism, at the same time she is undramatic and unromantic. It has been said that Jeanie Deans makes one understand Joan of Arc. Jeanie is the finest portrait ever made of the simple, pious, serene, intensely moral, and thoroughly substantial Scots peasantry. She is Scott's most impressive and satisfactory woman. Madge Wildfire is another Romantic creation like Meg Merrilies, but an added twist is her madness as a result of Staunton's perfidy. Although the Duke of Argyle, who aids Jeanie in London, is a true nobleman, Scott obviously favors the unpretentiously heroic Scottish peasants to the aristocratic survivors in a mundane world. Perhaps Scott's greatness rests chiefly in his realization of grandeur in realism. The novel should have ended with Jeanie's successful mission, but even with the inferior drawn-out conclusion, it is a notable claimant for "best Scott novel."

Rob Roy (1817) (A) is set during the Jacobite uprising of 1715. Rob Roy was a nickname for Robert MacGregor Campbell, the real-life Scottish Robin Hood.

Frank Osbaldistone, showing little aptitude for his father's mercantile enterprises, is sent to his uncle, Sir Hildebrand Osbaldistone. En route, his fellow traveler, Morris, is robbed. Morris accuses Frank before a squire, but Rob Roy dramatically appears to force Morris to tell the truth. Frank is drawn to the vivacious Diana Vernon, niece of Sir Hildebrand. Rob Roy aids Frank in saving his father's funds, endangered by "The Fifteen." Sir Hildebrand's son Rashleigh plays an equivocating game in politics, finance, and personal life, trying to seize Diana; but Rob Roy kills him in a fight. Frank becomes master of his uncle's mansion and marries Diana, although she is a Roman Catholic and he is a Presbyterian.

Essentially a loose picaresque account, this work is dreadfully slow in getting underway. Scott apparently could not decide whether he was writing a romance or another version of the *Waverley* theme. The Von Flotow operatic version, like many readers, assumes that the significant portion of the work is the melodrama in Scotland with the picturesque Highland bandit. Improperly developed is the theme of feudal honor and loyalty in Sir Hildebrand and Diana versus modern mercantilism in Osbaldistone's father and business associates. Frank incongruously is a "man of feeling" belonging to Scott's own generation, accepting the new order while trying to preserve virtues of the old. Diana is perhaps Scott's most vivacious and attractive heroine, his one success in the portraiture of a gentlewoman. Andrew Fairservice, Frank's Sancho Panza, is a comic masterpiece, and Bailie Nicol Jarvie is the shrewd bourgeois rock of common sense and practicality, a foil to the vanishing heroic world of Rob Roy and to the idealistic Frank; he is the one character perfectly sure of himself and of the future that will belong to his class.

The Bride of Lammermoor (1819) (A) belongs to the third series of *Tales of My Landlord*. The germ of the story (similar to the Romeo and Juliet theme) is derived from an unauthenticated Scottish legend. Scott arbitrarily chooses the time of William III as setting.

Edgar, Master of Ravenswood, is last and poorest of a proud Scottish line of nobles. His enemy, Lord Ashton, now holds Ravenswood Castle, while Edgar is reduced to the Gothic ruin of Wolf's Crag. Edgar and Lucy Ashton, daughter of the Lord Keeper, pledge eternal love. While Lord Ashton agrees, the imperious Lady Ashton demurs and compels her weak daughter to marry the Laird of Bucklaw. When Edgar learns of Lucy's marriage, he challenges the Ashton men to duel. On her wedding night Lucy stabs her husband to death and goes mad. Galloping to the duel, Edgar and his horse are suddenly sucked into quicksand.

Critics debate whether this is the masterpiece of the Gothic novel or the first truly tragic novel in English. Certainly it is the first poetic novel in English. Not parts or characters alone, as in previous works, but the entire novel is conceived poetically. It is a ballad tragedy, a conscious artist's reproduction of the stark intensity of the tragic medieval ballads. Clouded skies, wild scenery, and the ruined castle of the last Ravenswood form an unrelenting background of somber threat. Scott invests objects such as the coin broken by the lovers and the interloping raven with the intensity of poetic symbolism. Over all is the curse of the house of Ravenswood. Unlike the other Scott novels, this does not fall into occasional pedestrianism or arid antiquarianism, and again, unlike most of his other novels, this is tightly constructed. The hero and the heroine are the dominant figures, not the often perfunctory lovers of other novels. Lucy is a passive, sentimental young lady, graceful and tearful. Edgar is darkly impressive and stately, but he too is driven by fate. No other Scott novel is so sunless and so pessimistic. Donizetti was able to take the story almost intact from the novel to form his sweeping, emotional opera. Though not typical Scott, this may be his best novel; it is certainly his most Romantic and most remarkable.

A Legend of Montrose (1819) (A) was included with the previous novel in the third series of *Tales of My Landlord*. It is based upon one episode of the 1644 Highland campaign for Charles I against the Covenanters, and resembles Alexandre Dumas more than Scott. Montrose, the royalist leader, is only a shadow, for Scott found such intellectuality and rationalism not to his taste. The professional soldier Dugald Dalgetty carries the work. No other author has so plumbed the strange but intelligible mind of the mercenary trooper.

Ivanhoe (1819) (C) was Scott's first novel to break from a Scottish setting and the first to be set in medieval times (England during the reign of Richard I, 1189–99). It has consistently proved the most popular Scott novel.

Wilfred of Ivanhoe had gone with Richard I on the Crusades because his father, Cedric the Saxon, had opposed the youth's marriage to Rowena, Cedric's lovely ward. Ivanhoe returns to his father's home disguised as a palmer to find the unscrupulous knight Brian de Bois-Guilbert, who was plotting to rob the wealthy Jew, Isaac of York. In knightly disguise, Ivanhoe wins at the lists in Ashby de la Zouche but faints afterward from wounds. Isaac and his daughter, Rebecca, bear off the wounded Ivanhoe but are captured by Bois-Guilbert. An assault upon the Norman castle of Torquilstone by Robin Hood and the returned Richard I releases the prisoners, but Bois-Guilbert escapes with Rebecca as captive. She is to be burned as a sorceress, but Ivanhoe fights as her champion, killing Bois-Guilbert. Richard I reassumes his proper rule, Ivanhoe marries Rowena, and Isaac and Rebecca seek greater happiness in distant Grenada.

Waverley created the historical novel; *Ivanhoe* gave it dimensions. The Scottish historical novels were set in times that were still a living memory to Scots. With *Ivanhoe,* Scott lifted the curtain upon a distant past and made it live. Nevertheless, generations of readers have misconstrued English history from this novel. Scott's theme is antagonism between Saxon and Norman in England of the late 12th century. Such hostility, however, was never as sharp as Scott suggests, and, moreover, it existed all through Western society, not on racial or linguistic grounds, but on the restiveness of the serfs under their oppressive landlords. The actions and characters ascribed to the only historic personalities, John and Richard, are imaginary or disputable. Robin Hood, though wholly unhistoric, is not even interpreted in line with his character as set forth in the ballads. Scott's hero, Ivanhoe, who wears all the medieval trappings and knows the ritual of the joust, thinks like a genteel contemporary of the author. Wamba and Gurth are more interesting than their betters, but they are still not the richly convincing peasants of the Scottish novels. And the dialogue, which is shrewdly concocted to give an air of quaint distance, is a language never used by human beings. *Ivanhoe* is a marvelous feat of imaginative recreation, but too many have erroneously accepted this novel as history instead of art.

The Monastery (1820) (C) was a failure. Supposedly the time is the early years of the reign of Elizabeth I, but the chronology is hopelessly confused. The theme is the downfall of the religious house at Melrose Abbey, but while the medieval trappings of the Church aroused Scott's sympathies, he did not truly understand Catholicism or the concept of monasticism. The supernatural element in the White Lady of Avenel borders upon farce. Redeeming features in the book are the spectacle of Moray's army on the Glasgow Road, some descriptions of the Scotish countryside where Scott lived at Abbotsford, and some robust Scottish peasants as vividly alive as only Scott can portray them.

The Abbot (1820) (C) treats of a brief period in the life of Mary Queen of Scots: her imprisonment in Lochleven Castle, her escape in 1568, and her flight to England after the Protestant forces won the battle of Langside near Glasgow.

The impetuous Roland Graeme, a foundling educated by Lady Avenel, loves Catherine Seyton, lady-in-waiting to Mary. Graeme aids the queen in her escape from Lochleven (historically it was William Douglas who helped her). Graeme is revealed as the rightful heir of the Avenels and marries Catherine. The abbot is Father Ambrose, head of Kennaquhair Monastery and brother of the knight of Avenel.

Graeme is one of Scott's less interesting heroes, while Catherine is the most hoydenish of his heroines, a rival to Diana Vernon. Both are overshadowed by the queen, for whom Scott had a romantic Scottish devotion. Mary is his best portrait of a historic woman; she is not merely the personification of grace and beauty, but highly intelligent and courageous also. Unlike later historical novelists, Scott avoids analyzing her but lets her reveal herself in speech. Seldom distinguished in depicting noble ladies, Scott convincingly demonstrates Mary's powerful allure.

Kenilworth (1821) (C), with its two predecessors, constitutes a 16th-century trio. The moderate success of *The Abbot* caused Scott's publisher to call for a novel on Mary's adversary, Elizabeth I.

Rejecting the worthy Edmund Tressilian, Amy Robsart, daughter of Sir Hugh Robsart of Devon, secretly weds the Earl of Leicester, favorite of Elizabeth I. To avoid the queen's displeasure, Leicester conceals Amy at Cumnor Place. Suspecting that Varney, an accomplice of Leicester, is seducing Amy, Tressilian appeals to the queen. Varney persuades Leicester to pawn off Amy upon the queen as Varney's wife. Amy refuses the deception and persuades Leicester to acknowledge her. Berated by the queen, Leicester is amenable to Varney's claims of improper relations between Amy and Tressilian. Leicester permits Varney to murder Amy, Tressilian and Sir Walter Raleigh arriving too late.

Though full of historical inaccuracies, this is one of Scott's best plots and probably the best novel outside of the Scottish pieces. Elizabeth lacks the glamour of Mary, but she is a mighty queen and a genuinely jealous woman. Scott accepts the standard English appraisal of Elizabeth, and the portrait is sure but not subtle. Though not the Dudley of history, Leicester is believably weak and charming, and Sussex, the bluff, forthright type admired by Scott, is admirably drawn. Documents of the age say little about Amy; so Scott imagines her as a ballad heroine depicted by Mickle (the novelist printed Mickle's ballad of Amy in the 1831 edition). Scott's narrative wizardry reaches its height in the meeting of Elizabeth, Amy, and Leicester in the garden of Kenilworth. Probably no other novel has so effectively evoked the surface pageantry and sparkle of Elizabeth's reign.

The Pirate (1821) (A) arose from Scott's 1814 visit to the Orkneys and Shetlands, during which he learned of the early 18th-century pirate John Gow, who menaced the islands. Scott tried unsuccessfully to create a magnificent Romantic novel out of the character of Cleveland, the exciting figure from a tropical world cast onto the northern islands. However, the scenic descriptions of these remote and misty isles are probably the best in Scott's novels.

The Fortunes of Nigel (1822) (C) is set in London a year after the accession (1603) of James I to the English throne. The fortunes of Nigel Olifaunt are confused and not very important, which is unfortunate, for if Scott had constructed a good plot here, he might have produced his masterpiece. Early Stuart London, from the king's court to the underworld, is brought to life with the vividness of Ben Jonson, and in the figure of James I Scott achieves his supreme re-creation of a historic personage. With remarkable subtlety the novelist limns a bizarre but wholly credible man: vain, ridiculous, superstitious, cowardly, but also somehow dignified, impressive, honest to his lights, and delightfully whimsical. The royal mixture of broad Scots and pedantic Latin produces a unique and wonderful speech. Scott's creative imagination has produced a man consonant with the historic facts and, where they appear simply preposterous, has formed a wholly plausible human being.

Peveril of the Peak (1823) (C) is Scott's longest and probably poorest novel. Set primarily in 1678 during the pretended Popish Plot but rambling over twenty years, it displays meager comprehension of the period. Some historical characters are interestingly reconstructed (Buckingham, Colonel Blood, Charles II) and the humbler imaginary characters are good (Mrs. Deborah, Lance, the jailers), but no portraits are monumental.

Quentin Durward (1823) (D) broke new ground for Scott, who left his native islands altogether for a brilliant novel of France during the reign of Louis XI (1461–83). As in *The Fortunes of Nigel,* Scott employed the handy device of a young Scottish hero abroad.

A young Scottish archer, Quentin Durward, joins the Scottish Guards of Louix XI to be with his uncle, Le Balafré. The scheming French monarch entrusts to Quentin two vassals of the Duke of Burgundy, the lovely Isabelle de Croye and her aunt. Quentin innocently obeys orders to conduct the women to the Bishop of Liège, not knowing that the king has planned for William de la March, a powerful brigand, to seize Isabelle. Quentin outwits the brigands and brings the women to the bishop. William attacks Liège castle, murdering the bishop, but Quentin and Isabelle escape. Isabelle seeks the protection of the Duke of Burgundy, who offers her to William's conqueror. Quentin succeeds and wins his princess as reward.

While Scott imperfectly understands the French, he knows all the accouterments and décor of the 15th century. The surface color and pictorial quality of this work almost equal *Ivanhoe.* The action is stirringly conceived and well executed, from the opening hazards through the man-traps of Plessis-les-Tours until Quentin obtains the jewel of his dreams, although in the process many liberties are taken with French history.

Scott shrewdly picks the quarrel between Louis XI and Charles the Bold, Duke of Burgundy, to exemplify the downfall of feudal chivalry beneath the selfish greed of modern times, as symbolized in the king. The author righteously condemns the unscrupulous French ruler, but the detailed treatment shows Scott's fascination with the wily Louis. Only James I, in *The Fortunes of Nigel,* surpasses this portrait of a historic character. The Quixotic idealism of Quentin is countered by the sharp grasp of actualities stated by the ambassador Crèvecoeur and the guardsman Balafré. Such perceptions give to this and other Scott historical novels a sense of genuine life often missing in the superb spectacles of Dumas. Awkwardly claiming a special upbringing for Quentin, Scott admits that his hero is a "man of feeling" incongruous to the 15th century. European reception of the novel exceeded even the English enthusiasm. Scott was at the apex of his fame, recovering from the failure of *Peveril of the Peak.*

St. Ronan's Well (1823) (B) is set in Scott's own time, in an imaginary resort town a few miles up the Tweed river from Abbotsford. The author tries to join a melodramatic account of deceit and mock-marriage to a satiric comedy of manners about rich idlers. The tragedy of Clara Mowbray, entangled in a supposed marriage to the dissolute Etherington, is hopelessly bungled because Scott's publisher insisted upon damaging revisions that render the central plot ridiculous. Unique in Scott is the work's pervading theme of life's irony instead of life's splendid hopes. Fate and fortune here ignore the innocent and virtuous. This is an anti-Romantic novel in its picturing of trifling gentlefolk, petty, bickering, and mean-spirited. The Scots characters are good, especially Meg Dods, the termagant hostess of Cleikum Inn, expressing thorough disillusionment with her useless guests in robust, rhythmic Scots.

Redgauntlet (1824) (A), last of the Scottish novels, is based upon the unauthenticated legend that Bonnie Prince Charlie actually appeared in disguise in London of 1763 but, though recognized, was permitted to leave by a magnanimous George III, who felt securely in power and was unwilling to persecute a helpless rival. The story is told through letters exchanged by two young Scottish lawyers, Darsie Latimer and Alan Fairford (Scott himself).

Sir Alberick Redgauntlet paid with his life for his support of the Young Pretender in 1745. His daughter is carried off by his last-ditch Jacobite brother, while his son is brought up by Alberick's widow as

Darsie Latimer, ignorant of his origin. The surviving fanatical Red-gauntlet seizes Darsie and involves him in a conspiracy to support Bonnie Prince Charlie, secretly returned in disguise. Darsie's friend, Alan Fairford, tracks down the missing Darsie just as the conspirators are ready to spring their plot. Betrayed by Redgauntlet's servant, the plotters disperse, their cabal rendered preposterous by the generous clemency of George III. Redgauntlet accompanies the Pretender to France, ending his days in a monastery. Darsie, now Sir Arthur Red-gauntlet, supports the Hanoverians and bestows his sister's hand upon Alan.

Some lovers of Scott claim this as the novelist's best work. Though slow-moving for half the book, the plot is well constructed, fusing both private problems and the swirl of national destiny. The theme first expounded in *Waverley* suffuses the novel: the contest between old loyalties to a departed Scotland and new loyalties to the present world in which Scots now live. This is Scott's farewell to romantic Jacobitism, as symbolized by the courageous Scottish officer Colin Campbell, loyal to the Hanoverians, who enters the conspirators' circle unarmed and disperses them by the generous terms. The End of the Cause in the great final scene may contain Scott's best writing. Scott's own youthful amours are suggested in the account of the Lady of the Green Mantle (Margaret Belches). Scottish characters are again superb, notably Nanty Ewart, the smuggling captain, Poor Peter Peebles, the pedantic lawyer, and Joshua Geddes, the intrepid Quaker. Embedded in the letters is "Wandering Willie's Tale," an imaginative account of diablerie in melodic Scots supposedly from a blind fiddler. It is essentially poetic in the manner distinctly Scots since at least the "Makaris." Stevenson termed it the greatest short story in English, and no one can omit it from the dozen or so of the world's best short stories.

The Betrothed (1825) (C) was the first of the *Tales of the Cru-sades*. Set during the reign (1154–89) of Henry II in the Welsh border-land, the novel intended a combination of two struggles: Flemish settlers against the native Welsh, and local and personal ties against the crusad-ing urge. The account of the first struggle is passable, producing in Wilkin Flammock the sort of homespun figure in which Scott excelled. The second calls for psychological probings, not Scott's forte. The novelist wanted to burn this work but was persuaded that it would be carried by its accompanying novel.

The Talisman (1825) (D) completed *Tales of the Crusades*. Though set in the same era as *Ivanhoe,* the locale is Palestine as digested from *Historical Geography of the Holy Land*, by G. A. Smith. As usual, Scott brought in a Scotsman, Sir Kenneth. The novel is ringingly Romantic with fewer realistic touches than any other Scott novel. Richard I and Saladin are dashing figures in the grand manner, but they lack any subtlety of portraiture. The novel's continued popularity rests upon its appeal to chivalric poetry in the young.

Woodstock; or The Cavalier (1826) (C) revolves about the escape of Charles II after the battle of Worcester (1651). Though written in the midst of financial ruin and personal tragedy, the novel is surprisingly light-hearted. Roger Wildrake is an excellent study of the cavalier, but Scott could not get into the minds of the English parliamentarians as he could into the Covenanters of his own land. The plot is so well handled that Thackeray lifted much of it for *Henry Esmond*, simply renaming many of the characters. Dramatic episodes often display the familiar taut mastery of Scott. The major failing seems to arise from Scott's first and only attempt to make noted figures of English history his central characters. Both Charles II and Cromwell are satisfactory but not momentous characters.

Chronicles of the Canongate (1827) (A) first acknowledged Scott's authorship of the novels. The initial series consists of short stories supposedly written by Mr. Chrystal Croftangry, based upon tales of Mrs. Bethune Balliol, resident in the Canongate, Edinburgh. The narrator is the most interesting character, revealing a bitter-sweetness, a mellowing similar to Ivan Turgenev's. "The Highland Widow" depicts the disruption of Highland life after "The Forty-Five," with the wild and stubborn Elspeth MacTavish. "The Two Drovers" tells of Robin Oig's killing and stoic acceptance of penalty. Both pieces show unusual psychological skill, though, of course, they are about uncomplicated folk. "The Surgeon's Daughter" memorably sketches the country physician, Dr. Gideon Gray, mixing homey Middlemas with an exotic, second-hand India.

St. Valentine's Day; or, The Fair Maid of Perth (1828) (C) was the chief item in the second series of *Chronicles of the Canongate*. This is the darkest and wildest of Scott's novels, venturing far more than any other into the savage violence of medievalism, here in Perth, Scotland, around 1400.

The Duke of Rothsay, son of Robert III of Scotland, enlists Sir John Ramorny in an attempt to abduct Catherine Glover, "the fair maid of Perth." Armorer Henry Smith, in love with Catherine, rescues her, slashing off Ramorny's hand in the process. Believing that Rothsay betrayed him, Ramorny lures the duke to his death. Catherine is also sought by Conachar, head of clan Quhele. The dispute is settled by a pitched battle at North Inch between clan Quhele and clan Chattan (Smith's clan). Conachar flees from Smith in momentary cowardice and, in chagrin, commits suicide. At Catherine's insistence, Smith gives up fighting to marry her.

Smith is the most savage of all Scott's heroes, more genuinely medieval than the Ivanhoes and the Durwards. His wildness cannot remain under his control, and his untamable spirit is a world away from the Waverleys and the Osbaldistones. Conachar, by Scott's admission, is an expiation for the author's refusal to attend the funeral of his brother Daniel, accused of cowardice during a Jamaican slave uprising. Sympathetically, Scott here sees how as brave a fighter as Hector can suddenly lose his nerve. Except for the saintly Catherine and her Lollard instructor, Father Clement, who stand out in vivid contrast to their surroundings, there is no character to charm the sentimental reader. Scott's artificial romances of medievalism gained a huge audience; this sort of novel shows what he might have done if readers could have appreciated authentic medievalism. Expertly he evokes the feel of a walled medieval city, one of the English-speaking communities resolutely but precariously set in the outskirts of Highland Scotland, land of the Celt.

Anne of Geierstein (1829) (D) was an inferior sequel to *Quentin Durward,* carrying on the history of Charles the Bold, Duke of Burgundy. Three elements are inadequately blended: (1) politics (as in the discussion of Oxford and Charles) and war (stirring battle scenes of Granson and Murten); (2) Gothicism (as in the secret tribunal of the *Vehmgericht,* a late medieval tribunal common in Germany which met in secret and often usurped the functions of government); and (3) idyllic young love between Arthur and Anne.

Count Robert of Paris (1832) (D) was the initial piece in the fourth and last series of *Tales of My Landlord.* Gibbon is the chief source for this tale of the First Crusade and especially the plot concerning Nicephorus Briennius's attempt to dethrone his father-in-law, the Byzantine emperor Alexius Comnenus. However, the history is never transmuted into believable fiction.

Castle Dangerous (1832) (C), Scott's last novel, tells of the defense of Douglas Castle by Sir John de Walton in 1306 against the forces of Sir James Douglas and Robert the Bruce. All the events occur during rain squalls and leaden skies, appropriate to the mood of the dying novelist. The material was well in his domain, but Scott was too weary to rise to the challenge.

Jane Porter (1776–1850). A native of Durham in northern England, Jane Porter followed the lead of her novelist sister, Anna Maria Porter, and outstripped her.

The Scottish Chiefs (1810) proved one of the most popular novels of the 19th century and still has some appeal to juvenile readers. It deals with the Scottish hero William Wallace.

Outraged by his wife's murder in 1296 at the hands of English soldiers, Wallace rallies the Scottish nobles, especially the estimable Lord Mar, against Edward, the English monarch. Lady Mar makes advances to the handsome Wallace and, spurned by that honorable gentleman, thereafter proves his most implacable foe. Spectacular victories over the English insure Wallace's elevation to the regentship, followed by jealous bickerings among Scottish aristocrats. In the disguise of a harper, Wallace enters the court of Edward and persuades the Bruce to espouse his country's cause. The two hasten to France to rescue the abducted Helen Mar. Returning, Wallace finds that internal quarrels have destroyed his achievement. He is captured during Edward's second invasion and brutally executed.

Here is the Scott formula of high, colorful adventure with a valiant, pure hero. Absent, however, is Scott's sense of the transformations of history in the contest of old and new. Picturesque scenery and emotional fervor, especially in the lamentation for a lost but not forgotten leader, heighten the novel's bravura appeal. The work's superficiality and sentimentality have now generally denied it an adult audience.

Thomas Hope (c. 1770–1831). A wealthy London antiquary and art connoisseur, Thomas Hope traveled extensively in the Near East and produced a novel whose atmospheric authenticity annoyed Byron.

Anastasius, or Memoirs of a Greek (1819) suffers from too much pure narration and undigested sections of history and description. Supposedly, it is dictated by a dying soldier of fortune recounting his swashbuckling adventures throughout the 18th-century Levant. It is a belated specimen of the picaresque tale but without low comedy. Its hero is an attractive scoundrel, honestly self-critical and capable of some unselfish emotion. The exotic locale and exotic adventures appealed strongly to Romantic readers. The novel displays interesting parallels to *Don Juan,* and Byron may owe to Hope the germ of Leila and other elements in his long poem.

Mary Wollstonecraft Shelley née **Godwin** (1797–1851). Mary Shelley was the London-born daughter of two of the most remarkable persons of the era: her father was William Godwin, the philosopher; and her mother was Mary Wollstonecraft, the first great feminist in England (both of them are discussed in Chapter 5). In 1814 Mary eloped to the Continent with Shelley and married him in 1816 after the suicide of his first wife, Harriet Westbrook. After Shelley's death, she returned with her son to England in 1823. In 1824 she edited her husband's works, printing many previously unpublished poems and supplying valuable notes. She wrote several novels, most notably:

Frankenstein; or The Modern Prometheus (1818). During the summer of 1816 the Shelleys were frequently with Byron in Geneva. At a reading of ghost stories, Polidari, Byron's physician, suggested that everyone write a horror story. All tried, but Byron and Shelley soon discarded their attempts, and Polidari completed a rambling account, *The Vampire*. But Mary saw to completion the most famous horror novel in English.

Intent upon the creation of life from inanimate matter, the young scientist Frankenstein collects human remains from charnel houses. He fashions a living being that resembles a man but that is a powerful, ugly creature. Lonely because no human being can endure it, the creature demands that Frankenstein construct a wife for it. Frankenstein starts but breaks off his project when he contemplates a race of such monsters. The enraged creature slays the brother and the bride of Frankenstein, and the scientist determines to kill the monster. He tracks it to the far northern ice floes but dies of exposure. The monster disappears in the swirling snow.

This is a serious novel upon two significant concepts. Looking backward to 18th-century thought is the idea of "natural" man. Frankenstein's creature yearns for sympathy and love; it is transformed into a monster because everyone, including its creator, is repelled by it. Any living thing is inherently good; it is mistreatment that makes it "wicked." Looking ahead, this is the first significant apprehension in English that science will create a monster that can destroy science and possibly mankind.

The novel is also revelatory of the author's Romantic personality. Mary was torn between her strongly emotional nature and the rigid intellectual discipline imposed by her father. Therefore, the novel is her protest against Godwin's rationalistic handling of human beings, herself included. She feels that such treatment will destroy human values and human beings. Prominent, too, is Mary's morbid preoccupation with forthcoming disaster. Terrifying domestic tragedies were awaiting her, and one can sense in the novel a dire foreboding of, even a psychic urging to, disaster.

The Last Man (1826), though uneven and deficient in social and political foresight, is Mary's most remarkable novel. A devastating plague has exterminated all mankind by the year 2073 except for the poetic Adrian, modeled after Shelley. Born of the Romantic's self-imposed isolation and loneliness, this work is the prototype of stories about the last man on earth.

Charles Robert Maturin (mat'ū-rin) (1782–1824). Of French Huguenot ancestry and a native of Dublin, Charles Robert Maturin was educated locally at Trinity College and became the Anglican curate of St. Peter's, Dublin. His grandfather had succeeded Swift as dean of St. Patrick's. Maturin's play *Bertram* was performed by Kean in 1816 to wide applause with the exception of Coleridge, who was disappointed at the rejection of his own play. Maturin wrote several novels with sensational plots and, in his greatest work, produced the masterpiece of the Gothic novel:

Melmoth the Wanderer (1820) really consists of a series of tales locked together by the central figure of Melmoth, an amalgam of Faust, Mephistopheles, the Flying Dutchman, and the Wandering Jew.

The 17th-century Irish gentleman Melmoth has sold his soul to the devil in return for immortal life. In remorse, he wishes to slough off his horrible burden, but he may do so only if a fellow human being will accept it. Therefore, Melmoth appears to mortals who are undergoing fearful agonies. The Englishman Stanton meets him in a madhouse. The Spaniard Monçada is approached by Melmoth amid the tortures of the Inquisition. Immalee, another Haidée upon an island in the Indian Ocean, is treated by Melmoth as Gretchen was by Faust, but when he confronts her with the "unutterable condition" as she awaits execution for infanticide, she also refuses. Also demurring is the German musician Walberg, even as he and his family starve. Melmoth returns to his ancestral Irish home, darkly informing his contemporary descendant, John, that his long-delayed end is coming. Melmoth locks himself in a room that resounds with fearful struggles during the night. In the morning, John follows footprints to the edge of a great precipice overlooking the sea. There the footprints end.

The kaleidoscope of brilliant stories, ranging from the idyllic romance of Immalee to the bleak economic plight of Walberg, forms perhaps the most varied and intriguing novel in English. Maturin is the supreme master of atmosphere and suspense. He never descends to the pseudo-horrors of Mrs. Radcliffe or the obscenities of "Monk" Lewis. Tone and diction never fall below the high-pitched excitement and wonder of Romanticism. Maturin ingeniously alters the theme of the man who sells his soul to the devil; Melmoth is ceaselessly attempting deliverance, and his contemplated victims always read the full truth of the proposal in Melmoth's hell-ravaged eyes. The novel thrilled Byron, Scott, Rossetti, Thackeray, Stevenson, and Poe. The French were especially excited by the work, and Balzac wrote a sequel.

James Justinian Morier (mō′ri-êr or mor′i-ā) (c. 1780–1849). Morier was born in Smyrna, Turkey, son of the consul general of the Levant Company in Constantinople. After education at Harrow, he rejoined his family in Constantinople in 1807, in the same year entering the British diplomatic service. Until 1816 he served in the British embassy in Teheran, Persia. In 1812 and again in 1818 he published accounts of his experiences in Persia, the first full depictions of that country in English. After 1817 he devoted his time to writing except for a term as special commissioner in Mexico, 1824–26. A cosmopolite fluent in several languages, Morier wrote his last novel, *Martin Toutrond,* in French and then translated it himself in 1849.

The Adventures of Hajji Baba of Ispahan (1824) is a picaresque novel in a Persian locale. "Hajji" in Arabic means a pilgrim to Mecca and Medina, but Baba is a scamp unwarrantedly assuming this honorific.

In succession the hero is a barber, robber, servant, physician's assistant, aide to an executioner, religious fanatic, and tobacco broker. He survives the most dangerous and ludicrous escapades, to marry a rich widow, become a government official, and accompany the ambassador to England.

Baba's adventures are frequently quite realistic, but the gay rascality and exotic surroundings made a distinctly Romantic appeal. The authentic portrayal of Persian life and the amusing picture of Oriental bungling and chicanery caused the Persian ambassador in England to protest. A sequel in 1828, bringing Baba to England, was less successful. The sequel falls into the "foreign visitor" genre, using a perceptive observer from another culture to satirize European shortcomings. With Morier's work, this genre writes itself to extinction.

THE NON-ROMANTIC NOVELS OF THE PERIOD

Thomas Love Peacock (1785–1866). Born in Weymouth, Dorsetshire, Thomas Love Peacock was largely self-educated. His first publication was a thin volume of poetry in 1804. Upon a slender patrimony, Peacock enjoyed reading, writing, and study. In 1812 he made Shelley's acquaintance and became an intimate friend of the poet. In 1819 he was unexpectedly appointed to a post with the East India Company. Promptly he proposed by letter to Jane Gryffydh, of Elwys Vach, Wales, whom he had seen in 1811 but had not contacted since. After Jane's acceptance, Shelley remarked: "The affair is extremely like the denouement of one of your own novels." Thereafter Peacock lived with distinguished success in two worlds. He succeeded James Mill as the chief examiner of the East India Company in 1836 and in 1856 relinquished the position to John Stuart Mill. Without the spur of financial need, Peacock could issue short novels that were "caviar to the general" but stimulating to current intellectuals.

"Novel" may be a misleading term to apply to Peacock's works, for he is unconcerned with plot and only slightly interested in character. Ideas are his forte, and his pieces of fiction are essentially discussion novels. Each follows the same pattern: Peacock assembles a group of diverse extremists who battle over ideas in some of the most interesting and thought-provoking dialogue in English fiction. Peacock's specific distastes are evident—rotten boroughs, slavery, the universities, spiritualism, paper money, Malthusianism, etc.—but pervasive is his anti-Romantic hostility to illusion, pretense, and theory. Rather than espousing any positive position, he seems essentially a modern Lucian, a witty skeptic unconvinced by the dramatic "march of mind." In his rapier-like play of thought he resembles his son-in-law, George Meredith.

Headlong Hall (1816) assembles a group of faddists at the country house of Squire Headlong. The principal controversy ensues between Foster (the Godwinian or Shelleyan theorist), the perfectibilitarian, and Escot (probably Peacock himself for the sake of argument), the believer in the degeneration of mankind. The wild-eyed optimism of Foster is countered by some sober but witty analyses of current society. The Coleridge type of sesquipedalian mystic is amusingly portrayed in Panscope.

Melincourt (1817) is the longest Peacock work and the most farcical.

Tongue-in-cheek, Peacock accepts Monboddo's theory that the orang-utan is an underdeveloped form of man. Sir Oran Haut-Ton is a monkey who is caught, dressed in the best tailored garments, and coached to maintain a distinguished bearing. Though mute, he runs for Parliament and is elected by the rotten borough of Onevote. Not only Monboddo but unjust representation and the notorious uselessness of some members of Parliament are merrily ridiculed. The turncoat Romantics are sneeringly derided—Wordsworth as Mr. Paperstamp of Mainchance Villa (he had a sinecure as seller of revenue stamps) and Southey as Mr. Feathernest. Mr. Fax is a caricature of Malthus.

Nightmare Abbey (1818) is the most direct attack upon Romanticism. Shelley confessed that he was amused by his own portrait as Scythrop, which satirizes the poet even to his tug between Harriet (Marionetta) and Mary (Stella). Cypress is Byron, glowering in proper titanic and demoniacal fashion, finding exquisite joy only in bitterest despair. Flosky ("lover of shadows"—Coleridge) has appropriately named his son Emmanuel Kant Flosky and rapturously extols mystery as "the very key-stone of all that is beautiful in poetry, all that is sacred in faith, and all that is recondite in transcendental psychology." Glowry sums up for the Romantics in exhorting them: "Let us all be unhappy together."

Maid Marian (1822) is an anti-romance, a parody of the Robin Hood theme, but so charming that Planché turned it into a moderately successful opera. Peacock smiles at the "natural" man and the outlaws' exemplary republican society. Friar Tuck as the embodiment of laughter and witty common sense is probably Peacock's most memorable creation. It would be difficult to find another satire upon romance that so much itself breathes the air of graceful romance.

The Misfortunes of Elphin (1829) is a superb burlesque. Ostensibly it is a romantic tale from the Welsh, celebrating the great sea wall protecting the plain of Gwaelod and the absurd methods of those responsible for maintaining the wall. Actually it is a telling stab at the dilapidated conservatism of current English politics. The drunken prince Seithenyn is the prototype of all reactionaries oblivious to the needs of a new world and blindly insistent upon continuing an old rottenness unaltered. Peacock's position is not that of a revolutionary but rather of one like Burke, who recognizes the need for modification and improvement of existing institutions.

Crotchet Castle (1831) is the most finished in Peacock's unusual genre of the novel of pure talk. Mr. Chainmail is a ludicrous burlesque of Scott's penchant for ballads and medievalism, and Wordsworth and Southey briefly appear, respectively, as Wilful Wontsee and Rumblesack Shantsee (the prename alludes to the butt of sack which is a perquisite of the poet laureate). Numerous other dislikes of Peacock are aired—modern literature, newspaper mania, "the insane passion of the public for speed," modern science and the economists, the Industrial Revolution, and the stupidity of Columbus in discovering a new world to plague the old. Dr. Folliott is the nearest figure in the novels to the author himself: epicurean, humanist, intellectual, anti-Romantic, and man of the world.

Gryll Grange (1860), belated product of a septuagenarian, shows no diminution of strength and offers more of a plot than the other novels. Morgana Gryll, an heiress who persistently refuses all marriage proposals, is forced by accident to spend several days at the lonely tower of Algernon Falconer, a wealthy young man (modeled after Shelley) disinclined to matrimony by the solicitous attentions of seven foster sisters. A love affair inevitably develops, as it also does between Lord Curryfin and Alice Niphet. The most interesting character, Dr. Opimian, is another expositor of Peacock's sallies against modern inventions, reforms, education, and competitive examinations. The Peacock view of life appears summed up in Opimian's advice: "Whatever happens in this world, never let it spoil your dinner." Notable in this last novel are Peacock's capable women, intelligent, independent, and without contemporary prudishness.

NON-FICTION PROSE. *The Four Ages of Poetry* (1820) is a half-humorous attack upon poetry that elicited Shelley's famous *Defence of Poetry*. Peacock adapts the ancient concept of four ages to see in English poetry the iron age of medievalism, the golden age of Shakespeare, the silver age of Dryden and Pope, and the brass age of the current era. Peacock sees poetry as logical at an early stage of cultural development, for poetry is "the mental rattle that awakened the attention of intellect in the infancy of civil society." With the maturing of civilization, the poet is an anachronism, "a semi-barbarian in a civilized community." Peacock sneers at contemporary versifiers, the "egregious confraternity of rhymesters, known by the name of the Lake poets," and those of the Byron and Shelley type, who vent "querulous, egotistical rhapsodies, to express the writer's high dissatisfaction with the world and every thing in it." It is high time, he concludes, to discard poetry in favor of the work of serious thinkers and scientists.

Mary Russell Mitford (1787–1855). The only child of an Alresford, Hampshire, physician, Mary Russell Mitford proved quite precocious. Her earlier works were verse and drama, but by 1820 her father's extravagance forced her to novel writing to support her family. Haydon painted her portrait, Lamb asserted that nothing as fresh and true as her writing had appeared for a long time, Mrs. Browning called her "a sort of prose Crabbe in the sun," and Landor eloquently praised her shortly before her death. With all this acclaim, Mary Mitford lived and died in modest surroundings.

Our Village was serialized in *The Lady's Magazine* from 1819, amounting to three series by 1832. In many respects she resembles Jane Austen, proving an utterly faithful feminine reporter of small-town life, chiefly Three-Mile Cross, near Reading. All the local characters are there, and all the minor tragedies and triumphs of a quiet community. The author's clear observation and womanly humor save her from the current sentimentalism of many men as well as women writers. The stories are thin, but the dialogue rings authentically, and an entire hamlet becomes alive with atmosphere and color.

Chapter 9

The Essayists and Other
Prose Writers of the
Romantic Period (1800–1837)

THE BEGINNING OF MODERN MAGAZINES

The first decade of the 19th century inaugurated the Golden Age of English periodicals, which was to last until World War I. The sizable increase in literate readers, plus the intensified national and international concerns born of the Industrial Revolution and the Napoleonic era, stimulated English periodical writing at the century's outset. The foundation of these magazines, of course, rested upon the momentous development of English journals throughout the previous century, but the 18th-century periodicals had been handicapped for the following reasons:

(1) Essay periodicals had been one-man performances (*Spectator, Idler, etc.*) of relatively short duration. Though frequently of high quality, they may best be considered as one author's essays printed in installments.

(2) Edited publications (e.g. *Gentleman's Magazine*) had depended upon amateur contributions or the padding of poorly paid hacks. Much space was given to "chronicles" of births, deaths, promotions, bankruptcies, etc. Periodical writing did not provide a living for professional writers of real ability.

(3) Reviews (such as the *Critical* and the *Monthly*) had generally consisted of short, specific criticisms that were often little more than summaries of printed books or, for controversial writings, laborious point-by-point analysis and refutation.

(4) No periodical obtained the position of a sustained, high-quality

literary publication with a regular following. Apparently the reading public had not yet been created to support such a publication.

The Edinburgh Review and Critical Journal (1802–1929), founded by Sydney Smith, Francis Jeffrey, and Henry Brougham, inaugurated two important policies: (1) it would review only a few significant writings; (2) it would offer generous pay to editors and contributors. By restricting its compass and making no attempt to note everything printed, the *Edinburgh* brushed aside trivialities and encouraged reviews that were notable essays in themselves. By paying well, the magazine secured the services of professionals who up to 1837 included Scott, Hazlitt, Malthus, Henry Hallam, Macaulay, Carlyle, and Thomas Arnold. By 1818 the circulation was fourteen thousand copies with perhaps five times as many readers. As already mentioned, Brougham's slighting review of Byron's first volume of poetry elicited the famous satire *English Bards and Scotch Reviewers*. Though independent at the beginning, the *Edinburgh* quickly became a partisan publication, vigorously expressing Whig opinion; however, it may be said that with this periodical, modern English literary journalism was born.

The *Quarterly Review* (1809–   ) is the oldest English review still in existence and the most important reviewing publication in our literature. Although many Tories were involved in its inception, Scott (irked by the unfavorable reaction of the *Edinburgh* to *Marmion*) was its leading spirit, along with the satirist William Gifford, who was its first editor. The editorial policies of the *Edinburgh* were followed, though the *Quarterly* was staunchly Tory, with contributors up to 1837 including Scott (reviewing his own anonymous novels), Lamb, Southey, and Washington Irving. By 1818 its circulation equaled that of the *Edinburgh*. The massive influence of this publication is demonstrated by the old Lincolnshire squire who, in 1832, told Tennyson's father that the *Quarterly* was "the next book to God's *Bible*." Scores of imitators followed the *Edinburgh* and the *Quarterly,* but these two reviews dominated English letters in the 19th century as no periodicals have before or since. Their critical, political, and religious viewpoints made them speak for thousands of English readers; from the aloof heights of anonymity their magisterial finality was the definitive and unquestioned judgment for generations of readers.

Monthly Repository of Theology and General Literature (1806–37) was essentially an organ of the Unitarians. Its contributors included John Stuart Mill, Henry Crabb Robinson, Robert Browning, and

Ebenezer Elliott. It proved sympathetic to the Romantics, and in later issues it published much of the work of Leigh Hunt and Richard Hengist Horne. Both of the latter were among the publication's editors. This periodical introduced the previously unknown practice of signing many reviews, a practice widespread today.

Blackwood's Edinburgh Magazine (1817–   ), known familiarly to generations of literary men as *Maga,* is the oldest continuing purely literary journal in English. The original publisher, William Blackwood, entrusted the periodical to John Wilson, James Hogg, and John Lockhart. Contributions in the early years included Scott, Mackenzie, De Quincey, and Coleridge. The most ebullient of the current periodicals, this militantly Tory publication was famous for its "trumpet tone," scathingly denouncing liberals like Hunt and Hazlitt. By 1831 *Blackwood's* had discarded its heritage of 18th-century pot-pourri journals and emerged as the prototype of the modern literary magazine —consisting entirely of original articles, poetry, fiction, and reviews. Wilson enthusiastically asserted in "Noctes Ambrosianae" (*Blackwood's,* 1829): "Our current periodical literature teems with thought and feeling. . . . The whole surface of society is thus irrigated by a thousand streams."

The *London Magazine* (1819–29), in emulation of *Blackwood's,* was started by the brilliant John Scott. Under his tragically brief editorship, it enjoyed for its span the greatest literary triumphs of any English periodical. Scott here first published De Quincey's *Confessions of an English Opium-Eater,* Lamb's *Essays of Elia,* and Hazlitt's *Table Talk.* Its liberal but judicious criticism of Scott, Shelley, Keats, Byron, and Wordsworth puts to shame all other current reviewing. Attacks upon *Blackwood's* resulted in a challenge to a duel, in which J. C. Christie, representing the Scottish publication, killed Scott in 1821. Under Benthamite editorship, the periodical petered out.

The *New Monthly Magazine and Literary Journal* (1820–84) succeeded the *New Monthly,* founded in 1814. Under the editorship of the poet Thomas Campbell, it ignored politics for a purely literary approach. Campbell's "Last Man," which inspired Mary Shelley's novel, was first printed here, but in spite of some noted contributors (Hazlitt and Lamb) and commendable studies of the Romantics, its career was not the most distinguished.

The Liberal (1822) consisted of only four numbers edited by Hunt in Italy. It is the first significant "expatriate" literary publication in English. Shelley, along with Byron, had been instrumental in its founding, but Shelley died before the first issue appeared with Byron's *Vision of Judgment*. Some of Shelley's posthumous verse first saw print in this publication, and Hazlitt contributed some of his best essays.

The *Westminster Review* was started in 1824 by James Mill as a vehicle of Benthamism and liberal reform. It was the vociferous mouthpiece for all liberalism and exerted a strong influence, even though its circulation was always well below that of its famous rivals. Distinctly utilitarian, it tended to ignore mere literature or to scrutinize literary works solely from a "party line," anticipating the practice of some 20th-century periodicals. Amalgamation caused its retitling in 1836 as *London and Westminster Review*, continuing the same liberal viewpoint under the supervision of John Stuart Mill. At Mill's insistence, for the first time a periodical printed nothing but signed articles. The practice arose from Mill's refusal to accept responsibility for the statements of his father and others whose articles he disagreed with but felt obliged to publish. Once begun, the practice of signed articles became the policy of this journal, and eventually it became quite general. Another change, to *Westminster and Foreign Quarterly Review* in 1851 under John Chapman, started an even more famous course, notably with George Eliot.

THE REVIEWERS

Most of the Romantics were political radicals, a minority in an England reacting against the French Revolution. The pontifical *Edinburgh* was liberal only in the sense of the 18th-century Whigs; it was as hostile to republicanism as its Tory competitors. Further, both Whig and Tory publications were culturally conservative. Reviewing Southey's *Thalaba* in the first issue of the *Edinburgh*, Jeffrey laid down the dictum that he, his publication, and the *Quarterly* and *Blackwood's* would thereafter follow rather rigorously: "Poetry has this much, at least, in common with religion, that its standards were fixed long ago, by certain inspired writers, whose authority it is no longer lawful to call in question." Such dogmatism therefore rendered inevitable the consistently unsympathetic response of the great reviews to the new literature of the Romantics.

Sydney Smith (1771–1845). The "Smith of Smiths," Sydney Smith was born at Woodford, Essex, son of a feckless father and a beautiful French refugee mother. His father's haphazard finances caused Smith to elect the church as a career. As tutor to an English boy, Smith came to Edinburgh in 1798, where his wit and geniality made him central in the sparkling literary society of the "Athens of the North." Smith proposed the *Edinburgh Review* and supervised the first three issues. During the next twenty-five years he contributed about eighty articles to the publication. Through all his criticism breathes the un-Romantic distaste of anything extreme or mysterious. In London, Smith proved the most popular preacher of the time, and perhaps the most popular lecturer, speaking upon "moral philosophy" but displaying such wit and shrewdness in observation as to make the soberest topics delightful. Smith's liberalism militated against his advancement in the church until the return of the Whigs to power, when he became canon of St. Paul's.

Smith was a pious man but in many respects the epitome of the 18th-century English clergyman. He looked upon a cleric as a human being in a surplice and considered the Established Church as a division of the civil service. He therefore saw no incongruity in his position as the outstanding humorist, even buffoon, of the era. Some of the brilliant remarks credited to him are certainly apocryphal, but there is enough confirmation from the scores of authors who knew him (notably Rogers, in *Table Talk*) to make us profoundly regret that there was no Boswell to record the superlative talk of the great Smith.

Letters on the Subject of the Catholics . . . by Peter Plymley and *A Letter to the Electors upon the Catholic Question* (1807–08) have aged because their cause, Catholic Emancipation, has long since triumphed. Both are classics of fighting propaganda, blending wit and temper. There is no revolutionary or mystic theorist in Smith. In direct English fashion he appeals to common sense, fair play, and self-interest. He pleads for a tolerant spirit "to fling down no man's altar, to punish no man's prayer." Without the imaginative insight of Hazlitt, Smith displays the same ease and fluency in arguing a case. Smith's prose is a belated survivor of the best 18th-century brevity and naturalness.

Francis Jeffrey, Lord Jeffrey (1773–1850). Son of a deputy clerk in the court of session, Jeffrey was educated in his native Edinburgh, in Glasgow, and in Oxford. After a brief practice of law, he devoted himself essentially to editing and reviewing. Initially the *Edinburgh* was edited by a committee, but Jeffrey became the undisputed editor in 1803. Thomas Moore challenged him to a duel because of a hostile review in 1806, but the duel was averted, and the two men were later to be friends. Although Jeffrey formally relinquished editorship in 1829, he was the leading spirit of the publication until his death. He contributed approximately two hundred articles to the *Edinburgh*. Though unqualifiedly Whig in viewpoint, Jeffrey was less severe and less biased than many contemporary critics or his own stated principles would indicate.

Jeffrey's critical position was that of the 18th century, and exalted common sense, reason, and practicality. He therefore had no sympathy for the Romanticism of Scott, Wordsworth, Coleridge, and Shelley. *The Excursion,* he solemnly decided, "will never do"; the conclusion of the "Ode to Duty" was meaningless; the "Ode on Intimations of Immortality" was unintelligible; and Wordsworth was a genius too often seduced by the trivial and the absurd. The moderate praise that Jeffrey occasionally afforded to Byron, Scott, and Moore was carefully balanced with censure; however, Crabbe was one of his favorites. Toward the end of his career Jeffrey asserted that Rogers and Campbell were the only two poets of the era who would secure enduring fame. Comparing Jeffrey to Voltaire, Carlyle asserted that he was the most eminent of all English critics. Certainly Jeffrey proved one of the best editors of any English literary periodical. Macaulay feelingly called Jeffrey "as near perfection as any human being with whom I have been acquainted."

John Wilson Croker (1780–1857). A native of Galway, Ireland, Croker was first educated in a school conducted by the father of Sheridan Knowles, the dramatist. At Trinity College, Dublin, he was a schoolmate of Moore. Croker thereafter cultivated with equal facility a political career and literary criticism. A staunch Tory, Croker rose to be secretary of the admiralty. On the floor of Parliament, he several times locked horns with the brilliant Macaulay, and that scintillating Whig, stung by Croker's success, did much to blacken the reputation of Croker's writings. Croker is credited in his January 1830 article in the *Quarterly* with the first use of the word *Conservative* to designate the Tory party. After the Reform Bill, Croker refused to serve in Parliament, convinced that the nation was thoroughly ruined.

From 1811 until 1845 practically every issue of the *Quarterly* carried an article by Croker (a total of about 260) but, because the contributions were unsigned, it is impossible to establish the exact canon of his writings. Most famous is the review of Keats's *Endymion* in September 1818. Since Croker imperfectly understood the poem, disliked what he did understand, and detested the liberalism of Hunt (who encouraged Keats), he immediately assumed that the poem was atrocious. Croker was not always so wrong-headed, but he could never appreciate the Romantics, nurtured as he was in the Tory school of Pope.

Memoirs, Diaries, and Correspondence of the Right Hon. John Wilson Croker (1884) lacks the sprightly flavor of the Creevey papers, but it is the fullest and most informative picture of the English political world during the first half of the century, viewed through Tory eyes. Without inspiration, Croker writes lucidly and honestly, to the limit of his rigid Toryism.

John Gibson Lockhart (1794–1854). Son of the Kirk of Scotland clergyman at Cambusnethan, John Gibson Lockhart was educated at the universities of Glasgow and Oxford. As an undergraduate he was famed for practical jokes and witticisms. Briefly practicing law, he turned to writing for the newly established *Blackwood's* in 1817. In 1820 Lockhart married Scott's eldest daughter and for some time lived on Scott's estate in intimate association with the novelist. In 1825 he became editor of the *Quarterly,* holding this post until declining health forced his resignation in 1853. He died in the room next to that in which Scott died.

Lockhart has usually been stigmatized on the basis of his early reviews in *Blackwood's.* With sarcasm and grossly unfair prejudice he lashed out against the *Edinburgh* and Coleridge's *Biographia Literaria.* Here he concocted the label "Cockney School of Poets" to brand Hunt and Keats. The older Lockhart regretted these sallies as the injudicious cruelties of youth.

About a hundred articles he wrote for the *Quarterly* show perhaps the broadest perspective and largest spirit among the official reviewers of the age. Lockhart was the greatest stylist among them, occasionally resembling the cool, severe grace of Landor. With Wilson he shared the honor of full recognition of Wordsworth's accomplishment.

Life of Scott (seven volumes, 1836–38) is one of the monumental biographies of English, often considered second only to Boswell's life of Johnson. The mature Lockhart was in a rare position as biographer of the novelist. In addition to close family ties with Scott, Lockhart wholly shared his father-in-law's Tory politics, undogmatic Presbyterianism, gentlemanly attitude and position in life, and love of sports and tradition. Lockhart quite surpassed his father-in-law in careful scholarship. He was also a poet and novelist in his own right. The biography may well be termed the supreme portrait of a gentleman in English literature. The reader of Scott's works joyfully recognizes that this must indeed be the romancer and the realist who wrote *Marmion* and *The Heart of Midlothian*. The biography seems the final word until one examines Scott's *Journals* and finds depths that Lockhart did not plumb. The proceeds of the biography cleared up the financial obligations that Scott had so gallantly assumed.

THE GREAT ESSAYISTS OF THE PERIOD

The expansion of periodical literature created a large market for the professional writer and encouraged the extensive writing of essays (the short story had not yet arisen as a literary staple). From the welter of ephemeral writers emerged a trio of great Romantic essayists—Lamb, Hazlitt, and De Quincey. Except for Hazlitt, the essayists were not radicals like the Romantic poets. Even much of Hazlitt's writing is not politically revolutionary, for the periodical writer must be more respectful of the general reader's opinions than a poet need be. Consequently, the essayists enjoyed more popular approval than the poets, spoke to a wider audience, and actually did more to persuade the public to Romantic viewpoints. In contrast to these Romantic essayists stands Walter Savage Landor, who, in his prose and in his poetry, followed the classical tradition of English letters rather than the Romantic. Another essayist, Leigh Hunt, has been discussed in Chapter 7 because his links with the Romantic poets and his reputation as a poet make his appearance there more appropriate.

Charles Lamb (1775–1834). Following is a list of the more important events in the life of Charles Lamb.

1775: Born February 10 in the Inner Temple, London, where his father was confidential clerk to a lawyer, Samuel Salt.

1782–89: Educated at Christ's Hospital, where he formed a lifelong friendship with schoolmate Coleridge.

1791: Briefly worked as a clerk at the South Sea House.

1792: Started his thirty-three-year career as a clerk in the East India House. Facetiously termed the hundred mammoth folios of his clerical job his "true works."

1795–96: Briefly confined in a Hoxton madhouse perhaps as the aftermath of an unhappy love affair with Ann Simmons. Wrote Coleridge: "I am got somewhat rational now, and don't bite anyone. But mad I was."

1796: On September 21 his elder sister Mary, a mantua maker (dressmaker), stabbed their mother to death with scissors in an insane fit. For the rest of his life Lamb assumed responsibility for her, the two moving from one section of London to another as gossip dwelt upon her periodic seizures. At the age of twenty-three he was the sole support of a maniac sister, a dying aunt, and a prematurely senile father.

1797: Holidaying with Coleridge at Nether Stowey, he established a warm friendship with the Wordsworths.

1798: First published volume, *Blank Verse,* in collaboration with Charles Lloyd.

1801: Start of consistent prose contributions to periodicals.

1802: First published drama, *John Woodvil.* Extensive miscellaneous writings thereafter, alone and with Mary.

1819: Actress Fanny Kelley declined his proposal of marriage.

1820–23: Contributed *Essays of Elia* to *London Magazine.*

1825: Retired on pension of £450 per annum.

1833: Last Essays of Elia. With Mary and adopted daughter, Emma Isola, moved from Enfield to Edmonton. In July, Emma married Lamb's publisher, Edward Moxon.

1834: Died December 27 in Edmonton. Mary survived him until 1847.

VERSE. Lamb's earliest publications were poems, but he was insufficiently gifted in verse and wrote little in his mature years. "The Old Familiar Faces" (1798) is a wistful but painful personal poem upon his tragic deprivations. "Hester" (*1803,* 1818) is another wistful sentiment, here recording the untimely death of Hester Savoy, a Quaker goldsmith's daughter, whom Lamb, after her death, confessed to loving. Both pieces have become standard anthology selections.

DRAMA. Lamb's attempts at playwriting proved unsuccessful. He wrote two blank-verse plays: *John Woodvil* (1802), an imitation of the Elizabethans, though set in the Restoration period, which Southey branded as "delightful poetry badly put together"; and *The Wife's Trial; or, The Intruding Widow* (*1827,* 1828), based upon Crabbe's poem "The Confidant." His prose farce, *Mr. H.: or Beware a Bad Name* (*1805,* pub. 1813) hinges about the gentleman's unfortunate name—Mr. Hogsflesh; Henry Crabb Robinson relates how Lamb joined in the booing at the first and only performance in 1806. *The Pawnbroker's Daughter* (c. *1825,* 1830) is a two-act farce based upon the author's own essay "On the Inconvenience of Being Hanged."

CRITICAL ESSAYS. *Tales from Shakespeare. Designed for the Use of*

Young Persons (1807) was commissioned by Godwin, then publishing a "Juvenile Library." Twenty summaries pleasantly outline the plot and unobtrusively insinuate the moral implications. Mary prepared fourteen comedies and Charles six tragedies (*Romeo and Juliet, Hamlet, Othello, King Lear, Macbeth,* and *Timon of Athens*).

Specimens of English Dramatic Poets, Who Lived about the Time of Shakespeare (1808). With this work Lamb restored to popular reading numerous Renaissance dramas that previously had been rarely reprinted and that had aroused little but antiquarian interest. Shakespeare and Jonson had never been forgotten, but it required Lamb to awaken English readers to the hosts of other Renaissance playwrights.

The annotations and comments in this work caused the English critic A. C. Bradley, perhaps too enthusiastically, to term Lamb "the best critic of the nineteenth century." Although the late 18th century provided some predecessors, Lamb with this work printed Romantic criticism for the first time (leaning heavily upon Longinus of antiquity). Its distinctive features are:

(1) Evocation. The primary role of Romantic criticism is to make the reader sense and feel the experience of the work being examined. The critic wishes the reader to relive the dark horror of *The Duchess of Malfi* and the sunny fairyland of *The Old Wives Tale.* Perhaps we have become blasé about this word-picturing of past masterworks, but to Lamb's readers it was a new and exciting adventure.

(2) Allusions. The Romantic critic searches for similes and metaphors that will liken literary works to our experience and to our acquaintance with other literature. Typical is Lamb's reference to Heywood as a "prose Shakespeare." Such comparisons and figures of speech often heighten and clarify a reader's understanding, but they are also capable of creating irrelevance and mistaken analogy.

(3) Impressionistic response. To the Romantic critic, the ultimate criterion, of course, is how he is moved by what he reads. His standard is no authority, appealed to by Jeffrey, but his own spirit. Lamb offers unarguable personal judgment when he says of *The Revenger's Tragedy:* "I have never read it but my ears tingle, and I feel a hot blush overspread my cheeks." Lamb's Romantic criticism is intensely individualistic; its value lies solely upon our acceptance of the critic as a highly sensitive and perceptive being. To inspire credence in his dicta, this critic offers as credentials simply himself.

Whatever the deficiencies of himself or his critical approach, Lamb proved a notable innovator in literary criticism. Along with Coleridge he was instrumental in giving a new and enlarged province to criticism that was to influence the 19th century profoundly and to have its repercussions well into our own age.

"On the Tragedies of Shakespeare Considered with Reference to Their Fitness for Stage Representation" (1811) utters the famous and pernicious statement that the "plays of Shakespeare are less calculated for performance on a stage, than those of almost any dramatist whatever." The influence of Coleridge and Lamb for almost a century was to emphasize the closet reading of Shakespeare and to neglect the Shakespearean plays as living theater. Worthwhile, however, was Lamb's insistence upon the sheer poetry of Shakespeare and the merits of thoughtfully pondering his works long after the stage lights have dimmed.

"On the Artificial Comedy of the Last Century" (1822) is responsible for another misconception, the belief that Restoration comedy, in its depiction of a "land of cuckoldry, the Utopia of gallantry," truthfully "has no reference whatever to the world that is." Belonging to a later bourgeois society, the moral Lamb cannot conceive of the rococo aristocracy of the Restoration.

Lamb did little formal reviewing. He and Hazlitt used the same copy of *The Excursion* for review, but because Hazlitt was in his usual quarrelsome mood, the text was exchanged through a third party. Lamb highly praised this poem by Wordsworth but was dismayed to see how Gifford altered his review for publication in the *Quarterly* (1814). For the *New Times,* Lamb's review of the 1820 volume by Keats was printed without alteration. This was one of the first warm receptions for the youthful poet, even though Lamb and Keats had little personal regard for each other. Though highly praised, Lamb's review surprisingly values "Isabella" above the odes and everything else in the volume because "an ounce of feeling is worth a pound of fancy." To Lamb's Romantic temperament, poetry was to be judged strictly upon its amount of sentiment and emotion.

PERSONAL ESSAYS. On the basis of his personal essays Lamb has been termed "the prince of English essayists," and here lies the foundation for his lasting fame. His personal essays differ from those of his predecessors and claim originality on these counts:

(1) Unlike Montaigne, the originator of the personal essay, Lamb is concerned not so much with thought as with feeling. The great Frenchman intrigues us primarily by the spectacle of a powerful, independent mind exploring all phases of life with an inquisitive, penetrating in-

tellect. Lamb is absorbingly interested in the emotional aura of life.

(2) Unlike Steele, his greatest comparable predecessor in the English essay, Lamb is intent upon selling not simply his attitudes but his total self. Never before had an essayist so projected his own personality in every line. No previous English prose writer so thoroughly took his readers into his fullest confidence.

(3) Lamb added a vast dimension to English prose in making the personal essay essentially a lyric in prose. No previous prose writer could produce the charmingly personal appeal, the intensely private poetic emotion, of these essays.

Lamb disliked all dogmatists. He objected to moralists and reformers who try to dragoon man into any pattern. He was skeptical of ecclesiastics and impatient with any doctrinaire thinker. Books and men and life interested him in their eccentricity, variety, and surprise. He expected and did not shrink from the weakness and fallibility of all mankind. "I often shed tears in the motley Strand for fulness of joy at so much life." "I am determined to lead a merry life in the midst of sinners."

However, it is impossible to divorce Lamb's biography from his writings. Far more than Byron, he had cause in the series of family and personal tragedies to defy the gods and complain that the world was wrong and had wronged him. But behind the smiling, off-hand Elia is a monument of courage, one who did not advertise his achievement and would not ask the world to cut itself to his plan. Possibly no man, and certainly none with the pall of insanity hanging over him, has so determinedly deported himself with true sanity and wholesomeness.

Lamb's Romanticism was no escape from his life and from London. Nature, that deity of the Romantics, left him cold. When Wordsworth invited him to the Lake Country, he replied: "Separate from the pleasure of your company, I don't much care if I never see a mountain in my life." Rather his Romanticism consisted in reverie, in the glamorizing and sentimentalizing of his own past experience, a device that offered him a vital therapeutic effect to counter his omnipresent concerns. No other writer has draped such a hazy nostalgia over his past or founded so extensive an esthetic upon memory. He is also master of make-believe and fancy, giving to all a dreamy continuity.

And most important of all, Lamb forged from English prose a remarkable means of expression. Deceptively his prose seems an outpouring of vivacious conversation—perfect talk without any affectation.

Actually it supports subtle rhythms throughout and packs an allusiveness and connotation generally associated solely with poetry. Like lyric poetry, also, it is always emotionally charged.

Elia. Essays Which Have Appeared under that Signature in the London Magazine (1823). Lamb published his collected works in 1818, assuming that he had essentially rounded out his literary career. From 1820 to 1823, however, he produced for John Scott, distinguished editor of the *London Magazine,* a series of essays which would truly establish his reputation. The pseudonym *Elia* was the name of an Italian clerk in the South Sea House, where Lamb had first worked in his youth. Bridget and James Elia in the essays are Mary and John, brother and sister of the essayist. Most noted of these twenty-eight essays are:

"Recollections of the South-Sea House," first of the series, is a forty-five-year-old man's picture of the eccentric clerks he had known briefly at the age of seventeen. Though undoubtedly colored and modified, it is one of the most remarkable feats in literature of imaginative memory.

"Oxford in the Vacation" has immortalized an otherwise forgotten bibliophile, George Dyer, a former Christ's Hospital boy like Lamb. Only a man denied a dearly sought college education could paint so ideally the rare and rarefied joys of the academic life.

"Christ's Hospital Five-and-Thirty Years Ago" talks in the third person about the schoolboys Lamb and Coleridge. Schooldays were often rigorous and unpleasant in those times of regular thrashings and relentless inculcation of the classics, but Lamb plays upon his youth with a lambent smile and a sensuous reproduction of its trials and joys. Sometimes he confuses Coleridge's experiences with his own, and absolute accuracy may be doubted, but here unquestionably is the strange and wonderful boy who was later to write "Kubla Khan."

"The Two Races of Man" whimsically divides humanity into "the men who borrow and the men who lend." Lamb praises as superior those who borrow the riches of knowledge and experience contributed by others.

"New Year's Eve" reveals much of Lamb: his exquisite delight in memories of the past, his love of books, his wistful desire for friends, and his acceptance of daily duties and normal human contacts as the sustainers of life. The mild pessimism and undogmatic skepticism of this work aroused quite a few protests.

"Mrs. Battle's Opinions on Whist" is largely based upon Sarah Burney, wife of Admiral Burney and, like many 18th-century gentlefolk, an avid devotee of the card table. Mrs. Battle fought at cards with all the cool determination and reckless courage of a warrior, to emerge as perhaps the most interesting character ever depicted in a single essay. She re-enacts for Lamb the famous game in Pope's *The Rape of the Lock*.

"A Chapter on Ears" denies musical appreciation in Lamb and nonetheless displays considerable appreciation. Few prose pieces can so movingly create the effect of music. The title, of course, is purposely whimsical.

"Imperfect Sympathies" was originally titled "Jews, Quakers, Scotchmen, and Other Imperfect Sympathies." Lamb was greatly tolerant except against bigotry, fanaticism, and intolerance. Whenever a rigid system or dogma was presented to him, he automatically proclaimed the opposite. In his little world of acquaintance he, statesmanlike, sought always a balance of power.

"Witches, and Other Night Fears" shows Lamb's love of childhood and concern for the effects of the macabre upon infantile minds. He turns to the dream world of poetry, praising Coleridge's dream visions but resting his own case upon the glory of actual living instead of the wild imagination of the unconscious.

"My Relations" is nostalgia for family connections in childhood, especially for his spinster aunt, Hetty Lamb.

"Mackery End, in Hertfordshire" recounts the pleasures of Mary and Charles in their 1815 visit to Mackery End to renew acquaintance with cousins. Lamb's genius is demonstrated by just such joyous savoring of everyday, commonplace experiences.

"Dream Children: a Reverie" is an old bachelor's wistful dream of what might have been. His first love, Ann Simmons, appears as "Alice," wife of his dreams and mother of his dream children. It is the sort of lyricism that is Lamb's unique contribution to the essay.

"The Praise of Chimney-Sweepers" expounds a lonely man's outpouring of heart upon the poor urchins, sooty and grimy always from their miserable employment. Bringing joy to such blackened faces is the essayist's warmest joy.

"A Dissertation upon Roast Pig" is partly a spoof of travelers' tales and the rage for quaint orientalism. In the rich, sensuous pleasure of the physical, here pork, Lamb is a gay prose Keats.

The Last Essays of Elia (1833) consists of twenty-five pieces subsequent to Scott's editing of the *London Magazine*. Lamb was running out of enthusiasm for the task but still produced some of his best essays:

"Poor Relations" is the classic portrait of that unenviable tribe.

Lamb's abundant sympathy does not prevent him from clear portrayal of grinding poverty.

"Sanity of True Genius" is Lamb's contribution to the doctrine of the Romantic Imagination. Like Coleridge, he eschews fancy in favor of a true shaping power that reveals inner truth.

"The Superannuated Man" recounts the feelings of Lamb as he retires and must no longer be an active figure in the East India House with his professional cronies.

"Barbara S—" charmingly tells of an incident in the early life of Fanny Kelly when she resisted temptation and returned money given to her by mistake. Although Miss Kelly rejected Lamb's proposal of marriage, he bore her not the slightest grudge.

"Newspapers Thirty-Five Years Ago" amusingly pictures the journalistic life at the turn of the century. Always an exacting job, journalism becomes a heady and quixotic adventure in Lamb's reminiscences.

"The Wedding" was a favorite of Wordsworth. The occasion was the marriage of Sarah Burney's daughter. The happiness of the event contrasts with the loneliness of the old bachelor (we shall never know whether Lamb, as here stated, gave away the bride).

"Old China" is perhaps everyone's favorite Lamb essay. It excellently depicts Mary. Its theme is the contrast of their earlier simple joys in relative poverty against their greater burdens in present relative affluence.

"Confessions of a Drunkard" is a jest not to be taken seriously. Lamb poses as an inebriate in smiling self-depreciation, but his sins were the lightest of venality. The essay was actually issued in 1854 as a teetotaler tract but was withdrawn upon protest with the substitution of the "horrible" example of Hartley Coleridge.

"Popular Fallacies" is a delightful piece of tongue-in-cheek comment on old chestnuts such as "That handsome is as handsome does," "That we must not look a gift horse in the mouth," and "That you must love me and love my dog."

William Hazlitt (1778–1830). Following is a list of the more important events in the life of William Hazlitt.

1778: Born April 10 at Maidstone, son of a Unitarian clergyman.

1783–87: With parents in United States, in Philadelphia and near Boston.

1793–98: Attended Hackney Theological College (Unitarian) in Lon-

don but quit to read and study at Wem. Made acquaintance of Wordsworth and Coleridge.

1799–1802: Started life-long acquaintance with the Lambs. Studied
painting under his brother John.

1802: Studied painting at the Louvre, Paris.

1802–06: Painted portraits of Wordsworth, Coleridge, and Lamb but
abandoned painting for writing.

1805: First published book, *An Essay on the Principles of Human
Action.*

1806: Began pamphleteering for radical causes.

1808: Married Sarah Stoddart, friend of Mary Lamb, and settled
on wife's property at Winterslow, Salisbury.

1812: Delivered lectures at Russell Institution on "Rise and Progress
of Modern Philosophy."

1813: Parliamentary reporter and later drama critic for *Morning
Chronicle,* leading Whig newspaper. Began major journalistic career.

1817–19: Delivered lectures upon literature.

1819: Separated from wife, became infatuated with Sarah Walker,
servant girl in Southampton Building.

1822: Received a Scottish divorce from his first wife.

1824: Married Mrs. Isabella Bridgewater, who left him after a year's
honeymoon on the Continent.

1830: Died September 18 after protracted illness.

Hazlitt's last words were the incredible "Well, I've had a happy life."
This statement came from a man whose crowning work was to be *The
Life of Napoleon Buonaparte* (four volumes, 1828–30), which was a
miserable failure. This was a man who fearfully botched his domestic
life and who quarreled with everyone, even briefly with the amiable
Lamb. As Hazlitt himself admitted, he was so out of step that he was
the only Englishman who sorrowed at Napoleon's downfall. He was
virtually a party of one, reviled by all of the orthodox of the age and
viewed with suspicion by his fellow Romantics. Yet he had his undying
faith in the fight for human rights and freedom, and he nurtured
within himself the jealous pride of unwavering devotion to his independent principles. His steadfast refusal to be subservient to any man
or any organization gives to his writings a free judgment and an over-
all perspective missing in most of his contemporaries.

Much of Hazlitt's extensive journalism has been properly forgotten,
but even in his lesser pieces there is incessant energy and sharp intellectuality. His curt, incisive style has carried probably more of his

essays across the century than those of any of his fellows. Robert Louis Stevenson admitted: "We are mighty fine fellows nowadays, but we cannot write like William Hazlitt."

LITERARY CRITICISM. The principles of Romantic criticism implicit in Lamb are forcefully and directly stated by Hazlitt: "I say what I think; I think what I feel. I cannot help receiving certain impressions from things; and I have sufficient courage to declare (somewhat abruptly) what they are." The same methods employed by Lamb are utilized by Hazlitt: impressionistic response, allusion, and evocation. Understandably, however, where Lamb prefers the quaintness of Thomas Browne and the sweetness of Izaak Walton, Hazlitt is enthusiastic about the vigor of Donne and the murky glories of Ossian. Where Lamb seeks sentiment and emotion, Hazlitt looks for "gusto" (one of his favorite words). However, Hazlitt emphasizes the subjectivity of literature and praises the spectrum-like variety of appeals to every type of reader. He sees original genius as giving to each perception "its characteristic essence," but he denies Joshua Reynolds's theory of abstract idealization. Still clinging to an associationistic psychology, he fundamentally agrees with the Wordsworth and Coleridge concept of the Imagination; to him it is the "intuitive perception of the hidden analogies of things." On the whole, Hazlitt has left a body of criticism that in range, insight, and forceful expression is unmatched since Dryden.

Characters of Shakespeare's Plays (1817), though often challenged by the scholar, has proved the most popular and rewarding of all Shakespearean criticism to the general public. Unlike Coleridge, Hazlitt does not seek obscurities or subtle hints upon which to dilate. Rarely profound, Hazlitt is brilliantly receptive, making the reader believe that this or that character is indeed what the reader vaguely sensed but only Hazlitt could so sharply and incisively round. More than any other criticism, his allusions and evocations make the reader see the people about him today as precisely the same people delineated by Shakespeare. Hazlitt establishes the realization that "it is *we* who are Hamlet." His interpretation of Iago is today's interpretation, and he inaugurated the sympathetic interpretation of Shylock, which, although not wholly justified in Elizabethan terms, has dominated stage presentations ever since. From Lear to Imogen and from Falstaff to Desdemona, he has presented revealing psychological portraits in the most felicitous and delightful of Shakespearean criticism.

Lectures on the English Poets (1818) largely elaborates the scheme of Thomas Warton (discussed in Chapter 3). Hazlitt traces the course of English poetry from imagination (Elizabeth I), fancy (James I and Charles I), wit (Restoration and Queen Anne), commonplaces (George I and George II), to paradox and eclecticism (George III). He has little sympathy with the medieval material, except for Chaucer, but he is well grounded on the entire main line of English literature since Sidney. His is the first strong voice to resurrect the poetic memory of Marvell. He skips what he does not relish and speaks with infectious enthusiasm about his preferences. His viewpoint is strongly Romantic and anti-Augustan.

Lectures on the English Comic Writers (1819) actually includes studies of Montaigne and Cervantes, Le Sage and Hogarth. Hazlitt discriminates the laughable, the ludicrous, and the ridiculous. His preference in the comic drama is Restoration, and he considers Congreve the greatest comic genius of the English stage. Except for Scott's comments, Hazlitt is the first significant critic of the English novel (until the emergence of the Gothic novel, this form had been considered entirely comic). In fact, this work by Hazlitt is probably the first important critique of English prose and among the most delightful of all critical pieces.

Dramatic Literature of the Age of Elizabeth (1820), along with Lamb's *Specimens,* is significant in renewing interest in the host of Renaissance dramatists outside of Shakespeare and Jonson. Disliking the abnormal, Hazlitt cannot share Lamb's taste for Ford, but he is always perceptive, especially with Massinger, and Beaumont and Fletcher. His view of the Elizabethan era is essentially that of Warton but more Romantically shaded.

The Spirit of the Age; or Contemporary Portraits (1825) is often considered his best work. It offers twenty-five portraits of the personal character and writings of his contemporaries, most of them alive at the time. The less spectacular figures are best handled: Bentham, Godwin, Cobbett, Campbell, Crabbe, Hunt, and Lamb. The picture of his closest friend, Lamb, is one of the most dignified and balanced tributes ever paid to an intimate literary acquaintance. Literary quarrels caused a blistering attack upon William Gifford, and political differences dictated a virulent assault upon Southey. Hazlitt's deep-seated hostility to rank made him personally unsympathetic to Shelley and Byron, but he tried in literary judgment to do them justice, admitting that Byron had "intensity of power." He declared that he would not shake hands with the Tory Sir Walter Scott, but he would gladly kneel to the author of the Waverley novels. Landor was particularly pleased with this work. On the whole, it is doubtful whether any other critic has so agreed with posterity about his contemporary authors.

ART CRITICISM. Hazlitt's extensive training in and knowledge of painting established him as the only truly significant Romantic art critic and the best in this field during the 19th century before Ruskin. He never praised mere technical excellence in a painting but sought the imaginative spirit of the painter in the interpretation of Nature and life. His favorites were Rembrandt, Titian, Claude Lorrain, and Nicolas Poussin. Before Ruskin was born, Hazlitt proclaimed: "In landscape Turner has shown a knowledge of the effects of air and of powerful relief in objects which was never surpassed." With his customary independence, Hazlitt admired what he liked, not what tradition had sanctified. His critical approach here was identical with that of his literary criticism.

Sketches of the Principal Picture Galleries in England (1824) collects Hazlitt's art criticisms, especially those appearing in the *London Magazine*. "On the Pleasure of Painting" is his credo of art criticism. He finds painters as a class "the most lively observers of what passes in the world about them, and the closest observers of what passes in their own minds." One of his best appreciations appears in "On Hogarth's 'Marriage à la Mode,'" first printed in *The Examiner* (1814).

PERSONAL ESSAYS. Hazlitt assembled his personal essays in two major series, *Table Talk* (1821–22) and *The Plain Speaker* (1826). The essays discussed below are generally considered his best.

"On Reading Old Books" (*London Magazine,* 1821) is a delightful ramble through Hazlitt's personal choices—Temple, Fielding, Sterne, Rousseau, Keats, and the essayists. He dates his "insight into the mysteries of poetry" from the reading of *Lyrical Ballads.*

"On Going on a Journey" (*New Monthly Magazine,* 1822) develops the idea of the great adventure of Romantic travel, the opportunity to learn and to expand one's self. To travel is to escape one's limitations and to change ideas and opinions.

"The Fight" (*New Monthly Magazine,* 1822) was accepted by the editor-in-chief, Campbell, over the objections of his staff. Without any recourse to the slang of the fight ring or the clichés of sporting accounts, this is the unquestioned masterpiece of sports reporting. Hazlitt recounts a genuine boxing match between the favored Tom Hickman ("the Gasman") and the challenger and victor Bill Neate during the great age of English fisticuffs. All the reality of the prize ring is contained in this lusty word painting.

"On the Fear of Death" (*Table Talk,* 1822) is one of the noblest pronouncements ever made by a skeptic of immortality. There is ample richness in life itself, states Hazlitt, to be satisfied with it alone. The twofold meanings of life are its vivacious personal pleasures and the opportunity to serve the cause of mankind's betterment. Hazlitt is content to relinquish his own life on these terms: "I should like to see some prospect of good to mankind such as my life began with. I should like to leave some sterling work behind me. I should like to have some friendly hand to consign me to the grave. On these conditions I am ready, if not willing, to depart. I could then write on my tomb—Grateful and Contented."

"My First Acquaintance with Poets" (*The Liberal,* 1823) has consistently been the most famous Hazlitt essay. From the vantage point of forty-five years, Hazlitt looks back across a quarter of a century to 1798 when he first met Coleridge and Wordsworth, in all their glorious youth of poetry and liberalism. Although he now thinks of them as turncoats, he remembers the magic they once radiated. The eloquent vision of Coleridge and the primeval majesty of Wordsworth are nowhere else so vividly portrayed.

"Of Persons One Would Wish to Have Seen" (*New Monthly Magazine,* 1826) celebrates one of the many rich literary gatherings at Lamb's house. Lamb, Hunt, Hazlitt, and the other conversationalists discuss what figures of the past they would most like to meet. The tastes are revealingly personal, and the dialogue is liveliness itself.

"On the Feeling of Immortality in Youth" (*The Monthly Magazine,* 1827) sings of the gusto and poetry of young life in a stately prose that is veritable poetry. Hazlitt laments, as did Wordsworth, the departure of the vision splendid, but the recollections of abounding young life suffice in themselves to console him.

"On Disagreeable People" (*The Monthly Magazine,* 1827) pleasantly analyzes those we dislike. They all lack satisfaction with themselves or with others. If we embrace our own life experiences and love our fellows, even in their shortcomings, we ourselves shall always prove agreeable people.

Liber Amoris; or, The New Pygmalion ("Book of Love") (1823) is one of the most confessional works in English, and it was not really disguised by its anonymous publication. Hazlitt embarrassingly tells all about his infatuation with Sarah Walker, who intended only a mild flirtation but caused the break-up of Hazlitt's first marriage. Part I reports conversations between the essayist and Sarah Walker. Part II details the middle of the romance in letters slightly altered from the originals which were addressed to Peter George Patmore, father of the Victorian poet Coventry Patmore. Part III consists of letters supposedly sent to J. S. K. (John Sheridan Knowles, the dramatist who will be discussed later in the chapter), relating the wretched conclusion of the affair. Hazlitt made a frightful scene when he learned of Sarah Walker's sudden marriage to another, and only Lamb's diplomatic intervention prevented legal action. In one of the most psychologically impressive of personal revelations, Hazlitt lays bare his soul. The reader is hard put to it to decide which is more distressing: that a man should make such a fool of himself, or that he should let the world know all about it.

Thomas De Quincey (1785–1859). Following is a list of the more important events in the life of Thomas De Quincey.

1785: Born August 15 in Manchester, plain Thomas Quincey (the family added the aristocratic French article after 1792). Early bereaved by death in 1792 of his father, a well-to-do merchant.

1802: Ran away from Manchester Grammar School, wandered through Wales, and lived hand-to-mouth existence in London. Details of this period are unknown except through his own highly imaginative accounts. Deprivation permanently injured his health.

1803: Discovered by guardians and sent to Worcester College, Oxford.

1809: Leased Dove Cottage, Grasmere, after Wordsworth moved. Intimate with Wordsworth, Southey, and Wilson.

1813: Thoroughly addicted to opium.

1817: Married his rustic mistress, Margaret Simpson, thereby alienating Wordsworth.

1818–19: Edited Tory newspaper, *Westmorland Gazette*. Throughout his life he was conservative and untouched by the political radicalism infecting most Romantics.

1820: Residence in Edinburgh.

1821–25: London residence. Fame with *Confessions*.

1830: Settled in Edinburgh, becoming increasingly the eccentric solitary.

1859: Died December 8.

In person De Quincey was a strange, gnomish little man. During his lifetime he published only two separate volumes, a novel, *Klosterheim* (1832), and *The Logic of Political Economy* (1844), a work largely indebted to Ricardo. All his other writings were for periodicals, totaling about 215 essays. So ephemeral was most of his writing that less than one tenth has truly survived. His memorable works have endured less for their intrinsically meager content than for their remarkable style —the "impassioned" poetic prose culminating in the ornate style best known in Sir Thomas Browne, De Quincey's master. De Quincey employs every known rhetorical device to achieve majestic harmony and splendor in words. Usually he produces periodic sentences, holding the reader in suspense, with extended parentheses and sonorous convolutions, until the cadenced, "ful-orbed" conclusion. His vocabulary is melodiously Latinized, and seeks the most striking and varied effects. Allusions, picturesque figures of speech, elaborate personifications and apostrophes also weave a thick tapestry of emotion and sensation. Above all, De Quincey is more intent upon elaborate prose rhythms than any other English writer since the 17th century. Much of his prose could properly be printed as free verse; much falls into regular scansion, especially anapestic.

CRITICAL ESSAYS. "On the Knocking at the Gate in Macbeth" (*London Magazine,* 1823) is highly perceptive impressionistic Romantic criticism. The concern is with the powerful emotional impact upon the reader or viewer. De Quincey suggests that the drunken porter's pounding upon the gate provides necessary relief of tension and, especially, a return from the fiendish world of murder to the world of reality. It is distressing that De Quincey failed to continue such sensitive appraisals of literature.

Literary Reminiscences is the title given to a series of essays in *Tait's Edinburgh Magazine* (1834–40) upon De Quincey's associations with Wordsworth, Coleridge, and Southey. Though replete with fascinating anecdotes about the poets, these articles are unreliable as examinations of their subjects. They tell much more about De Quincey than they do about the poets. For example, De Quincey indulges in paroxysms of grief at the death (1812) of Kate Wordsworth and seeks at enormous length to justify his estrangement (1816) from William Wordsworth. Any reader will be beguiled by these personal glimpses (e.g. Wordsworth using a dirty butter knife to open the pages of a book), but he must go elsewhere for the truth about Wordsworth and Coleridge.

"Literature of Knowledge and Literature of Power" is all posterity has found worth retaining from De Quincey's review in the *North British Review* (1848) of Roscoe's edition of the works of Pope. The famous discrimination is between writings that offer factual information and knowledge and *belles lettres,* which move the reader emotionally.

HISTORICAL ESSAYS. "Revolt of the Tartars" (*Blackwood's Edinburgh Magazine,* 1837) is based upon a real historical event, the flight of the Kalmucks from Russian to Chinese territory, 1761–71. De Quincey brilliantly senses and conveys the human drama of mass migration across the vast emptiness of central Asia. Much of the detail is imagined, highly dubious from any scholar's viewpoint, but nevertheless superbly visualized.

"Joan of Arc" (*Tait's Edinburgh Magazine,* 1847) is more dramatized history, the passionate pleading to the reader's emotions that gripped sentimentalists of the 19th century. Even saints suffer from this barrage of rhetorical questions and exclamation points. So far as factual value goes, this and "Revolt of the Tartars" are the literature of power, not of knowledge.

AUTOBIOGRAPHICAL WRITINGS. *Confessions of an English Opium-Eater* first appeared in the *London Magazine* in 1821. In the next year a slightly revised version was published along with an appendix upon De Quincey's attempts to reduce his daily intake of opium. In 1856 the author extensively rewrote and published the piece, increasing it to twice its previous length. In all versions the work is divided into three sections:

I, "Preliminary confessions, or introductory narrative." De Quincey relates the story of his earlier years, but this portion probably belongs more to fiction than to authentic autobiography. In London he knew fearful hardships, and was befriended only by a sixteen-year-old prostitute, Ann (one of the many literary portraits of a soiled sisterhood with heart of gold). After a family acquaintance relieved his want, De Quincey searched for Ann but could never find her. She seems so much the product of a dream that perhaps she never did exist except in his mind.

II, The Pleasures of Opium. One Sunday, at the age of nineteen, while up in London from Oxford, De Quincey was tortured by neuralgia pains in his head. At the suggestion of a fellow student he relieved his agonies by taking laudanum, a tincture of opium. Then ensued the most gorgeous and delicious dreams of splendor and lush (though not erotic) beauty. Nothing before in English literature approaches this host of overpowering visions.

III, The Pains of Opium. Gradually opium rendered De Quincey incapable of action and appetite. Vainly he struggled to diminish his dosages. Visions of frightful, demoniacal horror assailed him—mammoth crushing structures, vast trampling armies, huge engulfing seas, all the loathsome reptiles and vermin of the East. Reading this horrendous account, Carlyle avowed: "This child hath been in hell." In dreams De Quincey again wandered the forlorn streets of London with Ann. In 1820 one vision of such devastating terror visited him as to elicit his refusal ever to sleep again. Fearing death if he did not abandon opium, De Quincey reduced his ration and eventually broke free of the habit, concluding an addiction of seventeen years. Later he was again to succumb to narcotic addiction.

In 1845 De Quincey explained the purpose of his work—"to reveal something of the grandeur which belongs *potentially* to human dreams." Like Coleridge, De Quincey was a dreamer who happened to take narcotics; he was dream-haunted even without opium, not solely because of it. It is difficult to choose between the first and the last version of this work. The final writing adds many magnificent and melodious passages but also clutters up the text with digressions and irrelevancies. Anthology editors always select the vivid poetic portions of this work, but there are many prosaic passages in both versions. In either version one finds an illuminating document of a sensitive, tortured Romantic, ill-equipped for the blows of normal existence, beset with dreadful anxiety, and seeking escape in an imaginative dream world.

Suspira de Profundis: Being a Sequel to the Confessions of an English Opium-Eater ("Sighs from the depths") was conceived by De Quincey as a continuation of the dream sequences of the *Confessions.* This work was in part a product of his fourth and last period (1840–48) of opium eating. Only six sections of what De Quincey confidently expected to be a long volume were completed. Five of these appeared in *Blackwood's* (1845), and a sixth ("The Daughter of Lebanon") was first printed in the collected edition of 1856. De Quincey attached considerable importance to this work, perhaps more than justified. He conceives of his pain and suffering as plumbing previously unchartered depths of knowledge about the meaning of life and death. Most notable of the author's prose poetry is "Levana and our Ladies of Sorrow." Levana is the Roman goddess of childbirth and protectress of children. She is accompanied in De Quincey's account by Mater Lachrymarum ("mother of tears"), Mater Suspiriorum ("mother of sighs"), and Mater Tenebrarum ("mother of shadows"). He suggests that these transcendental figures communicate the eternal mysteries to him, which he therefore records as by an automatic hand. No other work by De Quincey has such consistent poetic exaltation.

The English Mail-Coach (*Blackwood's,* 1849) was originally planned as part of the *Suspira* but grew and assumed, somewhat unusually for De Quincey, complete and rounded form of its own.

I, The Glory of Motion, is a paean to the great age of stage-coaching, viewed with nostalgia in the age of the railroad's triumph.

II, The Vision of Death, factually relates De Quincey's ride through Lancashire on the mail coach carrying the news of Waterloo. The thundering horses bear down upon a young man and woman in a frail gig. In the nick of time they avoid collision and the mail coach hurtles onward.

III, Dream-Fugue, imaginatively transforms the substance of the previous section into baroque splendor, with such visions as the dashing coach proceeding up the aisle of a vast cathedral, and marble statuary of the trumpeteer blowing his warning signal to the imperiled pair. De Quincey consciously strives for organ tones of sweeping lines and stupendous spectacles. Although such pieces were to influence later writers to ecstatic adventures in mere words, De Quincey is no "decadent," for every word or phrase is chosen for its clear specific reference as well as for its melodious effect.

In his later years De Quincey achieved probably his greatest sustained writing, demonstrating to the mid-19th century the dimensions of prose which make it a fit rival for all the qualities of poetry and music.

Walter Savage Landor (lan'der) (1775–1864). Walter Savage Landor was the eldest son of a Warwick physician. In 1763, after education at Rugby, he entered Trinity College, Oxford, where he became imbued with current Republicanism. His violent temper, a life-long handicap, caused him to shoot at the window of a Tory student and thereby get himself suspended. For over a decade he led a wandering life in Britain and on the Continent; in 1808 he fought with Spanish troops against the French at La Coruña, leading a regiment equipped at his own expense. He loved a charming Irish beauty, Sophia Jane Swift (the Ianthe of his poems), but as her husband obstinately refused to release her or to die, Landor perfunctorily married Julia Thuillier in 1811. When Swift conveniently died, Landor was inconveniently married. After years of waiting, Sophia remarried. Landor fled his creditors in 1814, and from 1821 until 1835 he resided in Florence, Italy. Leaving his wife in the latter year, he was again living in England from 1835 to 1858. Then he returned to Florence, where he died. Robert and Elizabeth Browning were his close friends in the later years.

Landor's span of years was fantastic. He was born before Cowper had published any verse, and he lived to see Swinburne establish a reputation. His own publications stretched across sixty-eight years from *Poems* (1795) to *Heroic Idylls* (1863). Had he lived no longer than Shelley or Keats, he would now be considered a minor Romantic. His first significant publication, *Gebir* (1798), is a blank-verse epic about the legendary Arabic founder of Gibraltar. *Count Julian: A Tragedy* (1812) was a Romantic closet drama derived in part from his Spanish experiences. But Landor's true ability lay neither in extended works nor in Romantic subjects. From early years a devoted student of classical literature, he found his metier in short chiseled poems, classically restrained. He frequently translated his English verse into Latin or wrote original Latin poems which he then put into English.

VERSE. The significant poetry of Landor runs in strange cross-current against the Romantic tendencies of his time and against his own pugnacious, explosive temperament (unforgettably caricatured as Boythorn in Dickens's *Bleak House*). His multitudinous successes in relatively short poems fall roughly into three categories:

(1) "Hellenics," a term which he coined to denote a moderately short narrative poem derived from ancient Greek history and mythology, and usually in blank verse. The effect is idyllic and statuesque rather than dynamic, resembling a series of exquisite illustrations upon ancient vases. Landor here is seeking, not for the beauty of luxuriance and activity cherished by the Romantics, but for the beauty of quiet restraint. "Cool purity" well describes this poetry in contrast to the lush Elizabethan reading of the Greeks or the Romantic exaltation of giant struggles in Hellas. Landor printed *Hellenics* in 1846, but he actually wrote "Hellenics" through much of his career. Although the severe classical beauty is rather evenly distributed throughout this work, best known are "Iphigeneia and Agamemnon," "The Hamadryad," and "Artemidora."

(2) Short epigrammatic poems seldom exceeding a dozen lines and often no more than four. Landor proves the best writer of such short pieces in English; he is rivaled only by Herrick. In his published writings scattered across half a century are scores of these gems—terse, perfect expressions of a single feeling weighted with the guarded memories of years and intellectually incisive. Their meticulous polishing of the last syllable and their extreme refining of emotion distinguish them from conventional English lyrics. One significant division includes classically disciplined sorrow for the brevity and pain of life and beauty, such as "Rose Aylmer," "Past Ruin'd Ilion," "Dirce," and "On Lucretia Borgia's Hair." Another important division is classical love po-

etry, masking sincere feeling with the air of calm imperturbability or an aristocratic smile, as in "It Often Comes into My Head," "You Smiled, You Spoke, and I Believed," and "One Year Ago My Path Was Green."

(3) The poetry of old age. Only Tennyson among English poets matches Landor in the poetic productivity of advanced years, but far more than Tennyson, Landor is the poetic voice of the aged. During his last twenty years Landor knew old age but never senility. The brief poems of these years are unique in their serene moderation, their placid resignation, as in "God Scatters Beauty," "Death Stands above Me," "I Strove with None," and "To My Ninth Decade."

PROSE. As mentioned before, Landor himself stated: "Poetry was always my amusement, prose my study and business." His prose far exceeded his verse in quantity and remains the chief basis for his continuing reputation.

Imaginary Conversations. Between 1824 and 1853 Landor printed a total of 152 "imaginary conversations" (to this number, kindred pieces such as *The Citation and Examination of William Shakespeare* might be added). The genre is Landor's own creation, leaning, however, upon the dialogues of Plato (Berkeley is the only other English writer to approximate the Platonic dialogues). Only two conditions govern the form: (1) presentation entirely in dialogue, with no narrative and no stage directions; (2) real persons exclusively, except for an occasional legendary or mythological character. Generally the conversation focuses upon a moment of powerful emotion just preceding climactic action. The purpose is not dramatic conflict but the revelation of character and ideas. Landor ranges through all Western history from "Peleus and Thetis" (parents of Achilles) to his own day (e.g. "Southey and Landor"), with only a few famous historical personages omitted. The general effect is of statuesque dignity, but Landor can be wickedly funny as in "Louis the Fourteenth and Père La Chaise" or savagely brutal as in "Empress Catherine and Princess Dashkoff." Landor considered "Dante and Beatrice" his best, while students of the Renaissance also praise "Filippo Lippi and Pope Eugenius IV" and "Henry VIII and Anne Boleyn." Perhaps he was most at home amidst his noble Greeks and Romans of antiquity, as "Marcellus and Hannibal," "Tiberius and Vipsania." Usually only two characters are involved, though occasionally additional figures are introduced into the conversation. The dialogues are wholly imaginary, with no insertion of quotations. There is no attempt at archaic language, but Landor seeks fidelity to the spirit of the era depicted and to known personality traits. He makes no attempt to hide his prejudices wherever he feels sincerely about the cause. His anti-clerical and anti-tyranny sentiments are strongly expressed, although he enters the scene in person only where he is a specified conversationalist. Some of the dialogues are bookish and others seem a bit fine-spun. In toto, however, they form a gallery of more extensive historical portraits than attempted by any other writer in English. Even without any real followers in his self-created genre of "imaginary conversations," Landor by these works added considerable dimensions to English prose. Along with contemporary prose writers like Lamb and De Quincey, he demonstrated that prose could be as imaginative and perhaps as potent as verse, and that it opened vistas of effects denied to verse.

Pericles and Aspasia (1836) was Landor's longest and most ambitious work. Its purpose was to portray the Golden Age of Athens, the consummate period of human achievement in Landor's eyes, through letters, chiefly those exchanged between Aspasia and Cleone, another intellectual lady. The task was too great even for a poet steeped in the classics. The initial thirty letters, relating the first meetings and first love between Aspasia and Pericles, are delicate masterpieces; thereafter a number of excellent things are lost in too much lecturing and unconvincing speeches from hallowed geniuses, but the concluding letter to Aspasia from the dying Pericles is the perfectly simple but magnificent ending of a great age.

Christopher North (pen name for **John Wilson**) (1785–1854). Son of a wealthy Paisley, Scotland, manufacturer, John Wilson was educated at Glasgow and Oxford. After failure as a gentleman farmer in the Lake Country of England, Wilson settled in Edinburgh and started contributing to the literary journals. From 1817 on, he was one of the main supports of *Blackwood's*. On the preposterous grounds that he was a Tory and therefore "right," Wilson was made professor of moral philosophy at Edinburgh University in 1819. Surprisingly, he turned out to be quite good at a profession for which he had no initial preparation.

In contrast with Jeffrey, Wilson was the most sympathetic to the Romantics among the writers for the great reviews. He proclaimed Wordsworth, along with Scott and Byron, as "one of the three great master-spirits of our day in the poetical world." In his favorable review of Tennyson's 1832 volume, Wilson was among the first to herald this rising star of poetry. De Quincey praised Wilson for "his large expansiveness of heart, and a certain air of noble frankness which overspread everything he said."

In 1822 *Blackwood's* started "Noctes Ambrosianae," a modification of the Platonic dialogues. Until 1825 these pieces were by various hands, but from 1825 until he broke off in 1835, Wilson was the sole author. The central figure of "Noctes Ambrosianae" is "The Ettrick Shepherd," based upon James Hogg but impressively developed by Wilson to the stature of a Falstaff-Socrates in the guise of a Scottish peasant. The range of subject matter is enormous, from literary philosophizing to men's beards, all treated with eloquence, much with rich Scottish humor. "The Ettrick Shepherd" carries the burden throughout, speaking in a racy and realistic dialect. "Christopher North" is largely prompter to the central character, but he often acts as chorus or the voice of the cultured world. Other participants in the conversations (including "the opium eater"—De Quincey) are minor.

OTHER PROSE WRITINGS OF THE PERIOD

Radical Propagandists

William Cobbett (1763–1835). A native of Farnham, Surrey, William Cobbett served as an enlisted man in the British army in Nova Scotia. He then started a stormy journalistic career in Philadelphia which saw him thrice sued for libel. Until the turn of the century he was a stout Tory, but by 1806 he had completed an about-face—to stun the age as a thunderous radical. Back in England after 1800, he started the publication of *Cobbett's Weekly Political Register,* which continued until his death. He was imprisoned from 1810 to 1812 and fined £1000 for attacks upon flogging in the army. From 1817 to 1819 he again resided in America. A resolute champion of reform, he became a member of Parliament from Oldham in the crucial year of 1832.

Always his was a sturdy proletarian voice—earthy, practical, prejudiced, often coarse but never dull. While Hunt was an intellectual radical editor speaking to the cultured and artistic, Cobbett was the people's editor, talking to them in their own home-spun idiom. He became the most beloved Englishman of his era in the hearts of the commonality, and the most hated by the gentry. Cobbett fulminated against privilege, landlords, "fundlords," the entrenched clergy, inadequate justice for the poor, and the Corn Laws. By parliamentary reform he hoped to eliminate government sinecures, corruption and waste, a huge national debt, and a standing army. Failing to understand the Industrial Revolution, he saw the future of England essentially in agriculture. A journalist like Defoe, he has the same power of direct, forceful language. For his early conservative work he chose the pseudonym of Peter Porcupine, a name that well suited his prickly invective.

Works of Peter Porcupine (1801), in twelve volumes, is a collection of his extensive early journalism, most of it in America. Here he is a conservative, savagely attacking the principles of Priestley, Paine, and all the radicals. His conservatism arises not from a philosophic basis but rather from the tenacity of the English people to hold on to an established way of life.

Rural Rides was published serially in the *Political Register* from 1821 to 1834. Cobbett made a selection that was issued in book form in 1830. Much of this work consists of angry tirades against the oppressors of the poor. Cobbett presents pictures of human deprivation and injustice in vivid colors of reality. He stubbornly refused to believe statistics and the census figures and was convinced that the population and total national wealth were rapidly declining. Although his quarrels are now long dead, the modern reader still finds wholly refreshing and engrossing his blunt, manly statements, his untiring vigor and homey shrewdness. In contrast to Defoe, making a similar tour a century before, Cobbett finds strife and confusion in England's green and pleasant land; however, most impressively different from Defoe is the boundless love Cobbett has for the English countryside.

Advice to Young Men (1829) is the type of grass-roots admonition that wise peasants give their sons, but only in Cobbett does it see print. This is a sort of "courtesy book," intended, however, not for a courtier like Castiglione's Renaissance work, but for the everyday farmer and tradesman. Cobbett offers advice for the successive stages of a man's life: youth, lover, husband, father, and citizen. In looking for a wife, Cobbett offers sage criteria: Does she walk firmly, not mincingly? Does she chew her food straightforwardly, with no nonsense? He advises choosing a pretty girl, for, obviously, the husband of a beauty will not have to expend much for her dressing and grooming. Besides, having a good-looking wife keeps a husband "pleased with his bargain." Also, he admonishes them to marry for love, not for money or ambition. If instead of a calculated, mercenary marriage, Napoleon had wed "the poorest and prettiest girl in all France," he "would in all probability have now been on an imperial throne, instead of being eaten by worms at the bottom of a very deep hole in St. Helena."

Robert Owen (1771–1858). "The Father of English Socialism" was born at Newtown, Montgomeryshire, Wales, son of the postmaster. Early reading of religious controversies convinced him that there was "something fundamentally wrong in all religions." In his early teens he was apprenticed to a fabric dealer, and by 1790 he was a successful cotton manufacturer in Manchester. He became a friend of John Dalton, the scientist, and talked on equal terms with Coleridge. In New Lanark, near Glasgow, in 1800 Owen started a model industrial community that soon became the talk of the world. Character, he insisted, is made by circumstances. Therefore he began with model homes and schools for the workers and their children, and sought an ideal factory system for all employees. New Lanark was transformed from a squalid mill town into a community of clean, comfortable houses with recreational facilities. Alcoholic beverages could not be sold, and special stores offered good merchandise at low prices. Working hours were reduced below the prevailing standard and wages were increased above usual rates. All profits over 5% were to be used for the benefit of employees; when Owen's partners demurred at this unheard-of practice, he got new partners. Visitors came from all parts of Europe and the Americas. Owen traveled through much of the British Isles and the United States as a crusading reformer. His socialistic community at New Harmony, Indiana, proved a failure. In the senility of advanced age he became rambling and addicted to spiritualism.

A New View of Society, or, Essays on the Formation of the Human Character (1813–14) consisted of four essays summing up his radical philosophy. Although Owen wrote many other works, this piece contains the essence of them all. Unlike most of the world's reformers, Owen was not advancing an untried theory but was essentially detailing what he had already accomplished at New Lanark. Insisting that "man's character is formed for, and not by, him," he claimed that society and not the poor should be blamed for the filth and vulgarity of the laboring classes. A proper environment would build proper people, and New Lanark provided just such an environment. Similar remolding of the social surroundings would eliminate from the world the horrors of unemployment, poverty, degradation, ignorance, and war. Owen aroused considerable hostility from the pious, for he attacked religion as blaming individual sinners instead of the genuine villain, inadequate social conditions. Owen envisaged further reforms: old-age and unemployment benefits, compulsory education, and a self-owned home with attached garden for every worker. While his articulate contemporaries were justifying the exploitation of labor for the increase of national wealth, Owen conceived of a society subordinating the machine to human needs and carrying the better physical life to every man.

The Physical and Social Sciences

While artistic intellectuals of the age were generally swayed by Romanticism, intellectuals who were physical or social scientists generally maintained a resolutely realistic position.

John Dalton (1766–1844). Born at Eaglesfield near Cockermouth in Cumberland, John Dalton was the son of a Quaker weaver. A brilliant and studious pupil, Dalton soon conducted his own school, while pursuing independent researches in mathematics and science. In 1793 he accepted a professorship in mathematics and natural philosophy at New College, Manchester, and published *Meteorological Observations and Essays* (1793), in which he first revealed his discovery that the aurora borealis was an electrical phenomenon. With this work he was the founder of meteorology as a science. His study of his own color-blindness was so impressive that for generations English and continental students termed the defect "Daltonism." Although his numerous works proclaiming momentous scientific discoveries and theories brought him international acclaim, Dalton lived an austere life of bachelorhood.

A New System of Chemical Philosophy (1808–27) transformed the philosophical concept of the atom (a theory at least as old as the ancient Greek philosopher Democritus) into a viable scientific hypothesis. Dalton suggested that every atom of a given element is identical in weight and form with every other atom of the same element, but the atoms of different elements will vary considerably in weight and form. Accordingly, he drew up the first table of atomic weights, originally including only twenty-one elements. He also prepared the first system of atomic notation, though his complicated symbols have since been superseded by the simpler notations of the Swedish chemist Berzelius. His "law of multiple proportions" still stands as the principle of atomic combinations that form the countless chemical compounds of the physical world. Although physicists have enormously expanded and modified the atomic theory since the days of Dalton, his work truly inaugurates the Atomic Age. Dalton's is competent technical writing with no pretensions whatever toward literary style.

Sir Charles Lyell (1797–1875). Though a native of Kinnordy, Forfarshire, Scotland, Charles Lyell was quickly taken by his parents to the south of England, where from childhood he displayed a fervent interest in geology. He interspersed his Oxford training with geological tours of the British Isles and Western Europe. His noted work, though initially meeting some challenge, established a distinguished reputation that by 1864 brought him a baronetcy and the presidency of the British Association. He encouraged the young Charles Darwin and vigorously praised Darwin's writings on evolution. Darwin said of Lyell: "I never forget that almost everything which I have done in science I owe to the study of his great works."

Principles of Geology, Being an Attempt to Explain the Former Changes of the Earth's Surface, by Reference to Causes Now in Operation (1830–33) was in part a popularizing of the concepts of James Hutton, whose *Theory of the Earth* (1795) had come too soon in time for general acceptance. Against his contemporary thinkers, who believed that the strata of the earth demonstrated a series of spectacular catastrophes, Lyell substantiated Hutton's contention that geological processes now constantly in operation can account for the varied geological formations of the past. There have been no horrendous cataclysms or monumental floods. All processes have been continuous and uniform. Lyell's greatest contribution lay in the interpretation of fossil remains, which he saw as clearly indicating a progression of ever-increasing complexity in organic life from the lowest strata to the highest, and he further revealed that organisms inhabiting the earth in earlier geological eras were often fantastically different from the living organisms of today. Lyell succeeded simultaneously in a huge synthesis and interpretation of his contemporary geological knowledge, and in a foundation for the later evolutionary works that were to rock the Victorian intellectual world. Eschewing all literary pretenses, the work is written in an admirably direct and cogent prose.

David Ricardo (re-kär′dō) (1772–1823). David Ricardo was the London-born son of a Jewish merchant-banker immigrating from the Netherlands. At fourteen he went to work for his father, and at twenty-two set up business for himself with capital of £800. When he retired in 1814 at the age of forty-two, his fortune was worth approximately £1,000,000. Ricardo became a Quaker in faith, and married a beautiful Quaker girl. During his later years as a Member of Parliament, he was known as "the man who educated Commons." Although he strongly supported parliamentary reform and Roman Catholic emancipation, even his most conservative opponents respected him. His name is usually coupled with that of Malthus, a close personal friend. Strangely enough, Malthus, the college professor, was hammering constantly at the realities of the world (and thereby gaining wide disfavor), while Ricardo, the practical man of affairs, was all theory. A belletristic quality still clings about Malthus's writings, but Ricardo and James Mill thoroughly discard any "literary" flavor.

Principles of Political Economy and Taxation (1817), according to De Quincey, "constructed what hitherto was but a collection of tentative discussions into a science of regular proportions, now first standing upon an eternal basis." Ricardo is generally recognized as the great formulator of "classic economics." The literary quality of Adam Smith and the sense of the bustling world of men that shone in *The Wealth of Nations* are here superseded by steely abstractions, as clean in line and sharp in structure as a Euclidian theorem. Ricardo postulates the "economic man," admittedly a non-existent theoretical being whose life is governed solely by profit and loss; this creature eternally seeks satisfaction of his material wants by trying to buy at the lowest price and sell his product or service at the highest price. The worker, a unit of productive energy, is bound by "the iron law of wages," Ricardo's dictum that a worker's pay will tend always to fall to the subsistence level. Any increase in wages will cause an automatic increase in the working population and thereby drive wages back to bleak subsistence. The employers of the workers are the capitalists, beings whose sole purpose is to secure profits and then reinvest them in a bid for still more profits. By free competition with each other, capitalists will erase the momentary high profits that a fortunate capitalist may briefly obtain by a new technique of manufacture or distribution. In the long run, the capitalist will show for his efforts a monetary return that will amount to his wages; profits beyond a capitalist's pay for his services will be wiped out by the incessant friction of competitors. The only real beneficiaries of the economic system in the long run are the landlords. Rent, as Ricardo saw it, was a special kind of return based upon the obvious fact that all land is not equally productive in minerals or agricultural crops. The soil of one field will yield more grain than another field into which the same amount of money and labor has been invested. With both landowners receiving the same price for grain, the owner of the more productive field will clearly receive more profit.

Like Adam Smith and Malthus, Ricardo assumed that the economic world would constantly expand. The demand for more food and raw materials would therefore bring into production more and more marginal land. Prices of raw materials and food would consequently climb because of the greater costs in extraction from marginal soil. The "iron law of wages" would compel higher pay for workers to maintain subsistence, and capitalists would be caught in the vise between higher rent and higher wages. Landowners would pocket the wealth produced by an expanding society, but no one else would benefit. Ricardo's theory sounds like a tragic reading of life without the life. While the humanists of the time were horrified, the hard-headed agreed that Ricardo had established economic truth upon irrefutable foundations.

James Mill (1773–1836). A shoemaker's son, James Mill was born at Northwater Bridge, Forfarshire, Scotland. He entered Edinburgh University in 1790, concentrating upon theological studies. Although licensed to preach in 1798, he became skeptical of all religion and moved to London in search of literary work in 1802. He became a friend of Ricardo and the first lieutenant of Bentham, with whom he founded the *Westminster Review* in 1824. His writings covered a wide field, always carrying the banner for Utilitarianism. His 1814 articles in the *Encyclopaedia Britannica* gave wide currency to Benthamism. Possibly his greatest work was his brilliant son, John Stuart Mill.

History of British India (1817) is the first real history of the Orient in English. Mill's scholarly labors over twenty years were indefatigable, but he was personally unacquainted with the area or its languages. As a thoroughgoing rationalist, he had no sympathy with the religion or customs of the East. Determined to strip away the glamour of the Orient, he wrote in a sparse, matter-of-fact style.

Elements of Political Economy (1821) largely derives from Ricardo, whom Mill highly esteemed. To counteract the unearned increment accruing to landowners solely because of increasing population and demand, Mill urges a graduated land tax. Sharing Malthus's fear of exploding population, he seeks humane means of limiting human numbers.

Analysis of the Phenomena of the Human Mind (1829) provided a "behavioristic" psychology for Utilitarianism. Based on Hartley's ideas, this is Mill's most important work, one that some have termed the most lucid book ever written upon psychology. Ignoring Berkeley and Hume, Mill began with the assumption of "sensations," valid perceptions of what he assumed is outward reality. "Ideas" are the after-effects of original sensations, joined by "association" in successive trains or clusters. When the human mind experiences inseparable associations of ideas, the result is "belief." The "identity" that men cherish is simply a "thread of consciousness" by which an individual's series of inseparable associations cause him to assert a belief in his own selfhood. The result of this wholly rationalistic and materialistic analysis was not skeptical pessimism but utilitarian optimism. All men start with the same potentials and are capable of limitless perfectibility. Proper education can minimize the unsatisfactory associations, maximize desirable clusters or trains of associations, and result in an ever-improving human being and human society.

Henry Hallam (1777–1859). Henry Hallam was the only son of the canon of Windsor. A precocious child, Hallam was composing sonnets at the age of ten. After training at Eton and Oxford, he practiced law until his father's death made him independently wealthy. Thereafter his life consisted of study and historical writing. His son, Arthur Henry Hallam, was Tennyson's close friend and the subject of *In Memoriam*. Of the historian's eleven children, only one daughter survived him.

View of the State of Europe during the Middle Ages (1818) was the first great history by an Englishman since Gibbon and really the first significant English study of medievalism outside of antiquarianism. Nine surveys, rather than a continuously flowing narrative, span a millennium from the fall of Rome until the 15th century. In modern fashion, Hallam has little interest in battles and pageantry; he searches for the growth of institutions, but unlike historians of our day, he is perfectly willing to make moral judgments. Legally minded, he weighs figures of the past for their contribution to the emergence of organized justice in a stable society.

The Constitutional History of England from the Accession of Henry VII to the Death of George II (1827) is tremendously important for establishing the Whig interpretation of English history, the dominant interpretation down to the present. This is the first work on modern English history that truly achieved international significance. Although Southey and other Tories sharply attacked the study, Hallam was a very moderate Whig who gravely demurred at the Reform Bill. His work is a sustained attack upon Tudor and Stuart despotism and praise for the Revolution of 1688. His ideal principles are the growth of civil liberties and toleration, and the balance of power between Parliament and monarch. While acknowledging their roles in the development of English freedoms, Hallam is highly critical of Henry VIII and Oliver Cromwell. "From unwillingness to excite the prejudices of modern politics," he cuts his survey short in the 18th century. While lucid, erudite, and structurally excellent, Hallam's writing lacks pictorial or exciting qualities.

Introduction to the Literature of Europe in the Fifteenth, Sixteenth, and Seventeenth Centuries (four volumes, 1837–39) is an encyclopedic survey of Western knowledge and thought as disseminated in print. It is the first real attempt in English at an intellectual history of modern times. Surprisingly, the moralistic Hallam is just to Machiavelli and Rabelais; but when he contemplates Spenser and Milton, he comes closest to eloquence.

THE THEATER (1800–1837)

During the first third of the 19th century the English stage was distinguished in theater and undistinguished in drama. From this age Edmund Kean, Charles Kemble, and William Macready are still considered among England's greatest actors, only a bit below David Garrick. Sarah Siddons reigned as the acknowledged queen of the theater, as highly regarded as any actress in English history.

"Legitimate" drama was performed at Covent Garden and Drury Lane, the only two London theaters licensed by patent. Bills regularly introduced in Parliament to break the monopoly were all defeated, the Fourth Theatre Bill passing in Commons but losing out in the House of Lords in 1833. Both patent theaters were destroyed by fire within a few months, Covent Garden in 1808 and Drury Lane the next year. In rebuilding, both structures were modernized to essentially the present physical appearance of the theater, reducing to a stub the forestage in front of the proscenium arch, removing the old proscenium doors and stage boxes, and introducing reserved seats. Acting sought increased realism, strengthened by fidelity to locale in stage settings (Kean insisted upon even botanical accuracy in scenery) and authenticity for costuming. The large dimensions of the two patent theaters demanded robust acting and glittering spectacle. Hazlitt objected that upper-gallery spectators could not hear the actors, and Scott, discussing a proposed Edinburgh theater in 1827, asked for a small structure "in which we can hear our old friends in comfort." In spite of their monopoly, the two licensed theaters were continually in financial difficulties, as good actors commanded high pay and the patronage of the theater was often spotty.

When Kemble reopened Covent Garden in 1809 at increased rates, the unruly audience started the "O. P. [Old Price] riots." The entire audience stood up and turned nothing but their backs to the stage. After about seventy thoroughly disturbed nights, the original prices were restored. The best seats in the early 19th-century theater were occupied by Regency society, often more intent upon demonstrating its fashionable presence and sportive spirit than upon watching the play. Real theatergoers increasingly gravitated toward the more subdued atmosphere at the opera houses. Middle-class persons seldom frequented the theater.

The bourgeois spirit was nonetheless manifesting itself in the drama, which bore no parallel to Restoration naughtiness. The Lord Chamberlain's censorship rigorously excluded any indecency or suggestiveness, any disrespectful reference to religion, or any criticism of the government.

"Illegitimate" drama was performed at minor London theaters, which numbered seven in 1800. Forbidden to offer the fare of Covent Garden and Drury Lane, these theaters ranged from melodrama to farce, with special emphasis upon gaudy spectacle. The Lyceum (later called The English Opera House) presented "Musical Glasses," "Phantasmagoria," and battle scenes with gas illumination. Sadler's Wells (termed the Aquatic Theatre in 1806) floated entire vessels in a huge tank for impressive staginess.

While theater flourished, drama floundered. With the high cost of performers and maintenance, managers provided only starving pay to aspiring dramatists. Many plays were hasty translations from the French or German, or hack writers' adaptations of novels, especially Scott's. Drudges turned out numerous farces and extravaganzas, all cut from the same comic cloth. Particularly popular at the minor houses were "burlettas," brief comic bits accompanied by music. Audience taste seems extraordinary to us in the wide vogue of travesties, chiefly of Shakespeare.

Great writing talent was available from the Romantics, but though every significant Romantic wrote drama, none really succeeded in creating actable plays. Byron, with an advantageous position as one of the committee of management of Drury Lane, had some of his plays actually staged; but his attempts at drama, like those of his fellow Romantics, belong to literature rather than to the theater. The notable failure of the Romantics to produce actable dramas may be explained thus: (1) The subjective approach of the Romantics prevented them from creating objective drama. (2) The Romantic gift was lyrical or contemplative rather than truly dramatic. (3) Exuberant, often long-winded, the Romantics could not master the condensation and incisive representation required for actual staging. (4) The Romantics refused to cater to current taste, and their dramatic styles tended to be anti-quarian or otherwise derivative.

Posterity has remembered, and that dimly, only one practicing dram-atist of the era—James Sheridan Knowles.

James Sheridan Knowles (nōlz) (1784–1862). A cousin of Rich-ard Brinsley Sheridan, James Sheridan Knowles was born in Cork, Ire-land. He served in the militia, studied medicine, taught school, and acted on the stage before producing his first successful play, *Caius Gracchus* (1815). Until 1843 he acted occasionally in his own plays and in the plays of others. In 1844 he became a Baptist preacher and abandoned the theater.

Virginius (1820) is founded upon the Appius and Virginia account, ultimately found in Dionysius of Halicarnassus. The best-known pre-vious version of the story appears in the Renaissance play *Appius and Virginia* (c. 1609), by John Webster.

By trumped-up documents, the evil Roman aristocrat Appius claims as a slave the beautiful Virginia, betrothed to Icilius. Rather than see her dishonored, her father, Virginius, stabs her with her consent and delivers her corpse to Appius. In madness, Virginius strangles the vile Appius.

The treatment is striking though essentially rhetorical, and the style is an attempt at the severely classical with the poise of high tragedy. Knowles's success springs largely from emphasis upon the domestic scenes between father and daughter.

And so we close, having, in dramatic literature, fallen rather pitifully from the heights of the age of Wycherley, Congreve, and Farquhar. The fact that the serious literary minds of the Romantic period were un-successful at making great stage plays seems indicative of the change that had come about in British thought between 1660 and 1837. For in drama one creates a microcosmic reflection of the world; but in a world of increasing complexity and accelerated change this image blurs. The function of mirroring society as a whole we find taken over increasingly by the novel, a more flexible and personal form which could be readily stretched to encompass a growing scientific knowledge and social unrest. In parallel fashion, satiric poetry, which presupposes an ordered society from which to establish a norm of behavior, gives way more and more to a completely personal lyrical poetry in which the standard for judging life is the poet's own feelings.

Index

Page numbers in **bold face** signify major references to the subject.